PLAYER
FOOTBALL
ANNUAL 2011-2012

EDITED BY
GLENDA ROLLIN AND JACK ROLLIN

headline

First published in 2011
by HEADLINE PUBLISHING GROUP

1

Apart from any use permitted under UK copyright law, this publication may only be reproduced, stored, or transmitted, in any form, or by any means, with prior permission in writing of the publishers or, in the case of reprographic production, in accordance with the terms of licences issued by the Copyright Licensing Agency.

Cataloguing in Publication Data is available from the British Library

ISBN 978 0 7553 6233 2

Typeset by Wearset Ltd, Boldon, Tyne and Wear

Printed and bound in the UK by Clays Ltd, St Ives plc

Headline's policy is to use papers that are natural, renewable and recyclable products and made from wood grown in sustainable forests. The logging and manufacturing processes are expected to conform to the environmental regulations of the country of origin.

HEADLINE PUBLISHING GROUP
An Hachette UK Company
338 Euston Road
London NW1 3BH

www.headline.co.uk
www.hachette.co.uk

CONTENTS

EDITORIAL

It was part of a book review in the *Times Literary Supplement* many years ago that made a succinct reference to power when it quoted: "The wrong sort of people are always in power because they would not be in power if they were not the wrong sort of people." Basically it gets you where you started – nowhere, which is just what has happened inside FIFA after a year of scandals.

While there were certainly question marks over the manner in which the England bid for the 2018 World Cup finals was carried out, even the slickest and most convincing presentation would not have landed us the prize because it was always going to be where Sepp Blatter wanted it – in Russia.

Extra time looked to have improved matters and bringing in heavyweight substitutes in the form of a future king of England, the current Prime Minister and a one-hundred-plus capped international footballer who was at least recognised all over the world, should have sealed it, but we know about casts that die.

If that was not enough, in the wake of it all came accusations and resignations from the world governing body and the farce to end all when just one candidate stood for election as head of FIFA. Blatter had played his usual blinder of course.

Interesting to note the voting from the first round which showed England 2 votes, Holland/Belgium 4, Spain/Portugal 7 and Russia 9, surely game, set and match already it would have seemed. Round two revealed Holland/Belgium 2 votes, Spain/Portugal 7 and Russia 13.

Neither FIFA nor UEFA are remotely interested in domestic football. In fact club football is only tolerated because it can furnish teams for the cups these two bodies organise that make millions of pounds for both of them. The growth of the two European tournaments, the Champions League and Europa League has been at the detriment of the bread and butter fare that provides the nucleus of players for Europe and internationals.

Both the FA Cup and the Carling Cup have suffered because the leading teams have long since treated them as second class. They have to save their best for Europe. Yes, there is still romance in the FA Cup in particular, but only at the lower levels. Yet oddly enough the attendances for the FA Cup have held up remarkably well over the last few years.

As to the Carling Cup it would benefit from being restructured to allow the lower division clubs a better deal. Combining the Johnstone's Paint Trophy with it would also reduce the number of matches played. If the re-vamped Carling Cup tournament started in 16 regional groups for the 48 associate member clubs, comprising three in each, with just one home and one away match to be played, it would cut out meaningless ties with the group winner guaranteed a home draw at the knock-out stage. Also every runner-up placed in the draw, too, plus the best eight bottom finishing ones. Only eight teams eliminated at this stage. The FA Cup cannot give every entry the sureness of one home gate.

These opening stages could be played pre-season – one such was played this season. The 24 Championship clubs would come in at the first knock-out round making 64 for the next round. The 32 survivors then take the five nearest bottom in the Premier League and the three promoted ones. Twenty teams left after that round plus the top dozen from the Premiership and so on. Any teams in Europe outside this quota – like Birmingham City this season – can be accounted for in advance. It would be a worthwhile companion to the world's oldest tournament.

As to prospects for England to qualify for Euro 2012, it is a small group of no great weight. Yet already points have been dropped at Wembley. The Under-21s failed to win a group game in Denmark – three draws for the Three Lions. For hopes of an enterprising generation to come this was not encouraging. But top players are required to play more matches outside domestic commitments.

The Under-21s had to fulfil 13 fixtures both friendly and competitive during the season which represents a quarter of it added onto European calls at club level. This, plus the home front league and cup requirements makes it an almost impossible situation in which to nurture talent.

At Under-17 level, the youngsters had an even more gruelling schedule that culminated in the FIFA U-17 World Cup. Naturally this went well into July before it came to a conclusion. Again added to other calls on their services, it is too much football.

England bowed out to Germany, not the first time at any level that this has happened of course, but there was at least a brave fight back from three down that just fell short. But too many times the skill of the Spaniards and the strength of the Germans and a mixture of both from Holland have proved our downfall.

Before even the domestic season opened the Under-20s were embarked on the FIFA Under-20 World Cup. Needless to say, the Champions League, Europa League and belief it or not the qualifying stages of the 2014 World Cup started in some areas before July was to old! And so it continues. Moreover, England has climbed in the FIFA ranks to fourth, so why the problem!

CLUB AND OTHER RECORDS 2010–2011

Accrington Stanley – Record League points 73.

Aldershot Town – Most capped player Anthony Straker Grenada with 5.

Aston Villa – Brad Friedel sets Premier League record with his 250th consecutive appearance.

Birmingham City – Kevin Phillips at 37 becomes the oldest Premier League outfield player and goalscorer.

Bournemouth – Steve Fletcher takes his record League appearances to 597.

Brighton & Hove Albion – Record League points 95.

Burnley – Graham Alexander reaches his 1000th career appearance.

Burton Albion – Jacques Maghoma adds to his appearances for DR Congo with his second cap.
Tom Parkes at 18 years and 8 days becomes the club's youngest player.

Bury – Ryan Lowe scores for club record 8th successive time.

Chelsea – Frank Lampard increases his total number of England caps to 86 of which 84 were earned with Chelsea.
Chelsea pays British record transfer fee of £50,000,000 for Fernando Torres from Liverpool.

Dagenham & Redbridge – Tony Roberts takes his record League appearances to 175.

Huddersfield Town – Record League points 87.

Liverpool – Steven Gerrard increases his number of England caps to 89.
Liverpool breaks transfer record for a British player paying £35,000,000 for Andy Carroll from Newcastle U.

Manchester United – Ryan Giggs overtakes Bobby Charlton's record number of 606 League appearances and takes his total to 613.
First Premier League club to reach 1500 points.
They also reach a record 19th Championship (12th in Premier League).

Millwall – Neil Harris adds to his club record by taking his total number of goals to 124.

Milton Keynes Dons – Dean Lewington takes his record number of League appearances to 301.

Morecambe – Jim Bentley takes his record number of League appearances to 146 and Stuart Drummond takes his goals total to 27.

Queens Park Rangers – Equals Record League points with 88.

Shrewsbury Town – Equals Record League points with 79.

Southampton – Record League points 92.

Wycombe W – Record League points 80.

Stranraer – Record win 9-0 v St Cuthberts Wanderers in Scottish Cup.

Bangor City – Breaks British record with 14th consecutive League win from season's start.

Jose Mourinho – completes 150th unbeaten home game for three clubs; Porto, Chelsea and Real Madrid.

Premier League – 2010–11 sees record number of goals scored; 1063.

LEAGUE REVIEW AND CLUB SECTION

Just scanning the bare facts of Manchester United's record-breaking 19th overall championship title and their twelfth in the Premier League, they achieved at least on paper the classic: win at home and draw away – a formula that was always considered to be a sure-fired way of gaining something special in a season.

Secure at Old Trafford to the extent that only one team West Bromwich Albion managed to leave with a point and surprisingly two goals, too, the away record was dominated by drawn affairs, ten of them no less. No other team in the leading four English divisions remained undefeated at home.

Sir Alex Ferguson again proved the master despite his penchant for tinkering with his team selection. Others did the same but he had a stronger squad from whom to choose. Of the 29 players used in the Premier League, none was ever-present. Javier Hernandez, the Mexican known as Chicarito, was considered the find of the season in attack. But the huge disappointment for Manchester United was being defeated by Barcelona in the Champions League final, when there appeared to be a something of a gulf between the Premier League's best and the one from La Liga.

However, the race for the domestic title went to the penultimate week and the relegation battle was not settled for two teams from a list of five in danger until the last day of the campaign.

On a wider scale 1,063 goals were scored, a Premier League record. But there was also an increase in the number of drawn matches to 111, twenty-five of which were goalless. Ever-present players dwindled overall to sixteen and only two outfield players Leighton Baines of Everton and Martin Skrtel from Liverpool remained on the pitch for the entire 3,420 minutes.

Mancunian joy was not confined to Old Trafford. Manchester City won the FA Cup beating Stoke City for the club's best season for more than thirty years. City finished third behind Chelsea who despite runners-up position found its manager Carlo Ancelotti losing his position at the end of the season and being hit by below expectations from £50m Fernando Torres. Inconsistent Arsenal disappointed, too, in fourth place and even lost the Carling Cup final to Birmingham City who suffered later as one of the three teams demoted.

Tottenham Hotspur slipped in the pecking order to fifth one place above Liverpool who just kept Merseyside rivals Everton four points behind them. Fulham in eighth place had the satisfaction of gaining another chance in the Europa League thanks to the team's disciplinary record via the fair play card.

Aston Villa had another change of management with Gerard Houllier retiring through ill health and at the season's end Alex McLeish moved over from Birmingham City to take charge. Sunderland finished tenth ahead of West Bromwich who installed Roy Hodgson as manager after his removal at Liverpool.

There was also a new man at the helm for Newcastle United in Alan Pardew and Stoke's season was brightened by reaching the FA Cup final of course. Bolton Wanderers succeeded in keeping out of trouble but Blackburn Rovers with Steve Kean taking Sam Allardyce's role had to sweat until the last week.

Wigan Athletic achieved the great escape on the final day at Ewood Park and despite defeat for Wolverhampton Wanderers in their last game, they also survived at the expense of Birmingham City and Blackpool in their first season back in the top bracket since 1971, finally succumbed, too.

West Ham United had been earlier casualties in this field. Replacing this trio were runaway leaders Queens Park Rangers accompanied by runners-up Norwich City in the second automatic slot and Swansea City through the play-offs.

Down from the Football League Championship went Preston North End, Sheffield United and Scunthorpe United. Up from League One Brighton & Hove Albion celebrated the anticipated move to a new ground with the title and Southampton after a slow start came up with them. From the play-offs free-scoring Peterborough United proved successful.

The quartet relegated: Dagenham & Redbridge, Bristol Rovers, Plymouth Argyle – hindered by a points-deduction – and Swindon Town. The three automatically promoted from League Two were Chesterfield as champions, Bury and Wycombe Wanderers while Stevenage made it a memorable season through the play-offs.

Lincoln City for the second time in their history found themselves relegated to the Conference along with Stockport County. Their replacements: record-breaking Crawley Town who won the honour of the best FA Cup performance and AFC Wimbledon.

Carlisle United defeated Brentford in the Johnstone's Paint Trophy to round up the domestic honours in England. So to Europe and apart from Manchester United's gallant attempt to defeat Barcelona once more, Arsenal went out in the knock-out round, Chelsea lost to United in the quarter-finals, Liverpool lacking in goals survived until the third round of the Europa League as did Manchester City.

Tottenham Hotspur did well in the Champions League accounting for AC Milan and Internazionale but discovered Real Madrid more than a match for them. The Premier League clubs also entered the 2011–12 season with an overall rise in season ticket prices, not the best way of appealing to many financially hard-pressed patrons.

BARCLAYS PREMIER LEAGUE 2010–2011

(P) Promoted into division at end of 2009–10 season.
(R) Relegated into division at end of 2009–10 season.

							Total					Home					Away					
		P	W	D	L	F	A	W	D	L	F	A	W	D	L	F	A	GD	Pts
1	Manchester U	38	23	11	4	78	37	18	1	0	49	12	5	10	4	29	25	41	80
2	Chelsea	38	21	8	9	69	33	14	3	2	39	13	7	5	7	30	20	36	71
3	Manchester C	38	21	8	9	60	33	13	4	2	34	12	8	4	7	26	21	27	71
4	Arsenal	38	19	11	8	72	43	11	4	4	33	15	8	7	4	39	28	29	68
5	Tottenham H	38	16	14	8	55	46	9	9	1	30	19	7	5	7	25	27	9	62
6	Liverpool	38	17	7	14	59	44	12	4	3	37	14	5	3	11	22	30	15	58
7	Everton	38	13	15	10	51	45	9	7	3	31	23	4	8	7	20	22	6	54
8	Fulham	38	11	16	11	49	43	8	7	4	30	23	3	9	7	19	20	6	49
9	Aston Villa	38	12	12	14	48	59	8	7	4	26	19	4	5	10	22	40	–11	48
10	Sunderland	38	12	11	15	45	56	7	5	7	25	27	5	6	8	20	29	–11	47
11	WBA (P)	38	12	11	15	56	71	8	6	5	30	30	4	5	10	26	41	–15	47
12	Newcastle U (P)	38	11	13	14	56	57	6	8	5	41	27	5	5	9	15	30	–1	46
13	Stoke C	38	13	7	18	46	48	10	4	5	31	18	3	3	13	15	30	–2	46
14	Bolton W	38	12	10	16	52	56	10	5	4	34	24	2	5	12	18	32	–4	46
15	Blackburn R	38	11	10	17	46	59	7	7	5	22	16	4	3	12	24	43	–13	43
16	Wigan Ath	38	9	15	14	40	61	5	8	6	22	34	4	7	8	18	27	–21	42
17	Wolverhampton W	38	11	7	20	46	66	8	4	7	30	30	3	3	13	16	36	–20	40
18	Birmingham C	38	8	15	15	37	58	6	8	5	19	22	2	7	10	18	36	–21	39
19	Blackpool (P)	38	10	9	19	55	78	5	5	9	30	37	5	4	10	25	41	–23	39
20	West Ham U	38	7	12	19	43	70	5	5	9	24	31	2	7	10	19	39	–27	33

LEADING GOALSCORERS 2010–2011

BARCLAYS PREMIER LEAGUE

	League	Carling Cup	FA Cup	Other	Total
Only goals scored in the same division are included.					
Carlos Tevez *(Manchester C)*	20	0	3	0	23
Dimitar Berbatov *(Manchester U)*	20	0	0	1	21
Robin Van Persie *(Arsenal)*	18	1	1	2	22
Darren Bent *(Aston Villa)*	17	2	1	0	20
(Includes 8 League goals, 2 Carling Cup goals and 1 FA Cup goal for Sunderland).					
Peter Odemwingie *(WBA)*	15	0	0	0	15
Javier Hernandez *(Manchester U)*	13	1	1	5	20
Dirk Kuyt *(Liverpool)*	13	0	0	2	15
Rafael Van der Vaart *(Tottenham H)*	13	0	0	2	15
Florent Malouda *(Chelsea)*	13	0	0	1	14
Dudley Campbell *(Blackpool)*	13	0	0	0	13
Andy Carroll *(Liverpool)*	13	0	0	0	13
(Includes 11 League goals for Newcastle U).					
Charlie Adam *(Blackpool)*	12	1	0	0	13
Clint Dempsey *(Fulham)*	12	1	0	0	13
Kevin Nolan *(Newcastle U)*	12	0	0	0	12

Other matches consist of European games, J Paint Trophy, Community Shield and Football League play-offs. Players listed in order of League goals total.

NPOWER CHAMPIONSHIP 2010–2011

			Total					Home					Away					
	P	W	D	L	F	A	W	D	L	F	A	W	D	L	F	A	GD	Pts
1 QPR	46	24	16	6	71	32	14	7	2	43	15	10	9	4	28	17	39	88
2 Norwich C (P)	46	23	15	8	83	58	13	6	4	47	30	10	9	4	36	28	25	84
3 Swansea C¶	46	24	8	14	69	42	15	5	3	41	11	9	3	11	28	31	27	80
4 Cardiff C	46	23	11	12	76	54	12	7	4	41	25	11	4	8	35	29	22	80
5 Reading	46	20	17	9	77	51	12	7	4	43	25	8	10	5	34	26	26	77
6 Nottingham F	46	20	15	11	69	50	13	8	2	43	22	7	7	9	26	28	19	75
7 Leeds U (P)	46	19	15	12	81	70	11	8	4	47	34	8	7	8	34	36	11	72
8 Burnley (R)	46	18	14	14	65	61	12	6	5	40	30	6	8	9	25	31	4	68
9 Millwall (P)	46	18	13	15	62	48	12	6	5	39	22	6	7	10	23	26	14	67
10 Leicester C	46	19	10	17	76	71	13	6	4	48	27	6	4	13	28	44	5	67
11 Hull C (R)	46	16	17	13	52	51	7	8	8	21	19	9	9	5	31	32	1	65
12 Middlesbrough	46	17	11	18	68	68	10	7	6	37	32	7	4	12	31	36	0	62
13 Ipswich T	46	18	8	20	62	68	10	3	10	33	37	8	5	10	29	31	−6	62
14 Watford	46	16	13	17	77	71	9	7	7	39	32	7	6	10	38	39	6	61
15 Bristol C	46	17	9	20	62	65	10	4	9	30	29	7	5	11	32	36	−3	60
16 Portsmouth (R)	46	15	13	18	53	60	8	9	6	31	26	7	4	12	22	34	−7	58
17 Barnsley	46	14	14	18	55	66	11	6	6	32	23	3	8	12	23	43	−11	56
18 Coventry C	46	14	13	19	54	58	9	5	9	27	26	5	8	10	27	32	−4	55
19 Derby Co	46	13	10	23	58	71	8	4	11	35	32	5	6	12	23	39	−13	49
20 Crystal Palace	46	12	12	22	44	69	11	6	6	28	24	1	6	16	16	45	−25	48
21 Doncaster R	46	11	15	20	55	81	7	9	7	26	31	4	6	13	29	50	−26	48
22 Preston NE	46	10	12	24	54	79	7	4	12	27	36	3	8	12	27	43	−25	42
23 Sheffield U	46	11	9	26	44	79	7	5	11	27	36	4	4	15	17	43	−35	42
24 Scunthorpe U	46	12	6	28	43	87	5	5	13	21	40	7	1	15	22	47	−44	42

¶Swansea C promoted via play-offs.

NPOWER CHAMPIONSHIP

	League	Carling Cup	FA Cup	Other	Total
Danny Graham (Watford)	23	2	1	0	26
Shane Long (Reading)	21	0	2	2	25
Grant Holt (Norwich C)	21	2	0	0	23
Scott Sinclair (Swansea C)	19	4	1	3	27
Luciano Becchio (Leeds U)	19	1	0	0	20
Adel Taarabt (QPR)	19	0	0	0	19
Jay Bothroyd (Cardiff C)	18	2	0	0	20
Max Gradel (Leeds U)	18	0	0	0	18
Steve Morison (Millwall)	15	2	0	0	17
Andy King (Leicester C)	15	0	1	0	16
Billy Sharp (Doncaster R)	15	0	1	0	16
Jay Rodriguez (Burnley)	14	0	1	0	15

NPOWER LEAGUE 1 2010–2011

	P	W	D	L	F	A	W	D	L	F	A	W	D	L	F	A	GD	Pts
			Total						Home					Away				
1 Brighton & HA	46	28	11	7	85	40	17	4	2	54	22	11	7	5	31	18	45	95
2 Southampton	46	28	8	10	86	38	16	4	3	44	13	12	4	7	42	25	48	92
3 Huddersfield T	46	25	12	9	77	48	12	8	3	38	21	13	4	6	39	27	29	87
4 Peterborough U¶ (R)	46	23	10	13	106	75	15	5	3	69	40	8	5	10	37	35	31	79
5 Milton Keynes D	46	23	8	15	67	60	14	5	4	35	23	9	3	11	32	37	7	77
6 Bournemouth (P)	46	19	14	13	75	54	13	5	5	47	24	6	9	8	28	30	21	71
7 Leyton Orient	46	19	13	14	71	62	12	6	5	37	25	7	7	9	34	37	9	70
8 Exeter C	46	20	10	16	66	73	12	5	6	40	31	8	5	10	26	42	−7	70
9 Rochdale (P)	46	18	14	14	63	55	9	8	6	36	30	9	6	8	27	25	8	68
10 Colchester U	46	16	14	16	57	63	12	7	4	38	30	4	7	12	19	33	−6	62
11 Brentford	46	17	10	19	55	62	9	5	9	24	28	8	5	10	31	34	−7	61
12 Carlisle U	46	16	11	19	60	62	9	7	7	34	26	7	4	12	26	36	−2	59
13 Charlton Ath	46	15	14	17	62	66	10	6	7	29	29	5	8	10	33	37	−4	59
14 Yeovil T	46	16	11	19	56	66	8	6	9	27	30	8	5	10	29	36	−10	59
15 Sheffield W (R)	46	16	10	20	67	67	10	5	8	38	29	6	5	12	29	38	0	58
16 Hartlepool U	46	15	12	19	47	65	9	6	8	32	32	6	6	11	15	33	−18	57
17 Oldham Ath	46	13	17	16	53	60	7	9	7	29	31	6	8	9	24	29	−7	56
17 Tranmere R	46	15	11	20	53	60	9	4	10	28	27	6	7	10	25	33	−7	56
19 Notts Co (P)	46	14	8	24	46	60	9	3	11	24	25	5	5	13	22	35	−14	50
20 Walsall	46	12	12	22	56	75	9	3	11	33	36	3	9	11	23	39	−19	48
21 Dagenham and R (P)	46	12	11	23	52	70	8	6	9	28	27	4	5	14	24	43	−18	47
22 Bristol R	46	11	12	23	48	82	6	7	10	24	35	5	5	13	24	47	−34	45
23 Plymouth Arg (R)	46	12	4	24	51	74	9	4	10	27	33	6	3	14	24	41	−23	42
24 Swindon T	46	9	14	23	50	72	5	9	9	20	27	4	5	14	30	45	−22	41

Plymouth Arg deducted 10 points. ¶Peterborough U promoted via play-offs.

LEADING GOALSCORERS 2010–2011

NPOWER LEAGUE 1

	League	Carling Cup	FA Cup	Other	Total
Craig Mackail-Smith *(Peterborough U)*	27	3	2	3	35
Glenn Murray *(Brighton & HA)*	22	0	0	0	22
Bradley Wright Phillipps *(Charlton Ath)*	22	0	0	0	22
(Includes 13 league goals for Plymouth Arg)					
Richard Lambert *(Southampton)*	21	0	0	0	21
Ashley Barnes *(Brighton & HA)*	18	0	2	0	20
Gary Jones *(Rochdale)*	17	2	0	0	19
Will Hoskins *(Bristol R)*	17	0	1	2	20
Jamie Cureton *(Exeter C)*	17	0	0	3	20
Jordan Rhodes *(Huddersfield T)*	16	1	1	4	22
George Boyd *(Peterborough U)*	15	2	0	0	17
Dean Bowditch *(Yeovil T)*	15	0	0	0	15
Lee Barnard *(Southampton)*	14	0	1	0	15

NPOWER LEAGUE 2 2010–2011

		P	W	D	L	F	A	W	D	L	F	A	W	D	L	F	A	GD	Pts
				Total						*Home*						*Away*			
1	Chesterfield	46	24	14	8	85	51	16	3	4	59	31	8	11	4	26	20	34	86
2	Bury	46	23	12	11	82	50	11	6	6	35	23	12	6	5	47	27	32	81
3	Wycombe W (R)	46	22	14	10	69	50	12	6	5	38	25	10	8	5	31	25	19	80
4	Shrewsbury T	46	22	13	11	72	49	11	9	3	36	18	11	4	8	36	31	23	79
5	Accrington S	46	18	19	9	73	55	15	5	3	53	24	3	14	6	20	31	18	73
6	Stevenage¶ (P)	46	18	15	13	62	45	9	11	3	37	24	9	4	10	25	21	17	69
7	Torquay U	46	17	18	11	74	53	10	8	5	36	22	7	10	6	38	31	21	68
8	Gillingham (R)	46	17	17	12	67	57	10	7	6	29	24	7	10	6	38	33	10	68
9	Rotherham U	46	17	15	14	75	60	10	8	5	41	26	7	7	9	34	34	15	66
10	Crewe Alex	46	18	11	17	87	65	13	6	4	49	18	5	5	13	38	47	22	65
11	Port Vale	46	17	14	15	54	49	11	7	5	32	22	6	7	10	22	27	5	65
12	Oxford U (P)	46	17	12	17	58	60	11	4	8	32	25	6	8	9	26	35	-2	63
13	Southend U (R)	46	16	13	17	62	56	10	7	6	37	28	6	6	11	25	28	6	61
14	Aldershot T	46	14	19	13	54	54	8	8	7	26	26	6	11	6	28	28	0	61
15	Macclesfield T	46	14	13	19	59	73	6	7	10	25	36	8	6	9	34	37	-14	55
16	Northampton T	46	11	19	16	63	71	8	9	6	40	33	3	10	10	23	38	-8	52
17	Cheltenham T	46	13	13	20	56	77	6	6	11	24	32	7	7	9	32	45	-21	52
18	Bradford C	46	15	7	24	43	68	10	3	10	27	30	5	4	14	16	38	-25	52
19	Burton Alb	46	12	15	19	56	70	9	8	6	36	31	3	7	13	20	39	-14	51
20	Morecambe	46	13	12	21	54	73	6	8	9	26	31	7	4	12	28	42	-19	51
21	Hereford U	46	12	17	17	50	66	4	11	8	23	30	8	6	9	27	36	-16	50
22	Barnet	46	12	12	22	58	77	8	5	10	30	35	4	7	12	28	42	-19	48
23	Lincoln C	46	13	8	25	45	81	7	4	12	18	41	6	4	13	27	40	-36	47
24	Stockport Co (R)	46	9	14	23	48	96	4	12	7	31	51	5	2	16	17	45	-48	41

Torquay U deducted 1 point. Hereford U deducted 3 points. ¶Stevenage promoted via play-offs.

NPOWER LEAGUE 2

	League	Carling Cup	FA Cup	Other	Total
Clayton Donaldson *(Crewe Alex)*	28	0	0	1	29
Ryan Lowe *(Bury)*	27	0	1	0	28
Cody McDonald *(Gillingham on loan from Norwich C)*.	25	0	0	0	25
Craig Davies *(Chesterfield)*	23	0	1	1	25
Adam Le Fondre *(Rotherham U)*	23	0	0	1	24
Barry Corr *(Southend U)*	18	1	2	0	21
Wesley Thomas *(Cheltenham T)*	18	0	1	0	19
Shaun Miller *(Crewe Alex)*	18	0	0	0	18
Jack Lester *(Chesterfield)*	17	0	0	0	17
Marc Richards *(Port Vale)*	16	0	2	2	20
Shaun Harrad *(Northampton T)*	16	1	2	0	19
(Includes 10 league goals, 1 Carling Cup and 2 FA Cup for Burton Alb)					
James Constable *(Oxford U)*	15	2	0	0	17
Ashley Grimes *(Lincoln C on loan from Millwall)*.	15	0	2	0	17
Jake Robinson *(Shrewbury T)*	15	1	0	0	16
(Includes 7 league goals on loan to Torquay U)					
Danny Whitaker *(Chesterfield)*	15	0	0	0	15

BARCLAYS PREMIER LEAGUE

HOME TEAM	Arsenal	Aston V	Birmingham C	Blackburn R	Blackpool	Bolton W	Chelsea	Everton	Fulham	Liverpool
Arsenal	—	1-2	2-1	0-0	6-0	4-1	3-1	2-1	2-1	1-1
Aston V	2-4	—	0-0	4-1	3-2	1-1	0-0	1-0	2-2	1-0
Birmingham C	0-3	1-1	—	2-1	2-0	2-1	1-0	0-2	0-2	0-0
Blackburn R	1-2	2-0	1-1	—	2-2	1-0	1-2	1-0	1-1	3-1
Blackpool	1-3	1-1	1-2	1-2	—	4-3	1-3	2-2	2-2	2-1
Bolton W	2-1	3-2	2-2	2-1	2-2	—	0-4	2-0	0-0	0-1
Chelsea	2-0	3-3	3-1	2-0	4-0	1-0	—	1-1	1-0	0-1
Everton	1-2	2-2	1-1	2-0	5-3	1-1	1-0	—	2-1	2-0
Fulham	2-2	1-1	1-1	3-2	3-0	3-0	0-0	0-0	—	2-5
Liverpool	1-1	3-0	5-0	2-1	1-2	2-1	2-0	2-2	1-0	—
Manchester C	0-3	4-0	0-0	1-1	1-0	1-0	1-0	1-2	1-1	3-0
Manchester U	1-0	3-1	5-0	7-1	4-2	1-0	2-1	1-0	2-0	3-2
Newcastle U	4-4	6-0	2-1	1-2	0-2	1-1	1-1	1-2	0-0	3-1
Stoke C	3-1	2-1	3-2	1-0	0-1	2-0	1-1	2-0	0-2	2-0
Sunderland	1-1	1-0	2-2	3-0	0-2	1-0	2-4	2-2	0-3	0-2
Tottenham H	3-3	2-1	2-1	4-2	1-1	2-1	1-1	1-1	1-0	2-1
WBA	2-2	2-1	3-1	1-3	3-2	1-1	1-3	1-0	2-1	2-1
West Ham U	0-3	1-2	0-1	1-1	0-0	1-3	1-3	1-1	1-1	3-1
Wigan Ath	2-2	1-2	2-1	4-3	0-4	1-1	0-6	1-1	1-1	1-1
Wolverhampton W	0-2	1-2	1-0	2-3	4-0	2-3	1-0	0-3	1-1	0-3

2010–2011 RESULTS

Manchester C	Manchester U	Newcastle U	Stoke C	Sunderland	Tottenham H	WBA	West Ham U	Wigan Ath	Wolverhampton W
0-0	1-0	0-1	1-0	0-0	2-3	2-3	1-0	3-0	2-0
1-0	2-2	1-0	1-1	0-1	1-2	2-1	3-0	1-1	0-1
2-2	1-1	0-2	1-0	2-0	1-1	1-3	2-2	0-0	1-1
0-1	1-1	0-0	0-2	0-0	0-1	2-0	1-1	2-1	3-0
2-3	2-3	1-1	0-0	1-2	3-1	2-1	1-3	1-3	2-1
0-2	2-2	5-1	2-1	1-2	4-2	2-0	3-0	1-1	1-0
2-0	2-1	2-2	2-0	0-3	2-1	6-0	3-0	1-0	2-0
2-1	3-3	0-1	1-0	2-0	2-1	1-4	2-2	0-0	1-1
1-4	2-2	1-0	2-0	0-0	1-2	3-0	1-3	2-0	2-1
3-0	3-1	3-0	2-0	2-2	0-2	1-0	3-0	1-1	0-1
—	0-0	2-1	3-0	5-0	1-0	3-0	2-1	1-0	4-3
2-1	—	3-0	2-1	2-0	2-0	2-2	3-0	2-0	2-1
1-3	0-0	—	1-2	5-1	1-1	3-3	5-0	2-2	4-1
1-1	1-2	4-0	—	3-2	1-2	1-1	1-1	0-1	3-0
1-0	0-0	1-1	2-0	—	1-2	2-3	1-0	4-2	1-3
0-0	0-0	2-0	3-2	1-1	—	2-2	0-0	0-1	3-1
0-2	1-2	3-1	0-3	1-0	1-1	—	3-3	2-2	1-1
1-3	2-4	1-2	3-0	0-3	1-0	2-2	—	3-1	2-0
0-2	0-4	0-1	2-2	1-1	0-0	1-0	3-2	—	2-0
2-1	2-1	1-1	2-1	3-2	3-3	3-1	1-1	1-2	—

NPOWER CHAMPIONSHIP

HOME TEAM	Barnsley	Bristol C	Burnley	Cardiff C	Coventry C	Crystal Palace	Derby Co	Doncaster R	Hull C	Ipswich T
Barnsley	—	4-2	1-2	1-2	2-1	1-0	1-1	2-2	1-1	1-1
Bristol C	3-3	—	2-0	3-0	1-2	1-1	2-0	1-0	3-0	0-1
Burnley	3-0	0-0	—	1-1	2-2	1-0	2-1	1-1	4-0	1-2
Cardiff C	2-2	3-2	1-1	—	2-0	0-0	4-1	4-0	2-0	0-2
Coventry C	3-0	1-4	1-0	1-2	—	2-1	2-1	2-1	0-1	1-1
Crystal Palace	2-1	0-0	0-0	1-0	2-0	—	2-2	1-0	0-0	1-2
Derby Co	0-0	0-2	2-4	1-2	2-2	5-0	—	1-3	0-1	1-2
Doncaster R	0-2	1-1	1-0	1-3	1-1	0-0	2-3	—	3-1	0-6
Hull C	2-0	2-0	0-1	0-2	0-0	1-1	2-0	3-1	—	1-0
Ipswich T	1-3	2-0	1-1	2-0	1-2	2-1	0-2	3-2	1-1	—
Leeds U	3-3	3-1	1-0	0-4	1-0	2-1	1-2	5-2	2-2	0-0
Leicester C	4-1	2-1	4-0	2-1	1-1	1-1	2-0	5-1	1-1	4-2
Middlesbrough	1-1	1-2	2-1	1-0	2-1	2-1	2-1	3-0	2-2	1-3
Millwall	2-0	0-0	1-1	3-3	3-1	3-0	2-0	1-0	4-0	2-1
Norwich C	2-1	3-1	2-2	1-1	2-2	1-2	3-2	1-1	0-2	4-1
Nottingham F	2-2	1-0	2-0	2-1	2-1	3-0	5-2	0-0	0-1	2-0
Portsmouth	1-0	3-1	1-2	0-2	0-3	1-0	1-1	2-3	2-3	0-0
Preston NE	1-2	0-4	1-2	0-1	2-1	4-3	1-2	0-2	0-2	1-0
QPR	4-0	2-2	1-1	2-1	2-1	2-1	0-0	3-0	1-1	2-0
Reading	3-0	4-1	2-1	1-1	0-0	3-0	2-1	4-3	1-1	1-0
Scunthorpe U	0-0	0-2	0-0	2-4	0-2	3-0	0-0	1-3	1-5	1-1
Sheffield U	2-2	3-2	3-3	0-2	0-1	3-2	0-1	2-2	2-3	1-2
Swansea C	1-0	0-1	1-0	0-1	2-1	3-0	0-0	3-0	1-1	4-1
Watford	1-0	1-3	1-3	4-1	2-2	1-1	3-0	2-2	1-2	2-1

2010–2011 RESULTS

	Leeds U	Leicester C	Middlesbrough	Millwall	Norwich C	Nottingham F	Portsmouth	Preston NE	QPR	Reading	Scunthorpe U	Sheffield U	Swansea C	Watford
	5-2	0-2	2-0	1-0	0-2	3-1	1-0	2-0	0-1	0-1	2-1	1-0	1-1	0-0
	0-2	2-0	0-4	0-3	0-3	2-3	2-1	1-1	1-1	1-0	2-0	3-0	0-2	0-2
	2-3	3-0	3-1	0-3	2-1	1-0	1-1	4-3	0-0	0-4	0-2	4-2	2-1	3-2
	2-1	2-0	0-3	2-1	3-1	0-2	3-0	1-1	2-2	2-2	1-0	1-1	0-1	4-2
	2-3	1-1	1-0	2-1	1-2	1-2	2-0	1-2	0-2	0-0	1-1	0-0	0-1	2-0
	1-0	3-2	1-0	0-1	0-0	0-3	4-1	1-0	1-2	3-3	1-2	1-0	0-3	3-2
	2-1	0-2	3-1	0-0	1-2	0-1	2-0	3-0	2-2	1-2	3-2	0-1	2-1	4-1
	0-0	1-1	2-1	2-1	3-1	1-1	0-2	1-1	0-1	0-3	3-0	2-0	1-1	1-1
	2-2	0-1	2-4	0-1	1-1	0-0	1-2	1-0	0-0	1-1	0-1	0-1	2-0	0-0
	2-1	3-0	3-3	2-0	1-5	0-1	0-2	2-1	0-3	1-3	2-0	3-0	1-3	0-3
	—	1-2	1-1	3-1	2-2	4-1	3-3	4-6	2-0	0-0	4-0	1-0	2-1	2-2
	2-2	—	0-0	4-2	2-3	1-0	0-1	1-0	0-2	1-2	3-1	2-2	2-1	4-2
	1-2	3-3	—	0-1	1-1	1-1	2-2	1-1	0-3	3-1	2-0	1-0	3-4	2-1
	3-2	2-0	2-3	—	1-1	0-0	0-1	4-0	2-0	0-0	3-0	0-1	0-2	1-6
	1-1	4-3	1-0	2-1	—	2-1	0-2	1-1	1-0	2-1	6-0	4-2	2-0	2-3
	1-1	3-2	1-0	1-1	1-1	—	2-1	2-2	0-0	3-4	5-1	1-1	3-1	1-0
	2-2	6-1	0-0	1-1	0-1	2-1	—	1-1	1-1	1-1	2-0	1-0	0-0	3-2
	1-2	1-1	1-3	0-0	0-1	1-2	1-0	—	1-1	1-1	2-3	3-1	2-1	3-1
	1-2	1-0	3-0	0-0	0-0	1-1	2-0	3-1	—	3-1	2-0	3-0	4-0	1-3
	0-0	3-1	5-2	2-1	3-3	1-1	2-0	2-1	0-1	—	1-2	2-3	0-1	1-1
	1-4	0-3	0-2	1-2	0-1	1-0	1-1	0-3	4-1	0-2	—	3-2	1-0	1-2
	2-0	0-1	1-2	1-1	1-2	2-1	1-0	1-0	0-3	1-1	0-4	—	1-0	0-1
	3-0	2-0	1-0	1-1	3-0	3-2	1-2	4-0	0-0	1-0	2-0	4-0	—	1-1
	0-1	3-2	3-1	1-0	2-2	1-1	3-0	2-2	0-2	1-1	0-2	3-0	2-3	—

NPOWER LEAGUE 1

HOME TEAM	Bournemouth	Brentford	Brighton & HA	Bristol R	Carlisle U	Charlton Ath	Colchester U	Dagenham & R	Exeter C	Hartlepool U
Bournemouth	—	3-1	1-0	2-1	2-0	2-2	1-2	3-0	3-0	0-1
Brentford	1-1	—	0-1	1-0	2-1	2-1	1-1	2-1	1-1	0-0
Brighton & HA	1-1	1-0	—	2-2	4-3	1-1	2-0	4-3	3-0	4-1
Bristol R	1-0	0-0	2-4	—	1-1	2-2	0-1	0-2	0-2	0-0
Carlisle U	1-0	2-0	0-0	4-0	—	3-4	4-1	0-2	2-2	1-0
Charlton Ath	1-0	0-1	0-4	1-1	1-3	—	1-0	2-2	1-3	0-0
Colchester U	2-1	0-2	1-1	2-1	1-1	3-3	—	2-2	5-1	3-2
Dagenham & R	1-2	4-1	0-1	0-3	3-0	2-1	1-0	—	1-1	1-1
Exeter C	2-0	2-4	1-2	2-2	2-1	1-0	2-2	2-1	—	1-2
Hartlepool U	2-2	3-0	3-1	2-2	0-4	2-1	1-0	0-1	2-3	—
Huddersfield T	2-2	4-4	2-1	0-1	2-0	3-1	0-0	2-1	0-1	0-1
Leyton Orient	2-2	1-0	0-0	4-1	0-0	1-3	4-2	1-1	3-0	1-0
Milton Keynes D	2-0	1-1	1-0	2-0	3-2	2-0	1-1	2-0	1-0	1-0
Notts Co	0-2	1-1	1-1	0-1	0-1	1-0	2-0	1-0	0-2	3-0
Oldham Ath	2-1	2-1	0-1	1-1	0-1	0-0	0-0	1-1	3-3	4-0
Peterborough U	3-3	2-1	0-3	3-0	6-0	1-5	1-1	5-0	3-0	4-0
Plymouth Arg	1-2	1-2	0-2	3-1	1-1	2-2	2-1	2-1	2-0	0-1
Rochdale	0-0	0-1	2-2	3-1	2-3	2-0	1-2	3-2	0-1	0-0
Sheffield W	1-1	1-3	1-0	6-2	0-1	2-2	2-1	2-0	1-2	2-0
Southampton	2-0	0-2	0-0	1-0	1-0	2-0	0-0	4-0	4-0	2-0
Swindon T	1-2	1-1	1-2	2-1	0-1	0-3	2-1	1-1	0-0	1-1
Tranmere R	0-3	0-3	1-1	0-1	2-1	1-1	1-0	2-0	4-0	0-1
Walsall	0-1	3-2	1-3	6-1	2-1	2-0	0-1	1-0	2-1	5-2
Yeovil T	2-2	2-0	0-1	0-1	1-0	0-1	4-2	1-3	1-3	0-2

2010–2011 RESULTS

Huddersfield T	Leyton Orient	Milton Keynes D	Notts Co	Oldham Ath	Peterborough U	Plymouth Arg	Rochdale	Sheffield W	Southampton	Swindon T	Tranmere R	Walsall	Yeovil T
1-1	1-1	3-2	3-3	3-0	5-1	3-0	1-2	0-0	1-3	3-2	1-2	3-0	2-0
0-1	2-1	0-2	1-1	1-3	2-1	2-0	1-3	1-0	0-3	0-1	2-1	1-2	1-2
2-3	5-0	2-0	1-0	2-1	3-1	4-0	2-2	2-0	1-2	2-1	2-0	2-1	2-0
0-1	0-3	1-2	2-1	1-0	2-2	2-3	2-1	1-1	0-4	3-1	0-1	2-2	2-1
2-2	0-1	4-1	1-0	2-2	0-1	1-1	1-1	0-1	3-2	0-0	2-0	1-3	0-2
0-1	3-1	1-0	1-0	1-1	3-2	2-0	3-1	1-0	1-1	2-4	1-1	0-1	3-2
0-3	3-2	1-3	2-1	1-0	2-1	1-1	1-0	1-1	0-2	2-1	3-1	2-0	0-0
1-1	2-0	0-1	3-1	0-1	0-2	0-1	0-1	1-1	1-3	2-1	2-2	1-1	2-1
1-4	2-1	1-1	3-1	2-0	2-2	1-0	1-0	5-1	1-2	1-0	1-1	2-1	2-3
0-1	0-1	0-1	1-1	4-2	2-0	2-0	0-2	0-5	0-0	2-2	1-1	2-1	3-1
—	2-2	4-1	3-0	0-0	1-1	3-2	2-1	1-0	2-0	0-0	0-0	1-0	4-2
1-2	—	2-2	2-0	1-0	2-1	2-0	2-1	4-0	0-2	3-0	0-3	0-0	1-5
1-3	2-3	—	2-1	0-0	1-0	1-3	1-1	1-4	2-0	2-1	2-0	1-1	3-2
0-3	3-2	2-0	—	0-2	0-1	2-0	1-2	0-2	1-3	1-0	0-1	1-1	4-0
1-0	1-1	1-2	3-0	—	0-5	4-2	1-2	2-3	0-6	2-0	0-0	1-1	0-0
4-2	2-2	2-1	2-3	5-2	—	2-1	2-1	5-3	4-4	5-4	2-1	4-1	2-2
2-1	1-4	1-0	1-1	0-2	0-3	—	0-1	3-2	1-3	1-0	1-3	2-0	0-0
3-0	1-1	1-4	1-0	1-1	2-2	1-1	—	2-1	2-0	3-3	3-2	3-2	0-1
0-2	1-0	2-2	0-1	0-0	1-4	2-4	2-0	—	0-1	3-1	4-0	3-0	2-2
4-1	1-1	3-2	0-0	2-1	4-1	0-1	0-2	2-0	—	4-1	2-0	3-1	3-0
1-0	2-2	0-1	1-2	0-2	1-1	2-3	1-1	2-1	1-0	—	0-0	0-0	0-1
0-2	1-2	4-2	0-1	1-2	1-0	1-0	1-1	3-0	2-0	0-2	—	3-3	0-1
2-4	0-2	1-2	0-3	1-1	1-3	2-1	0-0	1-1	1-0	1-2	1-4	—	0-1
1-1	2-1	1-0	2-1	1-1	0-2	1-0	0-1	0-2	1-1	3-3	3-1	1-1	—

NPOWER LEAGUE 2

HOME TEAM	Accrington S	Aldershot T	Barnet	Bradford C	Burton Alb	Bury	Cheltenham T	Chesterfield	Crewe Alex	Gillingham
Accrington S	—	0-0	3-1	3-0	3-1	1-0	2-4	2-2	3-2	7-4
Aldershot T	1-1	—	1-0	1-0	1-2	1-3	0-2	0-2	3-2	1-1
Barnet	2-0	1-2	—	0-2	0-0	1-1	3-1	2-2	2-1	1-2
Bradford C	1-1	2-1	1-3	—	1-1	1-0	3-1	0-1	1-5	1-0
Burton Alb	1-1	1-2	1-4	3-0	—	1-3	2-0	1-0	1-1	1-1
Bury	3-0	1-1	2-0	0-1	1-0	—	2-3	1-1	3-1	5-4
Cheltenham T	1-2	1-2	1-1	4-0	2-1	0-2	—	0-3	3-2	1-2
Chesterfield	5-2	2-2	2-1	2-2	1-2	2-3	3-0	—	5-5	3-1
Crewe Alex	0-0	3-1	7-0	2-1	4-1	3-0	8-1	2-0	—	1-1
Gillingham	3-1	2-1	2-4	2-0	1-0	1-1	1-1	0-2	1-3	—
Hereford U	1-1	2-2	1-2	1-1	0-0	0-3	1-1	3-0	1-0	0-0
Lincoln C	0-0	0-3	1-0	1-2	0-0	0-5	0-2	0-2	1-1	0-4
Macclesfield T	2-2	2-0	1-1	0-1	2-1	2-4	0-2	1-1	1-0	2-4
Morecambe	1-2	1-1	2-2	0-1	2-1	1-4	1-1	1-1	1-2	1-1
Northampton T	0-0	1-1	0-0	2-0	2-3	2-4	1-1	1-2	6-2	2-1
Oxford U	0-0	0-1	2-1	2-1	3-0	1-2	1-1	0-0	2-1	0-1
Port Vale	2-0	1-0	0-0	2-1	2-1	0-0	0-1	1-1	2-1	0-0
Rotherham U	2-0	1-0	0-0	0-0	3-3	0-0	6-4	1-0	3-1	0-1
Shrewsbury T	0-0	1-1	2-1	3-1	3-0	0-3	1-1	0-0	0-1	0-0
Southend U	1-1	0-0	2-1	4-0	1-1	1-1	1-2	2-3	0-2	2-2
Stevenage	2-2	2-2	4-2	2-1	2-1	3-3	4-0	0-0	1-1	2-2
Stockport Co	2-2	2-2	2-1	1-1	0-0	2-1	1-1	1-1	3-3	1-5
Torquay U	0-0	0-1	1-1	2-0	1-0	3-4	2-1	0-0	2-1	1-1
Wycombe W	1-2	2-2	4-2	1-0	4-1	1-0	2-1	1-2	2-0	1-0

2010–2011 RESULTS

Hereford U	Lincoln C	Macclesfield T	Morecambe	Northampton T	Oxford U	Port Vale	Rotherham U	Shrewsbury T	Southend U	Stevenage	Stockport Co	Torquay U	Wycombe W
4-0	3-0	3-0	1-1	3-1	0-0	3-0	2-3	1-3	3-1	1-0	3-0	1-0	1-1
1-2	2-2	0-0	2-1	1-1	1-2	1-2	2-2	3-0	1-0	1-1	1-0	1-0	0-0
2-0	4-2	1-0	1-2	4-1	2-2	1-0	1-4	1-1	0-2	0-3	1-3	0-3	0-1
1-0	1-2	0-1	0-1	1-1	5-0	0-2	2-1	1-2	0-2	1-0	3-2	0-3	1-0
3-0	3-1	3-2	3-2	1-1	0-0	0-0	2-4	0-0	3-1	0-2	2-1	3-3	1-2
1-1	1-0	2-2	1-0	1-1	3-0	0-1	1-1	1-0	1-0	3-0	0-1	1-2	1-3
0-3	1-2	0-1	1-1	1-0	1-1	0-0	1-1	0-1	0-2	1-0	2-1	2-2	1-2
4-0	2-1	2-1	0-2	2-1	1-2	2-0	5-0	4-3	2-1	1-0	4-1	1-0	4-1
0-1	1-1	1-1	2-1	2-0	1-1	2-1	0-1	1-2	1-0	0-1	2-0	3-3	3-0
0-0	0-1	2-4	1-1	1-0	0-0	3-0	3-1	2-0	0-0	1-0	2-1	1-1	0-2
—	0-1	2-2	2-1	1-1	0-2	1-1	0-1	0-2	1-3	1-4	3-0	2-2	0-0
3-1	—	2-1	2-0	0-2	3-1	1-0	0-6	1-5	2-1	0-1	0-0	0-2	1-2
1-1	1-1	—	2-0	2-0	3-2	0-3	0-2	0-1	0-0	0-4	0-2	3-3	0-1
1-1	1-2	1-2	—	1-2	0-3	1-0	0-0	1-0	2-1	0-0	5-0	2-1	0-3
3-4	2-1	0-1	3-3	—	2-1	0-0	2-2	2-3	2-1	2-0	2-0	2-2	1-1
0-2	2-1	2-1	4-0	3-1	—	2-1	2-1	3-1	0-2	1-2	0-1	0-2	2-2
1-1	2-1	2-1	7-2	1-1	1-2	—	1-0	1-0	1-1	1-3	1-2	1-2	2-1
0-0	2-1	1-1	0-1	2-2	2-1	5-0	—	1-3	1-2	1-1	4-0	3-1	3-4
4-0	2-0	4-1	1-3	3-1	3-0	2-2	1-0	—	1-1	1-0	2-0	1-1	1-1
4-0	1-0	4-1	2-3	1-1	2-1	1-3	1-0	0-2	—	1-0	1-1	2-1	3-2
0-1	2-1	2-2	2-0	0-1	0-0	1-0	3-0	1-1	1-1	—	3-1	0-0	0-2
0-5	3-4	1-4	0-2	2-2	2-1	0-5	3-3	0-4	2-1	2-2	—	1-1	0-0
1-3	2-0	1-3	3-1	3-0	3-4	0-0	1-1	5-0	1-1	2-0	2-0	—	0-0
2-1	2-2	1-2	2-0	2-2	0-0	1-1	1-0	2-2	3-1	0-1	2-0	1-3	—

ACCRINGTON STANLEY

FL CHAMPIONSHIP 2

Player	Ht	Wt	Birthplace	D.O.B.	Source
Barnett Charlie (M)	5 7	11 07	Liverpool	19 9 88	Tranmere R
Burton Alan (M)	6 0	11 00	Blackpool	22 2 91	Scholar
Cisak Aleksander (G)	6 3	14 11	Krakow	19 5 89	Leicester C
Craney Ian (M)	5 10	12 00	Liverpool	21 7 82	Huddersfield T
Dunbavin Ian (G)	6 2	10 10	Knowsley	27 5 80	Scarborough
Edwards Phil (D)	5 8	11 03	Kirkby	8 11 85	Wigan Ath
Gornell Terence (F)	5 11	12 04	Liverpool	16 12 89	Tranmere R
Hessey Sean (D)	5 11	12 08	Whiston	19 9 78	Macclesfield T
Jacobson Joe (D)	5 11	12 06	Cardiff	17 11 86	Oldham Ath
Joyce Luke (M)	5 11	12 03	Bolton	9 7 87	Carlisle U
Lindfield Craig (F)	6 0	10 05	Wirral	7 9 88	Macclesfield T
McConville Sean (F)	5 11	11 09	Burscough	6 3 89	Skelmersdale U
Murphy Peter (M)	6 0	11 10	Liverpool	13 2 90	Scholar
Procter Andy (M)	6 0	12 04	Lancashire	13 3 83	Gt Harwood T
Putterill Ray (M)	5 8	12 03	Liverpool	2 3 89	Liverpool
Ryan James (M)	5 8	11 08	Maghull	6 9 88	Liverpool
Winnard Dean (D)	5 9	10 04	Wigan	20 8 89	Blackburn R

League Appearances: Barnett, C. 31(9); Bateson, J. 12; Boulding, R. 6(9); Burton, A. 1; Cisak, A. 21; Craney, I. 22; Dunbavin, I. 25; Edwards, P. 44; Gornell, T. 40; Hessey, S. 40(1); Jacobson, J. 26; Joyce, L. 24(3); Lindfield, C. 2(14); Long, K. 11(4); McConville, S. 37(6); Murphy, P. 5(8); Owens, A. (3); Parkinson, A. 10(8); Procter, A. 42(1); Putterill, R. 11(13); Richardson, L. 3(8); Ryan, J. 45(1); Smyth, T. 3(1); Turner, C. (13); Winnard, D. 45.
Goals – League (73): Edwards 13 (11 pens), Gornell 13, McConville 13, Ryan 9, Craney 7, Procter 6, Barnett 2, Boulding 2, Jacobson 2, Parkinson 2, Hessey 1, Joyce 1, Richardson 1, Winnard 1.
Carling Cup (4): Hessey 1, Lindfield 1, Putterill 1, Turner 1.
FA Cup (3): Putterill 2, Ryan 1.
J Paint Trophy (1): Putterill 1.
Play-Offs (0).
Ground: The Fraser Eagle Stadium, Livingstone Road, Accrington, Lancashire BB5 5BX. Telephone: (0871) 434 1968.
Record Attendance: 13,181 v Hull C, Division 3 (N), 28 September 1948 (at Peel Park). 4,368 v Colchester U, FA Cup 1st rd, 3 January 2004 (at Fraser Eagle Stadium – Crown Inn).
Capacity: 5,057.
Manager: John Coleman.
Secretary: Hannah Bailey.
Most League Goals: 96, Division 3 (N), 1954–55.
Highest League Scorer in Season: George Stewart, 35, Division 3 (N), 1955–56; George Hudson, 35, Division 4, 1960–61.
Most League Goals in Total Aggregate: George Stewart, 136, 1954–58.
Most Capped Player: Romuald Boco, 19 (42), Benin.
Most League Appearances: Jim Armstrong, 260, 1927–34.
Honours: None.
Colours: All red.

AFC WIMBLEDON

FL CHAMPIONSHIP 2

Blackman Andre (D)	5 11	11 05	Lambeth	10 11 90	Bristol C
Brown Seb (G)	6 0	12 13	Sutton	24 11 89	Brentford
Gregory Steven (M)	6 1	12 08	Aylesbury	19 3 87	Hayes & Yeading U
Harris Ed (D)	6 1	13 05	Roehampton	3 11 90	QPR

Hatton Sam (M)	5 11	11 02	St Albans	7	2 88	Stevenage
Jackson Ryan (D)			Streatham	31	7 90	Youth
Johnson Brett (D)	6 1	13 01	Hammersmith	15	8 85	Brentford
Jolley Christian (M)			Aldershot	12	5 88	Kingstonian
Jones Reece (M)	6 1	11 09	London	22	7 92	Fulham
Kedwell Danny (F)	5 11	12 13	Gillingham	22	10 85	Grays Ath
Main Jon (F)	5 10	12 02	Greenwich	7	3 81	Tonbridge Angels
Minshull Lee (M)	6 2	14 07	Chatham	11	11 85	Tonbridge Angels
Moore Luke (F)	5 11	11 07	Gravesend	27	4 88	Ebbsfleet U
Moore Sammy (M)	5 8	10 00	Deal	7	9 87	Dover Ath
Nwokeji Mark (F)	5 11	11 05	London	30	1 82	Dagenham & R
Stuart Jamie (D)	5 10	11 00	Southwark	15	10 76	Rushden & D
Wellard Ricky (M)	5 11	9 13	Hammersmith	9	5 88	Ashford T
Yakubu Ismail (D)	5 11	11 13	Kano	8	4 85	Barnet
Yussuf Rashid (M)	6 1	12 06	Poplar	23	9 89	Gillingham

League Appearances: Blackman, 12(1); Broughton, 3(5); Brown, 45; Bush, 12(1); Franks, 15(9); Gregory, 41(1); Gwillim, 20; Harris, 15(1); Hatton, 40; Hudson, 11(3); Jackson, 23(14); Johnson, 21(2); Jolley, 22(10); Jones, 1(2); Kedwell, 43(2); Kiernan, 1(1); Main, 7(9); Minshull, 9(10); Mohamed, 6(1); Moore, S. 27(1); Moore, L. 19(14); Mulley, 19(3); Nwokeji, 6(12); Stuart, 18(3); Turner, 1; Wellard, 22(3); Yakubu, 26(1); Yussuff, 21(17).

Goals – League (83): Kedwell 23 (5 pens), Jolley 12, Moore L 7 (1 pen), Yussuff 6, Hatton 5 (1 pen), Moore S 5, Mulley 5, Johnson 4, Broughton 2, Franks 2, Jackson 2, Minshull 2, Wellard 2, Yakubu 2, Hudson 1, Mohamed 1, Nwokeji 1, Stuart 1.

FA Cup (4): Moore S 2, Harris 1, Nwokeji 1.

Ground: The Cherry Red Records Fans' Stadium, Kingsmeadow, Jack Goodchild Way, 422a Kingston Road, Kingston-Upon-Thames, Surrey KT1 3PB. Telephone: (0208) 547 3528.

Record Attendance: 4,722 (2009 v St Albans City, Blue Square Premier, 25 April 2009).

Capacity: 5,194.

Manager: Terry Brown.

Secretary: David Charles.

Inherited Records

Most League Goals: 97, Division 3, 1983–84.

Highest League Scorer in Season: Alan Cork, 29, 1983–84.

Most League Goals in Total Aggregate: Alan Cork, 145, 1977–92.

Most Capped Player: Kenny Cunningham, 40 (72), Republic of Ireland. .

Most League Appearances: Alan Cork, 430, 1977–92.

Honours: None.

Colours: All blue with gold shirt trimmings.

ALDERSHOT TOWN   FL CHAMPIONSHIP 2

Breimyr Henrik (M)	6 1	12 02	Stavanger	20	7 93	Reading
Connolly Reece (F)	6 0	11 09	Frimley	22	1 92	Scholar
Guttridge Luke (M)	5 6	9 07	Barnstaple	27	3 82	Northampton T
Herd Ben (D)	5 9	10 12	Welwyn	21	6 85	Shrewsbury T
Hylton Danny (F)	6 0	11 03	London	25	2 89	Youth
Jones Darren (D)	6 0	14 12	Newport	28	8 83	Hereford U
McGlashan Jermain (M)	5 7	10 00	Croydon	14	4 88	Ashford T
Mekki Adam (M)	5 9	11 00	Chester	24	6 92	Scholar
Morris Aaron (D)	6 1	12 05	Cardiff	30	12 89	Cardiff C
Rodman Alex (F)	6 2	12 08	Sutton Coldfield	15	12 87	Tamworth
Straker Anthony (D)	5 9	11 11	Ealing	23	9 88	Crystal Palace
Vincenti Peter (F)	6 2	11 13	Jersey	7	7 86	Stevenage
Young Jamie (G)	5 11	13 00	Brisbane	25	8 85	Wycombe W

League Appearances: Bergqvist, D. (1); Charles, A. 41; Connolly, R. (5); Fortune, C. 3(4); Grand, S. 6; Guttridge, L. 36(5); Halls, J. 16(7); Harding, B. 29(6); Henderson, L. 1; Herd, B. 43; Hylton, D. 24(9); Jackson, M. 4(5); Jarrett, A. 2(2); Jones, D. 42(1); Little, G. 13(1); McGlashan, J. 23(15); Medley, L. (4); Mekki, A. 2(6); Morgan, M. 19; Morris, A. 13(9); Ngo Baheng, W. (3); Panther, M. 20(3); Randall, J. (1); Rodman, A. 9(5); Sills, T. 8(11); Small, W. 18(11); Spencer, D. 9(9); Straker, A. 35(3); Vincent, J. 22(1); Vincenti, P. 22(1); Young, J. 46.

Goals – League (54): Guttridge 8, Vincenti 6, Charles 5 (1 pen), Hylton 5 (2 pens), Morgan 5, Rodman 5, Small 5, Spencer 4, Harding 2, Sills 2, Straker 2, Halls 1, Herd 1, Jones 1, Little 1, McGlashan 1.

Carling Cup (0).

FA Cup (2): Small 2.

J Paint Trophy (2): Hylton 1, Spencer 1.

Ground: The EBB Stadium at the Recreation Ground, High Street, Aldershot GU11 1TW. Telephone: 01252 320211.

Record Attendance: 19,138 v Carlisle U, FA Cup 4th rd (replay), 28 January 1970.

Capacity: 7,100.

Manager: Dean Holdsworth.

Secretary: Bob Green.

Most League Goals: 83, Division 4, 1963–64.

Highest League Scorer in Season: John Dungworth, 26, Division 4, 1978–79.

Most League Goals in Total Aggregate: Jack Howarth, 171, 1965–71 and 1972–77.

Most Capped Player: Anthony Straker, 5, Grenada.

Most League Appearances: Murray Brodie, 461, 1970–83.

Honours – Blue Square Premier League: Champions 2007–08. **Setanta Shield:** Winners 2008.

Colours: All red shirts with blue sleeves, red shorts with blue and white trim, red stockings with blue and white trim.

ARSENAL   FA PREMIERSHIP

Afobe Benik (F)	5 10	11 00	Leyton	12	2 93	Scholar
Almunia Manuel (G)	6 3	13 00	Pamplona	19	5 77	Celta Vigo
Aneke Chuks (M)	6 3	13 01	Newham	3	7 93	Scholar
Angha Martin (D)			Switzerland	22	1 94	Zurich
Arshavin Andrei (F)	5 8	9 11	St Petersburg	29	5 81	Zenit
Bartley Kyle (D)	5 11	11 00	Manchester	22	5 91	Scholar
Bendtner Nicklas (F)	6 2	13 00	Copenhagen	16	1 88	Scholar
Boateng Daniel (D)			London	2	9 92	Scholar
Botelho Pedro (D)	6 2	12 00	Salvador	14 12 89		Salamanca
Chamakh Maroune (F)	6 1	11 00	Tonnens	10	1 84	Bordeaux
Clichy Gael (D)	5 9	10 04	Toulouse	26	7 85	Cannes
Coquelin Francis (M)	5 10	11 08	Laval	13	5 91	Laval
Denilson (M)	5 10	11 00	Sao Paulo	16	2 88	Sao Paulo
Diaby Vassirki (M)	6 2	12 04	Paris	11	5 86	Auxerre
Djourou Johan (D)	6 3	13 01	Ivory Coast	18	1 87	Scholar
Eastmond Craig (D)	5 8	11 11	Wandsworth	9 12 90		Scholar
Ebecilio Kyle (M)			Holland	17	2 94	Feyenoord
Eboue Emmanuel (D)	5 10	10 03	Abidjan	4	6 83	Beveren
Edge Jamie (M)			Cheltenham	9	9 93	Scholar
Emmanuel-Thomas Jay (M)	5 9	11 05	Forest Gate	27 12 90		Scholar
Fabianski Lukasz (G)	6 3	13 01	Costrzyn nad Odra	18	4 85	Legia
Fabregas Francesc (M)	5 11	11 01	Vilessoc de Mar	4	5 87	Barcelona
Freeman Luke (F)	6 1	10 00	London	22	3 92	Gillingham
Frimpong Emanuel (M)	5 11	10 07	Ghana	10	1 92	Scholar
Galindo Samuel (M)	6 3	12 00	Santa Cruz	18	4 92	Real America

22

Player	Ht	Wt	Birthplace	D.O.B.	Previous Club
Gibbs Kieran (M)	5 10	10 02	Lambeth	26 9 89	Scholar
Hajrovic Sead (D)			Brugg	4 6 93	Scholar
Henderson Conor (M)	6 1	11 13	Sidcup	8 9 91	Scholar
Hoyte Gavin (D)	5 11	11 00	Waltham Forest	6 6 90	Scholar
Jenkinson Carl (D)	6 1	12 02	Buckhurst Hill	8 2 92	Charlton Ath
Koscielny Laurent (D)	6 1	11 11	Tulle	10 9 85	Lorient
Lansbury Henri (M)	6 0	13 04	Enfield	12 10 90	Scholar
Lehmann Jens (G)	6 4	13 05	Essen	10 11 69	Stuttgart
Mannone Vito (G)	6 0	11 08	Desio	2 3 88	Atalanta
Martinez Damian (G)	6 3	12 00	Argentina	2 9 92	Independiente
McDermott Sean (G)			Kristiansand	30 5 93	Scholar
Miquel Ignasi (D)	6 4	13 05	Barcelona	28 9 92	Scholar
Miyaichi Ryo (F)	6 0	11 02	Okazaki	14 12 92	Chukyodai
Monteiro Elton (D)			Switzerland	22 2 94	Scholar
Murphy Rhys (F)	6 1	11 13	Shoreham	6 11 90	Scholar
Nasri Samir (M)	5 9	11 11	Marseille	26 6 87	Marseille
Ozyakup Oguzhan (M)	5 10	11 00	Zaandam	23 9 92	AZ
Ramsey Aaron (M)	5 9	10 07	Caerphilly	26 12 90	Cardiff C
Rosicky Tomas (M)	5 11	11 06	Prague	4 10 80	Borussia Dortmund
Sagna Bakari (D)	5 10	11 05	Sens	14 2 83	Auxerre
Shea James (G)	5 11	12 00	Islington	16 6 91	Scholar
Silva Wellington (M)	5 6	10 00	Rio de Janeiro	6 1 93	Fluminense
Song Bilong Alexandre (M)	6 4	12 07	Douala	9 9 87	Bastia
Squillaci Sebastien (D)	6 0	11 13	Toulon	11 8 80	Sevilla
Sunu Gilles (F)	5 11	11 00	Chateauroux	30 3 91	Scholar
Szczesny Wojciech (F)	5 10	11 11	Warsaw	18 4 90	Scholar
Traore Armand (D)	6 1	12 12	Paris	8 10 89	Monaco
Van Persie Robin (F)	6 0	11 00	Rotterdam	6 8 83	Feyenoord
Vela Carlos (F)	5 9	10 05	Mexico	1 3 89	Celta Vigo
Vermaelen Thomas (D)	6 0	11 11	Kapellen	14 11 85	Ajax
Walcott Theo (F)	5 9	11 01	Compton	16 3 89	Southampton
Watt Sanchez (M)	5 11	12 00	London	14 2 91	Scholar
Wilshere Jack (M)	5 7	11 03	Stevenage	1 1 92	Scholar
Yennaris Nicholas (D)			Leytonstone	23 5 93	Scholar

League Appearances: Almunia, M. 8; Arshavin, A. 25(12); Bendtner, N. 3(14); Chamakh, M. 18(11); Clichy, G. 33; Denilson, 6(10); Diaby, V. 13(3); Djourou, J. 20(2); Eboue, E. 8(5); Emmanuel-Thomas, J. (1); Fabianski, L. 14; Fabregas, F. 22(3); Gibbs, K. 4(3); Koscielny, L. 30; Lehmann, J. 1; Nasri, S. 28(2); Ramsey, A. 5(2); Rosicky, T. 8(13); Sagna, B. 33; Song Billong, A. 30(1); Squillaci, S. 20(2); Szczesny, W. 15; Van Persie, R. 19(6); Vela, C. (4); Vermaelen, T. 5; Walcott, T. 19(9); Wilshere, J. 31(4).

Goals – League (72): Van Persie 18 (2 pens), Nasri 10 (1 pen), Walcott 9, Chamakh 7, Arshavin 6 (1 pen), Song Billong 4, Fabregas 3, Bendtner 2, Diaby 2, Koscielny 2, Djourou 1, Eboue 1, Ramsey 1, Sagna 1, Squillaci 1, Vela 1, Wilshere 1, own goals 2.

Carling Cup (14): Bendtner 3, Nasri 2 (2 pens), Walcott 2, Arshavin 1, Fabregas 1, Koscielny 1, Lansbury 1, Van Persie 1, own goals 2.

FA Cup (12): Bendtner 3 (1 pen), Fabregas 2 (2 pens), Chamakh 1, Clichy 1, Nasri 1, Rosicky 1, Sagna 1, Van Persie 1, own goals 2.

Champions League (21): Arshavin 3, Chamakh 3, Fabregas 3 (2 pens), Nasri 2, Van Persie 2 (1 pen), Vela 2, Walcott 2, Song Billong 1, Squillaci 1, Wilshere 1, own goal 1.

Ground: Emirates Stadium, Highbury House, 75 Drayton Park, Islington, London N5 1BU. Telephone: (0207) 619 5003.

Record Attendance: 73,295 v Sunderland, Div 1, 9 March 1935 (at Highbury). 73,707 v RC Lens, UEFA Champions League, 25 November 1998 (at Wembley). 60,162 v Manchester U, FA Premier League, 3 November 2007 (at Emirates).

Capacity: 60,361.

Manager: Arsène Wenger.
Secretary: David Miles.
Most League Goals: 127, Division 1, 1930–31.
Highest League Scorer in Season: Ted Drake, 42, 1934–35.
Most League Goals in Total Aggregate: Thierry Henry, 174, 1999–2007.
Most Capped Player: Thierry Henry, 81 (123), France.
Most League Appearances: David O'Leary, 558, 1975–93.
Honours – FA Premier League: Champions – 1997–98, 2001–02, 2003–04. **Football League:** Division 1 Champions – 1930–31, 1932–33, 1933–34, 1934–35, 1937–38, 1947–48, 1952–53, 1970–71, 1988–89, 1990–91. **FA Cup:** Winners – 1929–30, 1935–36, 1949–50, 1970–71, 1978–79, 1992–93, 1997–98, 2001–02, 2002–03, 2004–05. **Football League Cup:** Winners – 1986–87, 1992–93. **European Competitions: European Cup-Winners' Cup:** Winners – 1993–94. **Fairs Cup:** Winners – 1969–70.
Colours: Red shirts with white trim, white shorts, white stockings with red tops.

ASTON VILLA   FA PREMIERSHIP

Agbonlahor Gabriel (F)	5 11	12 05	Birmingham	13 10 86	Scholar
Albrighton Marc (M)	6 2	12 06	Sutton Coldfield	18 11 89	Scholar
Baker Nathan (D)	6 2	11 11	Worcester	23 4 91	Scholar
Bannan Barry (D)	5 10	10 08	Glasgow	1 12 89	Scholar
Bent Darren (F)	5 11	12 07	Wandsworth	6 2 84	Sunderland
Beye Habib (D)	6 0	12 06	Paris	19 10 77	Newcastle U
Clark Ciaran (D)	6 2	12 00	Harrow	26 9 89	Scholar
Collins James M (D)	6 2	14 05	Newport	23 8 83	West Ham U
Cuellar Carlos (D)	6 3	13 03	Madrid	23 8 81	Rangers
Delfouneso Nathan (F)	6 1	12 04	Birmingham	2 2 91	Scholar
Delph Fabian (D)	5 8	11 00	Bradford	5 5 91	Leeds U
Devine Daniel (M)			Dublin	8 5 93	Scholar
Downing Stewart (M)	5 11	10 04	Middlesbrough	22 7 84	Middlesbrough
Drennan Michael (F)			Kilkenny	1 1 94	Scholar
Dunne Richard (D)	6 2	15 10	Dublin	21 9 79	Manchester C
Friedel Brad (G)	6 3	14 00	Lakewood	18 5 71	Blackburn R
Gardner Gary (M)			Solihull	29 6 92	Scholar
Guzan Brad (G)	6 4	14 11	Home Glen	9 9 84	Chivas USA
Herd Chris (M)	5 9	11 04	Melbourne	4 4 89	Scholar
Heskey Emile (F)	6 2	13 12	Leicester	11 1 78	Wigan Ath
Hogg Jonathan (M)	5 7	10 05	Middlesbrough	6 12 88	Scholar
Ireland Stephen (F)	5 8	10 07	Cork	22 8 86	Manchester C
Johnson Daniel (M)	5 8	10 07	Kingston (Jam)	8 10 92	Scholar
Lichaj Eric (M)	5 11	12 07	Denvers Grove	17 11 88	Chicago Magic
Lowry Shane (D)	6 1	13 01	Perth	12 6 89	Scholar
Makoun Jean (M)	5 8	10 12	Yaounde	29 5 83	Lyon
Marshall Andrew (G)	6 2	13 07	Bury St Edmunds	14 4 75	Coventry C
Parish Elliot (G)	6 2	13 00	Northampton	20 5 90	Scholar
Petrov Stilian (M)	5 11	13 05	Montana	5 7 79	Celtic
Serrano Juan (M)			Spain	17 1 94	Espanyol
Siegrist Benjamin (G)	6 4	13 05	Basle	31 1 92	Scholar
Stieber Andras (M)			Sarvar	8 10 91	Scholar
Warnock Stephen (D)	5 7	11 09	Ormskirk	12 12 81	Blackburn R
Weimann Andreas (F)	6 2	11 13	Vienna	5 8 91	Scholar
Williams Derrick (D)			Germany	17 1 93	Scholar
Young Ashley (F)	5 6	9 06	Stevenage	9 7 85	Watford
Young Luke (D)	6 0	12 04	Harlow	19 7 79	Middlesbrough

League Appearances: Agbonlahor, G. 17(9); Albrighton, M. 20(9); Baker, N. 4; Bannan, B. 7(5); Bent, D. 16; Beye, H. 2(1); Bradley, M. (3); Carew, J. 6(4); Clark, C. 16(3);

Collins, James M 31(1); Cuellar, C. 10(2); Delfouneso, N. 2(9); Delph, F. 4(3); Downing,
S. 38; Dunne, R. 32; Friedel, B. 38; Herd, C. 1(5); Heskey, E. 11(8); Hogg, J. 5; Ireland, S.
6(4); Lichaj, E. 3(2); Makoun, J. 7; Milner, J. 1; Petrov, S. 23(4); Pires, R. 2(7); Reo-
Coker, N. 24(6); Sidwell, S. 1(3); Walker, K. 15; Warnock, S. 19; Weimann, A. (1); Young,
A. 34; Young, L. 23.

Goals – League (48): Bent 9, Downing 7, Young A 7 (4 pens), Albrighton 5, Agbonlahor 3, Clark 3, Collins, James M 3, Heskey 3, Delfouneso 1, Milner 1, Petrov 1, Walker
1, Young L 1, own goals 3.

Carling Cup (6): Heskey 2, Young A 2, Agbonlahor 1, Downing 1.

FA Cup (6): Albrighton 1, Clark 1, Delfouneso 1, Petkov 1, Pires 1, Walker 1.

Europa League (3): Agbonlahor 1, Bannan 1, Heskey 1.

Ground: Villa Park, Birmingham B6 6HE. Telephone: (0121) 327 2299.

Record Attendance: 76,588 v Derby Co, FA Cup 6th rd, 2 March 1946.

Capacity: 42,582.

Manager: Alex McLeish.

Secretary: Sharon Barnhurst.

Most League Goals: 128, Division 1, 1930–31.

Highest League Scorer in Season: 'Pongo' Waring, 49, Division 1, 1930–31.

Most League Goals in Total Aggregate: Harry Hampton, 215, 1904–15.

Most Capped Player: Steve Staunton 64 (102), Republic of Ireland.

Most League Appearances: Charlie Aitken, 561, 1961–76.

Honours – Football League: Division 1 Champions – 1893–94, 1895–96, 1896–97, 1898–99,
1899–1900, 1909–10, 1980–81. Division 2 Champions – 1937–38, 1959–60. Division 3
Champions – 1971–72. **FA Cup:** Winners – 1887, 1895, 1897, 1905, 1913, 1920, 1957. **Football
League Cup:** Winners – 1961, 1975, 1977, 1994, 1996. **European Competitions: European Cup:**
Winners – 1981–82. **European Super Cup:** Winners – 1982–83. **Intertoto Cup:** Winners – 2001,
2008.

Colours: Claret body, blue sleeve shirts, white shorts, sky blue stockings.

BARNET   FL CHAMPIONSHIP 2

Cox Sam (D)	5 7	10 00	Edgware	10 10 90	Tottenham H
Dennehy Darren (D)	6 3	11 11	Tralee	21 9 88	Cardiff C
Devera Joe (D)	6 2	12 00	Southgate	6 2 87	Scholar
Fraser Tom (M)	5 10	11 00	Brighton	5 12 87	Port Vale
Holmes Ricky (F)	6 2	11 11	Southend	19 6 87	Chelmsford C
Kamdjo Clovis (D)	5 11	12 02	Cameroon	15 12 90	Reading
Leach Daniel (D)	6 3	12 10	Redcliffe	5 1 86	Portland T
Marshall Mark (M)	5 7	10 07	Manchester (Jam)	9 5 86	Swindon T
McLeod Izale (F)	6 1	11 02	Birmingham	15 10 84	Charlton Ath
O'Brien Liam (G)	6 1	12 06	Brent	30 11 91	Portsmouth
Parkes Jordan (D)	6 0	12 00	Hemel Hempstead	26 7 89	Watford
Taylor Charlie (F)	6 2	11 13	London	1 12 85	Sutton U
Uddin Anwar (D)	5 11	11 10	Whitechapel	1 11 81	Dagenham & R

League Appearances: Adjeman-Pamboe, K. (1); Basey, G. 11; Byrne, M. 26(2); Cole, J.
31; Coulton, T. 1; Cox, S. 5(5); Deering, S. 14(2); Dennehy, D. 4(1); Devera, J. 43; Dob-
son, C. (1); Dunleavy, J. 1(2); Francomb, G. 13; Fraser, T. 10(5); Gallen, K. 6(1); Holmes,
R. 14(11); Hughes, M. 31(2); Jarvis, R. 12(10); Kabba, S. 23; Kamdjo, C. 28(4); Kelly, D.
(3); Leach, D. 14; Marshall, M. 45(1); McLeod, I. 25(4); Midson, J. 3(2); O'Brien, L. 7(1);
Parkes, J. 37(3); Parsons, M. 7(1); Poole, G. 6(4); Pulis, A. 4; Southam, G. 31(2); Stimson,
C. (6); Stirling, J. 5(1); Taylor, C. 2(16); Uddin, A. 28(2); Vilhete, M. 6(14); Walker, S. 7;
Walsh, P. 6(3).

Goals – League (58): McLeod 14 (3 pens), Kabba 11 (3 pens), Byrne 6, Marshall 6,
Walsh 3, Deering 2, Holmes 2, Hughes 2, Basey 1, Devera 1, Gallen 1, Kamdjo 1, Leach
1, Parkes 1, Poole 1, Southam 1 (1 pen), Taylor 1, Uddin 1, own goals 2.

Carling Cup (0).
FA Cup (0).
J Paint Trophy (1): Marshall 1.
Ground: Underhill Stadium, Barnet Lane, Barnet, Herts EN5 2DN. Telephone: (020) 8441 6932.
Record Attendance: 11,026 v Wycombe Wanderers, FA Amateur Cup 4th Round 1951–52.
Capacity: 5,345.
Manager: Lawrie Sanchez.
Most League Goals: 81, Division 4, 1991–92.
Highest League Scorer in Season: Dougie Freedman, 24, Division 3, 1994–95.
Most League Goals in Total Aggregate: Sean Devine, 47, 1995–99.
Most Capped Player: Ken Charlery, 4, St Lucia.
Most League Appearances: Lee Harrison, 270, 1996–2002, 2006–09.
Honours – Football League: GMVC: Winners – 1990–91. **Football Conference:** Winners – 2004–05. **FA Amateur Cup:** Winners 1945–46.
Colours: All black with amber trim.

BARNSLEY   FL CHAMPIONSHIP

Butterfield Jacob (D)	5 10	11 00	Manchester	10	6 90	Scholar
Clark Jordan (F)			Barnsley	22	9 93	Scholar
Dickinson Liam (F)	6 4	11 07	Salford	4	10 85	Brighton & HA
Doyle Nathan (D)	5 11	11 13	Derby	12	1 87	Hull C
Foster Stephen (D)	6 0	11 05	Warrington	10	9 80	Burnley
Gray Andy (F)	6 1	13 00	Harrogate	15	11 77	Charlton Ath
Hassell Bobby (D)	5 10	12 00	Derby	4	6 80	Mansfield T
Haynes Danny (F)	5 11	12 04	London	19	1 88	Bristol C
Lovre Goran (M)	6 3	12 13	Zagreb	23	3 82	Groningen
McEveley James (D)	6 1	13 03	Liverpool	11	2 85	Derby Co
Miller Kern (D)	5 9	11 03	Skegness	9	2 91	Lincoln C
Noble-Lazarus Reuben (F)	5 11	13 07	Huddersfield	16	8 93	Youth
O'Brien Jim (F)	6 0	11 11	Glasgow	28	9 87	Motherwell
Potter Luke (D)	6 2	12 07	Barnsley	13	7 89	Scholar
Preece David (G)	6 2	11 11	Sunderland	28	8 76	Odense
Rose Danny (F)			Barnsley	10	12 93	Scholar
Shackell Jason (D)	6 4	13 06	Stevenage	27	9 83	Wolverhampton W
Steele Luke (G)	6 2	12 00	Peterborough	24	9 84	WBA
Taylor Alastair (M)	6 1	10 06	Sheffield	13	9 91	Scholar

League Appearances: Arismendi, D. 24(7); Bennett, S. (4); Butterfield, J. 18(22); Clark, J. (4); Colace, R. 24(2); Devaney, M. 1(5); Dickinson, L. (3); Doyle, N. 35(8); Foster, S. 32(1); Gray, A. 24(10); Hammill, A. 25; Harewood, M. 9(1); Hassell, B. 34(3); Hayes, P. 2(5); Haynes, D. 20; Hill, M. 23; Hume, I. (1); Lovre, G. 19(2); McEveley, J. 15(2); McShane, P. 10; Mellis, J. 14(1); Newmann, J. (5); Noble-Lazarus, R. 1(6); Nouble, F. 4; O'Brien, J. 20(13); O'Connor, G. 19(3); Potter, L. 2(2); Rose, D. (1); Shackell, J. 44; Steele, L. 46; Taylor, A. (2); Trippier, K. 37(2); Wood, C. 4(3).

Goals – League (55): Hammill 8, Gray 7 (3 pens), Haynes 6, Harewood 4, O'Connor 4, Shackell 3, Butterfield 2, Doyle 2, Hill 2, Lovre 2, Mellis 2, Trippier 2, Arismendi 1, Colace 1, Foster 1, Hassell 1, McEveley 1, McShane 1, Noble-Lazarus 1, O'Brien 1, own goals 3.

Carling Cup (0).
FA Cup (0).
Ground: Oakwell Stadium, Grove Street, Barnsley, South Yorkshire S71 1ET. Telephone: (01226) 211 211.

Record Attendance: 40,255 v Stoke C, FA Cup 5th rd, 15 February 1936.
Capacity: 23,186.
Manager: Keith Hill.
General Manager/Secretary: Albert Donald Rowing.
Most League Goals: 118, Division 3 (N), 1933–34.
Highest League Scorer in Season: Cecil McCormack, 33, Division 2, 1950–51.
Most League Goals in Total Aggregate: Ernest Hine, 123, 1921–26 and 1934–38.
Most Capped Player: Gerry Taggart, 35 (50), Northern Ireland.
Most League Appearances: Barry Murphy, 514, 1962–78.
Honours – Football League: Division 3 (N) Champions – 1933–34, 1938–39, 1954–55.
FA Cup: Winners – 1912.
Colours: Red shirts with white trim, white shorts, red stockings.

BIRMINGHAM CITY   FL CHAMPIONSHIP

Asante Akwasi (F)	5 7	10 00	Amsterdam	6	9 92	Scholar
Beausejour Coliqueo (M)	5 10	12 08	Santiago	1	6 84	America
Butland Jack (G)	6 4	12 00	Clevedon	10	3 93	Scholar
Carr Stephen (D)	5 9	11 13	Dublin	29	8 76	Newcastle U
Dann Scott (D)	6 2	12 00	Liverpool	14	2 87	Coventry C
Davies Curtis (D)	6 2	11 13	Waltham Forest	15	3 85	Aston Villa
Doyle Colin (G)	6 5	14 05	Cork	12	8 85	Scholar
Fahey Keith (M)	5 10	12 07	Dublin	15	1 83	Aston Villa
Ferguson Barry (M)	5 7	9 10	Glasgow	2	2 78	Rangers
Foster Ben (G)	6 2	12 08	Leamington Spa	3	4 83	Manchester U
Gardner Craig (M)	5 10	11 13	Solihull	25	11 86	Aston Villa
Hubbins Luke (M)			Birmingham	11	9 91	Scholar
Jerome Cameron (F)	6 1	13 06	Huddersfield	14	8 86	Cardiff C
Jervis Jake (F)	6 3	12 13	Birmingham	17	9 91	Scholar
Jiranek Martin (D)	6 2	14 02	Liberec	25	5 79	Spartak Moscow
Johnson Roger (D)	6 3	11 00	Ashford	28	4 83	Cardiff C
Kerr Fraser (D)	6 3	13 03	Motherwell	17	1 93	Scholar
Michel (M)	6 0	11 05	Pola de Lena	9	11 85	Gijon
Murphy David (D)	6 1	12 03	Hartlepool	1	3 84	Hibernian
Mutch Jordon (M)	5 9	10 03	Birmingham	2	12 91	Derby Co
Ridgewell Liam (D)	5 10	10 03	Bexley	21	7 84	Aston Villa
Sammons Ashley (M)	5 8	11 02	Solihull	10	11 91	Scholar
Valles Enric (M)	6 2	13 01	Barcelona	1	3 90	NAC Breda
Zigic Nikola (F)	6 8	14 02	Backa Topola	25	9 80	Valencia

League Appearances: Beausejour, J. 9(8); Bentley, D. 9(4); Bowyer, L. 24(5); Carr, S. 38; Dann, S. 20; Davies, C. 2(4); Derbyshire, M. 4(9); Doyle, C. (1); Fahey, K. 19(5); Ferguson, B. 35; Foster, B. 38; Gardner, C. 25(4); Hleb, A. 13(6); Jerome, C. 30(4); Jiranek, M. 10; Johnson, R. 38; Larsson, S. 31(4); Martins, O. 3(1); McFadden, J. 3(1); Murphy, D. 3(7); Mutch, J. 3; O'Connor, G. 2(1); Parnaby, S. 5; Phillips, K. 5(9); Ridgewell, L. 36; Zigic, N. 13(12).
Goals – League (37): Gardner 8 (1 pen), Zigic 5, Bowyer 4, Larsson 4 (1 pen), Ridgewell 4, Jerome 3, Beausejour 2, Dann 2, Johnson 2, Fahey 1, Phillips 1.
Carling Cup (15): Zigic 3, Gardner 2, Bowyer 1, Derbyshire 1, Hleb 1, Johnson 1, Larsson 1 (pen), McFadden 1 (pen), Martins 1, Murphy 1, Phillips 1, Ridgewell 1.
FA Cup (12): Derbyshire 2, Jerome 2, Murphy 2, Phillips 2, Beausejour 1, Bentley 1, Martins 1, Parnaby 1.
Ground: St Andrews Stadium, Birmingham B9 4RL. Telephone: 0844 557 1875.
Record Attendance: 66,844 v Everton, FA Cup 5th rd, 11 February 1939.
Capacity: 30,079.
Manager: Chris Hughton.

Secretary: Julia Shelton.
Most League Goals: 103, Division 2, 1893–94 (only 28 games).
Highest League Scorer in Season: Joe Bradford, 29, Division 1, 1927–28.
Most League Goals in Total Aggregate: Joe Bradford, 249, 1920–35.
Most Capped Player: Maik Taylor, 50 (87), Northern Ireland.
Most League Appearances: Frank Womack, 491, 1908–28.
Honours – Football League: Division 2 Champions – 1892–93, 1920–21, 1947–48, 1954–55, 1994–95. **Football League Cup:** Winners – 1963, 2011. **Leyland Daf Cup:** Winners – 1991. **Auto Windscreens Shield:** Winners – 1995.
Colours: Blue shirts with white trim, white shorts, blue stockings.

BLACKBURN ROVERS   FA PREMIERSHIP

Aley Zach (M)	5 11	11 02	Fazakerley	17	8 91	Scholar
Andrews Keith (M)	6 0	12 04	Dublin	13	9 80	Milton Keynes D
Blackman Nick (F)	6 2	11 08	Whitefield	11 11 89		Macclesfield T
Bunn Mark (G)	6 0	12 02	Camden	16 11 84		Northampton T
Diouf El Hadji (F)	5 11	11 11	Dakar	15	1 81	Sunderland
Doran Aaron (M)	5 7	12 00	Ireland	13	5 91	Scholar
Dunn David (M)	5 9	12 03	Gt Harwood	27 12 79		Birmingham C
Emerton Brett (M)	6 1	13 05	Bankstown	22	2 79	Feyenoord
Formica Mauro (M)	5 9	10 01	Rosario	4	4 88	Newell's Old Boys
Givet Gael (D)	5 11	11 11	Arles	9 10 81		Marseille
Goulon Herold (M)	6 4	14 07	Paris	12	6 88	Middlesbrough
Grella Vince (M)	6 0	12 06	Melbourne	5 10 79		Torino
Gunning Gavin (D)	6 0	12 06	Dublin	26	1 91	Scholar
Hanley Grant (D)	6 2	12 00	Dumfries	20 11 91		Scholar
Hitchcock Tom (F)			Hemel Hempstead	1 10 92		Scholar
Hoilett David (M)	5 8	11 00	Ottowa	5	6 90	Scholar
Jones Phil (D)	5 11	11 02	Preston	21	2 92	Scholar
Kalinic Nikola (F)	6 2	12 11	Olin	5	1 88	Hajduk Split
Kean Jake (G)	6 4	11 09	Derby	4	2 91	Scholar
Knowles James (M)	5 9	11 00	Northern Ireland	6	4 93	Scholar
Lindsay Cameron (D)			New Zealand	21 12 92		Scholar
Linganzi Amine (M)	6 1	10 00	Alger	16 11 89		Saint Etienne
Lowe Jason (M)	6 0	12 08	Wigan	2	9 91	Scholar
Morris Josh (D)	5 9	10 01	Blackburn	30	9 91	Scholar
N'Zonzi Steven (M)	6 3	11 11	Paris	15 12 88		Amiens
Nelsen Ryan (D)	5 11	14 02	New Zealand	18 10 77		DC United
O'Connor Anthony (D)			Republic of Ireland	25 10 92		Scholar
Olsson Martin (D)	5 7	11 00	Sweden	17	5 88	Hogaborg
Pedersen Morten (F)	5 11	11 00	Vadso	8	9 81	Tromso
Pivkovski Filip (M)			Sweden	31	1 94	Scholar
Roberts Jason (F)	6 1	13 06	Park Royal	25	1 78	Wigan Ath
Robinson Paul (G)	6 1	14 07	Beverley	15 10 79		Tottenham H
Rochina Ruben (F)	5 11	11 00	Sagunto	23	3 91	Barcelona
Salgado Michel (D)	5 9	11 11	Galicia	22 10 75		Real Madrid
Samba Christopher (D)	6 5	13 03	Creteil	28	3 84	Hertha Berlin
Vastic Toni (F)			Austria	17	1 93	Scholar

League League Appearances: Andrews, K. 2(3); Biram Diouf, M. 17(9); Bunn, M. 2(1); Chimbonda, P. 3(3); Diouf, E. 18(2); Dunn, D. 17(10); Emerton, B. 24(6); Givet, G. 29; Goulon, H. 1(3); Grella, V. 4(1); Hanley, G. 5(2); Hoilett, D. 17(7); Jones, P. 24(2); Jones, J. 15; Kalinic, N. 15(3); Linganzi, A. (1); Lowe, J. (1); Morris, J. (4); Mwaruwari, B. 6(12); N'Zonzi, S. 13(8); Nelsen, R. 28; Olsson, M. 25(4); Pedersen, M. 27(8); Roberts, J. 13(12); Robinson, P. 36; Rochina, R. 1(3); Salgado, M. 36; Samba, C. 33; Santa Cruz, R. 7(2).

Goals – League (46): Hoilett 5, Kalinic 5, Roberts 5, Emerton 4, Pedersen 4, Samba 4, Biram Diouf 3, Mwaruwari 3, Nelsen 3, Dunn 2 (1 pen), Olsson 2, Givet 1, N'Zonzi 1, own goals 4.
Carling Cup (4): Biram Diouf 3, Givet 1.
FA Cup (2): Hoilett 1, Kalinic 1.
Ground: Ewood Park, Blackburn, Lancs BB2 4JF. Telephone: 0871 702 1875.
Record Attendance: 62,522 v Bolton W, FA Cup 6th rd, 2 March 1929.
Capacity: 31,367.
Manager: Steve Kean.
Secretary: Andrew Pincher.
Most League Goals: 114, Division 2, 1954–55.
Highest League Scorer in Season: Ted Harper, 43, Division 1, 1925–26.
Most League Goals in Total Aggregate: Simon Garner, 168, 1978–92.
Most Capped Player: Henning Berg, 58 (100), Norway.
Most League Appearances: Derek Fazackerley, 596, 1970–86.
Honours – FA Premier League: Champions – 1994–95. **Football League:** Division 1 Champions – 1911–12, 1913–14. Division 2 Champions – 1938–39. Division 3 Champions – 1974–75. **FA Cup:** Winners – 1884, 1885, 1886, 1890, 1891, 1928. **Football League Cup:** Winners – 2002. **Full Members' Cup:** Winners – 1986–87.
Colours: Blue and white halved shirts, white shorts, blue stockings.

BLACKPOOL   FL CHAMPIONSHIP

Adam Charlie (M)	6 1	12 00	Dundee	10 12 85	Rangers
Almond Louis (F)	5 11	12 00	Blackburn	15 8 90	Scholar
Basham Christopher (M)	5 11	12 08	Stafford	20 7 88	Bolton W
Campbell Dudley (F)	5 10	11 00	London	12 11 81	Leicester C
Clarke Billy (F)	5 7	10 01	Cork	13 12 87	Ipswich T
Crainey Stephen (D)	5 9	10 06	Glasgow	22 6 81	Leeds U
Eardley Neal (M)	5 11	11 10	Llandudno	6 11 88	Oldham Ath
Eastham Ashley (D)	6 3	12 06	Preston	22 3 91	Scholar
Evatt Ian (D)	6 3	13 12	Coventry	19 11 81	QPR
Gilks Matthew (G)	6 3	13 12	Rochdale	4 6 82	Norwich C
Grandin Elliot (F)	5 10	10 07	Caen	17 10 87	CSKA Sofia
Halstead Mark (G)	6 3	14 00	Blackpool	1 1 90	Scholar
Husband Stephen (M)	6 0	12 13	Dunfermline	29 10 90	Hearts
John-Baptiste Alex (D)	6 0	11 11	Sutton-in-Ashfield	31 1 86	Mansfield T
Ormerod Brett (F)	5 11	11 12	Blackburn	18 10 76	Preston NE
Phillips Matthew (M)	6 0	12 10	Aylesbury	13 3 91	Wycombe W
Southern Keith (M)	5 10	12 06	Gateshead	24 4 81	Everton
Sylvestre Ludovic (M)	6 0	11 09	Le Blanc-Mesnil	5 2 84	Mlada Boleslav
Taylor-Fletcher Gary (F)	5 11	12 06	Liverpool	4 6 81	Huddersfield T
Vaughan David (M)	5 7	11 00	Rhuddlan	18 2 83	Real Sociedad

League Appearances: Adam, C. 34(1); Basham, C. 1(1); Beattie, J. 5(4); Campbell, D. 30(1); Carney, D. 5(6); Cathcart, C. 28(2); Crainey, S. 31; Demontagnac, I. (1); Eardley, N. 30(1); Edwards, R. 1(1); Euell, J. 1(2); Evatt, I. 36(2); Gilks, M. 18; Grandin, E. 21(2); Halstead, M. (1); Harewood, M. 7(9); John-Baptiste, A. 19(2); Keinan, D. 3(3); Kingson, R. 19(1); Kornilenko, S. 3(3); Ormerod, B. 6(13); Phillips, M. 6(21); Puncheon, J. 6(5); Rachubka, P. 1(1); Reid, A. 2(3); Southern, K. 11(10); Sylvestre, L. 6(2); Taylor-Fletcher, G. 29(2); Varney, L. 24(6); Vaughan, D. 35.
Goals – League (55): Campbell 13, Adam 12 (7 pens), Taylor-Fletcher 6, Harewood 5, Varney 5, Puncheon 3, John-Baptiste 2, Vaughan 2, Cathcart 1, Eardley 1, Evatt 1, Grandin 1, Ormerod 1, Phillips 1, own goal 1.
Carling Cup (3): Adam 1 (pen), Ormerod 1, Sylvestre 1.
FA Cup (0).

Ground: Bloomfield Road, Seasiders Way, Blackpool FY1 6JJ. Telephone: (0871) 6221 953.
Record Attendance: 38,098 v Wolverhampton W, Division 1, 17 September 1955.
Capacity: 9,491.
Manager: Ian Holloway.
Secretary: Matt Williams.
Most League Goals: 98, Division 2, 1929–30.
Highest League Scorer in Season: Jimmy Hampson, 45, Division 2, 1929–30.
Most League Goals in Total Aggregate: Jimmy Hampson, 248, 1927–38.
Most Capped Player: Jimmy Armfield, 43, England.
Most League Appearances: Jimmy Armfield, 568, 1952–71.
Honours – Football League: Division 2 Champions – 1929–30. **FA Cup:** Winners – 1953.
Anglo-Italian Cup: Winners – 1971. **LDV Vans Trophy:** Winners – 2002, 2004.
Colours: Tangerine shirts with white trim, white shorts, tangerine stockings with white tops.

BOLTON WANDERERS   FA PREMIERSHIP

Al-Habsi Ali (G)	6 4	12 06	Oman	30 12 81	Lyn
Alonso Marcos (D)	6 2	13 05	Madrid	28 12 90	Real Madrid
Blake Robert (F)	5 9	12 00	Middlesbrough	4 3 76	Burnley
Bogdan Adam (G)	6 4	14 02	Budapest	27 9 87	Vasas
Cahill Gary (D)	6 2	12 06	Dronfield	19 12 85	Aston Villa
Connolly Mark (D)	6 1	12 01	Monaghan	16 12 91	Wolverhampton W
Davies Kevin (F)	6 0	12 10	Sheffield	26 3 77	Southampton
Davies Mark (M)	5 11	11 08	Wolverhampton	18 2 88	Wolverhampton W
Davis Sean (M)	5 10	12 00	Clapham	20 9 79	Portsmouth
Eaves Thomas (M)	6 3	13 07	Liverpool	14 1 92	Oldham Ath
Holden Stuart (M)	5 10	11 07	Aberdeen	1 8 85	Houston Dynamo
Jaaskelainen Jussi (G)	6 3	12 10	Mikkeli	19 4 75	VPS
Klasnic Ivan (F)	6 1	12 00	Hamburg	29 1 80	Nantes
Knight Zat (D)	6 6	15 02	Solihull	2 5 80	Aston Villa
Lainton Robert (G)	6 2	12 06	Ashton-under-Lyne	12 10 89	Scholar
Lee Chung Yong (M)	5 11	10 09	Seoul	2 7 88	FC Seoul
Muamba Fabrice (M)	6 1	11 10	Kinshasa	6 4 88	Birmingham C
O'Halloran Michael (F)	6 2	12 06	Glasgow	6 1 91	Scholar
Obadeyi Temitope (F)	5 10	11 09	Coventry	29 10 89	Scholar
Petrov Martin (F)	6 0	12 02	Vtazza	15 1 79	Manchester C
Ricketts Sam (D)	6 1	12 01	Aylesbury	11 10 81	Hull C
Robinson Paul (D)	5 9	11 12	Watford	14 12 78	WBA
Sampson Jack (F)			Wigan	14 4 93	Scholar
Steinsson Gretar (D)	6 2	12 04	Siglufjordur	9 1 82	AZ
Taylor Matthew (D)	5 11	12 03	Oxford	27 11 81	Portsmouth
Ward Daniel (F)	5 11	12 05	Bradford	11 12 91	Scholar
Wheater David (D)	6 5	12 12	Redcar	14 2 87	Middlesbrough

League Appearances: Alonso, M. 4; Blake, R. (8); Bogdan, A. 3(1); Cahill, G. 36; Cohen, T. 3(5); Davies, K. 38; Davies, M. 9(15); Elmander, J. 37; Gardner, R. 3(2); Holden, S. 26; Jaaskelainen, J. 35; Klasnic, I. (22); Knight, Z. 34; Lee, C. 25(6); Moreno, R. 4(13); Muamba, F. 32(4); O'Brien, A. 1(1); Petrov, M. 18(10); Ricketts, S. 14(3); Robinson, P. 35; Steinsson, G. 23; Sturridge, D. 11(1); Taylor, M. 22(14); Wheater, D. 5(2).
Goals – League (52): Elmander 10, Davies K 8 (4 pens), Sturridge 8, Klasnic 4, Cahill 3, Lee 3, Petrov 3, Holden 2, Taylor 2, Blake 1, Cohen 1, Davies M 1, Knight 1, Moreno 1, Muamba 1, Steinsson 1, own goals 2.
Carling Cup (1): Klasnic 1.
FA Cup (7): Davies K 2 (1 pen), Elmander 2, Klasnic 2, Lee 1.

Ground: The Reebok Stadium, Burnden Way, Lostock, Bolton BL6 6JW. Telephone: (0844) 871 2932. Fax: (01204) 673 773.
Record Attendance: 69,912 v Manchester C, FA Cup 5th rd, 18 February 1933 (at Burnden Park). 28,353 v Leicester C, FA Premier League, 23 December 2003 (at The Reebok Stadium).
Capacity: 28,101.
Manager: Owen Coyle.
Secretary: Simon Marland.
Most League Goals: 100, Division 1, 1996–97.
Highest League Scorer in Season: Joe Smith, 38, Division 1, 1920–21.
Most League Goals in Total Aggregate: Nat Lofthouse, 255, 1946–61.
Most Capped Player: Mark Fish, 34 (62), South Africa.
Most League Appearances: Eddie Hopkinson, 519, 1956–70.
Honours – Football League: Division 1 Champions – 1996–97. Division 2 Champions – 1908–09, 1977–78. Division 3 Champions – 1972–73. **FA Cup:** Winners – 1923, 1926, 1929, 1958. **Sherpa Van Trophy:** Winners – 1989.
Colours: White shirts with blue body trim, blue shorts, white stockings.

AFC BOURNEMOUTH   FL CHAMPIONSHIP 1

Player			Birthplace			Signed/Previous
Arter Harry (M)	5 9	11 07	Eltham	28 12 89	Woking
Baudry Mathieu (D)	6 2	12 08	Saint-Adresse	24 2 88	Troyes
Cooper Shaun (D)	5 10	10 05	Newport (IW)	5 10 83	Portsmouth
Cummings Warren (D)	5 9	11 08	Aberdeen	15 10 80	Chelsea
Feeney Liam (M)	5 10	12 02	Hammersmith	24 1 87	Salisbury C
Fletcher Steve (F)	6 2	14 09	Hartlepool	26 7 72	Crawley T
Garry Ryan (D)	6 0	11 05	Hornchurch	29 9 83	Arsenal
Hollands Danny (M)	6 0	12 00	Ashford	6 11 85	Chelsea
Ings Daniel (F)	5 10	11 07	Winchester	1 8 92	Scholar
Jalal Shwan (G)	6 2	14 02	Baghdad	14 8 83	Peterborough U
Lovell Stephen (F)	5 11	11 08	Amersham	6 12 80	Partick T
Molesley Mark (M)	6 1	12 07	Hillingdon	11 3 81	Grays Ath
Nelson Mitchell (D)	6 3	13 00	Lambeth	31 8 89	Tooting & Mitcham U
Partington Joe (M)	5 11	11 13	Portsmouth	1 4 90	Scholar
Pearce Jason (D)	5 11	12 00	Hampshire	6 12 87	Portsmouth
Pugh Marc (M)	5 11	11 04	Burnley	2 4 87	Hereford U
Purches Stephen (D)	5 11	11 13	Ilford	14 1 80	Leyton Orient
Robinson Anton (M)	5 9	10 03	Harrow	17 2 86	Weymouth
Stewart Jon (G)	6 2	13 01	London	13 3 89	Weymouth
Stockley Jayden (F)	6 2	12 07	Poole	10 10 93	School
Symes Michael (F)	6 3	12 04	Gt Yarmouth	31 10 83	Shrewsbury T
Taylor Lyle (F)	6 2	12 00	Staines	29 3 90	Concord R
Thomas Dan (G)	6 2	13 01	Poole	1 9 91	School
Wiggins Rhoys (D)	5 8	11 05	Uxbridge	4 11 87	Norwich C

League Appearances: Arter, H. 7(11); Bartley, M. 24(2); Baudry, M. 1(2); Bignall, N. 3(2); Bradbury, L. 8(6); Cooper, S. 33(3); Cummings, W. 9(5); Dalla Valle, L. 5(3); Feeney, L. 44(2); Fletcher, S. 7(31); Garry, R. 10; Hollands, D. 31(11); Ings, D. 21(5); Jalal, S. 43; Lovell. S. 5(2); McDermott, D. 6(3); McQuoid, J. 15(2); Molesley, M. (2); Partington, J. 2(3); Pearce, J. 46; Pitman, B. 2; Pugh, M. 40(1); Purches, S. 6(3); Robinson, A. 45; Smith, A. 38; Stewart, J. 3(1); Stockley, J. (4); Symes, M. 16(6); Taylor, L. 2(9); Wiggins, R. 34(1); Williamson, B. (4).
Goals – League (75): Pugh 12 (2 pens), McQuoid 9, Symes 8 (3 pens), Hollands 7, Ings 7 (1 pen), Fletcher 6, Robinson 5, Feeney 4, Pearce 3, Pitman 3, Dalla Valle 2, Garry 2, Wiggins 2, Bartley 1, Baudry 1, Lovell 1, McDermott 1, Smith 1.
Carling Cup (0).

FA Cup (6): McQuoid 3, Feeney 1, Fletcher 1, Pugh 1.
J Paint Trophy (0).
Play-Offs (4): Lovell 2 (1 pen), Ings 1, McDermott 1.
Ground: Dean Court, Kings Park, Bournemouth, Dorset BH7 7AF. Telephone: (01202) 726 300.
Record Attendance: 28,799 v Manchester U, FA Cup 6th rd, 2 March 1957.
Capacity: 10,375 (with temporary stand, 9,776 without).
Manager: Lee Bradbury.
Secretary: Neil Vacher (Football Administrator).
Most League Goals: 88, Division 3 (S), 1956–57.
Highest League Scorer in Season: Ted MacDougall, 42, 1970–71.
Most League Goals in Total Aggregate: Ron Eyre, 202, 1924–33.
Most Capped Player: Gerry Peyton, 7 (33), Republic of Ireland.
Most League Appearances: Steve Fletcher, 597, 1992–2007; 2008–.
Honours – Football League: Division 3 Champions – 1986–87. **Associate Members' Cup:** Winners – 1984.
Colours: Red shirts with thin black vertical stripes, black shorts, black stockings.

BRADFORD CITY   FL CHAMPIONSHIP 2

Bullock Lee (M)	6 0	11 04	Stockton	22	5 81	Hartlepool U
Dean Luke (F)	5 9	11 00	Bradford	1	8 89	Scholar
Flynn Michael (M)	5 10	13 04	Newport	17 10 80		Huddersfield T
Hanson James (F)	6 4	12 04	Bradford	9 11 87		Guiseley
Hunt Lewis (D)	5 11	12 09	Birmingham	25	8 82	Wycombe W
McLaughlin Jon (G)	6 2	13 00	Edinburgh	9	9 87	Harrogate Railway
O'Brien Luke (D)	5 9	12 01	Halifax	11	9 88	Scholar
Oliver Luke (D)	6 6	14 05	Hammersmith	1	5 84	Wycombe W
Osborne Leon (F)	5 10	10 10	Doncaster	28 10 89		Scholar
Ramsden Simon (D)	6 0	12 06	Bishop Auckland	17 12 81		Rochdale
Speight Jake (F)	5 7	11 02	Sheffield	28	9 85	Bury
Syers David (M)			Leeds	30 11 91		Guiseley
Threlfall Robbie (D)	5 11	11 00	Liverpool	25 11 88		Liverpool
Williams Steve (D)	6 4	13 04	Preston	24	4 87	Bamber Bridge

League Appearances: Adeyemi, T. 30(4); Brown, R. 3; Bullock, L. 22(4); Chilaka, C. (4); Cullen, M. 1(3); Daley, O. 22(4); Dean, L. (1); Dobie, S. 8(5); Doherty, T. 17(1); Duff, S. 14; Eckersley, R. 12; Ellison, K. 6(1); Evans, G. 28(8); Flett, A. (1); Flynn, M. 16(3); Gill, O. 4; Hanson, J. 31(5); Hendrie, L. 8(4); Hunt, L. 24; Kiernan, R. 6(2); McLaughlin, J. 25; Moult, L. 4(7); Neilson, S. 1; O'Brien, L. 37(5); Oliver, L. 41(1); Osborne, L. 10(12); Pidgeley, L. 21; Price, J. 6(4); Ramsden, S. 2; Rehman, Z. 5(3); Rowe, D. 1(1); Speight, J. 13(15); Stephenson, D. (1); Syers, D. 30(7); Threlfall, R. 16(4); Williams, S. 26(2); Worthington, J. 16.
Goals – League (43): Syers 8, Hanson 6, Adeyemi 5, Daley 5 (1 pen), Speight 4 (3 pens), Evans 3 (1 pen), Williams 3, Hendrie 2 (1 pen), Duff 1, Ellison 1, Hunt 1, Moult 1, Oliver 1, Osborne 1, Price 1.
Carling Cup (3): Hanson 1, Speight 1, Syers 1.
FA Cup (3): Hanson 2, Syers 1.
J Paint Trophy (0).
Ground: Coral Window Stadium, Valley Parade, Bradford, West Yorkshire BD8 7DY. Telephone: (01274) 773 355.
Record Attendance: 39,146 v Burnley, FA Cup 4th rd, 11 March 1911.
Capacity: 25,136.
Manager: Peter Jackson.
Football Club Secretary: Kath Brown.
Most League Goals: 128, Division 3 (N), 1928–29.

Highest League Scorer in Season: David Layne, 34, Division 4, 1961–62.
Most League Goals in Total Aggregate: Bobby Campbell, 121, 1981–84, 1984–86.
Most Capped Player: Jamie Lawrence, 19 (24), Jamaica.
Most League Appearances: Cec Podd, 502, 1970–84.
Honours – Football League: Division 2 Champions – 1907–08. Division 3 Champions – 1984–85. Division 3 (N) Champions – 1928–29. **FA Cup:** Winners – 1911.
Colours: Claret and amber striped shirts with claret sleeves, black shorts, black stockings.

BRENTFORD FL CHAMPIONSHIP 1

Alexander Gary (F)	6 0	13 04	Lambeth	15	8	79	Millwall
Balkestein Pim (D)	6 3	12 00	Gouda	29	4	87	Ipswich T
Bean Marcus (M)	5 11	11 06	Hammersmith	2	11	84	Blackpool
Blake Ryan (D)	5 10	10 10	Kingston	8	12	91	Scholar
Diagouraga Toumani (M)	6 2	11 05	Corbeil-Essones	10	6	87	Peterborough U
Forster Nicky (F)	5 9	11 05	Caterham	8	9	73	Brighton & HA
Grabban Lewis (F)	6 0	11 03	Croydon	12	1	88	Millwall
Hudson Kirk (F)	5 8	10 00	Rochford	12	12	86	Aldershot T
Lee Richard (G)	6 0	12 06	Oxford	5	10	82	Watford
Legge Leon (D)	6 1	11 02	London	28	4	85	Tonbridge Angels
MacDonald Charlie (F)	5 8	12 10	Southwark	13	2	81	Southend U
McCracken David (D)	6 2	11 06	Glasgow	16	10	81	Milton Keynes D
Moore Simon (G)	6 3	12 02	Isle of Wight	19	5	90	Farnborough T
O'Connor Kevin (F)	5 11	12 00	Blackburn	24	2	82	Trainee
Osborne Karleigh (M)	6 2	12 08	Southall	19	3	88	Scholar
Saunders Sam (M)	5 6	11 04	London	29	10	82	Dagenham & R
Spillane Michael (M)	5 9	11 10	Jersey	23	3	89	Norwich C
Weston Myles (F)	5 11	12 05	Lewisham	12	3	88	Notts Co
Wood Sam (M)	6 0	11 05	London	6	2	88	Bromley
Woodman Craig (D)	5 9	10 11	Tiverton	22	12	82	Wycombe W

League Appearances: Adams, N. 3(4); Alexander, G. 37(1); Balkestein, P. 17(3); Bean, M. 32(5); Bignall, N. 1(5); Byrne, N. 4(7); Carson, T. 1; Cort, C. (3); Diagouraga, T. 32; Forster, N. 6(12); Grabban, L. 13(9); Hacker, L. (1); Hamer, B. 10; Hudson, K. (2); Hunt, D. (3); Laird, M. 4; Lee, R. 22; Legge, L. 27(3); MacDonald, C. 28(2); McCarthy, A. 3; McCracken, D. 1(1); Moore, S. 9(1); Neilson, R. 15; O'Connor, K. 39(2); Osborne, K. 41(1); Reed, A. 8(3); Reeves, J. (1); Royce, S. 1(1); Saunders, S. 18(3); Schlupp, J. 6(3); Simpson, R. 11(16); Spillane, M. 18(6); Tudur Jones, O. 4(2); Weston, M. 33(9); Wood, S. 13(7); Woodman, C. 40(1); Wright, S. 9(2).

Goals – League (55): Alexander 9 (1 pen), MacDonald 9, Schlupp 6, Grabban 5 (1 pen), Simpson 4, Bean 3, Legge 3, Weston 3, O'Connor 2 (1 pen), Saunders 2, Balkestein 1, Diagouraga 1, Forster 1, Laird 1, Osborne 1, Spillane 1, Wood 1, Woodman 1, own goal 1.

Carling Cup (6): Simpson 2, Alexander 1, Bean 1, Wood 1, Woodman 1.
FA Cup (1): MacDonald 1.
J Paint Trophy (5): Alexander 2, Simpson 2, Saunders 1.
Ground: Griffin Park, Braemar Road, Brentford, Middlesex TW8 0NT. Telephone: 0845 3456 442.
Record Attendance: 38,678 v Leicester C, FA Cup 6th rd, 26 February 1949.
Capacity: 12,400.
Manager: Uwe Rosler.
Secretary: Lisa Hall.
Most League Goals: 98, Division 4, 1962–63.
Highest League Scorer in Season: Jack Holliday, 38, Division 3 (S), 1932–33.
Most League Goals in Total Aggregate: Jim Towers, 153, 1954–61.

Most Capped Player: John Buttigieg, 22 (98), Malta.
Most League Appearances: Ken Coote, 514, 1949–64.
Honours – Football League: Championship 2 Winners – 2008–09. Division 2
Champions – 1934–35. Division 3 Champions – 1991–92, 1998–99. Division 3 (S)
Champions – 1932–33. Division 4 Champions – 1962–63.
Colours: White shirts with red sleeves and black trim underneath, four separated red
vertical stripes on body, black shorts, black stockings.

BRIGHTON & HOVE ALBION — FL CHAMPIONSHIP

Name	Ht		Born date	Birthplace	Signed			From
Agdestein Torbjorn (F)	6 0	12 10	Norway	18	9	91	Stord
Ankergren Casper (G)	6 3	14 07	Koge	9	11	79	Leeds U
Barnes Ashley (F)	6 0	12 00	Bath	30	10	89	Plymouth Arg
Bennett Elliott (M)	5 9	10 11	Telford	18	12	88	Wolverhampton W
Brezovan Peter (G)	6 6	14 13	Bratislava	9	12	79	Swindon T
Bridcutt Liam (M)	5 9	11 07	Reading	8	5	89	Chelsea
Calderon Inigo (D)	5 10	12 02	Vitoria	4	1	82	Alaves
Caskey Jake (M)	5 10	10 00	Southend	1	6	94	Hull C
Cook Steve (D)	6 1	12 13	Hastings	19	4	91	Scholar
Dicker Gary (M)	6 0	12 00	Dublin	31	7	86	Stockport Co
Dunk Lewis (D)	6 3	12 02	Brighton	21	11	91	Scholar
El-Abd Adam (D)	5 10	13 05	Brighton	11	9	84	Scholar
Elphick Tommy (M)	5 11	11 07	Brighton	7	9	87	Scholar
Greer Gordon (D)	6 2	12 05	Glasgow	14	12	80	Swindon T
Kasim Yaser (M)			Baghdad	16	5	91	Scholar
McNulty Jim (D)	6 1	12 00	Liverpool	13	2	85	Stockport co
Murray Glenn (F)	6 1	12 12	Maryport	25	9	83	Rochdale
Noone Craig (M)	6 3	12 07	Southport	17	11	87	Plymouth Arg
Painter Marcos (D)	5 11	12 04	Solihull	17	8	86	Swansea C
Poke Michael (G)	6 1	13 12	Spelthorne	21	11	85	Southampton
Smith Jamie (M)	5 6	10 07	Leytonstone	16	9	89	Leytonstone
Sparrow Matt (M)	5 11	10 06	Wembley	3	10	81	Scunthorpe U
Tunnicliffe James (D)	6 4	12 03	Denton	17	1	89	Stockport Co
Walker Mitch (G)	6 2	13 00	St Albans	24	9	91	Scholar

League Appearances: Ankergren, C. 45; Barnes, A. 31(11); Battipiedi, A. 3(5); Baz, C.
(7); Bennett, E. 45(1); Brezovan, P. 1(1); Bridcutt, L. 31(6); Calderon, I. 44; Dicker, G.
38(8); Dunk, L. 2(3); El-Abd, A. 36(1); Elphick, T. 22(5); Greer, G. 32; Hart, G. (3); Holroyd, C. (3); Kasim, Y. 1; Kishishev, R. 21(11); LuaLua, K. 7(4); Murray, G. 38(4);
Navarro, A. 2(2); Noone, C. 10(13); Painter, M. 46; Sandaza, F. 3(12); Smith, J. 3(5); Spar-
row, M. 21(8); Taricco, M. 2(2); Wood, C. 22(7).
Goals – League (85): Murray 22, Barnes 18 (2 pens), Wood 8 (4 pens), Calderon 7, Ben-
nett 6, LuaLua 4, Sparrow 4, Dicker 3 (1 pen), Bridcutt 2, Noone 2, Sandaza 2, El-Abd
1, Elphick 1, Painter 1, own goals 4.
Carling Cup (0).
FA Cup (11): Barnes 2 (1 pen), Bennett 2, Sandaza 2, Sparrow 2, Calderon 1, Taricco 1,
Wood 1.
J Paint Trophy (0).
Ground: American Express Community Stadium, Village Way, Brighton BN1 9BL.
Telephone: (01273) 878 288.
Record Attendance: 36,747 v Fulham, Division 2, 27 December 1958 (at Goldstone
Ground). 8,691 v Leeds U, FL 1, 20 October 2007 (at Withdean).
Capacity: 8,850.
Manager: Gus Poyet.
Secretary: Derek J. Allan.
Most League Goals: 112, Division 3 (S), 1955–56.

Highest League Scorer in Season: Peter Ward, 32, Division 3, 1976–77.
Most League Goals in Total Aggregate: Tommy Cook, 114, 1922–29.
Most Capped Player: Steve Penney, 17, Northern Ireland.
Most League Appearances: 'Tug' Wilson, 509, 1922–36.
Honours – Football League: Championship 1 Winners – 2010–11. Division 2 Champions – 2001–02. Division 3 Champions – 2000–01. Division 3 (S) Champions – 1957–58. Division 4 Champions – 1964–65.
Colours: Blue and white striped shirts, white sleeves with blue trim, white shorts, white stockings.

BRISTOL CITY   FL CHAMPIONSHIP

Adomah Albert (F)	6 1	11 08	Harrow	13 12 87	Barnet
Campbell-Ryce Jamal (M)	5 7	12 03	Lambeth	6 4 83	Barnsley
Carey Louis (D)	5 10	12 09	Bristol	20 1 77	Trainee
Cisse Kalifa (M)	6 2	12 11	Orleans	1 9 84	Reading
Clarkson David (F)	5 10	10 03	Belshill	10 9 85	Motherwell
Edwards Joe (D)	5 8	11 07	Gloucester	31 10 90	Scholar
Elliott Marvin (M)	6 0	12 02	Wandsworth	15 9 84	Millwall
Fontaine Liam (D)	5 11	11 09	Beckenham	7 1 86	Fulham
Gerken Dean (G)	6 3	12 08	Rochford	22 5 85	Colchester U
Henderson Stephen (G)	6 3	11 00	Dublin	2 5 88	Aston Villa
Hunt Nicky (D)	6 1	13 07	Westhoughton	3 9 83	Bolton W
Jackson Marlon (F)	5 11	11 12	Bristol	6 12 90	Scholar
James David (G)	6 5	15 07	Welwyn	1 8 70	Portsmouth
Johnson Lee (M)	5 6	10 07	Newmarket	7 6 81	Hearts
Maynard Nicky (F)	5 11	11 00	Winsford	11 12 86	Crewe Alex
McAllister Jamie (D)	5 10	11 00	Glasgow	26 4 78	Hearts
Nyatanga Lewin (D)	6 2	12 08	Burton	18 8 88	Derby Co
Pitman Brett (F)	6 0	11 00	Jersey	31 1 88	Bournemouth
Ribeiro Christian (D)	5 11	12 02	Neath	14 12 89	Scholar
Skuse Cole (M)	6 1	11 05	Bristol	29 3 86	Scholar
Stead Jon (F)	6 3	13 03	Huddersfield	7 4 83	Ipswich T
Stewart Damion (D)	6 3	13 10	Jamaica	18 8 80	QPR
Wilson James (D)	6 2	11 05	Newport	26 2 89	Scholar
Woolford Martyn (M)	6 0	11 09	Castleford	13 10 85	Scunthorpe U

League Appearances: Adomah, A. 45(1); Akinde, J. (2); Campbell-Ryce, J. 21(10); Carey, L. 20(1); Caulker, S. 29; Cisse, K. 19(10); Clarkson, D. 17(17); Edwards, J. 1(1); Elliott, M. 46; Fontaine, L. 30(1); Gerken, D. 1; Haynes, D. 10(3); Hunt, N. 6(1); Jackson, M. (4); James, D. 45; Johnson, L. 14(6); Keogh, A. 4(5); Maynard, N. 11(2); McAllister, J. 33(1); Nyatanga, L. 18(2); Pitman, B. 21(18); Reid, B. (1); Ribeiro, C. 8(1); Rose, D. 13(4); Skuse, C. 25(5); Spence, J. 11; Sproule, I. 4(7); Stead, J. 24(3); Stewart, D. 18(3); Vokes, S. (1); Williams, G. (3); Williams, T. (1); Wilson, J. 2; Woolford, M. 10(5).
Goals – League (62): Pitman 13 (4 pens), Stead 9, Elliott 8, Clarkson 7 (2 pens), Maynard 6 (1 pen), Adomah 5, Campbell-Ryce 2, Caulker 2, Haynes 1, Johnson 1, Keogh 1, McAllister 1, Nyatanga 1, Skuse 1, Stewart 1, own goals 3.
Carling Cup (2): McAllister 1, Sproule 1.
FA Cup (0).
Ground: Ashton Gate Stadium, Bristol BS3 2EJ. Telephone: (0871) 222 6666.
Record Attendance: 43,335 v Preston NE, FA Cup 5th rd, 16 February 1935.
Capacity: 21,804.
Manager: Keith Millen.
Secretary: Michelle McDonald.
Most League Goals: 104, Division 3 (S), 1926–27.
Highest League Scorer in Season: Don Clark, 36, Division 3 (S), 1946–47.

Most League Goals in Total Aggregate: John Atyeo, 314, 1951–66.
Most Capped Player: Billy Wedlock, 26, England.
Most League Appearances: John Atyeo, 597, 1951–66.
Honours – Football League: Division 2 Champions – 1905–06. Division 3 (S) Champions – 1922–23, 1926–27, 1954–55. Welsh Cup: Winners – 1934. Anglo-Scottish Cup: Winners – 1977–78. Freight Rover Trophy: Winners – 1985–86. LDV Vans Trophy: Winners – 2002–03.
Colours: Red shirts with white trim, white shorts, red stockings.

BRISTOL ROVERS   FL CHAMPIONSHIP 2

Anthony Byron (D)	6 1	11 02	Newport	20	9	84	Cardiff C
Blizzard Dominic (M)	6 2	12 04	High Wycombe	2	9	83	Stockport Co
Brown Wayne (M)	5 9	12 05	Kingston	6	8	88	Fulham
Campbell Stuart (M)	5 10	10 08	Corby	9	12	77	Grimsby T
Clough Charlie (M)	6 0	12 04	Somerset	3	9	90	Scholar
Coles Danny (D)	6 1	11 05	Bristol	31	10	81	Hull C
Hoskins Will (F)	5 11	11 02	Nottingham	6	5	86	Watford
Jeffries Darren (M)			Swindon	25	10	93	Scholar
Lines Chris (M)	6 2	12 00	Bristol	30	11	85	Filton College
Osei-Kuffour Jo (F)	5 8	11 11	Edmonton	17	11	81	Bournemouth
Pell Harry (M)			Chadwell-St-Mary	21	10	91	Charlton Ath
Powell Lamar (F)			Bristol	3	9	93	Scholar
Reece Charlie (M)	5 11	11 03	Birmingham	8	9	88	Scholar
Richards Elliot (M)	5 9	11 09	New Tredegar	10	9	91	Scholar
Sawyer Gary (D)	6 0	11 08	Bideford	5	7	85	Plymouth Arg
Swallow Ben (M)	5 8	10 10	Cardiff	20	10	89	Scholar

League Appearances: Akinde, J. 9(5); Andersen, M. 19; Anthony, B. 36(1); Blizzard, D. 3(2); Bolger, C. 4(2); Brown, W. 12(13); Campbell, S. 37; Clarke, O. (1); Clough, C. 1(1); Coles, D. 37; Daniels, L. 9; Davies, S. 4(3); Duffy, D. (3); Green, M. 2; Harrison, E. (1); Hoskins, W. 41(2); Howe, R. 8(4); Hughes, J. 40(2); Ifil, J. 3; Kalala, J. 10(1); Lambe, R. 1(6); Lines, C. 41(1); Logan, C. 16; McCracken, D. 5(5); Osei-Kuffour, J. 33(9); Pell, H. 7(3); Powell, L. (1); Reece, C. 6(8); Regan, C. 19(2); Richards, E. 2(11); Sawyer, G. 37; Senda, D. 15; Swallow, B. 11(6); Tunnicliffe, J. 21(4); Williams, G. 17(2).
Goals – League (48): Hoskins 17 (1 pen), Hughes 10 (5 pens), Osei-Kuffour 6, Anthony 3, Brown 3, Lines 3, Williams 2, Howe 1, Richards 1, own goals 2.
Carling Cup (1): Lines 1.
FA Cup (1): Hoskins 1.
J Paint Trophy (9): Osei-Kuffour 3, Hoskins 2, Swallow 2, Hughes 1 (pen), Lines 1.
Ground: The Memorial Stadium, Filton Avenue, Horfield, Bristol BS7 0BF. Telephone: (0117) 909 6648.
Record Attendance: 38,472 v Preston NE, FA Cup 4th rd, 30 January 1960 (at Eastville). 9,464 v Liverpool, FA Cup 4th rd, 8 February 1992 (at Twerton Park). 12,011 v WBA, FA Cup 6th rd, 9 March 2008 (at Memorial Stadium).
Capacity: 11,626.
Manager: Paul Buckle.
Secretary: Rod Wesson.
Most League Goals: 92, Division 3 (S), 1952–53.
Highest League Scorer in Season: Geoff Bradford, 33, Division 3 (S), 1952–53.
Most League Goals in Total Aggregate: Geoff Bradford, 242, 1949–64.
Most Capped Player: Vitalijs Astafjevs, 31 (167), Latvia.
Most League Appearances: Stuart Taylor, 546, 1966–80.
Honours – Football League: Division 3 (S) Champions – 1952–53. Division 3 Champions – 1989–90.
Colours: Blue and white quarters, white shorts, white stockings.

Alexander Graham (D)	5 10	12 07	Coventry	10 10 71	Preston NE
Austin Charlie (F)	6 2	13 03	Hungerford	5 7 89	Swindon T
Bartley Marvyn (M)	6 1	12 04	Reading	4 7 86	Bournemouth
Bikey Andre (D)	6 0	12 08	Douala	8 1 85	Reading
Carlisle Clarke (D)	6 2	14 11	Preston	14 10 79	Watford
Cort Leon (D)	6 3	13 01	Bermondsey	11 9 79	Stoke C
Duff Michael (D)	6 1	11 08	Belfast	11 1 78	Cheltenham T
Eagles Chris (M)	5 10	11 07	Hemel Hempstead	19 11 85	Manchester U
Easton Brian (D)	6 0	12 00	Glasgow	5 3 88	Hamilton A
Eckersley Richard (D)	5 9	11 09	Worsley	12 3 89	Manchester U
Edgar David (D)	6 2	12 13	Ontario	19 5 87	Newcastle U
Elliott Wade (M)	5 10	10 03	Southampton	14 12 78	Bournemouth
Fletcher Wes (F)	5 11	12 06	Ormskirk	28 2 90	Scholar
Fox Danny (D)	5 11	12 06	Crewe	29 5 86	Celtic
Grant Lee (G)	6 3	13 01	Hemel Hempstead	27 1 83	Sheffield W
Harvey Alex-Ray (M)	5 7	10 09	Burnley	4 4 90	Scholar
Iwelumo Chris (F)	6 3	15 03	Coatbridge	1 8 78	Wolverhampton W
Jensen Brian (G)	6 4	16 09	Copenhagen	8 6 75	WBA
Knowles Dominic (F)			Oswaldtwistle	13 2 92	Scholar
Long Kevin (D)	6 3	13 01	Cork	18 8 90	Cork C
MacDonald Alex (F)	5 7	11 04	Warrington	14 4 90	Scholar
Marney Dean (M)	5 10	11 09	Barking	31 1 84	Hull C
McCann Chris (M)	6 1	11 11	Dublin	21 7 87	Scholar
Mears Tyrone (D)	5 11	11 10	Stockport	18 2 83	Derby Co
Paterson Martin (F)	5 9	10 11	Tunstall	13 5 87	Scunthorpe U
Rodriguez Jay (F)	6 0	12 00	Burnley	27 7 89	Scholar
Wallace Ross (M)	5 6	9 12	Dundee	23 5 85	Preston NE

League Appearances: Alexander, G. 15(17); Austin, C. 2(2); Bartley, M. 3(2); Bikey, A. 27(1); Carlisle, C. 33(2); Cork, J. 36(4); Cort, L. 3(1); Delfouneso, N. 7(4); Duff, M. 27(1); Duffy, S. 1; Eagles, C. 37(6); Easton, B. 11(1); Edgar, D. 3(4); Elliott, W. 37(7); Fox, D. 35; Grant, L. 25; Guidetti, J. 2(3); Iwelumo, C. 29(16); Jensen, B. 21; Marney, D. 34(2); McCann, C. 4; Mears, T. 44; Paterson, M. 7(4); Rodriguez, J. 37(5); Thompson, S. 2(27); Wallace, R. 24(16).
Goals – League (65): Rodriguez 14, Eagles 11 (4 pens), Iwelumo 11, Alexander 3 (3 pens), Cork 3, Marney 3, Wallace 3, Bikey 2, Elliott 2, Paterson 2, Thompson 2, Carlisle 1, Delfouneso 1, Duff 1, Easton 1, Guidetti 1, McCann 1, Mears 1, own goals 2.
Carling Cup (5): Carlisle 1, Eagles 1, Elliott 1, McDonald 1, Thompson 1 (pen).
FA Cup (8): Eagles 3, Alexander 1 (pen), Carlisle 1, Mears 1, Paterson 1, Rodriguez 1.
Ground: Turf Moor, Harry Potts Way, Burnley, Lancashire BB10 4BX. Telephone: 0871 221 1882.
Record Attendance: 54,775 v Huddersfield T, FA Cup 3rd rd, 23 February 1924.
Capacity: 22,610.
Manager: Eddie Howe.
Football Secretary: Pauline Scott.
Most League Goals: 102, Division 1, 1960–61.
Highest League Scorer in Season: George Beel, 35, Division 1, 1927–28.
Most League Goals in Total Aggregate: George Beel, 179, 1923–32.
Most Capped Player: Jimmy McIlroy, 51 (55), Northern Ireland.
Most League Appearances: Jerry Dawson, 522, 1907–28.
Honours – Football League: Division 1 Champions – 1920–21, 1959–60. Division 2 Champions – 1897–98, 1972–73. Division 3 Champions – 1981–82. Division 4 Champions – 1991–92. **FA Cup:** Winners – 1913–14. **Anglo-Scottish Cup:** Winners – 1978–79.
Colours: Claret shirts with blue sleeves, white shorts, claret stockings.

Austin Ryan (D)	6 3	13 07	Stoke	15 11 84	Crewe Alex
Boertien Paul (D)	5 10	11 02	Haltwhistle	21 1 79	Walsall
Bolder Adam (M)	5 9	10 08	Hull	25 10 80	Millwall
Corbett Andrew (M)	6 0	11 05	Worcester	20 2 82	Nuneaton B
Dyer Jack (M)			Sutton Coldfield	11 12 91	Aston Villa
Ellison James (F)	5 10	12 08	Liverpool	25 10 91	Liverpool
James Tony (D)	6 3	14 02	Cardiff	9 10 78	Weymouth
Legzdins Adam (G)	6 1	14 02	Stafford	28 11 86	Crewe Alex
Maghoma Jacques (M)	5 9	11 06	Lubumbashi	23 10 87	Tottenham H
McGrath John (M)	5 10	10 03	Limerick	27 3 80	Tamworth
Moore Darren (D)	6 2	15 07	Birmingham	22 4 74	Barnsley
Pearson Greg (F)	6 0	11 00	Birmingham	3 4 85	Bishop's Stortford
Penn Russell (M)	5 11	12 13	Dudley	8 11 85	Kidderminster H
Phillips Jimmy (M)	5 7	10 00	Stoke	20 9 89	Stoke C
Poole Kevin (G)	5 10	11 11	Bromsgrove	21 7 63	Derby Co
Preen Garyn (M)	5 11	12 06	Tredegar	25 10 91	Southampton
Stanton Nathan (D)	5 9	12 06	Nottingham	6 5 81	Rochdale
Webster Aaron (D)	6 2	12 02	Burton-on-Trent	19 12 80	Youth

League Appearances: Austin, R. 20(4); Boertien, P. 15(1); Bolder, A. 32(5); Collins, J. 9(1); Corbett, A. 36(4); Dyer, J. 4(1); Ellison, J. (2); Gilroy, K. (1); Grocott, K. (2); Harrad, S. 16(4); Hughes, B. 1; James, T. 25(2); Legzdins, A. 46; Maghoma, J. 39(2); Malone, S. 18(4); McGrath, J. 38(3); Moore, D. 32(2); Parkes, T. 4(1); Pearson, G. 16(19); Penn, R. 39(2); Phillips, J. 10(13); Preen, G. (1); Rodney, N. (3); Stanton, N. 23; Walker, R. 9(9); Webster, A. 38(4); Whaley, S. 1(2); Winnall, S. 12(7); Young, L. 9(10); Zola, C. 14(4).
Goals – League (56): Webster 11, Harrad 10 (2 pens), Winnall 7 (2 pens), Pearson 5 (2 pens), Collins 4, Maghoma 4, McGrath 3, Penn 3, Zola 3, Bolder 1, Corbett 1, Malone 1, Walker 1, own goals 2.
Carling Cup (1): Harrad 1.
FA Cup (7): Harrad 2, Webster 2, Collins 1, Maghoma 1, Zola 1.
J Paint Trophy (1): Walker 1.
Ground: Pirelli Stadium, Princess Way, Burton-on-Trent, Staffordshire DE13 0AR. Telephone: (01283) 565 938.
Record Attendance: 5,806 v Weymouth, Southern League Cup final 2nd leg 1964 (at Eton Park). 6,192 v Oxford U, Blue Square Premier, 17 April 2009 (at Pirelli Stadium).
Capacity: 6,350 (2,034 seated).
Manager: Paul Peschisolido.
Football Secretary: Fleur Robinson.
Most League Goals: 71, FL 2, 2009–10.
Highest League Scorer in Season: Shaun Harrad, 21, 2009–10.
Most League Goals in Total Aggregate: Shaun Harrad, 31, 2009–11.
Most Capped Player: Jacques Maghoma, 2, DR Congo.
Most League Appearances: John McGrath, 86, 2009–.
Honours: Conference: Champions – 2008–09. **Southern League Cup:** Winners – 1964, 1997, 2000. **Northern Premier League:** Champions – 2001–02. **Northern Premier League Shield:** 1983. **Challenge Cup:** Winners – 1983. **Birmingham Senior Cup:** Winners – 1954, 1997. **Staffordshire Senior Cup:** Winners – 1956. **Midland Floodlit Cup:** Winners – 1976.
Colours: Yellow shirts with black insert, black shorts, black stockings.

BURY

FL CHAMPIONSHIP 1

Belford Cameron (G)	6 1	11 10	Nuneaton	16 10 88	Coventry C
Bennett Kyle (F)	5 5	9 08	Telford	9 9 90	Wolverhampton W

Bishop Andy (F)	6 0	11 00	Stone	19 10 82	York C
Branagan Ritchie (G)	5 11	12 10	Gravesend	20 10 91	Bolton W
Futcher Ben (D)	6 7	12 05	Manchester	20 2 81	Peterborough U
Haworth Andrew (M)	5 11	11 10	Lancaster	28 11 88	Blackburn R
John-Lewis Lenell (M)	5 10	11 10	Hammersmith	17 5 89	Lincoln C
Jones Andrai (M)	5 11	10 10	Liverpool	1 1 92	Scholar
Jones Mike (M)	5 11	12 04	Birkenhead	15 8 87	Tranmere R
Lowe Ryan (F)	5 10	12 08	Liverpool	18 9 78	Chester C
Mozika Damien (M)	6 0	11 13	Corbeil-Essonnes	15 4 87	Chester C
Patel Krishnan (M)	5 7	11 00	Bolton	17 12 91	Scholar
Picken Phil (D)	5 9	10 07	Droylsden	12 11 85	Chesterfield
Rothwell Zach (M)	6 1	11 07	Bury	16 7 92	Scholar
Schumacher Steven (M)	5 10	11 00	Liverpool	30 4 84	Crewe Alex
Skarz Joe (D)	5 10	11 04	Huddersfield	13 7 89	Huddersfield T
Sodje Efe (D)	6 1	12 00	Greenwich	5 10 72	Gillingham
Sweeney Peter (M)	6 0	12 11	Glasgow	25 9 84	Grimsby T
Worrall David (M)	6 0	11 03	Manchester	12 6 90	WBA

League Appearances: Ajose, N. 22(6); Belford, C. 39; Bennett, K. 13(19); Bishop, A. 14(5); Branagan, R. 1(1); Carlton, D. (3); Eckersley, R. 3; Futcher, B. 6(5); Gunning, G. 2; Harrop, M. (3); Haworth, A. 20(20); Holroyd, C. 3(1); John-Lewis, L. 6(33); Jones, M. 37(5); Jones, A. (1); Lees, T. 45; Lowe, R. 46; McCarthy, L. (1); Mozika, D. 32(1); Picken, P. 38; Schumacher, S. 42(1); Skarz, J. 46; Sodje, E. 40; Sweeney, P. 18(7); Williams, O. 6; Worrall, D. 27(13).
Goals – League (82): Lowe 27 (4 pens), Ajose 13, Schumacher 9, Jones M 8, Bishop 4, Lees 4, Haworth 3, Sodje 3, Bennett 2, John-Lewis 2, Mozika 2, Worrall 2, Futcher 1, Holroyd 1, Skarz 1.
Carling Cup (0).
FA Cup (3): Lees 1, Lowe 1, Sodje 1.
J Paint Trophy (0).
Ground: Gigg Lane, Bury, Lancs BL9 9HR. Telephone: (08445) 790009.
Record Attendance: 35,000 v Bolton W, FA Cup 3rd rd, 9 January 1960.
Capacity: 11,669.
Manager: Richie Barker.
Secretary: Jill Neville.
Most League Goals: 108, Division 3, 1960–61.
Highest League Scorer in Season: Craig Madden, 35, Division 4, 1981–82.
Most League Goals in Total Aggregate: Craig Madden, 129, 1978–86.
Most Capped Player: Bill Gorman, 11 (13), Republic of Ireland and (4), Northern Ireland.
Most League Appearances: Norman Bullock, 506, 1920–35.
Honours – Football League: Division 2 Champions – 1894–95, 1996–97. Division 3 Champions – 1960–61. **FA Cup:** Winners – 1900, 1903.
Colours: Black and blue halved shirts, white shorts, black stockings

---

CARDIFF CITY   FL CHAMPIONSHIP

Blake Darcy (M)	5 10	12 05	New Tredegar	13 12 88	Scholar
Chopra Michael (F)	5 9	10 10	Newcastle	23 12 83	Sunderland
Gerrard Anthony (D)	6 2	13 07	Liverpool	6 2 86	Walsall
Gyepes Gabor (D)	6 3	13 01	Hungary	26 6 81	Northampton T
Heaton Tom (G)	6 1	13 12	Chester	15 4 86	Manchester U
Hudson Mark (D)	6 1	12 01	Guildford	30 3 82	Charlton Ath
Keinan Dekel (D)	6 0	11 09	Rosh Hanikra	15 9 84	Blackpool
Marshall David (G)	6 3	13 04	Glasgow	5 3 85	Norwich C
Matthews Adam (M)	5 10	11 02	Swansea	13 1 92	Scholar

McNaughton Kevin (D)	5 10	10 06	Dundee	28 8 82	Aberdeen
McPhail Steve (M)	5 10	13 03	Westminster	9 12 79	Barnsley
Meades Jonathan (D)	6 1	13 00	Cardiff	2 3 92	Scholar
Naylor Lee (D)	5 9	11 03	Walsall	19 3 80	Wolverhampton W
Parkin Jon (F)	6 4	13 07	Barnsley	30 12 81	Preston NE
Quinn Paul (D)	6 0	11 04	Wishaw	21 7 85	Motherwell
Taiwo Soloman (M)	6 1	13 02	Lagos	29 4 85	Dagenham & R
Whittingham Peter (M)	5 10	11 06	Nuneaton	8 9 84	Aston Villa
Wildig Aaron (M)	5 9	11 02	Hereford	26 1 90	Scholar

League Appearances: Bellamy, C. 34(1); Blake, D. 13(13); Bothroyd, J. 37; Burke, C. 31(13); Bywater, S. 8; Chopra, M. 25(7); Drinkwater, D. 7(2); Emmanuel-Thomas, J. 7(7); Gyepes, G. 16(5); Heaton, T. 27; Hudson, M. 39(1); Keinan, D. 18; Keogh, A. 11(5); Koumas, J. 5(18); Marshall, D. 11; Matthews, A. 2(6); McCormack, R. (2); McNaughton, K. 44; McPhail, S. 23(5); Naylor, L. 25(2); Olofinjana, S. 38(1); Parkin, J. 2(9); Quinn, P. 22(1); Rae, G. 2(5); Ramsey, A. 6; Riggott, C. 2; Samuel, J. 6; Whittingham, P. 45; Wildig, A. (2).

Goals – League (76): Bothroyd 18 (1 pen), Bellamy 11, Whittingham 11 (3 pens), Chopra 9, Olofinjana 6, Burke 5, Emmanuel-Thomas 2, Keinan 2, Keogh 2, Koumas 2, Naylor 2, Gyepes 1, Parkin 1, Quinn 1, Rae 1, Ramsey 1, own goal 1.

Carling Cup (5): Bothroyd 2, McCormack 2, Chopra 1.

FA Cup (1): Chopra 1.

Play-Offs (0).

Ground: Cardiff City Stadium, Leckwith Road, Cardiff CF11 8AZ. Telephone: (0845) 365 1115.

Record Attendance: 62,634, Wales v England, 17 October 1959 (at Ninian Park); 26,055 v Leicester C, FL C Play-Off semi-final 2nd leg 12 May 2010 (at Cardiff City Stadium).

Club Record Attendance: 57,893 v Arsenal, Division 1, 22 April 1953.

Capacity: 26,828.

Manager: Malky Mackay.

Secretary: Jason Turner.

Most League Goals: 95, Division 3, 2000–01.

Highest League Scorer in Season: Robert Earnshaw, 31, Division 2, 2002–03.

Most League Goals in Total Aggregate: Len Davies, 128, 1920–31.

Most Capped Player: Alf Sherwood, 39 (41), Wales.

Most League Appearances: Phil Dwyer, 471, 1972–85.

Honours – Football League: Division 3 (S) Champions – 1946–47; Division 3 Champions – 1992–93. **FA Cup:** Winners – 1926–27 (only occasion the Cup has been won by a club outside England). **Welsh Cup:** Winners – 22 times. **Charity Shield:** Winners 1927.

Colours: Blue shirts with yellow trim, white shorts, white stockings.

CARLISLE UNITED   FL CHAMPIONSHIP 1

Berrett James (M)	5 10	10 13	Halifax	13 1 89	Huddersfield T
Collin Adam (G)	6 2	12 00	Carlisle	9 12 84	Doncaster R
Curran Craig (F)	5 9	11 09	Liverpool	23 9 89	Tranmere R
Gillespie Mark (G)	6 3	13 07	Newcastle	27 3 92	Scholar
Livesey Danny (D)	6 3	13 01	Salford	31 12 84	Bolton W
Loy Rory (F)	5 10	10 07	Dumfries	19 3 88	Rangers
Madden Patrick (F)			Dublin	4 3 90	Bohemians
Michalik Lubomir (D)	6 4	13 00	Cadca	13 8 83	Leeds U
Murphy Peter (M)	5 10	12 10	Dublin	27 10 80	Blackburn R
Robson Matty (D)	5 10	11 02	Durham	23 1 85	Hartlepool U
Simek Frankie (D)	6 0	11 06	St Louis	13 10 84	Sheffield W
Taiwo Tom (M)	5 8	10 07	Leeds	27 2 90	Chelsea

| Thirlwell Paul (M) | 5 11 | 11 04 | Springwell Village | 13 | 2 79 | Derby Co |
| Zoko Francois (F) | 6 0 | 11 05 | Daloa | 13 | 9 83 | Ostend |

League Appearances: Arter, H. 2(3); Berrett, J. 46; Borrowdale, G. 1; Bowman, R. (3); Bridge-Wilkinson, M. (3); Chester, J. 18; Collin, A. 46; Cooper, L. 6; Cruise, T. 3; Curran, C. 36(9); Dudgeon, J. 1(1); Evans, C. 1; Grella, M. 7(3); Harte, I. 4; Hurst, K. (2); Kane, T. (1); Kavanagh, G. (1); Livesey, D. 5(5); Loy, R. 5(12); Madden, P. 1(12); Madine, G. 21; Marshall, B. 27(6); McDaid, S. 12; McKenna, B. (1); Michalik, L. 32; Murphy, P. 32(2); Noble, L. 18(3); Norwood, O. 4(2); Price, J. (3); Robson, M. 27(15); Simek, F. 46; Taiwo, T. 44(2); Thirlwell, P. 21(2); Wells, N. (3); Zoko, F. 40(4).

Goals – League (60): Berrett 10 (4 pens), Curran 8, Madine 8, Zoko 6, Grella 3, Marshall 3, Murphy 3, Noble 3, Chester 2, Harte 2 (1 pen), Michalik 2, Robson 2, Taiwo 2, Arter 1, Cooper 1, Loy 1, Thirlwell 1, own goals 2.

Carling Cup (0).

FA Cup (9): Madine 5, Zoko 3, Chester 1.

J Paint Trophy (13): Murphy 4, Marshall 2, Michalik 2, Chester 1, Price 1, Taiwo 1, Zoko 1, own goal 1.

Ground: Brunton Park, Warwick Road, Carlisle CA1 1LL. Telephone: (01228) 526 237.

Record Attendance: 27,500 v Birmingham C, FA Cup 3rd rd, 5 January 1957 and v Middlesbrough, FA Cup 5th rd, 7 February 1970.

Capacity: 16,981.

Manager: Greg Abbott.

Secretary: Sarah McKnight.

Most League Goals: 113, Division 4, 1963–64.

Highest League Scorer in Season: Jimmy McConnell, 42, Division 3 (N), 1928–29.

Most League Goals in Total Aggregate: Jimmy McConnell, 126, 1928–32.

Most Capped Player: Eric Welsh, 4, Northern Ireland.

Most League Appearances: Allan Ross, 466, 1963–79.

Honours – Football League: Division 3 Champions – 1964–65, 1994–95; Championship 2 Champions – 2005–06. **Auto Windscreen Shield:** Winners 1997. **Johnstone's Paint Trophy:** Winners – 2010–11.

Colours: Blue shirts with white and red trim, white shorts, white stockings.

CHARLTON ATHLETIC

FL CHAMPIONSHIP 1

Benson Paul (F)	6 1	11 01	Rochford	12	10 79	Dagenham & R
Davisson Benjamin (M)	5 7	11 00	Sidcup	23	10 91	Scholar
Doherty Gary (D)	6 3	13 13	Carndonagh	31	1 80	Norwich C
Elliot Rob (G)	6 3	14 10	Chatham	30	4 86	Scholar
Francis Simon (D)	6 0	12 06	Nottingham	16	2 85	Southend U
Jackson Johnnie (M)	6 1	12 00	Camden	15	8 82	Notts Co
Jenkinson Carl (D)	6 1	12 02	Buckhurst Hill	8	2 92	Scholar
Mambo Yado (D)	6 3	13 01	Kilburn	22	10 91	Scholar
McCormack Alan (M)	5 8	11 00	Dublin	10	1 84	Southend U
Solly Chris (D)	5 8	10 07	Chatham	20	1 91	Scholar
Wagstaff Scott (F)	5 10	10 03	Maidstone	31	3 90	Scholar
Wright-Phillips Bradley (M)	5 10	10 07	Lewisham	12	3 85	Plymouth Arg

League Appearances: Abbott, P. 10(7); Anyinsah, J. 14(5); Benson, P. 28(4); Bessone, F. 13; Dailly, C. 32; Doherty, G. 35(3); Eccleston, N. 8(13); Elliot, R. 35; Fortune, J. 12(4); Francis, S. 32(2); Fry, M. 20(5); Harriott, C. 1(2); Jackson, J. 29(1); Jenkinson, C. 7(1); Llera, M. 14(1); Martin, L. 14(6); McCormack, A. 18(6); Nouble, F. 4(5); Parrett, D. 9; Racon, T. 34(5); Reid, K. 13(19); Semedo, J. 42; Sodje, A. 1(14); Solly, C. 9(5); Stewart, M. 6(3); Sullivan, J. 4; Wagstaff, S. 35(5); Worner, R. 7(1); Wright-Phillips, B. 20(1).

Goals – League (62): Jackson 13 (6 pens), Benson 10, Wright-Phillips 9, Wagstaff 8, Anyinsah 3, Eccleston 3, Racon 3, Abbott 2, Martin 2, Fry 1, Llera 1, McCormack 1, Nouble 1, Parrett 1, Reid 1, Semedo 1, Sodje 1, Solly 1.

Carling Cup (3): Abbott 2, Martin 1.
FA Cup (6): Anyinsah 2, Jackson 1, Racon 1, Reid 1, Wagstaff 1.
J Paint Trophy (4): Racon 2, Abbott 1, Wagstaff 1.
Ground: The Valley, Floyd Road, Charlton, London SE7 8BL. Telephone: (020) 8333 4000.
Capacity: 27,111.
Record Attendance: 75,031 v Aston Villa, FA Cup 5th rd, 12 February 1938 (at The Valley).
Manager: Chris Powell.
Football Secretary: Chris Parkes.
Most League Goals: 107, Division 2, 1957–58.
Highest League Scorer in Season: Ralph Allen, 32, Division 3 (S), 1934–35.
Most League Goals in Total Aggregate: Stuart Leary, 153, 1953–62.
Most Capped Player: Jonatan Johansson, 42 (105), Finland.
Most League Appearances: Sam Bartram, 579, 1934–56.
Honours – Football League: Division 1 Champions – 1999–2000. Division 3 (S) Champions – 1928–29, 1934–35. **FA Cup:** Winners – 1947.
Colours: Red shirts with white trim, white shorts, white stockings with red tops.

CHELSEA   FA PREMIERSHIP

Player			Birthplace				Former club
Alex (D)	6 2	14 00	Niteroi	17	6	82	PSV Eindhoven
Anelka Nicolas (F)	6 1	13 03	Versailles	14	3	79	Bolton W
Ashton James (D)			Gravesend	2	10	92	Scholar
Benayoun Yossi (M)	5 10	11 00	Beer Sheva	6	6	80	Liverpool
Bertrand Ryan (D)	5 10	11 00	Southwark	5	8	89	Scholar
Borini Fabio (F)	5 10	11 02	Bentivoglio	23	3	91	Bologna
Bosingwa Jose (D)	6 0	12 08	Kinshasa	24	8	82	Porto
Bruma Jeffrey (D)	6 1	12 00	Rotterdam	13	11	91	Scholar
Cech Petr (G)	6 5	14 03	Plzen	20	5	82	Rennes
Clifford Billy (M)			Slough	18	10	92	Scholar
Clifford Conor (M)	5 8	10 08	Dublin	1	10	91	Scholar
Cole Ashley (D)	5 8	10 08	Stepney	20	12	80	Arsenal
Cork Jack (D)	6 0	10 12	Carshalton	25	6	89	Scholar
Deen-Conteh Aziz (D)			Bumpeh	14	1	93	Scholar
Delac Matej (G)	6 3	13 00	Vakuf-Uskoplje	20	8	92	Vitesse
Djalo Aliu (M)			Bissau	5	2	92	Scholar
Drogba Didier (F)	6 2	13 08	Abidjan	11	3	78	Marseille
Essien Michael (M)	5 10	13 06	Accra	3	12	82	Lyon
Gordon Ben (D)	5 11	12 06	Bradford	2	3	91	Scholar
Hilario (G)	6 2	13 05	San Pedro da Cova	21	10	75	Nacional
Ince Rohan (D)			Whitechapel	8	11	92	Scholar
Ivanovic Branislav (M)	6 0	12 04	Sremska Mitreovica	22	2	84	Lokomotiv Moscow
Kakuta Gael (F)	5 8	10 03	Lille	21	6	91	Lens
Kalas Tomas (D)	6 0	12 00	Olomouc	15	5	93	Sigma Olomouc
Kalou Salomon (F)	6 0	12 02	Oume	5	8	85	Feyenoord
Lalkovic Milan (F)			Kosice	9	12	92	Scholar
Lampard Frank (M)	6 0	14 01	Romford	20	6	78	West Ham U
Luiz David (D)	6 2	13 03	Sao Paulo	22	4	87	Benfica
Malouda Florent (M)	6 0	11 06	Cayenne	13	6	80	Lyon
Mancienne Michael (D)	6 0	11 09	Isleworth	8	1	88	Scholar
Matic Nemanja (M)	6 4	12 13	Sabac	1	8	88	Kosice
McEachran Josh (M)	5 10	10 03	Oxford	1	3	93	Scholar
Mellis Jacob (D)	6 0	11 08	Nottingham	8	1	91	Scholar
Mikel John Obi (M)	6 0	13 05	Jos	22	4	87	Lyn
Mitrovic Marko (F)			Malmo	27	6	92	Malmo

Paulo Ferreira (D)	6 0	11 13	Cascais	18	1 79	Porto
Phillip Adam (F)			Carshalton	19	6 91	Scholar
Prosenik Philipp (F)			Vienna	1	3 93	Scholar
Rajkovic Slobodan (D)	6 5	14 00	Belgrade	3	3 89	OFK Belgrade
Ramires (M)	5 11	10 03	Rio de Janeiro	24	3 87	Benfica
Sala Jacopo (M)	6 0	11 08	Bergamo	5	12 91	Scholar
Saville George (M)			Camberley	1	6 93	Scholar
Sturridge Daniel (F)	6 2	12 00	Manchester	1	9 89	Manchester C
Taylor Rhys (G)	6 2	12 08	Neath	7	4 90	Scholar
Terry John (D)	6 1	13 08	Barking	7	12 80	Trainee
Tore Gokhan (M)	5 9	11 09	Cologne	20	1 92	Leverkusen
Torres Fernando (F)	6 0	11 07	Madrid	20	3 84	Liverpool
Turnbull Ross (G)	6 4	15 00	Bishop Auckland	4	1 85	Middlesbrough
Van Aanholt Patrick (D)	5 9	10 08	S'Hertogenbosch	3	7 88	Ajax
Walker Sam (G)	6 5	14 00	Gravesend	2	10 91	Scholar
Zhirkov Yuri (M)	6 1	11 11	Tambov	20	8 83	CSKA Moscow

League Appearances: Alex, 12(3); Anelka, N. 27(5); Benayoun, Y. 1(6); Bertrand, R. (1); Bosingwa, J. 13(7); Bruma, J. 1(1); Cech, P. 38; Cole, A. 38; Drogba, D. 30(6); Essien, M. 32(1); Ivanovic, B. 32(2); Kakuta, G. 1(4); Kalou, S. 16(15); Lampard, F. 23(1); Luiz, D. 11(1); Malouda, F. 33(5); McEachran, J. 1(8); Mikel, J. 28; Paulo Ferreira, 12(9); Ramires, 22(7); Sturridge, D. (13); Terry, J. 33; Torres, F. 8(6); Zhirkov, Y. 6(6).
Goals – League (69): Malouda 13, Drogba 11 (2 pens), Kalou 10, Lampard 10 (4 pens), Anelka 6, Ivanovic 4, Essien 3, Terry 3, Alex 2, Luiz 2, Ramires 2, Benayoun 1, Torres 1, own goal 1.
Carling Cup (3): Anelka 2 (1 pen), Van Aanholt 1.
FA Cup (9): Lampard 3, Kalou 2, Sturridge 2, Anelka 1, own goal 1.
Champions League (17): Anelka 7 (1 pen), Drogba 2 (1 pen), Ivanovic 2, Sturridge 2, Essien 1, Malouda 1, Terry 1, Zhirkov 1.
Community Shield (1): Kalou 1.
Ground: Stamford Bridge, Fulham Road, London SW6 1HS. Telephone: 0871 984 1955.
Record Attendance: 82,905 v Arsenal, Division 1, 12 October 1935.
Capacity: 41,841.
Manager: Andre Villas-Boas.
Secretary: David Barnard.
Most League Goals: 103, FA Premier League, 2009–10.
Highest League Scorer in Season: Jimmy Greaves, 41, 1960–61.
Most League Goals in Total Aggregate: Bobby Tambling, 164, 1958–70.
Most Capped Player: Frank Lampard, 84 (86), England.
Most League Appearances: Ron Harris, 655, 1962–80.
Honours – FA Premier League: Champions – 2004–05, 2005–06, 2009–10. **Football League:** Division 1 Champions – 1954–55. Division 2 Champions – 1983–84, 1988–89. **FA Cup:** Winners – 1970, 1997, 2000, 2007, 2009, 2010. **Football League Cup:** Winners – 1964–65, 1997–98, 2004–05, 2006–07. **Full Members' Cup:** Winners – 1985–86. **Zenith Data Systems Cup:** Winners – 1989–90. **European Cup-Winners' Cup:** Winners – 1970–71, 1997–98. **Super Cup:** Winners – 1999.
Colours: Reflex blue shirt, reflex blue shorts, white stockings with blue trim.

CHELTENHAM TOWN   FL CHAMPIONSHIP 2

Andrew Danny (D)	5 11	11 06	Boston	23	12 90	Peterborough U
Bird David (M)	5 9	12 00	Gloucester	26	12 84	Cinderford T
Brown Scott P (G)	6 2	13 01	Wolverhampton	26	4 85	Bristol C
Elliott Steve (D)	6 1	14 00	Derby	29	10 78	Bristol R
Gallinagh Andy (D)	5 8	11 08	Sutton Coldfield	16	3 85	Stratford T
Goulding Jeff (F)	6 2	11 11	Sutton	13	5 84	Bournemouth

Haynes Kyle (D)	5 11	11 02	Wolverhampton	29 12 91	Scholar
Lewis Theo (F)	5 10	10 12	Oxford	10 8 91	Scholar
Low Josh (M)	6 2	14 03	Bristol	15 2 79	Peterborough U
Lowe Keith (D)	6 2	13 03	Wolverhampton	13 9 85	Hereford U
Pook Michael (M)	5 11	11 10	Swindon	22 10 85	Swindon T
Smikle Brian (M)	5 11	11 09	London	3 11 85	Kidderminster H
Thomas Wesley (F)	5 10	11 00	Barking	23 1 87	Dagenham & R

League Appearances: Andrew, D. 43; Artus, F. 21(8); Bird, D. 27(12); Brown, S. 46; Eastham, A. 8(1); Elito, M. 1(1); Elliott, S. 39(2); Gallinagh, A. 20(4); Goulding, J. 34(5); Green, M. 10(9); Haynes, K. 1; Jeffers, S. 3(19); Lewis, T. 8(14); Low, J. 28(2); Lowe, K. 36; Melligan, J. 14(13); Pack, M. 32(6); Pook, M. 25(4); Riley, M. 26; Shroot, R. 4(3); Smikle, B. 37(9); Thomas, W. 40(1); Thomson, J. 3(2); Walsh, P. (4); Watkins, M. (1).

Goals – League (56): Thomas 18, Goulding 10, Low 7, Andrew 4, Smikle 4, Artus 3, Gallinagh 2, Pack 2, Elliott 1, Jeffers 1, Lowe 1, Pook 1, Shroot 1, Thomson 1.

Carling Cup (1): Jeffers 1.

FA Cup (1): Thomas 1.

J Paint Trophy (0).

Ground: The Abbey Business Stadium, Whaddon Road, Cheltenham, Gloucestershire GL52 5NA. Telephone: (01242) 573 558.

Record Attendance: 10,389 v Blackpool, FA Cup 3rd rd, 13 January 1934 (at Cheltenham Athletic Ground). 8,326 v Reading, FA Cup 1st rd, 17 November 1956 (at Whaddon Road).

Capacity: 7,136.

Manager: Mark Yates.

Secretary: Paul Godfrey.

Most League Goals: 66, Division 3, 2001–02.

Highest League Scorer in Season: Julian Alsop, 20, Division 3, 2001–02.

Most League Goals in Total Aggregate: Julian Alsop, 39, 2000–03; 2009–10.

Most Capped Player: Grant McCann, 7 (33), Northern Ireland.

Most League Appearances: David Bird, 288, 2001–11.

Honours – Football Conference: Champions – 1998–99. **FA Trophy:** Winners – 1997–98.

Colours: All red with white trim.

CHESTERFIELD   FL CHAMPIONSHIP 1

Allott Mark (M)	5 11	11 07	Middleton	3 10 77	Oldham Ath
Boden Scott (F)	5 11	11 00	Sheffield	19 12 89	IFK Marlehamn
Bowery Jordan (F)	6 1	12 00	Nottingham	2 7 91	Scholar
Clay Craig (M)	5 11	11 07	Nottingham	5 5 92	Scholar
Darikwa Tendayi (M)			Nottingham	13 12 91	Scholar
Davies Craig (F)	6 2	13 05	Burton-on-Trent	9 1 86	Brighton & HA
Downes Aaron (D)	6 3	13 00	Mudgee	15 5 85	Frickley C
Ford Simon (D)	5 11	11 07	Newham	17 11 81	Kilmarnock
Gray Dan (M)	6 0	11 00	Mansfield	23 11 89	Scholar
Holden Dean (D)	6 1	12 04	Salford	15 9 79	Shrewsbury T
Lee Tommy (G)	6 2	12 00	Keighley	3 1 86	Macclesfield T
Lester Jack (F)	5 9	12 08	Sheffield	8 10 75	Nottingham F
Lowry Jamie (D)	6 0	12 04	Newquay	18 3 87	Scholar
Mattis Dwayne (M)	6 1	11 12	Huddersfield	31 7 81	Walsall
Morgan Dean (M)	5 11	13 00	Enfield	3 10 83	Milton Keynes D
Niven Derek (M)	6 0	12 02	Falkirk	12 12 83	Bolton W
Robertson Gregor (D)	6 0	12 04	Edinburgh	19 1 84	Rotherham U
Talbot Drew (F)	5 10	11 00	Barnsley	19 7 86	Luton T
Whitaker Danny (M)	5 10	11 00	Manchester	14 11 80	Oldham Ath

League Appearances: Allott, M. 33(3); Boden, S. 2(21); Bowery, J. 5(22); Breckin, I. 19(6); Clay, C. 1(2); Davies, C. 41; Djilali, K. 7(3); Forde, S. 31; Gray, D. 1(1); Griffiths, S. 28(1); Holden, D. 17; Hunt, J. 18(2); Lee, T. 46; Lester, J. 29(11); Lomax, K. 3(1); Lowry, J. (3); Mattis, D. 35(3); Morgan, D. 18(3); Morris, I. 13(6); Niven, D. 24(11); Page, R. (1); Robertson, G. 21; Smalley, D. 22(6); Talbot, D. 44; Vidal, J. 5(1); Whitaker, D. 43(3).

Goals – League (85): Davies 23, Lester 17, Whitaker 15 (8 pens), Smalley 12, Boden 3, Mattis 3, Talbot 3, Holden 2, Bowery 1, Clay 1, Djilali 1, Forde 1, Morgan 1, Morris 1, Niven 1.

Carling Cup (1): Mattis 1.

FA Cup (3): Boden 1, Bowery 1, Davies 1.

J Paint Trophy (4): Morgan 2, Bowery 1, Davies 1.

Ground: b2net stadium, 1866 Sheffield Road, Whittington Moor, Chesterfield S41 8NZ. Telephone: (01246) 209 765.

Record Attendance: 30,968 v Newcastle U, Division 2, 7 April 1939 (at Saltergate).

Capacity: 8,502.

Manager: John Sheridan.

Most League Goals: 102, Division 3 (N), 1930–31.

Highest League Scorer in Season: Jimmy Cookson, 44, Division 3 (N), 1925–26.

Most League Goals in Total Aggregate: Ernie Moss, 161, 1969–76, 1979–81 and 1984–86.

Most Capped Player: Walter McMillen, 4 (7), Northern Ireland; Mark Williams, 4 (30), Northern Ireland.

Most League Appearances: Dave Blakey, 613, 1948–67.

Honours – Football League: Championship 2 Winners – 2010–11. Division 3 (N) Champions – 1930–31, 1935–36. Division 4 Champions – 1969–70, 1984–85. **Anglo-Scottish Cup:** Winners – 1980–81.

Colours: Blue shirts with white trim, white shorts, white stockings.

COLCHESTER UNITED   FL CHAMPIONSHIP 1

Baldwin Pat (D)	6 3	12 07	City of London	12	11 82	Chelsea
Bender Thomas (M)	6 3	12 00	Harlow	19	1 93	Scholar
Bond Andy (M)	5 10	11 07	Wigan	16	3 86	Barrow
Coker Ben (D)	5 11	11 09	Cambridge	1	7 90	Bury T
Cousins Mark (G)	6 1	11 03	Chelmsford	9	1 87	Scholar
Gillespie Steven (F)	5 9	11 02	Liverpool	4	6 84	Cheltenham T
Heath Matt (D)	6 4	13 13	Leicester	1	11 81	Leeds U
Henderson Ian (F)	5 10	11 06	Thetford	25	1 85	Luton T
Izzet Kem (M)	5 7	10 05	Mile End	29	9 80	Charlton Ath
James Lloyd (M)	5 11	11 01	Bristol	16	2 88	Southampton
O'Toole John (M)	6 2	13 07	Harrow	30	9 88	Watford
Odejayi Kayode (F)	6 2	12 02	Ibadon	21	2 82	Barnsley
Okuonghae Magnus (D)	6 3	13 04	Nigeria	16	2 86	Dagenham & R
Pentney Carl (G)	6 0	12 00	Leicester	3	2 89	Leicester C
Perkins David (D)	5 6	11 06	St Asaph	21	6 82	Rochdale
Powell Conor (D)	5 10	11 13	Dublin	26	8 87	Bohemians
Rose Michael (D)	5 11	12 04	Salford	28	7 82	Swindon T
Vincent Ashley (F)	5 10	11 08	Oldbury	26	5 85	Cheltenham T
White John (M)	5 10	12 01	Maldon	26	7 86	Scholar
Williams Ben (G)	6 0	13 01	Manchester	27	8 82	Carlisle U
Wilson Brian (D)	5 10	11 00	Manchester	9	5 83	Bristol C
Wordsworth Anthony (M)	6 1	12 00	London	3	1 89	Scholar

League Appearances: Baldwin, P. 10(1); Beevers, L. 12(7); Bond, A. 36(7); Clarke, N. 18; Coker, B. 20; Cousins, M. 13(1); Gillespie, S. 11(7); Hackney, S. (1); Heath, M. 26(1); Henderson, I. 24(12); Henderson, L. (8); Izzet, K. 38(3); James, L. 17(11); Mooney, D.

37(2); O'Toole, J. 5(6); Odejayi, K. 18(26); Okuonghae, M. 14; Perkins, D. 36; Powell, C. 2; Reid, P. 17(1); Sanderson, J. (1); Smith, T. 6; Tierney, M. 12(1); Vilhjalmsson, M. (3); Vincent, A. 28(9); White, J. 15(7); Williams, B. 33; Williams, T. 7; Wilson, B. 25(1); Wordsworth, A. 26(9).

Goals – League (57): Henderson I 10 (1 pen), Gillespie 9, Mooney 9 (4 pens), Bond 7, Vincent 5, Wordsworth 5, Odejayi 4, Heath 2, Okuonghae 2, Perkins 1, Williams T 1, Wilson 1, own goal 1.

Carling Cup (3): Mooney 2, Henderson I 1.

FA Cup (5): Mooney 3 (1 pen), Bond 1, Wilson 1.

J Paint Trophy (0).

Ground: Weston Homes Community Stadium, United Way, Colchester, Essex CO4 5UP. Telephone: (01206) 755 100.

Record Attendance: 19,072 v Reading, FA Cup 1st rd, 27 November 1948 (at Layer Road). 10,064 v Norwich C, FL 1, 16 January 2010 (at Community Stadium).

Capacity: 10,000.

Manager: John Ward.

Football Secretary: Caroline Pugh.

Most League Goals: 104, Division 4, 1961–62.

Highest League Scorer in Season: Bobby Hunt, 38, Division 4, 1961–62.

Most League Goals in Total Aggregate: Martyn King, 130, 1956–64.

Most Capped Player: Bela Balogh, 2 (9), Hungary.

Most League Appearances: Micky Cook, 613, 1969–84.

Honours – GM Vauxhall Conference: Winners – 1991–92. **FA Trophy:** Winners: 1991–92.

Colours: Royal blue and white striped shirts with white sleeves, royal blue shorts, white stockings.

COVENTRY CITY FL CHAMPIONSHIP

Baker Carl (M)	6 2	12 06	Prescot	26 12 82	Stockport Co
Bell David (M)	5 10	11 05	Kettering	21 1 84	Norwich C
Cameron Nathan (D)	6 2	12 04	Birmingham	21 11 91	Scholar
Clarke Jordan (D)	6 0	11 02	Coventry	19 11 91	Scholar
Clingan Sammy (M)	5 11	11 06	Belfast	13 1 84	Norwich C
Cranie Martin (D)	6 1	12 09	Yeovil	23 9 86	Portsmouth
Deegan Gary (M)	5 9	11 11	Dublin	28 9 87	Bohemians
Eastwood Freddy (F)	5 11	12 04	Epsom	29 10 83	Wolverhampton W
Gunnarsson Aron (M)	5 9	11 00	Akureyri	22 9 89	AZ
Hussey Chris (D)	5 10	10 03	Hammersmith	2 1 89	AFC Wimbledon
Ireland Daniel (G)	6 2	13 00	Sydney	20 1 89	Academy
Jeffers Shaun (F)	6 1	11 03	Bedford	14 4 92	Scholar
Jutkiewicz Lukas (F)	6 1	12 11	Southampton	20 3 89	Everton
Keogh Richard (D)	6 0	11 02	Harlow	11 8 86	Carlisle U
King Marlon (F)	5 10	12 10	Dulwich	26 4 80	Wigan Ath
McPake James (D)	6 2	12 08	Bellshill	2 6 84	Livingston
McSheffrey Gary (F)	5 8	10 06	Coventry	13 8 82	Birmingham C
O'Donovan Roy (F)	5 10	11 07	Cork	10 8 85	Sunderland
Platt Clive (F)	6 4	12 07	Wolverhampton	27 10 77	Colchester U
Thomas Conor (M)			Coventry	29 10 93	Scholar
Turner Ben (D)	6 4	14 04	Birmingham	21 1 88	Scholar
Westwood Keiren (G)	6 1	13 10	Manchester	23 10 84	Carlisle U
Wilson Callum (M)	5 11	10 06	Coventry	27 2 92	Scholar
Wood Richard (D)	6 3	12 13	Wakefield	5 7 85	Sheffield W

League Appearances: Baker, C. 19(13); Bell, D. 20(2); Cameron, N. 22(3); Carsley, L. 25; Clarke, J. 12(9); Clingan, S. 26(2); Cranie, M. 32(4); Deegan, G. (1); Doyle, M. 15(3); Eastwood, F. 14(13); Gunnarsson, A. 37(5); Hussey, C. 8(3); Ireland, D. (1); Jutkiewicz,

46

L. 34(8); Keogh, R. 46; King, M. 24(4); McIndoe, M. (6); McPake, J. 11(1); McSheffrey, G. 30(3); O'Donovan, R. (2); O'Halloran, S. 10(1); Platt, C. 22(12); Quirke, M. 3(1); Turner, B. 14; Turner, I. 2; Ward, D. 4(1); Westwood, K. 41; Wilson, C. (1); Wood, R. 35(5).

Goals – League (54): King 12 (3 pens), Jutkiewicz 9 (3 pens), McSheffrey 8, Eastwood 5, Gunnarsson 4, Turner B 4, Platt 3, Bell 2, Baker 1, Clarke 1, Doyle M 1, Keogh 1, Wood 1, own goals 2.

Carling Cup (0).

FA Cup (4): Baker 1, Eastwood 1, King 1, Wood 1.

Ground: The Ricoh Arena, Phoenix Way, Foleshill, Coventry CV6 6GE. Telephone: (0844) 873 1883.

Record Attendance: 51,455 v Wolverhampton W, Division 2, 29 April 1967 (at Highfield Road). 31,407 v Chelsea, FA Cup 6th rd, 7 March 2009 (at Ricoh Arena).

Capacity: 32,609.

Manager: Andy Thorn.

Secretary: Pam Hindson.

Most League Goals: 108, Division 3 (S), 1931–32.

Highest League Scorer in Season: Clarrie Bourton, 49, Division 3 (S), 1931–32.

Most League Goals in Total Aggregate: Clarrie Bourton, 171, 1931–37.

Most Capped Player: Magnus Hedman, 44 (58), Sweden.

Most League Appearances: Steve Ogrizovic, 507, 1984–2000.

Honours – Football League: Division 2 Champions – 1966–67. Division 3 Champions – 1963–64. Division 3 (S) Champions 1935–36. **FA Cup:** Winners – 1986–1987.

Colours: Sky blue shirts with grey horizontal stripes, white shorts, sky blue stockings.

CRAWLEY TOWN   FL CHAMPIONSHIP 2

Brodie Richard (F)	6 2	12 13	Gateshead	8 7 87	York C
Bulman Dannie (M)	5 9	11 11	Ashford	24 1 79	Oxford U
Dance James (M)			Coleshill	15 3 87	Kettering T
Dempster John (D)	6 1	11 07	Kettering	1 4 83	Kettering T
Gibson Willie (M)	5 10	10 01	Dumfries	6 8 84	Dunfermline Ath
Howell Dean (M)	6 1	12 04	Burton-on-Trent	29 11 80	Aldershot T
Kuipers Michel (G)	6 2	14 02	Amsterdam	26 6 74	Brighton & HA
McFadzean Kyle (D)	6 1	13 03	Sheffield	20 2 87	Alfreton T
Mills Pablo (D)	5 11	11 05	Birmingham	27 5 84	Rotherham U
Neilson Scott (M)	6 2	12 10	Enfield	15 5 87	Bradford C
Shearer Scott (G)	6 3	11 09	Glasgow	15 2 81	Wrexham
Simpson Josh (M)	5 10	12 02	Cambridge	6 3 87	Peterborough U
Smith Ben (M)	5 9	11 09	Chelmsford	23 11 78	Hereford U
Torres Sergio (M)	6 2	12 04	Mar del Plata	11 7 81	Peterborough U
Tubbs Matt (F)	5 9	11 00	Bournemouth	15 7 84	Salisbury C
Wassmer Charlie (D)			London	21 3 91	Hayes & Yeading U
Wilson Glenn (D)	6 1	12 08	Lewisham	16 3 86	Rushden & D

League Appearances: Brodie, 25(13); Bulman, 31; Cogan, 2(1); Cook, 6(15); Dance, 2(5); Dempster, 8(2); Enver-Marum, 1(2); Flood, (3); Gibson, 11(3); Hall, 9(5); Howell, 35; Hunt, 22(3); Hutchinson, (1); Jordan, 5(2); Kuipers, 26; Malcolm, (3); Masterton, 12(1); McAllister, 27(14); McFadzean, 34(3); Mills, 32; Neilson, 23(4); Quinn, 11; Reason, (4); Rents, 4(1); Rusk, 9(7); Shearer, 15(1); Simpson, 20(6); Smith, 22(7); Torres, 34(5); Tubbs, 38(3); Wassmer, 10(2); Wilson, 32(7); Wright, (9).

Goals – League (93): Tubbs 37 (11 pens), McAllister 12 (1 pen), Brodie 11 (1 pen), Neilson 5, Smith 4, Torres 4, McFadzean 3, Mills 3, Simpson 3, Cook 2, Wassmer 2, Bulman 1, Dance 1, Dempster 1, Gibson 1, Howell 1, Hunt 1, Masterton 1.

47

FA Cup (13): Tubbs 3, McAllister 2, Smith 2, Torres 2, Brodie 1, Hall 1, Neilson 1, own goal 1.
Ground: Broadfield Stadium, Winfield Way, Crawley, West Sussex RH11 9RX. Telephone: (01293) 410 000.
Record Attendance: 4,522 v Weymouth, Dr Martens Premier League, 6 March 2004.
Capacity:
Manager: Steve Evans.
Secretary: Barry Munn.
Most League Goals (since 2007): 93, Blue Square Premier, 2010–11.
Highest League and Cup Scorer in Season (since 2007): Matt Tubbs, 40.
Most League and Cup Appearances (since 2007): Glenn Wilson, 164.
Honours: Blue Square Premier – Champions: 2010–11.
Colours: All red.

CREWE ALEXANDRA FL CHAMPIONSHIP 2

Artell David (D)	6 3	14 01	Rotherham	22 11 80	Morecambe
Bell Lee (M)	5 11	12 04	Crewe	26 1 83	Macclesfield T
Connerton Jordan (M)	5 11	12 05	Lancaster	2 10 89	Lancaster C
Davis Harry (D)	6 2	12 04	Burnley	24 9 91	Scholar
Dugdale Adam (D)	6 3	12 07	Liverpool	12 9 87	Scholar
Leitch-Smith A-Jay (F)	5 11	12 04	Crewe	6 3 90	Scholar
Martin Carl (D)	5 8	10 07	London	24 10 86	Wealdstone
Mellor Kelvin (D)	5 10	11 09	Copenhagen	5 4 90	Nantwich T
Miller Shaun (F)	5 10	11 08	Alsager	25 9 87	Scholar
Moore Byron (M)	6 0	10 06	Stoke	24 8 88	Scholar
Murphy Luke (M)	6 1	11 05	Macclesfield	21 10 89	Scholar
Phillips Steve (G)	6 1	11 10	Bath	6 5 78	Bristol R
Powell Nick (M)	6 0	10 05	Crewe	23 3 94	Scholar
Sarcevic Antoni (M)	5 10	11 00	Manchester	13 3 92	Woodley Sp
Shelley Danny (D)	5 9	10 08	Stoke	29 12 90	Scholar
Tootle Matt (D)	5 9	11 00	Crewe	11 10 90	Scholar
Westwood Ashley R (D)	5 10	11 00	Crewe	1 4 90	Scholar

League Appearances: Ada, P. 39(1); Artell, D. 40; Bell, L. 45; Blanchett, D. 38(1); Clayton, M. (2); Connerton, J. (1); Davis, H. (1); Donaldson, C. 42(1); Dugdale, A. 15(5); Grant, J. 16(9); Hughes, C. (1); Leitch-Smith, A. 5(11); Mellor, K. (1); Miller, S. 38(4); Mitchel-King, M. 9(5); Moore, B. 28(10); Murphy, L. 36(3); Phillips, S. 2(1); Powell, N. (17); Sarcevic, A. (6); Shelley, D. 17(8); Taylor, R. 44; Tootle, M. 36(3); Turton, O. (1); Westwood, Ashley R. 45(1); Westwood, Ashley M. 7(1); Zola, C. 4(2).
Goals – League (87): Donaldson 28 (5 pens), Miller 18, Moore 6, Shelley 6, Grant 5 (1 pen), Leitch-Smith 5, Westwood, Ashley R 5 (1 pen), Artell 4, Murphy 3, Ada 1, Bell 1, Dugdale 1, Sarcevic 1, Zola 1, own goals 2.
Carling Cup (1): own goal 1.
FA Cup (1): Westwood Ashley R. 1.
J Paint Trophy (5): Artell 1, Bell 1 (pen), Donaldson 1, Grant 1, own goal 1.
Ground: The Alexandra Stadium, Gresty Road, Crewe, Cheshire CW2 6EB. Telephone: (01270) 213 014.
Record Attendance: 20,000 v Tottenham H, FA Cup 4th rd, 30 January 1960.
Capacity: 10,107.
Manager: Dario Gradi MBE.
Most League Goals: 95, Division 3 (N), 1931–32.
Highest League Scorer in Season: Terry Harkin, 35, Division 4, 1964–65.
Most League Goals in Total Aggregate: Bert Swindells, 126, 1928–37.
Most Capped Player: Clayton Ince, 38 (79), Trinidad & Tobago.

Most League Appearances: Tommy Lowry, 436, 1966–78.
Honours – Welsh Cup: Winners – 1936, 1937.
Colours: Red shirts with white trim, white shorts, red stockings.

CRYSTAL PALACE   FL CHAMPIONSHIP

Ambrose Darren (M)	6 0	11 00	Harlow	29	2 84	Charlton Ath
Andrew Calvin (F)	6 0	12 11	Luton	19	12 86	Luton T
Barrett Adam (D)	5 10	12 00	Dagenham	29	11 79	Southend U
Cadogan Kieron (M)	6 4	12 07	Wandsworth	16	8 90	Scholar
Clyne Nathaniel (D)	5 9	10 07	London	5	4 91	Scholar
Djilali Kieran (M)	6 3	13 02	London	1	1 91	Scholar
Dorman Andy (M)	6 0	10 10	Chester	1	5 82	St Mirren
Easter Jermaine (F)	5 9	12 02	Cardiff	15	1 82	Milton Keynes D
Foderingham Wesley (G)	6 1	12 00	London	14	1 91	Fulham
Garvan Owen (M)	6 0	10 07	Dublin	29	1 88	Ipswich T
Hills Lee (D)	5 10	11 11	Croydon	3	4 90	Scholar
Holland Jack (D)	6 3	12 02	Bromley	1	3 92	Scholar
Holness Charlie (D)	5 11	13 01	Lewisham	9	2 92	Scholar
Iversen Steffen (F)	6 1	12 07	Oslo	10	11 76	Rosenborg
Marrow Alex (M)	6 1	13 00	Ashton	21	1 90	Blackburn R
McCarthy Patrick (D)	6 2	13 07	Dublin	31	5 83	Charlton Ath
Moxey Dean (D)	6 2	11 00	Exeter	14	1 86	Derby Co
N'Diaye Alassane (M)	6 4	14 02	Audincourt	25	2 90	Scholar
O'Keefe Stuart (M)	5 8	10 00	Eye	4	3 91	Southend U
Parsons Matthew (D)	5 10	11 09	London	25	12 91	Scholar
Pinney Nathaniel (F)	6 0	12 05	South Norwood	16	11 90	Scholar
Price Lewis (G)	6 3	13 05	Bournemouth	19	7 84	Derby Co
Scannell Sean (F)	5 9	11 07	Cork	21	3 89	Scholar
Speroni Julian (G)	6 0	11 00	Buenos Aires	18	5 79	Dundee
Williams Jon (M)			Pembury	9	10 93	Scholar
Wright David (D)	5 11	11 01	Warrington	1	5 80	Ipswich T
Wynter Alex (M)	6 0	13 04	Beckenham	15	9 93	Youth
Zaha Wilfred (F)	5 11	10 05	Ivory Coast	10	11 92	Scholar

League Appearances: Agustien, K. 6(2); Ambrose, D. 27(1); Andrew, C. 1(12); Barrett, A. 5(2); Bennett, J. 10(3); Cadogan, K. 7(9); Clyne, N. 46; Counago, P. 17(13); Danns, N. 36(1); Davids, E. 6; Davis, C. 17(7); Dikgacoi, K. 13; Djilali, K. 10(4); Dorman, A. 14(6); Easter, J. 6(8); Gardner, A. 26(2); Garvan, O. 26; Iversen, S. 11(6); Lee, A. 3; Marrow, A. 20(1); McCarthy, P. 43; Moxey, D. 17; N'Diaye, A. 4(8); O'Keefe, S. 1(3); Obika, J. (7); Parsons, M. 2; Price, L. 1; Scannell, S. 5(14); Sekajja, I. (1); Speroni, J. 45; Vaughan, J. 28(2); Wright, D. 27(1); Zaha, W. 26(15).
Goals – League (44): Vaughan 9 (2 pens), Danns 8 (2 pens), Ambrose 7 (2 pens), Garvan 3, Counago 2, Iversen 2, Scannell 2, Bennett 1, Cadogan 1, Dikgacoi 1, Dorman 1, Easter 1, Gardner 1, Lee 1, McCarthy 1, Moxey 1, Sekajja 1, Zaha 1.
Carling Cup (2): Lee 1, own goal 1.
FA Cup (1): Danns 1.
Ground: Selhurst Park Stadium, Whitehorse Lane, London SE25 6PU. Telephone: (020) 8768 6000.
Record Attendance: 51,482 v Burnley, Division 2, 11 May 1979 (at Selhurst Park).
Capacity: 26,225.
Manager: Dougie Freedman.
Assistant Secretary: Christine Dowdeswell.
Most League Goals: 110, Division 4, 1960–61.

Highest League Scorer in Season: Peter Simpson, 46, Division 3 (S), 1930–31.
Most League Goals in Total Aggregate: Peter Simpson, 153, 1930–36.
Most Capped Player: Aleksandrs Kolinko, 23 (86), Latvia.
Most League Appearances: Jim Cannon, 571, 1973–88.
Honours – Football League: Division 1 – Champions 1993–94. Division 2 Champions – 1978–79. Division 3 (S) 1920–21. **Zenith Data Systems Cup:** Winners – 1991.
Colours: Red and blue striped shirts, blue shorts, blue stockings.

DAGENHAM & REDBRIDGE　　　FL CHAMPIONSHIP 2

Arber Mark (D)	6 1	11 09	Johannesburg	9 10 77	Peterborough U
Bingham Billy (D)	5 11	11 02	London	15 7 90	Crystal Palace
Doe Scott (D)	6 0	11 06	Reading	6 11 88	Weymouth
Gain Peter (M)	5 9	11 07	Hammersmith	11 11 76	Peterborough U
Green Danny J (M)			Harlow	4 8 90	Billericay T
Green Danny R (M)	5 11	12 00	Harlow	9 7 88	Northampton T
Gwillim Gareth (D)	5 11	12 06	Farnborough	9 2 83	Histon
Ilesanmi Femi (D)			Southwark	18 4 91	Ashford T
Lewington Christopher (G)	6 1	12 00	Sidcup	23 8 88	Leatherhead
McCrory Damien (D)	6 2	12 10	Limerick	22 2 90	Plymouth Arg
Nurse Jon (F)	5 9	12 04	Barbados	28 3 81	Stevenage B
Ogogo Abu (D)	5 8	10 02	Epsom	3 11 89	Arsenal
Okus Conor (M)			London	15 9 91	West Ham U
Osborn Alexander (F)			Walthamstow	25 7 93	Grays Ath
Reynolds Duran (D)			Boston	27 9 91	Southend U
Roberts Tony (G)	6 0	14 11	Bangor	4 8 69	QPR
Scannell Damian (M)	5 10	11 07	Croydon	28 4 85	Southend U
Scott Josh (F)	6 1	12 00	London	10 5 85	Hayes & Yeading
Tomlin Gavin (F)	6 0	12 02	Brentford	21 8 83	Yeovil T
Vincelot Romain (M)	5 9	11 02	Poitiers	29 10 85	Gueugnon
Walsh Phil (F)	6 3	13 04	Hartlepool	4 2 84	Dorchester T
Wilkinson Luke (D)	6 2	11 09	Bristol	2 12 91	Portsmouth

League Appearances: Akinde, J. 8(1); Antwi, W. 9(2); Arber, M. 44; Benson, P. 3; Bingham, B. 4(2); Brown, K. 3; Currie, D. 12(10); Doe, S. 38; Elito, M. 8(2); Gain, P. 35(2); Green, Danny 41; Green, Danny J (3); Gwillim, G. (2); Ifil, P. 13(1); Ilesanmi, F. 24(1); Lancaster, C. (4); Lee, O. 4(1); Lewington, C. 3; Lewis, S. 7(3); McCrory, D. 22(1); Morgan, M. 5(7); Nurse, J. 24(14); Ogogo, A. 33; Palsson, V. 2; Pinney, N. (1); Roberts, T. 43; Savage, B. 21(15); Scannell, D. 14(6); Scott, J. 8(8); Taiwo, S. 16(2); Tomlin, G. 16(3); Vincelot, R. 46; Walsh, P. (3).
Goals – League (52): Vincelot 12, Green, Danny 11 (5 pens), Nurse 10, Savage 3, Akinde 2, Arber 2, Elito 2, Scannell 2, Tomlin 2, Antwi 1, Currie 1, Ogogo 1, Scott 1, own goals 2.
Carling Cup (1): McCrory 1.
FA Cup (3): Green, Danny 2 (1 pen), Taiwo 1.
J Paint Trophy (0).
Ground: The London Borough of Barking and Dagenham Stadium, Victoria Road, Dagenham, Essex RM10 7XL. Telephone: (0208) 592 1549.
Record Attendance: 4,791 v Shrewsbury T, FL 2, 2 May 2009.
Capacity: 6,007.
Manager: John L. Still.
Secretary: Terry Grover.
Most League Goals in Total Aggregate: 77, FL 2, 2008–09.
Highest League Scorer in Season: Paul Benson, 28, Conference, 2006–07.
Most League Goals in Total Aggregate: 40, Paul Benson, 2007–.
Most Capped Player: Jon Nurse, 4, Barbados.

Most League Appearances: Tony Roberts, 175, 2007–.
Honours – Conference: Champions – 2006–07. **Isthmian League (Premier):** Champions 1999–2000.
Colours: Red shirts with blue sleeves and red trim, blue shorts, blue stockings.

DERBY COUNTY   FL CHAMPIONSHIP

Name	Ht	Wt	Birthplace	Birthdate	From
Addison Miles (D)	6 2	13 03	Newham	7 1 89	Scholar
Anderson Russell (D)	5 11	10 09	Aberdeen	25 10 78	Sunderland
Atkins Ross (G)	6 0	13 00	Derby	3 11 89	Scholar
Bailey James (M)	6 0	12 05	Bollington	18 9 88	Crewe Alex
Ball Callum (F)	6 1	10 03	Leicester	8 10 92	Scholar
Barker Shaun (D)	6 2	12 08	Nottingham	19 9 82	Blackpool
Brayford John (D)	5 8	11 02	Stoke	29 12 87	Crewe Alex
Bueno Alberto (F)	5 10	10 03	Madrid	20 3 88	Valladolid
Buxton Jake (D)	6 1	13 05	Sutton-in-Ashfield	4 3 85	Burton Alb
Bywater Stephen (G)	6 2	12 08	Manchester	7 6 81	West Ham U
Connolly Ryan (M)	5 10	10 06	Castlebar	13 1 92	Scholar
Croft Lee (M)	5 11	13 00	Wigan	21 6 85	Norwich C
Cywka Tomasz (M)	5 10	11 09	Gliwice	27 6 88	Wigan Ath
Davies Ben (M)	5 7	12 03	Birmingham	27 5 81	Notts Co
Davies Steve (F)	6 0	12 00	Liverpool	29 12 87	Tranmere R
Deeney Saul (G)	6 1	11 07	Derry	23 3 83	Burton Alb
Dillon Kealan (F)			Republic of Ireland	21 2 94	Scholar
Doyle Conor (F)	6 2	12 04	Mckinney	13 10 91	Creighton Univ
Fielding Frank (G)	5 11	12 00	Blackburn	4 4 88	Scholar
Green Paul (M)	5 9	10 02	Pontefract	10 4 83	Doncaster R
Hendrick Jeff (M)	6 1	11 11	Dublin	31 1 92	Scholar
Leacock Dean (D)	6 2	12 04	Croydon	10 6 84	Fulham
Martin David (M)	5 9	10 10	Erith	3 6 85	Millwall
Morch Mats (G)			Norway		
O'Brien Mark (D)	5 11	12 02	Dublin	20 11 92	Cherry Orchard
Pearson Stephen (M)	6 1	11 11	Lanark	2 10 82	Celtic
Pringle Ben (M)	5 8	11 09	Newcastle	27 5 89	Ilkeston T
Roberts Gareth (D)	5 8	11 12	Wrexham	6 2 78	Doncaster R
Severn James (G)	6 4	14 11	Nottingham	10 10 91	Scholar
Varney Luke (F)	5 11	11 00	Leicester	28 9 82	Charlton Ath
Ward Jamie (M)	5 5	9 04	Birmingham	12 5 86	Sheffield U

League Appearances: Addison, M. 10(11); Anderson, R. 4(7); Atkins, R. 1; Ayala, D. 16(1); Bailey, J. 32(4); Ball, C. 1(4); Barker, S. 42(1); Brayford, J. 46; Bueno, A. 25(4); Buxton, J. (1); Bywater, S. 22; Commons, K. 25(1); Cywka, T. 21(10); Davies, S. 14(6); Davies, B. 10(3); Doyle, C. 5(9); Fielding, F. 16; Green, P. 36; Hendrick, J. (4); Hulse, R. 1; Jones, B. 7; Kuqi, S. 8(4); Leacock, D. 22(3); Martin, D. (2); Moore, L. 9(4); Moxey, D. 20(2); Noble, R. (1); O'Brien, M. (2); Pearson, S. 21(9); Porter, C. 6(12); Pringle, B. 3(12); Roberts, G. 24(2); Robinson, T. 8(5); Savage, R. 37(3); Severn, J. (1); Varney, L. 1; Ward, J. 13.

Goals – League (58): Commons 13 (2 pens), Bueno 5, Davies S 5, Ward 5 (1 pen), Cywka 4, Moore 4, Savage 4 (4 pens), Green 2, Kuqi 2, Moxey 2, Porter 2, Robinson 2, Bailey 1, Barker 1, Brayford 1, Davies B 1, Hulse 1, Leacock 1, Pearson 1, own goal 1.
Carling Cup (0).
FA Cup (1): Addison 1.
Ground: Pride Park Stadium, Derby DE24 8XL. Telephone: 0871 472 1884.
Record Attendance: 41,826 v Tottenham H, Division 1, 20 September 1969 (at Baseball Ground). 33,597 England v Mexico, 25 May 2001 (at Pride Park).
Capacity: 33,597.

Manager: Nigel Clough.
Secretary: Clare Morris.
Most League Goals: 111, Division 3 (N), 1956–57.
Highest League Scorer in Season: Jack Bowers, 37, Division 1, 1930–31; Ray Straw, 37 Division 3 (N), 1956–57.
Most League Goals in Total Aggregate: Steve Bloomer, 292, 1892–1906 and 1910–14.
Most Capped Player: Deon Burton, 42 (59), Jamaica.
Most League Appearances: Kevin Hector, 486, 1966–78 and 1980–82.
Honours – Football League: Division 1 Champions – 1971–72, 1974–75. Division 2 Champions – 1911–12, 1914–15, 1968–69, 1986–87. Division 3 (N) Champions – 1956–57. **FA Cup:** Winners – 1945–46. **Texaco Cup:** Winners 1972.
Colours: White shirts with black trim, black shorts with white trim, white stockings with black trim.

DONCASTER ROVERS   FL CHAMPIONSHIP

Burge Ryan (M)	5 10	10 03	Cheltenham	12 10 88	Barnet
Chambers James (D)	5 10	11 11	West Bromwich	20 11 80	Leicester C
Coppinger James (F)	5 7	10 03	Middlesbrough	10 1 81	Exeter C
Dumbuya Mustapha (D)	5 7	11 00	Sierra Leone	7 8 87	Grays Ath
Fairhust Waide (F)	5 10	10 07	Sheffield	7 5 89	Scholar
Friend George (D)	6 2	13 01	Dorchester	19 10 87	Wolverhampton W
Gillett Simon (M)	5 6	11 07	Oxford	6 11 85	Southampton
Hayter James (F)	5 9	10 13	Newport (IW)	9 4 79	Bournemouth
Hird Samuel (D)	5 7	10 12	Askern	7 9 87	Leeds U
Keegan Paul (M)	5 11	11 05	Dublin	5 7 84	Bohemians
Lockwood Adam (D)	6 0	12 07	Wakefield	26 10 81	Yeovil T
Martis Shelton (D)	6 0	11 11	Willemstad	29 11 82	WBA
O'Connor James (D)	5 10	12 05	Birmingham	20 11 84	Bournemouth
Oster John (M)	5 9	10 08	Boston	8 12 78	Crystal Palace
Sharp Billy (F)	5 9	11 00	Sheffield	5 2 86	Sheffield U
Shiels Dean (F)	5 11	9 10	Magherfelt	1 2 85	Hibernian
Stock Brian (M)	5 11	11 02	Winchester	24 12 81	Preston NE
Sullivan Neil (G)	6 2	12 00	Sutton	24 2 70	Leeds U
Wilson Mark (M)	5 11	12 00	Scunthorpe	9 2 79	Dallas
Woods Gary (G)	6 1	11 00	Kettering	1 10 90	Manchester U
Woods Martin (M)	5 11	11 13	Airdrie	1 1 86	Rotherham U

League Appearances: Brooker, S. 1(12); Burge, R. (1); Chambers, J. 6(1); Coppinger, J. 38(2); Dumbuya, M. 17(6); Euell, J. 7(5); Fairhurst, W. (2); Friend, G. 30(2); Gillett, S. 21(1); Hayter, J. 28(4); Healy, D. 6(2); Hird, S. 20(12); Keegan, P. 9(1); Kilgallon, M. 7(5); Lockwood, A. 13(3); Martis, S. 24(2); Mason, R. 5(10); Mills, J. 17(1); Moussa, F. 14; O'Connor, J. 34; Oster, J. 41; Sharp, B. 27(2); Shiels, D. 15(18); Souza, D. 3(5); Stock, B. 31(6); Sullivan, N. 30(1); Thomas, W. 17(4); Webster, B. 1(6); Wilson, M. 15(13); Woods, G. 16; Woods, M. 13(2).
Goals – League (55): Sharp 15 (4 pens), Hayter 9, Coppinger 7, Euell 3, Shiels 3, Healy 2, Mills 2, Moussa 2, O'Connor 2, Stock 2, Brooker 1, Friend 1, Gillett 1, Lockwood 1, Martis 1, Woods M 1, own goals 2.
Carling Cup (1): Payne 1.
FA Cup (2): Hayter 1, Sharp 1.
Ground: Keepmoat Stadium, Stadium Way, Lakeside, Doncaster, South Yorkshire DN4 5JW. Telephone: (01302) 764 664.
Record Attendance: 37,149 v Hull C, Division 3 (N), 2 October 1948 (at Belle Vue). 15,001 v Leeds U, FL 1, 1 April 2008 (at Keepmoat Stadium).
Capacity: 15,231.
Manager: Sean O'Driscoll.
Chief Executive/Secretary: David Morris.

Most League Goals: 123, Division 3 (N), 1946–47.
Highest League Scorer in Season: Clarrie Jordan, 42, Division 3 (N), 1946–47.
Most League Goals in Total Aggregate: Tom Keetley, 180, 1923–29.
Most Capped Player: Len Graham, 14, Northern Ireland.
Most League Appearances: Fred Emery, 417, 1925–36.
Honours – Football League: Division 3 Champions – 2003–04. Division 3 (N) Champions – 1934–35, 1946–47, 1949–50. Division 4 Champions – 1965–66, 1968–69.
J Paint Trophy: Winners – 2006–07. **Football Conference:** Champions – 2002–03.
Colours: Red and white hooped shirts, red sleeves with black trim, black shorts with red trim, black stockings with red tops.

EVERTON   FA PREMIERSHIP

Anichebe Victor (F)	6 1	13 00	Nigeria	23 4 88	Scholar
Arteta Mikel (M)	5 9	10 08	San Sebastian	26 3 82	Real Sociedad
Baines Leighton (D)	5 8	11 00	Liverpool	11 12 84	Wigan Ath
Barkley Ross (M)	6 2	12 00	Liverpool	5 12 93	Scholar
Baxter Jose (F)	5 10	11 07	Bootle	7 2 92	Academy
Beckford Jermaine (F)	6 2	13 02	London	9 12 83	Leeds U
Bidwell Jake (D)	6 0	11 00	Southport	21 3 93	Scholar
Bilyaletdinov Diniyar (F)	6 1	11 11	Moscow	27 2 85	Lokomotiv Moscow
Cahill Tim (M)	5 10	10 12	Sydney	6 12 79	Millwall
Coleman Seamus (D)	6 4	12 00	Donegal	11 10 88	Sligo R
Davies Adam (G)			Rinteln	17 7 92	Scholar
Distin Sylvain (D)	6 3	14 06	Bagnolet	16 12 77	Portsmouth
Duffy Shane (D)	6 4	12 00	County Derry	1 1 92	Scholar
Fellaini Marouane (M)	6 4	13 05	Brussels	22 11 87	Standard Liege
Forrester Anton (F)			Liverpool	11 2 94	Scholar
Forshaw Adam (M)	6 1	11 00	Liverpool	8 10 91	Scholar
Garbutt Luke (D)	5 10	11 07	Harrogate	21 5 93	Scholar
Gueye Magaye (F)	5 10	11 07	Nogent-sur-Marne	6 7 90	Strasbourg
Hammar Johan (D)			Malmo	22 2 94	Malmo
Heitinga John (D)	5 11	11 05	Alphen aan den Rijn	15 11 83	Atletico Madrid
Hibbert Tony (D)	5 9	11 05	Liverpool	20 2 81	Trainee
Hope Hallam (F)			Manchester	17 3 94	Scholar
Howard Tim (G)	6 3	14 12	North Brunswick	6 3 79	Manchester U
Jagielka Phil (D)	6 0	13 01	Manchester	17 8 82	Sheffield U
McAleny Conor (F)			Liverpool	12 8 92	Scholar
Mucha Jan (G)	6 2	12 00	Bela nad Cirochou	5 12 82	Legia
Mustafi Shkodran (D)	6 0	11 07	Bad Hersfeld	17 4 92	Hamburg
Neville Phil (M)	5 11	12 00	Bury	21 1 77	Manchester U
Nsiala Aristote (D)	6 4	14 09	Congo	25 3 92	Scholar
Orenuga Femi (M)			London	18 3 93	Southend U
Osman Leon (F)	5 8	10 09	Billinge	17 5 81	Trainee
Roberts Connor (G)			Wrexham	8 12 92	Scholar
Rodwell Jack (D)	6 2	12 08	Birkdale	11 3 91	Scholar
Saha Louis (F)	6 1	12 08	Paris	8 8 78	Manchester U
Silva Joao (F)	6 2	12 08	Vila das Aves	21 5 90	Aves
Vaughan James (F)	5 11	12 08	Birmingham	14 7 88	Scholar
Vellios Apostolos (F)	6 3	12 06	Salonika	8 1 92	Iraklis
Wallace James (M)	5 11	13 00	Fazackerly	19 12 91	Scholar
Yakubu Ayegbeni (F)	6 0	14 07	Benin City	22 11 82	Middlesbrough
Yobo Joseph (D)	6 1	13 00	Kano	6 9 80	Marseille

League Appearances: Anichebe, V. 8(8); Arteta, M. 29; Baines, L. 38; Baxter, J. (1); Beckford, J. 14(18); Bilyaletdinov, D. 10(16); Cahill, T. 22(5); Coleman, S. 25(9); Distin, S. 38; Fellaini, M. 19(1); Forshaw, A. (1); Gueye, M. 2(3); Heitinga, J. 23(4); Hibbert, T.

17(3); Howard, T. 38; Jagielka, P. 31(2); Neville, P. 31; Osman, L. 20(6); Pienaar, S. 18; Rodwell, J. 14(10); Saha, L. 14(8); Vaughan, J. (1); Vellios, A. (3); Yakubu, A. 7(7).
Goals – League (51): Cahill 9, Beckford 8, Saha 7, Baines 5 (3 pens), Coleman 4, Osman 4, Arteta 3, Bilyaletdinov 2, Distin 2, Fellaini 1, Heitinga 1, Jagielka 1, Neville 1, Pienaar 1, Yakubu 1, own goal 1.
Carling Cup (6): Beckford 1 (pen), Coleman 1, Fellaini 1, Osman 1, Rodwell 1, Saha 1.
FA Cup (7): Baines 2, Saha 2, Beckford 1, Coleman 1, Fellaini 1.
Ground: Goodison Park, Goodison Road, Liverpool L4 4EL. Telephone: (0871) 663 1878.
Record Attendance: 78,299 v Liverpool, Division 1, 18 September 1948.
Capacity: 40,158.
Manager: David Moyes.
Secretary: David Harrison.
Most League Goals: 121, Division 2, 1930–31.
Highest League Scorer in Season: William Ralph 'Dixie' Dean, 60, Division 1, 1927–28 (All-time League record).
Most League Goals in Total Aggregate: William Ralph 'Dixie' Dean, 349, 1925–37.
Most Capped Player: Neville Southall, 92, Wales.
Most League Appearances: Neville Southall, 578, 1981–98.
Honours – Football League: Division 1 Champions – 1890–91, 1914–15, 1927–28, 1931–32, 1938–39, 1962–63, 1969–70, 1984–85, 1986–87. Division 2 Champions – 1930–31. **FA Cup:** Winners – 1906, 1933, 1966, 1984, 1995. **European Competitions: European Cup-Winners' Cup:** Winners – 1984–85.
Colours: Blue shirts with white trim, white shorts, white stockings.

EXETER CITY   FL CHAMPIONSHIP 1

Player			Birthplace		Birthdate	Previous club
Archibald-Henville Troy (D)	6 2	13 03	Newham	4	11 88	Tottenham H
Bennett Scott (D)	5 10	12 10	Truro	30	11 90	Scholar
Cureton Jamie (F)	5 8	10 07	Bristol	28	8 75	Norwich C
Dawson Aaron (M)	5 10	10 10	Exmouth	24	3 92	Scholar
Duffy Richard (D)	5 9	10 03	Swansea	30	8 85	Millwall
Dunne James (M)	5 11	10 12	Farnborough	18	9 89	Arsenal
Frear Elliott (F)	5 8	10 01	Exeter	11	9 90	Scholar
Furzer Jack (D)	5 11	12 02	Exeter	17	2 92	Scholar
Golbourne Scott (M)	5 8	11 08	Bristol	29	2 88	Reading
Jones Billy (D)	6 1	11 05	Chatham	26	3 83	Crewe Alex
Keats Noah (M)	5 9	11 05	Weymouth	17	2 92	Scholar
Krysiak Artur (G)	6 1	12 00	Lodz	11	8 89	Birmingham C
Logan Richard (F)	6 0	12 05	Bury St Edmunds	4	1 82	Weymouth
Nardiello Daniel (F)	5 11	11 04	Coventry	22	10 82	Blackpool
Noble David (M)	6 0	12 04	Hitchin	2	2 82	Bristol C
O'Flynn John (F)	5 11	11 11	Cobh	11	7 82	Barnet
Sercombe Liam (M)	5 10	10 10	Exeter	25	4 90	Youth
Shephard Chris (M)	6 3	13 03	Exeter	2	6 90	Youth
Taylor Matt (D)	6 1	12 04	Ormskirk	30	1 82	Team Bath
Tully Steve (D)	5 9	11 00	Paignton	10	2 80	Weymouth

League Appearances: Archibald-Henville, T. 32(4); Bennett, S. (1); Cozic, B. 4(7); Cureton, J. 34(7); Duffy, R. 41(1); Dunne, J. 36(6); Edwards, R. 6(3); Golbourne, S. 42(2); Hamer, B. 18; Harley, R. 40(2); Jones, B. 27(2); Jones, P. 18; Krysiak, A. 10; Logan, R. 22(18); Nardiello, D. 15(15); Nichols, T. (1); Noble, D. 29(7); Norwood, J. 1; O'Flynn, J. 22(9); Sercombe, L. 38(4); Stewart, M. 2(6); Taylor, M. 26(2); Thomson, J. 1(15); Tisdale, P. (1); Tully, S. 42(1).
Goals – League (66): Cureton 17, Logan 11, Harley 10 (4 pens), Nardiello 10, O'Flynn 6 (1 pen), Sercombe 3, Duffy 2, Golbourne 2, Taylor 2, Archibald-Henville 1, Dunne 1, Tully 1.

Carling Cup (2): Harley 2.
FA Cup (0).
J Paint Trophy (12): Cureton 3, Harley 3, Nardiello 3 (1 pen), Duffy 1, O'Flynn 1, own goal 1.
Ground: St James Park, Stadium Way, Exeter EX4 6PX. Telephone: (01392) 411 243.
Record Attendance: 20,984 v Sunderland, FA Cup 6th rd (replay), 4 March 1931.
Capacity: 8,830.
Manager: Paul Tisdale.
Club Secretary: Mike Radford.
Most League Goals: 88, Division 3 (S), 1932–33.
Highest League Scorer in Season: Fred Whitlow, 33, Division 3 (S), 1932–33.
Most League Goals in Total Aggregate: Tony Kellow, 129, 1976–78, 1980–83, 1985–88.
Most Capped Player: Dermot Curtis, 1 (17), Eire.
Most League Appearances: Arnold Mitchell, 495, 1952–66.
Honours – Division 3 (S) Cup: Winners 1934.
Colours: Red and white striped shirts, red sleeves, white shorts, white stockings.

FULHAM   FA PREMIERSHIP

Name			Birthplace				Previous club
Baird Chris (D)	5 10	11 11	Ballymoney	25	2	82	Southampton
Barroilhet Richard (F)	6 2	11 13	Westminster	29	8	92	Academy
Bettinelli Marcus (G)			London	24	5	92	Academy
Briggs Matthew (D)	6 1	11 12	Wandsworth	6	3	91	Scholar
Burn Daniel (D)	6 6	14 00	Blyth	9	5	92	Darlington
Cosgrove Jonathan (F)			Northern Ireland	12	1	93	Scholar
Dalla Valle Lauri (F)	5 11	12 00	Kontiolahti	14	9	91	Liverpool
Davies Simon (M)	5 10	11 07	Haverfordwest	23	10	79	Everton
Dembele Mousa (F)	5 9	10 01	Wilrijk	17	7	87	AZ
Dempsey Clinton (M)	6 1	12 02	Nacogdoches	9	3	83	New England R
Dikgacoi Kagisho (M)	5 11	12 10	Brandfort	24	11	84	Lamontville GA
Duff Damien (F)	5 9	12 06	Ballyboden	2	3	79	Newcastle U
Etheridge Neil (G)	6 3	14 00	Enfield	7	2	90	Scholar
Etuhu Dickson (M)	6 2	13 04	Kano	8	6	82	Sunderland
Frei Kerim (M)			Fledkirch	19	11	93	Scholar
Gameiro Corey (F)			Wollongong	7	2	93	Academy
Greening Jonathan (M)	5 11	11 00	Scarborough	2	1	79	WBA
Halliche Rafik (D)	6 2	12 02	Algiers	2	9	86	Benfica
Hangeland Brede (D)	6 4	13 05	Houston	20	6	81	FC Copenhagen
Harris Courtney (M)			London	7	9	91	Scholar
Hoesen Danny (F)	6 1	12 00	Kerkrade	15	1	91	Fortuna Sittard
Hughes Aaron (D)	6 0	11 02	Cookstown	8	11	79	Aston Villa
Johnson Andy (F)	5 7	10 09	Bedford	10	2	81	Everton
Joronen Jesse (G)			Finland	21	3	93	Scholar
Kacaniklic Alex (M)	5 11	10 05	Sweden	13	8	91	Liverpool
Kelly Stephen (D)	6 0	12 04	Dublin	6	9	83	Birmingham C
Marquez-Sanchez Christian (D)			Barcelona	13	1	93	Scholar
Marsh-Brown Keanu (F)	5 11	12 04	Hammersmith	10	8	92	Scholar
Minkwitz Ronny (M)			Duisburg	9	12	93	Stuttgart
Murphy Danny (M)	5 10	11 09	Chester	18	3	77	Tottenham H
Peniket Richard (F)			Bromsgrove	4	3	93	Scholar
Riise Bjorn Helge (M)	5 10	11 11	Alesund	21	6	83	Lillestrom
Salcido Carlos (D)	5 8	11 00	Ocotlan	2	4	80	PSV Eindhoven
Schwarzer Mark (G)	6 4	14 07	Sydney	6	10	72	Middlesbrough
Senderos Philippe (D)	6 1	13 10	Geneva	14	2	85	Arsenal
Sidwell Steven (M)	5 10	11 00	Wandsworth	14	12	82	Aston Villa
Smith Alex (D)	5 9	10 00	London	31	10	91	Scholar
Stockdale David (G)	6 3	13 04	Leeds	20	9	85	Darlington

Trotta Marcello (F)			Santa Maria Capua	29	9	92	Napoli
Zamora Bobby (F)	6 1	11 11	Barking	16	1	81	West Ham U
Zuberbuhler Pascal (G)	6 5	15 00	Frauenfeld	8	1	71	Neuchatel Xamax

League Appearances: Baird, C. 25(4); Briggs, M. 3; Davies, S. 25(5); Dembele, M. 22(2); Dempsey, C. 35(2); Dikgacoi, K. (1); Duff, D. 22(2); Etuhu, D. 23(5); Gera, Z. 10(17); Greening, J. 6(4); Gudjohnsen, E. 4(6); Halliche, R. (1); Hangeland, B. 37; Hughes, A. 38; Johnson, A. 15(12); Johnson, E. 1(10); Kakuta, G. 2(5); Kamara, D. 7(3); Kelly, S. 8(2); Konchesky, P. 1; Murphy, D. 37; Pantsil, J. 15(1); Riise, B. (3); Salcido, C. 22(1); Schwarzer, M. 31; Senderos, P. 3; Sidwell, S. 10(2); Stockdale, D. 7; Zamora, B. 9(5).

Goals – League (49): Dempsey 12 (1 pen), Hangeland 6, Zamora 5 (1 pen), Davies 4, Duff 4, Dembele 3, Johnson A 3, Baird 2, Etuhu 2, Kamara 2, Sidwell 2, Gera 1, Hughes 1, Kakuta 1, own goal 1.

Carling Cup (6): Gera 2, Zamora 2, Dembele 1, Dempsey 1.

FA Cup (10): Kamara 3, Murphy 2 (2 pens), Dembele 1, Etuhu 1, Gera 1, Greening 1, Hangeland 1.

Ground: Craven Cottage, Stevenage Road, London SW6 6HH. Telephone: 0870 442 1222.

Record Attendance: 49,335 v Millwall, Division 2, 8 October 1938.

Capacity: 26,600.

Manager: Martin Jol.

Secretary: Darren Preston.

Most League Goals: 111, Division 3 (S), 1931–32.

Highest League Scorer in Season: Frank Newton, 43, Division 3 (S), 1931–32.

Most League Goals in Total Aggregate: Gordon Davies, 159, 1978–84, 1986–91.

Most Capped Player: Johnny Haynes, 56, England.

Most League Appearances: Johnny Haynes, 594, 1952–70.

Honours – Football League: Division 1 Champions – 2000–01. Division 2 Champions – 1948–49, 1998–99. Division 3 (S) Champions – 1931–32. **European Competitions: Intertoto Cup:** Winners – 2002.

Colours: White shirts with black trim, black shorts, white stockings.

GILLINGHAM   FL CHAMPIONSHIP 2

Akinfenwa Adebayo (F)	5 11	13 07	Nigeria	10	5	82	Northampton T
Barcham Andy (F)	5 8	10 11	Basildon	16	12	86	Tottenham H
Essam Connor (D)	6 0	12 00	Chatham	9	7	92	Scholar
Fuller Barry (D)	5 10	11 10	Ashford	25	9	84	Stevenage B
Jackman Danny (D)	5 4	10 00	Worcester	3	1	83	Northampton T
King Simon (D)	6 0	13 00	Oxford	11	4	83	Barnet
Lawrence Matt (D)	6 1	12 12	Northampton	19	6	74	Crystal Palace
Maher Kevin (M)	6 0	12 13	Ilford	17	10	76	Oldham Ath
Oli Dennis (F)	6 0	12 00	Newham	28	1	84	Grays Ath
Palmer Chris (M)	5 7	11 00	Derby	16	10	83	Walsall
Payne Jack (M)	5 9	9 02	Gravesend	5	12	91	Scholar
Payne Stefan (F)			Lambeth	10	8	91	Sutton U
Rance Dean (M)			Maidstone	14	5	91	Scholar
Richards Garry (D)	6 3	13 00	Romford	11	6	86	Southend U
Rooney Luke (M)	5 8	11 07	Southwark	28	12	90	Scholar
Spiller Danny (M)	5 8	11 00	Maidstone	10	10	81	Dagenham & R
Weston Curtis (M)	5 11	11 09	Greenwich	24	1	87	Leeds U

League Appearances: Aborah, S. (1); Akinfenwa, A. 40(4); Barcham, A. 18(6); Bentley, M. 15(10); Cronin, L. 7; Davies, C. 1; Fuller, B. 40(2); Gowling, J. 21(1); Inkango, B. 1(4); Jackman, D. 15(2); Julian, A. 39; Kennedy, C. 3; King, S.(1); Lawrence, M. 41(2); Lee, C. 4; Maher, K. 36; Martin, J. 12(5); McCammon, M. (5); McDonald, C. 41; Miller, Ashley

(1); Nutter, J. 32(2); Oli, D. 3(18); Palmer, C. 18; Payne, J. 25(6); Payne, S. 1(15); Richards, G. 15(2); Rooney, L. 2(21); Sinclair, T. 17(3); Spiller, D. 23(7); Weston, C. 29(4); Whelpdale, C. 4; White, A. (1).

Goals – League (67): McDonald 25, Akinfenwa 11 (2 pens), Barcham 6, Palmer 4 (1 pen), Weston 4, Whelpdale 3, Bentley 2, Gowling 2, Spiller 2, Jackman 1, Lee 1, Martin 1, Nutter 1, Oli 1, Payne J 1, Rooney 1, own goal 1.

Carling Cup (1): Palmer 1.

FA Cup (0).

J Paint Trophy (0).

Ground: KRBS Priestfield Stadium, Redfern Avenue, Gillingham, Kent ME7 4DD. Telephone: (01634) 300 000.

Record Attendance: 23,002 v QPR, FA Cup 3rd rd, 10 January 1948.

Capacity: 11,440.

Manager: Andy Hessenthaler.

Secretary: Gwen Poynter.

Most League Goals: 90, Division 4, 1973–74.

Highest League Scorer in Season: Ernie Morgan, 31, Division 3 (S), 1954–55; Brian Yeo, 31, Division 4, 1973–74.

Most League Goals in Total Aggregate: Brian Yeo, 135, 1963–75.

Most Capped Player: Mamady Sidibe, 7 (14), Mali.

Most League Appearances: John Simpson, 571, 1957–72.

Honours – Football League: Division 4 Champions – 1963–64.

Colours: Blue shirts with white sleeves, blue shorts, blue stockings.

HARTLEPOOL UNITED   FL CHAMPIONSHIP 1

Player			Birthplace				Previous club
Austin Neil (D)	5 10	11 09	Barnsley	26	4	83	Darlington
Boyd Adam (F)	5 9	10 12	Hartlepool	25	5	82	Leyton Orient
Brown James (F)	5 11	11 00	Newcastle	3	1	87	Cramlington J
Collins Sam (D)	6 2	14 03	Pontefract	5	6	77	Hull C
Flinders Scott (G)	6 4	13 00	Rotherham	12	6	86	Crystal Palace
Hartley Peter (D)	6 0	12 06	Hartlepool	3	4	88	Sunderland
Haslam Steven (M)	5 11	10 10	Sheffield	6	9	79	Bury
Holden Darren (M)			Krugersdorp	27	8	93	Scholar
Horwood Evan (D)	6 0	10 06	Billingham	10	3	86	Carlisle U
Humphreys Richie (M)	5 11	12 07	Sheffield	30	11	77	Cambridge U
Johnson Paul (D)			Sunderland	5	4	92	Scholar
Larkin Colin (F)	5 9	11 07	Dundalk	27	4	82	Northampton T
Liddle Gary (D)	6 1	12 06	Middlesbrough	15	6	86	Middlesbrough
Monkhouse Andrew (M)	6 2	12 06	Leeds	23	10	80	Swindon T
Rafferty Andy (G)	5 10	12 00	Sidcup	27	5	88	Guisborough T
Sweeney Anthony (M)	6 0	11 07	Stockton	5	9	83	Scholar

League Appearances: Austin, N. 24; Behan, D. 1(12); Bjornsson, A. 3(15); Boyd, A. 9(10); Brown, J. 17(9); Collins, S. 42; Donaldson, R. 11(1); Flinders, S. 26; Fredriksen, J. (1); Gamble, J. 25(5); Hartley, P. 38(2); Haslam, S. 22(7); Holden, D. 1; Horwood, E. 44(1); Humphreys, R. 14(11); Johnson, P. 1; Kean, J. 19; Larkin, C. 15(15); Liddle, G. 42; Mackay, M. 1(2); McSweeney, L. 24(22); Monkhouse, A. 43(1); Murray, P. 35(1); Poole, J. (3); Rafferty, A. 1; Rowbotham, J. 1; Sweeney, A. 38(2); Yantorno, F. 9(8).

Goals – League (47): Sweeney 9, Monkhouse 7, Liddle 6, Boyd 3 (1 pen), Larkin 3, Austin 2 (1 pen), Collins 2, Hartley 2, Horwood 2, Humphreys 2, McSweeney 2, Brown 1, Flinders 1, Gamble 1, Murray 1, Poole 1, own goals 2.

Carling Cup (2): Boyd 1 (pen), Brown 1.

FA Cup (6): Sweeney 4, Brown 1, Humphreys 1.

J Paint Trophy (6): Behan 1, Horwood 1, McSweeney 1, Monkhouse 1, Sweeney 1, Yantorno 1.

Ground: Victoria Park, Clarence Road, Hartlepool TS24 8BZ. Telephone: (01429) 272 584.
Record Attendance: 17,426 v Manchester U, FA Cup 3rd rd, 5 January 1957.
Capacity: 7,630.
First Team Coach: Mick Wadsworth.
Senior Administrator: Maureen Smith.
Most League Goals: 90, Division 3 (N), 1956–57.
Highest League Scorer in Season: William Robinson, 28, Division 3 (N), 1927–28; Joe Allon, 28, Division 4, 1990–91.
Most League Goals in Total Aggregate: Ken Johnson, 98, 1949–64.
Most Capped Player: Ambrose Fogarty, 1 (11), Republic of Ireland.
Most League Appearances: Wattie Moore, 447, 1948–64.
Honours: None.
Colours: Broad blue and white striped shirts with blue sleeves, blue shorts, white stockings.

HEREFORD UNITED   FL CHAMPIONSHIP 2

Bartlett Adam (G)	6 0	11 11	Newcastle	27	2 86	Kidderminster H
Canham Sean (F)	6 1	13 01	Exeter	26	9 84	Notts Co
Colbeck Joe (M)	5 10	10 12	Bradford	29	11 86	Oldham Ath
Connor Dan (G)	6 2	13 00	Dublin	31	1 89	St Patricks Ath
Featherstone Nicky (F)	5 6	11 02	North Ferriby	22	9 88	Hull C
Fleetwood Stuart (F)	5 10	12 07	Gloucester	23	4 86	Charlton Ath
Green Ryan (D)	5 7	10 10	Cardiff	20	10 80	Bristol R
Kovacs Janos (D)	6 4	14 10	Budapest	11	9 85	Lincoln C
Lunt Kenny (M)	5 10	10 05	Runcorn	20	11 79	Sheffield W
McQuilkin James (F)	5 8	11 10	Belfast	9	1 89	Zlin
Townsend Michael (D)	6 1	13 12	Walsall	17	5 86	Cheltenham T
Weir Tyler (M)	5 10	11 08	Gloucester	21	10 90	Scholar

League Appearances: Bartlett, A. 46; Bauza, G. 9(3); Canham, S. 7(9); Colbeck, J. 40(4); Fairhurst, W. 10(6); Featherstone, N. 20(7); Fleetwood, S. 36(7); Green, R. 40(1); Gwynne, S. 3(3); Heath, J. 26; James, T. 6; Jervis, J. 3(1); Kanoute, S. (1); Kovacs, J. 21(4); Leslie, S. 10(1); Lund, M. 1(1); Lunt, K. 38(4); Malsom, S. 1(3); Manset, M. 18(3); McQuilkin, J. 31(7); Ngo Baheng, W. (2); Patulea, A. (6); Pell, H. 5(2); Price, J. 1(3); Purdie, R. 18(7); Rabihou, A. 1(2); Rose, R. 32(2); Stam, S. 10; Stratford, D. 2(5); Thompson, O. 5(1); Townsend, M. 42(1); Valentine, R. 16; Webster, B. 2; Weir, T. 2(2); Werling, D. 4(2).
Goals – League (50): Fleetwood 14, Manset 7, Colbeck 5, Fairhurst 3, McQuilkin 3, Purdie 3 (1 pen), Bauza 2 (1 pen), Canham 2, Kovacs 2, Leslie 2, Rose 2, Featherstone 1, Green 1, Townsend 1, own goals 2.
Carling Cup (0).
FA Cup (13): Manset 6 (1 pen), Fleetwood 4, Purdie 2, Rose 1.
J Paint Trophy (0).
Ground: Athletic Ground, Edgar Street, Hereford HR4 9JU. Telephone: (08442) 761 939.
Record Attendance: 18,114 v Sheffield W, FA Cup 3rd rd, 4 January 1958.
Capacity: 7,149.
Manager: Jamie Pitman.
Most League Goals: 86, Division 3, 1975–76.
Highest League Scorer in Season: Dixie McNeil, 35, 1975–76.
Most League Goals in Total Aggregate: Stewart Phillips, 93, 1980–88, 1990–91.
Most Capped Player: Trevor Benjamin, 2, Jamaica.
Most League Appearances: Mel Pejic, 412, 1980–92.
Honours – Football League: Division 3 Champions – 1975–76. **Welsh Cup:** Winners – 1990.
Colours: White shirts with black trim, black shorts, white stockings.

HUDDERSFIELD TOWN   FL CHAMPIONSHIP 1

Allinson Lloyd (G)	6 2	13 00	Leeds	7 9 93	Academy
Arfield Scott (M)	5 10	10 01	Dechmont	1 11 88	Falkirk
Atkinson Chris (M)	6 1	11 13	Huddersfield	13 2 92	Scholar
Bennett Ian (G)	6 0	12 10	Worksop	10 10 71	Sheffield U
Cadamarteri Danny (F)	5 7	13 05	Bradford	12 10 79	Dundee U
Chippendale Aiden (M)	5 8	10 10	Bradford	24 5 92	Scholar
Clarke Nathan (D)	6 2	12 00	Halifax	30 11 83	Scholar
Clarke Peter (D)	6 0	12 00	Southport	3 1 82	Southend U
Clarke Tom (D)	5 11	12 02	Halifax	21 12 87	Scholar
Gudjonsson Joey (M)	5 9	12 04	Akranes	25 5 80	Burnley
Hunt Jack (D)	5 9	11 02	Rothwell	6 12 90	Scholar
Kay Antony (D)	5 11	11 08	Barnsley	21 10 82	Tranmere R
Lee Alan (F)	6 2	13 09	Galway	21 8 78	Crystal Palace
McCombe Jamie (D)	6 5	12 05	Scunthorpe	1 1 83	Bristol C
Naysmith Gary (D)	5 9	12 01	Edinburgh	16 11 78	Sheffield U
Novak Lee (F)	6 0	12 04	Newcastle	28 9 88	Gateshead
Peltier Lee (D)	5 10	12 00	Liverpool	11 12 86	Yeovil T
Pilkington Anthony (M)	5 11	12 00	Manchester	3 11 87	Stockport Co
Rhodes Jordan (F)	6 1	11 03	Oldham	5 2 90	Ipswich T
Ridehalgh Liam (D)	5 10	11 05	Halifax	20 4 91	Scholar
Roberts Gary (F)	5 10	11 09	Chester	18 3 84	Ipswich T
Simpson Robbie (F)	6 1	11 11	Stevenage	15 3 85	Coventry C
Smithies Alex (G)	6 1	10 01	Huddersfield	25 3 90	Scholar
Spencer James (F)	6 1	13 00	Leeds	13 12 91	Scholar

League Appearances: Afobe, B. 14(14); Arfield, S. 33(7); Atkinson, C. 2; Bennett, I. 24; Cadamarteri, D. 2(9); Carey, G. 18(1); Chippendale, A. (1); Clarke, N. 1; Clarke, T. 3(2); Clarke, P. 46; Croft, L. (3); Garner, J. 10(6); Gudjonsson, J. 29(8); Hunt, J. 14(5); Johnson, D. 14(2); Jordan, S. 6; Kadar, T. 2; Kay, A. 21(6); Kilbane, K. 23(1); Lee, A. 17(11); McCombe, J. 31(3); Naysmith, G. 13(1); Novak, L. 12(19); Peltier, L. 38; Pilkington, A. 30(1); Rhodes, J. 27(10); Ridehalgh, L. 15(5); Roberts, G. 34(3); Robinson, T. (1); Smithies, A. 22; Ward, D. 5(2).

Goals – League (77): Rhodes 16, Pilkington 10, Roberts 9 (2 pens), Afobe 5, McCombe 5, Novak 5, Arfield 4, Clarke P 4, Cadamarteri 3, Kay 3, Ward 3, Carey 2, Gudjonsson 2, Kilbane 1, Clarke T 1, Hunt 1, Peltier 1, own goal 1.

Carling Cup (2): Rhodes 1, own goal 1.

FA Cup (11): Roberts 3, Afobe 1, Arfield 1, Kay 1, Lee 1, McCombe 1, Peltier 1, Pilkington 1, Rhodes 1.

J Paint Trophy (13): Rhodes 4, Pilkington 3, Afobe 2, Lee 2, Arfield 1, Carey 1.

Play-Offs (4): Kay 1, Kilbane 1, Peltier 1, Ward 1.

Ground: The Galpharm Stadium, Stadium Way, Leeds Road, Huddersfield HD1 6PX. Telephone: 0870 4444 677.

Record Attendance: 67,037 v Arsenal, FA Cup 6th rd, 27 February 1932 (at Leeds Road); 23,678 v Liverpool, FA Cup 3rd rd, 12 December 1999 (at Alfred McAlpine Stadium).

Capacity: 24,554.

Manager: Lee Clark.

Secretary: Ann Hough.

Most League Goals: 101, Division 4, 1979–80.

Highest League Scorer in Season: Sam Taylor, 35, Division 2, 1919–20; George Brown, 35, Division 1, 1925–26.

Most League Goals in Total Aggregate: George Brown, 142, 1921–29; Jimmy Glazzard, 142, 1946–56.

Most Capped Player: Jimmy Nicholson, 31 (41), Northern Ireland.

Most League Appearances: Billy Smith, 520, 1914–34.
Honours – Football League: Division 1 Champions – 1923–24, 1924–25, 1925–26. Division 2 Champions – 1969–70. Division 4 Champions – 1979–80. **FA Cup:** Winners – 1922.
Colours: Blue and white striped shirts, white shorts, blue stockings.

HULL CITY   FL CHAMPIONSHIP

Atkinson William (M)	5 10	10 07	Beverley	14 10 88	Scholar
Barmby Nick (M)	5 7	11 03	Hull	11 2 74	Leeds U
Bullard Jimmy (M)	5 10	11 05	Newham	23 10 78	Fulham
Cairney Tom (M)	6 0	11 05	Nottingham	20 1 91	Scholar
Chester James (D)	5 11	11 04	Warrington	23 1 89	Manchester U
Cooper Liam (D)	6 2	13 07	Hull	30 8 91	Scholar
Cullen Mark (F)	5 9	11 11	Ashington	24 4 92	Scholar
Dawson Andy (D)	5 10	11 02	Northallerton	20 10 78	Scunthorpe U
Devitt Jamie (F)	5 10	10 05	Dublin	6 6 90	Scholar
Fryatt Matty (F)	5 10	11 00	Nuneaton	5 3 86	Leicester C
Ghilas Kamel (F)	5 10	11 00	Marseille	9 3 84	Celta Vigo
Harper James (M)	5 10	11 02	Chelmsford	9 11 80	Sheffield U
Holohan Gavan (M)			Republic of Ireland	15 12 91	Academy
Kilbane Kevin (M)	6 1	13 05	Preston	1 2 77	Wigan Ath
Koren Robert (M)	5 10	11 03	Ljubljana	20 9 80	WBA
McLean Aaron (F)	5 9	10 10	Hammersmith	25 5 83	Peterborough U
McShane Paul (D)	6 0	11 05	Wicklow	6 1 86	Sunderland
Olofinjana Seyi (M)	6 4	11 10	Lagos	30 6 80	Stoke C
Oxley Mark (G)	5 11	11 05	Sheffield	2 6 90	Rotherham U
Rosenior Liam (D)	5 10	11 05	Wandsworth	9 7 84	Reading
Simpson Jay (F)	5 11	13 04	Enfield	1 12 88	Arsenal
Stewart Cameron (M)	5 8	11 05	Manchester	8 4 91	Manchester U

League Appearances: Akpan, H. 1(1); Amoo, D. 1(6); Ashbee, I. 19; Atkinson, W. 3(1); Ayala, D. 12; Barmby, N. 8(23); Belaid, T. 3(5); Bostock, J. 8(3); Bullard, J. 5(3); Cairney, T. 16(6); Chester, J. 21; Cooper, L. 2; Cullen. M.(13); Dawson, A. 45; Devitt, J. 7(9); Duke, M. 20(1); Evans, C. 17(1); Fagan, C. 4(1); Folan, C. 2(1); Fryatt, M. 21(1); Garcia, R. 16(9); Gardner, A. 2; Gerrard, A. 41; Guzan, B. 16; Harper, J. 27(1); Hobbs, J. 9(4); Kilbane, K. 11(3); Koren, R. 39(1); Mannone, V. 10; McLean, A. 18(5); McShane, P. 13(6); Rosenior, L. 26; Simpson, J. 19(13); Solano, N. 6(5); Stewart, C. 14; Vine, R. 4(1); Zayatte, K. 16.
Goals – League (52): Fryatt 9 (3 pens), Koren 7, Simpson 6 (1 pen), Barmby 5, Gerrard 5, Evans 3, McLean 3, Bostock 2, Bullard 2 (1 pen), Garcia 2, Amoo 1, Ashbee 1, Ayala 1, Cairney 1, Chester 1, Harper 1, Kilbane 1, own goal 1.
Carling Cup (1): Cullen 1.
FA Cup (2): Barmby 2.
Ground: The Circle, The KC Stadium, Walton Street, Hull, East Yorkshire HU3 6HU. Telephone: (01482) 504 600.
Record Attendance: KC Stadium: 25,512 v Sunderland, FL C, 28 October 2007. Booth-ferry Park: 55,019 v Manchester U, FA Cup 6th rd, 26 February 1949.
Capacity: 25,404.
Manager: Nigel Pearson.
Football Secretary: Phil Hough.
Most League Goals: 109, Division 3, 1965–66.
Highest League Scorer in Season: Bill McNaughton, 39, Division 3 (N), 1932–33.
Most League Goals in Total Aggregate: Chris Chilton, 193, 1960–71.
Most Capped Player: Theo Whitmore, 28 (105), Jamaica.
Most League Appearances: Andy Davidson, 520, 1952–67.
Honours – Football League: Division 3 (N) Champions – 1932–33, 1948–49. Division 3 Champions – 1965–66.
Colours: Black and amber striped shirts, black shorts, amber stockings with black hoops.

Ainsley Jack (D)	5 11	11 00	Ipswich	17 9 90	Scholar
Carson Josh (M)	5 9	11 00	Ballymena	3 6 93	Scholar
Civelli Luciano (M)	6 2	13 01	Capital Federal	6 10 86	Banfield
Delaney Damien (D)	6 3	14 00	Cork	20 7 81	QPR
Drury Andy (M)	5 11	12 06	Chatham	26 11 83	Luton T
Eastman Tom (D)	6 3	13 12	Colchester	21 10 91	Scholar
Edwards Carlos (M)	5 8	11 02	Port of Spain	24 10 78	Sunderland
Fulop Marton (G)	6 6	14 07	Budapest	3 5 83	Sunderland
Griffiths Jamie (M)	5 11	9 13	Bury St Edmunds	4 1 92	Scholar
Healy Colin (M)	6 1	12 13	Cork	14 3 80	Cork C
Hourihane Conor (M)	5 11	9 11	Cork	2 2 91	Sunderland
Hyam Luke (M)	5 10	11 05	Ipswich	24 10 91	Scholar
Kennedy Mark (D)	5 11	11 09	Dublin	15 5 76	Cardiff C
Leadbitter Grant (M)	5 9	11 06	Sunderland	7 1 86	Sunderland
Lee-Barrett Arran (G)	6 2	14 01	Ipswich	28 2 84	Hartlepool U
Martin Lee (M)	5 10	10 03	Taunton	9 2 87	Manchester U
Murray Ronan (F)	5 7	11 00	Mayo	12 9 91	Scholar
O'Connor Shane (M)	5 9	11 08	Cork	14 4 90	Liverpool
Peters Jaime (M)	5 7	10 12	Toronto	4 5 87	Moor Green
Priskin Tamas (F)	6 2	13 03	Komarno	27 9 86	Watford
Scotland Jason (F)	5 8	11 10	Morvant	18 2 79	Wigan Ath
Smith Tommy (D)	6 2	12 02	Macclesfield	31 3 90	Scholar
Wickham Connor (F)	6 0	14 01	Ipswich	31 3 93	Scholar

League Appearances: Ainsley, J. (1); Brown, T. 6(6); Bullard, J. 16; Carson, J. 8(1); Civelli, L. (9); Colback, J. 13; Delaney, D. 32; Drury, A. 4(8); Dyer, K. 1(3); Eastman, T. 8(1); Edwards, C. 42(3); Fallon, R. 4(2); Fulop, M. 35; Healy, C. 7(9); Hyam, L. 8(2); Kennedy, M. 24(2); Lambe, R. (2); Leadbitter, G. 44; Lee-Barrett, A. 7; Livermore, J. 8(4); Martin, L. 15(1); McAuley, G. 39; Murphy, B. 4; Murray, R. 1(7); Norris, D. 35(1); O'Connor, S. 2(3); O'Dea, D. 17(3); Peters, J. 12(11); Priskin, T. 18(14); Scotland, J. 32(7); Smith, T. 22; Stead, J. 2(1); Townsend, A. 11(2); Walters, J. 1; Wickham, C. 24(13); Zuiverloon, G. 4.

Goals – League (62): Scotland 10, Wickham 9 (1 pen), Norris 8, Bullard 5, Leadbitter 5 (4 pens), Priskin 4, Carson 3, Edwards 3, Smith 3, Delaney 2, Healy 2, McAuley 2, Fallon 1, Peters 1, Stead 1, Townsend 1, own goals 2.

Carling Cup (11): Norris 3, Priskin 3, Delaney 1, Edwards 1, Leadbitter 1 (pen), McAuley 1, Murray 1.

FA Cup (0).

Ground: Portman Road, Ipswich, Suffolk IP1 2DA. Telephone: (01473) 400 500.

Record Attendance: 38,010 v Leeds U, FA Cup 6th rd, 8 March 1975.

Capacity: 30,311.

Manager: Paul Jewell.

Secretary: Sally Webb.

Most League Goals: 106, Division 3 (S), 1955–56.

Highest League Scorer in Season: Ted Phillips, 41, Division 3 (S), 1956–57.

Most League Goals in Total Aggregate: Ray Crawford, 204, 1958–63 and 1966–69.

Most Capped Player: Allan Hunter, 47 (53), Northern Ireland.

Most League Appearances: Mick Mills, 591, 1966–82.

Honours – Football League: Division 1 Champions – 1961–62. Division 2 Champions – 1960–61, 1967–68, 1991–92. Division 3 (S) Champions – 1953–54, 1956–57. **FA Cup:** Winners – 1977–78. **European Competitions: UEFA Cup:** Winners – 1980–81.

Colours: Blue shirts with white trim, white shorts, blue stockings.

LEEDS UNITED

FL CHAMPIONSHIP

Becchio Luciano (F)	6 2	13 05	Cordoba	28 12 83	Merida
Bessone Frede (D)	5 11	11 13	Cordoba	23 1 84	Swansea C
Bromby Leigh (D)	5 11	11 06	Dewsbury	2 6 80	Watford
Bruce Alex (D)	6 0	11 06	Norwich	28 9 84	Ipswich T
Clayton Adam (M)	5 9	11 11	Manchester	14 1 89	Manchester C
Connolly Paul (D)	6 0	11 09	Liverpool	29 9 83	Derby Co
Gradel Max (M)	5 9	11 00	Abidjan	30 11 87	Ivory Coast
Grella Mike (F)	5 11	12 02	Glen Cove	23 1 87	Duke Univ
Hatfield Will (M)			Liversedge	10 10 91	Scholar
Howson Jonathan (M)	5 11	12 01	Leeds	21 5 88	Scholar
Lees Tom (D)	6 1	12 02	Warwick	28 11 90	Youth
McCann Joe (M)			Leeds	11 10 92	Scholar
McCormack Ross (F)	5 9	11 00	Glasgow	18 8 86	Cardiff C
Nunez Ramon (M)	5 7	10 00	Tegucigalpa	14 11 85	Cruz Azul
O'Brien Andy (D)	6 2	11 13	Harrogate	29 6 79	Bolton W
Parker Ben (D)	5 11	11 06	Pontefract	8 11 87	Scholar
Payne Sanchez (M)			Leeds	31 1 92	Scholar
Paynter Billy (F)	6 1	14 01	Liverpool	13 7 84	Swindon T
Sam Lloyd (F)	5 10	11 00	Leeds	27 9 84	Charlton Ath
Schmeichel Kasper (G)	6 1	13 00	Copenhagen	5 11 86	Notts Co
Snodgrass Robert (F)	6 0	12 02	Glasgow	7 9 87	Livingston
Somma Davide (F)	6 1	12 13	Johannesburg	26 3 85	San Jose E
White Aidan (D)	5 7	10 00	Leeds	10 10 91	Scholar

League Appearances: Bannan, B. 3(4); Becchio, L. 34(7); Bessone, F. 6; Bromby, L. 9(4); Brown, J. 3(1); Bruce, A. 21; Clayton, A. (4); Collins, N. 20(1); Connolly, P. 30; Faye, A. 6(2); Gradel, M. 38(3); Grella, M. (1); Higgs, S. 6; Howson, J. 46; Hughes, A. 5(5); Johnson, B. 40(5); Kilkenny, N. 29(8); Kisnorbo, P. (1); Lichaj, E. 16; Livermore, J. 4(1); McCartney, G. 32; McCormack, R. 6(15); Naylor, R. 13(2); Nunez, R. (2); O'Brien, A. 30; Parker, B. 1(1); Paynter, B. 8(14); Sam, L. 7(11); Schmeichel, K. 37; Snodgrass, R. 34(3); Somma, D. 12(17); Watt, S. 9(13); White, A. 1(1).
Goals – League (81): Becchio 19, Gradel 18 (2 pens), Somma 11, Howson 10, Snodgrass 6, Johnson 5, McCormack 2, O'Brien 2, Sam 2, Bruce 1, Kilkenny 1, Naylor 1, Paynter 1, Watt 1, own goal 1.
Carling Cup (5): Becchio 1, Howson 1, Kilkenny 1 (pen), Sam 1, Somma 1.
FA Cup (2): Johnson 1, Snodgrass 1 (pen).
Ground: Elland Road, Leeds, West Yorkshire LS11 0ES. Telephone: (0871) 334 1919.
Record Attendance: 57,892 v Sunderland, FA Cup 5th rd (replay), 15 March 1967.
Capacity: 39,457.
Manager: Simon Grayson.
Most League Goals: 98, Division 2, 1927–28.
Highest League Scorer in Season: John Charles, 42, Division 2, 1953–54.
Most League Goals in Total Aggregate: Peter Lorimer, 168, 1965–79 and 1983–86.
Most Capped Player: Lucas Radebe, 58 (70), South Africa.
Most League Appearances: Jack Charlton, 629, 1953–73.
Honours – Football League: Division 1 Champions – 1968–69, 1973–74, 1991–92. Division 2 Champions – 1923–24, 1963–64, 1989–90. **FA Cup:** Winners – 1972. **Football League Cup:** Winners – 1967–68. **European Competitions: European Fairs Cup:** Winners – 1967–68, 1970–71.
Colours: White shirts, white shorts, white stockings with yellow trim.

Abe Yuki (M)	5 9	12 02	Chiba	6	9 81	Urawa
Bamba Souleymane (D)	6 3	14 02	Ivry-sur-Seyne	13	1 85	Hibernian
Berner Bruno (M)	6 1	12 13	Zurich	21	11 77	Blackburn R
Bolger Cian (D)			Co. Kildare	12	3 92	Scholar
Chamberlain Elliott (M)			Wales	29	4 92	Scholar
Crncic Leon (F)	6 1	11 09	Slovenia	2	3 90	Aluminij
Dyer Lloyd (M)	5 8	10 03	Birmingham	13	9 82	Milton Keynes D
Gallagher Paul (F)	6 1	11 00	Glasgow	9	8 84	Blackburn R
Hobbs Jack (D)	6 3	13 05	Portsmouth	18	8 88	Liverpool
Howard Steve (F)	6 3	15 00	Durham	10	5 76	Derby Co
Kennedy Tom (D)	5 10	11 01	Bury	24	6 85	Rochdale
Kermorgant Yann (F)	6 0	13 03	Vannes	8	11 81	Reims
King Andy (M)	6 0	11 10	Luton	29	10 88	Scholar
Lamey Michael (D)	6 1	12 06	Amsterdam	29	11 79	Arminia Bielefeld
Logan Conrad (G)	6 0	14 09	Letterkenny	18	4 86	Scholar
Moreno Jose (D)	6 1	12 10	Urgeses	19	8 81	Guimaraes
Moussa Franck (M)	5 8	10 08	Brussels	24	9 87	Southend U
N'Guessan Dany (M)	6 0	12 13	Ivry-sur-Seine	11	8 87	Lincoln C
Neilson Robbie (D)	6 0	13 01	Paisley	19	6 80	Hearts
Oakley Matthew (M)	5 10	12 06	Peterborough	17	8 77	Derby Co
Parkes Tom (D)	6 3	12 05	Leicester	15	1 92	Scholar
Schlupp Jeffrey (F)	5 8	11 00	Hamburg	23	12 92	Youth
Vassell Darius (F)	5 9	13 00	Birmingham	13	6 80	Ankaragucu
Waghorn Martyn (F)	5 9	13 01	South Shields	23	1 90	Sunderland
Warburton Jack (M)			Enfield	27	4 93	Youth
Weale Chris (G)	6 2	13 03	Yeovil	9	2 82	Bristol C
Wellens Richard (M)	5 9	11 06	Manchester	26	3 80	Doncaster R

League Appearances: Abe, Y. 25(11); Bamba, S. 16; Bednar, R. 4(1); Berner, B. 15(2); Bruma, J. 10(1); Campbell, D. 3; Cunningham, G. 13; Davies, C. 12; Dyer, L. 18(17); Fryatt, M. 5(7); Gallagher, P. 32(9); Hobbs, J. 23(3); Howard, S. 11(18); Ikeme, C. 5; Kamara, D. 5(2); Kennedy, T. 1; King, A. 44(1); Kirkland, C. 3; Lamey, M. 2(2); Logan, C. 2(1); Mee, B. 15; Miguel Vitor, 13(2); Moreno, J. 3; Morrison, M. 10(1); Moussa, F. 2(6); N'Guessan, D. 3(2); Naughton, K. 34; Neilson, R. 7; Oakley, M. 22(12); Ricardo, 8; Tunchev, A. (2); Van Aanholt, P. 12; Vassell, D. 26(5); Waghorn, M. 11(19); Weale, C. 28(1); Wellens, R. 44(1); Yakubu, A. 19(1).

Goals – League (76): King A 15, Yakubu 11, Gallagher 10 (4 pens), Naughton 5, Howard 4 (2 pens), Vassell 4, Waghorn 4, Dyer 3, Miguel Vitor 3, Bamba 2, Bruma 2, Fryatt 2, Kamara 2, Oakley 2, Wellens 2, Abe 1, Berner 1, Campbell 1, Moussa 1, Van Aanholt 1.

Carling Cup (9): Fryatt 2, Wellens 2, Dyer 1, Howard 1 (pen), Morrison 1, Neilson 1, own goal 1.

FA Cup (4): Bamba 1, Dyer 1, Gallagher 1 (pen), King 1.

Ground: Walkers Stadium, Filbert Way, Leicester LE2 7FL. Telephone: 0844 815 6000.

Record Attendance: 47,298 v Tottenham H, FA Cup 5th rd, 18 February 1928 (at Filbert Street). 32,148 v Manchester U, FA Premier League, 26 December 2003 (at Walkers Stadium).

Capacity: 32,500 (all seated).

Manager: Sven-Göran Eriksson.

Secretary: Andrew Neville.

Most League Goals: 109, Division 2, 1956–57.

Highest League Scorer in Season: Arthur Rowley, 44, Division 2, 1956–57.

Most League Goals in Total Aggregate: Arthur Chandler, 259, 1923–35.

Most Capped Player: John O'Neill, 39, Northern Ireland.

Most League Appearances: Adam Black, 528, 1920–35.
Honours – Football League: Championship 1 Winners – 2008–09. Division 2 Champions – 1924–25, 1936–37, 1953–54, 1956–57, 1970–71, 1979–80. **Football League Cup:** Winners – 1964, 1997, 2000.
Colours: Blue shirts with white trim, white shorts, blue stockings with white trim.

LEYTON ORIENT   FL CHAMPIONSHIP 1

Argent Jake (F)			Enfield	9 12 91	Scholar
Beautyman Harry (M)			Newham	1 4 92	Youth
Butcher Lee (G)			Waltham Forest	11 10 88	Tottenham H
Cestor Mike (D)			Paris	30 4 92	Youth
Chambers Adam (M)	5 10	11 08	Sandwell	20 11 80	Kidderminster H
Chorley Ben (D)	6 3	13 02	Sidcup	30 9 82	Tranmere R
Cox Dean (M)	5 4	9 08	Cuckfield	12 8 87	Brighton & HA
Daniels Charlie (M)	6 1	12 12	Harlow	7 9 86	Tottenham H
Dawson Stephen (M)	5 9	11 09	Dublin	4 12 85	Bury
Forbes Terrell (D)	5 11	12 07	Southwark	17 8 81	Yeovil T
Jones Jamie (G)	6 2	14 05	Kirkby	18 2 89	Everton
Omozusi Elliott (D)	5 11	12 09	Hackney	15 12 88	Fulham
Porter George (F)	5 10	12 00	London	27 6 92	Cray W
Revell Alex (F)	6 3	13 00	Cambridge	7 7 83	Wycombe W
Smith Jimmy (M)	6 0	10 03	Newham	7 1 87	Chelsea
Spring Matthew (M)	5 11	12 05	Harlow	17 11 79	Charlton Ath
Tehoue Jonathan (F)	5 8	11 06	Paris	3 5 84	Alfortville
Whing Andrew (D)	6 0	12 00	Birmingham	20 9 84	Brighton & HA

League Appearances: Barrett, A. 14; Brown, A. 4(1); Brown, J. 3; Butcher, L. 8(1); Carroll, T. 8(4); Cestor, M. 2; Chambers, A. 23(6); Chorley, B. 28(1); Cox, D. 44(1); Crowe, J. 5(7); Daniels, C. 41(1); Dawson, S. 39(1); Forbes, T. 32(2); Frampton, A. 1; Jarvis, R. 3(8); Jones, J. 35; Kane, H. 9(9); Liddle, M. 1; M'Poku, P. 9(18); McGleish, S. 27(12); Omozusi, E. 39(1); Patulea, A. (1); Porter, G. (1); Revell, A. 35(4); Smith, J. 25(6); Spring, M. 39; Tehoue, J. 9(23); Walker, J. (11); Whing, A. 23(1).
Goals – League (71): Revell 13, McGleish 12 (2 pens), Cox 11, Smith 7, Tehoue 7, Kane 5, Chorley 3 (2 pens), Dawson 2, Forbes 2, Jarvis 2, M'Poku 2, Spring 2, Whing 2, own goal 1.
Carling Cup (2): Jarvis 1, Revell 1.
FA Cup (17): McGleish 6, Tehoue 4, Revell 2, Smith 2, Chorley 1 (pen), M'Poku 1, own goal 1.
J Paint Trophy (1): Cox 1.
Ground: Matchroom Stadium, Brisbane Road, Leyton, London E10 5NF. Telephone: 0871 310 1881.
Record Attendance: 34,345 v West Ham U, FA Cup 4th rd, 25 January 1964.
Capacity: 9,300.
Manager: Russell Slade.
Secretary: Lindsey Martin.
Most League Goals: 106, Division 3 (S), 1955–56.
Highest League Scorer in Season: Tom Johnston, 35, Division 2, 1957–58.
Most League Goals in Total Aggregate: Tom Johnston, 121, 1956–58, 1959–61.
Most Capped Players: Tunji Banjo, 7 (7), Nigeria; John Chiedozie, 7 (9), Nigeria; Tony Grealish, 7 (45), Republic of Ireland.
Most League Appearances: Peter Allen, 432, 1965–78.
Honours – Football League: Division 3 Champions – 1969–70. Division 3 (S) Champions – 1955–56.
Colours: Red shirts with white insert and striped sleeves, red shorts, red stockings.

LINCOLN CITY   BLUE SQUARE PREMIER

Anyon Joe (G)	6 1	12 11	Poulton-le-Fylde	29 12 86	Port Vale
Carayol Mustapha (F)	5 10	11 11	Gambia	10 4 90	Torquay U
Fuseini Ali (M)	5 6	9 10	Ghana	7 12 88	Millwall
Hone Daniel (D)	6 2	12 00	Croydon	15 9 89	Scholar
Hutchinson Andrew (F)	5 7	12 00	Lincoln	10 5 92	Scholar
Hutchinson Ben (F)	5 11	12 07	Nottingham	27 11 87	Celtic
McCallum Gavin (M)	5 9	12 00	Mississauga	24 8 87	Hereford U
O'Keefe Josh (M)	6 1	11 05	Whalley	22 12 88	Walsall
Watts Adam (D)	6 2	12 06	London	4 3 88	Fulham

League Appearances: Anderson, J. 19(3); Anyon, J. 21; Broughton, D. 9(14); Carayol, M. 24(9); Carson, T. 16; Clapham, J. 21(4); Facey, D. 26(6); Fuseini, A. 15(3); Gowling, J. 4; Green, P. 14(3); Grimes, A. 24(3); Hone, D. 25(1); Howell, L. 23(2); Hoyte, G. 11(1); Hughton, C. 17(5); Hunt, S. 14; Hutchinson, A. (5); Hutchinson, B. 26(10); Jarrett, A. 19(3); Kanyuka, P. 2(4); Kelly, J. 21; Keltie, C. 16(2); Kerr, S. 10(6); Kilbey, T. 6(1); McCallum, G. 24(12); Musselwhite, P. (1); O'Keefe, J. 33(4); Parish, E. 9; Pearce, I. 3(1); Spencer, S. 2(8); Swaibu, M. 12; Turner, S. (2); Watts, A. 40.
Goals – League (45): Grimes 15 (2 pens), Hutchinson B 4 (1 pen), O'Keefe 4, Carayol 3, Facey 3, McCallum 3, Hughton 2, Hunt 2, Swaibu 2, Clapham 1, Green 1, Howell 1, Jarrett 1, Watts 1, own goals 2.
Carling Cup (0).
FA Cup (6): Grimes 2, Carayol 1, Clapham 1, Facey 1, Jarrett 1.
J Paint Trophy (0).
Ground: Sincil Bank Stadium, Sincil Bank, Lincoln LN5 8LD. Telephone: (01522) 880 011.
Record Attendance: 23,196 v Derby Co, League Cup 4th rd, 15 November 1967.
Capacity: 10,120.
Manager: Steve Tilson.
Football Secretary: Fran Martin.
Most League Goals: 121, Division 3 (N), 1951–52.
Highest League Scorer in Season: Allan Hall, 41, Division 3 (N), 1931–32.
Most League Goals in Total Aggregate: Andy Graver, 143, 1950–55 and 1958–61.
Most Capped Player: Gareth McAuley, 5 (30), Northern Ireland.
Most League Appearances: Grant Brown, 407, 1989–2002.
Honours – Football League: Division 3 (N) Champions – 1931–32, 1947–48, 1951–52. Division 4 Champions – 1975–76. **GM Vauxhall Conference:** Champions – 1987–88.
Colours: Red and white striped shirts, black shorts, red stockings.

LIVERPOOL   FA PREMIERSHIP

Adorian Krisztian (F)			Budapest	19 1 93	Scholar
Agger Daniel (D)	6 2	12 06	Hvidovre	12 12 84	Brondby
Amoo David (F)	5 10	12 03	London	23 4 91	Scholar
Aquilani Alberto (M)	6 0	12 03	Rome	7 7 84	Roma
Aurelio Fabio (M)	5 10	11 11	Sao Carlos	24 9 79	Valencia
Ayala Daniel (D)	6 3	13 01	Seville	7 11 90	Sevilla
Bouzanis Dean (G)	6 1	13 05	Sydney	2 10 90	Sydney
Bruna Gerardo (M)	5 8	10 02	Mendoza	29 1 91	Real Madrid
Carragher Jamie (D)	5 9	12 01	Liverpool	28 1 78	Trainee
Carroll Andy (F)	6 4	11 00	Gateshead	6 1 89	Newcastle U
Coady Conor (D)	6 1	11 05	Liverpool	25 2 93	Scholar
Cole Joe (M)	5 9	11 09	Romford	8 11 81	Chelsea
Darby Stephen (D)	6 1	11 11	Liverpool	6 10 88	Scholar
Degen Philipp (D)	6 0	12 10	Holstein	15 2 83	Bor Dortmund

Eccleston Nathan (F)	5 10	12 00	Manchester	30	12 90	Scholar
El Zhar Nabil (F)	5 9	11 05	Rabat	27	8 86	St Etienne
Emilsson Kristjan (M)			Sweden	26	4 93	Scholar
Flanagan John (D)			Liverpool	1	1 93	Scholar
Gerrard Steven (M)	6 0	12 05	Whiston	30	5 80	Trainee
Gulacsi Peter (G)	6 3	13 01	Budapest	6	5 90	MTK Budapest
Hansen Martin (G)	6 2	12 07	Denmark	15	6 90	Scholar
Ince Thomas (F)	5 10	10 05	Liverpool	30	1 92	Scholar
Insua Emiliano (D)	5 10	12 08	Buenos Aires	7	1 89	Boca Juniors
Johnson Glen (D)	6 0	13 04	Greenwich	23	8 84	Portsmouth
Jones Brad (G)	6 3	12 01	Armadale	19	3 82	Middlesbrough
Jovanovic Milan (M)	6 0	11 07	Belgrade	18	4 83	Standard Liege
Kelly Martin (D)	6 3	12 02	Bolton	27	4 90	Scholar
Kohlert Nicolaj (F)	5 10	11 00	Denmark	21	1 93	Esbjerg
Konchesky Paul (D)	5 10	11 07	Barking	15	5 81	Fulham
Kuyt Dirk (F)	6 0	12 02	Katwijk	22	7 80	Feyenoord
Kyrgiakos Sotirios (D)	6 3	14 06	Megalochori	23	7 79	AEK Athens
Lucas (M)	5 10	11 09	Dourados	9	1 87	Gremio
Mavinga Chrys (D)	5 10	10 03	Meaux	26	5 91	Paris St Germain
Meireles Raul (M)	5 10	10 12	Oporto	17	3 83	Porto
Mendy Emmanuel (D)	5 7	11 09	Medina Gounass	30	3 90	Murcia
N'Gog David (F)	6 3	12 04	Gennevillers	1	4 89	Paris St Germain
N'Goo Michael (F)			London	23	10 92	Southend U
Pacheco Daniel (F)	5 6	10 07	Malaga	5	1 91	Barcelona
Palsson Victor (M)	6 1	12 00	Iceland	30	4 91	Aarhus
Reina Jose (G)	6 2	14 06	Madrid	31	8 82	Villarreal
Roberts Michael (M)			Liverpool	5	12 91	Scholar
Robinson Jack (D)	5 11	10 08	Warrington	1	9 93	Scholar
Rodriguez Maxi (M)	5 11	12 06	Rosario	2	1 81	Atletico Madrid
Sama Stephen (D)			Cameroon	5	3 93	Scholar
Shelvey Jonjo (M)	6 1	11 02	Romford	27	2 92	Charlton Ath
Silva Toni (M)			Guinea-Bissau	15	9 93	Scholar
Skrtel Martin (D)	6 3	12 10	Hamdlova	15	12 84	Zenit
Sokolik Jakub (D)	5 6	10 00	Prague	28	8 93	Scholar
Spearing Jay (D)	5 6	11 00	Wirral	25	11 88	Scholar
Stephens James (G)			Wotton-under-Edge	24	8 93	Scholar
Suarez Luis (F)	5 11	12 10	Salto	24	1 87	Ajax
Suso (M)	5 8	10 12	Cadiz	19	11 93	Cadiz
Wilson Danny (D)	6 2	12 06	Livingston	27	12 91	Rangers
Wisdom Andre (D)			Leeds	9	5 93	Scholar

League Appearances: Agger, D. 12(4); Babel, R. 1(8); Carragher, J. 28; Carroll, A. 5(2); Cole, J. 9(11); Eccleston, N. (1); Fabio Aurelio, 7(7); Flanagan, J. 7; Gerrard, S. 20(1); Johnson, G. 28; Jovanovic, M. 5(5); Kelly, M. 10(1); Konchesky, P. 15; Kuyt, D. 32(1); Kyrgiakos, S. 10(6); Lucas, 32(1); Mascherano, J. 1; N'Gog, D. 9(16); Pacheco, D. (1); Poulsen, C. 9(3); Raul Meireles, 32(1); Reina, J. 38; Robinson, J. 1(1); Rodriguez, M. 24(4); Shelvey, J. (15); Skrtel, M. 38; Spearing, J. 10(1); Suarez, L. 12(1); Torres, F. 22(1); Wilson, D. 1(1).

Goals – League (59): Kuyt 13 (5 pens), Rodriguez 10, Torres 9, Raul Meireles 5, Gerrard 4 (1 pen), Suarez 4, Carroll 2, Cole 2, Johnson 2, Kyrgiakos 2, N'Gog 2, Skrtel 2, Babel 1, own goal 1.

Carling Cup (2): Jovanovic 1, N'Gog 1.

FA Cup (0).

Europa League (16): N'Gog 5 (1 pen), Gerrard 4 (2 pens), Kuyt 2, Babel 1, Cole 1, Jovanovic 1, Lucas 1, own goal 1.

Ground: Anfield Stadium, Anfield Road, Liverpool L4 0TH. Telephone: (0151) 260 1433.

Record Attendance: 61,905 v Wolverhampton W, FA Cup 4th rd, 2 February 1952.
Capacity: 45,522.
Manager: Kenny Dalglish.
Secretary: Ian Silvester.
Most League Goals: 106, Division 2, 1895–96.
Highest League Scorer in Season: Roger Hunt, 41, Division 2, 1961–62.
Most League Goals in Total Aggregate: Roger Hunt, 245, 1959–69.
Most Capped Player: Steven Gerrard, 89, England.
Most League Appearances: Ian Callaghan, 640, 1960–78.
Honours – Football League: Division 1 – Champions 1900–01, 1905–06, 1921–22, 1922–23, 1946–47, 1963–64, 1965–66, 1972–73, 1975–76, 1976–77, 1978–79, 1979–80, 1981–82, 1982–83, 1983–84, 1985–86, 1987–88, 1989–90 (Liverpool have a record number of 18 League Championship wins). Division 2 Champions – 1893–94, 1895–96, 1904–05, 1961–62. **FA Cup:** Winners – 1965, 1974, 1986, 1989, 1992, 2001, 2006. **League Cup:** Winners – 1981, 1982, 1983, 1984, 1995, 2001, 2003. **League Super Cup:** Winners 1985–86. **European Competitions: European Cup:** Winners – 1976–77, 1977–78, 1980–81, 1983–84. **Champions League:** Winners – 2004–05. **UEFA Cup:** Winners – 1972–73, 1975–76, 2001. **Super Cup:** Winners – 1977, 2005.
Colours: All red with white trim.

MACCLESFIELD TOWN   FL CHAMPIONSHIP 2

Barnett Tyrone (F)			Stevenage	28	10	85	Huddersfield T
Bencherif Hamza (D)	5 9	12 03	Paris	9	2	88	Nottingham F
Bolland Paul (M)	5 10	10 12	Bradford	23	12	79	Grimsby T
Brisley Shaun (M)	6 2	12 02	Stockport	6	5	90	Scholar
Brown Nat (D)	6 2	12 05	Sheffield	15	6	81	Lincoln C
Chalmers Lewis (M)	6 0	12 04	Manchester	4	2	86	Aldershot T
Cudworth Jack (G)			Preston	11	9	90	Rhyl
Daniel Colin (M)	5 11	11 06	Crewe	15	2	88	Crewe Alex
Diagne Tony (D)			Meulan	17	9	90	Nottingham F
Draper Ross (M)	6 3	15 05	Wolverhampton	20	10	88	Hednesford T
Hamshaw Matt (M)	5 10	11 08	Rotherham	1	1	82	Notts Co
Morgan Paul (D)	6 0	11 05	Belfast	23	10	78	Bury
Mukendi Vinny (F)	6 2	12 00	Bury	12	3	92	Scholar
Reid Izak (M)	5 5	10 05	Sheffield	08	7	87	Scholar
Roberts Adam (M)	5 9	10 07	Manchester	30	12	91	Scholar
Sinclair Emile (F)	6 0	11 04	Leeds	20	12	87	Nottingham F
Thomas Michael (M)	6 1	11 00	Manchester	12	8	92	Scholar
Tremarco Carl (D)	5 8	11 11	Liverpool	11	10	85	Tranmere R
Veiga Jose Manuel (G)	6 2	12 13	Lisbon	18	12	76	Hereford U
Wedgbury Samuel (M)			Oldbury	26	2	89	Sheffield U

League Appearances: Barnett, T. 45; Bencherif, H. 36(5); Bolland, P. 31(1); Brisley, S. 12(2); Brown, N. 44; Butcher, R. 5(2); Chalmers, L. 22(8); Daniel, C. 36(7); Diagne, T. 19(1); Draper, R. 34(6); Gray, D. 18(3); Hamshaw, M. 18(10); Hewitt, E. 1; Lowe, M. (1); Morgan, P. 27(1); Mukendi, V. 8(13); Nsiala, A. 10; Reid, I. 34(3); Roberts, A. (2); Sappleton, R. 1(9); Sinclair, E. 26(5); Tremarco, C. 20(5); Veiga, J. 46; Wedgbury, S. 13(10).
Goals – League (59): Barnett 13, Bencherif 11, Daniel 8, Draper 5, Sinclair 5, Bolland 2, Brown 2, Chalmers 2 (2 pens), Hamshaw 2, Butcher 1, Diagne 1, Gray 1, Mukendi 1, Reid 1, Sappleton 1, Wedgbury 1, own goals 2.
Carling Cup (3): Brown 1, Daniel 1, Mukendi 1.
FA Cup (4): Brown 1, Daniel 1, Nsiala 1, Sinclair 1.
J Paint Trophy (3): Mukendi 1, own goals 2.
Ground: Moss Rose Ground, London Road, Macclesfield, Cheshire SK11 7SP. Telephone: (01625) 264 686.
Record Attendance: 9,008 v Winsford U, Cheshire Senior Cup 2nd rd, 4 February 1948.

Capacity: 6,141.
Manager: Gary Simpson.
Company Secretary: Barrie Darcey.
Most League Goals: 66, Division 3, 1999–2000.
Highest League Scorer in Season: Jon Parkin, 22, FL 2, 2004–05.
Most League Goals in Total Aggregate: Matt Tipton, 50, 2002–05; 2006–07; 2009–10.
Most Capped Player: George Abbey, 10, Nigeria.
Most League Appearances: Darren Tinson, 263, 1997–2003.
Honours: Vauxhall Conference: Champions – 1994–5, 1996–7. **FA Trophy:** Winners – 1969–70, 1970–71.
Colours: Blue shirts with white design, white shorts, blue stockings.

MANCHESTER CITY   FA PREMIERSHIP

Name			Birthplace				Previous Club
Abu Mohammed (M)			Ghana	14	11	91	SC Accra
Adebayor Emmanuel (F)	6 4	11 08	Lome	26	2	84	Arsenal
Assulin Gai (M)			Nahariya	9	4	91	Barcelona
Balotelli Mario (F)	6 2	13 08	Palermo	12	8	90	Internazionale
Barry Gareth (M)	5 11	12 06	Hastings	23	2	81	Aston Villa
Bellamy Craig (F)	5 9	10 12	Cardiff	13	7	79	West Ham U
Benali Ahmad (M)			Libya	7	2	92	Scholar
Boateng Jerome (D)	6 3	14 02	Berlin	3	9	88	Hamburg
Boyata Anga (M)	6 2	12 00	Uccle	8	9	90	Scholar
Bridge Wayne (D)	5 10	12 13	Southampton	5	8	80	Chelsea
Bunn Harry (F)			Oldham	25	11	92	Scholar
Caicedo Felipe (F)	6 1	12 08	Guayaquil	5	9	88	Basle
Chantler Chris (D)	5 8	11 00	Cheadle Hulme	16	12	90	Scholar
Cunningham Greg (D)	6 0	11 00	Cammore	31	1	91	Scholar
De Jong Nigel (D)	5 8	11 05	Amsterdam	30	11	84	Hamburg
Dzeko Edin (F)	6 3	12 08	Doboj	17	3	86	Wolfsburg
Elabdellaoui Omar (M)			Norway	5	12	91	Scholar
Given Shay (G)	6 0	13 03	Lifford	20	4	76	Newcastle U
Gonzalez David (G)	6 4	13 01	Medellin	20	7	82	Huracan
Guidetti John (F)	5 11	12 06	Stockholm	15	4	92	Scholar
Hart Joe (G)	6 5	14 05	Shrewsbury	19	4	87	Shrewsbury T
Helan Jeremy (M)			France	9	5	92	Rennes
Henshall Alex (M)			Swindon	15	2	94	Swindon T
Huws Emyr (M)			Wales	30	9	93	Scholar
Ibrahim Abdisalam (M)	6 0	11 02	Guriceel	4	5	91	Scholar
Jo (F)	5 9	11 00	Sao Paulo	20	3	87	CSKA Moscow
Johansen Eirik (G)			Norway	12	7	92	Scholar
Johnson Adam (M)	5 8	10 00	Sunderland	14	7	87	Middlesbrough
Johnson Michael (M)	6 0	12 07	Urmston	3	3	88	Scholar
Karius Loris (G)	6 2	11 11	Biberach	22	6	93	Scholar
Kolarov Aleksandar (D)	6 2	13 05	Belgrade	10	11	85	Lazio
Kompany Vincent (D)	6 3	13 05	Uccle	10	4	86	Hamburg
Lescott Joleon (D)	6 2	13 00	Birmingham	16	8	82	Everton
McDermott Donal (M)	6 6	12 00	Dublin	19	10	89	Scholar
McGivern Ryan (D)	5 10	11 07	Newry	8	1	90	Scholar
Mee Ben (D)	5 11	11 09	Manchester	21	9	89	Scholar
Milner James (M)	5 9	11 00	Leeds	4	1	86	Aston Villa
Morrissey Conor (D)			Republic of Ireland	13	4	93	Scholar
Nielsen Gunnar (G)	6 3	14 00	Faeroes	7	10	86	Blackburn R
Nimely-Tchuimeni Alex (F)	5 11	11 03	Monrovia	11	5	91	Cotonsport
Onuoha Nedum (D)	6 2	12 04	Warri	12	11	86	Scholar
Razak Abdul (M)			Abidjan	11	11	92	Crystal Palace
Richards Micah (D)	5 11	13 00	Birmingham	24	6	88	Scholar

Santa Cruz Roque (F)	6 2	13 12	Asuncion	16	8 81	Blackburn R
Silva David (F)	5 7	10 07	Arguineguin	8	1 86	Valencia
Taylor Stuart (G)	6 5	13 07	Romford	28	11 80	Aston Villa
Tevez Carlos (F)	5 8	11 11	Cuidadela	5	2 84	Manchester U
Toure Kolo (D)	5 10	13 08	Sokuora Bouake	19	3 81	Arsenal
Toure Yaya (M)	6 3	14 02	Sokuora Bouake	13	5 83	Barcelona
Trippier Keiran (D)	5 10	11 00	Bury	19	9 90	Scholar
Veseli Frederic (D)	6 0	12 08	Switzerland	22	11 92	Scholar
Wabara Reece (D)			Stoke Heath	28	12 91	Scholar
Weiss Vladimir (M)	5 8	11 02	Bratislava	30	11 89	Academy
Wright-Phillips Shaun (F)	5 5	10 01	Lewisham	25	10 81	Chelsea
Zabaleta Pablo (D)	5 8	10 12	Buenos Aires	16	1 85	Espanyol

League Appearances: Adebayor, E. 2(6); Balotelli, M. 12(5); Barry, G. 31(2); Boateng, J. 14(2); Boyata, A. 5(2); Bridge, W. 1(2); De Jong, N. 30(2); Dzeko, E. 8(7); Hart, J. 38; Jo, 3(9); Johnson, A. 15(16); Kolarov, A. 20(4); Kompany, V. 37; Lescott, J. 20(2); McGivern, R. (1); Milner, J. 23(9); Razak, A. (1); Richards, M. 16(2); Santa Cruz, R. (1); Silva, D. 30(5); Tevez, C. 30(1); Toure, K. 21(1); Toure, Y. 35; Vieira, P. 4(11); Wabara, R. (1); Wright-Phillips, S. 2(5); Zabaleta, P. 21(5).

Goals – League (60): Tevez 20 (5 pens), Toure Y 8, Balotelli 6 (2 pens), Johnson A 4, Silva 4, Lescott 3, Barry 2, Dzeko 2, Vieira 2, Zabaleta 2, Adebayor 1 (1 pen), De Jong 1, Kolarov 1, Richards 1, Toure K 1, own goals 2.

Carling Cup (1): Jo 1.

FA Cup (18): Tevez 3, Toure Y 3, Vieira 3, Dzeko 2, Richards 2, Balotelli 1, Johnson A 1, Kolarov 1, Milner 1, Silva 1.

Europa League (18): Adebayor 4, Balotelli 3, Dzeko 2, Jo 2, Johnson A 2, Boyata 1, Kolarov 1, Silva 1, Toure Y 1, Wright-Phillips 1.

Ground: The City of Manchester Stadium, SportCity, Manchester M11 3FF. Telephone: 0870 062 1894.

Record Attendance: 84,569 v Stoke C, FA Cup 6th rd, 3 March 1934 (at Maine Road, British record for any game outside London or Glasgow). 47,370 v Tottenham H, FA Premier League, 5 May 2010 (at City of Manchester Stadium).

Capacity: 47,726.

Manager: Roberto Mancini.

Secretary: Rebecca Firth.

Most League Goals: 108, Division 2, 1926–27, 108, Division 1, 2001–02.

Highest League Scorer in Season: Tommy Johnson, 38, Division 1, 1928–29.

Most League Goals in Total Aggregate: Tommy Johnson, 158, 1919–30.

Most Capped Player: Colin Bell, 48, England.

Most League Appearances: Alan Oakes, 565, 1959–76.

Honours – Football League: Division 1 Champions – 1936–37, 1967–68, 2001–02. Division 2 Champions – 1898–99, 1902–03, 1909–10, 1927–28, 1946–47, 1965–66. **FA Cup:** Winners – 1904, 1934, 1956, 1969, 2011. **Football League Cup:** Winners – 1970, 1976. **European Competitions: European Cup-Winners' Cup:** Winners – 1969–70.

Colours: Sky blue shirts with white detail, white shorts with sky blue detail, white stockings with sky blue tops.

MANCHESTER UNITED   FA PREMIERSHIP

Ajose Nicholas (F)	5 8	11 00	Bury	7	10 91	Scholar
Amos Ben (G)	6 2	13 00	Macclesfield	10	4 90	Scholar
Anderson (M)	5 8	10 07	Porto Alegre	13	4 88	Porto
Bebe (F)	6 3	11 11	Heualva-Cacem	12	7 90	Guimaraes
Berbatov Dimitar (F)	6 2	12 06	Blagoevgrad	30	1 81	Tottenham H
Biram Diouf Mame (F)	6 1	11 13	Dakar	16	12 87	Molde
Brady Robert (F)			Belfast	14	1 92	Scholar
Brown Reece (D)			Manchester	1	11 91	Scholar

Name			Birthplace			Previous
Brown Wes (D)	6 1	13 11	Manchester	13 10 79		Scholar
Carrick Michael (M)	6 2	13 03	Wallsend	28 7 81		Tottenham H
Cleverley Tom (M)	5 8	10 07	Basingstoke	12 8 89		Scholar
Cofie John (F)			Aboso	21 1 93		Scholar
De Laet Ritchie (D)	6 1	12 02	Antwerp	28 11 88		Stoke C
Drinkwater Daniel (M)	5 10	11 00	Manchester	5 3 90		Scholar
Dudgeon Joe (D)	5 9	11 11	Leeds	26 11 90		Scholar
Evans Corry (M)	5 8	10 12	Belfast	30 7 90		Scholar
Evans Jonny (D)	6 2	12 02	Belfast	3 1 88		Scholar
Evra Patrice (D)	5 8	11 10	Dakar	15 5 81		Monaco
Fabio (D)	5 8	10 03	Rio de Janeiro	9 7 90		Fluminense
Ferdinand Rio (D)	6 2	13 12	Peckham	7 11 78		Leeds U
Fletcher Darren (M)	6 0	13 01	Edinburgh	1 2 84		Scholar
Fornasier Michele (D)			Vittorio Veneto	22 8 93		Scholar
Gibson Darron (M)	6 0	12 04	Londonderry	25 10 87		Scholar
Giggs Ryan (F)	5 11	11 00	Cardiff	29 11 73		School
Gill Oliver (D)	6 2	12 13	Frimley	15 9 90		Scholar
Hernandez Javier (F)	5 8	9 11	Guadalajara	1 6 88		Guadalajara
James Matthew (M)	5 10	11 08	Bacup	22 7 91		Scholar
Johnstone Sam (G)			Preston	25 3 93		Scholar
Keane William (F)			Stockport	11 11 93		Scholar
King Joshua (F)	6 1	13 03	Oslo	15 1 92		Scholar
Kuszczak Tomasz (G)	6 3	13 03	Krosno Odrzansia	20 3 82		WBA
Lindegaard Anders (G)	6 4	12 08	Odense	13 4 84		Aalesund
Macheda Federico (F)	6 0	11 13	Rome	22 8 91		Scholar
Massacci Alberto (D)			Siena	27 5 93		Empoli
McGinty Sean (D)			Maidstone	11 8 93		Charlton Ath
Morrison Ravel (M)	5 8	11 01	Wythenshawe	2 2 93		Scholar
Nani (M)	5 9	10 04	Amadora	17 11 86		Sporting Lisbon
Norwood Oliver (M)			Burnley	12 4 91		Scholar
O'Shea John (D)	6 3	12 10	Waterford	30 4 81		Waterford
Obertan Gabriel (F)	6 1	12 06	Pantin	26 2 89		Bordeaux
Owen Michael (F)	5 8	10 12	Chester	14 12 79		Newcastle U
Park Ji-Sung (M)	5 9	11 06	Seoul	25 2 81		PSV Eindhoven
Petrucci Davide (F)	6 0	11 12	Rome	5 10 91		Scholar
Pogba Paul (M)			Lagny-sur-Marne	15 3 93		Scholar
Rafael (D)	6 3	12 08	Petropolis	9 7 90		Fluminense
Rooney Wayne (F)	5 10	12 04	Liverpool	24 10 85		Everton
Smalling Chris (D)	6 4	14 02	Greenwich	22 11 89		Fulham
Thorpe Tom (D)			Manchester	13 1 93		Scholar
Tunnicliffe Ryan (M)	5 11	12 07	Bury	30 12 92		Scholar
Valencia Luis (M)	5 10	12 04	Lago Agrio	5 8 85		Wigan Ath
Van Velzen Gyliano (F)			Holland	14 4 94		Scholar
Vermijl Marnick (D)	5 11	11 12	Belgium	13 1 92		Standard Liege
Vidic Nemanja (D)	6 1	13 02	Uzice	21 10 81		Spartak Moscow
Welbeck Daniel (F)	6 1	11 07	Manchester	26 11 90		Scholar
Wootton Scott (D)			Birkenhead	12 9 91		Scholar

League Appearances: Anderson, 14(4); Bebe, (2); Berbatov, D. 24(8); Brown, W. 4(3); Carrick, M. 23(5); Evans, J. 11(2); Evra, P. 34(1); Fabio, 5(6); Ferdinand, R. 19; Fletcher, D. 24(2); Gibson, D. 6(6); Giggs, R. 19(6); Hargreaves, O. 1; Hernandez, J. 15(12); Kuszczak, T. 5; Macheda, F. 2(5); Nani, 31(2); Neville, G. 3; O'Shea, J. 18(2); Obertan, G. 3(4); Owen, M. 1(10); Park, J. 13(2); Rafael, 15(1); Rooney, W. 25(3); Scholes, P. 16(6); Smalling, C. 11(5); Valencia, L. 8(2); Van der Sar, E. 33; Vidic, N. 35.

Goals – League (78): Berbatov 20, Hernandez 13, Rooney 11 (3 pens), Nani 9, Park 5, Vidic 5, Fletcher 2, Giggs 2, Owen 2, Anderson 1, Evra 1, Fabio 1, Macheda 1, Scholes 1, Valencia 1, own goals 3.

Carling Cup (8): Owen 2, Park 2, Bebe 1, Gibson 1, Hernandez 1, Smalling 1.
FA Cup (6): Brown 1, Fabio 1, Giggs 1 (pen), Hernandez 1, Owen 1, Rooney 1.
Champions League (19): Hernandez 4, Rooney 4 (1 pen), Anderson 3, Fletcher 1, Gibson 1, Giggs 1, Nani 1, Obertan 1, Park 1, Valencia 1, own goal 1.
Community Shield (3): Berbatov 1, Hernandez 1, Valencia 1.
Ground: Old Trafford, Sir Matt Busby Way, Manchester M16 0RA. Telephone: (0161) 868 8000.
Record Attendance: 76,962 Wolverhampton W v Grimsby T, FA Cup semi-final, 25 March 1939.
Club Record Attendance: 76,098 v Blackburn R, FA Premier League, 31 March 2007.
Capacity: 75,769.
Manager: Sir Alex Ferguson CBE.
Secretary: John Alexander.
Most League Goals: 103, Division 1, 1956–57 and 1958–59.
Highest League Scorer in Season: Dennis Viollet, 32, 1959–60.
Most League Goals in Total Aggregate: Bobby Charlton, 199, 1956–73.
Most Capped Player: Bobby Charlton, 106, England.
Most League Appearances: Ryan Giggs, 613, 1991–.
Honours – FA Premier League: Champions – 1993–94, 1995–96, 1996–97, 1998–99, 1999–2000, 2000–01, 2002–03, 2006–07, 2007–08, 2008–09, 2010–11. **Football League:** Division 1 Champions – 1907–8, 1910–11, 1951–52, 1955–56, 1956–57, 1964–65, 1966–67. Division 2 Champions – 1935–36, 1974–75. **FA Cup:** Winners – 1909, 1948, 1963, 1977, 1983, 1985, 1990, 1994, 1996, 1999, 2004. **Football League Cup:** Winners – 1991–92, 2006, 2009, 2010. **European Competitions: European Cup:** Winners – 1967–68. **Champions League:** Winners – 1998–99, 2007–08. **European Cup-Winners' Cup:** Winners – 1990–91. **Super Cup:** Winners – 1991. **Inter-Continental Cup:** Winners – 1999. **FIFA Club World Cup:** Winners – 2008.
Colours: Red shirts with black chevron, white shorts with red side panels, black stockings.

MIDDLESBROUGH   FL CHAMPIONSHIP

Name			Birthplace				Previous club
Atkinson David (D)			Shildon	27	4	93	Scholar
Bailey Nicky (M)	5 10	12 06	Hammersmith	10	6	84	Charlton Ath
Bates Matthew (D)	5 10	12 03	Stockton	10	12	86	Scholar
Bennett Joe (D)	5 10	10 04	Rochdale	28	3	90	Scholar
Boyd Kris (F)	6 0	13 01	Irvine	18	8	83	Rangers
Coyne Danny (G)	6 0	13 00	Prestatyn	27	8	73	Tranmere R
Digard Didier (M)	6 0	11 13	Gisors	12	7	86	Paris St Germain
Dolan Matthew (M)			Hartlepool	11	2	93	Scholar
Emnes Marvin (M)	5 9	10 06	Rotterdam	27	5	88	Sparta Rotterdam
Franks Jonathan (M)	5 9	11 03	Stockton	8	4	90	Scholar
Gibson Ben (D)			Nunthorpe	15	1	93	Scholar
Grounds Jonathan (D)	6 1	13 10	Ingleby Barwick	2	2	88	Scholar
Halliday Andrew (M)	5 8	10 07	Glasgow	11	10	91	Livingston
Hines Sebastian (M)	6 2	12 04	Wetherby	29	5	88	Scholar
Hoyte Justin (D)	5 11	11 00	Waltham Forest	20	11	84	Arsenal
Kink Tarmo (F)	6 0	11 09	Tallinn	6	10	85	Gyor
Lita Leroy (F)	5 7	11 12	DR Congo	28	12	84	Reading
McDonald Scott (F)	5 7	12 07	Dandenorg	21	8	83	Celtic
McMahon Anthony (D)	5 10	11 04	Bishop Auckland	24	3	86	Scholar
McManus Stephen (D)	6 2	13 00	Lanark	10	9	82	Celtic
Miller Lee (F)	6 0	11 07	Lanark	18	5	83	Aberdeen
Park Cameron (M)			Middlesbrough	6	7	92	Scholar
Pilatos Bruno (D)			Angola	30	3	93	Scholar
Ripley Connor (G)			Middlesbrough	13	2	93	Scholar
Robson Barry (M)	5 11	12 00	Aberdeen	7	11	78	Celtic

Smallwood Richard (M)			Redcar	29 12 90	Scholar
Steele Jason (G)	6 2	12 13	Bishop Auckland	18 8 90	Scholar
Thomson Kevin (M)	6 2	11 05	Edinburgh	14 10 84	Rangers
Weldon Paul (D)			Sunderland	27 11 91	Scholar
Williams Luke (F)	6 1	11 06	Middlesbrough	11 6 93	Scholar
Williams Rhys (D)	6 2	11 05	Perth	14 7 88	Scholar
Zemmama Merouane (M)	5 8	10 05	Rabat	7 10 83	Hibernian

League Appearances: Arca, J. 27(5); Bailey, N. 28(6); Bates, M. 31; Bennett, J. 28(3); Boyd, K. 18(9); Coyne, D. 1; Davies, A. 5(1); Emnes, M. 18(5); Flood, W. 1(4); Franks, J. 1(3); Gibson, B. (1); Grounds, J. 5(1); Haas, M. 1(1); Halliday, A. 5(7); Hines, S. 14; Hoyte, J. 14(3); Kilgallon, M. 2; Kink, T. 8(13); Lita, L. 28(10); McDonald, S. 34(4); McMahon, T. 28(6); McManus, S. 22(2); Miller, L. (1); O'Neil, G. 17(1); Park, C. (4); Reach, A. (1); Ripley, C. (1); Robson, B. 29(3); Smallwood, R. 7(6); Smith, P. 10; Steele, J. 35; Tavares, M. 10(3); Taylor, A. 20(1); Thomson, K. 18(1); Wheater, D. 24; Williams, R. 10(2); Williams, L. 5(1); Zemmama, M. 2(7).

Goals – League (68): Lita 12 (2 pens), McDonald 12, Boyd 6, Robson 5 (1 pen), Kink 4, Arca 3 (1 pen), Bates 3, Emnes 3, Taylor 3, Wheater 3, McMahon 2, Grounds 1, Halliday 1, Hines 1, McManus 1, Reach 1, Smallwood 1, Williams R 1, Zemmama 1, own goals 4.

Carling Cup (3): McDonald 2, Arca 1.

FA Cup (1): O'Neil 1.

Ground: Riverside Stadium, Middlesbrough TS3 6RS. Telephone: (0844) 499 6789.

Record Attendance: 53,536 v Newcastle U, Division 1, 27 December 1949 (at Ayresome Park). 34,814 v Newcastle U, FA Premier League, 5 March 2003 (at Riverside Stadium).

Capacity: 35,100.

Manager: Tony Mowbray.

Secretary: Karen Nelson.

Most League Goals: 122, Division 2, 1926–27.

Highest League Scorer in Season: George Camsell, 59, Division 2, 1926–27 (Second Division record).

Most League Goals in Total Aggregate: George Camsell, 325, 1925–39.

Most Capped Player: Wilf Mannion, 26, England.

Most League Appearances: Tim Williamson, 563, 1902–23.

Honours – Football League: Division 1 Champions 1994–95. Division 2 Champions 1926–27, 1928–29, 1973–74. **Football League Cup:** Winners – 2004, 2009. **Amateur Cup:** Winners – 1895, 1898. **Anglo-Scottish Cup:** Winners – 1975–76.

Colours: Red shirts with white design and one white sleeve, white shorts with red trim, white stockings.

MILLWALL   FL CHAMPIONSHIP

Abdou Nadjim (M)	5 10	11 02	Martigues	13 7 84	Plymouth Arg
Barron Scott (D)	5 9	9 08	Preston	2 9 85	Ipswich T
Batt Shaun (M)	6 3	12 08	Harlow	22 2 87	Peterborough U
Bouazza Hamer (F)	5 10	12 01	Evry	22 2 85	Blackpool
Craig Tony (D)	6 0	10 03	Greenwich	20 4 85	Crystal Palace
Dunne Alan (D)	5 10	10 13	Dublin	23 8 82	Trainee
Forde David (G)	6 3	13 06	Galway	20 12 79	Cardiff C
Hackett Chris (M)	6 0	11 06	Oxford	1 3 83	Hearts
Harris Neil (F)	5 11	12 09	Orsett	12 7 77	Nottingham F
Henry James (M)	6 1	11 11	Reading	10 6 89	Reading
Marquis John (F)	6 1	11 03	Millwall	16 5 92	Scholar
McQuoid Joshua (F)	5 9	10 10	Southampton	15 12 89	Bournemouth
Mildenhall Steve (G)	6 4	14 01	Swindon	13 5 78	Southend U
Mkandawire Tamika (D)	6 1	12 03	Malawi	28 5 83	Leyton Orient

Morison Steve (F)	6 2	13 07	Enfield	29	8	83	Stevenage B
O'Brien Aiden (F)			Republic of Ireland	4	10	93	Scholar
Purse Darren (D)	6 2	12 08	Stepney	14	2	77	Sheffield W
Robinson Paul (D)	6 1	11 09	Barnet	7	1	82	Scholar
Robinson Theo (F)	5 9	10 03	Birmingham	22	1	89	Huddersfield T
Smith Jack (D)	5 11	11 05	Hemel Hempstead	14	10	83	Swindon T
Trotter Liam (M)	6 2	12 02	Ipswich	24	8	88	Ipswich T
Ward Darren (D)	6 3	14 03	Kenton	13	9	78	Wolverhampton W

League Appearances: Abdou, N. 30(4); Andrew, C. 3; Barron, S. 35(3); Berthel Askou, J. 1; Bouazza, H. 3(9); Carter, D. 5(5); Craig, T. 21(3); Dunne, A. 38(1); Eastmond, C. 4(2); Forde, D. 46; Grabban, L. 1; Hackett, C. 7(9); Harris, N. 7(19); Henry, J. 39(3); Hughes-Mason, K. (1); Laird, M. (1); Lisbie, K. 10(10); Marquis, J. 5(6); McQuoid, J. 7(4); Mkandawire, T. 34(1); Morison, S. 40; Puncheon, J. 7; Purse, D. 9(4); Robinson, P. 35(2); Robinson, T. 8(3); Rowlands, M. (1); Schofield, D. 20(11); Shittu, D. 9; Smith, J. 9; Townsend, A. 11; Trotter, L. 34(1); Ward, D. 28(3).

Goals – League (62): Morison 15 (1 pen), Trotter 7 (2 pens), Henry 5 (1 pen), Puncheon 5, Lisbie 4, Marquis 4, Robinson P 3, Robinson T 3, Barron 2, Harris 2, Schofield 2, Townsend 2, Bouazza 1, McQuoid 1, Mkandawire 1, Purse 1, Smith 1 (1 pen), Ward 1, own goals 2.

Carling Cup (5): Morison 2 (1 pen), Dunne 1, Harris 1, Trotter 1.

FA Cup (1): Schofield 1.

Ground: The Den, Zampa Road, London SE16 3LN. Telephone: (020) 7232 1222.

Record Attendance: 48,672 v Derby Co, FA Cup 5th rd, 20 February 1937 (at The Den, Cold Blow Lane). 20,093 v Arsenal, FA Cup 3rd rd, 10 January 1994 (at The Den, Bermondsey).

Capacity: 19,734.

Manager: Kenny Jackett.

Secretary: Yvonne Haines.

Most League Goals: 127, Division 3 (S), 1927–28.

Highest League Scorer in Season: Richard Parker, 37, Division 3 (S), 1926–27.

Most League Goals in Total Aggregate: Neil Harris, 124, 1995–2004; 2006–11.

Most Capped Player: Eamonn Dunphy, 22 (23), Republic of Ireland.

Most League Appearances: Barry Kitchener, 523, 1967–82.

Honours – Football League: Division 2 Champions – 1987–88, 2000–01. Division 3 (S) Champions – 1927–28, 1937–38. Division 4 Champions – 1961–62. **Football League Trophy:** Winners – 1982–83.

Colours: All blue with white detail on shirts.

MILTON KEYNES DONS   FL CHAMPIONSHIP 1

Baldock George (M)	5 9	10 07	Buckingham	26	1	93	Youth
Baldock Sam (F)	5 7	10 07	Buckingham	15	3	89	Scholar
Chadwick Luke (M)	5 11	11 08	Cambridge	18	11	80	Norwich C
Chicksen Adam (D)	5 8	11 09	Coventry	27	9	91	Scholar
Collins Charlie (F)	6 0	11 11	Hammersmith	22	11	91	Scholar
Doumbe Stephen (D)	6 1	12 05	Paris	28	10	79	Plymouth Arg
Flanagan Tom (D)	6 2	11 05	Hammersmith	21	10	91	Scholar
Gleeson Stephen (M)	6 2	11 00	Dublin	3	8	88	Wolverhampton W
Guy Lewis (F)	5 10	10 07	Penrith	27	8	85	Doncaster R
Ibehre Jabo (F)	6 2	13 13	Islington	28	1	83	Walsall
Leven Peter (M)	5 11	12 13	Glasgow	27	9	83	Chesterfield
Lewington Dean (D)	5 11	11 07	Kingston	18	5	84	Scholar
MacKenzie Gary (D)	6 3	13 01	Lanark	15	10	85	Dundee
Martin David (G)	6 1	13 04	Romford	22	1	86	Liverpool
Powell Daniel (F)	5 11	13 03	Luton	12	3	91	Scholar

League Appearances: Amoo, D. (3); Balanta, A. 12(6); Baldock, S. 20(10); Baldock, G. 1(1); Carrington, M. 7(5); Chadwick, L. 39(5); Chicksen, A. 5(9); Clayton, A. 1(5); Collins, C. (1); Doumbe, S. 42(2); Easter, J. 11(3); Flanagan, T. 2; Gleeson, S. 35(1); Guy, L. 20(14); Hamann, D. 12; Howell, L. (1); Hughes, S. 2(4); Ibehre, J. 19(23); Johnson, J. 2(5); Leven, P. 40; Lewington, D. 42; MacKenzie, G. 24(2); Marsh-Brown, K. 12(5); Martin, D. 43; McIndoe, M. 8; O'Hanlon, S. 28(4); Powell, Daniel 23(6); Searle, S. 3; Stirling, J. (4); Vine, R. 12(5); Wilbraham, A. 5(5); Woodards, D. 36(1).

Goals – League (67): Baldock S 12 (1 pen), Powell, Daniel 9, Leven 8 (5 pens), Balanta 6, Doumbe 5, O'Hanlon 4, Ibehre 3, Lewington 3, Carrington 2, Gleeson 2, Guy 2, MacKenzie 2, Marsh-Brown 2, Wilbraham 2, Clayton 1, Johnson 1, Vine 1, Woodards 1, own goal 1.

Carling Cup (7): Easter 2, Ibehre 2, Baldock S 1, Guy 1, Wilbraham 1.

FA Cup (1): Guy 1.

J Paint Trophy (1): Chadwick 1.

Play-Offs (3): Balanta 1, Baldock S. 1, Powell.

Ground: Stadiummk, Stadium Way West, Milton Keynes MK1 1ST. Telephone: (01908) 622 922.

Record Attendance: 8,306 v Tottenham H, League Cup 3rd rd, 25 October 2006 (at National Hockey Stadium). 20,222 for England U21 v Bulgaria U21, 16 November 2007 and 17,717 v Leicester C, FL 1, 28 February 2009 (both at Stadiummk).

Capacity: 21,189.

Manager: Karl Robinson.

Head of Football Operations: Kirstine Nicholson.

Most League Goals: 83, FL 1, 2008–09.

Highest League Scorer in Season: Izale McLeod, 21, 2006–07.

Most League Goals in Total Aggregate: Izale McLeod, 54, 2004–07.

Most Capped Player: Ali Gerba (29), Canada.

Most League Appearances: Dean Lewington, 301, 2004–.

Honours – Football League: Championship 2 Champions – 2007–08. Division 4 Champions – 1982–83. **FA Cup:** Winners – 1987–88. **Johnstone's Paint Trophy:** Winners – 2007–08.

Colours: White shirts with black sleeves, white shorts, white stockings with black tops.

MORECAMBE   FL CHAMPIONSHIP 2

Bentley Jim (D)	6 1	12 00	Liverpool	11 6 76	Telford U
Charnock Kieran (D)	6 1	13 07	Preston	3 8 84	Torquay U
Cowperthwaite Niall (D)	5 11	11 00	Barrow	28 1 92	Youth
Drummond Stuart (M)	6 2	13 08	Preston	11 12 75	Shrewsbury T
Fleming Andy (M)	6 1	12 00	Liverpool	1 4 87	Wrexham
Haining Will (D)	6 0	11 02	Glasgow	2 10 82	St Mirren
Hunter Garry (M)	5 7	10 03	Morecambe	1 1 85	Scholar
Jevons Phil (F)	5 11	12 00	Liverpool	1 8 79	Huddersfield T
McCready Chris (D)	6 1	12 05	Ellesmere Port	5 9 81	Northampton T
Parrish Andy (D)	6 0	11 00	Bolton	22 6 88	Bury
Roche Barry (G)	6 5	14 08	Dublin	6 4 82	Chesterfield
Rundle Adam (F)	5 8	11 02	Durham	8 7 84	Chesterfield
Scott Paul (D)	5 11	12 00	Wakefield	5 11 79	Bury
Stanley Craig (M)	6 0	12 06	Coventry	3 3 83	Hereford U
Wilson Laurence (M)	5 10	10 09	Huyton	10 10 86	Chester C

League Appearances: Aley, Z. 1(1); Anyon, J. 4; Bentley, J. 7(1); Brown, S. 19(13); Capaldi, T. 17(1); Carlton, D. 11(5); Charnock, K. 20(1); Cowperthwaite, N. 6(1); Drummond, S. 39(2); Duffy, M. 16(6); Fleming, A. 23(7); Haining, W. 12; Hendrie, S. 1(6); Holdsworth, A. 12(3); Hunter, G. 27(6); Hurst, K. 21; Jevons, P. 27(11); McCready, C. 35(1); McLachlan, F. 1; Moss, D. 4; Mullin, P. 15(11); Parrish, A. 41; Roche, B. 42; Rundle,

A. 8(9); Scott, P. 6(2); Shuker, C. 12(15); Spencer, J. 20(12); Stanley, C. 21(1); Wainwright, N. 1(4); Wilson, L. 37(1).

Goals – League (54): Jevons 8 (3 pens), Spencer 8, Drummond 6, McCready 4, Mullin 4, Brown 3, Carlton 3, Wilson 3 (3 pens), Fleming 2, Hurst 2, Shuker 2, Stanley 2, Bentley 1, Charnock 1, Cowperthwaite 1, Haining 1, Holdsworth 1, Hunter 1, own goal 1.

Carling Cup (3): Fleming 2, Jevons 1.

FA Cup (0).

J Paint Trophy (0).

Ground: Globe Arena, Christie Way, Westgate, Morecambe LA4 4TB. Telephone: (01524) 598 393.

Record Attendance: 9,383 v Weymouth, FA Cup 3rd rd, 6 January 1962 (at Christie Park). 5,003 v Burnley, Lge Cup 2nd rd, 24 August 2010 (at Globe Arena).

Capacity: 6,402.

Player-Manager: Jim Bentley.

Secretary: Neil Marsdin.

Most League Goals: 73, FL 2, 2009–10.

Highest League Scorer in Season: Phil Jevons, 18, 2009–10.

Most League Goals in Total Aggregate: Stuart Drummond, 27, 2007–.

Most League Appearances: Jim Bentley, 146, 2007–.

Honours – Conference: Promoted to Football League (play-offs) 2006–07. **Presidents Cup:** Winners – 1991–92. **FA Trophy:** Winners 1973–74. **Lancs Senior Cup:** Winners 1967–68. **Lancs Combination:** Champions – 1924–25, 1961–62, 1962–63, 1967–68. **Lancs Combination Cup:** Winners – 1926–27, 1945–46, 1964–65, 1966–67, 1967–68. **Lancs Junior Cup:** Winners – 1927, 1928, 1962, 1963, 1969, 1986, 1987, 1994, 1996, 1999, 2004.

Colours: Red shirts with black trim, white shorts, red stockings.

NEWCASTLE UNITED

FA PREMIERSHIP

Player	Ht	Wt	Birthplace		DOB	Previous club
Adjei Samuel (F)	6 1	12 00	Ghana	18	1 92	Jonkoping
Airey Philip (F)	5 11	10 05	Newcastle	14	11 91	Scholar
Alnwick Jak (G)			Hexham	17	6 93	Scholar
Ameobi Foluwashola (F)	6 3	11 13	Zaria	12	10 81	Scholar
Ameobi Sam (F)	6 3	10 04	Newcastle	1	5 92	Scholar
Barton Joey (M)	5 11	12 05	Huyton	2	9 82	Manchester C
Ben Arfa Hatem (M)	5 8	10 08	Clamart	7	3 87	Marseille
Best Leon (F)	6 1	13 03	Nottingham	19	9 86	Coventry C
Coloccini Fabricio (D)	6 0	12 04	Cordoba	22	1 82	La Coruna
Donaldson Ryan (F)	5 9	11 00	Newcastle	1	5 91	Scholar
Dummett Paul (D)	5 10	10 02	Newcastle	26	9 91	Scholar
Edmundsson Joan (F)			Faeroes	26	7 91	B68
Ferguson Shane (D)	5 9	10 01	Derry	12	7 91	Scholar
Folan Stephen (M)	6 1	12 01	Galway	14	1 92	Scholar
Forster Fraser (G)	6 4	14 00	Newcastle	17	3 88	Scholar
Gosling Dan (M)	6 0	11 00	Brixham	2	2 90	Everton
Guthrie Danny (M)	5 9	11 06	Shrewsbury	18	4 87	Liverpool
Gutierrez Jonas (M)	6 0	11 07	Saenz Pena	5	7 82	Mallorca
Harper Steve (G)	6 2	13 10	Easington	14	3 75	Seaham Red Star
Henderson Jeff (D)	6 1	12 01	Ashington	9	12 91	Scholar
Inman Bradden (M)	5 9	11 03	Adelaide	10	12 91	Scholar
Jose Enrique (D)	6 0	12 00	Valencia	23	1 86	Villarreal
Kadar Tamas (D)	6 0	12 10	Veszprem	14	3 90	Zalaegerszegi
Krul Tim (G)	6 2	11 08	Den Haag	3	4 88	Den Haag
Lovenkrands Peter (F)	5 11	11 02	Copenhagen	29	1 80	Schalke
LuaLua Kazenga (F)	5 11	12 00	Kinshasa	10	12 90	Scholar
McDermott Greg (M)	5 10	10 00	Liverpool	18	10 91	Scholar
Moyo Yven (M)			France	15	3 92	Sochaux
Newton Conor (M)	5 11	11 00	Newcastle	17	10 91	Scholar

Nolan Kevin (M)	6 0	14 00	Liverpool	24	6 82	Bolton W
Perch James (D)	5 11	11 05	Mansfield	29	9 85	Nottingham F
Ranger Nile (F)	6 2	13 03	London	11	4 91	Southampton
Richardson Michael (M)			Newcastle	17	3 92	Scholar
Routledge Wayne (M)	5 6	11 02	Sidcup	7	1 85	QPR
Simpson Danny (D)	5 8	11 10	Salford	4	1 87	Manchester U
Smith Alan (F)	5 10	12 04	Rothwell	28	10 80	Manchester U
Soderberg Ole (G)	6 0	14 03	Norrkoping	20	7 90	BK Hacken
Spear Aaron (F)			Plymouth	29	4 93	Scholar
Tavernier James (D)	5 9	11 00	Bradford	31	10 91	Scholar
Taylor Ryan (M)	,5 8	10 04	Liverpool	19	8 84	Wigan Ath
Taylor Steven (D)	6 1	13 01	Greenwich	23	1 86	Scholar
Tiote Cheik (M)	5 11	12 06	Yamoussoukro	21	6 86	Twente
Tozer Ben (D)	6 1	13 05	Plymouth	1	3 90	Swindon T
Vuckic Haris (F)	6 2	12 02	Ljubljana	21	8 92	Domzale
Williamson Mike (D)	6 4	13 03	Stoke	8	11 83	Portsmouth
Xisco (F)	6 0	13 03	Palma	26	6 86	La Coruna
Zamblera Fabio (F)	6 3	14 09	Atalanta	7	4 90	Atalanta

League Appearances: Ameobi, Shola 21(7); Ameobi, Sam (1); Barton, J. 32; Ben Arfa, H. 3(1); Best, L. 9(2); Campbell, S. 4(3); Carroll, A. 18(1); Coloccini, F. 35; Ferguson, S. 3(4); Gosling, D. (1); Guthrie, D. 11(3); Gutierrez, J. 34(3); Harper, S. 18; Ireland, S. (2); Jose Enrique, 36; Krul, T. 20(1); Kuqi, S. (6); Lovenkrands, P. 18(7); LuaLua, K. (2); Nolan, K. 30; Perch, J. 9(4); Ranger, N. 1(23); Routledge, W. 10(7); Simpson, D. 30; Smith, A. 7(4); Taylor, R. 3(2); Taylor, S. 12(2); Tiote, C. 26; Williamson, M. 28(1); Xisco, (2).

Goals – League (56): Nolan 12 (1 pen), Carroll 11, Ameobi, Shola 6 (2 pens), Best 6, Lovenkrands 6, Barton 4 (2 pens), Gutierrez 3, Taylor S 3, Coloccini 2, Ben Arfa 1, Tiote 1, own goal 1.

Carling Cup (7): Ameobi 3, Taylor R 2, Lovenkrands 1, Ranger 1.

FA Cup (1): Barton 1.

Ground: St James' Park, Newcastle-upon-Tyne NE1 4ST. Telephone: (0191) 201 8400.

Record Attendance: 68,386 v Chelsea, Division 1, 3 September 1930.

Capacity: 52,387.

Manager: Alan Pardew.

Most League Goals: 98, Division 1, 1951–52.

Highest League Scorer in Season: Hughie Gallacher, 36, Division 1, 1926–27.

Most League Goals in Total Aggregate: Jackie Milburn, 177, 1946–57.

Most Capped Player: Shay Given, 82 (113), Republic of Ireland.

Most League Appearances: Jim Lawrence, 432, 1904–22.

Honours – Football League: Division 1 – Champions 1904–05, 1906–07, 1908–09, 1926–27, 1992–93. Division 2 Champions – 1964–65. FL C – Champions 2009–10. **FA Cup:** Winners – 1910, 1924, 1932, 1951, 1952, 1955. **Texaco Cup:** Winners – 1973–74, 1974–75. **European Competitions: European Fairs Cup:** Winners – 1968–69. **Anglo-Italian Cup:** Winners – 1973. **Intertoto Cup:** Winners – 2006.

Colours: Black and white striped shirts, black shorts with white trim, black stockings with white trim.

NORTHAMPTON TOWN FL CHAMPIONSHIP 2

Built Michael (D)	5 10	11 00	Hamilton	12	11 92	Youth
Dunn Chris (G)	6 5	13 11	Hammersmith	23	10 87	Scholar
Gilligan Ryan (M)	5 10	11 07	Swindon	18	1 87	Watford
Harrad Shaun (F)	5 10	12 04	Nottingham	11	12 84	Burton Alb
Holt Andy (M)	6 1	12 07	Stockport	21	5 78	Wrexham
Jacobs Michael (M)	5 9	11 08	Northampton	23	3 92	Scholar

Johnson John (D)	6 0	12 00	Middlesbrough	16	9 88	Middlesbrough
McKay Billy (F)	5 9	10 01	Corby	22	10 88	Leicester C
Purcell Tadhg (F)	5 11	11 08	Dundrum	9	2 85	Darlington
Walker Paul (G)	5 10	10 10	Wales	18	4 92	Scholar
Wedderburn Nathaniel (M)	6 1	13 05	Wolverhampton	30	6 91	Stoke C

League Appearances: Bauza, G. 9(1); Beckwith, D. 35(2); Collis, S. 3(1); Davis, L. 32(1); Dunn, C. 39; Gilligan, R. 20(2); Guinan, S. 5(6); Hall, M. 21(3); Harrad, S. 18; Harris, S. 1(3); Herbert, C. 1(14); Holt, A. 32(7); Jacobs, M. 33(8); Jansson, O. 4; Jarvis, R. 3; Johnson, J. 38; Kaziboni, G. (2); King, C. 3(4); Laurent, F. 3(3); McKay, B. 24(10); McKenzie, L. 17(10); Ofori-Twumasi, N. 11; Osman, A. 37(1); Parker, J. 3; Purcell, T. 1(3); Reckord, J. 4(3); Rodgers, P. 15(10); Thornton, K. 16(9); Tozer, B. 28(3); Uwezu, M. 2(2); Walker, J. 19; Walker, P. (1); Webster, B. 8; Wedderburn, N. 21(10).

Goals – League (63): McKenzie 10 (2 pens), Johnson 7, Harrad 6 (3 pens), Holt 6, Thornton 6 (1 pen), Jacobs 5, McKay 5, Bauza 4, Beckwith 3, Osman 3, Tozer 3, Davis 2, Gilligan 1, Guinan 1 (1 pen), Uwezu 1.

Carling Cup (8): Jacobs 2, McKay 2, Davis 1, Holt 1, Thornton 1, own goal 1.

FA Cup (5): Guinan 1, Jacobs 1, Johnson 1, McKay 1, Thornton 1.

J Paint Trophy (0).

Ground: Sixfields Stadium, Upton Way, Northampton NN5 5QA. Telephone: (01604) 683 700.

Capacity: 7,300.

Record Attendance: 24,523 v Fulham, Division 1, 23 April 1966 (at County Ground). 7,557 v Manchester C, Division 2, 26 September 1998 (at Sixfields Stadium).

Manager: Gary Johnson.

Secretary: Norman Howells.

Most League Goals: 109, Division 3, 1962–63 and Division 3 (S), 1952–53.

Highest League Scorer in Season: Cliff Holton, 36, Division 3, 1961–62.

Most League Goals in Total Aggregate: Jack English, 135, 1947–60.

Most Capped Player: Edwin Lloyd Davies, 12 (16), Wales.

Most League Appearances: Tommy Fowler, 521, 1946–61.

Honours – Football League: Division 3 Champions – 1962–63. Division 4 Champions – 1986–87.

Colours: Claret shirts, white shorts, white stockings.

NORWICH CITY   FA PREMIERSHIP

Adeyemi Thomas (M)	6 1	12 04	Norwich	24	10 91	Scholar
Barnett Leon (D)	6 0	12 04	Stevenage	30	11 85	WBA
Crofts Andrew (D)	5 10	12 09	Chatham	29	5 84	Brighton & HA
Daley Luke (F)	6 3	12 00	Northampton	10	11 89	Scholar
Dawkin Josh (M)	5 9	10 12	Huntingdon	16	1 92	Scholar
Drury Adam (D)	5 10	11 08	Cottenham	29	8 78	Peterborough U
Fox David (M)	5 9	11 08	Leek	13	12 83	Colchester U
Francomb George (D)	5 11	11 07	London	8	9 91	Scholar
Holt Grant (F)	6 1	14 02	Carlisle	12	4 81	Shrewsbury T
Hoolahan Wes (M)	5 6	10 03	Dublin	10	8 83	Blackpool
Hughes Stephen (M)	5 10	11 04	Motherwell	14	11 82	Motherwell
Jackson Simeon (F)	5 10	10 12	Kingston (Jam)	28	3 87	Gillingham
Johnson Oli (F)	5 11	12 04	Wakefield	6	11 87	Stockport Co
Lappin Simon (M)	5 11	9 06	Glasgow	25	1 83	St Mirren
Martin Chris (F)	6 2	12 06	Norwich	4	11 88	Scholar
Martin Russell (D)	6 0	11 06	Brighton	4	1 86	Peterborough U
McDonald Cody (F)	5 10	11 03	Norwich	30	5 86	Dartford
McNamee Anthony (M)	5 6	10 00	Kensington	13	7 84	Swindon T
Rudd Declan (G)	6 3	12 06	Norwich	16	1 91	Scholar
Ruddy John (G)	6 3	12 07	St Ives	24	10 86	Everton

Smith Korey (M)	5 9	11 01	Welwyn	31	1 91	Scholar
Smith Steven (D)	5 8	10 08	Bellshill	30	4 85	Rangers
Steer Jed (G)	6 2	14 00	Norwich	23	9 92	Scholar
Surman Andrew (M)	5 10	11 06	Johannesburg	20	8 86	Wolverhampton W
Tierney Marc (D)	5 11	11 04	Manchester	7	9 85	Colchester U
Tudur Jones Owain (M)	6 2	12 00	Bangor	15	10 84	Swansea C
Ward Elliott (D)	6 2	13 00	Harrow	19	1 85	Coventry C
Whitbread Zak (D)	6 2	12 07	Houston	4	3 84	Millwall
Wilbraham Aaron (F)	6 3	12 04	Knutsford	21	10 79	Milton Keynes D

League Appearances: Barnett, L. 25; Berthel Askou, J. 2(3); Crofts, A. 44; Daley, L. (1); Drury, A. 19(1); Edwards, R. (3); Fox, D. 30(2); Gill, M. (4); Holt, G. 44(1); Hoolahan, W. 36(5); Hughes, S. (1); Jackson, S. 20(18); Johnson, O. (4); Lansbury, H. 15(8); Lappin, S. 20(7); Martin, C. 21(9); Martin, R. 46; McNamee, A. 5(12); Nelson, M. 7(1); Pacheco, D. 3(3); Rudd, D. 1; Ruddy, J. 45; Smith, K. 19(9); Smith, S. 5(2); Surman, A. 19(3); Tierney, M. 14(2); Tudur Jones, O. 1(1); Vokes, S. 1(3); Ward, E. 39; Whitbread, Z. 20(2); Wilbraham, A. 5(7).

Goals – League (83): Holt 21 (3 pens), Jackson 13, Hoolahan 10 (4 pens), Crofts 8, Martin R 5, Lansbury 4, Martin C 4, Surman 3, Nelson 2, Pacheco 2, Barnett 1, Drury 1, Fox 1, Vokes 1, Ward 1, Whitbread 1, Wilbraham 1, own goals 4.

Carling Cup (5): Holt 2, Martin C 2, Berthel Askou 1.

FA Cup (0).

Ground: Carrow Road, Norwich NR1 1JE. Telephone: (01603) 760 760.

Record Attendance: 25,037 v Sheffield W, FA Cup 5th rd, 16 February 1935 (at The Nest). 43,984 v Leicester C, FA Cup 6th rd, 30 March 1963 (at Carrow Road).

Capacity: 26,034.

Manager: Paul Lambert.

Secretary: Kevan Platt.

Most League Goals: 99, Division 3 (S), 1952–53.

Highest League Scorer in Season: Ralph Hunt, 31, Division 3 (S), 1955–56.

Most League Goals in Total Aggregate: Johnny Gavin, 122, 1945–54, 1955–58.

Most Capped Player: Mark Bowen, 35 (41), Wales.

Most League Appearances: Ron Ashman, 592, 1947–64.

Honours – Football League: Division 1 Champions – 2003–04, 2009–10. Division 2 Champions – 1971–72, 1985–86. Division 3 (S) Champions – 1933–34. **Football League Cup:** Winners – 1962, 1985.

Colours: Yellow shirts with green trim, green shorts, yellow stockings.

NOTTINGHAM FOREST   FL CHAMPIONSHIP

Anderson Paul (M)	5 9	10 04	Leicester	23	7 88	Liverpool
Bamford Patrick (M)			Newark	5	9 93	Academy
Blackstock Dexter (F)	6 2	13 00	Oxford	20	5 86	QPR
Byrne Neill (D)			Port Marnock	2	2 93	Scholar
Camp Lee (G)	5 11	11 11	Derby	22	8 84	QPR
Chambers Luke (D)	6 1	11 13	Kettering	28	9 85	Northampton T
Cohen Chris (M)	5 11	10 11	Norwich	5	3 87	Yeovil T
Darlow Karl (G)	6 1	12 05	Northampton	8	10 90	Scholar
Earnshaw Robert (F)	5 8	10 10	Mulfulira	6	4 81	Derby Co
Findley Robbie (F)	5 9	11 11	Phoenix	4	8 85	Real Salt Lake
Freeman Kieron (D)			Bestwood	21	3 92	Scholar
Garner Joe (F)	5 10	11 02	Blackburn	12	4 88	Carlisle U
Gunter Chris (D)	5 11	11 02	Newport	21	7 89	Tottenham H
Lascelles Jamaal (D)	6 2	13 01	Derby	11	11 93	Scholar
Lynch Joel (D)	6 1	12 10	Eastbourne	3	10 87	Brighton & HA
Majewski Radoslaw (M)	5 7	10 06	Pruszkow	15	12 86	Polonia Warsaw

McCleary Garath (F)	5 10	12 06	Oxford	15	5 87	Bromley
McGoldrick David (F)	6 1	11 10	Nottingham	29	11 87	Southampton
McGugan Lewis (M)	5 9	11 06	Long Eaton	25	10 88	Scholar
McKenna Paul (M)	5 7	11 12	Eccleston	20	10 77	Preston NE
Moloney Brendan (M)	6 1	11 02	Enfield	18	1 89	Scholar
Morgan Wes (D)	6 2	14 00	Nottingham	21	1 84	Scholar
Moussi Guy (M)	6 1	12 11	Bondy	23	1 85	Angers
Smith Paul (G)	6 3	14 00	Epsom	17	12 79	Southampton
Tudgay Marcus (F)	5 10	12 04	Worthing	3	2 83	Sheffield W
Tyson Nathan (F)	5 10	10 02	Reading	4	5 82	Wycombe W
Watson Karlton (D)			Peterborough	30	4 92	Scholar
Wilson Kelvin (D)	6 2	12 12	Nottingham	3	9 85	Preston NE

League Appearances: Adebola, D. 4(25); Anderson, P. 27(9); Bennett, J. (3); Bertrand, R. 19; Blackstock, D. 13(4); Boyd, K. 7(3); Camp, L. 46; Chambers, L. 43(1); Cohen, C. 41(1); Darlow, K. (1); Earnshaw, R. 26(8); Findley, R. (2); Gunter, C. 40(3); Konchesky, P. 14(1); Lynch, J. 8(4); Majewski, R. 21(5); McCleary, G. 7(11); McGoldrick, D. 10(11); McGugan, L. 34(6); McKenna, P. 30(2); Moloney, B. 5(1); Morgan, W. 46; Moussi, G. 25(6); Ramsey, A. 2(3); Rodney, N. (3); Tudgay, M. 19(3); Tyson, N. 11(19); Wilson, K. 8(2).

Goals – League (69): McGugan 13 (3 pens), Earnshaw 8, Tudgay 7, Boyd 6 (2 pens), Chambers 6, Blackstock 5 (1 pen), McGoldrick 5, Anderson 3, Adebola 2, Cohen 2, Majewski 2, McCleary 2, McKenna 2, Tyson 2, Konchesky 1, Morgan 1, own goals 2.

Carling Cup (1): Thornhill 1.

FA Cup (4): Adebola 1, Anderson 1, Chambers 1, McGoldrick 1.

Play-Offs (1): Earnshaw 1.

Ground: The City Ground, Nottingham NG2 5FJ. Telephone: (0115) 982 4444.

Record Attendance: 49,946 v Manchester U, Division 1, 28 October 1967.

Capacity: 30,576.

Manager: Steve McClaren.

Most League Goals: 110, Division 3 (S), 1950–51.

Highest League Scorer in Season: Wally Ardron, 36, Division 3 (S), 1950–51.

Most League Goals in Total Aggregate: Grenville Morris, 199, 1898–1913.

Most Capped Player: Stuart Pearce, 76 (78), England.

Most League Appearances: Bob McKinlay, 614, 1951–70.

Honours – Football League: Division 1 – Champions 1977–78, 1997–98. Division 2 Champions – 1906–07, 1921–22. Division 3 (S) Champions – 1950–51. **FA Cup:** Winners – 1898, 1959. **Football League Cup:** Winners – 1977–78, 1978–79, 1988–89, 1989–90. **Anglo-Scottish Cup:** Winners – 1976–77. **Simod Cup:** Winners – 1989. **Zenith Data Systems Cup:** Winners – 1991–92. **European Competitions: European Cup:** Winners – 1978–79, 1979–80. **Super Cup:** Winners – 1979.

Colours: Red shirt with white trim, white shorts, red stockings.

NOTTS COUNTY   FL CHAMPIONSHIP 1

Bishop Neil (M)	6 1	12 10	Stockton	7	8 81	Barnet
Brandy Febien (F)	5 5	10 00	Manchester	4	2 89	Manchester U
Burch Rob (G)	6 2	12 13	Yeovil	8	10 83	Lincoln C
Burgess Ben (F)	6 3	14 04	Buxton	9	11 81	Blackpool
Chilvers Liam (D)	6 2	12 03	Chelmsford	6	11 81	Preston NE
Edwards Mike (D)	6 1	13 01	North Ferriby	25	4 80	Grimsby T
Harley Jon (D)	5 8	10 03	Maidstone	26	9 79	Watford
Hawley Karl (F)	5 8	12 02	Walsall	6	12 81	Preston NE
Hughes Lee (F)	5 10	12 00	Smethwick	22	5 76	Oldham Ath
Hunt Steve (D)	6 1	13 05	Southampton	11	11 84	Colchester U

Judge Alan (F)	5 6	11 03	Dublin	11 11 88	Blackburn R
Nelson Stuart (G)	6 1	12 12	Stroud	17 9 81	Norwich C
Pearce Krystian (D)	6 1	13 05	Birmingham	5 1 90	Huddersfield T
Ravenhill Ricky (M)	5 10	11 02	Doncaster	16 1 81	Darlington
Sodje Sam (D)	6 0	12 00	Greenwich	29 5 79	Charlton Ath
Spicer John (M)	5 11	11 07	Romford	13 9 83	Doncaster R
Westcarr Craig (F)	5 11	11 04	Nottingham	29 1 85	Kettering T

League Appearances: Bishop, N. 42(1); Brandy, F. 5(4); Burch, R. 14(1); Burgess, B. 8(9); Chilvers, L. 17(4); Clifford, C. 5(4); Darby, S. 23; Davies, B. 22; Demba-Nyren, N. 5(7); Edwards, M. 36(1); Gobern, L. (5); Gow, A. 12(4); Harley, J. 39; Hawley, K. 12(12); Hughes, L. 24(7); Hunt, S. 3(1); Ince, T. 3(3); Jervis, J. 1(9); Judge, A. 17(2); Lee, G. 14(4); Martin, D. 7(3); McDonald, K. 10(1); Miller, L. 5(1); Nelson, S. 32(1); Nicholas, G. (1); Pearce, K. 26(1); Ravenhill, R. 31(3); Regan, C. 4; Rodgers, L. (4); Smith, K. 6(7); Sodje, S. 5(6); Spicer, J. 15(8); Sproule, I. 4(1); Thompson, J. 23(2); Westcarr, C. 36(5); Wholey, J. (1).
Goals – League (46): Hughes 13 (1 pen), Westcarr 12 (1 pen), Davies 5, Ince 2, Miller 2, Spicer 2, Bishop 1, Burgess 1, Demba-Nyren 1, Edwards 1, Gow 1 (1 pen), Judge 1, Pearce 1, Smith 1, own goals 2.
Carling Cup (5): Smith 2, Davies 1, Hughes 1, Spicer 1.
FA Cup (8): Hughes 2, Bishop 1, Davies 1 (pen), Pearce 1, Rodgers 1, Westcarr 1, own goal 1.
J Paint Trophy (1): Davies 1.
Ground: Meadow Lane Stadium, Meadow Lane, Nottingham NG2 3HJ. Telephone: (0115) 952 9000.
Record Attendance: 47,310 v York C, FA Cup 6th rd, 12 March 1955.
Capacity: 20,300.
Manager: Martin Allen.
Secretary and General Manager: Tony Cuthbert.
Most League Goals: 107, Division 4, 1959–60.
Highest League Scorer in Season: Tom Keetley, 39, Division 3 (S), 1930–31.
Most League Goals in Total Aggregate: Les Bradd, 125, 1967–78.
Most Capped Player: Kevin Wilson, 15 (42), Northern Ireland.
Most League Appearances: Albert Iremonger, 564, 1904–26.
Honours – Football League: Division 2 Champions – 1896–97, 1913–14, 1922–23. Division 3 Champions – 1997–98. Division 3 (S) Champions – 1930–31, 1949–50. Division 4 Champions – 1970–71; FL 2 Champions – 2009–10. **FA Cup:** Winners – 1893–94. **Anglo-Italian Cup:** Winners – 1995.
Colours: Black and white striped shirts, black shorts, black stockings.

OLDHAM ATHLETIC   FL CHAMPIONSHIP 1

Bembo Leta Djenny (F)	5 10	11 05	Kinshasa	9 11 91	Scholar
Black Paul (D)	6 0	12 10	Middleton	18 1 90	Scholar
Brooke Ryan (M)	6 1	11 07	Crewe	4 10 90	Scholar
Evina Cedric (D)	5 11	12 08	Cameroon	16 11 91	Arsenal
Feeney Warren (F)	5 8	12 04	Belfast	17 1 81	Cardiff C
Furman Dean (M)	6 0	11 08	Cape Town	22 6 88	Bradford C
Lee Kieran (D)	6 1	12 00	Tameside	22 6 88	Manchester U
McGrath Phillip (M)	5 9	10 01	Co. Down	7 4 92	Glenavon
Millar Kirk (M)	5 9	10 07	Belfast	7 7 92	Linfield
Morais Filipe (M)	5 9	11 10	Lisbon	21 11 85	St Johnstone
Smalley Deane (M)	6 0	11 10	Chadderton	5 9 88	Scholar
Stephens Dale (M)	5 11	11 06	Bolton	12 12 87	Bury
Taylor Chris (M)	5 11	11 00	Oldham	20 12 86	Scholar

League Appearances: Alessandra, L. 10(9); Amos, B. 16; Bembo-Lita, D. 2(1); Black, P. 28(1); Brill, D. 30; Brooke, R. 2(11); Burns, R. 1; Christophe, J. (1); Dickov, P. (2); Dik-aba, R. 1; Evina, C. 24(3); Feeney, W. 13(10); Furman, D. 42; Gregan, S. (1); Hazell, R. 33; Jacobson, J. (1); Jarrett, J. 7(1); Jones, R. 21(10); Kelly, D. 1(12); Lee, K. 43; Lowe, J. 7; M'Voto, J. 25(2); Mantom, S. 3(1); McGrath, P. (1); Millar, K. (5); Morais, F. 20(3); Reid, R. 11(8); Smalley, D. (3); Stephens, D. 34; Tarkowski, J. 7(2); Taylor, C. 41(1); Todd, A. 5(1); Tounkara, O. 40(4); Trotman, N. 15(3); White, A. 19(5); Winchester, C. 5(1).

Goals – League (53): Taylor 11, Stephens 9 (3 pens), Tounkara 7, Furman 5, White 4, Morais 3, Evina 2, Lee 2, Lowe 2 (1 pen), M'Voto 2, Reid 2, Alessandra 1, Jones 1, Kelly 1, Winchester 1.

Carling Cup (1): Bembo-Leta 1.

FA Cup (2): Feeney 1, Stephens 1 (pen).

J Paint Trophy (0).

Ground: Boundary Park, Furtherwood Road, Oldham OL1 2PA. Telephone: (0161) 624 4972.

Record Attendance: 46,471 v Sheffield W, FA Cup 4th rd, 25 January 1930.

Capacity: 13,624.

Manager: Paul Dickov.

Chief Executive/Secretary: Alan Hardy.

Most League Goals: 95, Division 4, 1962–63.

Highest League Scorer in Season: Tom Davis, 33, Division 3 (N), 1936–37.

Most League Goals in Total Aggregate: Roger Palmer, 141, 1980–94.

Most Capped Player: Gunnar Halle, 24 (64), Norway.

Most League Appearances: Ian Wood, 525, 1966–80.

Honours – Football League: Division 2 Champions – 1990–91, Division 3 (N) Champions – 1952–53. Division 3 Champions – 1973–74.

Colours: Blue shirts with white sleeves, white shorts, white stockings.

OXFORD UNITED   FL CHAMPIONSHIP 2

Batt Damien (D)	5 10	11 07	Hoddesdon	16 9 84	Grays Ath
Chapman Adam (M)	5 10	11 00	Doncaster	29 11 89	Sheffield U
Clarke Ryan (G)	6 3	12 13	Bristol	30 4 82	Salisbury C
Clist Simon (M)	5 9	11 00	Shaftesbury	13 6 81	Forest Green R
Constable James (F)	6 2	12 13	Malmesbury	4 10 84	Shrewsbury T
Craddock Tom (F)	5 11	11 10	Durham	14 10 86	Luton T
Deering Sam (M)	5 6	11 00	London	26 2 91	Charlton Ath
Green Francis (F)	5 9	11 05	Derby	23 4 80	Kettering T
Hall Asa (M)	6 2	11 09	Sandwell	29 11 86	Luton T
Heslop Simon (M)	5 11	11 00	York	1 5 87	Barnsley
Kinniburgh Steven (D)	6 0	11 00	Glasgow	13 6 89	Partick T
McLaren Paul (M)	6 0	13 04	High Wycombe	17 11 76	Tranmere R
Payne Josh (M)	6 0	11 09	Basingstoke	25 11 90	Doncaster R
Potter Alfie (M)	5 7	9 06	Islington	1 1 89	Kettering T
Purkiss Ben (D)	6 2	11 00	Sheffield	1 4 84	York C
Tonkin Anthony (D)	511	12 02	Newlyn	17 1 80	Cambridge U
Worley Harry (D)	6 3	13 00	Warrington	25 11 88	Leicester C
Wright Jake (D)	5 10	11 07	Keighley	11 3 86	Brighton & HA

League Appearances: Baker, R. (6); Batt, D. 27(1); Bulman, D. 4(1); Burge, R. 5; Clarke, R. 46; Clist, S. 16(7); Cole, M. (4); Constable, J. 35(9); Craddock, T. 36(3); Creighton, M. 5(2); Deering, S. (6); Doble, R. 1(2); Franks, L. 4(1); Futcher, B. 6; Green, M. 9(8); Hackney, S. 2(11); Hall, A. 34(7); Hanson, M. (2); Heslop, S. 30(8); Kinniburgh, W. 10(1); MacLean, S. 26(5); McLaren, P. 24; Midson, J. 11(10); Payne, J. 23(5); Philliskirk, D. (1); Potter, A. 16(22); Purkiss, B. 19(4); Sangare, 2(2); Tonkin, A. 37(2); Worley, H. 41(2); Wotton, P. 4; Wright, J. 33(2).

Goals – League (58): Constable 15, Craddock 14 (3 pens), MacLean 6 (1 pen), Midson 6, Hall 4, Heslop 3, Potter 2, Clist 1, Green 1, McLaren 1, Payne 1, Worley 1, own goals 3.

Carling Cup (6): Constable 2, Heslop 2, Green 1, Midson 1.

FA Cup (0).

J Paint Trophy (0).

Ground: The Kassam Stadium, Grenoble Road, Oxford OX4 4XP. Telephone: (01865) 337 700.

Record Attendance: 22,730 v Preston NE, FA Cup 6th rd, 29 February 1964 (at Manor Ground). 12,243 v Leyton Orient, FL 2, 6 May 2006 (at The Kassam Stadium).

Capacity: 12,500.

Manager: Chris Wilder.

General Manager/Club Secretary: Mick Brown.

Most League Goals: 91, Division 3, 1983–84.

Highest League Scorer in Season: John Aldridge, 30, Division 2, 1984–85.

Most League Goals in Total Aggregate: Graham Atkinson, 77, 1962–73.

Most Capped Player: Jim Magilton, 18 (52), Northern Ireland.

Most League Appearances: John Shuker, 478, 1962–77.

Honours – Football League: Division 2 Champions – 1984–85. Division 3 Champions – 1967–68, 1983–84. **Football League Cup:** Winners – 1985–86.

Colours: Yellow shirts, blue shorts, blue stockings.

PETERBOROUGH UNITED   FL CHAMPIONSHIP

Ball David (F)	6 0	11 08	Whitefield	14 12 89	Manchester C
Basey Grant (D)	6 2	13 12	Farnborough	30 11 88	Barnet
Bennett Ryan (D)	6 0	12 05	Orsett	6 3 90	Grimsby T
Boyd George (M)	5 10	11 07	Stevenage	2 10 85	Stevenage B
Davies Arron (M)	5 9	11 00	Cardiff	22 6 84	Yeovil T
Frecklington Lee (M)	5 8	11 00	Lincoln	8 9 85	Lincoln C
Geohaghon Exodus (D)	6 7	11 11	Birmingham	27 2 85	Kettering T
Green Dominic (F)	5 6	11 02	London	5 7 89	Dagenham & R
Griffiths Scott (D)	5 9	11 09	London	27 11 85	Dagenham & R
Hibbert Dave (F)	6 2	12 00	Eccleshall	28 1 86	Shrewsbury T
Langmead Kelvin (D)	6 1	12 00	Coventry	23 3 85	Shrewsbury T
Lee Charlie (M)	5 11	11 07	Whitechapel	5 1 87	Tottenham H
Lewis Joe (G)	6 5	12 10	Bury St Edmunds	6 10 87	Norwich C
Little Mark (D)	6 1	12 10	Worcester	20 8 88	Wolverhampton W
Mackail-Smith Craig (F)	6 3	12 04	Hertford	25 2 84	Dagenham & R
McCann Grant (M)	5 10	11 00	Belfast	14 4 80	Scunthorpe U
Mills Danny (F)	6 3	13 00	Peterborough	27 11 91	Crawley T
Newell Joe (M)			Birmingham	15 3 93	Scholar
Rowe Thomas (M)	5 11	12 11	Manchester	1 5 89	Stockport Co
Taylor Paul (M)	5 11	11 02	Liverpool	4 11 87	Chester C
Tomlin Lee (F)	5 11	11 09	Leicester	12 1 89	Rushden & D
Wesolowski James (D)	5 8	11 11	Sydney	25 8 87	Leicester C
Whelpdale Chris (M)	6 0	12 08	Harold Wood	27 1 87	Billericay T
Zakuani Gaby (D)	6 1	12 13	DR Congo	31 5 86	Fulham

League Appearances: Ball, D. 7(12); Basey, G. 5(2); Bennett, R. 32(2); Boyd, G. 42(1); Clayton, A. 6(1); Davies, A. 12(10); Frecklington, L. 3(6); Gill, M. 4; Hibbert, D. (7); Jones, P. 1; Kennedy, T. 14; Langmead, K. 28(4); Lee, C. 26(8); Lewis, J. 45; Little, M. 32(3); Mackail-Smith, C. 44(1); McCann, G. 34(4); McLean, A. 19; Mendez-Laing, N. 8(25); Newell, J. 1(1); Nyatanga, L. 3; Obika, J. (1); Ofori-Twumasi, N. 6(5); Piergianni, C. (1); Rowe, T. 32(3); Taylor, P. (1); Tomlin, L. 31(6); Wesolowski, J. 23(9); Whelpdale, C. 16(6); Williams, M. 3; Zakuani, G. 29(1).

Goals – League (106): Mackail-Smith 27, Boyd 15, McLean 10 (1 pen), McCann 9 (5 pens), Tomlin 8 (1 pen), Ball 5, Mendez-Laing 5, Rowe 5, Bennett 4, Langmead 3, Wesolowski 2, Zakuani 2, Basey 1, Davies 1, Frecklington 1, Hibbert 1, Lee 1, Obika 1, Whelpdale 1, own goals 4.
Carling Cup (7): Mackail-Smith 3, Boyd 2, Bennett 1, McLean 1.
FA Cup (9): Tomlin 3, Mackail-Smith 2, McLean 2, Langmead 1, McCann 1 (pen).
J Paint Trophy (2): Little 1, McLean 1.
Play-Offs (7): Mackail-Smith 3, McCann 3 (1 pen), Rowe 1.
Ground: London Road Stadium, London Road, Peterborough PE2 8AL. Telephone: (01733) 563 947.
Record Attendance: 30,096 v Swansea T, FA Cup 5th rd, 20 February 1965.
Capacity: 15,460.
Manager: Darren Ferguson.
Director of Football and Club Secretary: Barry Fry.
Most League Goals: 134, Division 4, 1960–61.
Highest League Scorer in Season: Terry Bly, 52, Division 4, 1960–61.
Most League Goals in Total Aggregate: Jim Hall, 122, 1967–75.
Most Capped Player: Craig Morgan, 19 (23), Wales.
Most League Appearances: Tommy Robson, 482, 1968–81.
Honours – Football League: Division 4 Champions – 1960–61, 1973–74.
Colours: Blue shirts with white design, white shorts, white stockings.

PLYMOUTH ARGYLE　　　　　FL CHAMPIONSHIP 2

Arnason Kari (D)	6 3	13 10	Reykjavik	13 10 82	Aarhus
Bhasera Onismor (D)	5 9	11 13	Mutare	7 12 86	Kaizer Chiefs
Bolasie Yannick (M)	6 2	13 02	DR Congo	24 5 89	Barnet
Chenoweth Oliver (G)					Scholar
Fletcher Carl (M)	5 10	11 07	Camberley	7 4 80	Crystal Palace
Johnson Damien (M)	5 9	11 09	Lisburn	18 11 78	Birmingham C
Larrieu Romain (G)	6 2	13 00	Mont-de-Marsan	31 8 76	ASOA Valence
Mason Joe (F)	5 9	11 11	Peverell	13 5 91	Scholar
N'Gala Bondz (D)	6 0	12 03	Newham	13 9 89	West Ham U
Nelson Curtis (D)		·	Newcastle-u-Lyme	21 5 93	Scholar
Patterson Rory (F)	5 11	10 12	Strabane	16 7 84	Coleraine
Walton Simon (D)	6 1	13 05	Sherburn-in-Elmet	13 9 87	QPR
Zubar Stephane (D)			Pointe-a-Pitre	9 10 86	Vaslui

League Appearances: Arnason, K. 39(1); Bhasera, O. 28(1); Bolasie, Y. 25(10); Button, D. 29(1); Clark, C. 18(4); Clifford, C. 7; Duguid, K. 19(7); Fallon, R. 25(3); Fletcher, C. 37(1); Harper-Penman, G. (2); Johnson, R. 15(2); Larrieu, R. 17(1); MacLean, S. 4(3); Mason, J. 26(8); Molyneux, L. 7(2); N'Gala, B. 23(3); Nelson, C. 32(3); Noone, C. 16(1); Parrett, D. 5(3); Paterson, J. 21(7); Patterson, R. 21(14); Peterlin, A. 9(3); Rickard, M. (1); Seip, M. 16(1); Stephens, J. 2(3); Summerfield, L. 4(3); Timar, K. 7(2); Walton, S. 6(1); Wright-Phillips, B. 17; Young, L. 2(3); Zubar, S. 29.
Goals – League (51): Wright-Phillips 13, Bolasie 7 (1 pen), Mason 7, Fallon 4, Patterson 4, Noone 3, Fletcher 2, Johnson R 2, Zubar 2, Arnason 1, Bhasera 1, Clark 1, N'Gala 1, Parrett 1, Summerfield 1, Walton 1.
Carling Cup (0).
FA Cup (0).
J Paint Trophy (3): Clark 1, MacLean 1, Noone 1.
Ground: Home Park, Plymouth, Devon PL2 3DQ. Telephone: (01752) 562 561.
Record Attendance: 43,596 v Aston Villa, Division 2, 10 October 1936.
Capacity: 21,118.
Manager: Peter Reid.
Most League Goals: 107, Division 3 (S), 1925–26 and 1951–52.

Highest League Scorer in Season: Jack Cock, 32, Division 3 (S), 1926–27.
Most League Goals in Total Aggregate: Sammy Black, 180, 1924–38.
Most Capped Player: Moses Russell, 20 (23), Wales.
Most League Appearances: Kevin Hodges, 530, 1978–92.
Secretary: Carole Rowntree.
Honours – Football League: Division 2 Champions – 2003–04. Division 3 (S) Champions – 1929–30, 1951–52. Division 3 Champions – 1958–59, 2001–02.
Colours: Dark green shirts with white design, white shorts, white stockings with green design.

PORTSMOUTH   FL CHAMPIONSHIP

Ashdown Jamie (G)	6 1	13 05	Reading	30 11 80	Reading
Ben Haim Tal (D)	5 11	11 09	Rishon Le Zion	31 3 82	Manchester C
Ciftci Nadir (F)	6 1	13 00	Karacan	12 2 92	Scholar
Hreidarsson Hermann (D)	6 3	12 12	Reykjavik	11 7 74	Charlton Ath
Kanu Nwankwo (F)	6 5	13 00	Owerri	1 8 76	WBA
Kitson David (F)	6 3	12 07	Hitchin	21 1 80	Stoke C
Lawrence Liam (M)	5 11	12 06	Retford	14 12 81	Stoke C
Magri Sam (D)			Malta	30 3 94	Scholar
Mokoena Aaron (D)	6 2	14 00	Johannesburg	25 11 80	Blackburn R
Mullins Hayden (D)	5 11	11 12	Reading	27 3 79	West Ham U
Ricardo Rocha (D)	6 0	12 08	Braga	3 10 78	Standard Liege
Tsovolos Billy (M)			Australia	1 8 93	Scholar
Walshe Carl (F)			Dublin	7 10 92	Scholar
Ward Joel (D)	6 2	11 13	Portsmouth	29 10 89	Scholar

League Appearances: Ashdown, J. 46; Brown, M. 20(1); Ciftci, N. 4(15); Cotterill, D. 12(3); De Laet, R. 22; Dickinson, C. 23(13); Gregory, P. (1); Halford, G. 33; Hogg, J. 19; Hreidarsson, H. 20(8); Hughes, R. 5(6); Kanu, N. 13(19); Kilbey, T. (2); Kitson, D. 35; Lawrence, L. 28(3); Mokoena, A. 29(8); Mullins, H. 45; Nugent, D. 44; Pack, M. (1); Ricardo Rocha, 26(3); Ritchie, M. 2(3); Smith, T. 3; Sonko, I. 16(7); Utaka, J. 23(2); Ward, J. 33(9); Webber, D. 1(7); Wilson, M. 4.
Goals – League (53): Nugent 13, Kitson 8, Lawrence 7 (5 pens), Halford 5 (1 pen), Utaka 3, Ward 3, Brown 2, Kanu 2, Mokoena 2, Mullins 2, Ciftci 1, Cotterill 1, Hreidarsson 1, Sonko 1, own goals 2.
Carling Cup (4): Brown 1, Ciftci 1, Lawrence 1, Nugent 1.
FA Cup (1): Kilbey 1.
Ground: Fratton Park, Frogmore Road, Portsmouth, Hampshire PO4 8RA. Telephone: (02392) 731 204.
Record Attendance: 51,385 v Derby Co, FA Cup 6th rd, 26 February 1949.
Capacity: 20,688.
Manager: Steve Cotterill.
Secretary: Paul Weld.
Most League Goals: 97, Division 1, 2002–03.
Highest League Scorer in Season: Guy Whittingham, 42, Division 1, 1992–93.
Most League Goals in Total Aggregate: Peter Harris, 194, 1946–60.
Most Capped Player: Jimmy Dickinson, 48, England.
Most League Appearances: Jimmy Dickinson, 764, 1946–65.
Honours – Football League: Division 1 Champions – 1948–49, 1949–50, 2002–03. Division 3 (S) Champions – 1923–24. Division 3 Champions – 1961–62, 1982–83.
FA Cup: Winners – 1939, 2008.
Colours: Blue shirts with white trim, white shorts, red stockings.

PORT VALE   FL CHAMPIONSHIP 2

Collins Lee (D)	6 1	11 10	Telford	23 9 83	Wolverhampton W
Dodds Louis (F)	5 10	12 04	Leicester	8 10 86	Leicester C
Griffith Anthony (M)	6 0	12 00	Huddersfield	28 10 86	Doncaster R
Haldane Lewis (F)	6 0	11 03	Trowbridge	13 3 85	Bristol R
Loft Doug (M)	6 0	12 01	Maidstone	25 12 86	Brighton & HA
Martin Chris (G)	6 0	13 05	Mansfield	21 7 90	Scholar
McCombe John (D)	6 2	13 00	Pontefract	7 5 85	Hereford U
Morsy Sam (M)	5 9	12 06	Wolverhampton	10 9 91	Scholar
Owen Gareth (D)	6 1	11 07	Cheadle	21 9 82	Stockport Co
Richards Justin (F)	5 11	11 00	Sandwell	16 10 80	Cheltenham T
Richards Marc (F)	6 2	12 06	Wolverhampton	8 7 82	Barnsley
Rigg Sean (F)	5 9	12 01	Bristol	1 10 88	Bristol R
Taylor Rob (F)	5 7	11 05	Nuneaton	16 1 85	Nuneaton B
Tomlinson Stuart (G)	6 1	11 02	Chester	10 5 85	Crewe Alex
Yates Adam (D)	5 10	10 07	Stoke	28 5 83	Morecambe

League Appearances: Bell-Baggie, A. (3); Blizzard, D. 1; Brown, K. (4); Collins, L. 41(1); Cox, K. (1); Davis, J. (1); Dodds, L. 14(19); Fraser, T. 7(5); Geohaghon, E. 11(1); Griffith, A. 36(4); Haldane, L. 14(9); Johnson, J. 1(5); Lloyd, R. (1); Loft, D. 24(5); Malbon, A. (2); Martin, C. 12(2); McCombe, J. 42; Morsy, S. 12(4); O'Shea, J. 5; Owen, G. 35(1); Pope, T. 10(3); Richards, M. 37(3); Richards, J. 37(5); Rigg, S. 16(9); Roberts, G. 30(5); Sawyers, R. (1); Speight, J. 1(3); Sutton, R. 5(6); Taylor, R. 21(15); Taylor, K. 15(5); Tomlinson, S. 34(2); Yates, A. 45(1).

Goals – League (54): Richards M 16 (5 pens), Richards J 9 (2 pens), Dodds 7, McCombe 4, Pope 3, Rigg 3, Collins 2, Roberts 2, Griffith 1, Loft 1, Morsy 1, O'Shea 1, Owen 1, Speight 1, Taylor R 1, own goal 1.

Carling Cup (3): Richards J 2, Rigg 1.

FA Cup (8): Richards J 2, Richards M 2 (1 pen), Taylor R 2, McCombe 1, Rigg 1.

J Paint Trophy (4): Richards M 2, Richards J 1, own goal 1.

Ground: Vale Park, Hamil Road, Burslem, Stoke-on-Trent ST6 1AW. Telephone: (01782) 655 800.

Record Attendance: 22,993 v Stoke C, Division 2, 6 March 1920 (at Recreation Ground). 49,768 v Aston Villa, FA Cup 5th rd, 20 February 1960 (at Vale Park).

Capacity: 18,982.

Manager: Micky Adams.

Secretary: Bill Lodey.

Most League Goals: 110, Division 4, 1958–59.

Highest League Scorer in Season: Wilf Kirkham 38, Division 2, 1926–27.

Most League Goals in Total Aggregate: Wilf Kirkham, 154, 1923–29, 1931–33.

Most Capped Player: Chris Birchall, 22 (37), Trinidad & Tobago.

Most League Appearances: Roy Sproson, 761, 1950–72.

Honours – Football League: Division 3 (N) Champions – 1929–30, 1953–54. Division 4 Champions – 1958–59. **Autoglass Trophy:** Winners – 1993. **LDV Vans Trophy:** Winners – 2001.

Colours: White shirts with black trim, black shorts with white trim, white stockings.

PRESTON NORTH END   FL CHAMPIONSHIP 1

Arestidou Andreas (G)	6 2	13 00	London	6 12 89	Shrewsbury T
Ashbee Ian (M)	6 1	13 07	Birmingham	6 9 76	Hull C
Barton Adam (M)	5 11	12 01	Blackburn	7 1 91	Scholar
Coutts Paul (M)	5 9	11 11	Aberdeen	22 7 88	Peterborough U
Douglas Jamie (M)	5 11	12 00	Belfast	4 7 92	Scholar
Gray David (D)	5 11	11 02	Edinburgh	4 5 88	Manchester U

Hayes Paul (F)	6 0	12 12	Dagenham	20 9 83	Scunthorpe U
Hume Iain (F)	5 7	11 02	Brampton	31 10 83	Barnsley
Jones Billy (M)	5 11	13 00	Shrewsbury	24 3 87	Crewe Alex
Lonergan Andrew (G)	6 2	13 00	Preston	19 10 83	Scholar
Mayor Danny (M)	6 0	11 13	Preston	18 10 90	Scholar
McLaughlin Conor (D)	6 0	11 02	Belfast	26 7 91	Scholar
Mellor Neil (F)	6 0	14 00	Sheffield	4 11 82	Liverpool
Miller George (M)	5 9	12 02	Eccleston	25 11 91	Scholar
Morgan Craig (D)	6 0	11 04	St Asaph	18 6 85	Peterborough U
Nicholson Barry (M)	5 7	9 01	Dumfries	24 8 78	Aberdeen
Parry Paul (M)	5 11	12 12	Chepstow	19 8 80	Cardiff C
Proctor Jamie (F)	6 2	12 03	Preston	25 3 92	Scholar
Russell Darel (M)	5 10	11 09	Mile End	22 10 80	Norwich C
St Ledger-Hall Sean (D)	6 0	11 09	Birmingham	28 12 84	Peterborough U
Treacy Keith (M)	6 0	13 02	Dublin	13 9 88	Blackburn R
Wright Bailey (D)	5 9	13 05	Melbourne	28 7 92	Scholar

League Appearances: Ashbee, I. 19; Barton, A. 24(9); Brown, C. 12(4); Brown, W. 12(1); Carter, D. 13(1); Clarke, L. 5(1); Cort, L. 13; Coutts, P. 17(6); Davidson, C. 17(1); De Laet, R. 5; Devine, D. 2; Douglas, J. (2); Ellington, N. 7(11); Gardner, R. 4; Gray, D. 12(10); Hayes, P. 11(12); Hume, I. 29(2); James, M. 10; Johnson, E. 15(1); Jones, B. 43; Khumalo, B. 6; King, J. 6(2); Leather, S. 2; Linganzi, A. 1; Lonergan, A. 29; Mayor, D. 5(16); McLaughlin, C. 5(2); Middleton, D. (2); Miller, G. (1); Morgan, C. 30(1); Nicholson, B. 18(4); Parkin, J. 16(3); Parry, P. 6(17); Proctor, J. (5); Pugh, D. 5; Russell, D. 21(4); St Ledger-Hall, S. 31; Tonge, M. 5; Treacy, K. 33(5); Turner, I. 17; Wright, B. (2).

Goals – League (54): Hume 12 (1 pen), Parkin 7, Treacy 7, Jones 6, Nicholson 4, Davidson 3 (3 pens), Ellington 2, Hayes 2, Morgan 2, Barton 1, Brown C 1, Clarke 1, Coutts 1, Proctor 1, St Ledger-Hall 1, Tonge 1, own goals 2.

Carling Cup (8): Hayes 2 (1 pen), Treacy 2, Coutts 1, Davidson 1 (pen), James 1, King 1.

FA Cup (1): Carter 1.

Ground: Deepdale Stadium, Sir Tom Finney Way, Deepdale, Preston PR1 6RU. Telephone: (0844) 856 1964.

Record Attendance: 42,684 v Arsenal, Division 1, 23 April 1938.

Capacity: 23,408.

Manager: Phil Brown.

Secretary: Janet Parr.

Most League Goals: 100, Division 2, 1927–28 and Division 1, 1957–58.

Highest League Scorer in Season: Ted Harper, 37, Division 2, 1932–33.

Most League Goals in Total Aggregate: Tom Finney, 187, 1946–60.

Most Capped Player: Tom Finney, 76, England.

Most League Appearances: Alan Kelly, 447, 1961–75.

Honours – Football League: Division 1 Champions – 1888–89 (first champions), 1889–90. Division 2 Champions – 1903–04, 1912–13, 1950–51, 1999–2000. Division 3 Champions – 1970–71, 1995–96. **FA Cup:** Winners – 1889, 1938.

Colours: White shirts, blue shorts, white stockings.

QUEENS PARK RANGERS   FA PREMIERSHIP

Agyemang Patrick (F)	6 1	12 00	Walthamstow	29 9 80	Preston NE
Alberti Matteo (M)	5 10	11 05	Chievo Verona	4 8 88	Chievo Verona
Andrade Bruno (M)	5 9	11 09	Sao Bernardo	2 10 93	Scholar
Balanta Angelo (F)	5 10	11 11	Colombia	1 7 90	Scholar
Borrowdale Gary (D)	6 0	12 01	Sutton	16 7 85	Coventry C
Buzsaky Akos (M)	5 11	11 09	Hungary	7 5 82	Plymouth Arg
Cerny Radek (G)	6 1	14 02	Prague	18 2 74	Tottenham H
Clarke Leon (F)	6 2	14 02	Birmingham	10 2 85	Sheffield W

Connolly Matthew (D)	6 1	11 03	Barnet	24	9	87	Arsenal
Cook Lee (M)	5 8	11 10	Hammersmith	3	8	82	Fulham
Derry Shaun (M)	5 10	10 13	Nottingham	6	12	77	Crystal Palace
Doughty Michael (M)			Westminster	20	11	92	Scholar
Ehmer Max (M)			Frankfurt	3	2	92	Scholar
Ephraim Hogan (F)	5 9	10 06	Islington	31	3	88	West Ham U
Faurlin Alejandro (M)	6 1	12 06	Argentina	9	8	86	Instituto
German Antonio (F)	5 10	12 03	London	26	12	91	Scholar
Gorkss Kaspars (D)	6 3	13 05	Riga	6	11	81	Blackpool
Hall Fitz (D)	6 3	13 00	Leytonstone	20	12	80	Wigan Ath
Harriman Michael (D)			Republic of Ireland	23	10	92	Scholar
Hill Clint (D)	6 0	11 06	Liverpool	19	10	78	Crystal Palace
Hulse Rob (F)	6 1	12 04	Crewe	25	10	79	Derby Co
Kenny Paddy (G)	6 1	14 00	Halifax	17	5	78	Sheffield U
Leigertwood Mikele (D)	6 1	11 04	Enfield	12	11	82	Sheffield U
Mackie Jamie (F)	5 8	11 00	Dorking	22	9	85	Plymouth Arg
Orr Bradley (D)	6 0	11 11	Liverpool	1	11	82	Bristol C
Parmenter Taylor (D)			Bromley	9	9	92	Scholar
Pellicori Alessandro (F)	5 11	11 11	Cosenza	27	2	81	Avellino
Putnins Elvijs (G)			Latvia	12	4	91	FK Auda
Rowlands Martin (M)	5 9	10 10	Hammersmith	8	2	79	Brentford
Shittu Dan (D)	6 2	16 03	Lagos	2	9	80	Millwall
Smith Tommy (F)	5 8	11 04	Hemel Hempstead	22	5	80	Portsmouth
Sutherland Frankie (M)	5 9	10 00	Republic of Ireland	6	12	93	Scholar
Taarabt Adel (M)	5 9	10 12	Berre-l'Etange	24	5	89	Tottenham H
Tofas Georgios (F)	5 11	11 02	Paralimni	17	6	89	Anorthosis
Vaagan Moen Petter (F)	5 11	11 13	Hamar	5	2	84	Brann
Vine Rowan (F)	5 11	12 10	Basingstoke	21	9	82	Birmingham C

League Appearances: Agyemang, P. (19); Andrade, B. (1); Borrowdale, G. (1); Buzsaky, A. 9(10); Cerny, R. 2; Chimbonda, P. (3); Clarke, L. 2(11); Connolly, M. 33(3); Derry, S. 45; Ephraim, H. 19(9); Faurlin, A. 40; German, A. (2); Gorkss, K. 42; Hall, F. 12(7); Helguson, H. 32(2); Hill, C. 44; Hulse, R. 12(9); Kenny, P. 44; Leigertwood, M. (9); Mackie, J. 25; Miller, I. 4(8); Orr, B. 29(4); Parker, J. (1); Ramage, P. (4); Routledge, W. 20; Rowlands, M. (4); Shittu, D. 5(2); Smith, T. 23(10); Taarabt, A. 43(1); Tofas, G. (1); Vaagan Moen, P. 1(6); Walker, K. 20.

Goals – League (71): Taarabt 19 (6 pens), Helguson 13 (5 pens), Mackie 9, Smith 6 (1 pen), Routledge 5, Ephraim 3, Faurlin 3, Gorkss 3, Agyemang 2, Hill 2, Hulse 2, Hall 1, Miller 1, Orr 1, own goal 1.
Carling Cup (1): German 1.
FA Cup (0).
Ground: Loftus Road Stadium, South Africa Road, Shepherds Bush, London W12 7PJ. Telephone: (020) 8743 0262.
Record Attendance: 41,097 v Leeds U, FA Cup 3rd rd, 9 January 1932 (at White City). 35,353 v Leeds U, Division 1, 27 April 1974 (at Loftus Road).
Capacity: 18,682.
Manager: Neil Warnock.
Most League Goals: 111, Division 3, 1961–62.
Highest League Scorer in Season: George Goddard, 37, Division 3 (S), 1929–30.
Most League Goals in Total Aggregate: George Goddard, 172, 1926–34.
Most Capped Player: Alan McDonald, 52, Northern Ireland.
Most League Appearances: Tony Ingham, 519, 1950–63.
Honours – Football League: Championship Champions – 2010–11. Division 2 Champions – 1982–83. Division 3 (S) Champions – 1947–48. Division 3 Champions – 1966–67. **Football League Cup:** Winners – 1966–67.
Colours: Blue and white hooped shirts, white shorts, white stockings.

Andersen Mikkel (G)	6 5	12 08	Herlev	17 12 88	AB Copenhagen
Antonio Michail (M)	6 0	11 11	London	28 3 90	Tooting & M
Bignall Nicholas (F)	5 10	11 12	Reading	11 7 90	Scholar
Church Simon (F)	6 0	13 04	Wycombe	10 12 88	Scholar
Cummings Shaun (D)	6 0	11 10	Hammersmith	25 2 89	Chelsea
D'Ath Lawson (M)	5 9	12 02	Oxford	24 12 92	Scholar
Federici Adam (G)	6 2	14 02	Nowra	31 1 85	
Gage Ethan (D)	5 11	12 00	Cochrane	8 5 91	Vancouver Whitecaps
Griffin Andy (D)	5 9	10 10	Billinge	7 3 79	Stoke C
Gunnarsson Brynjar (M)	6 1	12 01	Reykjavik	16 10 75	Watford
Hamer Ben (G)	5 11	12 04	Reading	20 11 87	Crawley T
Harte Ian (D)	5 11	12 06	Drogheda	31 8 77	Carlisle U
Howard Brian (M)	5 8	11 00	Winchester	23 1 83	Sheffield U
Hunt Noel (F)	5 8	11 05	Waterford	26 12 82	Dundee U
Karacan Jem (M)	5 10	11 13	Lewisham	21 2 89	Scholar
Kebe Jimmy (M)	6 2	11 07	Vitry-sur-Seine	19 1 84	Boulogne
Locke Simon (G)			Newbury	15 10 91	Scholar
Long Shane (F)	5 10	11 02	Kilkenny	22 1 87	Cork C
Manset Mathieu (F)	6 1	13 08	Metz	5 8 89	Hereford U
McAnuff Jobi (M)	5 11	11 05	Edmonton	9 11 81	Watford
McCarthy Alex (G)	6 1	11 12	Reading	3 12 89	Scholar
Mills Matthew (D)	6 3	12 12	Swindon	14 7 86	Doncaster R
Morrison Sean (D)	6 4	14 00	Plymouth	8 1 91	Swindon T
Obita Jordan (F)	5 11	11 08	Oxford	8 12 93	Scholar
Pearce Alex (D)	6 0	11 10	Reading	9 11 88	Scholar
Robson-Kanu Hal (F)	5 7	11 08	Hammersmith	21 5 89	
Tabb Jay (M)	5 7	10 00	Tooting	21 2 84	Coventry C
Taylor Jake (M)	5 10	12 01	Ascot	1 12 91	Scholar
Walcott Jacob (F)			Abingdon	26 6 92	Scholar
Williams Marcus (D)	5 8	10 07	Doncaster	8 4 86	Scunthorpe U

League Appearances: Antonio, M. 2(19); Armstrong, C. 6(1); Church, S. 14(23); Cummings, S. 10; Federici, A. 34; Griffin, A. 33; Gunnarsson, B. 10(2); Harte, I. 40; Howard, B. 19(5); Hunt, N. 19(14); Ingimarsson, I. 12(1); Karacan, J. 39(1); Kebe, J. 34(2); Khizanishvili, Z. 21(1); Leigertwood, M. 21(1); Long, S. 44; Manset, M. 4(9); McAnuff, J. 40; McCarthy, A. 12(1); Mills, M. 38; Pearce, A. 20(1); Rasiak, G. (1); Robson-Kanu, H. 12(15); Sigurdsson, G. 4; Tabb, J. 15(6); Taylor, J. (1); Williams, M. 3.

Goals – League (77): Long 21 (6 pens), Harte 11 (4 pens), Hunt 10, Kebe 9, Church 5, Robson-Kanu 5, McAnuff 4, Karacan 3, Manset 2, Mills 2, Sigurdsson 2, Antonio 1, Leigertwood 1, Pearce 1.

Carling Cup (4): Mills 2, Rasiak 1, Robson-Kanu 1.

FA Cup (4): Long 2, Leigertwood 1, Mills 1.

Play-Offs (5): Long 2 (1 pen), McAnuff 1, Mills 1, own goal 1.

Ground: Madejski Stadium, Junction 11, M4, Reading, Berkshire RG2 0FL. Telephone: (0118) 968 1100.

Record Attendance: 33,042 v Brentford, FA Cup 5th rd, 19 February 1927 (at Elm Park). 24,122 v Aston Villa, FA Premier League, 10 February 2007 (at Madejski Stadium).

Capacity: 24,082.

Manager: Brian McDermott.

Secretary: Sue Hewett.

Most League Goals: 112, Division 3 (S), 1951–52.

Highest League Scorer in Season: Ronnie Blackman, 39, Division 3 (S), 1951–52.

Most League Goals in Total Aggregate: Ronnie Blackman, 158, 1947–54.

Most Capped Player: Kevin Doyle, 26 (41), Republic of Ireland.
Most League Appearances: Martin Hicks, 500, 1978–91.
Honours – Football League: Championship Champions – 2005–06. Division 2 Champions – 1993–94. Division 3 Champions – 1985–86. Division 3 (S) Champions – 1925–26. Division 4 Champions – 1978–79. **Simod Cup:** Winners – 1987–88.
Colours: Blue and white hooped shirts, blue shorts, blue stockings.

ROCHDALE   FL CHAMPIONSHIP 1

Adams Nicholas (F)	5 10	11 00	Bolton	16 10 86		Brentford
Akpa Akpro Jean-Louis (F)	6 0	10 12	Toulouse	4 1 85		Grimsby T
Barry-Murphy Brian (M)	5 10	13 01	Cork	27 7 78		Bury
Done Matt (M)	5 10	10 04	Oswestry	22 6 88		Hereford U
Edwards Matty (G)	6 2	12 11	Liverpool	22 8 90		Leeds U
Elding Anthony (F)	6 1	12 02	Boston	16 4 82		Crewe Alex
Holness Marcus (D)	6 0	12 02	Oldham	8 12 88		Scholar
Jones Gary (M)	5 11	12 05	Birkenhead	3 6 77		Barnsley
Kennedy Jason (M)	6 1	13 02	Stockton	11 9 86		Darlington
O'Grady Chris (F)	6 3	12 02	Nottingham	25 1 86		Leicester C
Thompson Joe (M)	6 0	9 07	Rochdale	5 3 89		Scholar
Widdowson Joe (D)	6 0	12 00	Forest Gate	28 3 89		Grimsby T
Wiseman Scott (D)	6 0	11 06	Hull	9 10 85		Darlington

League Appearances: Adams, N. 25(5); Akpa Akpro, J. 8(24); Andre, H. (1); Atkinson, W. 15(6); Barry-Murphy, B. 31(1); Daniels, L. 1; Dawson, C. 44(1); Dickinson, L. 7(7); Done, M. 16(17); Edwards, M. (1); Elding, A. 9(8); Flynn, M. (1); Goodall, A. 3(2); Grant, R. 5(1); Gray, R. (2); Holness, M. 46; Jones, G. 45(1); Kennedy, J. 44(1); Kennedy, T. 6; Lillis, J. 23; O'Grady, C. 45(1); Redshaw, J. (2); Smalley, D. (3); Thompson, Joe 19(13); Thompson, Josh 11(1); Tutte, A. 5(2); Widdowson, J. 30(4); Williams, O. 22; Williams, R. 9; Wiseman, S. 37.
Goals – League (63): Jones 17 (7 pens), Dawson 10, O'Grady 9, Done 5, Akpa Akpro 4, Kennedy J 4, Elding 3, Atkinson 2, Grant 2, Thompson, Joe 2, Gray 1, Holness 1, Thompson, Josh 1, own goals 2.
Carling Cup (3): Jones 2, Elding 1.
FA Cup (2): Dawson 1, Elding 1.
J Paint Trophy (1): Done 1.
Ground: Spotland Stadium, Willbutts Lane, Rochdale OL11 5DS. Telephone: (0844) 826 1907.
Record Attendance: 24,231 v Notts Co, FA Cup 2nd rd, 10 December 1949.
Capacity: 9,223.
Manager: Steve Eyre.
Chief Executive/Secretary: Colin Garlick.
Most League Goals: 105, Division 3 (N), 1926–27.
Highest League Scorer in Season: Albert Whitehurst, 44, Division 3 (N), 1926–27.
Most League Goals in Total Aggregate: Reg Jenkins, 119, 1964–73.
Most Capped Player: Leo Bertos, 6 (39), New Zealand.
Most League Appearances: Gary Jones, 379, 1998–2001; 2003–.
Honours: None.
Colours: Black and blue striped shirts, white shorts, blue stockings with black tops.

ROTHERHAM UNITED   FL CHAMPIONSHIP 2

Annerson Jamie (G)	6 2	13 02	Sheffield	21 6 88		Sheffield U
Bradley Mark (D)	6 0	11 05	Dudley	14 1 88		Walsall
Cresswell Ryan (D)	5 9	10 05	Rotherham	22 12 87		Bury
Harrison Danny (M)	5 11	12 04	Liverpool	4 11 82		Tranmere R

Law Nicky (M)	5 10	11 06	Nottingham	29	3 88	Sheffield U
Le Fondre Adam (F)	5 9	11 04	Stockport	2	12 86	Rochdale
Marshall Marcus (F)	5 10	11 06	Hammersmith	7	10 89	Blackburn R
Mullins John (D)	5 11	12 07	Hampstead	6	11 85	Stockport Co
Newey Tom (D)	5 10	10 02	Sheffield	31	10 82	Bury
Pope Tom (F)	6 3	11 03	Stoke	27	8 85	Crewe Alex
Taylor Jason (M)	6 1	11 03	Ashton-under-Lyne	28	1 87	Stockport Co
Taylor Ryan (F)	6 2	10 10	Rotherham	4	5 88	Scholar
Thomas-Moore Ian (F)	5 11	12 00	Birkenhead	26	8 76	Tranmere R
Tonge Dale (D)	5 10	10 06	Doncaster	7	5 85	Barnsley
Warne Paul (M)	5 10	11 07	Norwich	8	5 73	Yeovil T
Warrington Andy (G)	6 3	12 13	Sheffield	10	6 76	Bury

League Appearances: Annerson, J. 8(1); Ashworth, L. 3(6); Atkinson, W. 3; Banks, O. (1); Bradley, M. 14(7); Brogan, S. 1; Coid, D. 9; Cresswell, R. 21(1); Daley, O. 2(6); Elliott, T. 4(2); Ellison, K. 20(3); Fenton, N. 31(1); Geohaghon, E. 14; Green, J. 5(2); Harrison, D. 23(7); Henderson, L. 5(6); Holden, D. 4(2); Kennedy, C. 4(1); Law, N. 44; Le Fondre, A. 40(5); Marshall, M. 26(10); Mullins, J. 35; Newey, T. 38; Pope, T. 9(9); Randall, M. 3(7); Taylor, J. 37(5); Taylor, R. 30(4); Thomas-Moore, I. 11(1); Tonge, D. 21(2); Warne, P. 3(8); Warrington, A. 38.

Goals – League (75): Le Fondre 23 (2 pens), Taylor R 11, Taylor J 5, Cresswell 4, Harrison 4, Law 4, Ellison 3, Fenton 3, Marshall 3, Thomas-Moore 3 (1 pen), Atkinson 1, Banks 1, Daley 1, Geohaghon 1, Mullins 1, Pope 1, Randall 1, Warne 1, own goals 4.

Carling Cup (1): Marshall 1.

FA Cup (0).

J Paint Trophy (5): Bradley 1, Cresswell 1, Ellison 1 (pen), Le Fondre 1, Taylor R 1.

Ground: Don Valley Stadium, Worksop Road, Sheffield, South Yorkshire S9 3TL. Telephone: (08444) 140 737.

Record Attendance: 25,170 v Sheffield U, Division 2, 13 December 1952 (at Millmoor); 7,082 v Aldershot T, FL 2 Play-offs semi-final 2nd leg, 19 May 2010 (at Don Valley).

Capacity: 25,000.

Manager: Andy Scott.

Chief Operating Officer: Paul Douglas.

Most League Goals: 114, Division 3 (N), 1946–47.

Highest League Scorer in Season: Wally Ardron, 38, Division 3 (N), 1946–47.

Most League Goals in Total Aggregate: Gladstone Guest, 130, 1946–56.

Most Capped Player: Shaun Goater, 14 (36), Bermuda.

Most League Appearances: Danny Williams, 459, 1946–62.

Honours – Football League: Division 3 Champions – 1980–81. Division 3 (N) Champions – 1950–51. Division 4 Champions – 1988–89. **Auto Windscreens Shield:** Winners – 1996.

Colours: Red shirts with white design, white shorts, red stockings.

SCUNTHORPE UNITED   FL CHAMPIONSHIP 1

Byrne Cliff (D)	6 0	12 11	Dublin	27	4 82	Sunderland
Canavan Niall (D)	6 3	12 00	Leeds	11	4 91	Scholar
Collins Michael (M)	6 0	11 00	Halifax	30	4 86	Huddersfield T
Dagnall Chris (F)	5 8	12 03	Liverpool	15	4 86	Rochdale
Duffy Mark (M)	5 9	11 05	Liverpool	7	10 85	Morecambe
Godden Matt (F)	6 1	12 03	Canterbury	29	7 91	Scholar
Grant Robert (M)	5 11	12 00	Blackpool	27	3 87	Accrington S
Hughes Andy (M)	5 11	12 01	Stockport	2	1 78	Leeds U
Jones Rob (D)	6 7	12 02	Stockton	30	11 79	Hibernian
Lillis Joshua (G)	6 2	12 09	Scunthorpe	24	6 87	Scholar
Nelson Michael (D)	6 2	13 03	Gateshead	15	3 82	Norwich C

Nolan Eddie (D)	6 0	13 05	Waterford	5 8 88	Preston NE
O'Connor Michael (M)	6 1	11 08	Belfast	6 10 87	Crewe Alex
Raynes Michael (D)	6 4	12 00	Wythenshawe	15 10 87	Stockport Co
Reid Paul (D)	6 2	11 08	Carlisle	18 2 82	Colchester U
Slocombe Sam (G)	6 0	11 11	Scunthorpe	5 6 88	Bottesford T
Thompson Gary (M)	6 0	14 02	Kendal	24 11 80	Morecambe
Togwell Sam (D)	5 11	12 04	Beaconsfield	14 10 84	Barnsley
Wright Andrew (M)	6 1	13 07	Southport	15 1 85	West Virginia Univ

League Appearances: Byrne, C. 20(1); Canavan, N. 6(2); Collins, M. 19(13); Cowan-Hall, P. (1); Dagnall, C. 31(6); Duffy, M. 19(3); Forte, J. 18(6); Garner, J. 17(1); Godden, M. (5); Gordon, B. 13(1); Grant, R. 7(20); Hughes, A. 18(1); Ibrahim, A. 4(7); Jones, R. 13(1); Lillis, J. 15; McClenahan, T. (1); McDonald, K. 3(2); McNulty, J. 5(1); Miller, L. 12(6); Mirfin, D. 23; Murphy, J. 29; N'Guessan, D. 3; Nelson, M. 20; Nolan, E. 32(3); Nunez, R. 8; O'Connor, M. 25(7); Raynes, M. 15(7); Reid, P. 12; Sears, F. 9; Slocombe, S. (2); Thompson, G. 4(8); Togwell, S. 34(2); Warner, T. 2; Williams, M. 5; Woolford, M. 18(6); Wright, A. 16(4); Wright, J. 31(5).

Goals – League (43): O'Connor 8 (4 pens), Garner 6 (2 pens), Woolford 6, Dagnall 5, Forte 3, Mirfin 3, Nunez 3, Byrne 2, Collins 1, Duffy 1, Jones 1, McDonald 1, Miller 1, N'Guessan 1, Thompson 1.

Carling Cup (8): Dagnall 2, Woolford 2, Collins 1, Forte 1, O'Connor 1 (pen), Wright J 1.

FA Cup (1): Collins 1.

Ground: Glanford Park, Doncaster Road, Scunthorpe DN15 8TD. Telephone: (0871) 221 1899.

Record Attendance: 23,935 v Portsmouth, FA Cup 4th rd, 30 January 1954 (at Old Showground). 9,077 v Manchester U, League Cup 3rd rd, 22 September 2010 (at Glanford Park).

Capacity: 9,088.

Manager: Alan Knill.

Most League Goals: 88, Division 3 (N), 1957–58.

Highest League Scorer in Season: Barrie Thomas, 31, Division 2, 1961–62.

Most League Goals in Total Aggregate: Steve Cammack, 110, 1979–81, 1981–86.

Most Capped Player: Grant McCann, 10 (33), Northern Ireland.

Most League Appearances: Jack Brownsword, 595, 1950–65.

Honours – Football League: FL 1 Champions – 2006–07; Division 3 (N) Champions – 1957–58.

Colours: Claret shirts with light blue sleeves, white shorts, claret stockings.

SHEFFIELD UNITED   FL CHAMPIONSHIP 1

Aksalu Mihkel (G)	6 3	12 06	Kuressaare	7 11 84	Flora
Bogdanovic Daniel (F)	6 2	11 02	Misurata	26 3 80	Barnsley
Collins Neill (D)	6 3	12 07	Irvine	2 9 83	Leeds U
Conneely Seamus (D)			London	9 7 88	Galway U
Cresswell Richard (F)	6 0	13 00	Bridlington	20 9 77	Stoke C
Doyle Micky (M)	5 10	11 00	Dublin	8 7 81	Coventry C
Ertl Johannes (D)	6 2	12 08	Graz	13 11 82	Crystal Palace
Evans Ched (F)	6 0	12 00	Rhyl	28 12 88	Manchester C
Henderson Darius (F)	6 3	14 03	Sutton	7 9 81	Watford
Kennedy Terry (D)			Barnsley	14 11 93	Scholar
Lowton Matt (M)	5 11	12 04	Chesterfield	9 6 89	Scholar
Maguire Harry (D)			Sheffield	5 3 93	Scholar
McAllister David (M)	5 10	11 09	Dublin	29 12 88	St Patrick's Ath
Montgomery Nick (M)	5 8	12 08	Leeds	28 10 81	Scholar

Morgan Chris (D)	6 0	13 06	Barnsley	9 11 77	Barnsley
Quinn Stephen (M)	5 6	9 08	Dublin	4 4 86	Scholar
Simonsen Steve (G)	6 2	12 08	South Shields	3 4 79	Stoke C
Slew Jordan (F)	6 3	12 11	Sheffield	7 9 92	Scholar
Taylor Andy (D)	5 11	11 07	Blackburn	14 3 86	Tranmere R
Williamson Lee (D)	5 10	10 04	Derby	7 6 82	Watford
Yeates Mark (F)	5 8	13 03	Dublin	11 1 85	Middlesbrough

League Appearances: Bartley, K. 21; Batth, D. (1); Bent, M. 4(7); Bogdanovic, D. 12(20); Britton, L. 22(2); Calve, J. 16(2); Collins, N. 14; Cresswell, R. 30(5); De Laet, R. 4(2); Doyle, M. 16; Ertl, J. 25(3); Evans, C. 26(8); Harriott, M. (2); Henderson, D. Jordan, S. 14(1); Kennedy, T. (1); Kozluk, R. 2(6); Long, G. 1; Lowry, S. 17; Lowton, M. 21(11); Maguire, H. 4(1); Mattock, J. 12(1); McAllister, D. 1(1); Montgomery, N. 34(1); Morgan, C. 8; Nosworthy, N. 31(1); Parrino, E. 7(1); Philliskirk, D. (3); Quinn, S. 33(4); Reid, A. 8(1); Riise, B. 9(4); Simonsen, S. 43(2); Slew, J. 5(2); Taylor, A. 7(2); Tonne, E. (2); Vokes, S. 4(2); Ward, J. 13(6); Williamson, L. 14(2); Wright, R. 2; Yeates, M. 18(17).
Goals – League (44): Evans 9 (1 pen), Bogdanovic 5 (3 pens), Cresswell 5 (1 pen), Yeates 5, Lowton 4, Williamson 3, Henderson 2, Reid 2, Slew 2, Calve 1, Kozluk 1, McAllister 1, Quinn 1, Riise 1, Vokes 1, own goal 1.
Carling Cup (0).
FA Cup (1): Ward 1 (pen).
Ground: Bramall Lane Ground, Cherry Street, Bramall Lane, Sheffield S2 4SU. Telephone: (0871) 995 1899.
Record Attendance: 68,287 v Leeds U, FA Cup 5th rd, 15 February 1936.
Capacity: 32,500.
Manager: Danny Wilson.
Secretary: Donna Fletcher.
Most League Goals: 102, Division 1, 1925–26.
Highest League Scorer in Season: Jimmy Dunne, 41, Division 1, 1930–31.
Most League Goals in Total Aggregate: Harry Johnson, 205, 1919–30.
Most Capped Player: Billy Gillespie, 25, Northern Ireland.
Most League Appearances: Joe Shaw, 629, 1948–66.
Honours – Football League: Division 1 Champions – 1897–98. Division 2 Champions – 1952–53. Division 4 Champions – 1981–82. **FA Cup:** Winners – 1899, 1902, 1915, 1925.
Colours: Red and white striped shirts with red sleeves, black shorts, black stockings.

SHEFFIELD WEDNESDAY   FL CHAMPIONSHIP 1

Beevers Mark (D)	6 4	13 00	Barnsley	21 11 89	Scholar
Buxton Lewis (D)	6 1	13 11	Newport (IW)	10 12 83	Stoke C
Coke Giles (M)	6 0	11 11	London	3 6 86	Northampton T
Heffernan Paul (F)	5 10	11 00	Dublin	29 12 81	Doncaster R
Jameson Aaron (G)	6 3	13 00	Sheffield	7 11 89	Scholar
Johnson Jermaine (M)	6 0	12 08	Kingston	25 6 80	Bradford C
Johnson Reda (D)	6 2	13 10	Marseille	21 3 88	Plymouth Arg
Jones Daniel (D)	6 2	13 00	Wordsley	14 7 86	Wolverhampton W
Madine Gary (F)	6 1	12 00	Gateshead	24 8 90	Carlisle U
Modest Nathan (F)	5 9	12 02	Sheffield	29 9 91	Scholar
Morrison Clinton (F)	6 0	12 00	Tooting	14 5 79	Coventry C
Morrison Michael (D)	6 0	12 00	Bury St Edmunds	3 3 88	Leicester C
O'Connor James (M)	5 8	11 00	Dublin	1 9 79	Burnley
O'Donnell Richard (G)	6 2	13 05	Sheffield	12 9 89	Scholar
Otsemobor Jon (D)	5 10	12 07	Liverpool	23 3 83	Southampton
Palmer Liam (M)			Worksop	19 9 91	Scholar
Potter Darren (M)	6 0	10 08	Liverpool	21 12 84	Wolverhampton W
Reynolds Mark (D)	5 11	10 07	Motherwell	7 5 87	Motherwell

Sedgwick Chris (M)	5 11	11 10	Sheffield	28	4 80	Preston NE
Spurr Tommy (D)	6 1	11 05	Leeds	13	9 87	Scholar
Teale Gary (F)	5 11	12 02	Glasgow	21	7 78	Derby Co
Weaver Nick (G)	6 4	14 07	Sheffield	2	3 79	Burnley

League Appearances: Batth, D. 10; Beevers, M. 27(1); Buxton, L. 29(1); Coke, G. 22(5); Heffernan, P. 3(14); Hinds, R. 4; Jameson, A. 2; Johnson, J. 15(11); Johnson, R. 15(1); Jones, D. 13(12); Jones, R. 8; Madine, G. 20(2); Mellor, N. 24(9); Miller, T. 29(5); Morrison, C. 22(13); Morrison, M. 12; O'Brien, J. 3(1); O'Connor, J. 25(11); O'Donnell, R. 8(1); Osbourne, I. 9(1); Otsemobor, J. 13(2); Palmer, L. 4(5); Potter, D. 22(11); Purse, D. 22; Reynolds, M. 7; Sedgwick, C. 24(9); Spurr, T. 26; Teale, G. 37(4); Tudgay, M. 15(2); Weaver, N. 36.

Goals – League (67): Mellor 13, Miller 9 (4 pens), Morrison C 6, Madine 5, Coke 4, Johnson J 4, Sedgwick 4, Heffernan 3, Johnson R 3, Potter 3, Beevers 2, O'Connor 2, Teale 2, Tudgay 2 (1 pen), Buxton 1, Jones R 1, own goals 3.

Carling Cup (3): Coke 1, Mellor 1, Tudgay 1.

FA Cup (15): Morrison C 5 (2 pens), Mellor 2, Miller 2 (2 pens), Teale 2, Beevers 1, Johnson J 1, Potter 1, Spurr 1.

J Paint Trophy (9): Mellor 4 (1 pen), O'Connor 2, Purse 1, Teale 1, Tudgay 1.

Ground: Hillsborough, Sheffield S6 1SW. Telephone: (0871) 995 1867.

Record Attendance: 72,841 v Manchester C, FA Cup 5th rd, 17 February 1934.

Capacity: 39,812.

Manager: Gary Megson.

Most League Goals: 106, Division 2, 1958–59.

Highest League Scorer in Season: Derek Dooley, 46, Division 2, 1951–52.

Most League Goals in Total Aggregate: Andrew Wilson, 199, 1900–20.

Most Capped Player: Nigel Worthington, 50 (66), Northern Ireland.

Most League Appearances: Andrew Wilson, 501, 1900–20.

Honours – Football League: Division 1 Champions – 1902–03, 1903–04, 1928–29, 1929–30. Division 2 Champions – 1899–1900, 1925–26, 1951–52, 1955–56, 1958–59. **FA Cup:** Winners – 1896, 1907, 1935. **Football League Cup:** Winners – 1990–91.

Colours: Blue and white striped shirts, black shorts, blue stockings.

SHREWSBURY TOWN   FL CHAMPIONSHIP 2

Ainsworth Lionel (F)	5 9	9 10	Nottingham	1	10 87	Huddersfield T
Bradshaw Tom (F)	5 8	11 02	Shrewsbury	27	7 92	Aberystwyth T
Cansdell-Sherriff Shane (D)	5 11	11 08	Sydney	10	11 82	Tranmere R
Collins James (F)	6 2	13 08	Coventry	1	12 90	Aston Villa
Elder Nathan (F)	6 1	13 12	Hornchurch	5	4 85	Brentford
Goldson Connor (D)			York	18	12 92	Scholar
Grandison Jermaine (D)	6 4	13 03	Birmingham	15	12 90	Coventry C
Harrold Matt (F)	6 1	11 10	Leyton	25	7 84	Wycombe W
Leslie Steve (M)	5 11	12 10	Shrewsbury	5	11 87	Scholar
McAllister Sean (M)	5 8	10 07	Bolton	15	8 87	Sheffield W
Neal Chris (G)	6 2	12 04	St Albans	23	10 85	Preston NE
Sharps Ian (D)	6 3	14 07	Warrington	23	10 80	Rotherham U
Smith Benjamin (G)	6 1	12 11	Newcastle	5	9 86	Doncaster R
Taylor Jon (M)	5 11	12 04	Liverpool	23	12 89	Youth
Wright Mark (M)	5 11	11 00	Wolverhampton	24	2 82	Bristol R
Wroe Nicky (M)	5 11	10 02	Sheffield	28	9 85	Torquay U

League Appearances: Ainsworth, L. 21(12); Bradshaw, T. 13(13); Bright, K. (1); Canavan, N. 3; Cansdell-Sherriff, S. 39(2); Collins, J. 22(2); Davis, D. 19; Disley, C. 22(2); Geohaghon, E. 2; Goldson, C. 1(2); Grandison, J. 13; Harrold, M. 28(13); Holden, D. 11(2);

Leslie, S. 9(9); Lomax, K. (1); McAllister, S. 15(3); McIntyre, K. 18(13); Neal, C. 21(1); Neal, L. (2); O'Donnell, D. 4(1); Obadeyi, T. 7(2); Raven, D. 22(2); Robinson, J. 20(2); Sadler, M. 46; Sharps, I. 43; Smith, B. 25; Taylor, J. 19(1); Tutte, A. 2; Van den Broek, B. (11); Wright, M. 43(2); Wroe, N. 18.

Goals – League (72): Wright 14, Ainsworth 9, Collins 8, Harrold 8, Robinson 8, Bradshaw 6, Taylor J 6, Wroe 3 (2 pens), Cansdell-Sherriff 2, Davis 2, Disley 2, McIntyre 1, Sharps 1, own goals 2.

Carling Cup (5): Harrold 1, Leslie 1, O'Donnell 1, Robinson 1, own goal 1.

FA Cup (0).

J Paint Trophy (1): Leslie 1.

Play-Offs (0).

Ground: Greenhous Meadow, Oteley Road, Shrewsbury SY2 6ST. Telephone: (01743) 289 177.

Record Attendance: 18,917 v Walsall, Division 3, 26 April 1961 (at Gay Meadow); 8,429 v Bury, FL 2 Play-off semi-final, 7 May 2009 (at ProStar Stadium).

Capacity: 10,000.

Manager: Graham Turner.

Secretary/General Manager: Jonathan Harris.

Most League Goals: 101, Division 4, 1958–59.

Highest League Scorer in Season: Arthur Rowley, 38, Division 4, 1958–59.

Most League Goals in Total Aggregate: Arthur Rowley, 152, 1958–65 (thus completing his League record of 434 goals).

Most Capped Player: Jimmy McLaughlin, 5 (12), Northern Ireland; Bernard McNally, 5, Northern Ireland.

Most League Appearances: Mickey Brown, 418, 1986–91; 1992–94; 1996–2001.

Honours – Football League: Division 3 Champions – 1978–79, 1993–94. **Welsh Cup:** Winners – 1891, 1938, 1977, 1979, 1984, 1985.

Colours: All blue with yellow and red design.

SOUTHAMPTON   FL CHAMPIONSHIP

Name	Ht	Wt	Birthplace	Birthdate	Signed From
Barnard Lee (F)	5 10	10 10	Romford	18 7 84	Southend U
Bialkowski Bartosz (G)	6 3	12 10	Braniewo	6 7 87	Gornik Zabrze
Butterfield Danny (D)	5 10	11 06	Boston	21 11 79	Crystal Palace
Chaplow Richard (M)	5 9	9 03	Accrington	2 2 85	Preston NE
Connolly David (F)	5 9	11 00	Willesden	6 6 77	Sunderland
Davis Kelvin (G)	6 1	14 09	Bedford	29 9 76	Sunderland
Dean Harlee (M)	6 0	11 10	Basingstoke	26 7 91	Dagenham & R
Dickson Ryan (M)	5 10	11 05	Saltash	14 12 86	Brentford
Do Prado Guilherme (F)	6 2	12 04	Sao Paulo	31 12 81	Cesena
Doble Ryan (M)			Blaenavon	1 2 91	Scholar
Fonte Jose (D)	6 2	12 08	Penafiel	22 12 83	Crystal Palace
Forecast Tommy (G)	6 2	12 08	Newham	15 10 86	Tottenham H
Forte Jonathan (M)	6 0	12 02	Sheffield	25 7 86	Scunthorpe U
Gobern Oscar (M)	5 11	10 10	Birmingham	26 1 91	Scholar
Hammond Dean (M)	6 0	11 09	Hastings	7 3 83	Colchester U
Harding Dan (D)	6 0	11 11	Gloucester	23 12 83	Ipswich T
Holmes Lee (M)	5 8	10 06	Mansfield	2 4 87	Derby Co
Jaidi Radhi (D)	6 2	14 00	Tunis	30 8 75	Birmingham C
Lallana Adam (M)	5 8	11 06	Southampton	10 5 88	Scholar
Lambert Ricky (F)	6 2	14 08	Liverpool	16 2 82	Bristol R
Martin Aaron (D)	6 3	11 13	Newport (IW)	29 9 89	Eastleigh
Mills Joseph (F)	5 9	11 00	Swindon	30 10 89	Scholar
Oxlade-Chamberlain Alex (M)	5 11	11 00	Portsmouth	15 8 93	Scholar
Puncheon Jason (M)	5 9	12 05	Croydon	26 6 86	Plymouth Arg
Racine Aaron (D)			Rustington	30 10 91	Scholar

Reeves Ben (D)	5 10	10 07	Verwood	19 11 91	Scholar
Richardson Frazer (D)	5 11	11 12	Rotherham	29 10 82	Charlton Ath
Saville Jack (D)	6 3	12 00	Frimley	2 4 91	Scholar
Schneiderlin Morgan (M)	5 11	11 11	Zellwiller	8 11 89	Strasbourg
Seaborne Danny (D)	6 0	11 10	Barnstaple	5 3 87	Exeter C
Seidi Alberto (F)			Guinea-Bissau	20 11 92	Guinea-Bissau
Stephens Jack (D)			Torpoint	27 1 94	Plymouth Arg

League Appearances: Barnard, L. 24(12); Bignall, N. (3); Butterfield, D. 32(2); Chaplow, R. 27(6); Connolly, D. 8(7); Davis, K. 46; Dickson, R. 15(8); Do Prado, G. 23(11); Fonte, J. 43; Forte, J. 2(8); Gobern, O. 1(10); Hammond, D. 40(1); Harding, D. 35(1); Holmes, L. (7); Jaidi, R. 31; Lallana, A. 30(6); Lambert, R. 45; Martin, A. 4(4); Mills, J. (2); N'Guessan, D. 2(4); Oxlade-Chamberlain, A. 27(7); Puncheon, J. 15; Richardson, F. 14(7); Schneiderlin, M. 23(4); Seaborne, D. 14(10); Stephens, D. 5(1); Wotton, P. (2).

Goals – League (86): Lambert 21 (8 pens), Barnard 14, Do Prado 9, Oxlade-Chamberlain 9, Lallana 8, Fonte 7, Chaplow 4, Hammond 4, Connolly 3, Jaidi 3, Forte 2, Dickson 1, Gobern 1.

Carling Cup (2): Lallana 1, Oxlade-Chamberlain 1.

FA Cup (8): Do Prado 2, Lallana 2, Barnard 1, Chaplow 1, Connolly 1, Gobern 1.

J Paint Trophy (0).

Ground: St Mary's Stadium, Britannia Road, Southampton SO14 5FP. Telephone: (0845) 688 9448.

Record Attendance: 31,044 v Manchester U, Division 1, 8 October 1969 (at The Dell). 32,151 v Arsenal, FA Premier League, 29 December 2003 (at St Mary's).

Capacity: 32,689.

Manager: Nigel Adkins B.Sc (Hons).

Football Secretary: Ros Wheeler.

Most League Goals: 112, Division 3 (S), 1957–58.

Highest League Scorer in Season: Derek Reeves, 39, Division 3, 1959–60.

Most League Goals in Total Aggregate: Mike Channon, 185, 1966–77, 1979–82.

Most Capped Player: Peter Shilton, 49 (125), England.

Most League Appearances: Terry Paine, 713, 1956–74.

Honours – Football League: Division 3 (S) Champions – 1921–22. Division 3 Champions – 1959–60. **FA Cup:** Winners – 1975–76. **Johnstone's Paint Trophy:** Winners – 2009–10.

Colours: White shirts with diagonal red stripe, white shorts, black stockings.

SOUTHEND UNITED   FL CHAMPIONSHIP 2

Barker Chris (D)	6 2	13 08	Sheffield	2 3 80	Plymouth Arg
Clohessy Sean (D)	5 11	12 07	Croydon	12 12 86	Salisbury C
Corr Barry (F)	6 3	12 07	Co. Wicklow	2 4 85	Exeter C
Coughlan Graham (D)	6 2	13 07	Dublin	18 11 74	Shrewsbury T
Crawford Harry (F)	6 1	12 04	Saffron Walden	10 12 91	Scholar
Easton Craig (M)	5 11	11 03	Bellshill	26 2 79	Swindon T
Ferdinand Kane (D)	6 1	13 07	Newham	7 10 92	Scholar
Gilbert Peter (D)	5 11	12 00	Newcastle	31 7 83	Northampton T
Grant Anthony (M)	5 10	11 01	Lambeth	4 6 87	Chelsea
Hall Ryan (M)	5 10	10 04	Dulwich	4 1 88	Bromley
James-Lewis Merrick (M)			Southend	21 5 92	Scholar
Mohsni Bilel (D)	6 3	11 11	Paris	21 7 87	Sainte Genevieve
Morris Glenn (G)	6 0	12 03	Woolwich	20 12 83	Leyton Orient
Paterson Matthew (F)	5 10	10 10	Glasgow	18 10 89	Southampton
Phillips Mark (D)	6 2	11 00	Lambeth	27 1 82	Brentford
Prosser Luke (D)	6 2	12 04	Enfield	28 5 88	Port Vale
Sawyer Lee (M)	5 10	10 03	Leytonstone	10 9 89	Barnet
Sturrock Blair (F)	5 10	12 09	Dundee	25 8 81	Mansfield T

League Appearances: Asante, K. 1(8); Barker, C. 43; Clohessy, S. 46; Comminges, M. 4(3); Corr, B. 32(9); Coughlan, G. 28(5); Crawford, H. 5(18); Easton, C. 32; Evans, R. 13; Fairhurst, W. 2(1); Ferdinand, K. 19(3); German, A. 3(1); Gilbert, P. 26; Grant, A. 41(2); Hall, R. 36(5); Herd, J. 6(3); Jarvis, N. (6); Midson, J. 4; Mohsni, B. 21(2); Morris, G. 33; Nesbitt, T. (2); Paterson, M. 4(7); Phillips, M. 3(2); Prosser, L. 14(3); Sawyer, L. 7(10); Simpson, J. 17; Soares, L. 17(14); Spencer, S. 1(4); Stevens, J. 1; Sturrock, B. 34(9); Timlin, M. 8; Woodyard, A. 3; Zaaboub, S. 2(1).

Goals – League (62): Corr 18 (3 pens), Hall 9, Grant 8, Sturrock 6, Mohsni 5, Easton 4, Crawford 2 (1 pen), Ferdinand 2, Midson 2, Asante 1, Clohessy 1, Prosser 1, Simpson 1, Timlin 1, own goal 1.

Carling Cup (4): Paterson 2 (1 pen), Corr 1, Easton 1.

FA Cup (4): Corr 2, German 1 (pen), Simpson 1.

J Paint Trophy (3): Paterson 2, Soares 1.

Ground: Roots Hall Stadium, Victoria Avenue, Southend-on-Sea, Essex SS2 6NQ. Telephone: (01702) 304 050.

Record Attendance: 22,862 v Tottenham H, FA Cup 3rd rd replay, 11 January 1936 (at Southend Stadium). 31,090 v Liverpool, FA Cup 3rd rd, 10 January 1979 (at Roots Hall).

Capacity: 12,260.

Manager: Paul Sturrock.

Secretary: Mrs Helen Norbury.

Most League Goals: 92, Division 3 (S), 1950–51.

Highest League Scorer in Season: Jim Shankly, 31, 1928–29; Sammy McCrory, 1957–58, both in Division 3 (S).

Most League Goals in Total Aggregate: Roy Hollis, 122, 1953–60.

Most Capped Player: George Mackenzie, 9, Eire.

Most League Appearances: Sandy Anderson, 452, 1950–63.

Honours – Football League: Championship 1 Champions – 2005–06. Division 4 Champions – 1980–81.

Colours: Navy blue shirts with white collar, navy blue shorts, white stockings.

STEVENAGE   FL CHAMPIONSHIP 1

Player			Birthplace			Previous club
Ashton Jon (D)	6 2	13 05	Nuneaton	4 10 82	Grays Ath
Bayes Ashley (G)	6 1	13 05	Lincoln	19 4 72	Crawley T
Beardsley Chris (F)	6 0	12 02	Derby	28 2 84	Kettering T
Bostwick Michael (D)	6 4	14 00	London	17 5 88	Ebbsfleet U
Bridges David (M)	6 0	11 13	Huntingdon	22 9 82	Kettering T
Byrom Joel (M)	6 0	12 04	Oswaldtwistle	14 9 86	Northwich Vic
Charles Darius (M)	6 1	13 05	Ealing	10 12 87	Ebbsfleet U
Day Chris (G)	6 2	13 05	Walthamstow	28 7 75	Millwall
Foster Luke (D)	6 2	12 08	Mexborough	8 9 85	Mansfield T
Griffin Charlie (F)	6 0	12 08	Bath	25 6 79	Salisbury C
Harrison Byron (F)			Wandsworth	15 6 87	Carshalton Ath
Henry Ronnie (D)	5 11	11 11	Hemel Hempstead	2 1 84	Tottenham H
Laird Scott (D)	5 9	11 09	Taunton	15 5 88	Plymouth Arg
Long Stacy (M)	5 8	10 01	Bromley	11 1 85	Ebbsfleet U
May Ben (F)	6 3	12 12	Gravesend	10 3 84	Scunthorpe U
Mousinho John (M)	6 1	12 07	Buckingham	30 4 86	Wycombe W
Murphy Darren (M)	6 0	11 11	Cork	28 7 85	Cork C
Odubade Yemi (F)	5 7	11 07	Lagos	4 7 84	Oxford U
Reid Craig (F)	5 10	11 10	Coventry	17 12 85	Newport Co
Roberts Mark (D)	6 1	11 13	Northwich	16 10 83	Northwich Vic
Sinclair Robert (D)	5 10	11 02	Bedford	29 8 89	Luton T
Wilson Lawrie (D)	5 10	11 02	Collier Row	11 9 87	Colchester U
Winn Peter (M)	6 0	11 09	Cleethorpes	19 12 88	Scunthorpe U

League Appearances: Ashton, J. 37(1); Atieno, 1; Beardsley, C. 14(9); Bostwick, M. 41; Boylan, L. (1); Bridges, D. 8(11); Byrom, J. 5(2); Charles, D. 20(8); Daley, L. (2); Day, C. 46; Dixon, T. (1); Foster, L. 16(7); Griffin, C. 13(2); Harrison, B. 11(9); Henry, R. 42; Holroyd, C. 12; Kuqi, N. (1); Laird, S. 42(2); Long, S. 19(3); May, B. 7(13); Mousinho, J. 36(2); Murphy, D. 1(4); O'Shea, J. 5; Odubade, Y. 5(10); Reid, C. 14(6); Roberts, M. 42; Sills, T. 1; Sinclair, R. 14(13); Vincenti, P. 1(4); Walker, J. 1; Williams, M. (1); Wilson, L. 39(3); Winn, P. 13(15).

Goals – League (62): Mousinho 7 (3 pens), Harrison 8, Holroyd 6, Roberts 6, Wilson 5, Laird 4 (1 pen), Griffin 3, Bostwick 2, Charles 2, Long 2, Reid 2 (1 pen), Sinclair 2, Winn 2, Ashton 1, Beardsley 1, Bridges 1, Foster 1, May 1, Odubade 1, Vincenti 1, own goals 4.

Carling Cup (1): Murphy 1.

FA Cup (7): Charles 2, Bostwick 1, Odubade 1, Walker 1, Winn 1, own goal 1.

J Paint Trophy (0).

Play-Offs (4): Beardsley 1, Byrom 1, Long 1, Mousinho 1.

Ground: Lamex Stadium, Broadhall Way, Stevenage, Herts SG2 8RH. Telephone: 01438 223223.

Record Attendance: 6,489 v Kidderminster H, Conference, 25 January 1997.

Capacity: 6,546.

Manager: Graham Westley.

Secretary: Roger Austin.

Most League Goals: 62, FL 2, 2010–11.

Highest League Scorer in Season: Byron Harrison, 8, 2010–11.

Most League Goals in Total Aggregate: Byron Harrison, 8, 2010–11.

Most League Appearances: Chris Day, 46, 2010–11.

Honours: Blue Square Premier League: Champions – 2009–10.

Colours: White shirts, red shorts, red stockings with white tops.

STOCKPORT COUNTY   BLUE SQUARE PREMIER

Glennon Matty (G)	6 2	14 08	Stockport		8 10 78	Bradford C
Halls Andy (D)	6 0	12 02	Altrincham		20 4 92	Scholar
Lynch Mark (D)	5 11	11 03	Manchester		2 9 81	Rotherham U
Mainwaring Matty (M)	5 11	12 02	Salford		28 3 90	Preston NE
Rowe Daniel (M)	6 0	11 12	Wythenshawe		9 3 92	Bolton W
Tansey Greg (M)	6 1	12 03	Huyton		21 11 88	Scholar
Turnbull Paul (F)	5 10	11 07	Stockport		23 1 89	Scholar

League Appearances: Aldred, T. 7; Assoumani, M. 34(2); Brown, A. 17; Conlon, B. 5(4); Darkwah, C. (6); Demontagnac, I. 7; Doble, R. 3; Donnelly, G. 23; Elding, A. 18(3); Fisher, T. 6(20); Fletcher, W. 8(1); Glennon, M. 36; Goodall, A. 13; Grieve, M. 3; Griffin, A. 42(3); Halls, A. 17(2); Husband, S. 5; Lynch, M. 30(1); Mainwaring, M. 9(2); McLoughlin, I. 5; O'Donnell, D. 7; Paterson, M. 9(1); Pilkington, D. 1(5); Poole, D. 22(7); Proctor, J. 4(3); Pulis, A. 9(1); Rose, J. 13(2); Rowe, D. 7(10); Salem, Y. 2(3); Simpson, J. 11(8); Swailes, D. 13; Tansey, G. 30(8); Turnbull, P. 39(2); Vincent, J. 13(6); Wallace, J. 14; Williams, O. 5; Williams, R. 19(3).

Goals – League (48): Tansey 10 (5 pens), Donnelly 8, Turnbull 5, Elding 3, Paterson 3, Demontagnac 2, Husband 2, Poole 2, Assoumani 1, Brown 1, Doble 1, Fisher 1, Fletcher 1, Griffin 1, Pulis 1, Rowe 1, Wallace 1, Williams R 1, own goals 3.

Carling Cup (0).

FA Cup (2): Griffin 1, Tansey 1.

J Paint Trophy (0).

Ground: Edgeley Park, Hardcastle Road, Edgeley, Stockport, Cheshire SK3 9DD. Telephone: (0161) 286 8888 (ext 257).

Record Attendance: 27,833 v Liverpool, FA Cup 5th rd, 11 February 1950.

Capacity: 10,641.

Manager: Dietmar Hamman.
Business Operations Manager: Rachael Moss.
Most League Goals: 115, Division 3 (N), 1933–34.
Highest League Scorer in Season: Alf Lythgoe, 46, Division 3 (N), 1933–34.
Most League Goals in Total Aggregate: Jack Connor, 132, 1951–56.
Most Capped Player: Jarkko Wiss, 9 (45), Finland.
Most League Appearances: Andy Thorpe, 489, 1978–86, 1988–92.
Honours – Football League: Division 3 (N) Champions – 1921–22, 1936–37. Division 4 Champions – 1966–67.
Colours: Reflex blue shirts with one broad white band, reflex blue shorts, white stockings.

STOKE CITY   FA PREMIERSHIP

Arismendi Diego (M)	6 2	12 13	Montevideo	25	1 88	Nacional
Begovic Asmir (G)	6 5	13 01	Trebinje	20	6 87	Portsmouth
Collins Danny (D)	6 2	11 13	Buckley	6	8 80	Sunderland
Cuvelier Florent (M)			Belgium	12	9 92	Portsmouth
Davies Andrew (D)	6 2	12 03	Stockton	17	12 84	Southampton
Delap Rory (M)	6 0	11 10	Sutton Coldfield	6	7 76	Sunderland
Diao Salif (M)	6 1	12 08	Kedougou	10	2 77	Liverpool
Dickinson Carl (D)	6 0	12 00	Swadlincote	31	3 87	Scholar
Etherington Matthew (M)	5 10	10 12	Truro	14	8 81	West Ham U
Fuller Ricardo (F)	6 3	13 03	Kingston	31	10 79	Southampton
Higginbotham Danny (D)	6 1	12 03	Manchester	29	12 78	Sunderland
Huth Robert (D)	6 3	14 07	Berlin	18	8 84	Middlesbrough
Jones Kenwyne (F)	6 2	13 06	Point Fortin	5	10 84	Sunderland
Lund Matthew (M)	6 0	11 13	Stockport	21	11 90	Crewe Alex
Marshall Ben (F)	5 11	11 13	Salford	29	3 91	Crewe Alex
Moult Louis (F)	6 0	13 05	Stoke	14	5 92	Scholar
Nash Carlo (G)	6 5	14 01	Bolton	13	9 73	
Pennant Jermaine (M)	5 9	10 06	Nottingham	15	1 83	Liverpool
Pugh Danny (M)	6 0	12 10	Manchester	19	10 82	Preston NE
Shawcross Ryan (D)	6 3	13 03	Chester	4	10 87	Manchester U
Shotton Ryan (D)	6 3	13 05	Stoke	30	9 88	Scholar
Sidibe Mamady (F)	6 4	12 02	Bamako	18	12 79	Gillingham
Soares Tom (M)	6 0	11 04	Reading	10	7 86	Crystal Palace
Sorensen Thomas (G)	6 5	14 00	Odense	12	6 76	Aston Villa
Tonge Michael (M)	6 0	11 10	Manchester	7	4 83	Sheffield U
Walters Jon (F)	6 0	12 06	Birkenhead	20	9 83	Ipswich T
Whelan Glenn (M)	5 11	12 07	Dublin	13	1 84	Sheffield W
Whitehead Dean (M)	5 11	12 06	Abingdon	12	1 82	Sunderland
Wilkinson Andy (D)	5 11	11 00	Stone	6	8 84	Scholar
Wilson Marc (M)	6 2	12 07	Belfast	17	8 87	Portsmouth

League Appearances: Begovic, A. 28; Carew, J. 7(3); Collins, D. 23(2); Delap, R. 33(4); Diagne-Faye, A. 12(2); Diao, S. 3(5); Etherington, M. 30(2); Fuller, R. 9(19); Gudjohnsen, E. (4); Higginbotham, D. 9(1); Huth, R. 35; Jones, K. 33(1); Pennant, J. 26(3); Pugh, D. 5(5); Shawcross, R. 36; Shotton, R. (2); Sidibe, M. (2); Sorensen, T. 10; Tonge, M. (2); Tuncay, S. 5(9); Walters, J. 27(9); Whelan, G. 14(15); Whitehead, D. 31(6); Wilkinson, A. 21(1); Wilson, M. 21(7).
Goals – League (46): Jones 9, Huth 6, Walters 6 (1 pen), Etherington 5 (2 pens), Fuller 4, Pennant 3, Delap 2, Higginbotham 2, Whitehead 2, Carew 1, Diagne-Faye 1, Shawcross 1, Tuncay 1, Wilson 1, own goals 2.
Carling Cup (5): Jones 2, Higginbotham 1, Tuncay 1, Walters 1.
FA Cup (14): Walters 5, Huth 3, Carew 1, Etherington 1, Higginbotham 1, Jones 1, Shawcross 1, Tuncay 1.

Ground: Britannia Stadium, Stanley Matthews Way, Stoke-on-Trent ST4 4EG. Telephone (0871) 663 2008.
Record Attendance: 51,380 v Arsenal, Division 1, 29 March 1937 (at Victoria Ground). 28,218 v Everton, Division 2, 5 January 2002 (at Britannia Stadium).
Capacity: 28,383.
Manager: Tony Pulis.
Club Secretary: Eddie Harrison.
Most League Goals: 92, Division 3 (N), 1926–27.
Highest League Scorer in Season: Freddie Steele, 33, Division 1, 1936–37.
Most League Goals in Total Aggregate: Freddie Steele, 142, 1934–49.
Most Capped Player: Gordon Banks, 36 (73), England.
Most League Appearances: Eric Skeels, 506, 1958–76.
Honours – Football League: Division 2 Champions – 1932–33, 1962–63, 1992–93. Division 3 (N) Champions – 1926–27. **Football League Cup:** Winners – 1971–72. **Autoglass Trophy:** Winners – 1992. **Auto Windscreens Shield:** Winners – 2000.
Colours: Red and white striped shirts with red sleeves and shoulders, white shorts, white stockings.

SUNDERLAND   FA PREMIERSHIP

Adams Blair (D)	5 11	11 05	South Shields	8	9 91	Scholar
Angeleri Marcos (D)	6 0	10 10	Buenos Aires	4	7 83	Estudiantes
Bagnall Liam (D)	5 11	10 04	Newry	17	5 92	Scholar
Bardsley Phillip (D)	5 11	11 13	Salford	28	6 85	Manchester U
Bramble Titus (D)	6 2	13 10	Ipswich	31	7 81	Wigan Ath
Campbell Frazier (F)	5 11	12 04	Huddersfield	13	9 87	Manchester U
Carson Trevor (G)	6 0	14 11	Downpatrick	5	3 88	Scholar
Cattermole Lee (M)	5 10	11 13	Stockton	21	3 88	Wigan Ath
Colback Jack (M)	5 9	11 05	Newcastle	24 10	89	Scholar
Cook Jordan (M)	5 10	10 10	Hetton-le-Hole	20	3 90	Scholar
Egan John (D)	6 1	11 11	Cork	20 10	92	Scholar
Ferdinand Anton (D)	6 2	11 00	Peckham	18	2 85	West Ham U
Fletcher Matthew (F)	6 0	12 00	Sydney	1	6 92	Scholar
Gordon Craig (G)	6 4	12 02	Edinburgh	31 12	82	Hearts
Gyan Asamoah (F)	5 11	12 08	Accra	22 11	85	Rennes
Henderson Jordan (M)	6 0	10 07	Sunderland	17	6 90	Scholar
Kilgallon Matthew (D)	6 1	12 10	York	8	1 84	Sheffield U
Knott Billy (M)	5 8	11 02	Canvey Island	28 11	92	Scholar
Laing Louis (D)	5 11	12 00	Newcastle	6	9 93	Scholar
Liddle Michael (D)	5 6	11 00	London	25 12	89	Scholar
Lynch Craig (F)	5 9	10 01	Durham	25	3 92	Scholar
Malbranque Steed (M)	5 7	11 07	Mouscron	6	1 80	Tottenham H
McCartney George (D)	5 11	11 02	Belfast	29	4 81	West Ham U
Meyler David (M)	6 3	13 03	Cork	25	5 89	Cork C
Mignolet Simon (G)	6 4	13 10	St Truiden	6	3 88	St Truiden
Noble Liam (M)	5 9	10 05	Newcastle	8	5 91	Scholar
Noble Ryan (F)	6 0	11 00	Sunderland	11	6 91	Scholar
Nosworthy Nayron (D)	6 0	12 08	Brixton	11 10	80	Gillingham
Pickford Jordan (G)			Washington	7	3 94	Scholar
Reed Adam (M)	5 5	10 03	Hartlepool	8	5 91	Scholar
Richardson Kieran (M)	5 9	11 13	Greenwich	21 10	84	Manchester U
Riveros Cristian (M)	5 10	11 13	Saldivar	16 10	82	Cruz Azul
Sessegnon Stephane (M)	5 8	11 05	Allahe	1	6 84	Paris St Germain
Tounkara Oumare (M)	6 1	12 08	France	25	5 90	Sedan
Turner Michael (D)	6 4	13 05	Lewisham	9 11	83	Hull C

League Appearances: Al-Muhammadi, A. 26(10); Angeleri, M. (2); Bardsley, P. 32(2); Bent, D. 20; Bramble, T. 22(1); Campbell, F. 3; Cattermole, L. 22(1); Colback, J. 6(5); Cook, J. (3); Da Silva, P. 1; Ferdinand, A. 23(4); Gordon, C. 15; Gyan, A. 20(11); Henderson, J. 37; Laing, L. (1); Lynch, C. (2); Malbranque, S. 24(11); Mensah, J. 15(3); Meyler, D. 4(1); Mignolet, S. 23; Muntari, S. 7(2); Noble, R. (3); Onuoha, N. 31; Reid, A. (2); Richardson, K. 23(3); Riveros, C. 5(7); Sessegnon, S. 13(1); Turner, M. 15; Waghorn, M. (2); Welbeck, D. 21(5); Zenden, B. 10(17).

Goals – League (45): Gyan 10, Bent 8 (3 pens), Welbeck 6, Richardson 4, Bardsley 3, Henderson 3, Sessegnon 3 (1 pen), Zenden 2, Muntari 1, Onuoha 1, Riveros 1, own goals 3.

Carling Cup (3): Bent 2, Gyan 1.

FA Cup (1): Bent 1 (pen).

Ground: Stadium of Light, Sunderland, Tyne and Wear SR5 1SU. Telephone: (0871) 911 1200.

Record Attendance: 75,118 v Derby Co, FA Cup 6th rd replay, 8 March 1933 (at Roker Park). 48,353 v Liverpool, FA Premier League, 13 April 2002 (at Stadium of Light). FA Premier League figure (46,062).

Capacity: 49,000.

Manager: Steve Bruce.

Club Secretary: Margaret Byrne.

Most League Goals: 109, Division 1, 1935–36.

Highest League Scorer in Season: Dave Halliday, 43, Division 1, 1928–29.

Most League Goals in Total Aggregate: Charlie Buchan, 209, 1911–25.

Most Capped Player: Charlie Hurley, 38 (40), Republic of Ireland.

Most League Appearances: Jim Montgomery, 537, 1962–77.

Honours – Football League: Championship – Winners – 2004–05, 2006–07. Division 1 Champions – 1891–92, 1892–93, 1894–95, 1901–02, 1912–13, 1935–36, 1995–96, 1998–99. Division 2 Champions – 1975–76. Division 3 Champions – 1987–88. **FA Cup:** Winners – 1937, 1973.

Colours: Red and white striped shirts, black shorts, black stockings with red tops.

SWANSEA CITY   FA PREMIERSHIP

Agustien Kemy (M)	5 10	11 05	Tilburg	2	6 86	AZ
Alfei Daniel (D)	5 11	12 02	Swansea	23	2 92	Scholar
Allen Joe (M)	5 6	9 10	Carmarthen	14	3 90	Scholar
Beattie Craig (F)	6 0	11 07	Glasgow	16	1 84	WBA
Bodde Ferrie (M)	5 10	12 06	Delft	4	5 82	Den Haag
Britton Leon (M)	5 6	10 00	Merton	16	9 82	West Ham U
Cornell David (G)	5 11	11 07	Swansea	28	3 91	Scholar
Cotterill David (M)	5 9	11 02	Cardiff	4	12 87	Sheffield U
De Vries Dorus (G)	6 1	12 08	Beverwijk	29	12 80	Dunfermline Ath
Dobbie Stephen (F)	5 10	11 00	Glasgow	5	12 82	Queen of the S
Donnelly Scott (M)	5 8	11 10	Hammersmith	25	12 87	Aldershot T
Dyer Nathan (M)	5 5	9 00	Trowbridge	29	11 87	Southampton
Gower Mark (M)	5 11	11 12	Edmonton	5	10 78	Southend U
Harley Ryan (M)	5 11	11 00	Bristol	22	1 85	Exeter C
Lucas Lee (M)	5 11	11 08	Aberdare	10	6 92	Scholar
MacDonald Shaun (M)	6 1	11 04	Swansea	17	6 88	Scholar
Monk Garry (D)	6 1	13 00	Bedford	6	3 79	Barnsley
Moore Luke (F)	5 11	11 13	Birmingham	13	2 86	WBA
Orlandi Andrea (M)	6 0	12 01	Barcelona	3	8 84	Barcelona B
Pintado Gorka (F)	5 11	11 11	San Sebastian	24	3 78	Grenada
Pratley Darren (M)	6 1	11 00	Barking	22	4 85	Fulham
Rangel Angel (D)	5 11	11 09	Tortosa	28	10 82	Terrassa
Richards Jazz (M)	6 1	12 04	Swansea	12	4 91	Scholar

Sinclair Scott (F)	5 10	10 00	Bath	26	3	89	Chelsea
Tate Alan (D)	6 1	13 05	Easington	2	9	82	Manchester U
Taylor Neil (D)	5 9	10 02	Ruthin	7	2	89	Wrexham
Thomas Casey (M)	5 9	10 09	Port Talbot	14	11	90	Scholar
Walsh Joe (D)	5 11	11 00	Cardiff	15	5	92	Scholar
Williams Ashley (D)	6 0	11 02	Wolverhampton	23	8	84	Stockport Co

League Appearances: Agustien, K. 3(5); Alfei, D. (1); Allen, J. 30(10); Beattie, C. 9(13); Borini, F. 8(1); Britton, L. 10(7); Cotterill, D. 10(4); De Vries, D. 46; Dobbie, S. 23(18); Donnelly, S. (1); Dyer, N. 45(1); Easter, J. 2(4); Emnes, M. 3(1); Gower, M. 37(3); Kuqi, S. (2); Lopez, J. 1(2); Lucas, L. (1); Monk, G. 27(2); Moore, L. 11(4); Nouble, F. 2(4); Orlandi, A. 13(7); Pintado, G. (1); Pratley, D. 28(6); Priskin, T. (4); Rangel, A. 37(1); Richards, J. 6; Serran, A. 5(6); Sinclair, S. 39(4); Tate, A. 39(1); Taylor, N. 25(4); Van der Gun, C. 1(9); Williams, A. 46.

Goals – League (69): Sinclair 19 (7 pens), Dobbie 9, Pratley 9, Borini 6, Beattie 4, Moore 3, Williams 3, Allen 2, Dyer 2, Emnes 2, Gower 2, Rangel 2, Britton 1, Cotterill 1 (1 pen), Easter 1, Nouble 1, Priskin 1, Van der Gun 1.

Carling Cup (9): Sinclair 4, Kuqi 2, Van der Gun 2, Pratley 1.

FA Cup (5): Van der Gun 2, Monk 1, Pratley 1, Sinclair 1.

Play-Offs (7): Sinclair 3 (2 pens), Dobbie 2, Britton 1, Pratley 1.

Ground: Liberty Stadium, Morfa, Landore, Swansea SA1 2FA. Telephone: (01792) 616 600.

Record Attendance: 32,796 v Arsenal, FA Cup 4th rd, 17 February 1968 (at Vetch Field). 19,288 v Yeovil T, FL 1, 11 November 2005 (at Liberty Stadium).

Capacity: 20,520.

Manager: Brendan Rodgers.

Secretary: Jackie Rockey.

Most League Goals: 90, Division 2, 1956–57.

Highest League Scorer in Season: Cyril Pearce, 35, Division 2, 1931–32.

Most League Goals in Total Aggregate: Ivor Allchurch, 166, 1949–58, 1965–68.

Most Capped Player: Ivor Allchurch, 42 (68), Wales.

Most League Appearances: Wilfred Milne, 585, 1919–37.

Honours – Football League: Championship 1 – Winners – 2007–08, Division 3 Champions – 1999–2000. Division 3 (S) Champions – 1924–25, 1948–49. **Autoglass Trophy:** Winners – 1994, 2006. **Football League Trophy:** Winners – 2006. **Welsh Cup:** Winners – 11 times.

Colours: All white.

SWINDON TOWN   FL CHAMPIONSHIP 2

Amankwaah Kevin (D)	6 1	12 12	Harrow	19	5	82	Swansea C
Benyon Elliot (F)	5 9	10 01	Wycombe	29	8	87	Torquay U
Bodin Billy (M)			Swindon	24	3	92	Youth
Caddis Paul (D)	5 7	10 07	Irvine	19	4	88	Celtic
Evans Will (D)			Cricklade	19	10	91	Scholar
Ferry Simon (M)	5 9	11 00	Dundee	11	1	88	Celtic
Flint Aden (D)	6 2	12 00	Birmingham	11	7	89	Alfreton T
Kennedy Callum (M)	6 1	12 10	Cheltenham	6	1	89	Scholar
Lescinel Jean-Francois (M)	6 2	12 04	Cayenne	2	10	86	Guingamp
Lucas David (G)	6 1	13 07	Preston	23	11	77	Leeds U
McGovern John-Paul (M)	5 10	12 02	Glasgow	3	10	80	Milton Keynes D
Pavett Jordan (F)			Enfield	16	12	91	Redbridge
Prutton David (M)	5 10	13 00	Hull	12	9	81	Colchester U
Ritchie Matt (M)	5 8	11 00	Gosport	10	9	89	Portsmouth
Scott Mark (M)	5 9	12 04	Cheltenham	14	3	86	Scholar
Smith Phil (G)	6 0	15 02	Harrow	14	12	79	Crawley T

Thompson Nathan (D)   9 11 90 Scholar
Timlin Michael (M)   5 8   11 08 Lambeth   19 3 85 Fulham

League Appearances: Amankwaah, K. 17(2); Andrew, C. 9(1); Austin, C. 20(1); Ball, D. 7(11); Benyon, E. 7(5); Bodin, B. 2(3); Caddis, P. 36(2); Clark, M. (1); Cuthbert, S. 38(3); Dossevi, T. 16(11); Douglas, J. 38(1); Ferry, S. 18(3); Flint, A. 2(1); Frampton, A. 23; Grella, M. 6(1); Kennedy, C. 2(1); Lescinel, J. 16(2); Lucas, D. 20(1); McGovern, J. 30(8); Morrison, S. 19; N'Diaye, A. 2(4); O'Brien, A. 8(13); Obika, J. 3(2); Pericard, V. 11(7); Prutton, D. 31(10); Ritchie, M. 35(1); Rose, M. 27(8); Sheehan, A. 17(4); Smith, P. 26(1); Storey, M. (2); Thompson, N. 2(1); Timlin, M. 18(4).
Goals – League (50): Austin 12 (2 pens), Ritchie 7, Morrison 4, Dossevi 3, McGovern 3, Prutton 3, Rose 3, Ball 2, Cuthbert 2, Pericard 2, Timlin 2, Andrew 1, Benyon 1, Caddis 1, Douglas 1, Grella 1, Lescinel 1, Sheehan 1.
Carling Cup (1): McGovern 1.
FA Cup (7): Austin 3, McGovern 1, Morrison 1, Pericard 1, Ritchie 1.
J Paint Trophy (6): Pericard 3, Austin 2, Ball 1.
Ground: The County Ground, County Road, Swindon, Wiltshire SN1 2ED. Telephone: 0871 423 6433.
Record Attendance: 32,000 v Arsenal, FA Cup 3rd rd, 15 January 1972.
Capacity: 14,700.
Manager: Paulo Di Canio.
Secretary: Louise Fletcher.
Most League Goals: 100, Division 3 (S), 1926–27.
Highest League Scorer in Season: Harry Morris, 47, Division 3 (S), 1926–27.
Most League Goals in Total Aggregate: Harry Morris, 216, 1926–33.
Most Capped Player: Rod Thomas, 30 (50), Wales.
Most League Appearances: John Trollope, 770, 1960–80.
Honours – Football League: Division 2 Champions – 1995–96. Division 4 Champions – 1985–86. **Football League Cup:** Winners – 1968–69, 2007–08. **Anglo-Italian Cup:** Winners – 1970.
Colours: Red shirts with white inserts, red shorts with white inserts, red stockings with white inserts.

TORQUAY UNITED   FL CHAMPIONSHIP 2

Bevan Scott (G)   6 6 · 15 04 Southampton   19 9 79 Shrewsbury T
Branston Guy (D)   6 1   15 01 Leicester   9 1 79 Kettering T
Ellis Mark (D)   6 2   12 04 Plymouth   30 9 88 Bolton W
Halpin Saul (M)   6 1   12 00 Truro   31 5 91 Youth
Kee Billy (F)   5 9   11 04 Leicester   1 12 90 Leicester C
Lathrope Damon (M)   5 8   10 02 Stevenage   28 10 89 Norwich C
Macklin Lloyd (M)   5 9   12 03 Camberley   2 8 91 Swindon T
Mansell Lee (M)   5 9   10 10 Gloucester   23 9 82 Oxford U
Nicholson Kevin (M)   5 8   11 05 Derby   2 10 80 Forest Green R
O'Kane Eunan (M)   5 8   13 04 Co. Derry   10 7 90 Coleraine
Robertson Chris (D)   6 3   11 09 Dundee   11 10 86 Sheffield U
Rowe-Turner Lathaniel (D) 6 1   13 00 Leicester   12 11 89 Leicester C
Stevens Danny (F)   5 10 11 07 Enfield   26 11 86 Luton T
Yeoman Ashley (M)   5 10 12 01 London   25 2 92 Scholar
Zebroski Chris (F)   6 1   11 07 Swindon   29 10 86 Wycombe W

League Appearances: Benyon, E. 22(1); Bevan, S. 37; Branston, G. 45; Carlisle, W. 3(7); Charnock, K. 1(3); Ellis, M. 24(3); Gilligan, R. (5); Gritton, M. 3(9); Halpin, S. (4); Hemmings, A. 4(5); Kee, B. 17(23); Lathrope, D. 10(8); Macklin, L. 3(7); Mansell, L. 45; Murray, R. 4(3); Nicholson, K. 42(2); O'Kane, E. 31(14); Oastler, J. 17(8); Potter, D. 9; Pringle, B. 5; Robertson, C. 40(3); Robinson, J. 22; Rose, R. 2(3); Rowe-Turner, L. 4(4); Senda, D. 2; Stanley, C. 19; Stevens, D. 19(18); Tomlin, G. 12; Wroe, N. 20; Zebroski, C. 44.

Goals – League (74): Zebroski 14, Benyon 13 (1 pen), Kee 9, Robinson 7 (2 pens), O'Kane 6, Tomlin 4, Nicholson 3, Stevens 3, Wroe 3 (1 pen), Branston 2, Ellis 2, Robertson 2, Murray 1, Rose 1, Rowe-Turner 1, Stanley 1, own goals 2.
Carling Cup (0).
FA Cup (3): Benyon 1, Kee 1 (pen), O'Kane 1.
J Paint Trophy (0).
Play-Offs (2): O'Kane 1, Zebroski 1.
Ground: Plainmoor Ground, Torquay, Devon TQ1 3PS. Telephone: (01803) 328 666.
Record Attendance: 21,908 v Huddersfield T, FA Cup 4th rd, 29 January 1955.
Capacity: 6,117.
Manager: Martin Ling.
Secretary: Ann Sandford.
Most League Goals: 89, Division 3 (S), 1956–57.
Highest League Scorer in Season: Sammy Collins, 40, Division 3 (S), 1955–56.
Most League Goals in Total Aggregate: Sammy Collins, 204, 1948–58.
Most Capped Player: Tony Bedeau, 4, Grenada.
Most League Appearances: Dennis Lewis, 443, 1947–59.
Honours: None.
Colours: All yellow with blue inserts.

TOTTENHAM HOTSPUR FA PREMIERSHIP

Alnwick Ben (G)	6 0	12 09	Prudhoe	1	1 87	Sunderland
Assou-Ekotto Benoit (D)	5 10	11 00	Douala	24	3 84	Lens
Bale Gareth (D)	6 0	11 10	Cardiff	16	7 89	Southampton
Bassong Sebastien (D)	6 2	11 07	Paris	9	7 86	Newcastle U
Bentley David (F)	5 10	11 03	Peterborough	27	8 84	Blackburn R
Bostock John (M)	5 10	11 11	Romford	13	10 91	Crystal Palace
Button David (G)	6 3	13 00	Stevenage	27	2 89	Scholar
Byrne Nathan (D)			St Albans	5	6 92	Scholar
Carroll Tommy (M)			Watford	28	5 92	Scholar
Caulker Steven (D)	6 3	12 00	Feltham	29	12 91	Scholar
Corluka Vedran (D)	6 3	13 03	Zagreb	9	2 86	Manchester C
Crouch Peter (F)	6 7	13 03	Macclesfield	30	1 81	Portsmouth
Cudicini Carlo (G)	6 1	12 08	Milan	6	9 73	Chelsea
Dawkins Simon (F)	5 10	11 01	Edgware	1	12 87	Scholar
Dawson Michael (D)	6 2	12 02	Northallerton	18	11 83	Nottingham F
Defoe Jermain (F)	5 7	10 04	Beckton	7	10 82	Portsmouth
Fredericks Ryan (M)			London	10	10 92	Scholar
Gallas William (D)	6 0	12 12	Asnieres	17	8 77	Arsenal
Giovani (F)	5 8	12 03	Monterrey	11	5 89	Barcelona
Gomes Heurelho (G)	6 3	12 13	Joao Pinheiro	15	2 81	PSV Eindhoven
Huddlestone Tom (M)	6 2	11 02	Nottingham	28	12 86	Derby Co
Hutton Alan (D)	6 1	11 05	Glasgow	30	11 84	Rangers
Jansson Oscar (G)	6 0	12 13	Orebro	23	12 90	Karlslund
Jenas Jermaine (M)	5 11	11 00	Nottingham	18	2 83	Newcastle U
Kaboul Younes (D)	6 2	13 07	St-Julien-en-Genevois	4	1 86	Portsmouth
Kane Harry (F)			Walthamstow	28	7 93	Scholar
Keane Robbie (F)	5 9	12 06	Dublin	8	7 80	Leeds U
Khumalo Bongani (D)	6 2	12 13	Manzini	6	1 87	Supersport U
King Ledley (D)	6 2	14 05	Bow	12	10 80	Trainee
Kranjcar Niko (M)	6 1	12 13	Zagreb	13	8 84	Portsmouth
Lennon Aaron (M)	5 6	10 03	Leeds	16	4 87	Leeds U
Livermore Jake (M)	5 9	12 08	Enfield	14	11 89	Scholar
Loungo Massimo (M)			Australia	25	9 92	Rushden & D
Mason Ryan (M)	5 9	10 00	Enfield	13	6 91	Scholar

Modric Luka (M)	5 8	10 03	Zadar	9	9 85	Dinamo Zagreb
Mpuku Paul-Jose (M)	5 8	10 03	Kinshasa	19	4 92	Scholar
Naughton Kyle (D)	5 11	11 07	Sheffield	11	11 88	Sheffield U
Nicholson Jake (M)			Harrow	19	7 92	Scholar
O'Hara Jamie (M)	5 11	12 04	Dartford	25	9 86	Scholar
Obika Jonathan (F)	6 0	12 00	Enfield	12	9 90	Scholar
Oyenuga Kudus (F)	5 9	11 00	Walthamstow	18	3 93	Scholar
Palacios Wilson (D)	5 10	11 11	La Ceiba	29	7 84	Wigan Ath
Parrett Dean (M)	5 10	11 04	Hampstead	16	11 91	Scholar
Pavlyuchenko Roman (F)	6 2	12 04	Mostovskoy	15	12 81	Spartak Moscow
Pienaar Steven (M)	5 10	10 06	Westbury	17	3 82	Everton
Ranieri Mirko (G)			Italy	8	2 92	Perugia
Rose Danny (M)	5 8	11 11	Doncaster	2	7 90	Scholar
Sandro (M)	6 2	11 11	Riachinho	15	3 89	Internacional
Smith Adam (D)	5 8	10 05	Leytonstone	29	4 91	Scholar
Townsend Andros (M)	6 0	12 00	Whipps Cross	16	7 91	Scholar
Van der Vaart Rafael (M)	5 9	11 09	Heemskerk	11	2 83	Real Madrid
Walker Kyle (D)	5 10	11 07	Sheffield	28	5 90	Sheffield U

League Appearances: Assou-Ekotto, B. 30; Bale, G. 29(1); Bassong, S. 7(5); Bentley, D. 1(1); Corluka, V. 13(2); Crouch, P. 20(14); Cudicini, C. 8; Dawson, M. 24; Defoe, J. 16(6); Gallas, W. 26(1); Giovani, (3); Gomes, H. 30; Huddlestone, T. 13(1); Hutton, A. 19(2); Jenas, J. 14(5); Kaboul, Y. 19(2); Keane, R. 2(5); King, L. 6; Kranjcar, N. 2(11); Lennon, A. 25(9); Modric, L. 32; Palacios, W. 16(5); Pavlyuchenko, R. 18(11); Pienaar, S. 5(3); Rose, D. 4; Sandro, 11(8); Van der Vaart, R. 28; Walker, K. (1).
Goals – League (55): Van der Vaart 13 (4 pens), Pavlyuchenko 9, Bale 7, Crouch 4, Defoe 4, Lennon 3, Modric 3 (1 pen), Huddlestone 2, Hutton 2, Kranjcar 2, Bassong 1, Dawson 1, Kaboul 1, Sandro 1, own goals 2.
Carling Cup (1): Keane 1.
FA Cup (3): Defoe 2, Townsend 1.
Champions League (25): Crouch 7 (1 pen), Pavlyuchenko 4 (2 pens), Bale 4, Defoe 3, Van der Vaart 2, Bassong 1, Kaboul 1, Modric 1, own goals 2.
Ground: White Hart Lane, Bill Nicholson Way, 748 High Road, Tottenham, London N17 0AP. Telephone: (0844) 499 5000.
Record Attendance: 75,038 v Sunderland, FA Cup 6th rd. 5 March 1938.
Capacity: 36,534.
Manager: Harry Redknapp.
Secretary: Darren Eales.
Most League Goals: 115, Division 1, 1960–61.
Highest League Scorer in Season: Jimmy Greaves, 37, Division 1, 1962–63.
Most League Goals in Total Aggregate: Jimmy Greaves, 220, 1961–70.
Most Capped Player: Pat Jennings, 74 (119), Northern Ireland.
Most League Appearances: Steve Perryman, 655, 1969–86.
Honours – Football League: Division 1 Champions – 1950–51, 1960–61. Division 2 Champions – 1919–20, 1949–50. **FA Cup:** Winners – 1901 (as non-League club), 1921, 1961, 1962, 1967, 1981, 1982, 1991. **Football League Cup:** Winners – 1970–71, 1972–73, 1998–99, 2007–08. **European Competitions: European Cup-Winners' Cup:** Winners – 1962–63. **UEFA Cup:** Winners – 1971–72, 1983–84.
Colours: White shirts with black and yellow trim, black shorts, white stockings.

TRANMERE ROVERS   FL CHAMPIONSHIP 1

Akins Lucas (F)	5 10	11 07	Huddersfield	25	2 89	Hamilton A
Bakayogo Zoaumana (D)	5 9	10 08	Paris	11	8 86	Millwall
Coughlin Andy (G)	6 3	14 04	Bootle	31	1 93	Scholar
Cresswell Aaron (D)	5 7	10 05	Liverpool	15	12 89	Scholar

Goodison Ian (D)	6 1	12 06	St James (Jam)	21 11 72	Seba U
Jennings Dale (M)	5 7	11 00	Liverpool	21 12 92	Scholar
Labadie Joss (M)	5 7	11 02	London	31 8 90	WBA
Mahon Alan (M)	5 8	12 03	Dublin	4 4 78	Burnley
McChrystal Mark (D)	6 1	13 07	Derry	25 6 84	Derry C
McGurk Adam (F)	5 9	12 13	St Helier	24 1 89	Aston Villa
Power Max (M)	5 11	12 03	Wirral	27 7 93	Scholar
Showunmi Enoch (F)	6 3	14 11	Kilburn	21 4 82	Leeds U
Taylor Ash (M)	6 0	12 00	Chester	2 9 89	Scholar
Welsh John (M)	5 7	12 02	Liverpool	10 1 84	Hull C

League Appearances: Akins, L. 23(10); Bakayogo, Z. 15(12); Blanchard, M. 14(6); Broomes, M. 5; Brown, K. 1(3); Cathalina, T. 6(1); Collister, J. 7; Cresswell, A. 42(1); Darville, L. 8(1); Elford-Alliyu, L. 13(3); Fraughan, R. 4(10); Goodison, I. 40; Gornell, T. 3; Grandison, J. 6(2); Gulacsi, P. 12; Jennings, D. 25(4); Kay, M. 22; Labadie, J. 29(5); Mantom, S. 2; McChrystal, M. 21(2); McGurk, A. 3(18); McLaren, P. 6; Mendy, A. 11(1); Morrow, S. 2(3); Nielsen, G. 2; Robinson, A. 9(6); Showunmi, E. 43; Taylor, A. 23(3); Thomas-Moore, I. 15(4); Warner, T. 25; Weir, R. 16(2); Welsh, J. 41; Wood, N. 5(6); Wootton, S. 7.

Goals – League (53): Showunmi 11, Thomas-Moore 7 (4 pens), Jennings 6, Elford-Alliyu 5, Cresswell 4, Goodison 4, Welsh 4, McGurk 3, Akins 2, Labadie 2, Bakayogo 1, Kay 1, Mendy 1, Wootton 1, own goal 1.

Carling Cup (2): Goodison 1, Showunmi 1.

FA Cup (3): Cresswell 1, Goodison 1, Thomas-Moore 1.

J Paint Trophy (2): Showunmi 1, Thomas-Moore 1.

Ground: Prenton Park, Prenton Road West, Birkenhead, Merseyside CH42 9PY. Telephone: (0871) 221 2001.

Record Attendance: 24,424 v Stoke C, FA Cup 4th rd, 5 February 1972.

Capacity: 16,587.

Manager: Les Parry.

Chief Executive/Secretary: Mick Horton.

Most League Goals: 111, Division 3 (N), 1930–31.

Highest League Scorer in Season: Bunny Bell, 35, Division 3 (N), 1933–34.

Most League Goals in Total Aggregate: Ian Muir, 142, 1985–95.

Most Capped Player: John Aldridge, 30 (69), Republic of Ireland.

Most League Appearances: Harold Bell, 595, 1946–64 (incl. League record 401 consecutive appearances).

Honours – Football League: Division 3 (N) Champions – 1937–38. **Welsh Cup:** Winners – 1935. **Leyland Daf Cup:** Winners – 1990.

Colours: White shirts, white shorts, blue and white hooped stockings.

WALSALL   FL CHAMPIONSHIP 1

Bowerman George (F)	5 10	10 07	Wordsley	6 11 91	Scholar
Butler Andy (D)	6 0	13 00	Doncaster	4 11 83	Huddersfield T
Gray Julian (M)	6 1	11 00	Lewisham	21 9 79	Barnsley
Grigg Will (M)	5 11	11 00	Solihull	3 7 91	Stratford T
Lancashire Oliver (D)	6 1	11 10	Basingstoke	13 12 88	Southampton
Ledesma Emmanuel (M)	5 11	12 02	Quilmes	24 5 88	Crotone
Macken Jon (F)	5 11	12 04	Manchester	7 9 77	Barnsley
Nicholls Alex (F)	5 10	11 00	Stourbridge	19 12 87	Scholar
Paterson Jamie (F)	5 9	10 07	Coventry	20 12 91	Scholar
Richards Matt (D)	5 8	11 00	Harlow	26 12 84	Ipswich T
Smith Manny (D)	6 2	12 03	Birmingham	8 11 88	Scholar
Taundry Richard (D)	5 9	12 10	Walsall	15 2 89	Scholar
Westlake Darryl (D)	5 9	11 00	Sutton Coldfield	1 3 91	Scholar

League Appearances: Bevan, D. 4; Brain, J. 16; Butler, A. 31; Byfield, D. 8(11); Cook, J. 6(2); Davies, A. 3; Davis, D. 7; Devaney, M. 4; Dickinson, L. 2(2); Gbarssin, M. 8(1); Gill, M. 8; Gray, J. 42(1); Grigg, W. 8(20); Jones, S. 9(4); Laird, M. 8; Lancashire, O. 28(1); Ledesma, E. 5(5); Lescott, A. 34; Macken, J. 35(4); Marshall, P. 12(6); McDonald, C. 7(7); McGivern, R. 15; Nicholls, A. 26(11); Paterson, J. 2(12); Price, J. 4(1); Reid, R. 13(5); Richards, M. 46; Smith, M. 23(2); Taundry, R. 26(2); Walker, J. 26; Westlake, D. 26(2); Williams, T. 14.

Goals – League (56): Gray 10, Macken 9, Richards 8, Nicholls 5, Butler 4, Grigg 4, Reid 3, Byfield 2, Gill 2, Smith 2, Cook 1, Devaney 1, Ledesma 1, Lescott 1, Marshall 1, Westlake 1, Williams 1.

Carling Cup (0).

FA Cup (3): Reid 2, Richards 1.

J Paint Trophy (1): Reid 1.

Ground: Banks's Stadium, Bescot Crescent, Walsall WS1 4SA. Telephone: (01922) 622 791. Fax: (01922) 613 202.

Record Attendance: 25,453 v Newcastle U, Division 2, 29 August 1961 (at Fellows Park). 11,049 v Rotherham U, Division 1, 9 May 2004 (at Bescot Stadium).

Capacity: 11,300.

Manager: Dean Smith.

Secretary: Roy Whalley.

Most League Goals: 102, Division 4, 1959–60.

Highest League Scorer in Season: Gilbert Alsop, 40, Division 3 (N), 1933–34 and 1934–35.

Most League Goals in Total Aggregate: Tony Richards, 184, 1954–63; Colin Taylor, 184, 1958–63, 1964–68, 1969–73.

Most Capped Player: Mick Kearns, 15 (18), Republic of Ireland.

Most League Appearances: Colin Harrison, 467, 1964–82.

Honours – Football League: FL 2 Champions – 2006–07. Division 4 Champions – 1959–60.

Colours: Red shirts with black trim, red shorts, red stockings with black tops.

WATFORD   FL CHAMPIONSHIP

Name (Position)			Birthplace				Previous Club
Aldred Tom (D)	6 2	13 02	Bolton	11	9	90	Carlisle U
Bennett Dale (D)	5 11	12 02	Watford	6	1	90	Scholar
Bond Jonathan (G)			Hemel Hempstead	19	5	93	Scholar
Bonham Jack (G)			Republic of Ireland	14	9	93	Scholar
Bryan Michael (M)	5 8	10 00	Wexford	21	2	90	Scholar
Buckley Will (F)	6 0	13 00	Burnley	12	8	88	Rochdale
Cowie Don (M)	5 5	8 05	Inverness	15	2	83	Inverness CT
Deeney Troy (F)	5 11	12 00	Chelmsley	29	6	88	Walsall
Doyley Lloyd (D)	5 10	12 05	Whitechapel	1	12	82	Scholar
Eustace John (M)	5 11	11 12	Solihull	3	11	79	Stoke C
Gilmartin Rene (G)	6 5	13 06	Dublin	31	5	87	Walsall
Graham Danny (F)	5 11	12 05	Gateshead	12	8	85	Carlisle U
Hodson Lee (D)			Watford	2	10	91	Scholar
Jenkins Ross (M)	5 11	12 06	Watford	9	11	90	Scholar
Kiernan Robert (D)	6 1	11 13	Watford	13	1	91	Scholar
Loach Scott (G)	6 1	13 01	Nottingham	27	5	88	Lincoln C
Mariappa Adrian (D)	5 10	11 12	Harrow	3	10	86	Scholar
Massey Gavin (F)	5 11	11 06	Watford	14	10	92	Scholar
McGinn Stephen (M)	5 9	10 00	Glasgow	2	12	88	St Mirren
Mingoia Piero (M)			Enfield	20	10	91	Scholar
Murray Sean (M)			Abbots Langley	11	10	93	Scholar
Oshodi Eddie (D)	6 3	12 07	Brentford	14	1	92	Scholar
Sordell Marvin (F)	5 9	12 06	Brent	17	2	91	Scholar

106

Taylor Martin (D)	6 4	15 00	Ashington	9 11 79	Birmingham C
Thompson Adam (D)	6 2	12 10	Harlow	28 9 92	Scholar
Walker Josh (M)	5 11	11 13	Newcastle	21 2 89	Middlesbrough
Whichelow Matt (M)			Islington	28 9 91	Scholar

League Appearances: Bennett, D. 5(5); Bryan, M. 4(1); Buckley, W. 27(6); Cowie, D. 37; Deeney, T. 17(19); Doyley, L. 36; Drinkwater, D. 3(9); Eustace, J. 41; Graham, D. 45; Hoban, T. (1); Hodson, L. 26(3); Jenkins, R. 13(6); Loach, S. 46; Mariappa, A. 45; Massey, G. (3); McGinn, S. 24(5); Mingoia, P. 2(3); Murray, S. 1(1); Mutch, J. 21(2); Sordell, M. 25(18); Taylor, M. 46; Taylor, A. 19; Thompson, A. 7(3); Townsend, A. 2(1); Walker, J. (5); Weimann, A. 10(8); Whichelow, M. 4(15).

Goals – League (77): Graham 23 (1 pen), Sordell 12, Eustace 6, Taylor M 6, Mutch 5, Buckley 4, Cowie 4, Weimann 4, Deeney 3, Whichelow 3, McGinn 2, Hodson 1, Jenkins 1, Mariappa 1, Taylor A 1, Thompson 1.

Carling Cup (4): Graham 2, Deeney 1, Sordell 1.

FA Cup (4): Sordell 2, Graham 1, Mingoia 1.

Ground: Vicarage Road Stadium, Vicarage Road, Watford, Hertfordshire WD18 0ER. Telephone: 0844 856 1881.

Record Attendance: 34,099 v Manchester U, FA Cup 4th rd (replay), 3 February 1969.

Capacity: 19,920.

Manager: Sean Dyche.

Secretary: Michelle Ives.

Most League Goals: 92, Division 4, 1959–60.

Highest League Scorer in Season: Cliff Holton, 42, Division 4, 1959–60.

Most League Goals in Total Aggregate: Luther Blissett, 148, 1976–83, 1984–88, 1991–92.

Most Capped Player: John Barnes, 31 (79), England and Kenny Jackett, 31, Wales.

Most League Appearances: Luther Blissett, 415, 1976–83, 1984–88, 1991–92.

Honours – Football League: Division 2 Champions – 1997–98. Division 3 Champions – 1968–69. Division 4 Champions – 1977–78.

Colours: Yellow shirts with red and black trim, black shorts, yellow stockings.

WEST BROMWICH ALBION   FA PREMIERSHIP

Bednar Roman (F)	6 3	13 03	Prague	26 3 83	Hearts
Berahino Saido (F)			Burundi	4 8 93	Scholar
Borja Valero (M)	5 9	11 07	Madrid	12 1 85	Mallorca
Brunt Chris (M)	6 1	13 04	Belfast	14 12 84	Sheffield W
Carson Scott (G)	6 3	14 00	Whitehaven	3 9 85	Liverpool
Cech Marek (D)	6 0	11 09	Trebisov	26 1 83	Porto
Cox Simon (F)	5 10	10 12	Reading	28 4 87	Swindon T
Daniels Luke (G)	6 1	12 10	Bolton	5 1 88	Manchester U
Dawson Craig (D)	6 0	12 04	Rochdale	6 5 90	Radcliffe Bor
Dorrans Graham (F)	5 9	11 07	Glasgow	5 5 87	Livingston
Downing Paul (D)	6 1	12 06	Taunton	26 10 91	Scholar
Elford-Alliyu Lateef (F)	5 8	11 00	Ibadan	1 6 92	Hereford U
Fortune Marc-Antoine (F)	6 0	11 13	Cayenne	2 7 81	Celtic
Gayle Cameron (D)			Birmingham	22 11 92	Scholar
Hurst James (D)			Sutton Coldfield	31 1 92	Portsmouth
Jara Gonzalo (D)	5 10	12 02	Chile	29 8 85	Colo Colo
Mantom Samuel (M)			Stourbridge	20 2 92	Scholar
Mattock Joe (D)	5 11	12 05	Leicester	15 5 90	Leicester C
Miller Ishmael (F)	6 3	14 00	Manchester	5 3 87	Manchester C
Morrison James (M)	5 10	10 06	Darlington	25 5 86	Middlesbrough
Mulumbu Youssef (M)	5 9	10 03	Kinshasa	25 1 87	Paris St Germain
Myhill Boaz (G)	6 3	14 06	Modesto	9 11 82	Hull C

Odemwingie Peter (F)	6 0	11 09	Tashkent	15	7 81	Lokomotiv Moscow
Olsson Jonas (D)	6 4	12 08	Landskrona	10	3 83	NEC Nijmegen
Pablo (D)	6 3	13 07	Madrigueras	3	8 81	Atletico Madrid
Reid Steven (M)	6 0	12 07	Kingston	10	3 81	Blackburn R
Sawyers Romaine (M)	5 9	11 00	Birmingham	11	10 90	Scholar
Scharner Paul (D)	6 3	12 09	Scheibbs	11	3 80	Wigan Ath
Shorey Nicky (D)	5 9	10 08	Romford	19	2 81	Aston Villa
Tamas Gabriel (D)	6 2	12 02	Brasov	9	11 83	Dinamo Bucharest
Tchoyi Somen (M)	6 3	13 10	Douala	29	3 83	Salzburg
Thomas Jerome (M)	5 9	11 09	Wembley	23	3 83	Portsmouth
Thorne George (M)	6 2	13 01	Chatham	4	1 93	Scholar
Wood Chris (F)	6 3	12 10	Auckland	7	12 91	Waikato

League Appearances: Barnes, G. 1(13); Bednar, R. 1(3); Brunt, C. 34; Carson, S. 32; Cech, M. 14(1); Cox, S. 8(11); Dorrans, G. 16(5); Fortune, M. 14(11); Hurst, J. 1; Jara, G. 24(5); Meite, A. 10; Miller, I. (6); Morrison, J. 26(5); Mulumbu, Y. 34; Myhill, B. 6; Odemwingie, P. 29(3); Olsson, J. 24; Pablo, 8(2); Reid, S. 13(10); Scharner, P. 33; Shorey, N. 25(3); Tamas, G. 22(4); Tchoyi, S. 7(16); Thomas, J. 32(1); Thorne, G. (1); Vela, C. 3(5); Wood, C. (1); Zuiverloon, G. 1(1).
Goals – League (56): Odemwingie 15 (2 pens), Mulumbu 7, Tchoyi 6, Brunt 4 (2 pens), Morrison 4, Scharner 4, Thomas 3, Fortune 2, Vela 2, Cox 1, Dorrans 1, Jara 1, Olsson 1, Pablo 1, Reid 1, own goals 3.
Carling Cup (8): Cox 3, Pablo 1, Reid 1, Tchoyi 1, Wood 1, Zuiverloon 1.
FA Cup (0).
Ground: The Hawthorns, West Bromwich, West Midlands B71 4LF. Telephone: 0871 271 1100.
Record Attendance: 64,815 v Arsenal, FA Cup 6th rd, 6 March 1937.
Capacity: 28,003.
Head Coach: Roy Hodgson.
Legal Counsel/Secretary: Richard Garlick.
Most League Goals: 105, Division 2, 1929–30.
Highest League Scorer in Season: William 'Ginger' Richardson, 39, Division 1, 1935–36.
Most League Goals in Total Aggregate: Tony Brown, 218, 1963–79.
Most Capped Player: Stuart Williams, 33 (43), Wales.
Most League Appearances: Tony Brown, 574, 1963–80.
Honours – Football League: Division 1 Champions – 1919–20. Championship winners – 2007–08. Division 2 Champions – 1901–02, 1910–11. **FA Cup:** Winners – 1888, 1892, 1931, 1954, 1968. **Football League Cup:** Winners – 1965–66.
Colours: Navy blue and white striped shirts, white shorts, white stockings.

WEST HAM UNITED   FA CHAMPIONSHIP

Abdullah Ahmed (F)			Saudi Arabia	12	11 91	Scholar
Ba Demba (F)	6 2	12 13	Sevres	25	5 85	Hoffenheim
Barrera Pablo (M)	5 9	10 03	Tlalnepantla	21	6 87	UNAM
Boa Morte Luis (F)	5 9	12 06	Lisbon	4	8 77	Fulham
Boffin Ruud (G)	6 5	13 07	St Truiden	5	11 87	MVV
Cole Carlton (F)	6 3	14 02	Croydon	12	11 83	Chelsea
Collison Jack (M)	6 0	13 10	Watford	2	10 88	Scholar
Da Costa Manuel (D)	6 1	12 12	Saint-Max	6	5 86	Sampdoria
Faubert Julien (M)	5 10	11 08	Le Havre	1	8 83	Bordeaux
Fry Matt (D)	6 1	12 02	Ebbsfleet	26	9 90	Scholar
Green Robert (G)	6 3	14 09	Chertsey	18	1 80	Norwich C
Hines Zavon (F)	5 10	10 07	Jamaica	27	12 88	Scholar
Hitzlsperger Thomas (M)	6 0	11 12	Munich	5	4 82	Lazio

Ilunga Herita (D)	5 11	11 09	Kinshasa	25	2 82	Toulouse
Kovac Radoslav (D)	6 2	12 04	Sumperk	27	11 79	Spartak Moscow
Kurucz Peter (G)	6 2	13 09	Budapest	30	5 88	Ujpest
Lee Oliver (M)	5 11	12 07	London	11	7 91	Scholar
Lletget Sebastian (M)	5 10	10 11	San Francisco	3	9 92	California
Montano Cristian (F)	5 11	12 00	Colombia	11	12 91	Scholar
Noble Mark (M)	5 11	12 00	West Ham	8	5 87	Scholar
Nouble Frank (F)	6 3	12 08	Marseille	24	9 91	Chelsea
O'Neil Gary (M)	5 10	11 00	Bromley	18	5 83	Middlesbrough
Parker Scott (M)	5 9	11 10	Lambeth	13	10 80	Newcastle U
Piquionne Frederic (F)	6 2	12 00	New Caledonia	8	12 78	Portsmouth
Reid Winston (D)	6 3	13 10	North Shore	3	7 88	Midtjylland
Sanchez Sergio (D)			Spain	20	9 92	Barcelona
Sears Freddie (F)	5 8	10 01	Hornchurch	27	11 89	Scholar
Spence Jordan (M)	5 11	11 13	Woodford	24	5 90	Scholar
Stanislas Junior (M)	6 0	12 00	Kidbrooke	26	11 89	Scholar
Stech Marek (G)	6 3	14 00	Prague	28	1 90	Scholar
Tomkins James (D)	6 3	11 10	Basildon	29	3 89	Scholar

League Appearances: Ba, D. 10(2); Barrera, P. 6(8); Behrami, V. 6(1); Ben Haim, T. 8; Boa Morte, L. 19(3); Boffin, R. 1; Bridge, W. 15; Cole, C. 21(14); Collison, J. 2(1); Da Costa, M. 14(2); Diamanti, A. (1); Dyer, K. 8(3); Faubert, J. 7(2); Gabbidon, D. 24(2); Green, R. 37; Hines, Z. 4(5); Hitzlsperger, T. 11; Ilunga, H. 10(1); Jacobsen, L. 22(2); Keane, R. 5(4); Kovac, R. 7(6); McCarthy, B. (6); Noble, M. 25(1); Nouble, F. (2); O'Neil, G. 7(1); Obinna, V. 17(8); Parker, S. 30(2); Piquionne, F. 26(8); Reid, W. 3(4); Sears, F. 9(2); Spector, J. 10(4); Spence, J. 2; Stanislas, J. 4(2); Tomkins, J. 18(1); Upson, M. 30.
Goals – League (43): Ba 7, Piquionne 6 (1 pen), Cole 5, Parker 5, Noble 4 (4 pens), Obinna 3, Behrami 2, Hitzlsperger 2, Keane 2, Da Costa 1, Sears 1, Spector 1, Stanislas 1, Tomkins 1, own goals 2.
Carling Cup (13): Cole 4, Obinna 2, Parker 2, Spector 2, Da Costa 1, Noble 1, Piquionne 1.
FA Cup (11): Obinna 3 (1 pen), Cole 2, Piquionne 2, Hitzlsperger 1, Reid 1, Sears 1, Spector 1.
Ground: The Boleyn Ground, Upton Park, Green Street, London E13 9AZ. Telephone: (020) 8548 2748.
Record Attendance: 42,322 v Tottenham H, Division 1, 17 October 1970.
Capacity: 35,303.
Manager: Sam Allardyce.
Secretary: Peter Barnes.
Most League Goals: 101, Division 2, 1957–58.
Highest League Scorer in Season: Vic Watson, 42, Division 1, 1929–30.
Most League Goals in Total Aggregate: Vic Watson, 298, 1920–35.
Most Capped Player: Bobby Moore, 108, England.
Most League Appearances: Billy Bonds, 663, 1967–88.
Honours – Football League: Division 2 Champions – 1957–58, 1980–81. **FA Cup:** Winners – 1964, 1975, 1980. **European Competitions: European Cup-Winners' Cup:** Winners – 1964–65. **Intertoto Cup:** Winners – 1999.
Colours: Claret shirts with blue trim, white shorts, claret stockings.

WIGAN ATHLETIC   FA PREMIERSHIP

Alcaraz Antolin (D)	6 0	12 08	Roque Gonzalez	30	7 82	Club Brugge
Amaya Antonion (D)	6 3	13 07	Madrid	31	5 83	Rayo Vallecano
Boselli Mauro (F)	6 0	11 11	Capital Federal	22	5 85	Estudiantes
Boyce Emmerson (D)	6 0	12 06	Aylesbury	24	9 79	Crystal Palace
Breeze Jonathan (M)			Birkenhead	22	10 91	Scholar

Name	Height			Birthplace	D	M	Y	Club/Status
Buxton Adam (D)	6 1	12 10	Liverpool		12	5	92	Scholar
Caldwell Gary (D)	5 11	11 10	Stirling		12	4	82	Celtic
Di Santo Franco (F)	6 4	13 01	Mendoza		7	4	89	Chelsea
Diame Mohamed (M)	6 1	11 02	Creteil		14	6	87	Rayo Vallecano
Figueroa Maynor (D)	5 11	12 02	Jutiapa		2	5	83	Victoria La Ceiba
Gohouri Steve (D)	6 2	13 01	Treichville		8	2	81	Mgladbach
Golobart Roman (D)	6 4	13 10	Barcelona		21	3	92	Espanyol
Gomez Jordi (M)	5 10	11 09	Barcelona		24	5	85	Swansea C
Kirkland Chris (G)	6 5	14 05	Leicester		2	5	81	Liverpool
Langley Josh (M)			Warrington		13	8	92	Scholar
Lopez Adrian (D)	6 0	12 02	As Pontes		25	2	87	La Coruna
McArthur James (M)	5 6	9 13	Glasgow		7	10	87	Hamilton A
McCarthy James (M)	5 11	11 05	Glasgow		12	11	90	Hamilton A
McManaman Callum (F)	5 9	11 03	Huyton		25	4	91	Everton
Moses Victor (F)	5 10	11 07	Lagos		12	12	90	Crystal Palace
Mustoe Jordan (M)			Wirral		28	1	91	Scholar
N'Zogbia Charles (M)	5 9	11 00	Le Havre		28	5	86	Newcastle U
Nicholls Lee (G)			Huyton		5	10	92	Scholar
Redmond Daniel (D)			Liverpool		2	3	91	Scholar
Robinson Jordan (D)			Yarm		28	4	91	Middlesbrough
Rodallega Hugo (F)	5 11	11 05	El Carmelo		25	7	85	Necaxa
Rugg Jordan (M)			Liverpool		15	9	91	Scholar
Sammon Conor (F)	5 10	11 11	Dublin		13	4	87	Kilmarnock
Stam Ronnie (D)	5 9	11 00	Breda		18	6	84	Twente
Thomas Hendry (M)	5 11	12 08	La Ceiba		23	2	85	Olimpija
Watson Ben (M)	5 10	10 11	Camberwell		9	7	85	Crystal Palace

League Appearances: Al-Habsi, A. 34; Alcaraz, A. 34; Boselli, M. 5(3); Boyce, E. 20(2); Caldwell, G. 23; Caldwell, S. 8(2); Cleverley, T. 19(6); Di Santo, F. 9(16); Diame, M. 30(6); Figueroa, M. 32(1); Gohouri, S. 26(1); Gomez, J. 9(4); Kirkland, C. 4; McArthur, J. 3(15); McCarthy, J. 24; McManaman, C. (3); Moses, V. 8(13); N'Zogbia, C. 32(2); Piscu, 1; Pollitt, M. (1); Rodallega, H. 34(2); Sammon, C. 1(6); Stam, R. 17(8); Thomas, H. 22(2); Watson, B. 23(6).

Goals – League (40): N'Zogbia 9, Rodallega 9, Cleverley 3, McCarthy 3, Watson 3 (2 pens), Alcaraz 1, Di Santo 1, Diame 1, Figueroa 1, Gohouri 1, Gomez 1, Moses 1, Sammon 1, Stam 1, own goals 4.

Carling Cup (7): Gomez 2, Boselli 1, Moses 1, N'Zogbia 1, Watson 1 (pen), own goal 1.

FA Cup (3): Diame 2, McManaman 1.

Ground: The DW Stadium, Robin Park Complex, Newtown, Wigan, Lancashire WN5 0UZ. Telephone: (01942) 774 000.

Record Attendance: 27,526 v Hereford U, 12 December 1953 (at Springfield Park). 25,133 v Manchester U, FA Premier League, 11 May 2008 (at DW Stadium).

Capacity: 25,138.

Manager: Roberto Martinez.

Secretary: Stuart Hayton.

Most League Goals: 84, Division 3, 1996–97.

Highest League Scorer in Season: Graeme Jones, 31, Division 3, 1996–97.

Most League Goals in Total Aggregate: Andy Liddell, 70, 1998–2004.

Most Capped Players: Kevin Kilbane, 22 (110), Republic of Ireland; Henri Camara, 22 (99), Senegal.

Most League Appearances: Kevin Langley, 317, 1981–86, 1990–94.

Honours – Football League: Division 2 Champions – 2002–03. Division 3 Champions – 1996–97. **Freight Rover Trophy:** Winners – 1984–85. **Auto Windscreens Shield:** Winners – 1998–99.

Colours: Blue and white striped shirts with blue sleeves, blue shorts, white stockings.

Name			Birthplace			Previous club
Batth Danny (D)	6 3	13 05	Brierley Hill	21	9 90	Scholar
Berra Christophe (D)	6 1	12 10	Edinburgh	31	1 85	Hearts
Davis David (M)	5 8	12 03	Smethwick	20	2 91	Scholar
Doherty Matt (M)			Dublin	16	1 92	Portsmouth
Doyle Kevin (F)	5 11	12 06	Adamstown	18	9 83	Reading
Ebanks-Blake Sylvan (F)	5 10	13 04	Cambridge	29	3 86	Plymouth Arg
Edwards Dave (M)	5 11	11 04	Shrewsbury	3	2 86	Luton T
Elokobi George (D)	5 10	13 02	Cameroon	31	1 86	Colchester U
Fletcher Steven (F)	6 1	12 00	Shrewsbury	26	3 87	Burnley
Foley Kevin (D)	5 9	11 11	Luton	1	11 84	Luton T
Gorman Johnny (M)	5 9	11 00	Sheffield	26	10 92	Scholar
Griffiths Leigh (F)	5 7	10 01	Leith	20	8 90	Dundee
Guedioura Adlene (M)	6 1	12 08	La Roche-sur-Yon	12	11 85	Charleroi
Halford Greg (D)	6 4	12 10	Chelmsford	8	12 84	Sunderland
Hammill Adam (M)	5 11	11 07	Liverpool	25	1 88	Barnsley
Hemmings Ashley (M)	5 8	11 06	Wolverhampton	3	3 91	Scholar
Hennessey Wayne (G)	6 0	11 06	Anglesey	24	1 87	Scholar
Henry Karl (M)	6 0	11 02	Wolverhampton	26	11 82	Stoke C
Hunt Steve (M)	5 9	10 10	Port Laoise	1	8 80	Hull C
Ikeme Carl (G)	6 2	13 09	Sutton Coldfield	8	6 86	Scholar
Jarvis Matthew (M)	5 8	11 10	Middlesbrough	22	5 86	Gillingham
Keogh Andy (F)	6 0	11 00	Dublin	16	5 86	Scunthorpe U
Kightly Michael (F)	5 9	11 09	Basildon	24	1 86	Grays Ath
Maierhofer Stefan (F)	6 8	14 11	Gablitz	16	8 82	Rapid Vienna
Malone Scott (D)	6 2	11 11	Rowley Regis	25	3 91	Scholar
McCarey Aaron (G)			Monaghan	14	1 92	Monaghan U
Mendez-Laing Nathaniel (M)	5 10	11 12	Birmingham	15	4 92	Scholar
Milijas Nenad (M)	6 2	13 09	Belgrade	30	4 83	Red Star Belgrade
Mouyokolo Steven (D)	6 3	13 08	Mellin	24	11 87	Hull C
Reckord Jamie (D)	5 10	11 12	Wolverhampton	9	3 92	Scholar
Spray James (F)	6 0	12 01	Birmingham	2	12 92	Scholar
Stearman Richard (D)	6 2	10 08	Wolverhampton	19	8 87	Leicester C
Vokes Sam (F)	6 1	13 10	Southampton	21	10 89	Bournemouth
Ward Stephen (F)	5 11	12 01	Dublin	20	8 85	Bohemians
Winnall Sam (F)	5 9	11 04	Wolverhampton	19	1 91	Scholar
Zubar Ronald (D)	6 1	12 08	Guadeloupe	20	9 85	Marseille

League Appearances: Bent, M. (3); Berra, C. 31(1); Craddock, J. 14(1); Doyle, K. 25(1); Ebanks-Blake, S. 11(19); Edwards, D. 12(3); Elokobi, G. 23(4); Fletcher, S. 15(14); Foley, K. 30(3); Guedioura, A. 4(6); Hahnemann, M. 14; Halford, G. (2); Hammill, A. 7(3); Hennessey, W. 24; Henry, K. 28(1); Hunt, S. 14(6); Jarvis, M. 34(3); Jones, D. 11(1); Keogh, A. (1); Kightly, M. 1(3); Mancienne, M. 13(3); Milijas, N. 20(3); Mouyokolo, S. 2(2); Mujangi Bia, G. (1); O'Hara, J. 13(1); Stearman, R. 27(4); Van Damme, J. 4(2); Vokes, S. (2); Ward, S. 27(7); Zubar, R. 14(1).

Goals – League (46): Fletcher 10 (1 pen), Ebanks-Blake 7, Doyle 5 (2 pens), Jarvis 4, Hunt 3, O'Hara 3, Elokobi 2, Foley 2, Milijas 2, Craddock 1, Edwards 1, Guedioura 1, Jones 1, Van Damme 1, Ward 1, Zubar 1, own goal 1.

Carling Cup (8): Doyle 2, Milijas 2 (2 pens), Elokobi 1, Fletcher 1, Foley 1, Stearman 1.

FA Cup (7): Bia 1, Doyle 1, Fletcher 1, Hunt 1 (pen), Jarvis 1, Jones 1, Milijas 1.

Ground: Molineux Stadium, Waterloo Road, Wolverhampton WV1 4QR. Telephone: (0871) 222 2220.

Record Attendance: 61,315 v Liverpool, FA Cup 5th rd, 11 February 1939.

Capacity: 28,565.

Manager: Mick McCarthy.

Secretary: Richard Skirrow.
Most League Goals: 115, Division 2, 1931–32.
Highest League Scorer in Season: Dennis Westcott, 38, Division 1, 1946–47.
Most League Goals in Total Aggregate: Steve Bull, 250, 1986–99.
Most Capped Player: Billy Wright, 105, England (70 consecutive).
Most League Appearances: Derek Parkin, 501, 1967–82.
Honours – Football League: Championship Winners – 2008–09. Division 1 Champions – 1953–54, 1957–58, 1958–59. Division 2 Champions – 1931–32, 1976–77. Division 3 (N) Champions – 1923–24. Division 3 Champions – 1988–89. Division 4 Champions – 1987–88. **FA Cup:** Winners – 1893, 1908, 1949, 1960. **Football League Cup:** Winners – 1973–74, 1979–80. **Texaco Cup:** Winners – 1971. **Sherpa Van Trophy:** Winners – 1988.
Colours: Gold shirts with black trim, black shorts, gold stockings.

WYCOMBE WANDERERS   FL CHAMPIONSHIP 1

Name				Birthplace				Previous club
Ainsworth Gareth (M)	5 10	12 06	Blackburn	10	5	73	QPR
Arnold Steven (G)	6 1	13 02	Welham Green	22	8	89	Grays Ath
Beavon Stuart (F)	5 7	10 10	Reading	5	5	84	Weymouth
Betsy Kevin (M)	6 1	11 02	Woking	20	3	78	Southend U
Bloomfield Matt (M)	5 9	11 00	Ipswich	8	2	84	Ipswich T
Bull Nikki (G)	6 2	12 08	Hastings	2	10	81	Brentford
Foster Danny (D)	5 10	12 10	Enfield	23	9	84	Brentford
Johnson Leon (D)	6 1	13 05	Shoreditch	10	5	81	Gillingham
Lewis Stuart (M)	5 10	11 06	Welwyn	15	10	87	Dagenham & R
McClure Matt (F)			Slough	17	11	91	Crystal Palace
McCoy Marvin (D)			Waltham Forest	2	10	88	Wealdstone
Rendell Scott (F)	6 1	13 00	Ashford	21	10	86	Peterborough U
Sandell Andy (D)	5 11	11 09	Calne	8	9	83	Aldershot T
Strevens Ben (M)	6 1	12 00	Edgware	24	5	80	Brentford
Westwood Chris (D)	5 11	12 10	Dudley	13	2	77	Peterborough U
Winfield Dave (D)	6 3	13 08	Aldershot	24	2	88	Aldershot T

League Appearances: Ainsworth, G. 39(4); Beavon, S. 30(7); Bennett, A. 16(1); Betsy, K. 41(4); Bloomfield, M. 30(4); Bull, N. 46; Davies, S. 5(3); Donnelly, S. 11(7); Federico, J. (1); Foster, D. 37(1); Johnson, L. 22(1); Kiernan, R. 2; Lewis, S. 24(1); McClure, M. (8); McCoy, M. 18(3); Montrose, L. 27(9); Murtagh, K. 1(6); Parker, J. (1); Phillips, M. 1(2); Pittman, J. 6(13); Rendell, S. 24(13); Sandell, A. 30(2); Scowen, J. (2); Straker, A. 2(2); Strevens, B. 36(4); Westwood, C. 24(3); Winfield, D. 34(3).
Goals – League (69): Rendell 14 (8 pens), Ainsworth 10, Sandell 7, Strevens 7, Betsy 6, Montrose 4, Pittman 4, Beavon 3, Bloomfield 3, Donnelly 3, Lewis 2, Winfield 2, Davies 1, Foster 1, Johnson 1, Westwood 1.
Carling Cup (1): Strevens 1.
FA Cup (5): Beavon 2, Rendell 2, Ainsworth 1.
J Paint Trophy (5): Rendell 3, Betsy 1, Davies 1.
Ground: Adams Park, Hillbottom Road, Sands, High Wycombe HP12 4HJ. Telephone: (01494) 472 100.
Record Attendance: 15,850 v St Albans C, FA Amateur Cup 4th rd, 25 February 1950 (at Loakes Park). 9,921 v Fulham, FA Cup 3rd rd, 9 January 2002 (at Adams Park).
Capacity: 10,000.
Manager: Gary Waddock.
Secretary: Keith Allen.
Most League Goals: 72, FL 2, 2005–06.
Highest League Goalscorer in Season: Scott McGleish, 25, 2007–08.
Most League Goals in Total Aggregate: Nathan Tyson, 42, 2004–06.
Most Capped Player: Mark Rogers, 7, Canada.
Most League Appearances: Steve Brown, 371, 1994–2004.

Honours – GM Vauxhall Conference: Winners – 1993. **FA Trophy:** Winners – 1991, 1993.
Colours: Light blue and dark blue quartered shirts, dark blue shorts, light blue stockings.

YEOVIL TOWN   FL CHAMPIONSHIP 1

Alcock Craig (D)	5 8	11 00	Truro	8	12 87	Scholar
Ayling Luke (D)	5 11	10 08	London	25	8 91	Arsenal
Bowditch Dean (F)	5 11	11 05	Bishop's Stortford	15	6 86	Ipswich T
Huntington Paul (D)	6 3	12 08	Carlisle	17	9 87	Stockport Co
Russell Alex (M)	5 10	11 07	Crosby	17	3 73	Bath C
Smith Nathan (D)	5 11	12 00	Enfield	11	1 87	Potters Bar T
Upson Edward (M)	5 10	11 07	Bury St Edmunds	21	11 89	Ipswich T
Virgo Adam (D)	6 2	13 12	Brighton	25	1 83	Brighton & HA
Welsh Andy (M)	5 8	10 03	Manchester	24	1 83	Blackpool
Williams Andy (F)	5 11	11 09	Hereford	14	8 86	Bristol R
Wotton Paul (D)	5 11	12 00	Plymouth	17	8 77	Southampton

League Appearances: Alcock, C. 19(7); Ayling, L. 31(6); Bowditch, D. 40(1); Calver, C. (6); Ehmer, M. 26(1); Freeman, L. 5(8); German, A. (4); Gibson, B. (4); Gritton, M. (2); Henderson, S. 33; Huntington, P. 40; Johnson, O. 16(1); Jones, N. 7(1); Kalala, J. 13(2); Kiernan, R. 1(2); Macdonald, S. 26; Obika, J. 11; Parkes, T. (1); Phillip, A. (3); Russell, A. 2(12); Smith, N. 35(5); Sproule, I. 2; Stam, S. 3; Stewart, C. 1(4); Sullivan, J. 13; Tudur Jones, O. 12(2); Tutte, A. 12(3); Upson, E. 15(8); Virgo, A. 28(5); Welsh, A. 31(3); Williams, A. 27(10); Williams, S. 23(13); Williams, G. 11(1); Wotton, P. 23.
Goals – League (56): Bowditch 15, Williams A 6, Huntington 5, Virgo 5 (2 pens), Macdonald 4 (1 pen), Welsh 4, Johnson 3, Obika 3, Freeman 2, Tutte 2, Williams S 2, Wotton 2 (1 pen), Alcock 1, Williams G 1, own goal 1.
Carling Cup (0).
FA Cup (3): Williams A 2, Upson 1.
J Paint Trophy (1): Welsh 1.
Ground: Huish Park, Lufton Way, Yeovil, Somerset BA22 8YF. Telephone: (01935) 423 662.
Record Attendance: 16,318 v Sunderland, FA Cup 4th rd, 29 January 1949 (at Huish). 9,527 v Leeds U, FL 1, 25 April 2008 (at Huish Park).
Capacity: 9,665.
Manager: Terry Skiverton.
Secretary: Jean Cotton.
Most League Goals: 90, FL 2, 2004–05.
Highest League Goalscorer in Season: Phil Jevons, 27, 2004–05.
Most League Goals in Total Aggregate: Phil Jevons, 42, 2004–06.
Most Capped Player: Andrejs Stolcers, 1 (81) Latvia and Arron Davies, 1, Wales.
Most League Appearances: Terry Skiverton, 195, 2003–09.
Honours – Football League: Championship 2 – Winners 2004–05. **Football Conference:** Champions – 2002–03. **FA Trophy:** Winners 2001–02.
Colours: Green and white hooped shirts with green sleeves and black trim, white shorts, white stockings.

LEAGUE POSITIONS: FA PREMIER from 1992–93 and DIVISION 1 1985–86 to 1991–92

	2009–10	2008–09	2007–08	2006–07	2005–06	2004–05	2003–04	2002–03	2001–02	2000–01	1999–2000	1998–99	1997–98
Arsenal	3	4	3	4	4	2	1	2	1	2	2	2	1
Aston Villa	6	6	6	11	16	10	6	16	8	8	6	6	7
Barnsley	–	–	–	–	–	–	–	–	–	–	–	–	19
Birmingham C	9	–	19	–	18	12	10	13	–	–	–	–	–
Blackburn R	10	15	7	10	6	15	15	6	10	–	–	19	6
Bolton W	14	13	16	7	8	6	8	17	16	–	–	–	18
Bradford C	–	–	–	–	–	–	–	–	–	20	17	–	–
Burnley	18	–	–	–	–	–	–	–	–	–	–	–	–
Charlton Ath	–	–	–	19	13	11	7	12	14	9	–	18	–
Chelsea	1	3	2	2	1	1	2	4	6	6	5	3	4
Coventry C	–	–	–	–	–	–	–	–	–	19	14	15	11
Crystal Palace	–	–	–	–	–	18	–	–	–	–	–	–	20
Derby Co	–	–	20	–	–	–	–	–	–	19	17	16	8
Everton	8	5	5	6	11	4	17	7	15	16	13	14	17
Fulham	12	7	17	16	12	13	9	14	13	–	–	–	–
Hull C	19	17	–	–	–	–	–	–	–	–	–	–	–
Ipswich T	–	–	–	–	–	–	–	–	18	5	–	–	–
Leeds U	–	–	–	–	–	–	19	15	5	4	3	4	5
Leicester C	–	–	–	–	–	–	18	–	20	13	8	10	10
Liverpool	7	2	4	3	3	5	4	5	2	3	4	7	3
Luton T	–	–	–	–	–	–	–	–	–	–	–	–	–
Manchester C	5	10	9	14	15	8	16	9	–	18	–	–	–
Manchester U	2	1	1	1	2	3	3	1	3	1	1	1	2
Middlesbrough	–	19	13	12	14	7	11	11	12	14	12	9	–
Millwall	–	–	–	–	–	–	–	–	–	–	–	–	–
Newcastle U	–	18	12	13	7	14	5	3	4	11	11	13	13
Norwich C	–	–	–	–	–	19	–	–	–	–	–	–	–
Nottingham F	–	–	–	–	–	–	–	–	–	–	–	20	–
Notts Co	–	–	–	–	–	–	–	–	–	–	–	–	–
Oldham Ath	–	–	–	–	–	–	–	–	–	–	–	–	–
Oxford U	–	–	–	–	–	–	–	–	–	–	–	–	–
Portsmouth	20	14	8	9	17	16	13	–	–	–	–	–	–
QPR	–	–	–	–	–	–	–	–	–	–	–	–	–
Reading	–	–	18	8	–	–	–	–	–	–	–	–	–
Sheffield U	–	–	–	18	–	–	–	–	–	–	–	–	–
Sheffield W	–	–	–	–	–	–	–	–	–	–	19	12	16
Southampton	–	–	–	–	–	20	12	8	11	10	15	17	12
Stoke C	11	12	–	–	–	–	–	–	–	–	–	–	–
Sunderland	13	16	15	–	20	–	–	20	17	7	7	–	–
Swindon T	–	–	–	–	–	–	–	–	–	–	–	–	–
Tottenham H	4	8	11	5	5	9	14	10	9	12	10	11	14
Watford	–	–	–	20	–	–	–	–	–	–	20	–	–
WBA	–	20	–	–	19	17	–	19	–	–	–	–	–
West Ham U	17	9	10	15	9	–	–	18	7	15	9	5	8
Wigan Ath	16	11	14	17	10	–	–	–	–	–	–	–	–
Wimbledon	–	–	–	–	–	–	–	–	–	–	18	16	15
Wolverhampton W	15	–	–	–	–	–	20	–	–	–	–	–	–

1996-97	1995-96	1994-95	1993-94	1992-93	1991-92	1990-91	1989-90	1988-89	1987-88	1986-87	1985-86	
3	5	12	4	10	4	1	4	1	6	4	7	Arsenal
5	4	18	10	2	7	17	2	17	–	22	16	Aston Villa
–	–	–	–	–	–	–	–	–	–	–	–	Barnsley
–	–	–	–	–	–	–	–	–	–	–	21	Birmingham C
13	7	1	2	4	–	–	–	–	–	–	–	Blackburn R
–	20	–	–	–	–	–	–	–	–	–	–	Bolton W
–	–	–	–	–	–	–	–	–	–	–	–	Bradford C
–	–	–	–	–	–	–	–	–	–	–	–	Burnley
–	–	–	–	–	–	–	19	14	17	19	–	Charlton Ath
6	11	11	14	11	14	11	5	–	18	14	6	Chelsea
17	16	16	11	15	19	16	12	7	10	10	17	Coventry C
–	–	19	–	20	10	3	15	–	–	–	–	Crystal Palace
12	–	–	–	–	20	16	5	15	–	–	–	Derby Co
15	6	15	17	13	12	9	6	8	4	1	2	Everton
–	–	–	–	–	–	–	–	–	–	–	–	Fulham
–	–	–	–	–	–	–	–	–	–	–	–	Hull C
–	–	22	19	16	–	–	–	–	–	–	20	Ipswich T
11	13	5	5	17	1	4	–	–	–	–	–	Leeds U
9	–	21	–	–	–	–	–	–	–	20	19	Leicester C
4	3	4	8	6	6	2	1	2	1	2	1	Liverpool
–	–	–	–	–	20	18	17	16	9	7	9	Luton T
–	18	17	16	9	5	5	14	–	–	21	15	Manchester C
1	1	2	1	1	2	6	13	11	2	11	4	Manchester U
19	12	–	–	21	–	–	–	18	–	–	–	Middlesbrough
–	–	–	–	–	–	–	20	10	–	–	–	Millwall
2	2	6	3	–	–	–	–	20	8	17	11	Newcastle U
–	–	20	12	3	18	15	10	4	14	5	–	Norwich C
20	9	3	–	22	8	8	9	3	3	8	8	Nottingham F
–	–	–	–	–	21	–	–	–	–	–	–	Notts Co
–	–	–	21	19	17	–	–	–	–	–	–	Oldham Ath
–	–	–	–	–	–	–	–	–	21	18	18	Oxford U
–	–	–	–	–	–	–	–	–	19	–	–	Portsmouth
–	19	8	9	5	11	12	11	9	5	16	13	QPR
–	–	–	–	–	–	–	–	–	–	–	–	Reading
–	–	–	20	14	9	13	–	–	–	–	–	Sheffield U
7	15	13	7	7	3	–	18	15	11	13	5	Sheffield W
16	17	10	18	18	16	14	7	13	12	12	14	Southampton
–	–	–	–	–	–	–	–	–	–	–	–	Stoke C
18	–	–	–	–	–	19	–	–	–	–	–	Sunderland
–	–	–	22	–	–	–	–	–	–	–	–	Swindon T
10	8	7	15	8	15	10	3	6	13	3	10	Tottenham H
–	–	–	–	–	–	–	–	–	20	9	12	Watford
–	–	–	–	–	–	–	–	–	–	–	22	WBA
14	10	14	13	–	22	–	–	19	16	15	3	West Ham U
–	–	–	–	–	–	–	–	–	–	–	–	Wigan Ath
8	14	9	6	12	13	7	8	12	7	6	–	Wimbledon
–	–	–	–	–	–	–	–	–	–	–	–	Wolverhampton W

LEAGUE POSITIONS: DIVISION 1 from 1992–93, CHAMPIONSHIP from 2004–05 and DIVISION 2 1985–86 to 1991–92

	2009–10	2008–09	2007–08	2006–07	2005–06	2004–05	2003–04	2002–03	2001–02	2000–01	1999–2000	1998–99	1997–98
Aston Villa	–	–	–	–	–	–	–	–	–	–	–	–	–
Barnsley	18	20	18	20	–	–	–	–	23	16	4	13	–
Birmingham C	–	2	–	2	–	–	–	–	5	5	5	4	7
Blackburn R	–	–	–	–	–	–	–	–	–	2	11	–	–
Blackpool	6	16	19	–	–	–	–	–	–	–	–	–	–
Bolton W	–	–	–	–	–	–	–	–	–	3	6	6	–
Bournemouth	–	–	–	–	–	–	–	–	–	–	–	–	–
Bradford C	–	–	–	–	–	–	23	19	15	–	–	2	13
Brentford	–	–	–	–	–	–	–	–	–	–	–	–	–
Brighton & HA	–	–	–	–	24	20	–	23	–	–	–	–	–
Bristol C	10	10	4	–	–	–	–	–	–	–	–	24	–
Bristol R	–	–	–	–	–	–	–	–	–	–	–	–	–
Burnley	–	5	13	15	17	13	19	16	7	7	–	–	–
Bury	–	–	–	–	–	–	–	–	–	–	–	22	17
Cambridge U	–	–	–	–	–	–	–	–	–	–	–	–	–
Cardiff C	4	7	12	13	11	16	13	–	–	–	–	–	–
Carlisle U	–	–	–	–	–	–	–	–	–	–	–	–	–
Charlton Ath	–	24	11	–	–	–	–	–	–	–	1	–	4
Chelsea	–	–	–	–	–	–	–	–	–	–	–	–	–
Colchester U	–	–	24	10	–	–	–	–	–	–	–	–	–
Coventry C	19	17	21	17	8	19	12	20	11	–	–	–	–
Crewe Alex	21	–	–	–	22	21	18	–	22	14	19	18	11
Crystal Palace	–	15	5	12	6	–	6	14	10	21	15	14	–
Derby Co	14	18	–	3	20	4	20	18	–	–	–	–	–
Doncaster R	12	14	–	–	–	–	–	–	–	–	–	–	–
Fulham	–	–	–	–	–	–	–	–	–	1	9	–	–
Gillingham	–	–	–	–	–	22	21	11	12	13	–	–	–
Grimsby T	–	–	–	–	–	–	–	24	19	18	20	11	–
Huddersfield T	–	–	–	–	–	–	–	–	–	22	8	10	16
Hull C	–	–	3	21	18	–	–	–	–	–	–	–	–
Ipswich T	15	9	8	14	15	3	5	7	–	–	3	3	5
Leeds U	–	–	–	24	5	14	–	–	–	–	–	–	–
Leicester C	5	–	22	19	16	15	–	2	–	–	–	–	–
Luton T	–	–	–	23	10	–	–	–	–	–	–	–	–
Manchester C	–	–	–	–	–	–	–	–	1	–	2	–	22
Middlesbrough	11	–	–	–	–	–	–	–	–	–	–	–	2
Millwall	–	–	–	–	23	10	10	9	4	–	–	–	–
Newcastle U	1	–	–	–	–	–	–	–	–	–	–	–	–
Norwich C	–	22	17	16	9	–	1	8	6	15	12	9	15
Nottingham F	3	19	–	–	–	23	14	6	16	11	14	–	1
Notts Co	–	–	–	–	–	–	–	–	–	–	–	–	–
Oldham Ath	–	–	–	–	–	–	–	–	–	–	–	–	–
Oxford U	–	–	–	–	–	–	–	–	–	–	–	23	12
Peterborough U	24	–	–	–	–	–	–	–	–	–	–	–	–
Plymouth Arg	23	21	10	11	14	17	–	–	–	–	–	–	–
Port Vale	–	–	–	–	–	–	–	–	–	–	23	21	19
Portsmouth	–	–	–	–	–	–	–	1	17	20	18	19	20
Preston NE	17	6	15	7	4	5	15	12	8	4	–	–	–
QPR	13	11	14	18	21	11	–	–	–	23	10	20	21

1996–97	1995–96	1994–95	1993–94	1992–93	1991–92	1990–91	1989–90	1988–89	1987–88	1986–87	1985–86	
–	–	–	–	–	–	–	–	–	2	–	–	Aston Villa
2	10	6	18	13	16	8	19	7	14	11	12	Barnsley
10	15	–	22	19	–	–	–	23	19	19	–	Birmingham C
–	–	–	–	–	6	19	5	5	5	12	19	Blackburn R
–	–	–	–	–	–	–	–	–	–	–	–	Blackpool
1	–	3	14	–	–	–	–	–	–	–	–	Bolton W
–	–	–	–	–	–	–	22	12	17	–	–	Bournemouth
21	–	–	–	–	–	–	23	14	4	10	13	Bradford C
–	–	–	–	22	–	–	–	–	–	–	–	Brentford
–	–	–	–	–	23	6	18	19	–	22	11	Brighton & HA
–	–	23	13	15	17	9	–	–	–	–	–	Bristol C
–	–	–	–	24	13	13	–	–	–	–	–	Bristol R
–	–	22	–	–	–	–	–	–	–	–	–	Burnley
–	–	–	–	–	–	–	–	–	–	–	–	Bury
–	–	–	23	5	–	–	–	–	–	–	–	Cambridge U
–	–	–	–	–	–	–	–	–	–	–	–	Cardiff C
–	–	–	–	–	–	–	–	–	–	–	20	Carlisle U
15	6	15	11	12	7	16	–	–	–	–	2	Charlton Ath
–	–	–	–	–	–	–	–	1	–	–	–	Chelsea
–	–	–	–	–	–	–	–	–	–	–	–	Colchester U
–	–	–	–	–	–	–	–	–	–	–	–	Coventry C
–	–	–	–	–	–	–	–	–	–	–	–	Crewe Alex
6	3	–	1	–	–	–	–	3	6	6	5	Crystal Palace
–	2	9	6	8	3	–	–	–	–	1	–	Derby Co
–	–	–	–	–	–	–	–	–	–	–	–	Doncaster R
–	–	–	–	–	–	–	–	–	–	–	22	Fulham
–	–	–	–	–	–	–	–	–	–	–	–	Gillingham
22	17	10	16	9	19	–	–	–	–	21	15	Grimsby T
20	8	–	–	–	–	–	–	–	23	17	16	Huddersfield T
–	–	–	–	–	–	24	14	21	15	14	6	Hull C
4	7	–	–	–	1	14	9	8	8	5	–	Ipswich T
–	–	–	–	–	–	–	1	10	7	4	14	Leeds U
–	5	–	4	6	4	22	13	15	13	–	–	Leicester C
–	24	16	20	20	–	–	–	–	–	–	–	Luton T
14	–	–	–	–	–	–	–	2	9	–	–	Manchester C
–	–	1	9	–	2	7	21	–	3	–	21	Middlesbrough
–	22	12	3	7	15	5	–	–	1	16	9	Millwall
–	–	–	–	1	20	11	3	–	–	–	–	Newcastle U
13	16	–	–	–	–	–	–	–	–	–	1	Norwich C
–	–	–	2	–	–	–	–	–	–	–	–	Nottingham F
–	–	24	7	17	–	4	–	–	–	–	–	Notts Co
23	18	14	–	–	–	1	8	16	10	3	8	Oldham Ath
17	–	–	23	14	21	10	17	17	–	–	–	Oxford U
–	–	–	24	10	–	–	–	–	–	–	–	Peterborough U
–	–	–	–	–	22	18	16	18	16	7	–	Plymouth Arg
8	12	17	–	–	24	15	11	–	–	–	–	Port Vale
7	21	18	17	3	9	17	12	20	–	2	4	Portsmouth
–	–	–	–	–	–	–	–	–	–	–	–	Preston NE
9	–	–	–	–	–	–	–	–	–	–	–	QPR

LEAGUE POSITIONS: DIVISION 1 from 1992–93, CHAMPIONSHIP from 2004–05 and DIVISION 2 1985–86 to 1991–92 (cont.)

	2009-10	2008-09	2007-08	2006-07	2005-06	2004-05	2003-04	2002-03	2001-02	2000-01	1999-2000	1998-99	1997-98
Reading	9	4	–	–	1	7	9	4	–	–	–	–	24
Rotherham U	–	–	–	–	–	24	17	15	21	–	–	–	–
Scunthorpe U	20	–	23	–	–	–	–	–	–	–	–	–	–
Sheffield U	8	3	9	–	2	8	8	3	13	10	16	8	6
Sheffield W	22	12	16	9	19	–	–	22	20	17	–	–	–
Shrewsbury T	–	–	–	–	–	–	–	–	–	–	–	–	–
Southampton	–	23	20	6	12	–	–	–	–	–	–	–	–
Southend U	–	–	–	22	–	–	–	–	–	–	–	–	–
Stockport Co	–	–	–	–	–	–	–	–	24	19	17	16	8
Stoke C	–	–	2	8	13	12	11	21	–	–	–	–	23
Sunderland	–	–	–	1	–	1	3	–	–	–	–	1	3
Swansea C	7	8	–	–	–	–	–	–	–	–	–	–	–
Swindon T	–	–	–	–	–	–	–	–	–	–	24	17	18
Tranmere R	–	–	–	–	–	–	–	–	–	24	13	15	14
Walsall	–	–	–	–	–	–	22	17	18	–	22	–	–
Watford	16	13	6	–	3	18	16	13	14	9	–	5	–
WBA	2	–	1	4	–	–	2	–	2	6	21	12	10
West Ham U	–	–	–	–	–	6	4	–	–	–	–	–	–
Wigan Ath	–	–	–	–	–	2	7	–	–	–	–	–	–
Wimbledon	–	–	–	–	–	–	24	10	9	8	–	–	–
Wolverhampton W	–	1	7	5	7	9	–	5	3	12	7	7	9

LEAGUE POSITIONS: DIVISION 2 from 1992–93, LEAGUE 1 from 2004–05 and DIVISION 3 1985–86 to 1991–92

	2009-10	2008-09	2007-08	2006-07	2005-06	2004-05	2003-04	2002-03	2001-02	2000-01	1999-2000	1998-99	1997-98
Aldershot	–	–	–	–	–	–	–	–	–	–	–	–	–
Barnet	–	–	–	–	–	–	–	–	–	–	–	–	–
Barnsley	–	–	–	–	5	13	12	19	–	–	–	–	–
Birmingham C	–	–	–	–	–	–	–	–	–	–	–	–	–
Blackpool	–	–	–	3	19	16	14	13	16	–	22	14	12
Bolton W	–	–	–	–	–	–	–	–	–	–	–	–	–
Bournemouth	–	–	21	19	17	8	9	–	21	7	16	7	9
Bradford C	–	–	–	22	11	11	–	–	–	–	–	–	–
Brentford	9	–	–	24	3	4	17	16	3	14	17	–	21
Brighton & HA	13	16	7	18	–	–	4	–	1	–	–	–	–
Bristol C	–	–	–	2	9	7	3	3	7	9	9	–	2
Bristol R	11	11	16	–	–	–	–	–	–	21	7	13	5
Burnley	–	–	–	–	–	–	–	–	–	–	2	15	20
Bury	–	–	–	–	–	–	–	–	22	16	15	–	–
Cambridge U	–	–	–	–	–	–	–	–	24	19	19	–	–
Cardiff C	–	–	–	–	–	–	–	6	4	–	21	–	–
Carlisle U	14	20	4	8	–	–	–	–	–	–	–	–	23
Charlton Ath	4	–	–	–	–	–	–	–	–	–	–	–	–

1996–97	1995–96	1994–95	1993–94	1992–93	1991–92	1990–91	1989–90	1988–89	1987–88	1986–87	1985–86	
18	19	2	–	–	–	–	–	–	22	13	–	Reading
–	–	–	–	–	–	–	–	–	–	–	–	Rotherham U
–	–	–	–	–	–	–	–	–	–	–	–	Scunthorpe U
5	9	8	–	–	–	–	2	–	21	9	7	Sheffield U
–	–	–	–	–	–	3	–	–	–	–	–	Sheffield W
–	–	–	–	–	–	–	–	22	18	18	17	Shrewsbury T
–	–	–	–	–	–	–	–	–	–	–	–	Southampton
24	14	13	15	18	12	–	–	–	–	–	–	Southend U
–	–	–	–	–	–	–	–	–	–	–	–	Stockport Co
12	4	11	10	–	–	–	24	13	11	8	10	Stoke C
–	1	20	12	21	18	–	6	11	–	20	18	Sunderland
–	–	–	–	–	–	–	–	–	–	–	–	Swansea C
19	–	21	–	5	8	21	4	6	12	–	–	Swindon T
11	13	5	5	4	14	–	–	–	–	–	–	Tranmere R
–	–	–	–	–	–	–	–	24	–	–	–	Walsall
–	23	7	19	16	10	20	15	4	–	–	–	Watford
16	11	19	21	–	–	23	20	9	20	15	–	WBA
–	–	–	–	2	–	2	7	–	–	–	–	West Ham U
–	–	–	–	–	–	–	–	–	–	–	–	Wigan Ath
–	–	–	–	–	–	–	–	–	–	–	3	Wimbledon
3	20	4	8	11	11	12	10	–	–	–	–	Wolverhampton W

1996–97	1995–96	1994–95	1993–94	1992–93	1991–92	1990–91	1989–90	1988–89	1987–88	1986–87	1985–86	
–	–	–	–	–	–	–	–	24	20	–	–	Aldershot
–	–	–	24	–	–	–	–	–	–	–	–	Barnet
–	–	1	–	–	–	–	–	–	–	–	–	Barnsley
–	–	–	–	–	2	12	7	–	–	–	–	Birmingham C
7	3	12	20	18	–	–	23	19	10	9	12	Blackpool
–	–	–	–	2	13	4	6	10	–	21	18	Bolton W
16	14	19	17	17	8	9	–	–	–	1	15	Bournemouth
–	6	14	7	10	16	8	–	–	–	–	–	Bradford C
4	15	2	16	–	1	6	13	7	12	11	10	Brentford
–	23	16	14	9	–	–	–	–	2	–	–	Brighton & HA
5	13	–	–	–	–	2	11	5	6	9	–	Bristol C
17	10	4	8	–	–	–	1	5	8	19	16	Bristol R
9	17	–	6	13	–	–	–	–	–	–	–	Burnley
1	–	–	–	–	21	7	5	13	14	16	20	Bury
–	–	20	10	–	–	1	–	–	–	–	–	Cambridge U
–	–	22	19	–	–	–	21	16	–	–	22	Cardiff C
–	21	–	–	–	–	–	–	–	–	22	–	Carlisle U
–	–	–	–	–	–	–	–	–	–	–	–	Charlton Ath

	2009–10	2008–09	2007–08	2006–07	2005–06	2004–05	2003–04	2002–03	2001–02	2000–01	1999–2000	1998–99	1997–98
Cheltenham T	–	23	19	17	–	–	–	21	–	–	–	–	–
Chester C	–	–	–	–	–	–	–	–	–	–	–	–	–
Chesterfield	–	–	–	21	16	17	20	20	18	–	24	9	10
Colchester U	8	12	–	–	2	15	11	12	15	17	18	18	–
Crewe Alex	–	22	20	13	–	–	–	2	–	–	–	–	–
Darlington	–	–	–	–	–	–	–	–	–	–	–	–	–
Derby Co	–	–	–	–	–	–	–	–	–	–	–	–	–
Doncaster R	–	–	3	11	8	10	–	–	–	–	–	–	–
Exeter C	18	–	–	–	–	–	–	–	–	–	–	–	–
Fulham	–	–	–	–	–	–	–	–	–	–	–	1	6
Gillingham	21	–	22	16	14	–	–	–	–	–	3	4	8
Grimsby T	–	–	–	–	–	–	21	–	–	–	–	–	3
Hartlepool U	20	19	15	–	21	6	6	–	–	–	–	–	–
Hereford U	–	24	–	–	–	–	–	–	–	–	–	–	–
Huddersfield T	6	9	10	15	4	9	–	22	6	–	–	–	–
Hull C	–	–	–	–	–	2	–	–	–	–	–	–	–
Leeds U	2	4	5	–	–	–	–	–	–	–	–	–	–
Leiceser C	–	1	–	–	–	–	–	–	–	–	–	–	–
Leyton Orient	17	14	14	20	–	–	–	–	–	–	–	–	–
Lincoln C	–	–	–	–	–	–	–	–	–	–	–	23	–
Luton T	–	–	24	–	–	1	10	9	–	22	13	12	17
Macclesfield T	–	–	–	–	–	–	–	–	–	–	–	24	–
Manchester C	–	–	–	–	–	–	–	–	–	–	–	3	–
Mansfield T	–	–	–	–	–	–	–	23	–	–	–	–	–
Middlesbrough	–	–	–	–	–	–	–	–	–	–	–	–	–
Millwall	3	5	17	10	–	–	–	–	–	1	5	10	18
Newport Co	–	–	–	–	–	–	–	–	–	–	–	–	–
Northampton T	–	21	9	14	–	–	–	24	20	18	–	22	4
Norwich C	1	–	–	–	–	–	–	–	–	–	–	–	–
Nottingham F	–	–	2	4	7	–	–	–	–	–	–	–	–
Notts Co	–	–	–	–	–	–	23	15	19	8	8	16	–
Oldham Ath	16	10	8	6	10	19	15	5	9	15	14	20	13
Oxford U	–	–	–	–	–	–	–	–	–	24	20	–	–
Peterborough U	–	2	–	–	–	23	18	11	17	12	–	–	–
Plymouth Arg	–	–	–	–	–	–	1	8	–	–	–	–	22
Port Vale	–	–	23	12	13	18	7	17	14	11	–	–	–
Preston NE	–	–	–	–	–	–	–	–	–	–	1	5	15
QPR	–	–	–	–	–	–	2	4	8	–	–	–	–
Reading	–	–	–	–	–	–	–	–	2	3	10	11	–
Rotherham U	–	–	–	23	20	–	–	–	–	2	–	–	–
Rushden & D	–	–	–	–	–	22	–	–	–	–	–	–	–
Scunthorpe U	–	6	–	1	12	–	–	–	–	–	23	–	–
Sheffield U	–	–	–	–	–	–	–	–	–	–	–	–	–
Sheffield W	–	–	–	–	–	5	16	–	–	–	–	–	–
Shrewsbury T	–	–	–	–	–	–	–	–	–	–	–	–	–
Southampton	7	–	–	–	–	–	–	–	–	–	–	–	–
Southend U	23	8	6	–	1	–	–	–	–	–	–	–	24
Stockport Co	24	18	–	–	–	24	19	14	–	–	–	–	–
Stoke C	–	–	–	–	–	–	–	–	5	5	6	8	–

1996-97	1995-96	1994-95	1993-94	1992-93	1991-92	1990-91	1989-90	1988-89	1987-88	1986-87	1985-86	
–	–	–	–	–	–	–	–	–	–	–	–	Cheltenham T
–	–	23	–	24	18	19	16	8	15	15	–	Chester C
10	7	–	–	–	–	–	–	22	18	17	17	Chesterfield
–	–	–	–	–	–	–	–	–	–	–	–	Colchester U
6	5	3	–	–	–	22	12	–	–	–	–	Crewe Alex
–	–	–	–	–	24	–	–	–	–	23	13	Darlington
–	–	–	–	–	–	–	–	–	–	–	3	Derby Co
–	–	–	–	–	–	–	–	–	24	13	11	Doncaster R
–	–	–	22	19	20	16	–	–	–	–	–	Exeter C
–	–	–	21	12	9	21	20	4	9	18	–	Fulham
11	–	–	–	–	–	–	–	23	13	5	5	Gillingham
–	–	–	–	–	–	3	–	–	22	–	–	Grimsby T
–	–	–	23	16	11	–	–	–	–	–	–	Hartlepool U
–	–	–	–	–	–	–	–	–	–	–	–	Hereford U
–	–	5	11	15	3	11	8	14	–	–	–	Huddersfield T
–	24	8	9	20	14	–	–	–	–	–	–	Hull C
–	–	–	–	–	–	–	–	–	–	–	–	Leeds U
–	–	–	–	–	–	–	–	–	–	–	–	Leicester C
–	–	24	18	7	10	13	14	–	–	–	–	Leyton Orient
–	–	–	–	–	–	–	–	–	–	–	21	Lincoln C
3	–	–	–	–	–	–	–	–	–	–	–	Luton T
–	–	–	–	–	–	–	–	–	–	–	–	Macclesfield T
–	–	–	–	–	–	–	–	–	–	–	–	Manchester C
–	–	–	–	22	–	24	15	15	19	10	–	Mansfield T
–	–	–	–	–	–	–	–	–	–	2	–	Middlesbrough
14	–	–	–	–	–	–	–	–	–	–	–	Millwall
–	–	–	–	–	–	–	–	–	–	23	19	Newport Co
–	–	–	–	–	–	22	20	6	–	–	–	Northampton T
–	–	–	–	–	–	–	–	–	–	–	–	Norwich C
–	–	–	–	–	–	–	–	–	–	–	–	Nottingham F
24	4	–	–	–	–	–	3	9	4	7	8	Notts Co
–	–	–	–	–	–	–	–	–	–	–	–	Oldham Ath
–	2	7	–	–	–	–	–	–	–	–	–	Oxford U
21	19	15	–	–	6	–	–	–	–	–	–	Peterborough U
19	–	21	3	14	–	–	–	–	–	–	2	Plymouth Arg
–	–	–	2	3	–	–	–	3	11	12	–	Port Vale
15	–	–	–	21	17	17	19	6	16	–	–	Preston NE
–	–	–	–	–	–	–	–	–	–	–	–	QPR
–	–	–	1	8	12	15	10	18	–	–	–	Reading
23	16	17	15	11	–	23	9	–	21	14	14	Rotherham U
–	–	–	–	–	–	–	–	–	–	–	–	Rushden & D
–	–	–	–	–	–	–	–	–	–	–	–	Scunthorpe U
–	–	–	–	–	–	–	2	–	–	–	–	Sheffield U
–	–	–	–	–	–	–	–	–	–	–	–	Sheffield W
22	18	18	–	–	22	18	11	–	–	–	–	Shrewsbury T
–	–	–	–	–	–	–	–	–	–	–	–	Southampton
–	–	–	–	–	–	2	–	21	17	–	–	Southend U
2	9	11	4	6	5	–	–	–	–	–	–	Stockport Co
–	–	–	–	1	4	14	–	–	–	–	–	Stoke C

LEAGUE POSITIONS: DIVISION 2 from 1992–93, LEAGUE 1 from 2004–05 and DIVISION 3 1985–86 to 1991–92 (cont.)

	2009-10	2008-09	2007-08	2006-07	2005-06	2004-05	2003-04	2002-03	2001-02	2000-01	1999-2000	1998-99	1997-98
Sunderland	–	–	–	–	–	–	–	–	–	–	–	–	–
Swansea C	–	–	1	7	6	–	–	–	–	23	–	–	–
Swindon T	5	15	13	–	23	12	5	10	13	20	–	–	–
Torquay U	–	–	–	–	–	21	–	–	–	–	–	–	–
Tranmere R	19	7	11	9	18	3	8	7	12	–	–	–	–
Walsall	10	13	12	–	24	14	–	–	–	4	–	2	19
Watford	–	–	–	–	–	–	–	–	–	–	–	–	1
WBA	–	–	–	–	–	–	–	–	–	–	–	–	–
Wigan Ath	–	–	–	–	–	–	–	1	10	6	4	6	11
Wimbledon	12†	3†	–	–	22†	20†	–	–	–	–	–	–	–
Wolverhampton W	–	–	–	–	–	–	–	–	–	–	–	–	–
Wrexham	–	–	–	–	–	22	13	–	23	10	11	17	7
Wycombe W	22	–	–	–	–	24	18	11	13	12	19	14	–
Yeovil T	15	17	18	5	15	–	–	–	–	–	–	–	–
York C	–	–	–	–	–	–	–	–	–	–	–	21	16

†As Milton Keynes D

LEAGUE POSITIONS: DIVISION 3 from 1992–93, LEAGUE 2 from 2004–05 and DIVISION 4 1985–86 to 1991–92

	2009-10	2008-09	2007-08	2006-07	2005-06	2004-05	2003-04	2002-03	2001-02	2000-01	1999-2000	1998-99	1997-98
Accrington S	15	16	17	20	–	–	–	–	–	–	–	–	–
Aldershot T	6	15	–	–	–	–	–	–	–	–	–	–	–
Barnet	21	17	12	14	18	–	–	–	–	24	6	16	7
Blackpool	–	–	–	–	–	–	–	–	–	7	–	–	–
Bolton W	–	–	–	–	–	–	–	–	–	–	–	–	–
Boston U	–	–	–	23	11	16	11	15	–	–	–	–	–
Bournemouth	2	21	–	–	–	–	–	4	–	–	–	–	–
Bradford C	14	9	10	–	–	–	–	–	–	–	–	–	–
Brentford	–	1	14	–	–	–	–	–	–	–	–	1	–
Brighton & HA	–	–	–	–	–	–	–	–	–	1	11	17	23
Bristol R	–	–	–	6	12	12	15	20	23	–	–	–	–
Burnley	–	–	–	–	–	–	–	–	–	–	–	–	–
Burton Alb	13	–	–	–	–	–	–	–	–	–	–	–	–
Bury	9	4	13	21	19	17	12	7	–	–	–	–	–
Cambridge U	–	–	–	–	–	24	13	12	–	–	–	2	16
Cardiff C	–	–	–	–	–	–	–	–	–	2	–	3	21
Carlisle U	–	–	–	–	1	–	23	22	17	22	23	23	–
Cheltenham T	22	–	–	–	5	14	14	–	4	9	8	–	–
Chester C	–	23	22	18	15	20	–	–	–	–	24	14	14
Chesterfield	8	10	8	–	–	–	–	–	–	3	–	–	–
Colchester U	–	–	–	–	–	–	–	–	–	–	–	–	4

*Record expunged

	1996-97	1995-96	1994-95	1993-94	1992-93	1991-92	1990-91	1989-90	1988-89	1987-88	1986-87	1985-86
Sunderland	–	–	–	–	–	–	–	–	–	1	–	–
Swansea C	–	22	10	13	5	19	20	17	12	–	–	24
Swindon T	–	1	–	–	–	–	–	–	–	–	3	–
Torquay U	–	–	–	–	23	–	–	–	–	–	–	–
Tranmere R	–	–	–	–	–	–	5	4	–	–	–	–
Walsall	12	11	–	–	–	–	–	24	–	3	8	6
Watford	13	–	–	–	–	–	–	–	–	–	–	–
WBA	–	–	–	–	4	7	–	–	–	–	–	–
Wigan Ath	–	–	–	–	23	15	10	18	17	7	4	4
Wimbledon	–	–	–	–	–	–	–	–	–	–	–	–
Wolverhampton W	–	–	–	–	–	–	–	–	1	–	–	23
Wrexham	8	8	13	12	–	–	–	–	–	–	–	–
Wycombe W	18	12	6	–	–	–	–	–	–	–	–	–
Yeovil T	–	–	–	–	–	–	–	–	–	–	–	–
York C	20	20	9	5	–	–	–	–	–	23	20	7

	1996-97	1995-96	1994-95	1993-94	1992-93	1991-92	1990-91	1989-90	1988-89	1987-88	1986-87	1985-86
Accrington S	–	–	–	–	–	–	–	–	–	–	–	–
Aldershot T	–	–	–	–	–	*	23	22	–	–	6	16
Barnet	15	9	11	–	3	7	–	–	–	–	–	–
Blackpool	–	–	–	–	–	4	5	–	–	–	–	–
Bolton W	–	–	–	–	–	–	–	–	–	3	–	–
Boston U	–	–	–	–	–	–	–	–	–	–	–	–
Bradford C	–	–	–	–	–	–	–	–	–	–	–	–
Leeds U	–	–	–	–	–	–	–	–	–	–	–	–
Brentford	–	–	–	–	–	–	–	–	–	–	–	–
Brighton & HA	23	–	–	–	–	–	–	–	–	–	–	–
Bristol R	–	–	–	–	–	–	–	–	–	–	–	–
Burnley	–	–	–	–	–	1	6	16	16	10	22	14
Burton Alb	–	–	–	–	–	–	–	–	–	–	–	–
Bury	–	3	4	13	7	–	–	–	–	–	–	–
Cambridge U	10	16	–	–	–	–	6	8	15	11	22	–
Cardiff C	7	22	–	–	1	9	13	–	–	2	13	–
Carlisle U	3	–	1	7	18	22	20	8	12	23	–	–
Cheltenham T	–	–	–	–	–	–	–	–	–	–	–	–
Chester C	6	8	–	2	–	–	–	–	–	–	–	2
Chesterfield	–	–	3	8	12	13	18	7	–	–	–	–
Colchester U	8	7	10	17	10	–	–	24	22	9	5	6

	2009-10	2008-09	2007-08	2006-07	2005-06	2004-05	2003-04	2002-03	2001-02	2000-01	1999-2000	1998-99	1997-98
Crewe Alex	18	–	–	–	–	–	–	–	–	–	–	–	–
Dagenham & R	7	8	20	–	–	–	–	–	–	–	–	–	–
Darlington	24	12	6	11	8	8	18	14	15	20	4	11	19
Doncaster R	–	–	–	–	–	–	1	–	–	–	–	–	24
Exeter C	–	2	–	–	–	–	–	23	16	19	21	12	15
Fulham	–	–	–	–	–	–	–	–	–	–	–	–	–
Gillingham	–	5	–	–	–	–	–	–	–	–	–	–	–
Grimsby T	23	22	16	15	4	18	–	–	–	–	–	–	–
Halifax T	–	–	–	–	–	–	–	–	24	23	18	10	–
Hartlepool U	–	–	–	2	–	–	–	2	7	4	7	22	17
Hereford U	16	–	3	16	–	–	–	–	–	–	–	–	–
Huddersfield T	–	–	–	–	–	–	4	–	–	–	–	–	–
Hull C	–	–	–	–	–	–	2	13	11	6	14	21	22
Kidderminster H	–	–	–	–	–	23	16	11	10	16	–	–	–
Leyton Orient	–	–	–	–	3	11	19	18	18	5	19	6	11
Lincoln C	20	13	15	5	7	6	7	6	22	18	15	–	3
Luton T	–	24	–	–	–	–	–	–	2	–	–	–	–
Macclesfield T	19	20	19	22	17	5	20	16	13	14	13	–	2
Maidstone U	–	–	–	–	–	–	–	–	–	–	–	–	–
Mansfield T	–	–	23	17	16	13	5	–	3	13	17	8	12
Morecambe	4	11	11	–	–	–	–	–	–	–	–	–	–
Newport Co	–	–	–	–	–	–	–	–	–	–	–	–	–
Northampton T	11	–	–	–	2	7	6	–	–	–	3	–	–
Notts Co	1	19	21	13	21	19	–	–	–	–	–	–	1
Oxford U	–	–	–	–	23	15	9	8	21	–	–	–	–
Peterborough U	–	–	2	10	9	–	–	–	–	–	5	9	10
Plymouth Arg	–	–	–	–	–	–	–	–	1	12	12	13	–
Port Vale	10	18	–	–	–	–	–	–	–	–	–	–	–
Preston NE	–	–	–	–	–	–	–	–	–	–	–	–	–
Rochdale	3	6	5	9	14	9	21	19	5	8	10	19	18
Rotherham U	5	14	9	–	–	–	–	–	–	–	2	5	9
Rushden & D	–	–	–	24	22	–	1	6	–	–	–	–	–
Scarborough	–	–	–	–	–	–	–	–	–	–	–	24	6
Scunthorpe U	–	–	–	–	–	2	22	5	8	10	–	4	8
Shrewsbury T	12	7	18	7	10	21	–	24	9	15	22	15	13
Southend U	–	–	–	–	–	4	17	17	12	11	16	18	–
Stockport Co	–	–	4	8	22	–	–	–	–	–	–	–	–
Swansea C	–	–	–	–	–	3	10	21	20	–	1	7	20
Swindon T	–	–	–	3	–	–	–	–	–	–	–	–	–
Torquay U	17	–	–	24	20	–	3	9	19	21	9	20	5
Tranmere R	–	–	–	–	–	–	–	–	–	–	–	–	–
Walsall	–	–	–	1	–	–	–	–	–	–	–	–	–
Wigan Ath	–	–	–	–	–	–	–	–	–	–	–	–	–
Wimbledon	–	–	1†	4†	–	–	–	–	–	–	–	–	–
Wolverhampton W	–	–	–	–	–	–	–	–	–	–	–	–	–
Wrexham	–	–	24	19	13	–	–	3	–	–	–	–	–
Wycombe W	–	3	7	12	6	10	–	–	–	–	–	–	–
Yeovil T	–	–	–	–	–	1	8	–	–	–	–	–	–
York C	–	–	–	–	–	–	24	10	14	17	20	–	–

†As Milton Keynes D

1996–97	1995–96	1994–95	1993–94	1992–93	1991–92	1990–91	1989–90	1988–89	1987–88	1986–87	1985–86	
–	–	–	3	6	6	–	–	3	17	17	12	Crewe Alex
–	–	–	–	–	–	–	–	–	–	–	–	Dagenham & R
18	5	20	21	15	–	1	–	24	13	–	–	Darlington
19	13	9	15	16	21	11	20	23	–	–	–	Doncaster R
22	14	22	–	–	–	–	1	13	22	14	21	Exeter C
2	17	8	–	–	–	–	–	–	–	–	–	Fulham
–	2	19	16	21	11	15	14	–	–	–	–	Gillingham
–	–	–	–	–	–	–	2	9	–	–	–	Grimsby T
–	–	–	–	22	20	22	23	21	18	15	20	Halifax T
20	20	18	–	–	–	3	19	19	16	18	7	Hartlepool U
24	6	16	20	17	17	17	17	15	19	16	10	Hereford U
–	–	–	–	–	–	–	–	–	–	–	–	Huddersfield T
17	–	–	–	–	–	–	–	–	–	–	–	Hull C
–	–	–	–	–	–	–	–	–	–	–	–	Kidderminster H
16	21	–	–	–	–	–	–	6	8	7	5	Leyton Orient
9	18	12	18	8	10	14	10	10	–	24	–	Lincoln C
–	–	–	–	–	–	–	–	–	–	–	–	Luton T
–	–	–	–	–	–	–	–	–	–	–	–	Macclesfield T
–	–	–	–	–	18	19	5	–	–	–	–	Maidstone U
11	19	6	12	–	3	–	–	–	–	–	3	Mansfield T
–	–	–	–	–	–	–	–	–	–	–	–	Morecambe
–	–	–	–	–	–	–	–	24	–	–	–	Newport Co
4	11	17	22	20	16	10	–	–	–	1	8	Northampton T
–	–	–	–	–	–	–	–	–	–	–	–	Notts Co
–	–	–	–	–	–	–	–	–	–	–	–	Oxford U
–	–	–	–	–	–	4	9	17	7	10	17	Peterborough U
–	4	–	–	–	–	–	–	–	–	–	–	Plymouth Arg
–	–	–	–	–	–	–	–	–	–	–	4	Port Vale
–	1	5	5	–	–	–	–	–	–	2	23	Preston NE
14	15	15	9	11	8	12	12	18	21	21	18	Rochdale
–	–	–	–	–	2	–	–	1	–	–	–	Rotherham U
–	–	–	–	–	–	–	–	–	–	–	–	Rushden & D
12	23	21	14	13	12	9	18	5	12	–	–	Scarborough
13	12	7	11	14	5	8	11	4	4	8	15	Scunthorpe U
–	–	–	1	9	–	–	–	–	–	–	–	Shrewsbury T
–	–	–	–	–	–	3	–	–	3	9		Southend U
–	–	–	–	–	–	2	4	20	20	19	11	Stockport Co
5	–	–	–	–	–	–	–	–	6	12	–	Swansea C
–	–	–	–	–	–	–	–	–	–	–	1	Swindon T
21	24	13	6	19	–	7	15	14	5	23	24	Torquay U
–	–	–	–	–	–	–	–	2	14	20	19	Tranmere R
–	–	2	10	5	15	16	–	–	–	–	–	Walsall
1	10	14	19	–	–	–	–	–	–	–	–	Wigan Ath
–	–	–	–	–	–	–	–	–	–	–	–	Wimbledon
–	–	–	–	–	–	–	–	–	1	4	–	Wolverhampton W
–	–	–	–	2	14	24	21	7	11	9	13	Wrexham
–	–	–	4	–	–	–	–	–	–	–	–	Wycombe W
–	–	–	–	–	–	–	–	–	–	–	–	Yeovil T
–	–	–	–	4	19	21	13	11	–	–	–	York C

LEAGUE CHAMPIONSHIP HONOURS

FA PREMIER LEAGUE

Maximum points: 126

	First	Pts	Second	Pts	Third	Pts
1992–93	Manchester U	84	Aston Villa	74	Norwich C	72
1993–94	Manchester U	92	Blackburn R	84	Newcastle U	77
1994–95	Blackburn R	89	Manchester U	88	Nottingham F	77

Maximum points: 114

	First	Pts	Second	Pts	Third	Pts
1995–96	Manchester U	82	Newcastle U	78	Liverpool	71
1996–97	Manchester U	75	Newcastle U*	68	Arsenal*	68
1997–98	Arsenal	78	Manchester U	77	Liverpool	65
1998–99	Manchester U	79	Arsenal	78	Chelsea	75
1999–00	Manchester U	91	Arsenal	73	Leeds U	69
2000–01	Manchester U	80	Arsenal	70	Liverpool	69
2001–02	Arsenal	87	Liverpool	80	Manchester U	77
2002–03	Manchester U	83	Arsenal	78	Newcastle U	69
2003–04	Arsenal	90	Chelsea	79	Manchester U	75
2004–05	Chelsea	95	Arsenal	83	Manchester U	77
2005–06	Chelsea	91	Manchester U	83	Liverpool	82
2006–07	Manchester U	89	Chelsea	83	Liverpool*	68
2007–08	Manchester U	87	Chelsea	85	Arsenal	83
2008–09	Manchester U	90	Liverpool	86	Chelsea	83
2009–10	Chelsea	86	Manchester U	85	Arsenal	75
2010–11	Manchester U	80	Chelsea*	71	Manchester C	71

FOOTBALL LEAGUE CHAMPIONSHIP

Maximum points: 138

	First	Pts	Second	Pts	Third	Pts
2004–05	Sunderland	94	Wigan Ath	87	Ipswich T††	85
2005–06	Reading	106	Sheffield U	90	Watford	81
2006–07	Sunderland	88	Birmingham C	86	Derby Co	84
2007–08	WBA	81	Stoke C	79	Hull C	75
2008–09	Wolverhampton W	90	Birmingham C	83	Sheffield U††	80
2009–10	Newcastle U	102	WBA	91	Nottingham F††	79
2010–11	QPR	88	Norwich C	84	Swansea C*	80

DIVISION 1

Maximum points: 138

	First	Pts	Second	Pts	Third	Pts
1992–93	Newcastle U	96	West Ham U*	88	Portsmouth††	88
1993–94	Crystal Palace	90	Nottingham F	83	Millwall††	74
1994–95	Middlesbrough	82	Reading††	79	Bolton W	77
1995–96	Sunderland	83	Derby Co	79	Crystal Palace††	75
1996–97	Bolton W	98	Barnsley	80	Wolverhampton W††	76
1997–98	Nottingham F	94	Middlesbrough	91	Sunderland††	90
1998–99	Sunderland	105	Bradford C	87	Ipswich T††	86
1999–00	Charlton Ath	91	Manchester C	89	Ipswich T	87
2000–01	Fulham	101	Blackburn R	91	Bolton W	87
2001–02	Manchester C	99	WBA	89	Wolverhampton W††	86
2002–03	Portsmouth	98	Leicester C	92	Sheffield U††	80
2003–04	Norwich C	94	WBA	86	Sunderland††	79

FOOTBALL LEAGUE CHAMPIONSHIP 1

Maximum points: 138

2004–05	Luton T	98	Hull C	86	Tranmere R††	79
2005–06	Southend U	82	Colchester U	79	Brentford††	76
2006–07	Scunthorpe U	91	Bristol C	85	Blackpool	83
2007–08	Swansea C	92	Nottingham F	82	Doncaster R	80
2008–09	Leicester C	96	Peterborough U	89	Milton Keynes D††	87
2009–10	Norwich C	95	Leeds U	86	Millwall	85
2010–11	Brighton & HA	95	Southampton	92	Huddersfield T††	87

DIVISION 2

Maximum points: 138

1992–93	Stoke C	93	Bolton W	90	Port Vale††	89
1993–94	Reading	89	Port Vale	88	Plymouth Arg††	85
1994–95	Birmingham C	89	Brentford††	85	Crewe Alex††	83
1995–96	Swindon T	92	Oxford U	83	Blackpool††	82
1996–97	Bury	84	Stockport Co	82	Luton T††	78
1997–98	Watford	88	Bristol C	85	Grimsby T	72
1998–99	Fulham	101	Walsall	87	Manchester C	82
1999–00	Preston NE	95	Burnley	88	Gillingham	85
2000–01	Millwall	93	Rotherham U	91	Reading††	86
2001–02	Brighton & HA	90	Reading	84	Brentford*††	83
2002–03	Wigan Ath	100	Crewe Alex	86	Bristol C††	83
2003–04	Plymouth Arg	90	QPR	83	Bristol C††	82

FOOTBALL LEAGUE CHAMPIONSHIP 2

Maximum points: 138

2004–05	Yeovil T	83	Scunthorpe U*	80	Swansea C	80
2005–06	Carlisle U	86	Northampton T	83	Leyton Orient	81
2006–07	Walsall	89	Hartlepool U	88	Swindon T	85
2007–08	Milton Keynes D	97	Peterborough U	92	Hereford U	88
2008–09	Brentford	85	Exeter C	79	Wycombe W*	78
2009–10	Notts Co	93	Bournemouth	83	Rochdale	82
2010–11	Chesterfield	86	Bury	81	Wycombe W	80

DIVISION 3

Maximum points: 126

1992–93	Cardiff C	83	Wrexham	80	Barnet	79
1993–94	Shrewsbury T	79	Chester C	74	Crewe Alex	73
1994–95	Carlisle U	91	Walsall	83	Chesterfield	81

Maximum points: 138

1995–96	Preston NE	86	Gillingham	83	Bury	79
1996–97	Wigan Ath*	87	Fulham	87	Carlisle U	84
1997–98	Notts Co	99	Macclesfield T	82	Lincoln C	75
1998–99	Brentford	85	Cambridge U	81	Cardiff C	80
1999–00	Swansea C	85	Rotherham U	84	Northampton T	82
2000–01	Brighton & HA	92	Cardiff C	82	Chesterfield¶	80
2001–02	Plymouth Arg	102	Luton T	97	Mansfield T	79
2002–03	Rushden & D	87	Hartlepool U	85	Wrexham	84
2003–04	Doncaster R	92	Hull C	88	Torquay U*	81

* Won or placed on goal average (ratio)/goal difference.

†† Not promoted after play-offs. ¶ 9 pts deducted for irregularities.

FOOTBALL LEAGUE

Maximum points: a 44; *b* 60

1888–89a Preston NE	40	Aston Villa	29	Wolverhampton W	28
1889–90a Preston NE	33	Everton	31	Blackburn R	27
1890–91a Everton	29	Preston NE	27	Notts Co	26
1891–92b Sunderland	42	Preston NE	37	Bolton W	36

DIVISION 1 to 1991–92

Maximum points: a 44; *b* 52; *c* 60; *d* 68; *e* 76; *f* 84; *g* 126; *h* 120; *k* 114.

First	*Pts*	*Second*	*Pts*	*Third*	*Pts*
1892–93c Sunderland	48	Preston NE	37	Everton	36
1893–94c Aston Villa	44	Sunderland	38	Derby Co	36
1894–95c Sunderland	47	Everton	42	Aston Villa	39
1895–96c Aston Villa	45	Derby Co	41	Everton	39
1896–97c Aston Villa	47	Sheffield U*	36	Derby Co	36
1897–98c Sheffield U	42	Sunderland	37	Wolverhampton W*	35
1898–99d Aston Villa	45	Liverpool	43	Burnley	39
1899–1900d Aston Villa	50	Sheffield U	48	Sunderland	41
1900–01d Liverpool	45	Sunderland	43	Notts Co	40
1901–02d Sunderland	44	Everton	41	Newcastle U	37
1902–03d The Wednesday	42	Aston Villa*	41	Sunderland	41
1903–04d The Wednesday	47	Manchester C	44	Everton	43
1904–05d Newcastle U	48	Everton	47	Manchester C	46
1905–06e Liverpool	51	Preston NE	47	The Wednesday	44
1906–07e Newcastle U	51	Bristol C	48	Everton*	45
1907–08e Manchester U	52	Aston Villa*	43	Manchester C	43
1908–09e Newcastle U	53	Everton	46	Sunderland	44
1909–10e Aston Villa	53	Liverpool	48	Blackburn R*	45
1910–11e Manchester U	52	Aston Villa	51	Sunderland*	45
1911–12e Blackburn R	49	Everton	46	Newcastle U	44
1912–13e Sunderland	54	Aston Villa	50	Sheffield W	49
1913–14e Blackburn R	51	Aston Villa	44	Middlesbrough*	43
1914–15e Everton	46	Oldham Ath	45	Blackburn R*	43
1919–20f WBA	60	Burnley	51	Chelsea	49
1920–21f Burnley	59	Manchester C	54	Bolton W	52
1921–22f Liverpool	57	Tottenham H	51	Burnley	49
1922–23f Liverpool	60	Sunderland	54	Huddersfield T	53
1923–24f Huddersfield T*	57	Cardiff C	57	Sunderland	53
1924–25f Huddersfield T	58	WBA	56	Bolton W	55
1925–26f Huddersfield T	57	Arsenal	52	Sunderland	48
1926–27f Newcastle U	56	Huddersfield T	51	Sunderland	49
1927–28f Everton	53	Huddersfield T	51	Leicester C	48
1928–29f Sheffield W	52	Leicester C	51	Aston Villa	50
1929–30f Sheffield W	60	Derby Co	50	Manchester C*	47
1930–31f Arsenal	66	Aston Villa	59	Sheffield W	52
1931–32f Everton	56	Arsenal	54	Sheffield W	50
1932–33f Arsenal	58	Aston Villa	54	Sheffield W	51
1933–34f Arsenal	59	Huddersfield T	56	Tottenham H	49
1934–35f Arsenal	58	Sunderland	54	Sheffield W	49
1935–36f Sunderland	56	Derby Co*	48	Huddersfield T	48
1936–37f Manchester C	57	Charlton Ath	54	Arsenal	52
1937–38f Arsenal	52	Wolverhampton W	51	Preston NE	49

	First	Pts	Second	Pts	Third	Pts
1938–39f	Everton	59	Wolverhampton W	55	Charlton Ath	50
1946–47f	Liverpool	57	Manchester U*	56	Wolverhampton W	56
1947–48f	Arsenal	59	Manchester U*	52	Burnley	52
1948–49f	Portsmouth	58	Manchester U*	53	Derby Co	53
1949–50f	Portsmouth*	53	Wolverhampton W	53	Sunderland	52
1950–51f	Tottenham H	60	Manchester U	56	Blackpool	50
1951–52f	Manchester U	57	Tottenham H*	53	Arsenal	53
1952–53f	Arsenal*	54	Preston NE	54	Wolverhampton W	51
1953–54f	Wolverhampton W	57	WBA	53	Huddersfield T	51
1954–55f	Chelsea	52	Wolverhampton W*	48	Portsmouth*	48
1955–56f	Manchester U	60	Blackpool*	49	Wolverhampton W	49
1956–57f	Manchester U	64	Tottenham H*	56	Preston NE	56
1957–58f	Wolverhampton W	64	Preston NE	59	Tottenham H	51
1958–59f	Wolverhampton W	61	Manchester U	55	Arsenal*	50
1959–60f	Burnley	55	Wolverhampton W	54	Tottenham H	53
1960–61f	Tottenham H	66	Sheffield W	58	Wolverhampton W	57
1961–62f	Ipswich T	56	Burnley	53	Tottenham H	52
1962–63f	Everton	61	Tottenham H	55	Burnley	54
1963–64f	Liverpool	57	Manchester U	53	Everton	52
1964–65f	Manchester U*	61	Leeds U	61	Chelsea	56
1965–66f	Liverpool	61	Leeds U*	55	Burnley	55
1966–67f	Manchester U	60	Nottingham F*	56	Tottenham H	56
1967–68f	Manchester C	58	Manchester U	56	Liverpool	55
1968–69f	Leeds U	67	Liverpool	61	Everton	57
1969–70f	Everton	66	Leeds U	57	Chelsea	55
1970–71f	Arsenal	65	Leeds U	64	Tottenham H*	52
1971–72f	Derby Co	58	Leeds U*	57	Liverpool*	57
1972–73f	Liverpool	60	Arsenal	57	Leeds U	53
1973–74f	Leeds U	62	Liverpool	57	Derby Co	48
1974–75f	Derby Co	53	Liverpool*	51	Ipswich T	51
1975–76f	Liverpool	60	QPR	59	Manchester U	56
1976–77f	Liverpool	57	Manchester C	56	Ipswich T	52
1977–78f	Nottingham F	64	Liverpool	57	Everton	55
1978–79f	Liverpool	68	Nottingham F	60	WBA	59
1979–80f	Liverpool	60	Manchester U	58	Ipswich T	53
1980–81f	Aston Villa	60	Ipswich T	56	Arsenal	53
1981–82g	Liverpool	87	Ipswich T	83	Manchester U	78
1982–83g	Liverpool	82	Watford	71	Manchester U	70
1983–84g	Liverpool	80	Southampton	77	Nottingham F*	74
1984–85g	Everton	90	Liverpool*	77	Tottenham H	77
1985–86g	Liverpool	88	Everton	86	West Ham U	84
1986–87g	Everton	86	Liverpool	77	Tottenham H	71
1987–88h	Liverpool	90	Manchester U	81	Nottingham F	73
1988–89k	Arsenal*	76	Liverpool	76	Nottingham F	64
1989–90k	Liverpool	79	Aston Villa	70	Tottenham H	63
1990–91k	Arsenal†	83	Liverpool	76	Crystal Palace	69
1991–92g	Leeds U	82	Manchester U	78	Sheffield W	75

No official competition during 1915–19 and 1939–46; Regional Leagues operating.

* Won or placed on goal average (ratio)/goal difference.

† 2 pts deducted

Maximum points: a 44; b 56; c 60; d 68; e 76; f 84; g 126; h 132; k 138.

Year	Team	Pts	Team	Pts	Team	Pts
1892–93a	Small Heath	36	Sheffield U	35	Darwen	30
1893–94b	Liverpool	50	Small Heath	42	Notts Co	39
1894–95c	Bury	48	Notts Co	39	Newton Heath*	38
1895–96c	Liverpool*	46	Manchester C	46	Grimsby T*	42
1896–97c	Notts Co	42	Newton Heath	39	Grimsby T	38
1897–98c	Burnley	48	Newcastle U	45	Manchester C	39
1898–99d	Manchester C	52	Glossop NE	46	Leicester Fosse	45
1899–1900d	The Wednesday	54	Bolton W	52	Small Heath	46
1900–01d	Grimsby T	49	Small Heath	48	Burnley	44
1901–02d	WBA	55	Middlesbrough	51	Preston NE*	42
1902–03d	Manchester C	54	Small Heath	51	Woolwich A	48
1903–04d	Preston NE	50	Woolwich A	49	Manchester U	48
1904–05d	Liverpool	58	Bolton W	56	Manchester U	53
1905–06e	Bristol C	66	Manchester U	62	Chelsea	53
1906–07e	Nottingham F	60	Chelsea	57	Leicester Fosse	48
1907–08e	Bradford C	54	Leicester Fosse	52	Oldham Ath	50
1908–09e	Bolton W	52	Tottenham H*	51	WBA	51
1909–10e	Manchester C	54	Oldham Ath*	53	Hull C*	53
1910–11e	WBA	53	Bolton W	51	Chelsea	49
1911–12e	Derby Co*	54	Chelsea	54	Burnley	52
1912–13e	Preston NE	53	Burnley	50	Birmingham	46
1913–14e	Notts Co	53	Bradford PA*	49	Woolwich A	49
1914–15e	Derby Co	53	Preston NE	50	Barnsley	47
1919–20f	Tottenham H	70	Huddersfield T	64	Birmingham	56
1920–21f	Birmingham*	58	Cardiff C	58	Bristol C	51
1921–22f	Nottingham F	56	Stoke C*	52	Barnsley	52
1922–23f	Notts Co	53	West Ham U*	51	Leicester C	51
1923–24f	Leeds U	54	Bury*	51	Derby Co	51
1924–25f	Leicester C	59	Manchester U	57	Derby Co	55
1925–26f	Sheffield W	60	Derby Co	57	Chelsea	52
1926–27f	Middlesbrough	62	Portsmouth*	54	Manchester C	54
1927–28f	Manchester C	59	Leeds U	57	Chelsea	54
1928–29f	Middlesbrough	55	Grimsby T	53	Bradford PA*	48
1929–30f	Blackpool	58	Chelsea	55	Oldham Ath	53
1930–31f	Everton	61	WBA	54	Tottenham H	51
1931–32f	Wolverhampton W	56	Leeds U	54	Stoke C	52
1932–33f	Stoke C	56	Tottenham H	55	Fulham	50
1933–34f	Grimsby T	59	Preston NE	52	Bolton W*	51
1934–35f	Brentford	61	Bolton W*	56	West Ham U	56
1935–36f	Manchester U	56	Charlton Ath	55	Sheffield U*	52
1936–37f	Leicester C	56	Blackpool	55	Bury	52
1937–38f	Aston Villa	57	Manchester U*	53	Sheffield U	53
1938–39f	Blackburn R	55	Sheffield U	54	Sheffield W	53
1946–47f	Manchester C	62	Burnley	58	Birmingham C	55
1947–48f	Birmingham C	59	Newcastle U	56	Southampton	52
1948–49f	Fulham	57	WBA	56	Southampton	55
1949–50f	Tottenham H	61	Sheffield W*	52	Sheffield U*	52
1950–51f	Preston NE	57	Manchester C	52	Cardiff C	50
1951–52f	Sheffield W	53	Cardiff C*	51	Birmingham C	51
1952–53f	Sheffield U	60	Huddersfield T	58	Luton T	52

First	Pts	Second	Pts	Third	Pts
1953–54f Leicester C*	56	Everton	56	Blackburn R	55
1954–55f Birmingham C*	54	Luton T*	54	Rotherham U	54
1955–56f Sheffield W	55	Leeds U	52	Liverpool*	48
1956–57f Leicester C	61	Nottingham F	54	Liverpool	53
1957–58f West Ham U	57	Blackburn R	56	Charlton Ath	55
1958–59f Sheffield W	62	Fulham	60	Sheffield U*	53
1959–60f Aston Villa	59	Cardiff C	58	Liverpool*	50
1960–61f Ipswich T	59	Sheffield U	58	Liverpool	52
1961–62f Liverpool	62	Leyton Orient	54	Sunderland	53
1962–63f Stoke C	53	Chelsea*	52	Sunderland	52
1963–64f Leeds U	63	Sunderland	61	Preston NE	56
1964–65f Newcastle U	57	Northampton T	56	Bolton W	50
1965–66f Manchester C	59	Southampton	54	Coventry C	53
1966–67f Coventry C	59	Wolverhampton W	58	Carlisle U	52
1967–68f Ipswich T	59	QPR*	58	Blackpool	58
1968–69f Derby Co	63	Crystal Palace	56	Charlton Ath	50
1969–70f Huddersfield T	60	Blackpool	53	Leicester C	51
1970–71f Leicester C	59	Sheffield U	56	Cardiff C*	53
1971–72f Norwich C	57	Birmingham C	56	Millwall	55
1972–73f Burnley	62	QPR	61	Aston Villa	50
1973–74f Middlesbrough	65	Luton T	50	Carlisle U	49
1974–75f Manchester U	61	Aston Villa	58	Norwich C	53
1975–76f Sunderland	56	Bristol C*	53	WBA	53
1976–77f Wolverhampton W	57	Chelsea	55	Nottingham F	52
1977–78f Bolton W	58	Southampton	57	Tottenham H*	56
1978–79f Crystal Palace	57	Brighton & HA*	56	Stoke C	56
1979–80f Leicester C	55	Sunderland	54	Birmingham C*	53
1980–81f West Ham U	66	Notts Co	53	Swansea C*	50
1981–82g Luton T	88	Watford	80	Norwich C	71
1982–83g QPR	85	Wolverhampton W	75	Leicester C	70
1983–84g Chelsea*	88	Sheffield W	88	Newcastle U	80
1984–85g Oxford U	84	Birmingham C	82	Manchester C	74
1985–86g Norwich C	84	Charlton Ath	77	Wimbledon	76
1986–87g Derby Co	84	Portsmouth	78	Oldham Ath††	75
1987–88h Millwall	82	Aston Villa*	78	Middlesbrough	78
1988–89k Chelsea	99	Manchester C	82	Crystal Palace	81
1989–90k Leeds U*	85	Sheffield U	85	Newcastle U††	80
1990–91k Oldham Ath	88	West Ham U	87	Sheffield W	82
1991–92k Ipswich T	84	Middlesbrough	80	Derby Co	78

No official competition during 1915–19 and 1939–46; Regional Leagues operating.
* Won or placed on goal average (ratio)/goal difference.
†† Not promoted after play-offs.

DIVISION 3 to 1991–92

Maximum points: 92; 138 from 1981–82.

1958–59 Plymouth Arg	62	Hull C	61	Brentford*	57
1959–60 Southampton	61	Norwich C	59	Shrewsbury T*	52
1960–61 Bury	68	Walsall	62	QPR	60
1961–62 Portsmouth	65	Grimsby T	62	Bournemouth*	59
1962–63 Northampton T	62	Swindon T	58	Port Vale	54
1963–64 Coventry C*	60	Crystal Palace	60	Watford	58

	First	Pts	Second	Pts	Third	Pts
1964–65	Carlisle U	60	Bristol C*	59	Mansfield T	59
1965–66	Hull C	69	Millwall	65	QPR	57
1966–67	QPR	67	Middlesbrough	55	Watford	54
1967–68	Oxford U	57	Bury	56	Shrewsbury T	55
1968–69	Watford*	64	Swindon T	64	Luton T	61
1969–70	Orient	62	Luton T	60	Bristol R	56
1970–71	Preston NE	61	Fulham	60	Halifax T	56
1971–72	Aston Villa	70	Brighton & HA	65	Bournemouth*	62
1972–73	Bolton W	61	Notts Co	57	Blackburn R	55
1973–74	Oldham Ath	62	Bristol R*	61	York C	61
1974–75	Blackburn R	60	Plymouth Arg	59	Charlton Ath	55
1975–76	Hereford U	63	Cardiff C	57	Millwall	56
1976–77	Mansfield T	64	Brighton & HA	61	Crystal Palace*	59
1977–78	Wrexham	61	Cambridge U	58	Preston NE*	56
1978–79	Shrewsbury T	61	Watford*	60	Swansea C	60
1979–80	Grimsby T	62	Blackburn R	59	Sheffield W	58
1980–81	Rotherham U	61	Barnsley*	59	Charlton Ath	59
1981–82	Burnley*	80	Carlisle U	80	Fulham	78
1982–83	Portsmouth	91	Cardiff C	86	Huddersfield T	82
1983–84	Oxford U	95	Wimbledon	87	Sheffield U*	83
1984–85	Bradford C	94	Millwall	90	Hull C	87
1985–86	Reading	94	Plymouth Arg	87	Derby Co	84
1986–87	Bournemouth	97	Middlesbrough	94	Swindon T	87
1987–88	Sunderland	93	Brighton & HA	84	Walsall	82
1988–89	Wolverhampton W	92	Sheffield U*	84	Port Vale	84
1989–90	Bristol R	93	Bristol C	91	Notts Co	87
1990–91	Cambridge U	86	Southend U	85	Grimsby T*	83
1991–92	Brentford	82	Birmingham C	81	Huddersfield T	78

* Won or placed on goal average (ratio)/goal difference.

DIVISION 4 (1958–1992)
Maximum points: 92; 138 from 1981–82.

	First	Pts	Second	Pts	Third	Pts
1958–59	Port Vale	64	Coventry C*	60	York C	60
1959–60	Walsall	65	Notts Co*	60	Torquay U	60
1960–61	Peterborough U	66	Crystal Palace	64	Northampton T*	60
1961–62†	Millwall	56	Colchester U	55	Wrexham	53
1962–63	Brentford	62	Oldham Ath*	59	Crewe Alex	59
1963–64	Gillingham*	60	Carlisle U	60	Workington	59
1964–65	Brighton & HA	63	Millwall*	62	York C	62
1965–66	Doncaster R*	59	Darlington	59	Torquay U	58
1966–67	Stockport Co	64	Southport*	59	Barrow	59
1967–68	Luton T	66	Barnsley	61	Hartlepools U	60
1968–69	Doncaster R	59	Halifax T	57	Rochdale*	56
1969–70	Chesterfield	64	Wrexham	61	Swansea C	60
1970–71	Notts Co	69	Bournemouth	60	Oldham Ath	59
1971–72	Grimsby T	63	Southend U	60	Brentford	59
1972–73	Southport	62	Hereford U	58	Cambridge U	57
1973–74	Peterborough U	65	Gillingham	62	Colchester U	60
1974–75	Mansfield T	68	Shrewsbury T	62	Rotherham U	59
1975–76	Lincoln C	74	Northampton T	68	Reading	60
1976–77	Cambridge U	65	Exeter C	62	Colchester U*	59

	First	Pts	Second	Pts	Third	Pts
1977–78	Watford	71	Southend U	60	Swansea C*	56
1978–79	Reading	65	Grimsby T*	61	Wimbledon*	61
1979–80	Huddersfield T	66	Walsall	64	Newport Co	61
1980–81	Southend U	67	Lincoln C	65	Doncaster R	56
1981–82	Sheffield U	96	Bradford C*	91	Wigan Ath	91
1982–83	Wimbledon	98	Hull C	90	Port Vale	88
1983–84	York C	101	Doncaster R	85	Reading*	82
1984–85	Chesterfield	91	Blackpool	86	Darlington	85
1985–86	Swindon T	102	Chester C	84	Mansfield T	81
1986–87	Northampton T	99	Preston NE	90	Southend U	80
1987–88	Wolverhampton W	90	Cardiff C	85	Bolton W	78
1988–89	Rotherham U	82	Tranmere R	80	Crewe Alex	78
1989–90	Exeter C	89	Grimsby T	79	Southend U	75
1990–91	Darlington	83	Stockport Co*	82	Hartlepool U	82
1991–92§	Burnley	83	Rotherham U*	77	Mansfield T	77

Won or placed on goal average (ratio)/goal difference.

† Maximum points: 88 owing to Accrington Stanley's resignation. †† Not promoted after play-offs.

§ Maximum points: 126 owing to Aldershot being expelled.

DIVISION 3—SOUTH (1920–1958)

1920–21 Season as Division 3.

Maximum points: a 84; b 92.

	First	Pts	Second	Pts	Third	Pts
1920–21a	Crystal Palace	59	Southampton	54	QPR	53
1921–22a	Southampton*	61	Plymouth Arg	61	Portsmouth	53
1922–23a	Bristol C	59	Plymouth Arg*	53	Swansea T	53
1923–24a	Portsmouth	59	Plymouth Arg	55	Millwall	54
1924–25a	Swansea T	57	Plymouth Arg	56	Bristol C	53
1925–26a	Reading	57	Plymouth Arg	56	Millwall	53
1926–27a	Bristol C	62	Plymouth Arg	60	Millwall	56
1927–28a	Millwall	65	Northampton T	55	Plymouth Arg	53
1928–29a	Charlton Ath*	54	Crystal Palace	54	Northampton T*	52
1929–30a	Plymouth Arg	68	Brentford	61	QPR	51
1930–31a	Notts Co	59	Crystal Palace	51	Brentford	50
1931–32a	Fulham	57	Reading	55	Southend U	53
1932–33a	Brentford	62	Exeter C	58	Norwich C	57
1933–34a	Norwich C	61	Coventry C*	54	Reading*	54
1934–35a	Charlton Ath	61	Reading	53	Coventry C	51
1935–36a	Coventry C	57	Luton T	56	Reading	54
1936–37a	Luton T	58	Notts Co	56	Brighton & HA	53
1937–38a	Millwall	56	Bristol C	55	QPR*	53
1938–39a	Newport Co	55	Crystal Palace	52	Brighton & HA	49
1939–46	*Competition cancelled owing to war.*					
1946–47a	Cardiff C	66	QPR	57	Bristol C	51
1947–48a	QPR	61	Bournemouth	57	Walsall	51
1948–49a	Swansea T	62	Reading	55	Bournemouth	52
1949–50a	Notts Co	58	Northampton T*	51	Southend U	51
1950–51b	Nottingham F	70	Norwich C	64	Reading*	57
1951–52b	Plymouth Arg	66	Reading*	61	Norwich C	61
1952–53b	Bristol R	64	Millwall*	62	Northampton T	62
1953–54b	Ipswich T	64	Brighton & HA	61	Bristol C	56

First	Pts	Second	Pts	Third	Pts
1954–55b Bristol C	70	Leyton Orient	61	Southampton	59
1955–56b Leyton Orient	66	Brighton & HA	65	Ipswich T	64
1956–57b Ipswich T*	59	Torquay U	59	Colchester U	58
1957–58b Brighton & HA	60	Brentford*	58	Plymouth Arg	58

* Won or placed on goal average (ratio).

DIVISION 3—NORTH (1921–1958)

Maximum points: a 76; b 84; c 80; d 92.

First	Pts	Second	Pts	Third	Pts
1921–22a Stockport Co	56	Darlington*	50	Grimsby T	50
1922–23a Nelson	51	Bradford PA	47	Walsall	46
1923–24b Wolverhampton W	63	Rochdale	62	Chesterfield	54
1924–25b Darlington	58	Nelson*	53	New Brighton	53
1925–26b Grimsby T	61	Bradford PA	60	Rochdale	59
1926–27b Stoke C	63	Rochdale	58	Bradford PA	55
1927–28b Bradford PA	63	Lincoln C	55	Stockport Co	54
1928–29g Bradford C	63	Stockport Co	62	Wrexham	52
1929–30b Port Vale	67	Stockport Co	63	Darlington*	50
1930–31b Chesterfield	58	Lincoln C	57	Wrexham*	54
1931–32c Lincoln C*	57	Gateshead	57	Chester	50
1932–33b Hull C	59	Wrexham	57	Stockport Co	54
1933–34b Barnsley	62	Chesterfield	61	Stockport Co	59
1934–35b Doncaster R	57	Halifax T	55	Chester	54
1935–36b Chesterfield	60	Chester*	55	Tranmere R	55
1936–37b Stockport Co	60	Lincoln C	57	Chester	53
1937–38b Tranmere R	56	Doncaster R	54	Hull C	53
1938–39b Barnsley	67	Doncaster R	56	Bradford C	52
1939–46 . *Competition cancelled owing to war.*					
1946–47b Doncaster R	72	Rotherham U	64	Chester	56
1947–48b Lincoln C	60	Rotherham U	59	Wrexham	50
1948–49b Hull C	65	Rotherham U	62	Doncaster R	50
1949–50b Doncaster R	55	Gateshead	53	Rochdale*	51
1950–51d Rotherham U	71	Mansfield T	64	Carlisle U	62
1951–52d Lincoln C	69	Grimsby T	66	Stockport Co	59
1952–53d Oldham Ath	59	Port Vale	58	Wrexham	56
1953–54d Port Vale	69	Barnsley	58	Scunthorpe U	57
1954–55d Barnsley	65	Accrington S	61	Scunthorpe U*	58
1955–56d Grimsby T	68	Derby Co	63	Accrington S	59
1956–57d Derby Co	63	Hartlepools U	59	Accrington S*	58
1957–58d Scunthorpe U	66	Accrington S	59	Bradford C	57

* Won or placed on goal average (ratio).

PROMOTED AFTER PLAY-OFFS

(Not accounted for in previous section)

1986–87 Aldershot to Division 3.

1987–88 Swansea C to Division 3.

1988–89 Leyton Orient to Division 3.

1989–90 Cambridge U to Division 3; Notts Co to Division 2; Sunderland to Division 1.

1990–91 Notts Co to Division 1; Tranmere R to Division 2; Torquay U to Division 3.

1991–92 Blackburn R to Premier League; Peterborough U to Division 1.

1992–93 Swindon T to Premier League; WBA to Division 1; York C to Division 2.

1993–94 Leicester C to Premier League; Burnley to Division 1; Wycombe W to
Division 2.

1994–95 Huddersfield T to Division 1.

1995–96 Leicester C to Premier League; Bradford C to Division 1; Plymouth Arg to
Division 2.

1996–97 Crystal Palace to Premier League; Crewe Alex to Division 1; Northampton T
to Division 2.

1997–98 Charlton Ath to Premier League; Colchester U to Division 2.

1998–99 Watford to Premier League; Scunthorpe to Division 2.

1999–00 Peterborough U to Division 2.

2000–01 Walsall to Division 1; Blackpool to Division 2.

2001–02 Birmingham C to Premier League; Stoke C to Division 1; Cheltenham T to
Division 2.

2002–03 Wolverhampton W to Premier League; Cardiff C to Division 1;
Bournemouth to Division 2.

2003–04 Crystal Palace to Premier League; Brighton & HA to Division 1;
Huddersfield T to Division 2.

2004–05 West Ham U to Premier League; Sheffield W to Football League
Championship, Southend U to Football League Championship 1.

2005–06 Watford to Premier League; Barnsley to Football League Championship;
Cheltenham T to Football League Championship 1.

2006–07 Derby Co to Premier League; Blackpool to Football League Championship;
Bristol R to Football League Championship 1.

2007–08 Hull C to Premier League; Doncaster R to Football League Championship;
Stockport Co to Football League Championship 1.

2008–09 Burnley to Premier League; Scunthorpe U to Championship; Gillingham to
Championship 1.

2009–10 Blackpool to Premier League; Millwall to Championship; Dagenham & R to
Championship 1.

2010–11 Swansea C to Premier League; Peterborough U to Championship; Stevenage
to Championship 1.

RELEGATED CLUBS

FA PREMIER LEAGUE TO DIVISION 1

1992–93   Crystal Palace, Middlesbrough, Nottingham F
1993–94   Sheffield U, Oldham Ath, Swindon T
1994–95   Crystal Palace, Norwich C, Leicester C, Ipswich T
1995–96   Manchester C, QPR, Bolton W
1996–97   Sunderland, Middlesbrough, Nottingham F
1997–98   Bolton W, Barnsley, Crystal Palace
1998–99   Charlton Ath, Blackburn R, Nottingham F
1999–90   Wimbledon, Sheffield W, Watford
2000–01   Manchester C, Coventry C, Bradford C
2001–02   Ipswich T, Derby Co, Leicester C
2002–03   West Ham U, WBA, Sunderland
2003–04   Leicester C, Leeds U, Wolverhampton W

FA PREMIER LEAGUE TO FOOTBALL LEAGUE CHAMPIONSHIP

2004–05   Crystal Palace, Norwich C, Southampton
2005–06   Birmingham C, WBA, Sunderland
2006–07   Sheffield U, Charlton Ath, Watford
2007–08   Reading, Birmingham C, Derby Co
2008–09   Newcastle U, Middlesbrough, WBA
2009–10   Burnley, Hull C, Portsmouth
2010–11   Birmingham C, Blackpool, West Ham U

DIVISION 1 TO DIVISION 2

1898–99 Bolton W and Sheffield W
1899–1900 Burnley and Glossop
1900–01 Preston NE and WBA
1901–02 Small Heath and Manchester C
1902–03 Grimsby T and Bolton W
1903–04 Liverpool and WBA
1904–05 League extended. Bury and
        Notts Co, two bottom clubs in
        First Division, re-elected.
1905–06 Nottingham F and
        Wolverhampton W
1906–07 Derby Co and Stoke C
1907–08 Bolton W and Birmingham C
1908–09 Manchester C and Leicester
        Fosse
1909–10 Bolton W and Chelsea
1910–11 Bristol C and Nottingham F
1911–12 Preston NE and Bury
1912–13 Notts Co and Woolwich Arsenal
1913–14 Preston NE and Derby Co
1914–15 Tottenham H and Chelsea*
1919–20 Notts Co and Sheffield W
1920–21 Derby Co and Bradford PA
1921–22 Bradford C and Manchester U
1922–23 Stoke C and Oldham Ath
1923–24 Chelsea and Middlesbrough
1924–25 Preston NE and Nottingham F
1925–26 Manchester C and Notts Co
1926–27 Leeds U and WBA
1927–28 Tottenham H and Middlesbrough

1928–29 Bury and Cardiff C
1929–30 Burnley and Everton
1930–31 Leeds U and Manchester U
1931–32 Grimsby T and West Ham U
1932–33 Bolton W and Blackpool
1933–34 Newcastle U and Sheffield U
1934–35 Leicester C and Tottenham H
1935–36 Aston Villa and Blackburn R
1936–37 Manchester U and Sheffield W
1937–38 Manchester C and WBA
1938–39 Birmingham C and Leicester C
1946–47 Brentford and Leeds U
1947–48 Blackburn R and Grimsby T
1948–49 Preston NE and Sheffield U
1949–50 Manchester C and
        Birmingham C
1950–51 Sheffield W and Everton
1951–52 Huddersfield T and Fulham
1952–53 Stoke C and Derby Co
1953–54 Middlesbrough and Liverpool
1954–55 Leicester C and Sheffield W
1955–56 Huddersfield T and Sheffield U
1956–57 Charlton Ath and Cardiff C
1957–58 Sheffield W and Sunderland
1958–59 Portsmouth and Aston Villa
1959–60 Luton T and Leeds U
1960–61 Preston NE and Newcastle U
1961–62 Chelsea and Cardiff C
1962–63 Manchester C and Leyton Orient
1963–64 Bolton W and Ipswich T

1964–65 Wolverhampton W and Birmingham C
1965–66 Northampton T and Blackburn R
1966–67 Aston Villa and Blackpool
1967–68 Fulham and Sheffield U
1968–69 Leicester C and QPR
1969–70 Sunderland and Sheffield W
1970–71 Burnley and Blackpool
1971–72 Huddersfield T and Nottingham F
1972–73 Crystal Palace and WBA
1973–74 Southampton, Manchester U, Norwich C
1974–75 Luton T, Chelsea, Carlisle U
1975–76 Wolverhampton W, Burnley, Sheffield U
1976–77 Sunderland, Stoke C, Tottenham H
1977–78 West Ham U, Newcastle U, Leicester C
1978–79 QPR, Birmingham C, Chelsea
1979–80 Bristol C, Derby Co, Bolton W
1980–81 Norwich C, Leicester C, Crystal Palace
1981–82 Leeds U, Wolverhampton W, Middlesbrough
1982–83 Manchester C, Swansea C, Brighton & HA
1983–84 Birmingham C, Notts Co, Wolverhampton W
1984–85 Norwich C, Sunderland, Stoke C

1985–86 Ipswich T, Birmingham C, WBA
1986–87 Leicester C, Manchester C, Aston Villa
1987–88 Chelsea**, Portsmouth, Watford, Oxford U
1988–89 Middlesbrough, West Ham U, Newcastle U
1989–90 Sheffield W, Charlton Ath, Millwall
1990–91 Sunderland and Derby Co
1991–92 Luton T, Notts Co, West Ham U
1992–93 Brentford, Cambridge U, Bristol R
1993–94 Birmingham C, Oxford U, Peterborough U
1994–95 Swindon T, Burnley, Bristol C, Notts Co
1995–96 Millwall, Watford, Luton T
1996–97 Grimsby T, Oldham Ath, Southend U
1997–98 Manchester C, Stoke C, Reading
1998–99 Bury, Oxford U, Bristol C
1999–00 Walsall, Port Vale, Swindon T
2000–01 Huddersfield T, QPR, Tranmere R
2001–02 Crewe Alex, Barnsley, Stockport Co
2002–03 Sheffield W, Brighton & HA, Grimsby T
2003–04 Walsall, Bradford C, Wimbledon

** *Relegated after play-offs.*
* *Subsequently re-elected to Division 1 when League was extended after the War.*

FOOTBALL LEAGUE CHAMPIONSHIP TO FOOTBALL LEAGUE CHAMPIONSHIP 1

2004–05 Gillingham, Nottingham F, Rotherham U
2005–06 Crewe Alex, Millwall, Brighton & HA
2006–07 Southend U, Luton T, Leeds U
2007–08 Leicester C, Scunthorpe U, Colchester U
2008–09 Norwich C, Southampton, Charlton Ath
2009–10 Sheffield W, Plymouth Arg, Peterborough U
2010–11 Preston NE, Sheffield U, Scunthorpe U

DIVISION 2 TO DIVISION 3

1920–21 Stockport Co
1921–22 Bradford PA and Bristol C
1922–23 Rotherham Co and Wolverhampton W
1923–24 Nelson and Bristol C
1924–25 Crystal Palace and Coventry C
1925–26 Stoke C and Stockport Co
1926–27 Darlington and Bradford C
1927–28 Fulham and South Shields
1928–29 Port Vale and Clapton Orient
1929–30 Hull C and Notts Co

1930–31 Reading and Cardiff C
1931–32 Barnsley and Bristol C
1932–33 Chesterfield and Charlton Ath
1933–34 Millwall and Lincoln C
1934–35 Oldham Ath and Notts Co
1935–36 Port Vale and Hull C
1936–37 Doncaster R and Bradford C
1937–38 Barnsley and Stockport Co
1938–39 Norwich C and Tranmere R
1946–47 Swansea T and Newport Co
1947–48 Doncaster R and Millwall

1948–49 Nottingham F and Lincoln C
1949–50 Plymouth Arg and Bradford PA
1950–51 Grimsby T and Chesterfield
1951–52 Coventry C and QPR
1952–53 Southampton and Barnsley
1953–54 Brentford and Oldham Ath
1954–55 Ipswich T and Derby Co
1955–56 Plymouth Arg and Hull C
1956–57 Port Vale and Bury
1957–58 Doncaster R and Notts Co
1958–59 Barnsley and Grimsby T
1959–60 Bristol C and Hull C
1960–61 Lincoln C and Portsmouth
1961–62 Brighton & HA and Bristol R
1962–63 Walsall and Luton T
1963–64 Grimsby T and Scunthorpe U .
1964–65 Swindon T and Swansea T
1965–66 Middlesbrough and Leyton Orient
1966–67 Northampton T and Bury
1967–68 Plymouth Arg and Rotherham U
1968–69 Fulham and Bury
1969–70 Preston NE and Aston Villa
1970–71 Blackburn R and Bolton W
1971–72 Charlton Ath and Watford
1972–73 Huddersfield T and Brighton & HA
1973–74 Crystal Palace, Preston NE,
          Swindon T
1974–75 Millwall, Cardiff C, Sheffield W
1975–76 Oxford U, York C, Portsmouth
1976–77 Carlisle U, Plymouth Arg,
          Hereford U
1977–78 Blackpool, Mansfield T, Hull C
1978–79 Sheffield U, Millwall, Blackburn R
1979–80 Fulham, Burnley, Charlton Ath
1980–81 Preston NE, Bristol C, Bristol R
1981–82 Cardiff C, Wrexham, Orient
1982–83 Rotherham U, Burnley, Bolton W
1983–84 Derby Co, Swansea C, Cambridge U
1984–85 Notts Co, Cardiff C,

Wolverhampton W
1985–86 Carlisle U, Middlesbrough, Fulham
1986–87 Sunderland**, Grimsby T,
          Brighton & HA
1987–88 Huddersfield T, Reading, Sheffield
          U**
1988–89 Shrewsbury T, Birmingham C,
          Walsall
1989–90 Bournemouth, Bradford C,
          Stoke C
1990–91 WBA and Hull C
1991–92 Plymouth Arg, Brighton & HA,
          Port Vale
1992–93 Preston NE, Mansfield T,
          Wigan Ath, Chester C
1993–94 Fulham, Exeter C, Hartlepool U,
          Barnet
1994–95 Cambridge U, Plymouth Arg,
          Cardiff C, Chester C, Leyton
          Orient
1995–96 Carlisle U, Swansea C, Brighton &
          HA, Hull C
1996–97 Peterborough U, Shrewsbury T,
          Rotherham U, Notts Co
1997–98 Brentford, Plymouth Arg, Carlisle
          U, Southend U
1998–99 York C, Northampton T, Lincoln
          C, Macclesfield T
1999–00 Cardiff C, Blackpool, Scunthorpe
          U, Chesterfield
2000–01 Bristol R, Luton T, Swansea C,
          Oxford U
2001–02 Bournemouth, Bury, Wrexham,
          Cambridge U
2002–03 Cheltenham T, Huddersfield T,
          Mansfield T, Northampton T
2003–04 Grimsby T, Rushden & D, Notts
          Co, Wycombe W

FOOTBALL LEAGUE CHAMPIONSHIP 1 TO FOOTBALL LEAGUE CHAMPIONSHIP 2

2004–05 Torquay U, Wrexham, Peterborough U, Stockport Co
2005–06 Hartlepool U, Milton Keynes D, Swindon T, Walsall
2006–07 Chesterfield, Bradford C, Rotherham U, Brentford
2007–08 Bournemouth, Gillingham, Port Vale, Luton T
2008–09 Northampton T, Crewe Alex, Cheltenham T, Hereford U
2009–10 Gillingham, Wycombe W, Southend U, Stockport Co
2010–11 Dagenham & R, Bristol R, Plymouth Arg, Swindon T

DIVISION 3 TO DIVISION 4

1958–59 Rochdale, Notts Co,
          Doncaster R, Stockport Co
1959–60 Accrington S, Wrexham,
          Mansfield T, York C

1960–61 Chesterfield, Colchester U,
          Bradford C, Tranmere R
1961–62 Newport Co, Brentford,
          Lincoln C, Torquay U

138

1962–63 Bradford PA, Brighton & HA, Carlisle U, Halifax T

1963–64 Millwall, Crewe Alex, Wrexham, Notts Co

1964–65 Luton T, Port Vale, Colchester U, Barnsley

1965–66 Southend U, Exeter C, Brentford, York C

1966–67 Doncaster R, Workington, Darlington, Swansea T

1967–68 Scunthorpe U, Colchester U, Grimsby T, Peterborough U (demoted)

1968–69 Oldham Ath, Crewe Alex, Hartlepool, Northampton T

1969–70 Bournemouth, Southport, Barrow, Stockport Co

1970–71 Reading, Bury, Doncaster R, Gillingham

1971–72 Mansfield T, Barnsley, Torquay U, Bradford C

1972–73 Rotherham U, Brentford, Swansea C, Scunthorpe U

1973–74 Cambridge U, Shrewsbury T, Southport, Rochdale

1974–75 Bournemouth, Tranmere R, Watford, Huddersfield T

1975–76 Aldershot, Colchester U, Southend U, Halifax T

1976–77 Reading, Northampton T, Grimsby T, York C

1977–78 Port Vale, Bradford C, Hereford U, Portsmouth

1978–79 Peterborough U, Walsall, Tranmere R, Lincoln C

1979–80 Bury, Southend U, Mansfield T, Wimbledon

1980–81 Sheffield U, Colchester U, Blackpool, Hull C

1981–82 Wimbledon, Swindon T, Bristol C, Chester

1982–83 Reading, Wrexham, Doncaster R, Chesterfield

1983–84 Scunthorpe U, Southend U, Port Vale, Exeter C

1984–85 Burnley, Orient, Preston NE, Cambridge U

1985–86 Lincoln C, Cardiff C, Wolverhampton W, Swansea C

1986–87 Bolton W**, Carlisle U, Darlington, Newport Co

1987–88 Doncaster R, York C, Grimsby T, Rotherham U**

1988–89 Southend U, Chesterfield, Gillingham, Aldershot

1989–90 Cardiff C, Northampton T, Blackpool, Walsall

1990–91 Crewe Alex, Rotherham U, Mansfield T

1991–92 Bury, Shrewsbury T, Torquay U, Darlington

** *Relegated after play-offs.*

LEAGUE STATUS FROM 1986–1987

RELEGATED FROM LEAGUE	PROMOTED TO LEAGUE
1986–87 Lincoln C	Scarborough
1987–88 Newport Co	Lincoln C
1988–89 Darlington	Maidstone U
1989–90 Colchester U	Darlington
1990–91 —	Barnet
1991–92 —	Colchester U
1992–93 Halifax T	Wycombe W
1993–94 —	—
1994–95 —	—
1995–96 —	—
1996–97 Hereford U	Macclesfield T
1997–98 Doncaster R	Halifax T
1998–99 Scarborough	Cheltenham T
1999–2000 Chester C	Kidderminster H
2000–01 Barnet	Rushden & D
2001–02 Halifax T	Boston U
2002–03 Shrewsbury T, Exeter C	Yeovil T, Doncaster R
2003–04 Carlisle U, York C	Chester C, Shrewsbury T
2004–05 Kidderminster H, Cambridge U	Barnet, Carlisle U
2005–06 Oxford U, Rushden & D	Accrington S, Hereford U
2006–07 Boston U, Torquay U	Dagenham & R, Morecambe
2007–08 Mansfield T, Wrexham	Aldershot T, Exeter C
2008–09 Chester C, Luton T	Burton Alb, Torquay U
2009–10 Grimsby T, Darlington	Stevenage B, Oxford U
2010–11 Lincoln C, Stockport Co	Crawley T, AFC Wimbledon

Did You Know?

The Football League succeeded in organising regional fare during both world wars despite enormous difficulties. In 1914–15 the first year when hostilities had broken out, the official league programme was completed. But in 1939 the season that was three matches old was abandoned, though exactly the same fixtures were used when the competiton resumed in 1946. Unlike the Great War there was a transitional season 1945–46 to enable clubs to gradually return to normal and the FA Cup returned at the same time. In both war periods the use of guest players enabled clubs to sustain a viable standard of play when their own players were unavailable. In 1939–40 a War Cup competition was inaugurated and though the format changed, proved a successful addition to the programme. Also the start of the post-war boom in attendances had its roots in the latter stages of the Second World War.

LEAGUE TITLE WINS

FA PREMIER LEAGUE – Manchester U 12, Arsenal 3, Chelsea 3, Blackburn R 1.

FOOTBALL LEAGUE CHAMPIONSHIP – Sunderland 2, Newcastle U 1, QPR 1, Reading 1, WBA 1, Wolverhampton W 1.

LEAGUE DIVISION 1 – Liverpool 18, Arsenal 10, Everton 9, Sunderland 8, Aston Villa 7, Manchester U 7, Newcastle U 5, Sheffield W 4, Huddersfield T 3, Leeds U 3, Manchester C 3, Portsmouth 3, Wolverhampton W 3, Blackburn R 2, Burnley 2, Derby Co 2, Nottingham F 2, Preston NE 2, Tottenham H 2; Bolton W, Charlton Ath, Chelsea, Crystal Palace, Fulham, Ipswich T, Middlesbrough, Norwich C, Sheffield U, WBA 1 each.

FOOTBALL LEAGUE CHAMPIONSHIP 1 – Brighton & HA 1, Leicester C 1, Luton T 1, Norwich C 1, Scunthorpe U 1, Southend U 1, Swansea C 1.

LEAGUE DIVISION 2 – Leicester C 6, Manchester C 6, Birmingham C (one as Small Heath) 5, Sheffield W 5, Derby Co 4, Liverpool 4, Preston NE 4, Ipswich T 3, Leeds U 3, Middlesbrough 3, Notts Co 3, Stoke C 3, Aston Villa 2, Bolton W 2, Burnley 2, Bury 2, Chelsea 2, Fulham 2, Grimsby T 2, Manchester U 2, Millwall 2, Norwich C 2, Nottingham F 2, Tottenham H 2, WBA 2, West Ham U 2, Wolverhampton W 2; Blackburn R, Blackpool, Bradford C, Brentford, Brighton & HA, Bristol C, Coventry C, Crystal Palace, Everton, Huddersfield T, Luton T, Newcastle U, Plymouth Arg, QPR, Oldham Ath, Oxford U, Reading, Sheffield U, Sunderland, Swindon T, Watford, Wigan Ath 1 each.

FOOTBALL LEAGUE CHAMPIONSHIP 2 – Brentford 1, Carlisle U 1, Chesterfield 1, Milton Keynes D 1, Notts Co 1, Walsall 1, Yeovil T 1.

LEAGUE DIVISION 3 – Brentford 2, Carlisle U 2, Oxford U 2, Plymouth Arg 2, Portsmouth 2, Preston NE 2, Shrewsbury T 2; Aston Villa, Blackburn R, Bolton W, Bournemouth, Bradford C, Brighton & HA, Bristol R, Burnley, Bury, Cambridge U, Cardiff C, Coventry C, Doncaster R, Grimsby T, Hereford U, Hull C, Leyton Orient, Mansfield T, Northampton T, Notts Co, Oldham Ath, QPR, Reading, Rotherham U, Rushden & D, Southampton, Sunderland, Swansea C, Watford, Wigan Ath, Wolverhampton W, Wrexham 1 each.

LEAGUE DIVISION 4 – Chesterfield 2, Doncaster R 2, Peterborough U 2; Brentford, Brighton & HA, Burnley, Cambridge U, Darlington, Exeter C, Gillingham, Grimsby T, Huddersfield T, Lincoln C, Luton T, Mansfield T, Millwall, Northampton T, Notts Co, Port Vale, Reading, Rotherham U, Sheffield U, Southend U, Southport, Stockport Co, Swindon T, Walsall, Watford, Wimbledon, Wolverhampton W, York C 1 each.

DIVISION 3 (South) – Bristol C 3, Charlton Ath 2, Ipswich T 2, Millwall 2, Notts Co 2, Plymouth Arg 2, Swansea T 2; Brentford, Brighton & HA, Bristol R, Cardiff C, Coventry C, Crystal Palace, Fulham, Leyton Orient, Luton T, Newport Co, Norwich C, Nottingham F, Portsmouth, QPR, Reading, Southampton 1 each.

DIVISION 3 (North) – Barnsley 3, Doncaster R 3, Lincoln C 3, Chesterfield 2, Grimsby T 2, Hull C 2, Port Vale 2, Stockport Co 2; Bradford C, Bradford PA, Darlington, Derby Co, Nelson, Oldham Ath, Rotherham U, Scunthorpe U, Stoke C, Tranmere R, Wolverhampton W 1 each.

FOOTBALL LEAGUE PLAY-OFFS 2010–2011

ª *Denotes player sent off.*

CHAMPIONSHIP FIRST LEG

Nottingham F	(0) 0	Swansea C	(0) 0
Reading	(0) 0	Cardiff C	(0) 0

CHAMPIONSHIP SECOND LEG

Swansea C	(2) 3	Nottingham F	(0) 1
Cardiff C	(0) 0	Reading	(2) 3

CHAMPIONSHIP FINAL (at Wembley) Monday, 30 May 2011

Reading (0) 2 *(Allen 49 (og), Mills 57)*

Swansea C (3) 4 *(Sinclair 21 (pen), 22, 80 (pen), Dobbie 40)* 86,581

Reading: Federici; Griffin (Robson-Kanu), Harte, Karacan, Mills, Khizanishvili, Kebe, Leigertwood, Long, Hunt (Church), McAnuff.
Swansea C: De Vries; Rangel, Tate, Britton (Gower), Monk, Williams, Dyer, Allen (Moore), Borini, Dobbie (Pratley), Sinclair.
Unused substitute Tabb sent off at half-time.
Referee: P. Dowd (Staffordshire).

LEAGUE ONE FIRST LEG

Bournemouth	(0) 1	Huddersfield T	(1) 1
Milton Keynes D	(0) 3	Peterborough U	(1) 2

LEAGUE ONE SECOND LEG

Huddersfield T	(2) 3	Bournemouth	(1) 3
(aet; Huddersfield T won 4-2 on penalties.)			
Peterborough U	(1) 2	Milton Keynes D	(0) 0

LEAGUE ONE FINAL (at Old Trafford) Sunday, 29 May 2011

Huddersfield T (0) 0

Peterborough U (0) 3 *(Rowe 78, Mackail-Smith 80, McCann 85)* 48,410

Huddersfield T: Bennett; Hunt, Naysmith, Kilbane, Clarke P, Kay, Peltier, Arfield (Lee), Afobe (Rhodes), Ward (Cadamarteri), Roberts.
Peterborough U: Jones; Little, Basey (Lee), McCann, Zakuani, Bennett, Wesolowski, Rowe (Whelpdale), Mackail-Smith, Tomlin (Ball), Boyd.
Referee: S. Tanner (Somerset).

LEAGUE TWO FIRST LEG

Torquay U	(2) 2	Shrewsbury T	(0) 0
Stevenage	(2) 2	Accrington S	(0) 0

LEAGUE TWO SECOND LEG

Accrington S	(0) 0	Stevenage	(0) 1
Shrewsbury T	(0) 0	Torquay U	(0) 0

LEAGUE TWO FINAL (at Old Trafford) Saturday, 28 May 2011

Stevenage (1) 1 *(Mousinho 41)*

Torquay U (0) 0 11,484

Stevenage: Day; Henry, Laird, Mousinho, Roberts, Bostwick, Wilson, Byrom (Murphy), Charles (Beardsley), Reid (Harrison), Long.
Torquay U: Bevan; Mansell, Nicholson (Rowe-Turner), Robertson, Branston, Lathrope (Oastler), Robinson (Stevens), O'Kane, Kee, Tomlin, Zebroski.
Referee: D. Deadman (Cambridgeshire).

LEAGUE ATTENDANCES 2010–2011

FA BARCLAYCARD PREMIERSHIP ATTENDANCES

	Average Gate			Season 2010–11	
	2009–10	2010–11	+/–%	Highest	Lowest
Arsenal	59,927	60,025	+0.16	60,112	59,552
Aston Villa	38,573	37,193	–3.58	42,785	32,627
Birmingham City	25,246	25,461	+0.85	28,270	21,394
Blackburn Rovers	25,428	24,999	–1.69	29,867	21,848
Blackpool	8,611	15,779	+83.24	16,116	14,550
Bolton Wanderers	21,880	22,869	+4.52	26,881	18,139
Chelsea	41,422	41,435	+0.03	41,829	40,734
Everton	36,725	36,038	–1.87	39,673	31,808
Fulham	23,909	25,042	+4.74	25,694	23,222
Liverpool	42,863	42,820	–0.10	44,923	35,400
Manchester City	45,512	45,880	+0.81	47,393	43,077
Manchester United	74,864	75,109	+0.33	75,486	73,401
Newcastle United	43,387	47,717	+9.98	51,988	41,053
Stoke City	27,162	26,858	–1.12	27,566	25,019
Sunderland	40,355	40,011	–0.85	47,864	35,101
Tottenham Hotspur	35,794	35,703	–0.25	36,197	32,702
West Bromwich Albion	22,199	24,682	+11.19	26,196	22,846
West Ham United	33,683	33,492	–0.57	34,941	31,194
Wigan Athletic	18,006	16,812	–6.63	22,043	14,042
Wolverhampton Wanderers	28,365	27,695	–2.36	29,086	25,112

FOOTBALL LEAGUE CHAMPIONSHIP ATTENDANCES

	Average Gate			Season 2010–11	
	2009–10	2010–11	+/–%	Highest	Lowest
Barnsley	12,964	11,855	–8.55	20,309	10,250
Bristol City	14,600	14,604	+0.03	18,308	13,376
Burnley	20,653	14,930	–27.71	20,453	13,655
Cardiff City	20,717	23,193	+11.95	26,058	20,573
Coventry City	17,305	16,309	–5.76	28,184	12,292
Crystal Palace	14,770	15,390	+4.20	20,142	12,353
Derby County	29,230	25,892	–11.42	33,010	23,159
Doncaster Rovers	10,991	10,258	–6.67	14,312	7,921
Hull City	24,389	21,168	–13.21	24,110	19,714
Ipswich Town	20,840	19,614	–5.88	29,258	16,728
Leeds United	24,817	27,299	+10.00	33,622	20,747
Leicester City	23,942	23,666	–1.15	30,919	19,611
Middlesbrough	19,948	16,268	–18.45	23,550	13,712
Millwall	10,834	12,438	+14.81	16,724	8,937
Norwich City	24,671	25,386	+2.90	26,532	23,852
Nottingham Forest	23,831	23,274	–2.34	29,490	19,411
Portsmouth	18,249	15,707	–13.93	20,040	13,132
Preston North End	12,934	11,767	–9.02	18,417	8,994
Queens Park Rangers	13,348	15,635	+17.13	18,234	12,046
Reading	17,495	17,681	+1.06	23,677	14,029
Scunthorpe United	6,463	5,547	–14.17	8,122	4,190
Sheffield United	25,120	20,632	–17.87	23,728	17,496
Swansea City	15,407	15,507	+0.65	19,309	12,411
Watford	14,344	13,151	–8.32	15,538	10,620

Premiership and Football League attendance averages and highest crowd figures for 2010–11 are unofficial.

FOOTBALL LEAGUE CHAMPIONSHIP 1 ATTENDANCES

	Average Gate			Season 2010–11	
	2009–10	2010–11	+/–%	Highest	Lowest
AFC Bournemouth	5,719	7,103	+24.2	10,008	5,501
Brentford	6,017	5,172	–14.04	7,015	3,795
Brighton & Hove Albion	6,466	7,351	+13.69	8,416	6,474
Bristol Rovers	7,042	6,253	–11.2	8,340	4,829
Carlisle United	5,210	5,207	–0.06	7,412	3,354
Charlton Athletic	17,407	15,582	–10.48	24,767	12,797
Colchester United	5,529	4,246	–23.20	6,523	2,892
Dagenham & Redbridge	2,097	2,769	+32.05	4,446	1,907
Exeter City	5,832	5,393	–7.53	7,869	3,456
Hartlepool United	3,443	2,933	–14.81	4,084	2,289
Huddersfield Town	14,381	13,733	–4.51	17,024	11,462
Leyton Orient	4,937	4,581	–7.21	7,714	2,963
Milton Keynes Dons FC	10,289	8,512	–17.27	11,857	6,469
Notts County	7,352	6,586	–10.42	11,355	4,041
Oldham Athletic	4,630	4,392	–5.14	8,564	3,056
Peterborough United	8,913	6,449	–27.65	10,116	4,233
Plymouth Argyle	10,316	8,613	–16.51	14,347	4,960
Rochdale	3,443	3,537	+2.73	6,483	2,019
Sheffield Wednesday	23,179	17,817	–23.13	23,081	14,797
Southampton	20,982	22,160	+5.61	31,653	17,857
Swindon Town	8,389	8,457	+0.81	11,087	6,912
Tranmere Rovers	5,670	5,467	–3.58	12,249	4,110
Walsall	4,028	3,845	–4.54	6,015	2,072
Yeovil Town	4,664	4,291	–8.00	6,281	3,331

FOOTBALL LEAGUE CHAMPIONSHIP 2 ATTENDANCES

	Average Gate			Season 2010–11	
	2009–10	2010–11	+/–%	Highest	Lowest
Accrington Stanley	1,980	1,867	–5.71	2,815	1,356
Aldershot Town	3,085	2,487	–19.38	3,722	1,847
Barnet	2,059	2,249	+9.23	4,478	1,520
Bradford City	11,422	11,127	–2.58	15,332	10,392
Burton Albion	3,195	2,947	–7.76	4,321	1,904
Bury	3,028	3,313	+9.41	6,238	2,080
Cheltenham Town	3,185	2,980	–6.44	4,349	2,191
Chesterfield	3,849	6,972	+81.14	10,089	4,801
Crewe Alexandra	4,075	4,119	+1.08	7,183	3,171
Gillingham	6,335	5,230	–17.44	6,841	4,076
Hereford United	2,138	2,516	+17.68	3,942	1,444
Lincoln City	3,670	3,508	–4.41	7,932	2,261
Macclesfield Town	1,928	1,816	–5.81	3,915	1,067
Morecambe	2,262	2,647	+17.02	10,691	1,612
Northampton Town	4,375	4,604	+5.23	6,257	3,423
Oxford United	6,003	7,277	+21.22	9,440	6,004
Port Vale	5,079	5,532	+8.92	8,607	4,112
Rotherham United	3,817	3,667	–3.93	5,365	2,490
Shrewsbury Town	5,481	5,875	+7.19	8,817	4,343
Southend United	7,718	5,344	–30.76	6,622	4,499
Stevenage	2,589	2,899	+11.97	5,016	1,549
Stockport County	4,420	4,163	–5.81	5,470	3,335
Torquay United	2,855	2,630	–7.88	5,002	1,514
Wycombe Wanderers	5,544	4,495	–18.92	8,567	2,273

TRANSFERS 2010–2011

JUNE 2010

	From	To
7 Bailey, James J.	Crewe Alex	Derby Co
18 Batt, Shaun A.S.P.	Peterborough U	Millwall
9 Brayford, John R.	Crewe Alex	Derby Co
16 Connolly, Paul	Derby Co	Leeds U
24 Crofts, Andrew L.	Brighton & HA	Norwich C
4 Foster, Benjamin A.	Manchester U	Birmingham C
7 Fox, David L.	Colchester U	Norwich C
21 Hunt, Stephen	Hull C	Wolverhampton W
10 Kenny, Patrick	Sheffield U	QPR
29 Langmead, Kelvin S.	Shrewsbury T	Peterborough U
30 Little, Mark D.	Wolverhampton W	Peterborough U
19 Mackie, James C.	Plymouth Arg	QPR
26 Marney, Dean E.	Hull C	Burnley
1 Martin, David J.	Millwall	Derby Co
18 Mouyokolo, Steven	Hull C	Wolverhampton W
18 Shackell, Jason	Wolverhampton W	Barnsley
17 Sodje, Akpo	Sheffield W	Charlton Ath
24 Surman, Andrew R.E.	Wolverhampton W	Norwich C
25 Trotter, Liam A.	Ipswich T	Millwall

JULY 2010

	From	To
14 Adomah, Albert	Barnet	Bristol C
14 Aldred, Thomas M.	Carlisle U	Watford
22 Ashworth, Luke A.	Leyton Orient	Rotherham U
1 Ayling, Luke D.	Arsenal	Yeovil T
12 Bailey, Nicky F.	Charlton Ath	Middlesbrough
9 Barnes, Ashley L.	Plymouth Arg	Brighton & HA
9 Benayoun, Yossi S.	Liverpool	Chelsea
26 Berrett, James T.	Huddersfield T	Carlisle U
26 Bramble, Titus M.	Wigan Ath	Sunderland
30 Bruce, Alex S.	Ipswich T	Leeds U
13 Cisse, Kalifa	Reading	Bristol C
9 Collins, Michael A.	Huddersfield T	Scunthorpe U
7 Collins, Neill	Preston NE	Leeds U
21 Cresswell, Ryan A.	Bury	Rotherham U
1 Cuvelier, Florent	Portsmouth	Stoke C
16 Diagouraga, Toumani	Peterborough U	Brentford
2 Dickinson, Liam M.	Brighton & HA	Barnsley
9 Dickson, Ryan A.	Brentford	Southampton
14 Donnelly, Scott P.	Aldershot T	Swansea C
14 Eastwood, Simon C.	Huddersfield T	Oxford U
23 Fleetwood, Stuart K.W.	Charlton Ath	Hereford U
1 Fletcher, Steven K.	Burnley	Wolverhampton W
27 Foster, Danny	Brentford	Wycombe W
30 Francis, Simon C.	Southend U	Charlton Ath
7 Gilmartin, Rene	Walsall	Watford

1 Grant, Robert	Accrington S	Scunthorpe U
29 Gray, David P.	Manchester U	Preston NE
14 Green, Matthew J.	Torquay U	Oxford U
13 Greer, Gordon	Swindon T	Brighton & HA
27 Griffin, Andrew	Stoke C	Reading
22 Haworth, Andrew A.D.	Blackburn R	Bury
30 Henry, James	Reading	Millwall
23 Hourihane, Conor	Sunderland	Ipswich T
23 Hudson, Kirk I.	Aldershot T	Brentford
28 Huntington, Paul D.	Stockport Co	Yeovil T
8 Iwelumo, Christopher R.	Wolverhampton W	Burnley
16 Jackson, Simeon A.	Gillingham	Norwich C
29 Jutkiewicz, Lukas I.P.	Everton	Coventry C
1 Keogh, Richard J.	Carlisle U	Coventry C
9 Labadie, Joss C.	WBA	Tranmere R
24 McCallum, Gavin K.	Hereford U	Lincoln C
2 McCombe, Jamie P.	Bristol C	Huddersfield T
6 McCracken, David	Milton Keynes D	Brentford
26 McCready, Christopher J.	Northampton T	Morecambe
6 Morgan, Craig	Peterborough U	Preston NE
5 Perch, James R.	Nottingham F	Newcastle U
30 Platt, Clive L.	Colchester U	Coventry C
14 Potter, Alfie J.	Peterborough U	Oxford U
30 Pugh, Marc A.	Hereford U	AFC Bournemouth
20 Rendell, Scott D.	Peterborough U	Wycombe W
7 Richardson, Frazer	Charlton Ath	Southampton
5 Ruddy, John T.G.	Everton	Norwich C
9 Sharp, Billy L.	Sheffield U	Doncaster R
23 Skarz, Joseph P.	Huddersfield T	Bury
1 Smalling, Chris	Fulham	Manchester U
5 Spillane, Michael E.	Norwich C	Brentford
27 Strevens, Ben J.	Brentford	Wycombe W
20 Thomas, Wesley A.N.	Dagenham & R	Cheltenham T
5 Wallace, Ross	Preston NE	Burnley
23 Wesolowski, James	Leicester C	Peterborough U
6 Woodman, Craig A.	Wycombe W	Brentford

TEMPORARY TRANSFERS

14 Adeyemi, Thomas O. – Norwich C – Bradford C; 15 Al Habsi, Ali – Bolton W – Wigan Ath; 13 Arismendi, Hugo D. – Stoke C – Barnsley; 18 Balanta, Angelo J. – QPR – Milton Keynes D; 20 Ball, David M. – Manchester C – Swindon T; 15 Byrne, Mark – Nottingham F – Barnet; 2 Croft, Lee D. – Derby Co – Huddersfield T; 20 Daniels, Luke M. – WBA – Bristol R; 15 Elliott, Thomas J. – Leeds U – Rotherham U; 27 Franks, Leigh D. – Huddersfield T – Oxford U; 2 Freeman, Luke A. – Arsenal – Yeovil T; 21 Garner, Joseph A. – Nottingham F – Huddersfield T; 30 Gritton, Martin – Chesterfield – Torquay U; 15 Hatch, Liam M.A. – Peterborough U – Darlington; 16 Hone, Daniel – Lincoln C – Darlington; 2 James, Matthew – Manchester U – Preston NE; 28 Kiernan, Robert S. – Watford – Yeovil T; 6 Lillis, Joshua M. – Scunthorpe U – Rochdale; 28 Lisbie, Kevin A. – Ipswich T – Millwall; 16 McDonald, Cody – Norwich C – Gillingham;

16 McNulty, Jimmy – Brighton & HA – Scunthorpe U; 2 Mellor, Neil A. – Preston NE – Sheffield W; 5 Mendez-Laing, Nathaniel – Wolverhampton W – Peterborough U; 15 Morris, Ian – Scunthorpe U – Chesterfield; 21 Nielsen, Gunnar – Manchester C – Tranmere R; 7 Nolan, Edward W. – Preston NE – Scunthorpe U; 22 Nosworthy, Nyron – Sunderland – Sheffield U; 6 Sadler, Matthew – Watford – Shrewsbury T; 30 Soncko, Ibrahima – Stoke C – Portsmouth; 15 Spencer, James C. – Huddersfield T – Morecambe; 28 Sullivan, John D. – Millwall – Yeovil T; 5 Taylor, Rhys F. – Chelsea – Crewe Alex; 8 Thompson, O'Neil A.M.T. – Barnsley – Hereford U; 15 Tunnicliffe, James M. – Brighton & HA – Bristol R; 6 Walton, Simon W. – Plymouth Arg – Sheffield U; 16 Wright, Mark A. – Bristol R – Shrewsbury T

AUGUST 2010

2 Abbott, Pawel T.H.	Oldham Ath	Charlton Ath
20 Adams, Nicholas W.	Leicester C	Brentford
7 Ainsworth, Lionel G.R.	Huddersfield T	Shrewsbury T
6 Alexander, Gary G.	Millwall	Brentford
12 Basham, Christopher P.	Bolton W	Blackpool
31 Benson, Paul A.	Dagenham & R	Charlton Ath
5 Caddis, Paul	Celtic	Swindon T
31 Campbell, Dudley J.	Leicester C	Blackpool
6 Carayol, Mustapha L.	Torquay U	Lincoln C
12 Cathcart, Craig G.	Manchester U	Blackpool
31 Clayton, Adam S.	Manchester C	Leeds U
31 Dalla Valle, Lauri	Liverpool	Fulham.
31 Dawson, Craig	Rochdale	WBA
27 Dean, Harlee J.	Dagenham & R	Southampton
7 Deeney, Troy M.	Walsall	Watford
31 Di Santo, Francis M.	Chelsea	Wigan Ath
17 Doherty, Matthew J.	Portsmouth	Wolverhampton W
12 Eaves, Thomas J.	Oldham Ath	Bolton W
5 Ferry, Simon W.	Celtic	Swindon T
5 Fulop, Marton	Sunderland	Ipswich T
6 Garvan, Owen W.	Ipswich T	Crystal Palace
27 Gornell, Terence M.	Tranmere R	Accrington S
3 Grant, Lee A.	Sheffield W	Burnley
31 Harte, Ian P.	Carlisle U	Reading
31 Hulse, Robert W.	Derby Co	QPR
31 Hurst, James	Portsmouth	WBA
16 Ireland, Stephen	Manchester C	Aston Villa
31 Jacobsen, Lars	Blackburn R	West Ham U
6 Johnson, John J.	Middlesbrough	Northampton T
16 Jones, Bradley	Middlesbrough	Liverpool
30 Jones, Kenwyne J.	Sunderland	Stoke C
31 Kacaniklic, Alexander	Liverpool	Fulham
6 Kennedy, Mark J.	Cardiff C	Ipswich T
31 Konchesky, Paul M.	Fulham	Liverpool
25 Lee Alan D.	Crystal Palace	Huddersfield T
27 McCormack, Ross	Cardiff C	Leeds U
18 Milner, James P.	Aston Villa	Manchester C

2 Myhill, Boaz	Hull C	WBA
17 O'Keefe, Stuart A.A.	Southend U	Crystal Palace
3 Orr, Bradley J.	Bristol C	QPR
3 Payne, Stefan S.	Fulham	Gillingham
31 Phillips, Matthew	Wycombe W	Blackpool
23 Pitman, Brett D.	Bournemouth	Bristol C
3 Reid, Kyel R.	Sheffield U	Charlton Ath
23 Scotland, Jason K.	Wigan Ath	Ipswich T
9 Shorey, Nicholas	Aston Villa	WBA
19 Simpson, Jay-Alistaire F.	Arsenal	Hull C
11 Sinclair, Scott A.	Chelsea	Swansea C
26 Stead, Jonathan G.	Ipswich T	Bristol C
3 Stewart, Damion D.	QPR	Bristol C
6 Taarabt, Adel	Tottenham H	QPR
31 Waghorn, Martyn T.	Sunderland	Leicester C
23 Walker, Joshua	Middlesbrough	Watford
18 Walters, Jonathan R.	Ipswich T	Stoke C
5 Wiggins, Rhoys B.	Norwich C	AFC Bournemouth
31 Wilson, Marc D.	Portsmouth	Stoke C
3 Winfield, David T.	Aldershot T	Wycombe W

TEMPORARY TRANSFERS

27 Akinde, John J.A. – Bristol C – Bristol R; 31, Akinde, John J.A. – Ebbsfleet U – Bristol R; 3 Andersen, Mikkel – Reading – Bristol R; 13 Atkins, Ross M. – Derby Co – Tamworth; 5 Barker, Christopher A. – Plymouth Arg – Southend U; 26 Barnett, Leon P. – WBA – Norwich C; 10 Bartley, Kyle – Arsenal – Sheffield U; 20 Bell, Matthew – Port Vale – Newcastle T; 13 Bell-Baggie, Abdulai H. – Reading – Port Vale; 19 Bellamy, Craig D. – Manchester C – Cardiff C; 6 Bennett, Julian L. – Nottingham F – Crystal Palace; 31 Bent, Marcus N. – Birmingham C – Wolverhampton W; 5 Bertrand, Ryan – Chelsea – Nottingham F; 5 Bostock, John – Tottenham H – Hull C; 27 Brown, Christopher R. – Rochdale – Ashton U; 14 Brown, Kayledene – WBA – Tranmere R; 4 Button, David R.E. – Tottenham H – Plymouth Arg; 6 Carter, Darren A. – Preston NE – Millwall; 4 Chester, James G. – Manchester U – Carlisle U; 6 Clayton, Adam S. – Manchester C – Leeds U; 31 Cleverley, Thomas W. – Manchester U – Wigan Ath; 6 Cook, Andrew E. – Carlisle U – Barrow; 12 Cork, Jack F.P. – Chelsea – Burnley; 20 Counago, Pablo G. – Ipswich T – Crystal Palace; 26 Crawford, Harrison – Southend U – Dover Ath; 5 Darville, Liam T. – Leeds U – Tranmere R; 13 Davis, Harry S. – Crewe Alex – Stafford R; 31 Dawson, Craig – Bolton W – Rochdale; 6 Deeney, Troy M. – Walsall – Watford; 20 Demetriou, Stephen – Dagenham & R – Grays Ath; 13 Dickinson, Carl M. – Stoke City – Portsmouth; 6 Diouf, Mame Biram – Manchester U – Blackburn R; 6 Donnelly, Georgie J. – Plymouth Arg – Stockport Co; 10 Doyle, Colin – Birmingham C – Coventry C; 5 Drinkwater, Daniel N. – Manchester U – Cardiff C; 18 Fodor, Ferenc – Oldham Ath – Northwich Vic; 19 Foderingham, Wesley – Crystal Palace – Bromley; 5 Fry, Matthew – West Ham U – Charlton Ath; 31 Gardner, Anthony – Tottenham H – Crystal Palace; 3 Geohaghon, Exodus I. – Peterborough U – Rotherham U; 31 Gerrard, Anthony – Walsall – Hull C; 31 Grandison, Jermaine M. – Coventry C – Tranmere R; 14 Green, Daniel J. – Fulham – Braintree T; 13 Green, Dominic A. – Peterborough U – Rushden & D; 7 Griffiths, Scott R. – Peterborough U – Chesterfield; 13

Grimes, Jamie N. – Swansea C – Forest Green R; 5 Grof, David – Notts Co –
Tamworth; 31 Hamer, Benjamin J. – Reading – Brentford; 23 Hart, Danny –
Barnet – Thurrock; 20 Hector, Michael A.J. – Reading – Oxford C; 9 Highdale,
Sean – Liverpool – Oldham Ath; 5 Holden, Dean T.J. – Shrewsbury T –
Rotherham U; 13 Howe, Jermaine R. – Peterborough U – Rushden & D; 20
Hubbins, Luke A. – Birmingham C – Notts Co; 11 Hughes-Mason, Kiernan P. –
Millwall – Tooting & Mitcham U; 1 Hunt, Jack P. – Huddersfield T – Chesterfield;
26 Ikeme, Carl – WolverhamptonW – Leicester C; 14 Ilesanmi, Oluwafemi A.A. –
Dagenham & R – Histon; 6 Jansson, Oscar – Tottenham H – Northampton T; 6
Jeffers, Shaun E. – Coventry C – Cheltenham T; 6 Jervis, Jake M. – Birmingham C
– Notts Co; 5 Johnson, Damian M. – Plymouth Arg – Huddersfield T; 31 Judge,
Alan – Blackburn R – Notts Co; 25 Keogh, Andrew D. – Wolverhampton W –
Cardiff C; 31 Khizanishvili, Zurab – Blackburn R – Reading; 25 Kiernan, Robert
S. – Watford – Yeovil T; 20 Kilgallon, Matthew – Sunderland – Middlesbrough; 7
King, Joshua C.K. – Manchester U – Preston NE; 27 Kinsella, Sean W. –
Plymouth Arg – Bridgwater T; 23 Koranteng, Nathan P.K.T. – Peterborough U –
Rushden & D; 5 Koumas, Jason – Wigan Ath – Cardiff C; 3 Lees, Thomas J. –
Leeds U – Bury; 5 Liddle, Michael W. – Sunderland – Leyton Orient; 31 LuaLua,
Kazenga – Newcastle U – Brighton & HA; 13 Lynch, Christopher M. – Burnley –
Hyde U; 27 MacDonald, Shaun B. – Swansea C – Yeovil T; 26 Mancienne,
Michael I. – Chelsea – Wolverhampton W; 21 Marrow, Alexander J. – Blackburn
R – Crystal Palace; 31 Marshall, Ben – Stoke C – Carlisle U; 5 Martin, Alan –
Leeds U – Barrow; 7 Martin, Lee R. – Ipswich T – Charlton Ath; 13 Mason, Ryan
G. – Tottenham Hotspur – Doncaster R; 12 McCarthy, Alex S. – Reading –
Brentford; 12 McCrae, Romone C.A. – Barnet – Histon; 2 McGivern, Ryan –
Manchester C – Walsall; 12 McKeown, James K. – Peterborough U – Boston U;
13 Mellor, Kelvin – Crewe Alex – Stafford R; 31 Mendy, Arnaud – Derby Co –
Tranmere R; 31 Michalik, Lubomir – Bolton W – Carlisle U; 12 Mills, Daniel P. –
Peterborough U – Histon; 23 Mills, Gregory A. – Derby Co – Telford U; 20 Mills,
Jack I.A. – Reading – Oxford C; 5 Mooney, David – Reading – Colchester U; 20
Morgan, Kerry D. – Swansea C – Newport Co; 2 Moult, Louis E. – Stoke C –
Bradford C; 14 Mutch, Jordon J.E.S. – Birmingham C – Watford; 6 Mvoto, Yves
J.O. – Sunderland – Oldham Ath; 13 Norwood, James T. – Exeter C – Forest
Green R; 20 Obika, Jonathan – Tottenham H – Crystal Palace; 12 Offiong,
Richard – Carlisle U – Darlington; 24 Okus, Conor E. – Dagenham & R –
Thurrock; 10 Olofinjana, Seyi G. – Hull C – Cardiff C; 12 Onuoha, Chinedum –
Manchester C – Sunderland; 20 Osborn, Alexander S. – Dagenham & R – Grays
Ath; 31 Pack, Marlon – Portsmouth – Cheltenham T; 13 Parrett, Dean G. –
Tottenham H – Plymouth Arg; 31 Payne, Joshua J. – West Ham U – Oxford U; 19
Perkins, Lewis C. – Charlton Ath – Cray W; 5 Philliskirk, Daniel – Chelsea –
Oxford U; 13 Proctor, Jamie T. – Preston NE – Stockport Co; 19 Reid, Ruben J. –
WBA – Walsall; 20 Reynolds, Duran-Rhys – Dagenham & R – Grays Ath; 11
Scott, Mark J. – Swindon T – Swindon Super'e; 7 Shroot, Robin – Birmingham C
– Cheltenham T; 5 Simpson, Joshua R – Peterborough U – Southend U; 6
Simpson, Robbie – Coventry C – Brenford; 2 Stewart, Cameron R. – Manchester
U – Yeovil T; 30 Sullivan, John D. – Millwall – Yeovil T; 31 Taylor, Andrew D. –
Middlesbrough – Watford; 6 Tomlin, Lee M. – Rushden & D – Peterborough U; 6
Tounkara, Oumare – Sunderland – Oldham Ath; 13 Townsend, Andros –
Tottenham H – Ipswich T; 6 Trippier, Kieran J. – Manchester C – Barnsley; 27
Trott, Jordan R. – Plymouth Arg – Bridgwater T; 27 Tudur Jones, Owain –

Norwich C – Yeovil T; 14 Turner, Iain – Everton – Coventry C; 13 Tutte, Andrew W. – Manchester C – Rochdale; 27 Varney, Luke I. – Charlton Ath – Blackpool; 5 Vokes, Samuel M. – Wolverhampton W – Bristol C; 20 Walker, Joshua – Middlesbrough – Watford; 13 Walsh, Phillip – Dagenham & R – Barnet; 21 Waters, Aaron L.J. – QPR – Thurrock; 3 Watt, Herschel O.S. – Arsenal – Leeds U; 13 Welbeck, Daniel N.T.M. – Manchester U – Sunderland; 12 Wootton, Lee S. – Dagenham & R – Histon

SEPTEMBER 2010 TEMPORARY TRANSFERS

25 Ajose, Nicholas – Manchester U – Bury; 11 Ayala, Daniel S. – Liverpool – Hull C; 10 Brown, Jason R. – Blackburn R – Leeds U; 10 Brown, Lee J. – QPR – Hayes & Yeading U; 28 Brown, Reece – Manchester U – Bradford C; 30 Bulman, Dannie M. – Oxford U – Crawley T; 20 Byrne, Callum – Rochdale – Trafford; 24 Carlton, Daniel – Bury – Grimsby T; 27 Caulker, Steven R. – Tottenham H – Bristol C; 30 Chaplow, Richard D. – WBA – Southampton; 2 Clark, Gavin E. – Morecambe – Kendal T; 10 Clarke, Oliver A. – Bristol R – Gloucster C; 27 Clough, Charlie – Bristol R – Newport Co; 27 Connerton, James – Crewe Alex – Nantwich T; 17 Cook, Steve A. – Brighton & HA – Eastbourne Bor; 2 Cox, Elliott J. – QPR – Tooting & Mitcham U; 17 Daniels, Luke M. – WBA – Charlton Ath; 10 Davies, Scott M.E. – Reading – Wycombe W; 17 Davisson, Benjamin J. – Charlton Ath – Bromley; 9 Davis, David L. – Wolverhampton W – Walsall; 25 De Laet, Ritchie R.A. – Manchester U – Sheffield U; 28 Devlin, Conor – Manchester U – Hartlepool U; 10 Edwards, Joseph R. – Bristol C – Bath C; 17 Elliott, Christopher M. – Bradford C – Harrogate Rail; 6 Emery, Joshua S. – Cheltenham T – Cirencester T; 3 Fitchett, Daniel O. – Wycombe W – Oxford C; 24 Fitzsimons, Danny – QPR – Histon; 24 Fodor, Ferenc – Oldham Ath – Northwich Vic; 10 Frampton, Andrew J.K. – Millwall – Leyton Orient; 24 Gill, Matthew J. – Norwich C – Peterborough U; 28 Gill, Oliver D. – Manchester U – Bradford C; 17 Gulacsi, Peter – Liverpool – Tranmere R; 24 Harrison, Ryan A. – Bradford C – Harrogate Rail; 16 Henderson, Liam M. – Watford – Colchester U; 17 Henderson, Stephen – Bristol C – Yeovil T; 24 Holroyd, Christopher – Brighton & HA – Stevenage; 17 Hume, Iain E. – Barnsley – Preston NE; 10 Ings, Daniel W.J. – Bournemouth – Dorchester T; 16 Jackson, Marlon M. – Bristol C – Aldershot T; 24 Jarvis, Nathaniel S. – Cardiff C – Southend U; 10 John, Martin – Cardiff C – Newport Co; 16 Johnson, Jemal P. – Milton Keynes D – Port Vale; 28 Jones, Andrai R. – Bury – Altrincham; 10 Kean, Jacob K. – Blackburn R – Hartlepool U; 13 Kuqi, Shefki – Swansea C – Derby Co; 10 Lawrence, Liam – Stoke C – Portsmouth; 6 Lee, Jake A. – Cheltenham T – Cirencester T; 23 Livermore, Jake C. – Tottenham H – Ipswich T; 23 Mackreth, Jack – Tranmere R – Burscough; 23 McCartney, George – Sunderland – Leeds U; 17 Mambo, Yado M. – Charlton Ath – Eastbourne Bor; 13 Mills, Gregory A. – Derby Co – Telford U; 24 Moore, Luke I. – WBA – Derby Co; 24 M'Poku, Paul-Jose – Tottenham H – Leyton Orient; 27 Noble, Ryan – Sunderland – Derby Co; 16 Norwood, Oliver J. – Manchester U – Carlisle U; 17 Nouble, Frank H. – West Ham U – Swansea C; 10 O'Brien, Liam D. – Portsmouth – Eastbourne Bor; 11 O'Connor, Garry L.J. – Birmingham C – Barnsley; 3 O'Connor, Patrick J. – Millwall – Tooting & Mitcham U; 13 O'Donnell, Richard M. – Sheffield W – Grimsby T; 10 Patulea, Adrian M. – Leyton Orient – Hayes & Yeading U; 10 Robinson, Theo L.R. – Huddersfield T – Millwall; 13 Rose, Daniel L. – Tottenham H – Bristol C; 24 Sills, Timothy – Stevenage – Rushden & D; 23 Smalley, Deane A.M. – Oldham Ath – Rochdale;

23 Smith, Adam J. – Tottenham H – Bournemouth; 11 Smith, Thomas W. – Portsmouth – QPR; 16 Timlin, Michael A. – Swindon T – Southend U; 22 Tozer, Ben P.A. – Newcastle U – Northampton T; 7 Verma, Aman K. – Leicester C – Kidderminster H; 10 Vaughan, James O. – Everton – Crystal Palace; 28 Wainwright, Neil – Morecambe – Barrow; 17 Walcott, Jacob D. – Reading – Staines T; 14 Walker, Kyle A. – Tottenham H – QPR; 10 Ward, Daniel C. – Bolton W – Coventry C; 23 Waters, Aaron L.J. – QPR – Thurrock; 24 Watkins, Marley J. – Cheltenham T – Bath C; 17 Watson, Ben C. – Exeter C – Forest Green R; 9 Williams, Gavin J. – Bristol C – Yeovil T; 23 Wood, Christopher – WBA – Barnsley; 28 Woodley, Aaron R. – Oxford U – Oxford C; 30 Wootton, Scott J. – Manchester U – Tranmere R; 3 Yorke, Reece – Barnet – Harlow T

OCTOBER 2010 TEMPORARY TRANSFERS

15 Adams, Nicholas W. – Brentford – Rochdale; 7 Aksalu, Mihkel – Sheffield U – Mansfield T; 15 Alnwick, Ben R. – Tottenham H – Leeds U; 25 Beardsley, Jason C. – Macclesfield T – Eastwood T; 21 Beautyman, Harry H. – Leyton Orient – St Albans C; 8 Bignall, Nicholas C. – Reading – Southampton; 2 Blake, Ryan G. – Brentford – Woking; 22 Bowman, Ryan M. – Carlisle U – Workington; 15 Bridge-Wilkinson, Marc – Carlisle U – Darlington; 29 Bulmer, Niki-Lee – QPR – Hayes & Yeading U; 1 Chamberlain, Deale – Liverpool – Leeds U; 8 Clark, Robert J. – Doncaster R – Sheffield; 28 Clay, Craig W. – Chesterfield – Barrow; 22 Clifford, Conor – Chelsea – Plymouth Arg; 1 Coker, Ben – Colchester U – Chelmsford C; 18 Colback, Jack R. – Sunderland – Ipswich T; 15 Colgan, Nicholas V. – Grimsby T – Huddersfield T; 1 Collins, Dominic – Preston NE – Northwich Vic; 15 Collins, James S. – Aston Villa – Burton Alb; 22 Connolly, Reece W. – Aldershot T – Didcot T; 19 Cook, Steve A. – Brighton & HA – Mansfield T; 21 Cunningham, Gregory R. – Manchester C – Leicester C; 28 Darkwa, Tendayi D. – Chesterfield – Barrow; 6 Davies, Andrew J. – Stoke C – Walsall; 15 Davies, Curtis – Aston Villa – Leicester C; 18 Day, Rhys – Oxford U – Mansfield T; 7 Devaney, Martin T. – Barnsley – Walsall; 18 Emnes, Marvin – Middlesbrough – Swansea C; 29 Essam, Connor – Gillingham – Bishop's Stortford; 22 Evans, Corry J. – Manchester U – Carlisle U; 5 Evina, Cedric D. – Arsenal – Oldham Ath; 7 Fairhurst, Waide S. – Doncaster R – Southend U; 15 Fielding, Francis D. – Blackburn R – Derby Co; 15 Fletcher, Wesleigh J. – Burnley – Stockport Co; 29 Frampton, Andrew J.K. – Millwall – Swindon T; 9 Francomb, Georgie – Norwich C – Barnet; 22 Gallen, Kevin A. – Luton T – Barnet; 22 Gardner, Steven A. – Hull C – Harrogate T; 15 Gillespie, Mark J. – Carlisle U – Blyth Spartans; 28 Gowling, Joshua A.I. – Carlisle U – Lincoln C; 8 Grabban, Lewis J. – Millwall – Brentford; 29 Grandison, Jermaine M. – Coventry C – Tranmere R; 12 Grella, Michele – Leeds U – Carlisle U; 29 Grimes, Ashley J. – Millwall – Lincoln C; 19 Halford, Gregory – Wolverhampton W – Portsmouth; 22 Hall, Grant T. – Brighton & HA – Whitehawk; 29 Harris, Sebastian – Northampton T – Stafford R; 28 Hayes, Paul E. – Preston NE – Barnsley; 15 Head, Liam T. – Plymouth Arg – Forest Green R; 22 Hemmings, Ashley J. – Wolverhampton W – Torquay U; 21 Hill, Matthew C. – Wolverhampton W – Barnsley; 28 Howell, Luke A. – Milton Keynes D – Lincoln C; 29 Hoyte, Gavin A. – Arsenal – Lincoln C; 22 Jackson, Marlon M. – Bristol C – Aldershot T; 1 James, Anthony – Burton Alb – Hereford U; 1 Joyce, Daniel D. – Reading – Bedford T; 21 Kosylo, Matthew S.P. – Stockport Co – Woodley SP; 16 Lawrence, Liam – Stoke C – Portsmouth; 1 Locke, Simon J. – Reading – Croydon Ath; 15 Long, Kevin F. – Burnley – Accrington S; 30 McCartney, George –

Sunderland – Leeds U; 14 McDonald, Kevin – Burnley – Scunthorpe U; 29
McDonald, Rodney T. – Oldham Ath – Stafford R; 29 McLoughlin, Ian M. –
Ipswich T – Lowestoft T; 19 Mills, Joseph N. – Southampton – Doncaster R; 29
Moore, Luke I. – WBA – Derby Co; 7 Moore, Simon W. – Brentford –
Basingstoke T; 14 Naughton, Kyle – Tottenham H – Leicester C; 8 Nsiala,
Aristote – Everton – Macclesfield T; 8 Oastler, Joseph J. – QPR – Torquay U; 22
Obadeyi, Temitope – Bolton W – Shrewsbury T; 29 O'Brien, Andrew J. – Bolton
W – Leeds U; 27 Ollerenshaw, Joshua D. – Oldham Ath – Mossley; 27 O'Shea,
James – Birmingham C – Stevenage; 1 Parker, Joshua K.S. – QPR – Northampton
T; 29 Partington, Joseph M. – Bournemouth – Eastbourne Bor; 14 Pinney,
Nathaniel B. – Crystal Palace – Dagenham & R; 14 Poole, James A. – Manchester
C – Hartlepool U; 29 Porter, George – Leyton Orient – Lewes; 12 Price, Jason J. –
Carlisle U – Bradford C; 8 Pulis, Anthony J. – Southampton – Stockport Co; 29
Purdie, Robert J. – Oldham Ath – Hereford U; 27 Randall, Mark – Arsenal –
Rotherham U; 29 Reid, Andrew M. – Sunderland – Sheffield U; 5 Ritchie,
Matthew T. – Portsmouth – Swindon T; 6 Roe, Phillip M. – Sheffield U – Retford
T; 22 Rooney, Luke W. – Gillingham – Eastbourne Bor; 22 Rose, Romone A. –
QPR – Torquay U; 22 Sarcevic, Antoni – Crewe Alex – Chester; 19 Sears, Fred –
West Ham U – Scunthorpe U; 15 Severn, James A. – Derby Co – Tamworth; 16
Smith, Thomas W. – Portsmouth – QPR; 29 Speight, Jake C. – Bradford C – Port
Vale; 8 Stavrinou, Alexander M. – Charlton Ath – Cambridge U; 28 Taiwo,
Soloman O. – Cardiff C – Dagenham & R; 29 Thomas, Michael D. – Macclesfield
T – Mossley; 22 Vincenti, Peter I. – Stevenage – Mansfield T; 1 Vine, Rowan L. –
QPR – Hull C; 21 Walcott, Jacob D. – Reading – Staines T; 28 Whing, Andrew J. –
Brighton & HA – Leyton Orient; 26 White, Andrew J. – Gillingham – Margate; 29
Williams, Owain fon – Stockport Co – Bury; 1 Williams, Thomas A. – Bristol C –
Colchester U

NOVEMBER 2010 TEMPORARY TRANSFERS
5 Adams, Nathan M. – Lincoln C – Stamford; 2 Afobe, Benik – Arsenal –
Huddersfield T; 20 Ainsley, Jack W. – Ipswich T – Histon; 12 Aldred, Thomas M. –
Carlisle U – Stockport Co; 2 Allsop, Ryan – WBA – Stockport Co; 19 Andrew,
Calvin H. – Crystal Palace – Millwall; 11 Atkins, Ross M. – Derby Co –
Tamworth; 25 Atkinson, William H. – Hull C – Rotherham U; 13 Bassett, Kyle L.
– Exeter C – Bideford; 25 Batth, Daniel T. – Wolverhampton W – Sheffield U; 24
Bednar, Roman – WBA – Leicester C; 5 Belcher, Samuel M. – Wycombe W –
Hinckley U; 25 Bell-Baggie, Abdulai H. – Reading – Crawley T; 12 Bignall,
Nicholas C. – Reading – Bournemouth; 19 Brown, Jason R. – Blackburn R –
Leyton Orient; 8 Brown, Kayledene – WBA – Dagenham & R; 4 Byrne, Callum –
Rochdale – Mossley; 12 Chambers, Ashley R. – Leicester C – York C; 24
Charnock, Kieran J. – Peterborough U – Morecambe; 12 Chilaka, Chibuzor –
Bradford C – Bradford PA; 19 Clayton, Adam S. – Leeds U – Peterborough U; 12
Coid, Daniel J. – Blackpool – Rotherham U; 4 Coleman, Rory C. – Scunthorpe U
– Boston U; 24 Comminges, Miguel – Cardiff C – Carlisle U; 24 Cort, Leon T.A. –
Burnley – Preston NE; 25 Craney, Ian T.W. – Huddersfield T – Accrington S; 12
Creighton, Mark A. – Oxford U – Wrexham; 3 Cruise, Thomas D. – Arsenal –
Carlisle U; 2 Darby, Stephen – Liverpool – Notts Co; 5 Davisson, Benjamin J. –
Charlton Ath – Thurrock; 18 Deering, Sam – Oxford U – Newport Co; 17 De
Laet, Ritchie R.A. – Manchester U – Preston NE; 2 Dickinson, Liam M. –
Brighton & HA – Walsall; 25 Downing, Paul – WBA – Rotherham U; 25 Easter,

Jermaine M. – Milton Keynes D – Swansea C; 25 Eastham, Ashley – Blackpool – Carlisle U; 12 Eckersley, Richard J. – Burnley – Bradford C; 25 Elford-Alliyu, Lateef – WBA – Tranmere R; 11 Elito, Medy E. – Colchester U – Dagenham & R; 26 Ellison, James – Burton Alb – Stafford R; 25 Fallon, Rory M. – Plymouth Arg – Ipswich T; 4 Featherstone, Nicky L. – Hull C – Hereford U; 10 Federico, Jerome J. – Wycombe W – Woking; 4 Fitchett, Daniel O. – Wycombe W – Salisbury C; 11 Futcher, Benjamin P. – Bury – Oxford U; 2 Geohaghon, Exodus I. – Peterborough U – Shrewsbury T; 9 German, Antonio T. – QPR – Southend U; 4 Goodall, Alan J. – Rochdale – Newport Co; 16 Grant, Robert – Scunthorpe U – Rochdale; 25 Guidetti, John A. – Manchester C – Burnley; 26 Guinan, Stephen A. – Northampton – Forest Green R; 12 Gunning, Gavin – Blackburn R – Bury; 4 Healy MBE, David J. – Sunderland – Doncaster R; 25 Heath, Joseph – Exeter C – Hereford U; 12 Hector, Michael A.J. – Reading – Horsham; 24 Henderson, Liam M. – Watford – Colchester U; 24 Hill, Matthew C. – Wolverhampton W – Barnsley; 26 Hinton, Craig – Northampton T – Luton T; 16 Hoban, Patrick J. – Bristol C – Cleveland T; 18 Hooman, Harry J. – Shrewsbury T – Hinckley U; 26 Horne, Louis – Bradford C – Halifax T; 25 Hughes-Mason, Kiernan P. – Millwall – Tooting & Mitcham U; 24 Hussey, Christopher I. – Coventry C – Crewe Alex; 2 Ince, Thomas – Liverpool – Notts Co; 25 Jacobson, Joseph M. – Oldham Ath – Accrington S; 16 James-Lewis, Merrick A. – Southend U – Tooting & Mitcham U; 25 Jarvis, Ryan R. – Leyton Orient – Northampton T; 9 Jenkinson, Carl D. – Charlton Ath – Eastbourne Bor; 11 Jesionkowski, Jakub – Swindon T – Oxford C; 25 Johnson, Paul A. – Hartlepool U – Whitby T; 13 Keats, Noah J. – Exeter C – Bideford; 9 Kennedy, Callum E. – Swindon T – Gillingham; 1 Kennedy, Thomas G. – Leicester C – Rochdale; 16 Keohane, James C.J. – Bristol C – Cleveland T; 12 Kiernan, Robert S. – Watford – Bradford C; 12 King, Craig S. – Leicester C – Northampton T; 25 King, Joshua C.K. – Manchester U – Preston NE; 26 Kinsella, Sean – Plymouth Arg – Stafford R; 25 Kirkland, Christopher E. – Wigan Ath – Leicester C; 22 Lansbury, Henri G. – Arsenal – Norwich C; 20 Lawrence, Liam – Stoke C – Portsmouth; 12 Lee, Charlie – Peterborough U – Gillingham; 26 Lee, Jake A. – Cheltenham T – Bishop's Cleeve; 22 Leigertwood, Mikele B. – QPR – Reading; 22 Lewis, Stuart A. – Dagenham & R – Wycombe W; 26 Lindfield, Craig A. – Accrington S – Kidderminster H; 15 Livermore, Jake C. – Tottenham H – Ipswich T; 25 Locke, Simon J. – Reading – Dagenham & R; 2 Lomax, Kelvin – Oldham Ath – Chesterfield; 25 Lund, Matthew C. – Stoke C – Hereford U; 11 MacLean, Steven – Plymouth Arg – Oxford U; 12 McIndoe, Michael – Coventry C – Milton Keynes D; 23 McKenna, Jack S. – Bristol R – Chippenham T; 27 McPike, Mitchell L. – Birmingham C – Kidderminster H; 25 McQuoid, Joshua J.B. – Bournemouth – Millwall; 23 Mantom, Samuel S. – WBA – Tranmere R; 9 Midson, Jack W. – Oxford U – Southend U; 19 Miller, Lee A. – Middlesbrough – Notts Co; 19 Montgomery, Graeme – Dagenham & R – Hayes & Yeading U; 11 Nelson, Mitchell A. – Bournemouth – Eastbourne Bor; 12 N'Guessen, Diombo D-G. – Leicester C – Scunthorpe U; 9 Nicholls, Lee A. – Wigan Ath – Hartlepool U; 1 Nyatanga, Lewin J. – Bristol C – Peterborough U; 8 Oastler, Joseph J. – QPR – Torquay U; 8 O'Connor, Garry L.J. – Birmingham C – Barnsley; 25 O'Connor, Patrick J. – Millwall – Hampton & Richmond Bor; 25 Oshodi, Edward A.M.O.A. – Watford – Dagenham & R; 4 Palsson, Gudlaugur V. – AGF Aarhus – Dagenham & R; 23 Parker, Joshua K.S. – QPR – Wycombe W; 25 Parkes, Thomas P.W. – Leicester C – Yeovil T; 4 Pentney, Carl – Colchester U – Bath C; 15 Perkins, Lewis C. – Charlton Ath – Cray W; 15 Phillip, Adam – Chelsea – Yeovil

T; 26 Preen, Garyn V. – Burton Alb – Stafford R; 18 Pugh, Daniel A. – Stoke C – Preston NE; 19 Puncheon, Jason D.I. – Southampton – Millwall; 25 Ramsey, Aaron J. – Arsenal – Nottingham F; 26 Roberts, Adam J. – Macclesfield T – Northwich Vic; Roe, Philip – Sheffield W – Retford U; 12 Rowe, Daniel – Stockport Co – Northwich Vic; 5 Saville, Jack W. – Southampton – Stockport Co; 22 Seip, Marcel – Plymouth Arg – Charlton Ath; 19 Short, Lewis G.T. – Crewe Alex – Nantwich T; 2 Smalley, Deane A.M. – Oldham Ath – Chesterfield; 25 Smith, Thomas W. – Portsmouth – QPR; 26 Smyth, Thomas J. – Accrington S – Workington; 22 Sproule, Ivan – Bristol C – Yeovil T; 20 Stavrinou, Alexander M. – Charlton Ath – Cambridge U; 25 Stewart, Cameron R. – Manchester U – Hull C; 18 Tonge, Michael W.E. – Stoke C – Preston NE; 2 Tozer, Ben P.A. – Newcastle U – Northampton T; 25 Trotman, Neal A. – Preston NE – Oldham Ath; 4 Trott, Jordan R. – Plymouth Arg – Tiverton T; 25 Tudgay, Marcus – Sheffield W – Nottingham F; 5 Tuna, Tamer H. – Charlton Ath – Thurrock; 25 Tutte, Andrew W. – Manchester C – Shrewsbury T; 19 Verma, Aman K. – Leicester C – Darlington; 25 Vine, Rowan L. – QPR – Brentford; 25 Walker, Joshua – Watford – Stevenage; 25 Wallace, James R. – Everton – Bury; 2 Waters, Aaron L.J. – QPR – Thurrock; 18 Webster, Byron C. – Doncaster R – Hereford U; 12 Whelpdale, Christopher M. – Peterborough U – Gillingham; 18 White, Aidan P. – Leeds U – Oldham Ath; 12 Wilkinson, Luke A. – Dagenham & R – Boreham Wood; 19 Williams, Jonathan J. – Scunthorpe U – Boston U; 13 Williams, Marcus V. – Reading – Peterborough U; 4 Williams, Tom – Bristol C – Colchester U; 19 Wood, Chris – WBA – Brighton & HA; 25 Woods, Michael J. – Chelsea – Notts Co; 25 Wootton, Scott J. – Manchester U – Tranmere R; 9 Wotton, Paul A. – Southampton – Oxford U; 9 Wraighte, Christopher G. – Morecambe – Kendal T; 5 Yorke, Reece C. – Barnet – Wealdstone; 27 Zuiverloon, Gianni – Heerenveen – Ipswich T

DECEMBER 2010

31 Simpson, Joshua R.	Peterborough U	Crawley T

TEMPORARY TRANSFERS

10 Ambrusics, Robert – Leicester C – Stafford R; 31 Booth, George – Bristol R – Longwell Green; 23 Byrne, Callum – Rochdale – Mossley; 24 Clarke, Oliver A. – Bristol R – Mangotsfield U; 17 Collins, Dominic – Preston NE – Northwich Vic; 31 Cooper, Mark J. – Bristol R – Frome T; 3 Daniels, Luke M. – WBA – Rochdale; 11 Davisson, Benjamin J. – Charlton Ath – Hastings U; 10 Fitchett, Daniel O. – Wycombe W – Salisbury C; 28 Green, Daniel J. – Dagenham & R – Chelmsford C; 28 Green, Daniel J. – Dagenham & R – Boreham Wood; 2 Haynes, Kyle J. – Cheltenham T – Salisbury C; 10 Leonard, Ryan I. – Plymouth Arg – Weston-Super-Mare; 16 Mackreth, Jack – Tranmere R – Colwyn Bay; 17 Mambo, Yado M. – Charlton Ath – Staines T; 31 McKenna, Jack – Bristol R – Chippenham T; 18 Palmer, Edward G. – Torquay U – Tiverton T; 24 Raymond, Frankie J. – Reading – Horsham; 10 Ryan, Perry D. – Portsmouth – Bognor Regis T; 17 Wilkinson, Daniel P. – Hull C – Harrogate T; 18 Yeoman, Ashley S. – Torquay U – Tiverton T; 10 Yorke, Reece C. – Barnet – Harlow T

JANUARY 2011

1 Adams, Nicholas W.	Brentford	Rochdale
31 Austin, Charlie	Swindon T	Burnley
31 Ball, David M.	Manchester C	Peterborough U

154

1	Barnett, Leon P.	WBA	Norwich C
31	Bartley, Marvin C.	Bournemouth	Burnley
18	Bent, Darren A.	Sunderland	Aston Villa
31	Benyon, Elliot P.	Torquay U	Swindon T
20	Britton, Leon J.	Sheffield U	Swansea C
31	Carroll, Andrew T.	Newcastle U	Liverpool
1	Chaplow, Richard D.	Preston NE	Southampton
7	Charnock, Kieran J.	Torquay U	Morecambe
12	Chester, James G.	Manchester C	Hull C
7	Collins, James S.	Aston Villa	Shrewsbury T
31	Collins, Neill	Leeds U	Sheffield U
20	Davies, Benjamin J.	Notts Co	Derby Co
31	Davies, Curtis E.	Aston Villa	Birmingham C
26	Doyle, Michael P.	Coventry C	Sheffield U
20	Duffy, Mark J.	Morecambe	Scunthorpe U
14	Easter, Jermaine M.	Milton Keynes D	Crystal Palace
28	Evina, Cedric D.	Arsenal	Oldham Ath
31	Forte, Jonathan R.	Scunthorpe U	Southampton
2	Fryatt, Matthew C.	Leicester C	Hull C
31	Grandison, Jermaine M.	Coventry C	Shrewsbury T
20	Hammill, Adam	Barnsley	Wolverhampton W
26	Harley, Ryan	Exeter C	Swansea C
25	Harrad, Shaun	Burton Alb	Northampton T
20	Haynes, Danny L.	Bristol C	Barnsley
21	Hughes, Andrew J.	Leeds U	Scunthorpe U
1	Hume, Iain E.	Barnsley	Preston NE
5	Johnson, Reda	Plymouth Arg	Sheffield W
12	Judge, Alan	Blackburn R	Notts Co
31	Kalala, Jean-Paul K.	Yeovil T	Bristol R
22	Keinan, Dekel	Blackpool	Cardiff C
1	Lawrence, Liam	Stoke C	Portsmouth
17	Madine, Gary L.	Carlisle U	Sheffield W
24	Manset, Mathieu	Hereford U	Reading
5	Marrow, Alexander J.	Blackburn R	Crystal Palace
1	McLean, Aaron	Peterborough U	Hull C
5	McQuoid, Joshua J.	Bournemouth	Millwall
12	Moore, Luke I.	WBA	Swansea C
6	Morrison, Michael B.	Leicester C	Sheffield W
18	Morrison, Sean J.	Swindon T	Reading
31	Moxey, Dean	Derby Co	Crystal Palace
31	Nelson, Michael J.	Norwich C	Scunthorpe U
7	Nolan, Edward W.	Preston NE	Scunthorpe U
1	Noone, Craig	Plymouth Arg	Brighton & HA
4	O'Brien, Andrew J.	Bolton W	Leeds U
25	O'Neil, Gary P.	Middlesbrough	West Ham U
5	Parkin, Jonathan	Preston NE	Cardiff C
23	Payne, Joshua J.	Doncaster R	Oxford U
18	Pienaar, Steven	Everton	Tottenham H
31	Reid, Andrew M.	Sunderland	Blackpool
14	Reid, Paul M.	Colchester U	Scunthorpe U

28 Reid, Reuben J.	WBA	Oldham Ath
6 Ritchie, Matthew T.	Portsmouth	Swindon T
15 Robinson, Theo L.	Huddersfield T	Millwall
7 Sidwell, Steven J.	Aston Villa	Fulham
1 Smith, Thomas W.	Portsmouth	QPR
31 Stewart, Cameron R.	Manchester U	Hull C
27 Thomas-Moore, Ian R.	Tranmere R	Rotherham U
13 Tierney, Marc P.	Colchester U	Norwich C
31 Torres, Fernando J.	Liverpool	Chelsea
5 Tudgay, Marcus	Sheffield W	Nottingham F
13 Vincenti, Peter I.	Stevenage	Aldershot T
20 Wheater, David J.	Middlesbrough	Bolton W
1 Wilbraham, Aaron T.	Milton Keynes D	Norwich C
31 Woolford, Martyn	Scunthorpe U	Bristol C
7 Wright, Mark A.	Bristol R	Shrewsbury T
25 Wright-Phillips, Bradley	Plymouth Arg	Charlton Ath
31 Wroe, Nicholas	Torquay U	Shrewsbury T

TEMPORARY TRANSFERS

13 Adeyemi, Thomas O. – Norwich C – Bradford C; 27 Afobe, Benik – Arsenal – Huddersfield T; 6 Agard, Kieran R. – Everton – Peterborough U; 17 Akinde, John J.A. – Bristol C – Dagenham & R; 25 Amoo, David O. – Liverpool – Milton Keynes D; 7 Amos, Benjamin P. – Manchester U – Oldham Ath; 8 Atkinson, William H. – Hull C – Rochdale; 14 Barker, George J. – Brighton & HA – Lewes; 19 Bent, Marcus N. – Birmingham C – Sheffield U; 19 Berthel-Askou, Jens – Norwich C – Millwall; 31 Bessone, Federico L. – Leeds U – Charlton Ath; 31 Bignall, Nicholas C. – Reading – Brentford; 10 Blake, Ryan G. – Brentford – Ebbsfleet U; 18 Bolger, Cian T. – Leicester C – Bristol R; 7 Brogan, Stephen P. – Rotherham U – Stalybridge C; 24 Brown, Aaron A. – Leyton Orient – Stockport Co; 27 Brown, Christopher R. – Rochdale – Bamber Bridge; 21 Brown, Kayleden – WBA – Port Vale; 29 Brown, Lee J. – QPR – Hayes & Yeading; 27 Bullard, James R. – Hull C – Ipswich T; 27 Carroll, Thomas J. – Tottenham H – Leyton Orient; 21 Carson, Trevor – Sunderland – Lincoln C; 11 Cestor, Mike B. – Leyton Orient – Boreham Wood; 10 Chambers, Ashley R. – Leicester C – York C; 24 Clark, Gavin E. – Morecambe – Bamber Bridge; 28 Clarke, Leon M. – QPR – Preston NE; 27 Clarke, Nathan – Huddersfield T – Colchester U; 28 Clough, Charlie – Bristol R – Weymouth; 10 Coleman, Rory C. – Scunthorpe U – Boston U; 10 Cooper, Liam D.I. – Hull C – Carlisle U; 25 Cort, Leon T.A. – Burnley – Preston NE; 6 Cornell, David J. – Swansea C – Port Talbot; 6 Cullen, Mark – Hull C – Bradford C; 21 Daley, Luke A. – Norwich C – Stevenage; 5 Daniels, Luke M. – WBA – Bristol R; 21 Darby, Stephen – Liverpool – Notts Co; 21 Darley, Grant L.W. – Rotherham U – Ossett T; 28 Davies, Scott M.E. – Reading – Bristol R; 31 Davis, David L. – Wolverhampton W – Shrewsbury T; 13 De Laet, Ritchie R.A. – Manchester U – Portsmouth; 7 Demontagnac, Ishmel – Blackpool – Stockport Co; 6 Dickinson, Liam M. – Barnsley – Rochdale; 24 Donaldson, Ryan M. – Newcastle U – Hartlepool U; 1 Donnelly, Scott P. – Swansea C – Wycombe W; 31 Downing, Paul – WBA – Shrewsbury T; 28 Drinkwater, Daniel N. – Manchester U – Watford; 27 Dudgeon, Joseph P. – Manchester U – Carlisle U; 12 Dunleavy, John F. – Wolverhampton W – Barnet; 7 Eastham, Ashley – Blackpool – Cheltenham T; 25 Eastmond, Craig L. – Arsenal – Millwall; 14 Eccleston, Nathan

– Liverpool – Charlton Ath; 1 Ehmer, Maximillian A. – QPR – Yeovil T; 7 Elding, Anthony L. – Rochdale – Stockport Co; 13 Ellington, Nathan L. – Watford – Preston NE; 18 Emmanuel-Thomas, Jay-Aston – Arsenal – Cardiff C; 7 Essam, Connor – Gillingham – Bishop's Stortford; 14 Evans, Corry J. – Manchester U – Hull C; 7 Evina, Cedric D. – Arsenal – Oldham Ath; 28 Federico, Jerome J. – Wycombe W – Wealdstone; 6 Fitchett, Daniel O. – Wycombe W – Salisbury C; 31 Forecast, Tommy S. – Southampton – Eastbourne Bor; 6 Frampton, Andrew J. – Millwall – Swindon T; 7 Gardner, Anthony – Hull C – Crystal Palace; 31 Garner, Joseph A. – Nottingham F – Scunthorpe U; 24 Geohaghan, Exodus I. – Peterborough U – Port Vale; 21 Gill, Matthew J. – Norwich C – Walsall; 31 Gonzalez, David G. – Manchester C – Leeds U; 6 Gordon, Benjamin L. – Chelsea – Scunthorpe U; 20 Grand, Simon – Morecambe – Aldershot T; 14 Grandison, Jermaine M. – Coventry C – Shrewsbury T; 1 Gray, Daniel E. – Chesterfield – Macclesfield T; 31 Green, Matthew J. – Oxford U – Cheltenham T; 24 Greulich, Corey P. – Hartlepool U – Workington; 7 Grieve, Matthew A. – Newcastle U – Stockport Co; 31 Griffin, Charlie J. – Stevenage – Newport Co; 7 Griffiths, Scott R. – Peterborough U – Chesterfield; 14 Grimes, Ashley J. – Millwall – Lincoln C; 31 Grof, David A. – Notts Co – Mansfield T; 1 Guzan, Bradley E. – Aston Villa – Hull C; 31 Hackney, Simon J. – Colchester U – Oxford U; 28 Haining, William W. – Oldham Ath – Fleetwood T; 12 Halford, Gregory – Wolverhampton W – Portsmouth; 21 Hall, Grant T. – Brighton & HA – Lewes; 21 Hamer, Benjamin J. – Reading – Exeter C; 27 Harley, Ryan – Swansea C – Exeter C; 28 Hatfield, William H. – Leeds U – York C; 30 Heath, Joseph – Exeter C – Hereford U; 7 Henderson, Liam M. – Watford – Aldershot T; 4 Henderson, Stephen – Bristol C – Yeovil T; 25 Hogg, Jonathan – Aston Villa – Portsmouth; 17 Hooman, Harry J. – Shrewsbury T – Hinckley U; 28 Howe, Jermaine R. – Peterborough U – Bristol R; 11 Hudson, Kirk I. – Brentford – AFC Wimbledon; 1 Hunt, David J. – Brentford – Crawley T; 21 Hunt, Stephen J. – Notts Co – Lincoln C; 28 Hurst, Kevan – Carlisle U – Morecambe; 7 Husband, Stephen – Blackpool – Stockport Co; 7 Hutchinson, Andrew L. – Lincoln C – Harrogate T; 14 Ibrahim, Abdisalam – Manchester C – Scunthorpe U; 21 Jervis, Jake M. – Birmingham C – Hereford U; 14 Jesionkowski, Jakub – Swindon T – Oxford C; 31 Johnson, Edward – Fulham – Preston NE; 14 Johnson, Oliver T. – Norwich C – Yeovil T; 31 Jones, Paul – Exeter C – Peterborough U; 7 Judge, Alan – Blackburn R – Notts Co; 10 Kadar, Tamas – Newcastle U – Huddersfield T; 7 Kane, Harry – Tottenham H – Leyton Orient; 6 Kay, Michael J. – Sunderland – Tranmere R; 15 Keats, Noah J. – Exeter C – Barnstaple T; 21 Kelly, Danny M. – Barnet – Dover Ath; 14 Kelly, Julian J. – Reading – Lincoln C; 20 Kennedy, Thomas G. – Leicester C – Peterborough U; 31 Keogh, Andrew D. – Wolverhampton W – Bristol C; 1 Kilbane, Kevin D. – Hull C – Huddersfield T; 12 Kilgallon, Matthew – Sunderland – Doncaster R; 31 Konchesky, Paul M. – Liverpool – Nottingham F; 2 Koranteng, Nathan T. – Peterborough U – Boston U; 4 Laird, Marc J.P. – Millwall – Brentford; 25 Lansbury, Henri G. – Arsenal – Norwich C; 4 Lees, Thomas J. – Leeds U – Bury; 11 Leigertwood, Mikele – QPR – Reading; 27 Leonard, Ryan I. – Plymouth Arg – Tiverton T; 6 Lillis, Joshua M. – Scunthorpe U – Rochdale; 13 Linganzi, Amine K. – Blackburn R – Preston NE; 7 Locke, Simon J. – Reading – Basingstoke T; 31 Long, Kevin F. – Burnley – Accrington S; 13 Lowry, Shane T. – Aston Villa – Sheffield; 19 MacLean, Steven – Plymouth Arg – Oxford U; 7 Malone, Scott L. – Wolverhampton W – Burton Alb; 5 Malsom, Samual A. – Hereford U – Redditch U; 4 Mannone, Vito – Arsenal – Hull C; 21 Manset, Mathieu – Hereford U –

Reading; 31 Marsh-Brown, Keanu – Fulham – Milton Keynes D; 7 Marshall, Ben – Stoke C – Carlisle U; 21 Martin, David J. – Derby Co – Notts Co; 21 Martin, Ellis – Portsmouth – Havant & W'Ville; 21 Mason, Ryan G. – Tottenham H – Doncaster R; 13 Mattock, Joseph W. – WBA – Sheffield U; 14 McCartney, George – Sunderland – Leeds U; 18 McCracken, David – Brentford – Bristol R; 3 McCrae, Romone C. – Histon – Peterborough U; 31 McKenna, Jack S. – Bristol R – Chippenham T; 1 McLean, Aaron – Peterborough U – Hull C; 2 Mee, Benjamin – Manchester C – Leicester C; 31 Mellis, Jacob A. – Chelsea – Barnsley; 22 Miller, Ishmael A. – WBA – QPR; 28 Miller, Lee A. – Middlesbrough – Scunthorpe U; 3 Mills, Daniel P. – Histon – Peterborough U; 31 Mills, Joseph N. – Southampton – Doncaster R; 14 Modest, Nathan D. – Sheffield W – Darlington; 1 Montgomery, Graeme – Dagenham & R – Newport Co; 7 Mooney, David – Reading – Colchester U; 14 Morgan, Kerry D. – Swansea C – Newport Co; 7 Morgan, Marvin N. – Aldershot T – Dagenham & R; 31 Murtagh, Keiran Z. – Yeovil T – Woking; 11 Naughton, Kyle – Tottenham H – Leicester C; 26 N'Guessen, Diombo – Leicester C – Southampton; 31 Nicholls, Lee A. – Wigan Ath – Shrewsbury T; 11 Noble, Liam T. – Sunderland – Carlisle U; 1 Norwood, James T. – Exeter C – Eastbourne Bor; 31 Nouble, Frank H. – West Ham U – Barnsley; 7 Obika, Jonathan – Tottenham H – Peterborough U; 7 O'Connor, Patrick J. – Millwall – Hampton & Richmond Bor; 31 O'Donnell, Richard M. – Sheffield W – Alfreton T; 7 Okus, Conor E. – Dagenahm & R – Ebbsfleet U; 17 Ollerenshaw, Joshua D. – Oldham Ath – Salford C; 31 O'Neill, Luke M. – Leicester C – Kettering T; 20 O'Shea, James – Birmingham C – Port Vale; 30 Osbourne, Isaiah G. – Aston Villa – Sheffield W; 28 Oshodi, Edward A.M.O.A. – Watford – Rushden & D; 31 Pell, Harry D.B. – Bristol R – Hereford U; 31 Perkins, Lewis C. – Charlton Ath – Hastings U; 10 Philliskirk, Daniel – Chelsea – Sheffield U; 28 Pope, Thomas J. – Rotherham U – Port Vale; 31 Porter, George – Leyton Orient – Hastings U; 27 Preston, Daniel S. – Birmingham C – Hereford U; 28 Price, Jason J. – Carlisle U – Walsall; 7 Prosser, Luke B. – Southend U – Rushden & D; 31 Puncheon, Jason D.I. – Plymouth Arg – Blackpool; 15 Putnins, Elvijs – QPR – Boreham Wood; 28 Quirke, Michael J. – Coventry C – Nuneaton T; 24 Ramsey, Aaron J. – Arsenal – Cardiff C; 25 Rance, Dean J. – Gillingham – Maidstone U; 20 Roberts, Craig – Stockport Co – Lancaster C; 3 Rowe, James M. – Reading – Lewes; 31 Robinson, Jake D. – Brighton & HA – Torquay U; 21 Routledge, Wayne N. – Newcastle U – QPR; 11 Ryan, Perry D. – Portsmouth – Bognor Regis T; 6 Sadler, Matthew – Watford – Shrewsbury T; 21 Sawyers, Romaine – WBA – Port Vale; 30 Smalley, Deane A.M. – Oldham Ath – Chesterfield; 21 Smyth, Thomas J. – Accrington S – Workington; 28 Spencer, Damian M. – Cheltenham T – Eastbourne Bor; 5 Spencer, James C. – Huddersfield T – Morecambe; 31 Stanley, Craig – Morecambe – Torquay U; 7 Stockley, Jayden C. – Bournemouth – Dorchester T; 31 Straker, Anthony – Aldershot T – Wycombe W; 6 Tafazolli, Ryan S. – Southampton – Salisbury C; 1 Taiwo, Soloman O. – Cardiff C – Dagenham & R; 31 Taylor, Lyle J.A. – Bournemouth – Lewes; 7 Tejan-Sie, Thomas M. – Dagenham & R – Thurrock; 21 Thomas, Casey E. – Swansea C – Port Talbot; 20 Townsend, Andros – Tottenham H – Watford; 6 Tozer, Ben P.A. – Newcastle U – Northampton T; 11 Trippier, Kieran J. – Manchester C – Barnsley; 6 Trotman, Neal A. – Preston NE – Oldham Ath; 21 Tudur Jones, Owain – Norwich C – Brentford; 21 Tuna, Tamer H. – Charlton Ath – Aveley; 31 Tutte, Andrew W. – Manchester C – Yeovil T; 31 Van Aanholt, Patrick J. – Chelsea – Leicester C; 26 Vaughan, James O. – Everton – Crystal Palace; 31 Verma, Aman K. – Leicester C

– Darlington; 20 Vidal, Javan – Manchester C – Chesterfield; 15 Vine, Rowan L. – QPR – Milton Keynes D; 28 Walker, Joshua – Watford – Northampton T; 14 Walker, Mitchell C. – Brighton & HA – Welling U; 7 Walsh, Phillip – Dagenham & R – Cheltenham T; 18 Watson, Ben C. – Exeter C – Bath C; 24 Wedgbury, Samuel – Macclesfield T – Altrincham; 20 Weimann, Andreas – Aston Villa – Watford; 27 White, Aidan P. – Leeds U – Oldham Ath; 7 White, Andrew J. – Gillingham – Bishop's Stortford; 1 Wilbraham, Aaron T. – Milton Keynes D – Norwich C; 28 Wilson, Callum E. – Coventry C – Kettering T; 6 Wood, Chris – WBA – Brighton & HA; 25 Worthington, Jonathan A. – Oldham Ath – Bradford C; 1 Wotton, Paul A. – Southampton – Yeovil T; 14 Yakubu, Ayegbeni – Everton – Leicester C; 1 Yussuf, Abdillahie – Leicester C – Tamworth; 18 Zola, Calvin M. – Crewe Alex – Burton Alb

FEBRUARY 2011 TEMPORARY TRANSFERS

14 Allen-Djilali, Kieran S.L. – Crystal Palace – Chesterfield; 1 Almond, Louis J. – Blackpool – Barrow; 11 Ayala, Daniel S. – Liverpool – Derby Co; 8 Borrowdale, Gary I. – Coventry C – Carlisle U; 23 Broughton, Drewe O. – Lincoln C – AFC Wimbledon; 11 Bruma, Jeffrey K. – Chelsea – Leicester C; 21 Burton, Alan M. – Accrington S – Marine; 21 Byrne, Nathan W. – Tottenham H – Brentford; 12 Canham, Sean – Notts Co – Kidderminster H; 11 Chilaka, Chibuzor – Bradford C – Harrogate T; 11 Clifford, Conor – Chelsea – Notts Co; 28 Clough, Charlie – Bristol R – Bath C; 25 Coid, Daniel J. – Blackpool – Rotherham U; 21 Connolly, Reece W. – Aldershot T – Dorchester T; 18 Cotterill, David R.G.B. – Swansea C – Portsmouth; 15 Cowan-Hall, Paris D.J. – Scunthorpe U – Rushden & D; 10 Daley, Omar – Bradford C – Rotherham U; 22 Darley, Grant L.W. – Rotherham U – Boston U; 18 Davies, Andrew J. – Stoke C – Middlesbrough; 21 Davis, Harry S. – Crewe Alex – Curzon Ashton; 11 Dean, Harlee J. – Dagenham & R – Bishop's Stortford; 8 Deering, Sam – Oxford U – Barnet; 16 Dikagcoi, Kagisho – Fulham – Crystal Palace; 17 Doble, Ryan A. – Southampton – Stockport Co; 21 Edwards, Robert O. – Blackpool – Norwich C; 25 Elito, Medy E. – Colchester U – Cheltenham T; 10 Ellison, Kevin – Rotherham U – Bradford C; 18 Elliott, Christopher M. – Bradford C – Harrogate T; 17 Euell, Jason J. – Blackpool – Doncaster R; 11 Fairhurst, Waide S. – Doncaster R – Hereford U; 25 Fielding, Francis D. – Blackburn R – Derby Co; 22 Flanagan, Calum R. – Aston Villa – Kettering T; 1 Flanagan, Thomas M. – Milton Keynes D – Kettering T; 17 Foderingham, Wesley A. – Fulham – Boreham Wood; 26 Furzer, Jack L. – Exeter C – Bideford; 11 Garrod, Tony R. – Southampton – Bishop's Stortford; 10 German, Antonio T. – QPR – Yeovil T; 10 Gilligan, Ryan J. – Northampton T – Torquay U; 21 Green, Jamie P. – Rotherham U – Boston U; 25 Grella, Michele – Leeds U – Swindon T; 1 Grocutt, Kevin J. – Burton Alb – Vauxhall Motors; 4 Gwynne, Sam – Hereford U – Telford U; 26 Harewood, Marlon A. – Aston Villa – Barnsley; 28 Haynes, Kyle – Cheltenham T – Salisbury C; 15 Henderson, Liam M. – Watford – Rotherham U; 16 Hobbs, Jack – Leicester C – Hull C; 18 Holness, Charlie H.V. – Crystal Palace – Hampton & Richmond Bor; 25 Hooman, Harry J. – Shrewsbury T – Hinckley U; 11 Hughes, Stephen – Norwich C – Milton Keynes D; 25 Hughes-Mason, Kiernan P. – Millwall – Chelmsford C; 18 Jarrett, Albert O. – Lincoln C – Aldershot T; 16 Jeffers, Shaun E. – Coventry C – Cambridge U; 26 Jordan, Stephen R. – Sheffield U – Huddersfield T; 23 Kiernan, Robert S. – Watford – Wycombe W; 11 Kennedy, Callum E. – Swindon T – Rotherham U; 11 Lichaj, Eric J. – Aston Villa – Leeds U; 3 Locke, Simon J. – Reading –

159

Basingstoke T; 18 Logan, Conrad J. – Leicester C – Bristol R; 21 Mackreth, Jack – Tranmere R – Hyde U; 11 Malsom, Samual A. – Hereford U – Gloucester C; 17 Mantom, Samuel S. – WBA – Oldham Ath; 14 McCrae, Romone C.A. – Peterborough U – Kettering T; 11 McDonald, Kevin – Burnley – Notts Co; 22 McDonald, Rodney T. – Oldham Ath – Nantwich T; 25 McLoughlin, Ian M. – Ipswich T – Stockport Co; 17 McShane, Paul D. – Hull C – Barnsley; 28 Medley, Luke A.C. – Mansfield T – Aldershot T; 8 Mellor, Kelvin – Crewe Alex – Leek T; 14 Mills, Daniel P. – Peterborough U – Kettering T; 4 Mills, Gregory A. – Derby Co – Telford U; 19 Moussa, Franck – Leicester C – Doncaster R; 17 Neilson, Robbie – Leicester C – Brentford; 18 Nnamani, Jerry O. – Crystal Palace – Bromley; 8 Obika, Jonathan – Tottenham H – Swindon T; 11 O'Connor, Patrick J. – Millwall – Hampton & Richmond Bor; 9 Odubade, Yemi E. – Stevenage – Newport Co; 1 O'Neill, Luke M. – Leicester C – Kettering T; 25 Palmer, Edward G. – Torquay U – Weymouth; 10 Paterson, Matthew – Southend U – Stockport Co; 19 Payne, Stefan S. – Gillingham – Braintree T; 8 Pulis, Anthony J. – Southampton – Barnet; 4 Randall, Jack D. – Aldershot T – Didcot T; 11 Raymond, Frankie J. – Reading – Basingstoke T; 21 Reed, Adam M. – Sunderland – Brentford; 24 Regan, Carl A. – Bristol R – Notts Co; 15 Riise, Bjorn H.S. – Fulham – Sheffield U; 18 Roberts, Adam J. – Macclesfield T – Northwich Vic; 22 Robinson, Theo L.R. – Millwall – Derby Co; 25 Rowlands, Martin C. – QPR – Millwall; 23 Scott, Mark J. – Swindon T – Didcot T; 18 Shea, James – Arsenal – Southampton; 25 Shephard, Christopher J. – Exeter C – Salisbury C; 1 Smyth, Thomas J. – Accrington S – Workington; 15 Stockley, Jayden C. – AFC Bournemouth – Dorchester T; 7 Tavernier, James H. – Newcastle U – Gateshead; 11 Tejan-Sie, Thomas M. – Dagenham & R – Thurrock; 5 Thomas, Daniel – AFC Bournemouth – Dorchester T; 26 Thomson, Jake S. – Exeter C – Cheltenham T; 11 Turner, Iain – Everton – Preston NE; 15 Vokes, Samuel M. – Wolverhampton W – Sheffield U; 18 Wallace, James R. – Everton – Stockport Co; 16 Ward, Jamie J. – Sheffield U – Derby Co; 14 Weir, Robert J. – Sunderland – Tranmere R; 28 Weir, Tyler C. – Hereford U – Gloucester C; 10 Winnall, Sam T. – Wolverhampton W – Burton Alb

MARCH 2011 TEMPORARY TRANSFERS

10 Agustien, Germaine – Swansea C – Crystal Palace; 21 Akpan, Hope – Everton – Hull C; 17 Aley, Zachery G. – Blackburn R – Morecambe; 4 Alnwick, Ben R. – Tottenham H – Doncaster R; 1 Amoo, David O.S. – Liverpool – Hull C; 9 Andrew, Calvin H. – Crystal Palace – Swindon T; 7 Anyon, Joseph – Lincoln C – Morecambe; 4 Arter, Harry N. – AFC Bournemouth – Carlisle U; 7 Bannan, Barry – Aston Villa – Leeds U; 11 Barrett, Adam N. – Crystal Palace – Leyton Orient; 11 Bates, Jon-Jo D. – Dagenham & R – Maidenhead U; 3 Bateson, Jonathan A. – Accrington S – Altrincham; 16 Batth, Daniel T. – Wolverhampton W – Sheffield W; 23 Bell, Matthew – Port Vale – Newcastle T; 8 Bentley, Mark J. – Gillingham – Cambridge U; 18 Blizzard, Dominic J. – Bristol R – Port Vale; 17 Bond, Jonathan H. – Watford – Brackley T; 18 Borini, Fabio – Chelsea – Swansea C; 15 Bowerman, George O. – Walsall – Redditch U; 8 Boyd, Kris – Middlesbrough – Nottingham F; 31 Brown, Christopher R. – Rochdale – Hyde U; 3 Brown, Jason R. – Blackburn R – Cardiff C; 17 Burge, Ryan J. – Doncaster R – Oxford U; 31 Byrne, Callum – Rochdale – Hyde U; 2 Byrne, Mark – Nottingham F – Barnet; 4 Bywater Stephen – Derby Co – Cardiff C; 14 Calver, Craig – Yeovil T – Braintree T; 23 Canavan, Niall D.S. – Scunthorpe U – Shrewsbury T; 24

Canham, Sean – Hereford U – Kidderminster H; 24 Carson, Trevor – Sunderland – Brentford; 4 Cestor, Mike B. – Leyton Orient – Boreham Wood; 24 Clayton, Adam S. – Leeds U – Milton Keynes D; 8 Collis, Stephen P. – Peterborough U – Northampton T; 24 Cook, Jordan A. – Sunderland – Walsall; 4 Cooper, Liam D.I. – Hull C – Carlisle U; 11 Corcoran, Samuel J. – Colchester U – Lowestoft T; 24 Cosgrove, Jonathan G. – Fulham – Brentford; 25 Cox, Elliott J. – QPR – Histon; 4 Dalla Valle, Lauri – Liverpool – AFC Bournemouth; 31 Darley, Grant L.W. – Rotherham U – Frickley Ath; 31 Dean, Harlee J. – Southampton – Bishop's Stortofrd; 18 Dean, Luke A. – Bradford C – Ossett T; 8 Delfouneso, Nathan – Aston Villa – Burnley; 2 Doble, Ryan A. – Southampton – Oxford U; 31 Doughty, Michael E. – QPR – Woking; 24 Duffy, Shane P.M. – Everton – Burnley; 4 Duke, Matthew – Hull C – Derby Co; 11 Dyer, Kieron C. – West Ham U – Ipswich T; 14 Eckersley, Richard J. – Burnley – Bury; 18 Ellison, James – Burton Alb – Hednesford T – ; 21 Essam, Connor – Gillingham – Dover Ath; 8 Etheridge, Neil – Fulham – Charlton Ath; 3 Federico, Jerome J. – Wycombe W – Maidenhead U; 22 Flint, Aden – Swindon T – Alfreton T; 25 Foderingham, Wesley A. – Crystal Palace – Histon; 8 Gardner, Ricardo – Bolton W – Preston NE; 4 Gbarssin, Marc-Antoine – Carlisle U – Walsall; 15 Geddes, Sean A. – Walsall – Redditch U; 26 Green, Dominic A. – Dagenham & R – St Neots T; 8 Guzan, Bradley E. – Aston Villa – Hull C; 19 Harvey, Alex-Ray – Burnley – Fleetwood T; 8 Haynes, Kyle J. – Cheltenham T – Hednesford T; 11 Hendrie, Stuart S. – Morecambe – Tamworth; 22 Hickman, Alexander W. – Walsall – Redditch U; 25 Holland, Jack – Crystal Palace – Eastbourne Bor; 19 Holness, Charlie H.V. – Crystal Palace – Lewes; 11 Holroyd, Christopher – Brighton & HA – Bury; 31 Hutchinson, Andrew L. – Lincoln C – Lewes; 25 James-Lewis, Merrick – Southend U – Braintree T; 24 Jones, Bradley – Liverpool – Derby Co; 17 Jones, Robert W. – Scunthorpe U – Sheffield W; 21 Kamara, Diomansy – Fulham – Leicester C; 8 Kelly, Danny M. – Barnet – Eastbourne Bor; 24 Khumalo, Bongani – Tottenham H – Preston NE; 24 Kilbey, Thomas C. – Portsmouth – Lincoln C; 31 Kosylo, Matthew S.P. – Stockport Co – Salford C; 24 Laird, Marc J.P. – Millwall – Walsall; 22 Lancaster, Cameron P. – Tottenham H – Dagenham & R; 25 Lee, Jake A. – Cheltenham T – Thurrock; 24 Lee, Oliver R. – West Ham U – Dagenham & R; 24 Lennox, Joe M. – Bristol C – Bath C; 17 Leslie, Steven – Shrewsbury T – Hereford U; 24 Livermore, Jake C. – Tottenham H – Leeds U; 24 Lowe, Jason J. – Blackburn R – Oldham Ath; 10 Lowe, Matthew T. – Macclesfield T – Kidderminster H; 17 MacDonald, Shaun B. – Swansea C – Yeovil T; 30 Mackreth, Jack – Tranmere R – Chester C; 24 Mahon, Gavin A. – QPR – Crystal Palace; 7 Massey, Gavin A. – Watford – Wealdstone; 24 McDermott, Donal – Manchester C – AFC Bournemouth; 21 Midson, Jack W. – Oxford U – Barnet; 23 Morrison, Sean J. – Reading – Huddersfield T; 11 Murray, Ronan M. – Ipswich T – Torquay U; 18 Mvoto, Jean Y.O. – Sunderland – Oldham Ath; 14 N'Diaye, Alassane – Crystal Palace – Swindon T; 31 Nelson, Mitchell A. – AFC Bournemouth – Lewes; 24 Nicholls, Lee A. – Wigan Ath – Sheffield W; 11 Nouble, Frank H. – West Ham U – Charlton Ath; 24 Nunez, Ramon F. – Leeds U – Scunthorpe U; 17 Obika, Jonathan – Tottenham H – Yeovil T; 24 O'Brian, Joseph M. – Bolton W – Sheffield W; 29 O'Connor, Patrick J. – Millwall – Lewes; 8 Ofori-Twumasi, Seth N. – Peterborough U – Northampton T; 24 Pacheco, Daniel L. – Liverpool – Norwich C; 24 Parish, Elliott C. – Aston Villa – Lincoln C; 24 Parkes, Thomas P.W. – Leicester C – Burton Alb; 11 Parrett, Dean G. – Tottenham H – Charlton Ath; 3 Parsons, Matthew J. – Crystal Palace – Barnet; 11 Pentney, Carl – Colchester U – Chelmsford C; 25 Perkins, Lewis C. – Charlton

Ath – Aveley; 18 Pinney, Nathanel B. – Crystal Palace – Braintree T; 24 Price, Jason J. – Carlisle U – Hereford U; 4 Pringle, Ben P. – Derby Co – Torquay U; 24 Priskin, Tamas – Ipswich T – Swansea C; 31 Rance, Dean J.R. – Gillingham – Bishop's Stortford; 25 Raymond, Frankie J. – Reading – Basingstoke T; 8 Reckord, Jamie – Wolverhampton W – Northampton T; 29 Roberts, Craig – Stockport Co – Hyde U; 8 Rodney, Nialle – Nottingham F – Burton Alb; 1 Rundle, Adam – Morecambe – Gateshead; 24 Samuel, Jlloyd – Bolton W – Cardiff C; 14 Schlupp, Jeffrey – Leicester C – Brentford; 23 Short, Lewis G.T. – Crewe Alex – Northwich Vic; 29 Simpson, Jacob D. – Stockport Co – Hyde U; 8 Smith, Paul D. – Nottingham F – Middlesbrough; 17 Smith, Thomas J. – Ipswich T – Colchester U; 3 Spence, Jordan – West Ham U – Bristol C; 4 Sproule, Ivan – Bristol C – Notts Co; 21 Stam, Stefan – Yeovil T – Hereford U; 24 Stephens, Dale C. – Oldham Ath – Southampton; 24 Stirling, Jude B. – Milton Keynes D – Barnet; 17 Sullivan, John D. – Millwall – Charlton Ath; 31 Taylor, Lyle J.A. – AFC Bournemouth – Woking; 22 Taylor, Rhys F. – Chelsea – Crewe Alex; 31 Thomas, Aidan – Hereford U – Telford U; 31 Thomas, Daniel – AFC Bournemouth – Dorchester T; 24 Thompson-Lambe, Reginald – Ipswich T – Bristol R; 11 Tomlin, Gavin G. – Dagenham & R – Torquay U; 7 Townsend, Andros – Tottenham H – Millwall; 21 Vine, Rowan L. – QPR – Milton Keynes D; 24 Vokes, Samuel M. – Wolverhampton W – Norwich C; 24 Walker, Samuel C. – Chelsea – Barnet; 14 Ward, Daniel C. – Bolton W – Huddersfield T; 17 Webster, Byron C. – Doncaster R – Northampton T; 24 Welch, Joe – Histon – Stevenage; 30 Wilkinson, Daniel P. – Hull C – North Ferriby U; 5 Williams, Jonathan J. – Scunthorpe U – Brigg T; 24 Williams, Marcus V. – Reading – Scunthorpe U; 24 Wood, James R.F. – Manchester C – Exeter C; 11 Young, Lewis J. – Burton Alb – Forest Green R

APRIL 2011 TEMPORARY TRANSFERS

18 Byrne, Nathan – Tottenham H – Brentford; 3 Clough, Charlie – Bristol R – Bath C; 18 Connolly, Reece W. – Aldershot T – Dorchester T; 1 Davis, Harry S. – Crewe Alex – Curzon Ashton; 17 Djilai, Kieran – Crystal Palace – Chesterfield; 17 Fairhurst, Waide S. – Doncaster R – Hereford U; 27 Gwynne, Sam – Hereford U – AFC Telford U; 26 Moussa, Franck N. – Leicester C – Doncaster R; 17 Neilson, Robbie – Leicester C – Brentford; 1 O'Neill, Luke M. – Leicester C – Kettering T; 18 Reed, Adam – Sunderland – Brentford; 27 Shephard, Christopher – Exeter C – Salisbury C; 11 Turner, Iain R. – Everton – Preston NE; 3 Weir, Tyler – Hereford U – Gloucester C

MAY 2011

10 Fielding, Francis D.	Blackburn R	Derby Co
9 Ward, Jamie J.	Sheffield U	Derby Co

FOREIGN TRANSFERS 2010–2011

JULY/AUGUST 2010	From	To
Alcaraz, Antolin	Club Brugge	Wigan Ath
Al-Muhammadi, Ahmed	ENPPI	Sunderland
Barrera, Pablo	UNAM	West Ham U
Beausejour, Jean	America	Birmingham C
Ben Arfa, Hatem	Marseille	Newcastle U
Boateng, Jerome	Hamburg	Manchester C
Boselli, Mauro	Estudiantes	Wigan Ath
Chamakh, Marouane	Bordeaux	Arsenal
Dembele, Moussa	AZ	Fulham
Gohouri, Steve	Moenchengladbach	Wigan Ath
Grandin, Elliot	CSKA Sofia	Blackpool
Gyan, Asamoah	Rennes	Sunderland
Hernandez, Javier	Guadalajara	Manchester U
Jovanovic, Milan	Standard Liege	Liverpool
Keinan, Dekel	Maccabi Haifa	Blackpool
Kolarov, Aleksandar	Lazio	Manchester C
Koscielny, Laurent	Lorient	Arsenal
Linganzi, Amine	St Etienne	Blackburn Rovers
Mignolet, Simon	St Truiden	Sunderland
Mujangi Bia, Geoffrey	Charleroi	Wolverhampton W
Obinna, Victor	Internazionale	West Ham U
Odemwingie, Peter	Lokomotiv Moscow	WBA
Pablo	Atletico Madrid	WBA
Poulsen, Christian	Juventus	Liverpool
Ramires	Benfica	Chelsea
Raul Meireles	Porto	Liverpool
Reid, Winston	Midtjylland	West Ham U
Riveros, Cristian	Cruz Azul	Sunderland
Salcido, Carlos	PSV Eindhoven	Fulham
Silva, David	Valencia	Manchester C
Squillaci, Sebastien	Sevilla	Arsenal
Stam, Ronnie	Twente	Wigan Ath
Sylvestre, Ludovic	Mlada Boleslav	Blackpool
Tchoyi, Somen	Salzburg	WBA
Tiote, Cheik Ismael	Twente	Newcastle U
Toure, Yaya	Barcelona	Manchester C
Van der Vaart, Rafael	Real Madrid	Tottenham H
Zigic, Nikola	Valencia	Birmingham C

JANUARY/FEBRUARY 2011		
Ba, Demba	Hoffenheim	West Ham U
Ben Arfa, Hatem	Marseille	Newcastle U
Dzeko, Edin	Wolfsburg	Manchester C
Jones, Jermaine	Schalke	Blackburn R
Kornilenko, Sergei	Zenit	Blackpool
Lindegaard, Anders	Aalesund	Manchester U
Lopez, Adrian	La Coruna	Wigan Ath
Luiz, David	Benfica	Chelsea
Makoun, Jean	Lyon	Aston Villa
Rochina, Ruben	Barcelona	Blackburn R
Sessegnon, Stephane	Paris St Germain	Sunderland
Suarez, Luis	Ajax	Liverpool

MILESTONES 2010–2011

FEBRUARY
27   Carling Cup final: Birmingham City 2 Arsenal 1.

MARCH
20   CIS Insurance Cup final: Rangers 2 Celtic 1.

APRIL
 3   Johnstone's Paint Trophy: Carlisle United 1 Brentford 0.
 9   Livingston promoted to Scottish League Div 1.
      Crawley Town promoted to League Two as Blue Square Premier champions.
      Histon relegated from Blue Square Premier.
10   Stirling Albion relegated to Scottish League Div 2.
      Alba Challenge Cup final: Ross County 2 Queen of the South 0.
12   Brighton & Hove Albion promoted to Football League Championship.
16   Brighton & Hove Albion League One champions.
      Eastbourne Borough relegated from Blue Square Premier.
22   Chesterfield promoted to League One.
23   Arbroath promoted to Scottish League Div 2.
      Peterhead relegated to Scottish League Div 3.
25   Preston North End relegated to League One.
      Swindon Town relegated to League Two.
      Bury promoted to League One.
30   Queens Park Rangers Football League Champions.
      Sheffield United and Scunthorpe United relegated to League One.
      Stockport County relegated to Blue Square Premier.
      Dunfermline Athletic promoted to Scottish Premier League.
      Altrincham and Southport relegated from Blue Square Premier.
      Bangor City Welsh Premier League champions.

MAY
 2   Norwich City promoted to Premier League.
      Plymouth Argyle relegated to League Two.
 7   Southampton promoted to Championship.
      Wycombe Wanderers promoted to League One.
      Chesterfield become League Two champions.
      Dagenham & Redbridge relegated to League Two.
      Bristol Rovers relegated to League Two.
      Lincoln City relegated to Blue Square Premier.
      FA Trophy final: Darlington 1 Mansfield Town 0.
      Irish Cup final: Linfield 2 Crusaders 1.
 8   FA Vase final: Whitley Bay 3 Coalville Town 2.
      Welsh Cup final: Llanelli 4 Bangor City 1.
10   Hamilton Academical relegated to Scottish League Div 1.
14   Manchester United Premier League champions.
      FA Cup final: Manchester City 1 Stoke City 0.
      Cowdenbeath relegated to Scottish League Div 2.
      Alloa Athletic relegated to Scottish League Div 3.
15   West Ham United relegated to Football League Championship.
18   Europa League final: Porto 1 Braga 0.
21   Active Nation Scottish Cup final: Celtic 3 Motherwell 0.
      Blue Square Premier Play-off final: AFC Wimbledon 0 Luton Town 0
      (AFC Wimbledon win 4-3 on penalties and promoted to League Two).
      Women's FA Cup final: Arsenal 2 Bristol Academy 0.
22   Birmingham City and Blackpool relegated to Football League Championship.
      Ayr United promoted to Scottish League Div 1.
      Albion Rovers promoted to Scottish League Div 2.
28   Champions League final: Barcelona 3 Manchester United 1.
      League Two play-off final: Stevenage 1 Torquay United 0.
      (Stevenage promoted to League Two).
29   League One play-off final: Peterborough United 3 Huddersfield Town 0.
      (Peterborough United promoted to Championship).
30   Championship play-off final: Swansea City 4 Reading 2.
      (Swansea City promoted to Premier League).

THE FA CUP 2010–2011

FIRST ROUND

Rochdale	(0) 2	FC United of Manchester	(1) 3
Accrington S	(2) 3	Oldham Ath	(0) 2
AFC Wimbledon	(0) 0	Ebbsfleet U	(0) 0
Barnet	(0) 0	Charlton Ath	(0) 0
Bournemouth	(3) 5	Tranmere R	(2) 3
Brentford	(1) 1	Aldershot T	(1) 1
Brighton & HA	(0) 0	Woking	(0) 0
Bury	(1) 2	Exeter C	(0) 0
Cambridge U	(0) 0	Huddersfield T	(0) 0
Carlisle U	(5) 6	Tipton T	(0) 0
Chelmsford C	(2) 3	Hendon	(1) 2
Cheltenham T	(0) 1	Morecambe	(0) 0
Colchester U	(2) 4	Bradford C	(2) 3
Corby T	(1) 1	Luton T	(0) 1
Dagenham & R	(1) 1	Leyton Orient	(1) 1
Darlington	(1) 2	Bristol R	(1) 1
Dartford	(1) 1	Port Vale	(0) 1
Fleetwood T	(0) 1	Walsall	(1) 1
Forest Green R	(0) 0	Northampton T	(2) 3
Gillingham	(0) 0	Dover Ath	(2) 2
Guiseley	(0) 0	Crawley T	(2) 5
Harrow Bor	(0) 0	Chesterfield	(0) 2
Hartlepool U	(0) 0	Vauxhall Motors	(0) 0
Havant & Waterlooville	(0) 0	Droylsden	(0) 2
Hayes & Yeading U	(0) 1	Wycombe W	(0) 2
Hereford U	(4) 5	Hythe T	(1) 1
Lincoln C	(0) 1	Nuneaton T	(0) 0
Macclesfield T	(1) 2	Southend U	(1) 2
Mansfield T	(0) 0	Torquay U	(0) 1
Notts Co	(1) 2	Gateshead	(0) 0
Plymouth Arg	(0) 0	Swindon T	(2) 4
Rotherham U	(0) 0	York C	(0) 0
Rushden & D	(0) 0	Yeovil T	(0) 1
Southampton	(0) 2	Shrewsbury T	(0) 0
Stevenage	(0) 0	Milton Keynes D	(0) 0
Stockport Co	(1) 1	Peterborough U	(1) 1
Swindon Supermarine	(2) 2	Eastwood T	(0) 1
Tamworth	(1) 2	Crewe Alex	(0) 1
Burton Alb	(0) 1	Oxford U	(0) 0
Southport	(0) 2	Sheffield W	(1) 5

FIRST ROUND REPLAYS

Aldershot T	(1) 1	Brentford	(0) 0
Charlton Ath	(1) 1	Barnet	(0) 0
Huddersfield T	(0) 2	Cambridge U	(0) 1
Leyton Orient	(2) 3	Dagenham & R	(0) 2
Milton Keynes D	(0) 1	Stevenage	(0) 1
(aet; Stevenage won 7-6 on penalties.)			
Peterborough U	(1) 4	Stockport Co	(0) 1
Port Vale	(2) 4	Dartford	(0) 0
Southend U	(0) 2	Macclesfield T	(0) 2
(aet; Macclesfield T won 5-3 on penalties.)			
Vauxhall Motors	(0) 0	Hartlepool U	(0) 1

| Walsall | (0) 2 | Fleetwood T | (0) 0 |
| Woking | (0) 2 | Brighton & HA | (0) 2 |

(aet; Brighton & HA won 3-0 on penalties.)

Luton T	(2) 4	Corby T	(0) 2
York C	(0) 3	Rotherham U	(0) 0
Ebbsfleet U	(2) 2	AFC Wimbledon	(1) 3

(aet.)

SECOND ROUND

Crawley T	(0) 1	Swindon T	(0) 1
Port Vale	(1) 1	Accrington S	(0) 0
AFC Wimbledon	(0) 0	Stevenage	(1) 2
Brighton & HA	(0) 1	FC United of Manchester	(1) 1
Burton Alb	(2) 3	Chesterfield	(0) 1
Bury	(0) 1	Peterborough U	(2) 2
Carlisle U	(0) 3	Tamworth	(1) 2
Charlton Ath	(2) 2	Luton T	(1) 2
Colchester U	(1) 1	Swindon Supermarine	(0) 0
Darlington	(0) 0	York C	(1) 2
Dover Ath	(0) 2	Aldershot T	(0) 0
Hereford U	(1) 2	Lincoln C	(2) 2
Huddersfield T	(3) 6	Macclesfield T	(0) 0
Sheffield W	(2) 3	Northampton T	(0) 2
Southampton	(1) 3	Cheltenham T	(0) 0
Torquay U	(1) 1	Walsall	(0) 0
Wycombe W	(1) 3	Chelmsford C	(0) 1
Droylsden	(1) 1	Leyton Orient	(0) 1
Hartlepool U	(2) 4	Yeovil T	(2) 2
Notts Co	(3) 3	Bournemouth	(0) 1

SECOND ROUND REPLAYS

| Leyton Orient | (0) 8 | Droylsden | (1) 2 |

(aet.)

| Swindon T | (2) 2 | Crawley T | (1) 3 |

(aet.)

| FC United of Manchester | (0) 0 | Brighton & HA | (2) 4 |

(Played at Bury.)

| Luton T | (1) 1 | Charlton Ath | (1) 3 |
| Lincoln C | (2) 3 | Hereford U | (3) 4 |

THIRD ROUND

Arsenal	(0) 1	Leeds U	(0) 1
Blackburn R	(0) 1	QPR	(0) 0
Bolton W	(0) 2	York C	(0) 0
Brighton & HA	(2) 3	Portsmouth	(0) 1
Bristol C	(0) 0	Sheffield W	(0) 3
Burnley	(2) 4	Port Vale	(1) 2
Burton Alb	(0) 2	Middlesbrough	(0) 1
Coventry C	(2) 2	Crystal Palace	(0) 1
Doncaster R	(2) 2	Wolverhampton W	(1) 2
Fulham	(2) 6	Peterborough U	(0) 2
Huddersfield T	(2) 2	Dover Ath	(0) 0
Hull C	(0) 2	Wigan Ath	(1) 3
Millwall	(0) 1	Birmingham C	(3) 4

Norwich C	(0) 0	Leyton Orient	(1) 1
Preston NE	(1) 1	Nottingham F	(0) 2
Reading	(1) 1	WBA	(0) 0
Scunthorpe U	(0) 1	Everton	(2) 5
Sheffield U	(0) 1	Aston Villa	(2) 3
Southampton	(0) 2	Blackpool	(0) 0
Stevenage	(0) 3	Newcastle U	(0) 1
Stoke C	(1) 1	Cardiff C	(1) 1
Sunderland	(0) 1	Notts Co	(1) 2
Swansea C	(2) 4	Colchester U	(0) 0
Torquay U	(1) 1	Carlisle U	(0) 0
Watford	(0) 4	Hartlepool U	(1) 1
West Ham U	(1) 2	Barnsley	(0) 0
Chelsea	(3) 7	Ipswich T	(0) 0
Leicester C	(1) 2	Manchester C	(2) 2
Manchester U	(1) 1	Liverpool	(0) 0
Tottenham H	(0) 3	Charlton Ath	(0) 0
Crawley T	(1) 2	Derby Co	(0) 1
Wycombe W	(0) 0	Hereford U	(1) 1

THIRD ROUND REPLAYS

Cardiff C	(0) 0	Stoke C	(0) 2
(aet.)			
Manchester C	(3) 4	Leicester C	(1) 2
Wolverhampton W	(1) 5	Doncaster R	(0) 0
Leeds U	(1) 1	Arsenal	(2) 3

FOURTH ROUND

Aston Villa	(3) 3	Blackburn R	(1) 1
Birmingham C	(1) 3	Coventry C	(2) 2
Bolton W	(0) 0	Wigan Ath	(0) 0
Burnley	(1) 3	Burton Alb	(0) 1
Everton	(0) 1	Chelsea	(0) 1
Sheffield W	(1) 4	Hereford U	(1) 1
Southampton	(1) 1	Manchester U	(0) 2
Stevenage	(0) 1	Reading	(1) 2
Swansea C	(1) 1	Leyton Orient	(1) 2
Torquay U	(0) 0	Crawley T	(1) 1
Watford	(0) 0	Brighton & HA	(1) 1
Arsenal	(1) 2	Huddersfield T	(0) 1
Fulham	(4) 4	Tottenham H	(0) 0
Notts Co	(0) 1	Manchester C	(0) 1
West Ham U	(2) 3	Nottingham F	(2) 2
Wolverhampton W	(0) 0	Stoke C	(0) 1

FOURTH ROUND REPLAYS

Wigan Ath	(0) 0	Bolton W	(0) 1
Chelsea	(0) 1	Everton	(0) 1
(aet; Everton won 4-3 on penalties.)			
Manchester C	(1) 5	Notts Co	(0) 0

FIFTH ROUND

Birmingham C	(2) 3	Sheffield W	(0) 0
Manchester U	(1) 1	Crawley T	(0) 0

Stoke C	(3) 3	Brighton & HA	(0) 0
Fulham	(0) 0	Bolton W	(1) 1
Leyton Orient	(0) 1	Arsenal	(0) 1
West Ham U	(1) 5	Burnley	(0) 1
Everton	(0) 0	Reading	(1) 1
Manchester C	(2) 3	Aston Villa	(0) 0

FIFTH ROUND REPLAY

| Arsenal | (3) 5 | Leyton Orient | (0) 0 |

SIXTH ROUND

Birmingham C	(1) 2	Bolton W	(1) 3
Manchester U	(1) 2	Arsenal	(0) 0
Manchester C	(0) 1	Reading	(0) 0
Stoke C	(1) 2	West Ham U	(1) 1

SEMI-FINALS

| Manchester C | (0) 1 | Manchester U | (0) 0 |
| Bolton W | (0) 0 | Stoke C | (3) 5 |

THE FA CUP FINAL

Saturday, 14 May 2011

Manchester C (0) 1   Stoke C (0) 0

(at Wembley Stadium, attendance 88,643)

Manchester C: Hart; Richards, Kolarov, De Jong, Lescott, Kompany, Barry (Johnson A), Toure Y, Balotelli, Tevez (Zabaleta), Silva (Vieira).
Scorer: Toure Y 74.

Stoke C: Sorensen; Wilkinson, Wilson, Huth, Shawcross, Whelan (Pugh), Pennant, Delap (Carew), Jones, Walters, Etherington (Whitehead).

Referee: M. Atkinson (West Yorkshire).

Did You Know?

Of the four different actual FA Cup trophies that have existed since 1872 one was bought at Christie's in 2005 by David Gold, now the joint chairman of West Ham United, and generously loaned to the National Football Museum for display at Preston North End's Deepdale ground. The first trophy was stolen from the shoe shop window of William Shillcock when on display, too, in 1895. Aston Villa the then holders had to pay £25 for a replacement. The thief melted down the original for counterfeit coins! A replica cup was used until it was presented to FA President Lord Kinnaird in 1910 on completing 21 years as FA President. A larger size trophy was made in 1911 by Fattorini's a Bradford company and immediately won by Bradford City! Through usage and age this became too fragile and a subsequent replica was commissioned in 1992 and made by Toye, Kenning and Spencer with a back-up for emergencies.

PAST FA CUP FINALS

Details of one goalscorer is not available in 1878.

1872	The Wanderers............................1 *Betts*	Royal Engineers.............................0
1873	The Wanderers............................2 *Kinnaird, Wollaston*	Oxford University..........................0
1874	Oxford University.......................2 *Mackarness, Patton*	Royal Engineers.............................0
1875	Royal Engineers..........................1 *Renny-Tailyour*	Old Etonians...............................1* *Bonsor*
Replay	Royal Engineers..........................2 *Renny-Tailyour, Stafford*	Old Etonians.................................0
1876	The Wanderers............................1 *Edwards*	Old Etonians...............................1* *Bonsor*
Replay	The Wanderers............................3 *Wollaston, Hughes 2*	Old Etonians.................................0
1877	The Wanderers............................2 *Lindsay, Kenrick*	Oxford University.......................1* *Kinnaird (og)*
1878	The Wanderers............................3 *Kenrick 2, Kinnaird*	Royal Engineers.............................1 *Unknown*
1879	Old Etonians...............................1 *Clerke*	Clapham Rovers.............................0
1880	Clapham Rovers..........................1 *Lloyd-Jones*	Oxford University..........................0
1881	Old Carthusians..........................3 *Wyngard, Parry, Todd*	Old Etonians.................................0
1882	Old Etonians...............................1 *Anderson*	Blackburn Rovers..........................0
1883	Blackburn Olympic......................2 *Costley, Matthews*	Old Etonians...............................1* *Goodhart*
1884	Blackburn Rovers........................2 *Sowerbutts, Forrest*	Queen's Park, Glasgow.................1 *Christie*
1885	Blackburn Rovers........................2 *Forrest, Brown*	Queen's Park, Glasgow.................0
1886	Blackburn Rovers........................0	West Bromwich Albion.................0
Replay	Blackburn Rovers........................2 *Brown, Sowerbutts*	West Bromwich Albion.................0
1887	Aston Villa..................................2 *Hunter, Hodgetts*	West Bromwich Albion.................0
1888	West Bromwich Albion................2 *Woodhall, Bayliss*	Preston NE....................................1 *Dewhurst*
1889	Preston NE...................................3 *Dewhurst, J. Ross, Thompson*	Wolverhampton W........................0
1890	Blackburn Rovers........................6 *Walton, John Southworth,* *Lofthouse, Townley 3*	Sheffield W...................................1 *Bennett*
1891	Blackburn Rovers........................3 *Dewar, John Southworth,* *Townley*	Notts Co.......................................1 *Oswald*
1892	West Bromwich Albion................3 *Geddes, Nicholls, Reynolds*	Aston Villa....................................0
1893	Wolverhampton W.......................1 *Allen*	Everton..0

1894	Notts Co	4	Bolton W	1
	Watson, Logan 3		*Cassidy*	
1895	Aston Villa	1	West Bromwich Albion	0
	J. Devey			
1896	Sheffield W	2	Wolverhampton W	1
	Spiksley 2		*Black*	
1897	Aston Villa	3	Everton	2
	Campbell, Wheldon, Crabtree		*Boyle, Bell*	
1898	Nottingham F	3	Derby Co	1
	Cape 2, McPherson		*Bloomer*	
1899	Sheffield U	4	Derby Co	1
	Bennett, Beers, Almond, Priest		*Boag*	
1900	Bury	4	Southampton	0
	McLuckie 2, Wood, Plant			
1901	Tottenham H	2	Sheffield U	2
	Brown 2		*Bennett, Priest*	
Replay	Tottenham H	3	Sheffield U	1
	Cameron, Smith, Brown		*Priest*	
1902	Sheffield U	1	Southampton	1
	Common		*Wood*	
Replay	Sheffield U	2	Southampton	1
	Hedley, Barnes		*Brown*	
1903	Bury	6	Derby Co	0
	Ross, Sagar, Leeming 2, Wood, Plant			
1904	Manchester C	1	Bolton W	0
	Meredith			
1905	Aston Villa	2	Newcastle U	0
	Hampton 2			
1906	Everton	1	Newcastle U	0
	Young			
1907	Sheffield W	2	Everton	1
	Stewart, Simpson		*Sharp*	
1908	Wolverhampton W	3	Newcastle U	1
	Hunt, Hedley, Harrison		*Howey*	
1909	Manchester U	1	Bristol C	0
	A. Turnbull			
1910	Newcastle U	1	Barnsley	1
	Rutherford		*Tufnell*	
Replay	Newcastle U	2	Barnsley	0
	Shepherd 2 (1 pen)			
1911	Bradford C	0	Newcastle U	0
Replay	Bradford C	1	Newcastle U	0
	Speirs			
1912	Barnsley	0	West Bromwich Albion	0
Replay	Barnsley	1	West Bromwich Albion	0*
	Tufnell			
1913	Aston Villa	1	Sunderland	0
	Barber			
1914	Burnley	1	Liverpool	0
	Freeman			
1915	Sheffield U	3	Chelsea	0
	Simmons, Masterman, Kitchen			

Year	Winner	Score	Runner-up	Score
1920	Aston Villa *Kirton*	1	Huddersfield T	0*
1921	Tottenham H *Dimmock*	1	Wolverhampton W	0
1922	Huddersfield T *Smith (pen)*	1	Preston NE	0
1923	Bolton W *Jack, J.R. Smith*	2	West Ham U	0
1924	Newcastle U *Harris, Seymour*	2	Aston Villa	0
1925	Sheffield U *Tunstall*	1	Cardiff C	0
1926	Bolton W *Jack*	1	Manchester C	0
1927	Cardiff C *Ferguson*	1	Arsenal	0
1928	Blackburn Rovers *Roscamp 2, McLean*	3	Huddersfield T *A. Jackson*	1
1929	Bolton W *Butler, Blackmore*	2	Portsmouth	0
1930	Arsenal *James, Lambert*	2	Huddersfield T	0
1931	West Bromwich Albion *W.G. Richardson 2*	2	Birmingham *Bradford*	1
1932	Newcastle U *Allen 2*	2	Arsenal *John*	1
1933	Everton *Stein, Dean, Dunn*	3	Manchester C	0
1934	Manchester C *Tilson 2*	2	Portsmouth *Rutherford*	1
1935	Sheffield W *Rimmer 2, Palethorpe, Hooper*	4	West Bromwich Albion *Boyes, Sandford*	2
1936	Arsenal *Drake*	1	Sheffield U	0
1937	Sunderland *Gurney, Carter, Burbanks*	3	Preston NE *F. O'Donnell*	1
1938	Preston NE *Mutch (pen)*	1	Huddersfield T	0*
1939	Portsmouth *Parker 2, Barlow, Anderson*	4	Wolverhampton W *Dorsett*	1
1946	Derby Co *H. Turner (og), Doherty, Stamps 2*	4	Charlton Ath *H. Turner*	1*
1947	Charlton Ath *Duffy*	1	Burnley	0*
1948	Manchester U *Rowley 2, Pearson, Anderson*	4	Blackpool *Shimwell (pen), Mortensen*	2
1949	Wolverhampton W *Pye 2, Smyth,*	3	Leicester C *Griffiths*	1
1950	Arsenal *Lewis 2*	2	Liverpool	0
1951	Newcastle U *Milburn 2*	2	Blackpool	0

1952	Newcastle U 1	Arsenal 0
	G. Robledo	
1953	Blackpool 4	Bolton W 3
	Mortensen 3, Perry	*Lofthouse, Moir, Bell*
1954	West Bromwich Albion 3	Preston NE 2
	Allen 2 (1 pen), Griffin	*Morrison, Wayman*
1955	Newcastle U 3	Manchester C 1
	Milburn, Mitchell,	*Johnstone*
	Hannah	
1956	Manchester C 3	Birmingham C 1
	Hayes, Dyson, Johnstone	*Kinsey*
1957	Aston Villa 2	Manchester U 1
	McParland 2	*T. Taylor*
1958	Bolton W 2	Manchester U 0
	Lofthouse 2	
1959	Nottingham F 2	Luton T 1
	Dwight, Wilson	*Pacey*
1960	Wolverhampton W 3	Blackburn Rovers 0
	McGrath (og), Deeley 2	
1961	Tottenham H 2	Leicester C 0
	Smith, Dyson	
1962	Tottenham H 3	Burnley 1
	Greaves, Smith,	*Robson*
	Blanchflower (pen)	
1963	Manchester U 3	Leicester C 1
	Herd 2, Law	*Keyworth*
1964	West Ham U 3	Preston NE 2
	Sissons, Hurst, Boyce	*Holden, Dawson*
1965	Liverpool 2	Leeds U 1*
	Hunt, St John	*Bremner*
1966	Everton 3	Sheffield W 2
	Trebilcock 2, Temple	*McCalliog, Ford*
1967	Tottenham H 2	Chelsea 1
	Robertson, Saul	*Tambling*
1968	West Browmwich Albion 1	Everton 0*
	Astle	
1969	Manchester C 1	Leicester C 0
	Young	
1970	Chelsea 2	Leeds U 2*
	Houseman, Hutchinson	*Charlton, Jones*
Replay	Chelsea 2	Leeds U 1*
	Osgood, Webb	*Jones*
1971	Arsenal 2	Liverpool 1*
	Kelly, George	*Heighway*
1972	Leeds U 1	Arsenal 0
	Clarke	
1973	Sunderland 1	Leeds U 0
	Porterfield	
1974	Liverpool 3	Newcastle 0
	Keegan 2, Heighway	
1975	West Ham U 2	Fulham 0
	A. Taylor 2	
1976	Southampton 1	Manchester U 0
	Stokes	

Year	Winner	Score	Runner-up	Score
1977	Manchester U	2	Liverpool	1
	Pearson, J. Greenhoff		*Case*	
1978	Ipswich T	1	Arsenal	0
	Osborne			
1979	Arsenal	3	Manchester U	2
	Talbot, Stapleton, Sunderland		*McQueen, McIlroy*	
1980	West Ham U	1	Arsenal	0
	Brooking			
1981	Tottenham H	1	Manchester C	1*
	Hutchison (og)		*Hutchison*	
Replay	Totteham H	3	Manchester C	2
	Villa 2, Crooks		*MacKenzie, Reeves (pen)*	
1982	Tottenham H	1	QPR	1*
	Hoddle		*Fenwick*	
Replay	Tottenham H	1	QPR	0
	Hoddle (pen)			
1983	Manchester U	2	Brighton & HA	2*
	Stapleton, Wilkins		*Smith, Stevens*	
Replay	Manchester U	4	Brighton & HA	0
	Robson 2, Whiteside, Muhren (pen)			
1984	Everton	2	Watford	0
	Sharp, Gray			
1985	Manchester U	1	Everton	0*
	Whiteside			
1986	Liverpool	3	Everton	1
	Rush 2, Johnston		*Lineker*	
1987	Coventry C	3	Tottenham H	2*
	Bennett, Houchen, Mabbutt (og)		*C. Allen, Kilcline (og)*	
1988	Wimbledon	1	Liverpool	0
	Sanchez			
1989	Liverpool	3	Everton	2*
	Aldridge, Rush 2		*McCall 2*	
1990	Manchester U	3	Crystal Palace	3*
	Robson, Hughes 2		*O'Reilly, Wright 2*	
Replay	Manchester U	1	Crystal Palace	0
	Martin			
1991	Tottenham H	2	Nottingham F	1*
	Stewart, Walker (og)		*Pearce*	
1992	Liverpool	2	Sunderland	0
	Thomas, Rush			
1993	Arsenal	1	Sheffield W	1*
	Wright		*Hirst*	
Replay	Arsenal	2	Sheffield W	1*
	Wright, Linighan		*Waddle*	
1994	Manchester U	4	Chelsea	0
	Cantona 2 (2 pens), Hughes, McClair			
1995	Everton	1	Manchester U	0
	Rideout			
1996	Manchester U	1	Liverpool	0
	Cantona			
1997	Chelsea	2	Middlesbrough	0
	Di Matteo, Newton			

1998	Arsenal	2	Newcastle U	0
	Overmars, Anelka			
1999	Manchester U	2	Newcastle U	0
	Sheringham, Scholes			
2000	Chelsea	1	Aston Villa	0
	Di Matteo			
2001	Liverpool	2	Arsenal	1
	Owen 2		*Ljungberg*	
2002	Arsenal	2	Chelsea	0
	Parlour, Ljungberg			
2003	Arsenal	1	Southampton	0
	Pires			
2004	Manchester U	3	Millwall	0
	Ronaldo, Van Nistelrooy 2 (1 pen)			
2005	Arsenal	0	Manchester U	0*
	Arsenal won 5-4 on penalties			
2006	Liverpool	3	West Ham U	3*
	Cisse, Gerrard 2		*Carragher (og), Ashton, Konchesky*	
	Liverpool won 3-1 on penalties			
2007	Chelsea	1	Manchester U	0*
	Drogba			
2008	Portsmouth	1	Cardiff C	0
	Kanu			
2009	Chelsea	2	Everton	1
	Drogba, Lampard		*Saha*	

*After extra time

2010	Chelsea	1	Portsmouth	0
	Drogba			
2011	Manchester C	1	Stoke C	0
	Y. Toure			

FA CUP ATTENDANCES 1969–2011

	Total	No. of matches	Average per match		Total	No. of matches	Average per match
2010–11	1,996,935	150	13,313	1989–90	2,190,463	170	12,885
2009–10	1,884,421	151	12,480	1988–89	1,966,318	164	12,173
2008–09	2,131,669	163	13,078	1987–88	2,050,585	155	13,229
2007–08	2,011,320	152	13,232	1986–87	1,877,400	165	11,378
2006–07	2,218,846	158	14,043	1985–86	1,971,951	168	11,738
2005–06	1,966,638	160	12,291	1984–85	1,909,359	157	12,162
2004–05	1,999,752	146	13,697	1983–84	1,941,400	166	11,695
2003–04	1,870,103	149	12,551	1982–83	2,209,625	154	14,348
2002–03	1,850,326	150	12,336	1981–82	1,840,955	160	11,506
2001–02	1,809,093	148	12,224	1980–81	2,756,800	169	16,312
2000–01	1,804,535	151	11,951	1979–80	2,661,416	163	16,328
1999–2000	1,700,913	158	10,765	1978–79	2,604,002	166	15,687
1998–99	2,107,947	155	13,599	1977–78	2,594,578	160	16,216
1997–98	2,125,696	165	12,883	1976–77	2,982,102	174	17,139
1996–97	1,843,998	151	12,211	1975–76	2,759,941	161	17,142
1995–96	2,046,199	167	12,252	1974–75	2,968,903	172	17,261
1994–95	2,015,249	161	12,517	1973–74	2,779,952	167	16,646
1993–94	1,965,146	159	12,359	1972–73	2,928,975	160	18,306
1992–93	2,047,670	161	12,718	1971–72	3,158,562	160	19,741
1991–92	1,935,340	160	12,095	1970–71	3,220,432	162	19,879
1990–91	2,038,518	162	12,583	1969–70	3,026,765	170	17,805

SUMMARY OF FA CUP WINNERS SINCE 1872

Manchester United	11
Arsenal	10
Tottenham Hotspur	8
Aston Villa	7
Liverpool	7
Blackburn Rovers	6
Chelsea	6
Newcastle United	6
Everton	5
Manchester City	5
The Wanderers	5
West Bromwich Albion	5
Bolton Wanderers	4
Sheffield United	4
Wolverhampton Wanderers	4
Sheffield Wednesday	3
West Ham United	3
Bury	2
Nottingham Forest	2
Old Etonians	2
Portsmouth	2
Preston North End	2
Sunderland	2
Barnsley	1
Blackburn Olympic	1
Blackpool	1
Bradford City	1
Burnley	1
Cardiff City	1
Charlton Athletic	1
Clapham Rovers	1
Coventry City	1
Derby County	1
Huddersfield Town	1
Ipswich Town	1
Leeds United	1
Notts County	1
Old Carthusians	1
Oxford University	1
Royal Engineers	1
Southampton	1
Wimbledon	1

APPEARANCES IN FA CUP FINAL

Manchester United	18
Arsenal	17
Everton	13
Liverpool	13
Newcastle United	13
Aston Villa	10
Chelsea	10
West Bromwich Albion	10
Manchester City	9
Tottenham Hotspur	9
Blackburn Rovers	8
Wolverhampton Wanderers	8
Bolton Wanderers	7
Preston North End	7
Old Etonians	6
Sheffield United	6
Sheffield Wednesday	6
Huddersfield Town	5
Portsmouth	5
The Wanderers	5
West Ham United	5
Derby County	4
Leeds United	4
Leicester City	4
Oxford University	4
Royal Engineers	4
Southampton	4
Sunderland	4
Blackpool	3
Burnley	3
Cardiff City	3
Nottingham Forest	3
Barnsley	2
Birmingham City	2
Bury	2
Charlton Athletic	2
Clapham Rovers	2
Notts County	2
Queen's Park (Glasgow)	2
Blackburn Olympic	1
Bradford City	1
Brighton & Hove Albion	1
Bristol City	1
Coventry City	1
Crystal Palace	1
Fulham	1
Ipswich Town	1
Luton Town	1
Middlesbrough	1
Millwall	1
Old Carthusians	1
Queens Park Rangers	1
Stoke C.	1
Watford	1
Wimbledon	1

CARLING CUP 2010–2011

FIRST ROUND

Stevenage	(1) 1	Portsmouth	(2) 2
Aldershot T	(0) 0	Watford	(2) 3
Barnsley	(0) 0	Rochdale	(0) 1
Bradford C	(0) 2	Nottingham F	(1) 1
(aet.)			
Brentford	(2) 2	Cheltenham T	(0) 1
Carlisle U	(0) 0	Huddersfield T	(0) 1
Chesterfield	(0) 1	Middlesbrough	(2) 2
Crewe Alex	(1) 1	Derby Co	(0) 0
Doncaster R	(0) 1	Accrington S	(0) 2
(aet.)			
Exeter C	(0) 2	Ipswich T	(0) 3
(aet.)			
Hereford U	(0) 0	Colchester U	(2) 3
Leeds U	(3) 4	Lincoln C	(0) 0
Leicester C	(1) 4	Macclesfield T	(1) 3
Milton Keynes D	(0) 2	Dagenham & R	(1) 1
Morecambe	(1) 2	Coventry C	(0) 0
Northampton T	(2) 2	Brighton & HA	(0) 0
Norwich C	(2) 4	Gillingham	(1) 1
Oxford U	(4) 6	Bristol R	(1) 1
Peterborough U	(2) 4	Rotherham U	(1) 1
Plymouth Arg	(0) 0	Notts Co	(0) 1
QPR	(0) 1	Port Vale	(2) 3
Scunthorpe U	(0) 2	Oldham Ath	(1) 1
Sheffield W	(0) 1	Bury	(0) 0
Shrewsbury T	(2) 4	Charlton Ath	(3) 3
Southampton	(0) 2	Bournemouth	(0) 0
Southend U	(1) 3	Bristol C	(1) 2
(aet.)			
Stockport Co	(0) 0	Preston NE	(1) 5
Swansea C	(1) 3	Barnet	(0) 0
Swindon T	(1) 1	Leyton Orient	(0) 2
Walsall	(0) 0	Tranmere R	(1) 1
Wycombe W	(0) 1	Millwall	(1) 2
(aet.)			
Yeovil T	(0) 0	Crystal Palace	(0) 1
Cardiff C	(1) 4	Burton Alb	(1) 1
(aet)			
Hartlepool U	(1) 2	Sheffield U	(0) 0
Torquay U	(0) 0	Reading	(0) 1
(aet.)			

SECOND ROUND

Blackburn R	(1) 3	Norwich C	(0) 1
Bradford C	(0) 1	Preston NE	(1) 2
(aet.)			
Brentford	(1) 2	Hull C	(1) 1
Crewe Alex	(0) 0	Ipswich T	(0) 1
(aet.)			
Hartlepool U	(0) 0	Wigan Ath	(1) 3
Leeds U	(1) 1	Leicester C	(0) 2
Leyton Orient	(0) 0	WBA	(1) 2

Millwall	(2) 2	Middlesbrough	(0) 1
Milton Keynes D	(1) 4	Blackpool	(0) 3
(aet.)			
Morecambe	(1) 1	Burnley	(1) 3
Peterborough U	(0) 2	Cardiff C	(1) 1
Portsmouth	(0) 1	Crystal Palace	(0) 1
(aet; Portsmouth won 4-3 on penalties.)			
Reading	(1) 3	Northampton T	(1) 3
(aet; Northampton T won 4-2 on penalties.)			
Scunthorpe U	(1) 4	Sheffield W	(0) 2
Southampton	(0) 0	Bolton W	(1) 1
Stoke C	(2) 2	Shrewsbury T	(0) 1
Sunderland	(2) 2	Colchester U	(0) 0
Tranmere R	(1) 1	Swansea C	(0) 3
Watford	(0) 1	Notts Co	(0) 2
West Ham U	(0) 1	Oxford U	(0) 0
Wolverhampton W	(1) 2	Southend U	(0) 1
(aet.)			
Accrington S	(1) 2	Newcastle U	(1) 3
Everton	(2) 5	Huddersfield T	(1) 1
Fulham	(4) 6	Port Vale	(0) 0
Birmingham C	(1) 3	Rochdale	(1) 2

THIRD ROUND

Birmingham C	(3) 3	Milton Keynes D	(0) 1
Brentford	(1) 1	Everton	(1) 1
(aet; Brentford won 4-3 on penalties.)			
Burnley	(1) 1	Bolton W	(0) 0
Millwall	(0) 1	Ipswich T	(2) 2
Peterborough U	(1) 1	Swansea C	(2) 3
Portsmouth	(0) 1	Leicester C	(2) 2
Stoke C	(1) 2	Fulham	(0) 0
Sunderland	(1) 1	West Ham U	(1) 2
Tottenham H	(0) 1	Arsenal	(1) 4
(aet.)			
Wolverhampton W	(0) 4	Notts Co	(0) 2
(aet.)			
Aston Villa	(0) 3	Blackburn R	(1) 1
Chelsea	(1) 3	Newcastle U	(2) 4
Liverpool	(1) 2	Northampton T	(0) 2
(aet; Northampton T won 4-2 on penalties.)			
Scunthorpe U	(1) 2	Manchester U	(2) 5
WBA	(0) 2	Manchester C	(1) 1
Wigan Ath	(0) 2	Preston NE	(1) 1

FOURTH ROUND

Birmingham C	(0) 1	Brentford	(0) 1
(aet; Birmingham C won 4-3 on penalties.)			
Ipswich T	(2) 3	Northampton T	(1) 1
Leicester C	(0) 1	WBA	(1) 4
Manchester U	(0) 3	Wolverhampton W	(0) 2
Wigan Ath	(0) 2	Swansea C	(0) 0
Aston Villa	(0) 2	Burnley	(0) 1
(aet.)			
Newcastle U	(0) 0	Arsenal	(1) 4
West Ham U	(0) 3	Stoke C	(1) 1
(aet.)			

177

QUARTER-FINALS

Arsenal	(1) 2	Wigan Ath	(0) 0
West Ham U	(2) 4	Manchester U	(0) 0
Birmingham C	(1) 2	Aston Villa	(1) 1
Ipswich T	(0) 1	WBA	(0) 0

SEMI-FINALS FIRST LEG

West Ham U	(1) 2	Birmingham C	(0) 1
Ipswich T	(0) 1	Arsenal	(0) 0

SEMI-FINALS SECOND LEG

Arsenal	(0) 3	Ipswich T	(0) 0
Birmingham C	(0) 3	West Ham U	(1) 1

(aet.)

THE CARLING CUP FINAL

Sunday, 28 February 2011

Birmingham C (1) 2   Arsenal (1) 1

(at Wembley Stadium, attendance 88,851)

Arsenal: Szczesny; Sagna, Clichy, Song Billong, Djourou, Koscielny, Rosicky, Wilshere, Van Persie (Bendtner), Arshavin (Chamakh), Nasri.
Scorer: Van Persie 39.

Birmingham C: Foster; Carr, Ridgewell, Bowyer, Jiranek, Johnson, Larsson, Ferguson, Zigic (Jerome), Gardner (Beausejour), Fahey (Martins).
Scorers: Zigic 28, Martins 89.

Referee: M. Dean (Wirral).

Did You Know?

Aston Villa, the first winners of the League Cup in 1961 had to wait until the start of the following season before they could finish the two-legged final. Having done so they were required to defend their title within eight days! In half a century the cup has had some memorable finals initially played over two legs. In 1966 West Bromwich Albion came back to defeat a formidable West Ham United team which included the famous trio of Bobby Moore, Geoff Hurst and Martin Peters. Arsenal twice suffered defeats against lower opposition to Swindon Town in 1969 on a muddy Wembley pitch and in 1988 when Luton Town's Andy Dibble saved a penalty and they went on to score twice in the last seven minutes. Manager Ron Saunders led three different teams in three seasons: Norwich City, Manchester City and Aston Villa! Didier Drogba became the first player to score in three such finals.

PAST LEAGUE CUP FINALS

Played as two legs up to 1966

1961	Rotherham U	2	Aston Villa	0
	Webster, Kirkman			
	Aston Villa	3	Rotherham U	0*
	O'Neill, Burrows, McParland			
1962	Rochdale	0	Norwich C	3
	Lythgoe 2, Punton			
	Norwich C	1	Rochdale	0
	Hill			
1963	Birmingham C	3	Aston Villa	1
	Leek 2, Bloomfield		*Thomson*	
	Aston Villa	0	Birmingham C	0
1964	Stoke C	1	Leicester C	1
	Bebbington		*Gibson*	
	Leicester C	3	Stoke C	2
	Stringfellow, Gibson, Riley		*Viollet, Kinnell*	
1965	Chelsea	3	Leicester C	2
	Tambling, Venables (pen), McCreadie		*Appleton, Goodfellow*	
	Leicester C	0	Chelsea	0
1966	West Ham U	2	WBA	1
	Moore, Byrne		*Astle*	
	WBA	4	West Ham U	1
	Kaye, Brown, Clark, Williams		*Peters*	
1967	QPR	3	WBA	2
	Morgan R, Marsh, Lazarus		*Clark C 2*	
1968	Leeds U	1	Arsenal	0
	Cooper			
1969	Swindon T	3	Arsenal	1*
	Smart, Rogers 2		*Gould*	
1970	Manchester C	2	WBA	1*
	Doyle, Pardoe		*Astle*	
1971	Tottenham H	2	Aston Villa	0
	Chivers 2			
1972	Chelsea	1	Stoke C	2
	Osgood		*Conroy, Eastham*	
1973	Tottenham H	1	Norwich C	0
	Coates			
1974	Wolverhampton W	2	Manchester C	1
	Hibbitt, Richards		*Bell*	
1975	Aston Villa	1	Norwich C	0
	Graydon			
1976	Manchester C	2	Newcastle U	1
	Barnes, Tueart		*Gowling*	
1977	Aston Villa	0	Everton	0
Replay	Aston Villa	1	Everton	1*
	Kenyon (og)		*Latchford*	
Replay	Aston Villa	3	Everton	2*
	Little 2, Nicholl		*Latchford, Lyons*	
1978	Nottingham F	0	Liverpool	0*
Replay	Nottingham F	1	Liverpool	0
	Robertson (pen)			

1979	Nottingham F...........3	Southampton 2
	Birtles 2, Woodcock	Peach, Holmes
1980	Wolverhampton W 1	Nottingham F...........0
	Gray	
1981	Liverpool...........1	West Ham U 1*
	Kennedy A	Stewart (pen)
Replay	Liverpool...........2	West Ham U 1
	Dalglish, Hansen	Goddard
1982	Liverpool...........3	Tottenham H...........1*
	Whelan 2, Rush	Archibald
1983	Liverpool...........2	Manchester U 1*
	Kennedy A, Whelan	Whiteside
1984	Liverpool...........0	Everton...........0*
Replay	Liverpool...........1	Everton...........0
	Souness	
1985	Norwich C 1	Sunderland 0
	Chisholm (og)	
1986	Oxford U 3	QPR 0
	Hebberd, Houghton, Charles	
1987	Arsenal 2	Liverpool...........1
	Nicholas 2	Rush
1988	Luton T...........3	Arsenal 2
	Stein B 2, Wilson	Hayes, Smith
1989	Nottingham F...........3	Luton T...........1
	Clough 2, Webb	Harford
1990	Nottingham F...........1	Oldham Ath 0
	Jemson	
1991	Sheffield W 1	Manchester U 0
	Sheridan	
1992	Manchester U 1	Nottingham F...........0
	McClair	
1993	Arsenal 2	Sheffield W 1
	Merson, Morrow	Harkes
1994	Aston Villa 3	Manchester U 1
	Atkinson, Saunders 2 (1 pen)	Hughes
1995	Liverpool...........2	Bolton W 1
	McManaman 2	Thompson
1996	Aston Villa 3	Leeds U 0
	Milosevic, Taylor, Yorke	
1997	Leicester C 1	Middlesbrough...........1*
	Heskey	Ravanelli
Replay	Leicester C 1	Middlesbrough...........0*
	Claridge	
1998	Chelsea 2	Middlesbrough...........0*
	Sinclair, Di Matteo	
1999	Tottenham H...........1	Leicester C 0
	Nielsen	
2000	Leicester C 2	Tranmere R 1
	Elliott 2	Kelly
2001	Liverpool...........1	Birmingham C 1
	Fowler	Purse (pen)
	Liverpool won 5-4 on penalties.	
2002	Blackburn 2	Tottenham H...........1
	Jansen, Cole	Ziege

2003	Liverpool 2	Manchester U 0
	Gerrard, Owen	
2004	Middlesbrough 2	Bolton W 1
	Job, Zenden (pen)	*Davies*
2005	Chelsea 3	Liverpool..2*
	Gerrard (og), Drogba, Kezman	*Riise, Nunez*
2006	Manchester U 4	Wigan Ath 0
	Rooney 2, Saha, Ronaldo	
2007	Chelsea 2	Arsenal..1
	Drogba 2	*Walcott*
2008	Tottenham H..2	Chelsea 1*
	Berbatov, Woodgate	*Drogba*
2009	Manchester U 0	Tottenham H..0*

Manchester U won 4-1 on penalties.

2010	Manchester U 2	Aston Villa 1
	Owen, Rooney	*Milner (pen)*
2011	Birmingham C 2	Arsenal..1
	Zigic, Martins	*Van Persie*

*After extra time

LEAGUE CUP ATTENDANCES 1960–2011

	Total	No. of matches	Average per match		Total	No. of matches	Average per match
2010–11	1,197,917	93	12,881	1984–85	1,876,429	167	11,236
2009–10	1,376,405	93	14,800	1983–84	1,900,491	168	11,312
2008–09	1,329,753	93	14,298	1982–83	1,679,756	160	10,498
2007–08	1,332,841	94	14,179	1981–82	1,880,682	161	11,681
2006–07	1,098,403	93	11,811	1980–81	2,051,576	161	12,743
2005–06	1,072,362	93	11,531	1979–80	2,322,866	169	13,745
2004–05	1,313,693	93	14,216	1978–79	1,825,643	139	13,134
2003–04	1,267,729	93	13,631	1977–78	2,038,295	148	13,772
2002–03	1,242,478	92	13,505	1976–77	2,236,636	147	15,215
2001–02	1,076,390	93	11,574	1975–76	1,841,735	140	13,155
2000–01	1,501,304	154	9,749	1974–75	1,901,094	127	14,969
1999–2000	1,354,233	153	8,851	1973–74	1,722,629	132	13,050
1998–99	1,555,856	153	10,169	1972–73	1,935,474	120	16,129
1997–98	1,484,297	153	9,701	1971–72	2,397,154	123	19,489
1996–97	1,529,321	163	9,382	1970–71	2,035,315	116	17,546
1995–96	1,776,060	162	10,963	1969–70	2,299,819	122	18,851
1994–95	1,530,478	157	9,748	1968–69	2,064,647	118	17,497
1993–94	1,744,120	163	10,700	1967–68	1,671,326	110	15,194
1992–93	1,558,031	161	9,677	1966–67	1,394,553	118	11,818
1991–92	1,622,337	164	9,892	1965–66	1,205,876	106	11,376
1990–91	1,675,496	159	10,538	1964–65	962,802	98	9,825
1989–90	1,836,916	168	10,934	1963–64	945,265	104	9,089
1988–89	1,552,780	162	9,585	1962–63	1,029,893	102	10,097
1987–88	1,539,253	158	9,742	1961–62	1,030,534	104	9,909
1986–87	1,531,498	157	9,755	1960–61	1,204,580	112	10,755
1985–86	1,579,916	163	9,693				

JOHNSTONE'S PAINT TROPHY 2010–2011

NORTHERN SECTION FIRST ROUND

Hartlepool U	(0) 4	Northampton T	(0) 0
Macclesfield T	(1) 1	Morecambe	(0) 0
Oldham Ath	(0) 0	Shrewsbury T	(0) 1
Port Vale	(1) 2	Rochdale	(0) 1
Rotherham U	(0) 1	Lincoln C	(0) 0
Tranmere R	(0) 1	Accrington S	(0) 1

(Acccrington S won 5-3 on penalties; Accrington S withdrew from competition.)

Walsall	(1) 1	Chesterfield	(2) 2
Sheffield W	(2) 2	Notts Co	(1) 1

SOUTHERN SECTION FIRST ROUND

Aldershot T	(1) 2	Oxford U	(0) 0
Bournemouth	(0) 0	Torquay U	(0) 0

(Torquay U won 3-0 on penalties.)

Charlton Ath	(0) 1	Dagenham & R	(0) 0
Southampton	(0) 0	Swindon T	(1) 3
Southend U	(0) 0	Gillingham	(0) 0

(Southend U won 4-3 on penalties.)

Stevenage	(0) 0	Brentford	(1) 1
Yeovil T	(0) 1	Exeter C	(1) 3
Brighton & HA	(0) 0	Leyton Orient	(1) 1

NORTHERN SECTION SECOND ROUND

Bury	(0) 0	Shrewsbury T	(0) 0

(Bury won 6-5 on penalties.)

Carlisle U	(0) 2	Port Vale	(1) 2

(Carlisle U won 4-3 on penalties.)

Hartlepool U	(0) 1	Bradford C	(0) 0
Huddersfield T	(3) 3	Peterborough U	(0) 2
Macclesfield T	(2) 2	Crewe Alex	(2) 4
Burton Alb	(0) 1	Rotherham U	(0) 2
Sheffield W	(1) 2	Chesterfield	(1) 2

(Sheffield W won 8-7 on penalties.)

Tranmere R	(0) 0	Stockport Co	(0) 0

(Tranmere R won 4-3 on penalties.)

SOUTHERN SECTION SECOND ROUND

Barnet	(0) 1	Southend U	(1) 3
Bristol R	(0) 1	Aldershot T	(0) 0
Cheltenham T	(0) 0	Plymouth Arg	(1) 2
Colchester U	(0) 0	Wycombe W	(0) 2
Hereford U	(0) 0	Exeter C	(1) 3
Leyton Orient	(0) 0	Brentford	(0) 0

(Brentford won 5-4 on penalties.)

Milton Keynes D	(1) 1	Charlton Ath	(0) 2
Swindon T	(2) 2	Torquay U	(0) 0

NORTHERN SECTION QUARTER-FINALS

Bury	(0) 0	Tranmere R	(1) 1
Carlisle U	(1) 3	Crewe Alex	(0) 1
Rotherham U	(1) 2	Huddersfield T	(3) 5
Sheffield W	(2) 4	Hartlepool U	(1) 1

SOUTHERN SECTION QUARTER-FINALS

Plymouth Arg	(0) 1	Exeter C	(1) 2
Southend U	(0) 0	Charlton Ath	(1) 1

Swindon T	(1) 1	Brentford	(1) 1
(Brentford won 4-2 on penalties.)			
Wycombe W	(0) 3	Bristol R	(2) 6

NORTHERN SECTION SEMI-FINALS

| Carlisle U | (1) 3 | Sheffield W | (0) 1 |
| Tranmere R | (0) 0 | Huddersfield T | (1) 2 |

SOUTHERN SECTION SEMI-FINALS

Brentford	(0) 0	Charlton Ath	(0) 0
(Brentford won 3-1 on penalties.)			
Bristol R	(1) 2	Exeter C	(0) 2
(Exeter C won 5-4 on penalties.)			

NORTHERN SECTION FINAL FIRST LEG

| Carlisle U | (2) 4 | Huddersfield T | (0) 0 |

NORTHERN SECTION FINAL SECOND LEG

| Huddersfield T | (1) 3 | Carlisle U | (0) 0 |

SOUTHERN SECTION FINAL FIRST LEG

| Brentford | (0) 1 | Exeter C | (1) 1 |

SOUTHERN SECTION FINAL SECOND LEG

| Exeter C | (0) 1 | Brentford | (2) 2 |

JOHNSTONE'S PAINT TROPHY FINAL

Sunday, 3 April 2011

(at Wembley Stadium, attendance 40,476)

Brentford (0) 0   Carlisle U (1) 1

Brentford: Moore; Neilson, Woodman (O'Connor), Diagouraga■, Osborne, Legge, Saunders, Reed (Bean), Alexander, Schlupp, Weston (Grabban).

Carlisle U: Collin; Simek, Robson, Thirlwell, Michalik, Murphy, Marshall (Noble), Berrett, Curran, Zoko (Madden), Taiwo (Loy).

Scorer: Murphy 12.

Referee: G. Salisbury (Lancs).

THE FA COMMUNITY SHIELD 2010

Chelsea (0) 1   Manchester U (1) 3

At Wembley Stadium, 8 August 2010, attendance 84,623

Chelsea: Hilario; Paulo Ferreira (Zhirkov 79), Cole (Bruma 79), Mikel (Drogba 60), Terry, Ivanovic, Essien, Lampard, Anelka (Sturridge 61), Kalou, Malouda (Benayoun 73).

Scorer: Kalou 83.

Manchester United: Van der Sar; O'Shea, Fabio (Smalling 71), Carrick (Giggs 79), Evans J, Vidic, Valencia, Scholes (Fletcher 79), Owen (Nani 46), Rooney (Berbatov 46), Park (Hernandez 46).

Scorers: Valencia 41, Hernandez 76, Berbatov 90.

Referee: A. Marriner (West Midlands).

SCOTTISH LEAGUE TABLES 2010–2011

Clydesdale Bank Scottish

Premier League	P	W	D	L	F	A	W	D	L	F	A	W	D	L	F	A	GD	Pts
1 Rangers	38	30	3	5	88	29	14	2	3	43	14	16	1	2	45	15	59	93
2 Celtic	38	29	5	4	85	22	15	3	1	51	11	14	2	3	34	11	63	92
3 Hearts	38	18	9	11	53	45	9	5	5	27	21	9	4	6	26	24	8	63
4 Dundee U	38	17	10	11	55	50	13	1	5	34	22	4	9	6	21	28	5	61
5 Kilmarnock	38	13	10	15	53	55	6	4	9	26	31	7	6	6	27	24	-2	49
6 Motherwell	38	13	7	18	40	60	8	3	8	24	24	5	4	10	16	36	-20	46
7 Inverness CT (P)	38	14	11	13	52	44	7	4	8	25	24	7	7	5	27	20	8	53
8 St Johnstone	38	11	11	16	23	43	6	5	8	10	19	5	6	8	13	24	-20	44
9 Aberdeen	38	11	5	22	39	59	6	2	11	22	21	5	3	11	17	38	-20	38
10 Hibernian	38	10	7	21	39	61	5	6	8	21	29	5	1	13	18	32	-22	37
11 St Mirren	38	8	9	21	33	57	4	6	9	20	27	4	3	12	13	30	-24	33
12 Hamilton A	38	5	11	22	24	59	1	8	10	12	26	4	3	12	12	33	-35	26

Top 6 teams split after 33 games.

Irn-Bru Scottish

First Division	P	W	D	L	F	A	W	D	L	F	A	W	D	L	F	A	GD	Pts
1 Dunfermline Ath	36	20	10	6	66	31	11	6	1	39	14	9	4	5	27	17	35	70
2 Raith R	36	17	9	10	47	35	9	3	6	25	20	8	6	4	22	15	12	60
3 Falkirk (R)	36	17	7	12	57	41	9	3	6	32	22	8	4	6	25	19	16	58
4 Queen of the S	36	14	7	15	54	53	7	3	8	31	30	7	4	7	23	23	1	49
5 Partick Th	36	12	11	13	44	39	8	6	4	23	11	4	5	9	21	28	5	47
6 Dundee	36	19	12	5	54	34	11	7	0	29	13	8	5	5	25	21	20	44
7 Morton	36	11	10	15	39	43	7	5	6	18	17	4	5	9	21	26	-4	43
8 Ross Co	36	9	14	13	30	34	4	7	7	15	17	5	7	6	15	17	-4	41
9 Cowdenbeath (P)	36	9	8	19	41	72	5	4	9	21	31	4	4	10	20	41	-31	35
10 Stirling Alb (P)	36	4	8	24	32	82	2	4	12	17	39	2	4	12	15	43	-50	20

Dundee deducted 25 points.

Irn-Bru Scottish

Second Division	P	W	D	L	F	A	W	D	L	F	A	W	D	L	F	A	GD	Pts
1 Livingston (P)	36	25	7	4	79	33	13	5	0	41	14	12	2	4	38	19	46	82
2 Ayr U¶ (R)	36	18	5	13	62	55	11	3	4	28	21	7	2	9	34	34	7	59
3 Forfar Ath (P)	36	17	8	11	50	48	10	5	3	32	22	7	3	8	18	26	2	59
4 Brechin C	36	15	12	9	63	45	9	3	6	35	26	6	9	3	28	19	18	57
5 East Fife	36	14	10	12	77	60	8	3	7	42	30	6	7	5	35	30	17	52
6 Airdrie U (R)	36	13	9	14	52	60	5	7	6	24	29	8	2	8	28	31	-8	48
7 Dumbarton	36	11	7	18	52	70	7	3	8	33	29	4	4	10	19	41	-18	40
8 Stenhousemuir	36	10	8	18	46	59	7	3	8	28	26	3	5	10	18	33	-13	38
9 Alloa Ath	36	9	9	18	49	71	5	6	7	27	31	4	3	11	22	40	-22	36
10 Peterhead	36	5	11	20	47	76	5	5	8	27	32	0	6	12	20	44	-29	26

¶Ayr U promoted via play-offs.

Irn-Bru Scottish

Third Division	P	W	D	L	F	A	W	D	L	F	A	W	D	L	F	A	GD	Pts
1 Arbroath (R)	36	20	6	10	80	61	11	4	3	39	24	9	2	7	41	37	19	66
2 Albion R¶	36	17	10	9	56	40	9	4	5	25	16	8	6	4	31	24	16	61
3 Queen's Park	36	18	5	13	57	43	10	3	5	31	17	8	2	8	26	26	14	59
4 Annan Ath	36	16	11	9	58	45	8	5	5	32	25	8	6	4	26	20	13	59
5 Stranraer	36	15	12	9	72	57	10	4	4	39	25	5	8	5	33	32	15	57
6 Berwick R	36	12	13	11	62	56	7	7	4	38	31	5	6	7	24	25	6	49
7 Elgin City	36	13	6	17	53	63	8	2	8	30	29	5	4	9	23	34	-10	45
8 Montrose	36	10	7	19	47	61	6	4	8	28	27	4	3	11	19	34	-14	37
9 East Stirling	36	10	4	22	33	62	6	3	9	18	27	4	1	13	15	35	-29	34
10 Clyde (R)	36	8	8	20	37	67	4	5	9	23	31	4	3	11	14	36	-30	32

¶Albion R promoted via play-offs.

CLYDESDALE BANK SCOTTISH PREMIER LEAGUE RESULTS 2010–11

	Aberdeen	Celtic	Dundee U	Hamilton A	Hearts	Hibernian	Inverness CT	Kilmarnock	Motherwell	Rangers	St Johnstone	St Mirren
Aberdeen	—	0-3	1-1	4-0 1-0	0-1 0-0	4-2 0-1	1-2 1-0†	0-1 5-0	1-2	2-3 0-1	0-1 0-2†	2-0 0-1†
Celtic	9-0 1-0	—	1-1 4-1*	3-1 2-0	3-0 4-0	2-1 3-1	2-2	1-1	1-0 4-0*	1-3 3-0	2-0	4-0 1-0
Dundee U	3-1 3-1	1-2 1-3	—	2-1	2-0 2-1*	1-0 3-0	0-4 1-0	1-1 4-2*	2-0 4-0*	0-4	1-0 2-0	1-0 1-2
Hamilton A	0-1 1-1†	1-1	0-1 1-1	—	0-4 0-2	1-2 1-0†	1-3 1-2†	2-2 1-1	0-0	1-2 1-0	1-1 1-0	0-0
Hearts	5-0	2-0 0-3*	1-1 2-1	2-0	—	1-0	1-1	0-3 0-2	0-2 3-3*	1-2 1-0	1-1 1-0	3-0 3-2
Hibernian	1-2 1-3†	0-3	2-2	1-1 1-2	0-2 2-2	—	4-2 2-0†	2-1 2-1	2-1	0-3 0-2	0-0 1-2†	2-0 1-1†
Inverness CT	2-0 0-2	0-1 3-2	0-2	0-1 1-1	1-3 1-1	4-2 2-0†	—	1-3	1-2 3-0	1-1	1-1 2-0	1-2 1-0†
Kilmarnock	2-0	1-2 0-2* 0-4	1-2 1-1	3-0	1-2 2-2*	2-1	1-2 1-1	—	0-1 3-1	2-3 1-5*	1-1	2-1 2-0
Motherwell	1-1 2-1	0-1 2-0	2-1 2-1	0-1 1-0	1-0 4-0*	2-3 2-0	0-0	0-1 1-1*	—	1-4 0-5*	4-0	3-1 0-1
Rangers	2-0	0-2 0-0* 2-3	4-0 2-0* 2-3	4-0	1-0 4-0*	0-3	1-1 1-0	2-1 2-1	4-1 6-0	—	2-1 4-0	2-1
St Johnstone	0-1 0-0	0-3 0-1	0-0	2-0 1-0†	0-2	2-0 1-1	1-0 0-3†	0-3 0-0	0-2 1-0	0-2	—	2-1 0-0
St Mirren	2-1 3-2	0-1	1-1 1-1	2-2 0-1† 3-1	0-2	1-0 0-1	1-2 3-3	0-2	1-1	1-3 0-1	1-2 0-0†	—

*Splits after 33 games. Post-split matches, *top half, †bottom half.*

IRN BRU SCOTTISH LEAGUE—DIVISION ONE RESULTS 2010–2011

	Cowdenbeath	Dundee	Dunfermline Ath	Falkirk	Morton	Partick Th	Queen of S	Raith R	Ross Co	Stirling Alb
Cowdenbeath	—	2-1	0-4	0-0	2-2	2-1	1-3	1-2	0-2	5-1
	—	1-3	0-1	1-2	0-2	1-1	2-2	0-3	2-1	1-0
Dundee	3-0	—	2-2	2-0	2-1	2-1	1-0	0-0	0-0	2-0
	2-2	—	1-1	1-0	1-1	3-2	2-1	2-1	2-0	1-1
Dunfermline Ath	2-1	3-1	—	1-1	2-0	0-0	1-0	2-2	3-2	3-0
	5-0	0-0	—	3-0	1-3	0-0	6-1	2-1	1-1	4-1
Falkirk	5-1	3-3	0-1	—	2-1	2-3	3-1	0-0	0-1	3-0
	2-0	2-2	1-2	—	1-0	2-0	0-3	2-1	0-1	4-2
Morton	1-2	0-1	2-1	0-0	—	2-0	2-0	0-1	0-0	0-0
	3-0	1-3	0-2	2-2	—	1-0	0-4	0-0	2-1	2-0
Partick Th	1-0	1-0	0-2	1-0	0-0	—	3-1	0-0	1-1	1-2
	0-1	0-0	2-0	1-2	2-0	—	0-0	3-0	1-1	6-1
Queen of S	3-0	1-2	2-0	1-5	2-0	2-1	—	1-3	3-0	2-2
	2-2	3-0	1-3	0-1	1-4	3-3	—	0-2	0-1	4-1
Raith R	2-1	1-2	2-0	2-1	1-0	4-0	0-1	—	1-0	0-2
	2-2	2-1	2-1	1-2	2-2	0-2	0-1	—	1-1	2-1
Ross Co	1-1	0-3	0-0	0-1	2-2	0-2	1-1	0-0	—	3-1
	3-0	0-1	0-1	2-1	2-0	0-0	1-2	0-1	—	0-0
Stirling Alb	1-3	1-1	1-5	0-5	0-1	4-2	0-0	1-3	0-0	—
	3-4	0-1	1-1	1-2	3-2	0-3	0-2	1-2	0-2	—

186

IRN BRU SCOTTISH LEAGUE—DIVISION TWO RESULTS 2010–2011

	Airdrie U	Alloa Ath	Ayr U	Brechin C	Dumbarton	East Fife	Forfar Ath	Livingston	Peterhead	Stenhousemuir
Airdrie U	—	0-1 / 0-2	2-2 / 0-5	1-1 / 2-2	1-2 / 2-1	1-1 / 2-2	2-0 / 3-1	0-1 / 2-4	2-2 / 1-0	1-0 / 2-2
Alloa Ath	2-3 / 1-0	—	4-1 / 0-1	2-2 / 2-2	0-0 / 2-3	3-2 / 1-3	3-2 / 0-3	2-2 / 1-3	2-2 / 1-0	1-0 / 1-2
Ayr U	1-0 / 3-1	2-1 / 1-0	—	0-2 / 2-0	1-0 / 2-0	0-4 / 1-1	0-1 / 3-1	3-1 / 0-3	1-1 / 2-2	2-0 / 4-3
Brechin C	3-1 / 1-2	3-1 / 3-2	0-3 / 1-0	—	3-3 / 6-0	1-3 / 2-3	0-0 / 0-1	1-3 / 1-0	4-2 / 3-1	0-0 / 3-1
Dumbarton	1-3 / 1-1	4-1 / 2-2	3-2 / 1-2	1-3 / 1-2	—	4-1 / 4-2	1-2 / 0-0	1-2 / 0-3	3-0 / 5-2	1-0 / 0-1
East Fife	3-3 / 0-1	4-1 / 3-1	2-3 / 3-2	1-3 / 0-0	6-0 / 1-3	—	1-3 / 3-0	2-4 / 1-3	2-1 / 3-1	6-0 / 1-1
Forfar Ath	1-2 / 1-2	1-1 / 3-1	4-1 / 3-2	1-1 / 2-1	4-1 / 2-1	3-2 / 0-0	—	1-0 / 0-4	1-1 / 2-1	1-1 / 2-0
Livingston	2-1 / 2-0	3-3 / 4-0	0-0 / 3-2	2-0 / 0-0	2-0 / 1-1	1-1 / 4-3	2-0 / 3-0	—	1-0 / 5-1	4-1 / 2-1
Peterhead	5-1 / 2-4	1-0 / 4-1	2-4 / 1-2	0-5 / 1-1	1-0 / 1-2	2-2 / 0-2	1-2 / 1-1	0-0 / 3-0	—	2-2 / 0-3
Stenhousemuir	1-3 / 1-0	0-1 / 2-3	3-1 / 2-1	0-0 / 1-3	4-0 / 2-2	1-1 / 0-2	3-0 / 0-1	1-2 / 0-3	3-1 / 4-2	—

IRN BRU SCOTTISH LEAGUE—DIVISION THREE RESULTS 2010-2011

	Albion R	Annan Ath	Arbroath	Berwick R	Clyde	East Stirling	Elgin C	Montrose	Queen's Park	Stranraer
Albion R	—	0-0 0-0	0-2 3-0	2-2 0-1	3-1 1-1	1-0 2-0	3-1 2-0	3-1 0-2	2-1 1-2	1-2 1-0
Annan Ath	4-1 2-2	—	1-2 3-0	1-1 2-3	0-2 1-0	3-1 2-1	0-1 2-2	2-2 2-1	2-1 1-2	2-2 2-1
Arbroath	1-1 3-0	0-2 2-1	—	3-2 2-1	3-2 2-0	2-0 3-5	2-0 3-5	4-0 4-1	1-0 2-2	0-0 2-2
Berwick R	1-6 2-2	2-2 2-3	4-1 0-4	—	2-1 1-1	3-0 1-1	6-2 4-0	1-0 0-1	1-1 3-1	2-2 3-3
Clyde	1-2 0-1	0-2 0-2	1-1 0-3	1-4 2-0	—	1-2 2-0	1-1 3-3	2-0 1-1	2-3 0-2	2-2 4-2
East Stirling	0-0 1-2	1-5 2-0	1-3 2-5	0-0 1-0	0-0 2-0	—	0-2 2-1	2-1 1-2	0-1 3-2	0-1 0-2
Elgin C	2-2 1-1	2-0 2-3	3-5 3-2	1-2 3-2	0-1 0-1	0-2 2-1	—	3-2 1-0	4-2 0-1	1-2 2-1
Montrose	0-2 0-2	1-1 0-1	3-0 0-5	1-1 1-1	8-1 3-1	0-2 3-0	0-1 1-0	—	1-2 0-2	3-3 3-2
Queen's Park	0-1 2-1	3-0 0-1	5-2 1-1	0-2 1-0	0-1 4-0	2-0 2-0	1-1 1-0	1-0 4-1	—	1-3 3-3
Stranraer	3-2 1-3	2-2 1-1	4-1 3-4	1-1 3-1	3-1 3-0	4-1 2-0	2-1 1-2	1-2 2-2	1-0 2-1	—

ABERDEEN   PREMIER LEAGUE

Ground: Pittodrie Stadium, Aberdeen AB24 5QH (01224) 650400
Ground capacity: 21,421 (all seated). **Colours:** All red.
Manager: Craig Brown.
League Appearances: Aluko, S. 27(1); Anderson, M. (1); Blackman, N. 10(5); Considine, A. 26(1); Diamond, Z. 32; Folly, Y. 18; Foster, R. (1); Fraser, R. (2); Fyvie, F. 1(4); Grimmer, J. 1(1); Hansson, H. (1); Hartley, P. 23(1); Howard, M. 8(1); Ifil, J. 13(4); Jack, R. 26(4); Jarvis, D. (1); Langfield, J. 30(1); Low, N. (1); Mackie, D. 7(4); Magennis, J. 10(19); Maguire, C. 35; McArdle, R. 27(1); McNamee, D. 9(1); Megginson, M. 1(5); Milsom, R. 18; Paton, M. 4(6); Pawlett, P. 6(7); Robertson, C. 7(6); Shaughnessy, J. 1; Smith, S. 15(1); Velicka, A. 1(5); Vernon, S. 29(4); Vujadinovic, N. 13(5); Young, D. 20(9).
Goals – League (39): Vernon 10, Maguire 7 (2 pens), Hartley 4 (4 pens), Magennis 3, Aluko 2, Blackman 2, McArdle 2, Diamond 1, Folly 1, Jack 1, Mackie 1, Milsom 1, Pawlett 1, Velicka 1, Vujadinovic 1, own goal 1.
Scottish Cup (10): Maguire 4, Vernon 3, McArdle 1, Magennis 1, own goal 1.
CIS Cup (9): Hartley 4 (3 pens), Vernon 3, McArdle 1, Maguire 1.
Honours – Division 1: Champions – 1954–55, **Premier Division:** Champions – 1979–80, 1983–84, 1984–85. **Scottish Cup winners** 1947, 1970, 1982, 1983, 1984, 1986, 1990. **League Cup winners** 1956, 1977, 1986, 1990, 1996. **European Cup-Winners' Cup winners** 1983.

AIRDRIE UNITED   DIV. 2

Ground: Shyberry Excelsior Stadium, Airdrie ML6 8QZ (01236) 622000
Postal address: 60 St Enoch Square, Glasgow G1 4AG.
Ground capacity: 10,171. **Colours:** White shirts with red trim, white shorts, white stockings.
Manager: Jimmy Boyle.
League Appearances: Bain, J. 32; Blockley, N. 1(5); Burns, S. 1(2); Craig, C. 4(7); Devlin, R. 30; Donnelly, R. 10(7); Fairweather, A. 2(3); Ferguson, A. 3(3); Fisher, J. (1); Forrest, E. 9; Gemmill, S. 30; Gibson, S. 13; Goodall, G. 3(1); Grant, E. 19(1); Gray, D. 4(2); Hill, C. 5; Johnston, P. 26(2); Keast, F. 3(2); Lovering, P. 23(4); Macfarlane, N. 1; Mackay-Steven, G. 15(4); Malone, A. (1); McCord, R. 32; McGregor, H. 1(3); McKeown, S. 5; Morton, S. 3(6); Muir, G. 4(9); Owens, G. 11(1); Ridgers, M. 34; Sally, S. 1(17); Smith, G. 7(1); Stallard, K. 28; Stevenson, J. 20(7); Szpilcynski, A. 2; Wallace, R. 2(6); Watt, A. 12(3).
Goals – League (52): Gemmill 9, McCord 6 (2 pens), Donnelly 4, Morton 4, Owens 4, Wallace 3 (1 pen), Watt 3, Bain 2, Ferguson 2, Johnston 2, Lovering 2 (1 pen), Sally 2, Stevenson 2, Craig 1, Forrest 1, Gibson 1, Grant 1, own goals 3.
Scottish Cup (10): Gemmill 2, Mackay-Steven 2, Stevenson 2, Bain 1, Lovering 1, McCord 1, Sally 1.
CIS Cup (3): Gemmill 1, Grant 1, McCord 1.
Alba Challenge Cup (1): Muir 1 (pen).
Honours – Second Division: Champions – 2003–04. **League Challenge Cup winners** 2008–09.

ALBION ROVERS   DIV. 2

Ground: Cliftonhill Stadium, Main Street, Coatbridge ML5 3RB (01236) 606334
Ground capacity: 1249 (seated: 489). **Colours:** Yellow shirts with black trim, blue shorts, blue stockings.
Manager: Paul Martin.
League Appearances: Barnes, D. (1); Benton, A. 24(2); Boyle, C. 18(1); Canning, S. 31(1); Chaplain, S. 16(1); Donnelly, C. 35; Ferry, D. 5(7); Flynn, T. 11; Gaston, D. 25(1); Gemmell, J. 22(7); Gilmartin, J. 1(10); Hamilton, C. 17(10); Innes, P. 19(4); Kerr, H. 2(1);

Lawless, S. 11(14); Love, R. 36; Lumsden, T. 20; McCluskey, S. (1); McGowan, M. 36; McLeod, P. 9(6); Meechan, S. 1(1); Reid, A. 33; Smith, I. 3(15); Smith, D. (1); Stevenson, A. 21(11).
Goals – League (56): Love 10, Chaplain 8 (1 pen), Gemmell 6, Hamilton C 6, Boyle 4, Lawless 3, McLeod 3, Smith I 3, Stevenson 3 (3 pens), Canning 2, Donnelly 2, McGowan 2, Benton 1, Gilmartin 1, Innes 1, Lumsden 1.
Scottish Cup (0).
CIS Cup (0).
Alba Challenge Cup (1): Donnelly 1.
Play-Offs (7): Love 3, Gemmell 2, Chaplain 1, Donnelly 1.
Honours – Division II: Champions – 1933–34. **Second Division:** Champions 1988–89.

ALLOA ATHLETIC   DIV. 3

Ground: Recreation Park, Alloa FK10 1RY (01259) 722695
Ground capacity: 3100. **Colours:** Black shirts with gold hoops on front, black shorts, black stockings.
Player-Manager: Paul Hartley.
League Appearances: Bloom, J. 10(1); Brown, M. 19(2); Byrne, K. 6; Duffin, R. 1; Dunlop, M. 33; Ewings, J. 20; Ferguson, B. 7; Forrest, F. 3; Gibson, W. 32; Gormley, D. 10(5); Grant, J. 11(5); Hay, J. 5(12); Lister, J. 19(15); McAvoy, D. 1(2); McClune, D. 22(4); McDonald, K. 24(3); McGowan, M. 20(2); Motion, K. 10(3); Noble, S. 17(7); O'Brien, K. 1; Philp, R. 6; Pitman, S. (1); Prunty, B. 26(4); Robertson, S. 16; Scott, A. 16(13); Smith, D. 27(3); Taggart, N. 2(5); Thomson, J. (4); Walker, S. 31(1); Wilson, D. 1(4).
Goals – League (49): Prunty 8, Lister 7, McDonald 7 (4 pens), McGowan 7 (2 pens), Noble 6, Dunlop 3, Walker 3, Gibson 2, Gormley 2, Motion 2, Scott 1, Smith 1.
Scottish Cup (4): McDonald 3, Noble 1.
CIS Cup (2): Prunty 1, Tully 1.
Alba Challenge Cup (1): Walker 1.
Play-Offs (1): Scott 1.
Honours – Division II: Champions – 1921–22. **Third Division:** Champions – 1997–98.
League Challenge Cup winners 1999–2000.

ANNAN ATHLETIC   DIV. 3

Ground: Galabank, North Street, Annan DG12 5DQ (01461) 204108
Ground capacity: 3000 (426 seated). **Colours:** Black and gold striped shirts, black shorts, black stockings.
Manager: Harry Cairney.
League Appearances: Aitken, A. 29(1); Amaya, J. (2); Atkinson, J. (1); Bell, G. 2(12); Connolly, A. (2); Cox, D. 31(1); Docherty, M. 15(3); Felvus, B. 2(13); Gilfillan, B. 30(2); Halsman, J. 13; Harty, I. 30(1); Jack, M. 4(1); Jamieson, J. 8; Jardine, C. 21(5); MacBeth, J. 23(2); Macfarlane, N. 10(5); Mitchell, A. 1; Muirhead, A. 28(3); Neilson, K. 34(1); O'Connor, S. 22; Slattery, P. (1); Sloan, S. 31(5); Sloan, L. 1(4); Steele, J. 15(12); Summersgill, C. 27; Walker, P. 1(6); Watson, P. 18(1); Watson, J. (1).
Goals – League (58): Harty 14 (2 pens), O'Connor 8, Gilfillan 7, Neilson 5, Sloan S 5, Cox 4, Halsman 4, Muirhead 2, Bell 1, Docherty 1, Felvus 1, Jack 1, Jardine 1, Macfarlane 1, Steele 1, own goals 2.
Scottish Cup (9): Gilfillan 2, Harty 2, Aitken 1, Amaya 1, Halsman 1, MacBeth 1, Muirhead 1.
CIS Cup (0).
Alba Challenge Cup (2): Halsman 1, Muirhead 1.
Play-Offs (5): Gilfillan 2, Harty 1, Muirhead 1, Steele 1.
Honours – East of Scotland Premier League: Winners (4). **East of Scotland League Cup:** Winners (1). **East of Scotland Div 1:** Winners (1). **South of Scotland League:**

Winners (2). **South of Scotland League Cup:** Winners (4). **Scottish Challenge Cup South:** Winners (1). **Scottish Qualifying Cup South:** Winners (1).

ARBROATH DIV. 2

Ground: Gayfield Park, Arbroath DD11 1QB (01241) 872157
Ground capacity: 4165 (860 seated; 3305 standing). **Colours:** All maroon.
Manager: Paul Sheerin.
League Appearances: Burns, D. 1(1); Chisholm, R. 20(1); Deane, P. 1(4); Dimilta, D. 7(11); Doris, S. 25(5); Durnan, M. 9; Falkingham, J. 33(2); Gibson, K. 26(1); Griffin, D. 14(4); Hamilton, J. 4(3); Hill, D. 35; Malcolm, S. 24; McAnespie, K. 27; McCulloch, M. 8(1); McGowan, D. 8(24); McIlravey, M. (1); McManus, A. 11; McMullan, K. 30(1); Nimmo, I. (2); Rattray, A. 9; Ross, R. 1(4); Sheerin, P. 30(5); Sheerin, J. 2(12); Shields, J. 2(2); Sibanda, L. 5(6); Strachan, A. 12(4); Swankie, G. 35(1); Thomson, D. 5(1); Wedderburn, C. 12(4).
Goals – League (80): Swankie 22, Doris 16 (5 pens), Falkingham 9, Gibson 8, McGowan 6, Sheerin P 5 (1 pen), Strachan 3, Chisholm 2, Malcolm 2, McAnespie 2, Wedderburn 2, Durnan 1, Rattray 1, own goal 1.
Scottish Cup (3): Rattray 2, Doris 1.
CIS Cup (2): Sheerin P 1, Swankie 1.
Alba Challenge Cup (0).
Honours – Third Division: Champions – 2010-11.

AYR UNITED DIV. 1

Ground: Somerset Park, Ayr KA8 9NB (01292) 263435
Ground capacity: 10,185 (1597 seated). **Colours:** White shirts with thin black hoops, black shorts with white trim, white stockings.
Manager: Brian Reid.
League Appearances: Aitken, C. 1; Arbuckle, G. 1; Armstrong, G. (1); Bannigan, S. 15(2); Campbell, M. 29; Connolly, A. (2); Crawford, D. 18; Crawford II, D. 2(5); Donnelly, R. 6(1); Easton, W. 18(9); Keenan, D. 7(1); Lauchlan, J. 16; Main, A. 3; Malone, E. 28; Martin, A. 15; McCann, R. 21(2); McKay, D. 9(3); McKeown, S. 4; McLaughlin, S. 33; McLean, D. (1); McWilliams, R. (2); Moffat, R. 20(2); Paterson, R. (3); Reynolds, S. 4(3); Roberts, M. 30(2); Robertson, R. 8(13); Rodgers, A. 16(15); Shankland, M. (1); Smith, C. 29(1); Taggart, S. 2(4); Tiffoney, J. 24(5); Trouten, A. 31(1); Willis, P. 6; Woodburn, A. (4).
Goals – League (62): Roberts 21 (11 pens), Moffat 7, Trouten 5, Bannigan 4, McLaughlin 4, Rodgers 4 (2 pens), McCann 3, McKay 3, Easton 2, Robertson 2, Crawford II 1, Lauchlan 1, Malone 1, Smith 1, Willis 1, own goals 2.
Scottish Cup (7): Roberts 4 (3 pens), Rodgers 2, Bannigan 1.
CIS Cup (2): Connolly 1, McKeown 1.
Alba Challenge Cup (5): Rodgers 2, Campbell 1, Roberts 1, Trouten 1.
Play-Offs (10): Moffat 4, McCann 1, McLaughlin 1, Roberts 1, Rodgers 1, Trouten 1 (pen), own goal 1.
Honours – Division II: Champions – 1911–12, 1912–13, 1927–28, 1936–37, 1958–59, 1965–66. **Second Division:** Champions – 1987–88, 1996–97.

BERWICK RANGERS DIV. 3

Ground: Shielfield Park, Berwick-on-Tweed TD15 2EF (01289) 307424
Ground capacity: 4131. **Colours:** Black shirt with broad gold vertical stripes, black shorts, gold stockings.
Manager: Jimmy Crease.

League Appearances: Brazil, A. 15(18); Callaghan, S. 20; Currie, P. 29(1); Currie, L. 16; Ewart, J. 19(6); Gordon, K. 16(14); Grant, J. 16(2); Gray, D. 11(6); Greenhill, D. 26(4); Gribben, D. 28(3); Holms, R. (1); Kerr, G. (1); Little, I. 10(9); Malone, E. 1; McCaldon, I. 15(1); McLaren, F. 11(5); McLean, A. 36; McLeod, C. 26(1); McMullan, P. 12(1); Motion, K. (1); Neill, K. (2); Notman, S. 29; O'Connor, G. (1); O'Reilly, C. 15(6); Peat, M. 21; Ponton, A. 2(6); Roseburgh, S. 1; Smith, E. 16(2); Thomson, S. 5.

Goals – League (62): Gribben 17 (1 pen), Currie P 13 (2 pens), Gray 8, O'Reilly 6, Brazil 5, McLeod 3, Greenhill D 2, Little 2, Currie L 1, Gordon 1, McLean 1, Notman 1, Ponton 1, own goal 1.

Scottish Cup (5): McMullan 2, Brazil 1, Currie P 1, Greenhill D 1.

CIS Cup (0).

Alba Challenge Cup (1): McLean 1.

Honours – Second Division: Champions – 1978–79. **Third Division:** Champions – 2006–07.

BRECHIN CITY   DIV. 2

Ground: Glebe Park, Brechin DD9 6BJ (01356) 622856

Ground capacity: 3960. **Colours:** White shirts with red broad stripe, red shorts, red stockings.

Manager: Jim Weir.

League Appearances: Archdeacon, M. 1(8); Bolger, A. (3); Booth, C. 11; Byers, K. 19(6); Cook, A. 34(2); Docherty, M. 4(6); Fusco, G. 17(11); Gray, C. (1); Hill, D. 4; Janczyk, N. 31(2); King, C. 4(4); Kirkpatrick, J. 3(11); McAllister, R. 29; McBain, R. 11; McKay, D. 2(14); McKenna, D. 27(7); McLauchlan, G. 29; McLean, P. 25(2); Megginson, M. 9(5); Molloy, C. 34; Moyes, E. 33; Mulrooney, P. (2); Nelson, C. 33; Redman, J. 19(6); Scott, D. 3; Smith, B. 5(3); White, D. 9(2).

Goals – League (63): McAllister 19 (3 pens), McKenna 10, Molloy 8 (1 pen), Byers 4, Janczyk 4, Moyes 4, Redman 4, Booth 2, Megginson 2, Archdeacon 1, Bolger 1, Hill 1, King 1, McLauchlan 1, McLean 1.

Scottish Cup (13): McAllister 6 (1 pen), McKenna 4, Byers 2, Molloy 1.

CIS Cup (5): McAllister 3, McLauchlan 1, Molloy 1.

Alba Challenge Cup (3): Janczyk 1, McAllister 1, Moyes 1.

Play-Offs (6): Janczyk 1, Kirkpatrick 1, Megginson 1, Molloy 1, Redman 1, own goal 1.

Honours – Second Division: Champions – 1982–83, 1989–90, 2004–05. **Third Division:** Champions – 2001–02. **C Division:** Champions – 1953–54.

CELTIC   PREMIER LEAGUE

Ground: Celtic Park, Glasgow G40 3RE (0871) 226 1888

Ground capacity: 60,355 (all seated). **Colours:** Emerald green and white hooped shirts, white shorts with emerald green trim, whie stockings with emerald green trim.

Manager: Neil Lennon.

League Appearances: Brown, S. 26(2); Cha, D. 14(2); Commons, K. 11(3); Crosas, M. (1); Forrest, J. 15(4); Forster, F. 36; Fortune, M. 2; Hooiveld, J. 4(1); Hooper, G. 26; Izaguirre, E. 33; Juarez, E. 5(8); Kapo, O. 1(1); Kayal, B. 18(3); Ki, S. 18(8); Ledley, J. 26(3); Ljungberg, F. 1(6); Loovens, G. 13; Majstorovic, D. 32; Maloney, S. 15(6); McCourt, P. 8(17); McGinn, N. 6(5); Mulgrew, C. 20(3); Murphy, D. 9(9); Rogne, T. 14(2); Samaras, G. 16(6); Stokes, A. 22(7); Toshney, L. (1); Towell, R. (1); Wilson, M. 25; Zaluska, L. 2.

Goals – League (85): Hooper 20 (1 pen), Stokes 15 (4 pens), Commons 11 (1 pen), McCourt 6 (1 pen), Maloney 5, Forrest 3, Ki 3, Murphy 3 (2 pens), Samaras 3 (1 pen), Brown 2, Kayal 2, Ledley 2, McGinn 2, Wilson 2, Cha 1, Izaguirre 1, Loovens 1, Majstorovic 1, Rogne 1, own goal 1.

Scottish Cup (14): Ledley 3, Brown 2, Commons 2 (1 pen), Mulgrew 2, Ki 1, Majstorovic 1, Maloney 1, Wilson 1, own goal 1.

CIS Cup (14): Stokes 5 (2 pens), Samaras 3, Commons 1, Hooper 1, Ledley 1, McGinn 1, Mulgrew 1, Rogne 1.

Champions League (2): Hooper 1, Juarez 1.

Europa League (2): Juarez 1, Samaras 1.
Honours – Division I: Champions – 1892–93, 1893–94, 1895–96, 1897–98, 1904–05, 1905–06, 1906–07, 1907–08, 1908–09, 1909–10, 1913–14, 1914–15, 1915–16, 1916–17, 1918–19, 1921–22, 1925–26, 1935–36, 1937–38, 1953–54, 1965–66, 1966–67, 1967–68, 1968–69, 1969–70, 1970–71, 1971–72, 1972–73, 1973–74. **Premier Division:** Champions – 1976–77, 1978–79, 1980–81, 1981–82, 1985–86, 1987–88, 1997–98. **Premier League:** 2000–01, 2001–02, 2003–04, 2005–06, 2006–07, 2007–08. **Scottish Cup winners** 1892, 1899, 1900, 1904, 1907, 1908, 1911, 1912, 1914, 1923, 1925, 1927, 1931, 1933, 1937, 1951, 1954, 1965, 1967, 1969, 1971, 1972, 1974, 1975, 1977, 1980, 1985, 1988, 1989, 1995, 2001, 2004, 2005, 2007, 2011. **League Cup winners** 1957, 1958, 1966, 1967, 1968, 1969, 1970, 1975, 1983, 1998, 2000, 2001, 2004, 2006, 2009. **European Cup winners** 1967.

CLYDE   DIV. 3

Ground: Broadwood Stadium, Cumbernauld G68 9NE (01236) 451511
Ground capacity: 8006. **Colours:** White shirts with red trim, black shorts, red stockings.
Manager: Jim Duffy.
League Appearances: Allan, J. 6; Anson, S. 2; Brown, G. 14(1); Cochrane, H. 2(7); Connolly, K. 1; Dingwall, B. 6(3); Finlayson, K. 29(2); Girvan, G. 10(4); Gramovitl, A. 7(2); Gray, I. 11(1); Halliwell, B. 15; Henderson, M. 5(2); Hutchison, J. 15; Lithgow, A. 20(2); MacBeth, R. 5; McCluskey, J. 9; McCusker, M. 21; McGowan, N. 22(5); McMillan, R. 30; McMullan, P. 1; Miller, C. 4(1); Mills, S. 4(7); Mulrooney, P. 3(3); Park, A. 21(2); Paterson, N. 15(1); Sawyers, W. 10(10); Scullion, J. 18(1); Stevenson, C. 6(12); Stewart, J. 19(11); Strachan, A. 13; Sweeney, J. 25(5); Thomson, D. 1(4); Waddell, R. 26(5).
Goals – League (37): McCusker 11 (2 pens), Stewart 8 (2 pens), Lithgow 3, Paterson 3, Scullion 3, Mills 2, Sawyers 2, Dingwall 1, Finlayson 1, McCluskey 1, Strachan 1 (1 pen), Waddell 1.
Scottish Cup (1): Finlayson 1.
CIS Cup (4): McCusker 3, Strachan 1.
Alba Challenge Cup (1): Strachan 1.
Honours – Division II: Champions – 1904–05, 1951–52, 1956–57, 1961–62, 1972–73. **Second Division:** Champions – 1977–78, 1981–82, 1992–93, 1999–2000. **Scottish Cup winners** 1939, 1955, 1958. **League Challenge Cup winners** 2006–07.

COWDENBEATH   DIV. 2

Ground: Central Park, Cowdenbeath KY4 9QQ (01383) 610166
Ground capacity: 4370 (1431 seated). **Colours:** Royal blue shirts with white sleeves, white shorts, royal blue stockings.
Manager: Colin Cameron.
League Appearances: Adamson, K. 26; Armstrong, J. 21; Baxter, M. 26; Brett, D. 3(2); Byren, P. 2; Cameron, C. 25(1); Campbell, A. 13(4); Coult, L. 9(8); Crawford, S. 15(3); Dempster, J. 17(1); Fairbairn, B. 7(6); Ferguson, J. 4(3); Hay, D. 30; Linton, S. 28(5); Makel, L. 9(1); Malcolm, R. 2; Mbu, J. 8(1); McKenzie, M. 16(14); Miller, K. 7(2); Milne, L. (1); O'Brien, T. 10(3); Old, S. 4; Ramsay, M. 32(3); Robertson, J. 17(5); Roy, L. 6; Sibanda, L. 4(7); Smith, M. 3(2); Stewart, G. 16(16); Vauls, R. 6(2); Wilson, L. (1); Winter, C. 30.
Goals – League (41): Stewart 9, Ramsay 7 (2 pens), Campbell 5 (3 pens), Dempster 4, Fairbairn 3, Cameron 2, Crawford 2, Linton 2, McKenzie 2, Brett 1, Miller 1, Sibanda 1, own goals 2.
Scottish Cup (0).
CIS Cup (1): Ramsay 1.
Alba Challenge Cup (1): Armstrong 1.
Play-Offs (2): Coult 1, Linton 1.
Honours – Division II: Champions – 1913–14, 1914–15, 1938–39. **Third Division:** Champions – 2005–06.

DUMBARTON   DIV. 2

Ground: Strathclyde Homes Stadium, Castle Road, Dumbarton G82 1JJ (01389) 762569/767864
Ground capacity: 2025. **Colours:** All amber with black trim and white flashes.
Manager: Alan Adamson.
League Appearances: Brannan, K. 5(8); Campbell, R. 8(9); Carcary, D. 8(14); Chaplain, S. 5(4); Chisholm, I. 11(5); Cook, A. 4(5); Creaney, J. 25; Devlin, N. 21; Devlin, J. 2; Geggan, A. 33(1); Gilhaney, M. 24(5); Gordon, B. 32; Grindley, S. 30; Halsman, J. 13(1); Hunter, R. 1; Linsay, J. 2; Maxwell, P. 5(2); McGowan, M. 1; McLeish, C. 7(3); McManus, A. 8; McNiff, M. 24(3); McShane, J. 25(4); McStay, R. 25(5); Metcalf, R. 1(3); Nugent, P. 32; Smith, G. 1(3); Smith, S. 6; Walker, P. 24; Wallace, T. 3(1); White, M. 6; White , J. 1(7); Wilson, G. 3(1).
Goals – League (52): McShane 13, Gilhaney 9 (1 pen), Walker 9, Geggan 4, Carcary 3, Chaplain 2 (2 pens), Halsman 2, McLeish 2, McStay 2, Campbell 1, Cook 1 (1 pen), Maxwell 1, McNiff 1, own goals 2.
Scottish Cup (1): Geggan 1.
CIS Cup (1): Carcary 1.
Alba Challenge Cup (0).
Honours – Division I: Champions – 1890–91 (Shared), 1891–92. **Division II:** Champions – 1910–11, 1971–72. **Second Division:** Champions – 1991–92. **Third Division:** Champions – 2008–09. **Scottish Cup winners** 1883.

DUNDEE   DIV. 1

Ground: Dens Park, Dundee DD3 7JY (01382) 889966
Ground capacity: 11,760 (all seated). **Colours:** Navy blue shirts, white shorts, navy blue stockings.
Manager: Barry Smith.
League Appearances: Adams, J. 11; Bartlett, G. 2; Bayne, G. 1(1); Benedictis, K. 10; Brighton, T. 3; Douglas, R. 34; Forsyth, C. 26(7); Fox, S. 1(1); Gibson, J. 1; Grant, C. 2; Greacen, (1); Griffiths, L. 18; Harkins, G. 36; Higgins, S. 19(7); Hyde, J. 2; Irvine, G. 31; Kerr, B. 2; Kuqi, N. 3; Lockwood, M. 33; McCann, N. 2(1); McHale, P. 1(1); McIntosh, L. 7(5); McKeown, C. 34; McMenamin, C. 3(5); Misun, M 2; O'Donnell, S. 31(2); Paton, E. 3(1); Rennie, C. 4(2); Riley, N. 32(1); Robb, S. 1; Robertson, C. 2(1); Sansara, N. 1; Shimmin, D. 1; Stewart, J. 4(6); Tulleth, A. (3); Webster, G. 2(1); Weston, R. 29(1); Witteveen, D. 2(3).
Goals – League (54): Higgins 9, Forsyth 8, Griffiths 8, Harkins 5, Lockwood 5 (5 pens), McIntosh 4, Hyde 3, O'Donnell 3, Riley 3, Adams 1, Irvine 1, McCann 1, McKeown 1, McMenamin 1, Witteveen 1.
Scottish Cup (0).
CIS Cup (5): Griffiths 3 (1 pen), Riley 2.
Alba Challenge Cup (3): Griffiths 1, Higgins 1, McMenamin 1.
Honours – Division I: Champions – 1961–62. **First Division:** Champions – 1978–79, 1991–92, 1997–98. **Division II:** Champions – 1946–47. **Scottish Cup winners** 1910. **League Cup winners** 1952, 1953, 1974. **League Challenge Cup winners** 2009-10, **B&Q (Centenary) Cup winners** 1991.

DUNDEE UNITED   PREMIER LEAGUE

Ground: Tannadice Park, Dundee DD3 7JW (01382) 833166
Ground capacity: 14,223. **Colours:** Tangerine shirts with black trim, black shorts, tangerine stockings with black hoop.
Manager: Peter Houston.

League Appearances: Armstrong, S. 2(10); Buaben, P. 29(6); Cadamarteri, D. 2(8); Conway, C. 21(2); Daly, J. 18(11); Dillon, S. 34; Dixon, P. 28(2); Dods, D. 3; Douglas, B. 19(4); Dow, R. (1); Gomis, M. 32(2); Goodwillie, D. 37(1); Kenneth, G. 26(2); Kovacevic, M. 2; Myrie-Williams, J. (1); Pernis, D. 38; Robertson, S. 29(5); Robertson, D. 22(8); Russell, J. 21(9); Severin, S. 14(1); Shala, A. 1(9); Swanson, D. 9(12); Van der Meulen, T. 4(3); Watson, K. 27(2).

Goals – League (55): Goodwillie 17 (2 pens), Daly 9, Russell 9, Robertson D 4, Conway 3, Buaben 2, Douglas 2, Swanson 2, Dillon 1, Gomis 1, Kenneth 1, Severin 1, Shala 1, Watson 1, own goal 1.

Scottish Cup (5): Daly 2, Buaben 1, Dixon 1, Goodwillie 1.

CIS Cup (2): Goodwillie 1 (pen), own goal 1.

Europa League (1): Daly 1.

Honours – Premier Division: Champions – 1982–83. **Division II:** Champions – 1924–25, 1928–29. **Scottish Cup winners** 1994, 2010. **League Cup winners** 1980, 1981.

DUNFERMLINE ATHLETIC   PREMIER LEAGUE

Ground: East End Park, Dunfermline KY12 7RB (01383) 724295
Ground capacity: 12,509. **Colours:** Black and white striped shirts, white shorts, white stockings.
Player-Manager: Jim McIntyre.
League Appearances: Allison, K. (1); Bayne, G. 1(1); Bell, S. 10; Buchanan, L. 13(4); Burke, A. 5(3); Cardle, J. 23(9); Clarke, P. 14(17); Dowie, A. 24(2); Gibson, W. 12(3); Graham, D. 24(6); Graham, L. (1); Hardie, M. 12(2); Higgins, C. 17(4); Hyde, J. 1(1); Keddie, A. 25; Kirk, A. 29(2); Mason, G. 34; McCann, A. 35; McDougall, S. 16(19); McGregor, N. 3(2); Phinn, N. 11(6); Rutkiewicz, K. 12; Smith, C. 36; Thomson, R. 2(7); Willis, P. 5(3); Woods, C. 32.

Goals – League (66): Kirk 12 (1 pen), Clarke 9, Hardie 8 (2 pens), Gibson 6 (3 pens), Buchanan 5, Graham D 5, Cardle 4, Phinn 4, Bell 3, McDougall 3, Woods 3, Burke 1, Higgins 1, own goals 2.

Scottish Cup (7): Graham 2, Kirk 2, Clarke 1, Gibson 1 (pen), McDougall 1.

CIS Cup (10): Kirk 4, McDougall 2, Cardle 1, Willis 1, Woods 1, own goal 1.

Alba Challenge Cup (2): Kirk 2.

Honours – First Division: Champions – 1988–89, 1995–96, 2010-11. **Division II:** Champions – 1925–26. **Second Division:** Champions – 1985–86. **Scottish Cup winners** 1961, 1968.

EAST FIFE   DIV. 2

Ground: Bayview Park, Methil, Fife KY8 3RW (01333) 426323
Ground capacity: 1992. **Colours:** Gold shirts with black stripes, black shorts, gold stockings.
Manager: Stevie Crawford.
League Appearances: Baillie, S. 3; Brown, M. 29(1); Brown, R. 4(1); Byrne, K. 13(1); Campbell, S. 9(4); Cargill, S. (6); Crawford, S. 3(7); Deland, M. 4(1); Devlin, J. (1); Durie, S. 29(1); Fagan, S. (8); Hamilton, J. 7(2); Hislop, S. 31(5); Johnstone, C. 27(4); Linn, R. 34(1); McCulloch, M. 18; McGowan, D. 23; Muir, D. 33(2); Murdoch, S. 10; Newbigging, K. (1); Ovenstone, J. 29(3); Park, M. 18(1); Sloan, R. 17(2); Smart, J. 18(8); Tansey, P. (7); Wallace, R. 10(3); Weir, S. (1); Young, L. 27(7).

Goals – League (77): Linn 13, Johnstone 9, Wallace 8 (1 pen), Byrne 7, Sloan 7 (4 pens), Hislop 5, Crawford 4, Muir 4, Park 4, Durie 3, Smart 3, Young 3, Ovenstone 2, Hamilton 1, McCulloch 1, McGowan 1, own goals 2.

Scottish Cup (3): Hislop 1, Johnstone 1, Sloan 1 (pen).

CIS Cup (1): Linn 1.

Alba Challenge Cup (7): Byrne 1, Cargill 1, Crawford 1, Durie 1, Johnstone 1, Linn 1, Sloan 1 (pen).
Honours – Division II: Champions – 1947–48. **Third Division:** Champions – 2007–08.
Scottish Cup winners 1938. **League Cup winners** 1948, 1950, 1954.

EAST STIRLINGSHIRE   DIV. 3

Ground: Ochilview Park, Gladstone Road, Stenhousemuir FK5 4QL.
Postal Address: 202 Stirling Road, Larbert, Falkirk FK5 3NJ (01324) 557 862
Ground capacity: 3776 (626 seated). **Colours:** Black and white hooped shirts, black shorts, black and white hooped stockings.
Head Coach: John Coughlin.
League Appearances: Anderson, S. (4); Andrews, M. 36; Beveridge, S. 17(5); Cawley, K. 34(1); Donaldson, C. 23; Dunn, D. 28(4); Gibson, A. (1); Glasgow, J. (2); Grant, C. 11(2); Hay, P. 36; Jackson, S. 7; Johnston, S. 32(4); Kelly, D. 12(6); Kennedy, R. 1; Maguire, S. 25(5); Neil, J. 27(6); Richardson, D. 25(3); Scott, C. 3(7); Stevenson, J. 2(2); Team, F. (21); Tully, C. 14(2); Ure, D. 18(12); Walker, A. 16(2); Watts, K. 4(4); Weaver, P. 23(2); Wilkie, R. 2(9).
Goals – League (33): Cawley 8, Dunn 5 (1 pen), Maguire 5 (1 pen), Johnston 3, Neil 2, Stevenson 2, Beveridge 1, Kelly 1, Scott 1, Team 1, Walker 1, Weaver 1, own goals 2.
Scottish Cup (7): Cawley 4, Dunn 2, Weaver 1.
CIS Cup (1): Cawley 1.
Alba Challenge Cup (3): Cawley 1, Maguire 1 (pen), Richardson 1.
Honours – Division II: Champions – 1931–32. **C Division:** Champions – 1947–48.

ELGIN CITY   DIV. 3

Ground: Borough Briggs, Elgin IV30 1AP (01343) 551114
Ground capacity: 3927 (478 seated). **Colours:** Black and white striped shirts, black shorts, red stockings.
Manager: Ross Jack.
Scottish Cup (7): Gunn 3, Crooks 2, Millar 1, Wilson 1 (pen).
CIS Cup (3): Gunn 2 (1 pen), Millar 1.
Alba Challenge Cup (1): Gunn 1.
League Appearances: Bain, S. 11; Black, S. (1); Calder, J. 3; Cameron, B. 28(7); Crooks, J. 27(9); Dempsie, A. 30; Donnelly, P. 20; Duff, J. 24; Dunn, S. 2; Edwards, S. 10(7); Forbes, F. (2); Frizzel, C. 26(7); Gormley, D. 10(6); Gunn, C. 27(8); Inglis, J. 32; Jack, A. (1); Kaczan, P. 24(1); Lawrie, B. 2(11); MacDonald, N. 10(11); MacLeod, D. (1); Millar, P. 5(13); Nicolson, M. 27; Niven, D. 28; O'Donoghue, R. 35; Wilson, B. 15(10).
Goals – League (53): Crooks 13 (5 pens), Gunn 10 (1 pen), Gormley 6, Frizzel 4, Millar 3, O'Donoghue 3 (2 pens), Wilson 3 (2 pens), Cameron 2, Nicolson 2, Duff 1, Inglis J 1, Kaczan 1, MacDonald 1, MacLeod 1, Niven 1, own goal 1.
Honours – Nil.

FALKIRK   DIV. 1

Ground: Brockville Park, Falkirk FK1 5AX (01324) 624121
Ground capacity: 8000. **Colours:** Navy blue shirts with white seams, white shorts, white stockings.
Manager: Steven Pressley.
League Appearances: Alston, B. 3(4); Compton, J. 15(9); Deuchar, K. 4(11); Duffie, K. 19(4); Finnigan, C. 23(6); Flynn, R. 31(2); Fulton, J. (2); Higginbotham, K. 19(11); Khalis, M. 6(1); Kingsley, S. 1(2); Marr, J. 12(2); McLean, B. 31; McManus, T. 12(4); Millar, M. 28(2); Mitchell, C. 6(11); Moutinho, P. 6(4); Murdoch, S. 10(3); O'Brien, B. 31; Olejnik, R. 36; Perry, R. 9(3); Scobbie, T. 32(1); Stewart, M. 31(4); Twaddle, M. 31.

Goals – League (57): Stewart 15, McManus 7, Finnigan 6, Flynn 5, Millar 5 (4 pens), Compton 3, Deuchar 3, Higginbotham 2, McLean 2, Twaddle 2, Alston 1, Duffie 1, Marr 1, Murdoch 1, Scobbie 1, own goals 2.
Scottish Cup (2): Compton 1, Millar 1.
CIS Cup (6): Flynn 2, Stewart 2, Finnigan 1, Khalis 1.
Alba Challenge Cup (0).
Honours – Division II: Champions – 1935–36, 1969–70, 1974–75. **First Division:** Champions – 1990–91, 1993–94, 2002–03, 2004–05. **Second Division:** Champions – 1979–80. **Scottish Cup winners** 1913, 1957. **B&Q Cup winners** 1994. **League Challenge Cup winners** 1998, 2005.

FORFAR ATHLETIC   DIV. 2

Ground: Station Park, Carseview Road, Forfar DD8 3BT (01307) 463576
Ground capacity: 5177 (739 seated). **Colours:** Sky and navy blue hooped shirts, navy blue shorts, sky blue stockings.
Manager: Dick Campbell.
League Appearances: Allan, S. 4; Bishop, J. 27; Bolocheweckyj, M. 26(1); Brady, D. 9(6); Campbell, R. 24(9); Campbell, I. 27(1); Deasley, B. 19(15); Dow, R. 8(3); Duffy, N. 5(2); Fotheringham, M. 19(8); Gallacher, S. 29; Gibson, G. 16(16); Hilson, D. 27(2); Lunan, P. 7(2); McCulloch, M. 32(1); McLean, E. 2(1); McQuade, P. 5; Mowat, D. 22(3); Ross, G. 23; Sellars, B. 18(9); Smith, C. 3(10); Templeman, C. 29(5); Todd, A. 11; Tulloch, S. 4; Watson, P. (6).
Goals – League (50): Campbell R 11 (2 pens), Templeman 10 (1 pen), Fotheringham M 7 (1 pen), Bolocheweckyj 4, Deasley 3, Dow 3, Hilson 3, Gibson 2, Smith C 2, Allan 1, Brady 1, McQuade 1, Sellars 1, Todd 1.
Scottish Cup (1): Tod 1.
CIS Cup (3): Campbell I 1, Campbell R 1, Templeman 1.
Alba Challenge Cup (3): Deasley 1, Sellars 1, Templeman 1.
Play-Offs (4): Campbell R 1 (pen), Hilson 1, Sellars 1, Templeman 1.
Honours – Second Division: Champions – 1983–84. **Third Division:** Champions – 1994–95.

HAMILTON ACADEMICAL   DIV. 1

Ground: New Douglas Park, Cadzow Avenue, Hamilton ML3 0FT (01698) 368650
Ground capacity: 6078. **Colours:** Red and white hooped shirts, white shorts, white stockings.
Manager: Billy Reid.
League Appearances: Antoine-Curier, M. 10(3); Buchanan, D. 27(1); Canning, M. 23; Carrington, M. 6(6); Casalinuovo, D. 6(13); Cerny, T. 37; Chambers, J. 6(3); Crawford, A. 9(5); Devlin, M. 1; Elebert, D. 16(3); Elliott, T. 1(6); Gillespie, G. 8(9); Goodwin, J. 14; Gordon, Z. 2; Graham, A. 10(5); Hasselbaink, N. 21(6); Hopkirk, D. 2(3); Imrie, D. 35; Kilday, L. 4(1); Kirkpatrick, J. 2(3); Lyle, D. 1(3); McAlister, J. 15(4); McDonald, G. 22(3); McGlinchey, C. (1); McLaughlin, M. 21; McQueen, B. 1; Mensing, S. 30; Millar, K. (1); Murdoch, S. 1; Neil, A. 8(2); Paixao, F. 26(4); Paixao, M. 9(9); Ross, J. 2; Routledge, J. 22(2); Skelton, G. 14(2); Thomas, J. 1(2); Wildig, A. 2(1); Wilkie, K. 3(3).
Goals – League (24): Antoine-Curier 4 (2 pens), Imrie 4, Hasselbaink 3, Mensing 3 (1 pen), Paixao F 3, Buchanan 1, Chambers 1, McLaughlin 1, Paixao M 1, Routledge 1, own goals 2.
Scottish Cup (3): Antoine-Curier 1, Paixao, F 1, Hasselbaink 1.
CIS Cup (0).
Honours – First Division: Champions – 1985–86, 1987–88, 2007–08. **Division II:** Champions – 1903–04. **Division III:** Champions – 2000–01. **B&Q Cup winners** 1992, 1993.

HEART OF MIDLOTHIAN   PREMIER LEAGUE

Ground: Tynecastle Park, McLeod Street, Edinburgh EH11 2NL (0871) 663 1874
Ground capacity: 17,402. **Colours:** White shirts with maroon sleeves and side panels, white shorts with maroon side panels, maroon stockings with white tops.
Manager: Jim Jefferies.
League Appearances: Barr, D. 11(2); Black, I. 29(3); Bouzid, I. 31(1); Driver, A. 4(10); Elliot, C. 11(8); Elliott, S. 21(9); Glen, G. 2(9); Holt, J. (1); Jonsson, E. 29; Kello, M. 31; Kyle, K. 16(3); MacDonald, J. 7; McGowan, R. 3(5); Mrowiec, A. 26(4); Novikovas, A. 1(5); Obua, D. 7(6); Palazuelos, R. 31(2); Robinson , S. 1(3); Santana, S. 16(3); Skacel, R. 27(2); Smith, G. (1); Stevenson, R. 18(13); Templeton, D. 27(6); Thomson, J. 3(3); Thomson, C. 20(7); Wallace, L. 9; Webster, A. 9; Zaliukas, M. 28.
Goals – League (53): Skacel 13, Elliott 8, Kyle 7 (5 pens), Templeton 7, Stevenson 6, Elliot 4, Black 1, Glen 1, Novikovas 1, Thomson C 1 (1 pen), Zaliukas 1, own goals 3.
Scottish Cup (0).
CIS Cup (7): Kyle 3 (1 pen), Jonsson 1, Novikovas 1, Robinson 1, Santana 1.
Honours – Division I: Champions – 1894–95, 1896–97, 1957–58, 1959–60. **First Division:** Champions – 1979–80. **Scottish Cup winners** 1891, 1896, 1901, 1906, 1956, 1998, 2006. **League Cup winners** 1955, 1959, 1960, 1963.

HIBERNIAN   PREMIER LEAGUE

Ground: Easter Road Stadium, 12 Albion Place, Edinburgh EH7 5QG (0131) 661 2159
Ground capacity: 17,400. **Colours:** Green shirts with white sleeves, white shorts, white stockings.
Manager: Colin Calderwood.
League Appearances: Bamba, S. 16; Booth, C. 17; Brown, M. 26; Byrne, K. (3); De Graaf, E. 16(2); Dickoh, F. 27(1); Divis, J. 3; Duffy, D. 2(5); Galbraith, D. 8(14); Grounds, J. 13; Handling, D. (1); Hanlon, P. 30(3); Hart, M. 16(2); Hogg, C. 6(1); Horner, L. (1); McBride, K. 10(1); Miller, L. 30(3); Murray, I. 14(6); Nish, C. 11(9); Palsson, V. 15(1); Rankin, J. 14(3); Riordan, D. 28(5); Scott, M. 8(3); Smith, G. 3(1); Sodje, A. 13(2); Stack, G. 6; Stephens, D. 6(4); Stevenson, L. 11(8); Stokes, A. 3; Taggart, S. 2(1); Thicot, S. 4(3); Thornhill, M. 5(3); Towell, R. 15(1); Trakys, V. 4(5); Vas Te, R. 7(3); Wotherspoon, D. 26(9); Zemmama, M. 3(1).
Goals – League (39): Riordan 11, Sodje 6, Miller 5 (3 pens), Bamba 2, Dickoh 2, Hanlon 2, Hogg 2, Wotherspoon 2, Booth 1, Nish 1, Palsson 1 (1 pen), Rankin 1, Stevenson 1, Stokes 1, Vas Te 1.
Scottish Cup (0).
CIS Cup (1): Grounds 1.
Europa League (2): De Graaf 2.
Honours – Division I: Champions – 1902–03, 1947–48, 1950–51, 1951–52. **First Division:** Champions – 1980–81, 1998–99. **Division II:** Champions – 1893–94, 1894–95, 1932–33. **Scottish Cup winners** 1887, 1902. **League Cup winners** 1973, 1992, 2007.

INVERNESS CALEDONIAN THISTLE
PREMIER LEAGUE

Ground: Tulloch Caledonian Stadium, Stadium Road, Inverness IV1 1FF (01463) 715816
Ground capacity: 7780. **Colours:** Blue shirts with red stripes, blue shorts, blue stockings with red tops.
Manager: Terry Butcher.
League Appearances: Blumenshtein, G. 1(4); Cox, L. 25(2); Doran, A. 11(3); Duff, S. 34; Duncan, R. 20(4); Esson, R. 35; Foran, R. 30(2); Gillet, K. 12(1); Golabek, S. (2); Hayes, J. 23(1); Hogg, C. 10; Innes, C. 10(3); MacDonald, A. 2(8); McBain, R. (2); McCann, K. 8;

Morrison, G. 3(7); Munro, G. 34(1); Odhiambo, E. 18(14); Polworth, L. (1); Proctor, D. 7(3); Rooney, A. 37(1); Ross, N. 30(4); Sanchez, D. 3(6); Shinnie, G. 19; Sutherland, S. 9(20); Tokely, R. 34(1); Tuffey, J. 3.

Goals – League (52): Rooney 15 (5 pens), Foran 7, Hayes 6, Munro 4, Odhiambo 4, Doran 3, Duncan 2, Sutherland 2, Cox 1, Duff 1, Innes 1, MacDonald 1, McCann 1, Ross 1, Sanchez 1, Tokely 1, own goal 1.

Scottish Cup (8): Rooney 4 (1 pen), Foran 2, Hogg 1, Sanchez 1.

CIS Cup (6): Rooney 2 (1 pen), Cox 1, Munro 1, Odihambo 1, Tokely 1.

Honours – First Division: Champions – 2003–04, 2009-10. **Third Division:** Champions – 1996–97. **League Challenge Cup winners** 2004.

KILMARNOCK   PREMIER LEAGUE

Ground: Rugby Park, Kilmarnock KA1 2DP (01563) 525184

Ground capacity: 18,128. **Colours:** Blue shirts with white trim, blue shorts with white trim, blue stockings with white tops.

Manager: Kenny Shiels.

League Appearances: Agard, K. 3(5); Aubameyang, W. 4(2); Bell, C. 31; Berntsson, B. (4); Bryson, C. 33; Clancy, T. 19(2); Dayton, J. 7(3); Eremenko, A. 31; Fisher, G. (3); Forrester, H. 3(4); Fowler, J. 21(5); Gordon, B. 18; Gros, W. 8(3); Hamill, J. 31(1); Hay, G. 17(5); Invincibile, D. 3(4); Jaakkola, A. 7(1); Kelly, L. 30(2); McKenzie, R. (1); O'Leary, R. 3; Pascali, M. 34(1); Pursehouse, A. (1); Rui Miguel, M. 8(13); Sammon, C. 19(4); Silva, D. 17(12); Sissoko, M. 26(1); Taouil, M. 18(6); Wright, F. 27.

Goals – League (53): Sammon 15, Hamill 8 (6 pens), Kelly 7, Eremenko 4, Silva 4, Bryson 2, Dayton 2, Pascali 2, Rui Miguel 2, Agard 1, Aubameyang 1, Fowler 1, Gordon 1, Gros 1, Wright 1, own goal 1.

Scottish Cup (0).

CIS Cup (9): Sammon 3, Hamill 2 (1 pen), Kelly 1, Silva 1, Sissoko 1, Wright 1.

Honours – Division I: Champions – 1964–65. **Division II:** Champions – 1897–98, 1898–99. **Scottish Cup winners** 1920, 1929, 1997.

LIVINGSTON   DIV. 1

Ground: The Braidwood Motor Company Stadium, Almondvale Stadium Road, Livingston EH54 7DN (01506) 417 000

Ground capacity: 10,005. **Colours:** Yellow shirts, black shorts, yellow stockings.

Manager: Gary Bollan.

League Appearances: Barr, C. 33; Barr, R. 20(5); Bullock, T. 34; Conway, A. 6(7); Cowan, D. 8(1); De Vita, R. 15(16); Deuchar, K. 15(4); Docherty, R. 1; Fordyce, C. 3; Fox, L. 30(2); Gray, R. (1); Hamill, J. 22; Hastings, N. 1; Jacobs, Kyle 25(6); Jacobs, Keaghan 25(2); Jacobs, D. 11(1); Jamieson, D. 1; MacDonald, C. 4(2); Malone, C. 10(4); McDowall, C. 1; McNulty, M. (5); O'Byrne, M. 12; Russell, I. 31(3); Scougall, S. (2); Sinclair, D. 16(10); Talbot, J. 24(1); Watson, P. 33; Winters, R. 15(15).

Goals – League (79): Russell 22 (3 pens), De Vita 12, Deuchar 8, Fox 7, Winters 7 (1 pen), Jacobs, Keaghan 5, Barr R 4, Jacobs, Kyle 3, Sinclair 3, Barr C 2, Conway 1, Hamill 1, McNulty 1, Watson 1, own goals 2.

Scottish Cup (1): Russell 1.

CIS Cup (1): Russell 1.

Alba Challenge Cup (2): MacDonald 1, Sinclair 1.

Honours – First Division: Champions – 2000–01. **Second Division:** Champions – 1986–87, 1998–99, 2010–11. **Third Division:** Champions – 1995–96, 2009-10. **League Cup winners** 2004.

MONTROSE   DIV. 3

Ground: Links Park, Montrose DD10 8QD (01674) 673200
Ground capacity: 3292. **Colours:** All royal blue.
Player Manager: Steven Tweed.
League Appearances: Benedictus, K. 5; Bennett, S. 8; Boyle, M. 9(14); Cameron, D. 26; Campbell, A. 31; Collier, J. (1); Crawford, J. 18(1); Crighton, S. 31(2); Davidson, H. 18(3); Fleming, S. (2); Fraser, M. 1; Giordano, D. 3; Gonzalez, R. 14; Hegarty, C. 18(6); Masson, T. 13(2); McCord, R. 28(5); McNalley, S. 30(1); Milligan, F. 6(6); Murray, S. (1); Nicol, D. 9(14); Pope, G. 21(1); Sinclair, A. 31(4); Smith, N. 6(8); Stuart, D. (1); Thompson, C. 24(7); Tierce, S. 2(5); Tosh, P. 26(2); Tweed, S. 6; Watson, P. 2(6); Wood, S. 10.
Goals – League (47): Tosh 12 (6 pens), Thompson 5, McCord 4, Nicol 4 (2 pens), Boyle 3, Masson 3, Sinclair 3, Cameron 2, Campbell 2, Smith 2, Tierce 2, Crawford 1, Crighton 1, Hegarty 1, McNalley 1, Watson 1.
Scottish Cup (12): Tosh 6 (3 pens), Boyle 1, Hegarty 1, McCord 1, Pope 1, Sinclair 1, own goal 1.
CIS Cup (0).
Alba Challenge Cup (0).
Honours – Second Division: Champions – 1984–85.

MORTON   DIV. 1

Ground: Cappielow Park, Sinclair St, Greenock PA15 2TY (01475) 723571
Ground capacity: 11,612. **Colours:** Blue and white hooped shirts, blue shorts, blue stockings.
Manager: Allan Moore.
League Appearances: Bachirou, F. 16(3); Cregg, P. 1; Cuthbert, K. 9(1); Evans, G. 28; Fitzharris, S. 9(6); Graham, B. 16(12); Greacen, S. 2(1); Holmes, G. 14(11); Jenkins, A. 31(4); Kane, R. (2); Kean, S. 18(10); Kelbie, K. 1(7); Lyle, D. 16(4); MacGregor, D. 13; Malone, E. 1; McCaffrey, S. 34; McCarthy, S. 1(1); McKinlay, K. 23(2); Monti, C. 16(10); O'Brien, D. 24(6); Shepherd, N. (1); Smyth, M. 32(1); Stewart, C. 27(1); Tidser, M. 33(1); Toto, J. 3(1); Weatherson, P. 19(12); Young, D. 9(4).
Goals – League (39): Jenkins 8, Graham 7, Weatherson 6 (1 pen), O'Brien 5, Lyle 4 (1 pen), Kean 3, Monti 3 (3 pens), McCaffrey 1, Tidser 1, own goal 1.
Scottish Cup (10): Graham 4, Jenkins 2, Kean 1, Lyle 1, Monti 1 (pen), O'Brien 1.
CIS Cup (7): Kean 2, Weatherson 2, Holmes 1, Kelbie 1, Monti 1.
Alba Challenge Cup (1): Kelbie 1.
Honours – First Division: Champions – 1977–78, 1983–84, 1986–87. **Division II:** Champions – 1949–50, 1963–64, 1966–67. **Second Division:** Champions – 1994–95, 2006–07. **Third Division:** Champions 2002–03. **Scottish Cup winners** 1922.

MOTHERWELL   PREMIER LEAGUE

Ground: Fir Park, Motherwell ML1 2QN (01698) 333333
Ground capacity: 13,742. **Colours:** Amber shirts with claret hoop and trim, maroon shorts, amber stockings.
Manager: Stuart McCall.
League Appearances: Blackman, N. 15(3); Carswell, S. 3(1); Casagolda, E. 3(10); Craigan, S. 32(3); Fitzpatrick, M. 3(2); Forbes, R. 11(12); Gow, A. 9(6); Gunning, G. 12(2); Hammell, S. 26(5); Hateley, T. 36(2); Hollis, L. 1; Humphrey, C. 33(3); Hutchinson, S. 18(1); Jeffers, F. 8(2); Jennings, S. 30; Jones, S. 10(2); Lasley, K. 26; McHugh, R. (11); Meechan, S. (2); Murphy, J. 31(4); Page, J. 3(6); Pollock, J. (3); Randolph, D. 37; Reynolds, M. 19; Ross, M. 5(1); Saunders, S. 22(3); Smith, G. (1); Sutton, J. 25(10).
Goals – League (40): Blackman 10 (1 pen), Sutton 10 (2 pens), Murphy 6 (1 pen), Humphrey 3, Hateley 2 (1 pen), Gow 1, Hutchinson 1, Jeffers 1, Jones 1, Lasley 1, Saunders 1, own goals 3.

Scottish Cup (14): Sutton 6, Murphy 3, Craigan 1, Humphrey 1, Jeffers 1, Jennings 1, Jones 1.
CIS Cup (4): Page 2, Gow 1, Lasley 1.
Europa League (7): Murphy 3, Forbes 1, Hateley 1, Page 1, Sutton 1.
Honours – Division I: Champions – 1931–32. **First Division:** Champions – 1981–82, 1984–85. **Division II:** Champions – 1953–54, 1968–69. **Scottish Cup winners** 1952, 1991. **League Cup winners** 1951.

PARTICK THISTLE   DIV. 1

Ground: Firhill Stadium, Glasgow G20 7AL (0141) 579 1971
Ground capacity: 13,141. **Colours:** Yellow shirts with red design hoops, red shorts, black stockings.
Manager: Jackie McNamara.
League Appearances: Archibald, A. 27; Balatoni, C. 16(6); Bannigan, S. 1(1); Boyle, P. 35; Buchanan, L. 12(5); Burns, K. 1(1); Cairney, P. 24(5); Campbell, J. 6(6); Donnelly, S. 7(7); Doolan, K. 29(4); Erskine, C. 21(13); Flannigan, I. 22(7); Fox, S. 24; Fraser, S. (14); Grehan, M. 18(8); Halliwell, B. 10; Hardie, M. 4; Hodge, B. 13(3); Kinniburgh, W 4; Kinniburgh, W 19; Lochhead, K. (3); MacBeth, R. (1); Maxwell, I. 4; McGeough, R. (2); McGowan, R. 6(1); McGrotty, J. (1); McNamara, J. 15; Paton, P. 25(1); Robertson, J. 20; Rowson, D. 28(1); Scully, R. 1; Shepherd, G. 1; Stewart, T. 3(2).
Goals – League (44): Doolan 15 (3 pens), Erskine 7, Boyle 4, Flannigan 4, Buchanan 3 (1 pen), Fraser 2, Stewart 2, Balatoni 1, Campbell 1, Grehan 1, Hodge 1, Kinniburgh, W 1, Paton 1, Rowson 1.
Scottish Cup (6): Buchanan 1, Cairney 1, Donnelly 1, Doolan 1, Erskine 1, Grehan 1.
CIS Cup (1): Donnelly 1.
Alba Challenge Cup (8): Doolan 2, Boyle 1, Buchanan 1, Cairney 1, Kinniburgh 1, MacBeth 1, Rowson 1.
Honours – First Division: Champions – 1975–76, 2001–02. **Division II:** Champions – 1896–97, 1899–1900, 1970–71. **Second Division:** Champions 2000–01. **Scottish Cup winners** 1921. **League Cup winners** 1972.

PETERHEAD   DIV. 3

Ground: Balmoor Stadium, Balmoor Terrace, Peterhead AB42 1EU (01779) 478256
Ground capacity: 3250 (1000 seated). **Colours:** Navy blue shirts with royal blue sleeves, navy blue shorts, navy blue stockings.
Manager: John Sheran.
League Appearances: Anderson, S. 13(1); Bateman, J. 21(2); Bavidge, M. 30; Campbell, P. (2); Clark, N. 14(10); Donald, D. 33; Emslie, P. 23(4); Gethans, C. 11(15); Jarvie, P. 15(1); MacDonald, C. 30(3); Maclachlan, J. (1); Mann, R. 9; McVitie, N. 28(2); Moore, D. 11(5); Robertson, S. (1); Ross, S. 17(3); Ross, D. 19(7); Sharp, G. 25(6); Smith, Stuart 34; Smith, Stirling 13(1); Stephens, B. 2(4); Strachan, R. 23(6); Tosh, P. 4(2); Wyness, D. 21(7).
Goals – League (47): Wyness 8 (3 pens), Bavidge 7, Ross D 6, Clark 4, Gethans 4, Strachan 4 (2 pens), Anderson 2, Emslie 2, Sharp 2, Smith, Stuart 2, Tosh 2, Donald 1, MacDonald 1, own goals 2.
Scottish Cup (3): McVitie 1, Sharp 1, Strachan 1.
CIS Cup (1): Wyness 1.
Alba Challenge Cup (15): Wyness 4, Bavidge 3, Gethans 2, MacDonald 2, Emslie 1, Stuart Smith 1, own goals 2.
Honours – None.

QUEEN OF THE SOUTH   DIV. 1

Ground: Palmerston Park, Dumfries DG2 9BA (01387) 254853
Ground capacity: 6412. **Colours:** Royal blue shirts, white shorts, royal blue stockings.
Manager: Gus MacPherson.
League Appearances: Black, S. 1(3); Burns, P. 26; Carmichael, D. 15(13); Conroy, R. 11;
Degnan, S. 1(4); Harris, R. 30(1); Holmes, D. 29(1); Hutton, D. 25; Johnston, A. 25(1);
Lilley, D. 30(1); McGowan, J. 2(1); McGuffie, R. 32(2); McKenna, S. 29; McKenzie, R. 9;
McLaren, W. 28(4); McMenamin, C. 26; McShane, I. 3(10); O'Hear, K. (1); Orsi, D. 4(3);
Quinn, R. 16(2); Reid, C. 32; Reilly, G. (1); Robinson, L. 2; Scally, N. (4); Smylie, R. (5);
Weatherston, D. 18(11); Young, D. 2.
Goals – League (54): McMenamin 11, McLaren 9 (2 pens), Burns 5, Johnston 5, Weatherston 5, Carmichael 3, Conroy 3, McGuffie 3, Harris 2 (1 pen), Holmes 2, Quinn 2, Degnan 1, Lilley 1, Orsi 1, own goal 1.
Scottish Cup (1): McMenamin 1.
CIS Cup (9): Holmes 2 (1 pen), Carmichael 1, Harris 1 (pen), Johnston 1, McLaren 1, Quinn 1, Riley 1, Weatherston 1.
Alba Challenge Cup (10): Burns 4, Harris 1, Holmes 1, McGuffie 1, Reid 1, Weatherston 1, own goal 1.
Honours – Division II: Champions – 1950–51. **Second Division:** Champions – 2001–02.
League Challenge Cup winners 2003.

QUEEN'S PARK   DIV. 3

Ground: Hampden Park, Glasgow G42 9BA (0141) 632 1275
Ground capacity: 52,000. **Colours:** White shirts with thin black hoops, white shorts, white stockings.
Head Coach: Gardner Spiers.
League Appearances: Anderson, D. 32(1); Baillie, S. (1); Brough, J. 11; Burns, P. 2(1);
Capuano, G. 26(1); Daly, M. 17(12); Eagleshan, G. 9(4); Gallagher, P. 19(2); Hamilton, P.
1; Harkins, P. 8(5); Henry, J. 1(2); Lauchlan, G. 4(6); Little, R. 35; Longworth, J. 16(11);
McBride, M. 30(3); McGinn, P. 26; McPherson, G. 3(1); Meggatt, D. 30; Millen, A. 18;
Milne, A. 1; Murray, D. 17(8); O'Hara, M. 4(5); Quinn, T. 13(9); Sinclair, R. 3; Smith, C.
11(13); Strain, A. 32; Watt, I. 27(5).
Goals – League (57): Longworth 12, McBride M 8 (3 pens), Daly 6, Smith 6, Murray 4,
Quinn T 4, Watt 4, Brough 2, Meggatt 2, Capuano 1, Gallagher 1, Harkins 1, Lauchlan 1, Little 1, McGinn 1, O'Hara 1, own goals 2.
Scottish Cup (1): Brough 1.
CIS Cup (0).
Alba Challenge Cup (5): Eagleshan 3 (1 pen), McBride M 1, Watt 1.
Play-Offs (1): Smith 1.
Honours – Second Division: Champions – 1980–81. **Third Division:** Champions – 1999–2000. **Scottish Cup winners** 1874, 1875, 1876, 1880, 1881, 1882, 1884, 1886, 1890, 1893.

RAITH ROVERS   DIV. 1

Ground: Stark's Park, Pratt Street, Kirkcaldy KY1 1SA (01592) 263514
Ground capacity: 10,104 (all seated). **Colours:** Navy shirts with red flashings, navy blue shorts with red side flashings, navy blue stockings with red flashings.
Manager: John McGlynn.
League Appearances: Baird, J. 34(2); Callachan, R. (1); Campbell, M. 22(2); Davidson,
I. 29(2); Donaldson, R. (1); Dyer, W. 26(4); Ellis, L. 29; Ferry, M. 13(9); Hill, D. 8;
McBride, S. 18(4); McBride, K. 7; McGurn, D. 21(1); McKechnie, J. (1); McNeil, A.
15(1); Mole, J. 5(6); Murray, G. 36; Simmons, S. 26(3); Tade, G. 34(2); Wales, G. (7);
Walker, A. 34; Weir, G. 1(24); Williamson, I. 12(10); Wilson, C. 26(4).

Goals – League (47): Baird 13 (1 pen), Tade 8, Walker 7, Campbell 4, Ellis 3, Murray 3, Ferry 2, Mole 2, Simmons 2, Davidson 1, Dyer 1, Williamson 1.
Scottish Cup (2): Baird 1, Murray 1.
CIS Cup (7): Tade 3, Mole 2, Baird 1, Ferry 1.
Alba Challenge Cup (0).
Honours – First Division: Champions – 1992–93, 1994–95. **Second Division:** Champions – 2002–03, 2008–09. **Division II:** Champions – 1907–08, 1909–10 (Shared), 1937–38, 1948–49. **League Cup winners** 1995.

RANGERS   PREMIER LEAGUE

Ground: Ibrox Stadium, Glasgow G51 2XD (0871) 702 1972
Ground capacity: 51,082. **Colours:** Royal blue shirts with red and white trim, white shorts, black stockings with red tops.
Manager: Ally McCoist.
League Appearances: Alexander, N. 1; Bartley, K. 5; Beattie, J. 5(2); Bougherra, M. 31; Broadfoot, K. 5(3); Davis, S. 37; Diouf, E. 6(9); Edu, M. 27(6); Fleck, J. 3(10); Foster, R. 11(4); Healy, D. 2(6); Hutton, K. 1(6); Jelavic, N. 20(3); Kerkar, S. (1); Lafferty, K. 23(8); Loy, R. (1); McCulloch, L. 17(4); McGregor, A. 37; Miller, K. 17(1); Naismith, S. 28(3); Ness, J. 8(3); Papac, S. 34; Webster, A. 1; Weir, D. 37; Weiss, V. 17(6); Whittaker, S. 36; Wylde, G. 9(6).
Goals – League (88): Miller 21 (4 pens), Jelavic 16, Lafferty 11, Naismith 11, Weiss 5, Davis 4, Whittaker 4 (4 pens), Papac 3, Edu 2, Bartley 1, Bougherra 1, Diouf 1, Healy 1, own goals 7.
Scottish Cup (5): Whittaker 2 (2 pens), Lafferty 1, McCulloch 1, Ness 1.
CIS Cup (13): Jelavic 3, Lafferty 3, Naismith 3, Bougherra 1, Davis 1, Edu 1, Little 1.
Champions League (5): Jelavic 2, Edu 1, Miller 1, Naismith 1.
Europa League (3): Diouf 1, Edu 1, Whittaker 1.
Honours – Division I: Champions – 1890–91 (Shared), 1898–99, 1899–1900, 1900–01, 1901–02, 1910–11, 1911–12, 1912–13, 1917–18, 1919–20, 1920–21, 1922–23, 1923–24, 1924–25, 1926–27, 1927–28, 1928–29, 1929–30, 1930–31, 1932–33, 1933–34, 1934–35, 1936–37, 1938–39, 1946–47, 1948–49, 1949–50, 1952–53, 1955–56, 1956–57, 1958–59, 1960–61, 1962–63, 1963–64, 1974–75. **Premier Division:** Champions – 1975–76, 1977–78, 1986–87, 1988–89, 1989–90, 1990–91, 1991–92, 1992–93, 1993–94, 1994–95, 1995–96, 1996–97. **Premier League:** Champions – 1998–99, 1999–2000, 2002–03, 2004–05, 2008–09, 2009–10, 2010–11. **Scottish Cup winners** 1894, 1897, 1898, 1903, 1928, 1930, 1932, 1934, 1935, 1936, 1948, 1949, 1950, 1953, 1960, 1962, 1963, 1964, 1966, 1973, 1976, 1978, 1979, 1981, 1992, 1993, 1996, 1999, 2000, 2002, 2003, 2008, 2009. **League Cup winners** 1947, 1949, 1961, 1962, 1964, 1965, 1971, 1976, 1978, 1979, 1982, 1984, 1985, 1987, 1988, 1989, 1991, 1993, 1994, 1997, 1999, 2002, 2003, 2005, 2008, 2010, 2011. **European Cup-Winners' Cup winners** 1972.

ROSS COUNTY   DIV. 1

Ground: Victoria Park Stadium, Jubilee Road, Dingwall IV15 9QZ (01349) 860860
Ground capacity: 6700. **Colours:** Navy blue shirts with white sleeves, navy blue shorts with white flashes, navy blue stockings.
Manager: Derek Adam.
League Appearances: Barrowman, A. 22(6); Boyd, S. 33; Brittain, R. 32(2); Corcoran, M. 12(8); Craig, S. 11(7); Di Giacomo, P. 8(6); Fitzpatrick, M. 16(1); Flynn, J. 22(1); Gardyne, M. 25(5); Gartland, G. 3; Kettlewell, S. 18(6); Lawson, P. 25; Malin, J. (1); Marr, J. 9(4); McCormack, D. 15(1); McGovern, M. 36; Miller, G. 29(2); Milne, S. 11(2); Morrison, S. 21(3); Scott, M. 15(1); Smith, D. 2(5); Vigurs, I. 20(11); Wood, G. 11(15).
Goals – League (30): Barrowman 5, Boyd 3, Brittain 3 (2 pens), Flynn 3, Gardyne 3, Craig 2, Morrison 2, Vigurs 2, Wood 2, Corcoran 1, Di Giacomo 1, Lawson 1, Marr 1, Milne 1.
Scottish Cup (4): Barrowman 2, Craig 1, Miller 1.

CIS Cup (6): Barrowman 1, Brittain 1, Craig 1, Di Giacomo 1, Gardyne 1, Vigurs 1.
Alba Challenge Cup (11): Lawson 3, Barrowman 2, Scott 2, Gardyne 1, Morrison 1, Vigurs 1, own goal 1.
Honours – Second Division: Champions – 2007–08. **Third Division:** Champions – 1998–99.
League Challenge Cup winners 2007, 2011.

ST JOHNSTONE   PREMIER LEAGUE

Ground: McDiarmid Park, Crieff Road, Perth PH1 2SJ (01738) 459090
Ground capacity: 10,673. **Colours:** All royal blue with white trim.
Manager: Derek Adams.
League Appearances: Adams, J. 9(2); Anderson, S. 24(1); Caddis, L. 1(2); Craig, L. 29(5); Davidson, M. 33(1); Dobie, S. 1(3); Duberry, M. 32(1); Enckelman, P. 29; Gartland, G. 4(3); Grainger, D. 31(2); Haber, M. 5(6); Invincibile, D. 8(2); Jackson, A. 10(7); MacDonald, P. 14(10); MacKay, D. 32; May, S. 8(11); Maybury, A. 23(7); Millar, C. 29(1); Milne, S. 1(1); Moon, K. 4(2); Morris, J. 23; Myrie-Williams, J. 4(2); Novikovas, A. 1(5); Parkin, S. 17(4); Reynolds, S. (5); Robertson , J. 2(4); Rutkiewicz, K. 4(6); Samuel, C. 20(8); Smith, G. 9; Taylor, C. 11(10).
Goals – League (23): Craig 5 (2 pens), Parkin 4, Grainger 2, May 2, Samuel 2, Adams 1, Haber 1, Jackson 1, Moon 1, Taylor 1, own goals 3.
Scottish Cup (6): Craig 1, Davidson 1, Invincibile 1, MacDonald 1, Millar 1, Samuel 1.
CIS Cup (7): Davidson 2, Dobie 1, Haber 1, Millar 1, Morris 1 (pen), Parkin 1.
Honours – First Division: Champions – 1982–83, 1989–90, 1996–97, 2008–09. **Division II:** Champions – 1923–24, 1959–60, 1962–63. **League Challenge Cup winners** 2008.

ST MIRREN   PREMIER LEAGUE

Ground: St Mirren Park, Greenhill Road, Paisley PA3 1RU (0141) 889 2558
Ground capacity: 10,476 (all seated). **Colours:** Black and white striped shirts, black shorts, white stockings.
Manager: Danny Lennon.
League Appearances: Barron, D. 4(5); Brady, G. 3(2); Cregg, P. 18(4); Dargo, C. 14(8); Gallacher, P. 27; Goodwin, J. 16(1); Hegarty, N. 2(1); Higdon, M. 26(2); Lamont, M. (1); Love, A. (1); Lynch, S. 8(6); Mair, L. 22(2); McAusland, M. 24(1); McCluskey, J. (3); McGowan, P. 33; McGregor, D. 36; McKernon, A. (1); McLean, K. 10(9); McLennan, M. (1); McQuade, P. (5); Mooy, A. 7(6); Murray, H. 21(3); Potter, J. 32(2); Ramage, G. (1); Robb, S. 3; Samson, C. 11; Thomson, S. 25(2); Travner, J. 35(2); Van Zanten, D. 25(3); Wardlaw, G. 16(7).
Goals – League (33): Higdon 14 (3 pens), Thomson 5, Dargo 3 (1 pen), McGregor 3, Wardlaw 3, Lynch 2, McAusland 1, McGowan 1, Travner 1.
Scottish Cup (10): McGowan 4, Dargo 2, McQuade 2, Mooy 1, own goal 1.
CIS Cup (3): Higdon 1, McGowan 1, McGregor 1.
Honours – First Division: Champions – 1976–77, 1999–2000, 2005–06. **Division II:** Champions – 1967–68. **Scottish Cup winners** 1926, 1959, 1987.
League Challenge Cup winners 2005–06.

STENHOUSEMUIR   DIV. 2

Ground: Ochilview Park, Stenhousemuir FK5 4QL (01324) 562992
Ground capacity: 3776 (626 seated). **Colours:** All maroon.
Manager: Dave Irons.
League Appearances: Anderson, G. 30(2); Archdeacon, M. (1); Brown, A. 24(1); Clark, R. 11(4); Connachan, K. 1; Dalziel, S. 17(6); Devlin, M. 10; Dickson, S. 21(2); Fusco, S. 5(2); Gibb, S. 21(1); Gilmuir, B. 7(2); Hunter, M. (7); Love, A. 4(2); Lyle, W. 35; Lynch, S. 11(6); McCluskey, C. 12(1); McLennan, J. 2(1); Motion, K. 8(3); Murray, S. 32; Paton, E.

18; Plenderleith, G. (10); Quinn, P. 15(8); Scullion, P. 5(3); Sloane, L. 2(7); Smith, J. 23; Stirling, A. 10(10); Strachan, A. 1; Thom, G. 23(3); Thomson, S. 5; Thomson, I. 31; Williams, A. 12(5).
Goals – League (46): Anderson 7, Williams 6 (1 pen), Clark 5 (2 pens), Dalziel 5, Lynch 4, Devlin 3, Murray 3, Paton 3 (1 pen), Quinn 3, Smith 2, Hunter 1, Lyle 1, Plenderleith 1, Scullion 1, Thom 1.
Scottish Cup (10): Clark 3 (1 pen), Williams 3, Dalziel 1, Smith 1, Stirling 1, own goal 1.
CIS Cup (1): Anderson 1.
Alba Challenge Cup (8): Williams 3, Anderson 1, Dalziel 1, Motion 1, Quinn 1, own goal 1.
Honours – Second Division: Champions – 2009–10. **League Challenge Cup winners** 1996.

STIRLING ALBION   DIV. 2

Ground: The Doubletree, Dunblane Stadium, Springkerse, Stirling FK7 7UJ (01786) 450399
Ground capacity: 3808. **Colours:** All red with white trim.
Manager: Jocky Scott.
League Appearances: Aitken, C. 24(3); Allison, B. 23(2); Ashe, D. (1); Borris, R. 22(5); Brass, G. (1); Brighton, T. 10(3); Brown, J. 18; Buist, S. 26; Christie, S. 20(2); Colquhoun, D. 1(3); Comvalius, S. 1(5); Corrigan, M. 20(2); Currie, L. 2; Doyle, M. 17(2); Flood, J. 4(1); Forsyth, R. 25(1); Gibson, A. 11(8); Gilhaney, M. (1); Hamill, J. (1); Heeking, J. 14; Kane, J. 15(11); Kirwan, R. (1); McDonald, G. 7(1); McHale, P. 22(1); Mullen, M. 13(12); Reidford, C. 16; Robertson, S. 30(2); Smith, G. 31(3); Stirling, S. 2(8); Taggart, N. 5(6); Welsh, S. 15(2); Witteveen, D. 2; Yohan, M. (1).
Goals – League (32): Smith 11 (1 pen), Aitken 5 (3 pens), Mullen 4, Borris 2, Stirling 2 (1 pen), Flood 1, Forsyth 1, Gibson 1, Kane 1, McHale 1, Robertson 1, Welsh 1, Witteveen 1.
Scottish Cup (1): Smith 1.
CIS Cup (1): Taggart 1.
Alba Challenge Cup (1): Devine 1.
Honours – Division II: Champions – 1952–53, 1957–58, 1960–61, 1964–65. **Second Division:** Champions – 1976–77, 1990–91, 1995–96, 2009–10.

STRANRAER   DIV. 3

Ground: Stair Park, Stranraer DG9 8BS (01776) 703271
Ground capacity: 5600. **Colours:** Royal blue shirts, white shorts, royal blue stockings.
Manager: Keith Knox.
League Appearances: Agnew, S. 36; Aitken, S. (1); Bouadji, R. 4; Cochrane, A. 2(5); Gallacher, D. 26; Gallagher, G. 35; Kennedy, R. 7; Kurakins, A. 18(1); Malcolm, C. 34; Marshall, R. 4; McAuliffe, D. 5(1); McColm, S. 18(17); McInnes, P. (1); Mitchell, David 32; Mitchell, G. 4(7); Mitchell, Danny 24(8); Moore, M. 11(17); Murphy, P. 30(1); Nicoll, K. 20(5); Noble, S. 19(5); One, A. 24(11); Sharp, L. 20(5); Winter, S. 23(5).
Goals – League (72): One 17, Malcolm 15, Agnew 13 (3 pens), Winter 8, McColm 4, Gallacher 3, Moore 3, Murphy 3, Bouadji 2, Kennedy 1, Mitchell G 1, Nicoll 1, Noble 1.
Scottish Cup (17): Malcolm 6, One 5, Agnew 2 (1 pen), Gallacher 1, Moore 1, Murphy 1, Winter 1.
CIS Cup (1): McColm 1.
Alba Challenge Cup (1): Malcolm 1.
Honours – Second Division: Champions – 1993–94, 1997–98. **Third Division:** Champions – 2003–04. **League Challenge Cup winners** 1997.

SCOTTISH LEAGUE HONOURS

*On goal average (ratio)/difference. †Held jointly after indecisive play-off.
‡Won on deciding match. ††Held jointly. ¶Two points deducted for fielding ineligible
player. Competition suspended 1940–45 during war; Regional Leagues operating.
‡‡Two points deducted for registration irregularities. §Not promoted after play-offs.

PREMIER LEAGUE

Maximum points: 108

	First	Pts	Second	Pts	Third	Pts
1998–99	Rangers	77	Celtic	71	St Johnstone	57
1999–00	Rangers	90	Celtic	69	Hearts	54

Maximum points: 114

	First	Pts	Second	Pts	Third	Pts
2000–01	Celtic	97	Rangers	82	Hibernian	66
2001–02	Celtic	103	Rangers	85	Livingston	58
2002–03	Rangers*	97	Celtic	97	Hearts	63
2003–04	Celtic	98	Rangers	81	Hearts	68
2004–05	Rangers	93	Celtic	92	Hibernian*	61
2005–06	Celtic	91	Hearts	74	Rangers	73
2006–07	Celtic	84	Rangers	72	Aberdeen	65
2007–08	Celtic	89	Rangers	86	Motherwell	60
2008–09	Rangers	86	Celtic	82	Hearts	59
2009–10	Rangers	87	Celtic	81	Dundee U	63
2010–11	Rangers	93	Celtic	92	Hearts	63

PREMIER DIVISION

Maximum points: 72

	First	Pts	Second	Pts	Third	Pts
1975–76	Rangers	54	Celtic	48	Hibernian	43
1976–77	Celtic	55	Rangers	46	Aberdeen	43
1977–78	Rangers	55	Aberdeen	53	Dundee U	40
1978–79	Celtic	48	Rangers	45	Dundee U	44
1979–80	Aberdeen	48	Celtic	47	St Mirren	42
1980–81	Celtic	56	Aberdeen	49	Rangers*	44
1981–82	Celtic	55	Aberdeen	53	Rangers	43
1982–83	Dundee U	56	Celtic*	55	Aberdeen	55
1983–84	Aberdeen	57	Celtic	50	Dundee U	47
1984–85	Aberdeen	59	Celtic	52	Dundee U	47
1985–86	Celtic*	50	Hearts	50	Dundee U	47

Maximum points: 88

	First	Pts	Second	Pts	Third	Pts
1986–87	Rangers	69	Celtic	63	Dundee U	60
1987–88	Celtic	72	Hearts	62	Rangers	60

Maximum points: 72

	First	Pts	Second	Pts	Third	Pts
1988–89	Rangers	56	Aberdeen	50	Celtic	46
1989–90	Rangers	51	Aberdeen*	44	Hearts	44
1990–91	Rangers	55	Aberdeen	53	Celtic*	41

Maximum points: 88

	First	Pts	Second	Pts	Third	Pts
1991–92	Rangers	72	Hearts	63	Celtic	62

	First	Pts	Second	Pts	Third	Pts
1992–93	Rangers	73	Aberdeen	64	Celtic	60
1993–94	Rangers	58	Aberdeen	55	Motherwell	54

Maximum points: 108

	First	Pts	Second	Pts	Third	Pts
1994–95	Rangers	69	Motherwell	54	Hibernian	53
1995–96	Rangers	87	Celtic	83	Aberdeen*	55
1996–97	Rangers	80	Celtic	75	Dundee U	60
1997–98	Celtic	74	Rangers	72	Hearts	67

FIRST DIVISION

Maximum points: 52

	First	Pts	Second	Pts	Third	Pts
1975–76	Partick Th	41	Kilmarnock	35	Montrose	30

Maximum points: 78

	First	Pts	Second	Pts	Third	Pts
1976–77	St Mirren	62	Clydebank	58	Dundee	51
1977–78	Morton*	58	Hearts	58	Dundee	57
1978–79	Dundee	55	Kilmarnock*	54	Clydebank	54
1979–80	Hearts	53	Airdrieonians	51	Ayr U*	44
1980–81	Hibernian	57	Dundee	52	St Johnstone	51
1981–82	Motherwell	61	Kilmarnock	51	Hearts	50
1982–83	St Johnstone	55	Hearts	54	Clydebank	50
1983–84	Morton	54	Dumbarton	51	Partick Th	46
1984–85	Motherwell	50	Clydebank	48	Falkirk	45
1985–86	Hamilton A	56	Falkirk	45	Kilmarnock	44

Maximum points: 88

	First	Pts	Second	Pts	Third	Pts
1986–87	Morton	57	Dunfermline Ath	56	Dumbarton	53
1987–88	Hamilton A	56	Meadowbank Th	52	Clydebank	49

Maximum points: 78

	First	Pts	Second	Pts	Third	Pts
1988–89	Dunfermline Ath	54	Falkirk	52	Clydebank	48
1989–90	St Johnstone	58	Airdrieonians	54	Clydebank	44
1990–91	Falkirk	54	Airdrieonians	53	Dundee	52

Maximum points: 88

	First	Pts	Second	Pts	Third	Pts
1991–92	Dundee	58	Partick Th*	57	Hamilton A	57
1992–93	Raith R	65	Kilmarnock	54	Dunfermline Ath	52
1993–94	Falkirk	66	Dunfermline Ath	65	Airdrieonians	54

Maximum points: 108

	First	Pts	Second	Pts	Third	Pts
1994–95	Raith R	69	Dunfermline Ath*	68	Dundee	68
1995–96	Dunfermline Ath	71	Dundee U*	67	Morton	67
1996–97	St Johnstone	80	Airdrieonians	60	Dundee*	58
1997–98	Dundee	70	Falkirk	65	Raith R*	60
1998–99	Hibernian	89	Falkirk	66	Ayr U	62
1999–00	St Mirren	76	Dunfermline Ath	71	Falkirk	68
2000–01	Livingston	76	Ayr U	69	Falkirk	56
2001–02	Partick Th	66	Airdrieonians	56	Ayr U	52
2002–03	Falkirk	81	Clyde	72	St Johnstone	67
2003–04	Inverness CT	70	Clyde	69	St Johnstone	57

	First	Pts	Second	Pts	Third	Pts
2004–05	Falkirk	75	St Mirren*	60	Clyde	60
2005–06	St Mirren	76	St Johnstone	66	Hamilton A	59
2006–07	Gretna	66	St Johnstone	65	Dundee*	53
2007–08	Hamilton A	76	Dundee	69	St Johnstone	58
2008–09	St Johnstone	65	Partick Th	55	Dunfermline Ath	51
2009–10	Inverness CT	73	Dundee	61	Dunfermline Ath	58
2010–11	Dunfermline Ath	70	Raith R	60	Falkirk	58

SECOND DIVISION

Maximum points: 52

	First	Pts	Second	Pts	Third	Pts
1975–76	Clydebank*	40	Raith R	40	Alloa Ath	35

Maximum points: 78

	First	Pts	Second	Pts	Third	Pts
1976–77	Stirling Alb	55	Alloa Ath	51	Dunfermline Ath	50
1977–78	Clyde*	53	Raith R	53	Dunfermline Ath	48
1978–79	Berwick R	54	Dunfermline Ath	52	Falkirk	50
1979–80	Falkirk	50	East Stirling	49	Forfar Ath	46
1980–81	Queen's Park	50	Queen of the S	46	Cowdenbeath	45
1981–82	Clyde	59	Alloa Ath*	50	Arbroath	50
1982–83	Brechin C	55	Meadowbank Th	54	Arbroath	49
1983–84	Forfar Ath	63	East Fife	47	Berwick R	43
1984–85	Montrose	53	Alloa Ath	50	Dunfermline Ath	49
1985–86	Dunfermline Ath	57	Queen of the S	55	Meadowbank Th	49
1986–87	Meadowbank Th	55	Raith R*	52	Stirling Alb*	52
1987–88	Ayr U	61	St Johnstone	59	Queen's Park	51
1988–89	Albion R	50	Alloa Ath	45	Brechin C	43
1989–90	Brechin C	49	Kilmarnock	48	Stirling Alb	47
1990–91	Stirling Alb	54	Montrose	46	Cowdenbeath	45
1991–92	Dumbarton	52	Cowdenbeath	51	Alloa Ath	50
1992–93	Clyde	54	Brechin C*	53	Stranraer	53
1993–94	Stranraer	56	Berwick R	48	Stenhousemuir*	47

Maximum points: 108

	First	Pts	Second	Pts	Third	Pts
1994–95	Morton	64	Dumbarton	60	Stirling Alb	58
1995–96	Stirling Alb	81	East Fife	67	Berwick R	60
1996–97	Ayr U	77	Hamilton A	74	Livingston	64
1997–98	Stranraer	61	Clydebank	60	Livingston	59
1998–99	Livingston	77	Inverness CT	72	Clyde	53
1999–00	Clyde	65	Alloa Ath	64	Ross County	62
2000–01	Partick Th	75	Arbroath	58	Berwick R*	54
2001–02	Queen of the S	67	Alloa Ath	59	Forfar Ath	53
2002–03	Raith R	59	Brechin C	55	Airdrie U	54
2003–04	Airdrie U	70	Hamilton A	62	Dumbarton	60
2004–05	Brechin C	72	Stranraer	63	Morton	62
2005–06	Gretna	88	Morton§	70	Peterhead*§	57
2006–07	Morton	77	Stirling Alb	69	Raith R§	62
2007–08	Ross Co	73	Airdrie U	66	Raith R§	60
2008–09	Raith R	76	Ayr U	74	Brechin C§	62

	First	Pts	Second	Pts	Third	Pts
2009–10	Stirling Alb*	65	Alloa Ath§	65	Cowdenbeath	59
2010–11	Livingston	82	Ayr U*	59	Forfar§	59

THIRD DIVISION
Maximum points: 108

	First	Pts	Second	Pts	Third	Pts
1994–95	Forfar Ath	80	Montrose	67	Ross Co	60
1995–96	Livingston	72	Brechin C	63	Caledonian Th	57
1996–97	Inverness CT	76	Forfar Ath*	67	Ross Co	67
1997–98	Alloa Ath	76	Arbroath	68	Ross Co*	67
1998–99	Ross Co	77	Stenhousemuir	64	Brechin C	59
1999–00	Queen's Park	69	Berwick R	66	Forfar Ath	61
2000–01	Hamilton A*	76	Cowdenbeath	76	Brechin C	72
2001–02	Brechin C	73	Dumbarton	61	Albion R	59
2002–03	Morton	72	East Fife	71	Albion R	70
2003–04	Stranraer	79	Stirling Alb	77	Gretna	68
2004–05	Gretna	98	Peterhead	78	Cowdenbeath	51
2005–06	Cowdenbeath*	76	Berwick R§	76	Stenhousemuir§	73
2006–07	Berwick R	75	Arbroath§	70	Queen's Park	68
2007–08	East Fife	88	Stranraer	65	Montrose§	59
2008–09	Dumbarton	67	Cowdenbeath§	63	East Stirling§	61
2009–10	Livingston	78	Forfar Ath	63	East Stirling§	61
2010–11	Arbroath	66	Albion R	61	Queen's Park*§	59

DIVISION 1 to 1974–75
Maximum points: a 36; b 44; c 40; d 52; e 60; f 68; g 76; h 84.

	First	Pts	Second	Pts	Third	Pts
1890–91a	Dumbarton††	29	Rangers††	29	Celtic	21
1891–92b	Dumbarton	37	Celtic	35	Hearts	34
1892–93a	Celtic	29	Rangers	28	St Mirren	20
1893–94a	Celtic	29	Hearts	26	St Bernard's	23
1894–95a	Hearts	31	Celtic	26	Rangers	22
1895–96a	Celtic	30	Rangers	26	Hibernian	24
1896–97a	Hearts	28	Hibernian	26	Rangers	25
1897–98a	Celtic	33	Rangers	29	Hibernian	22
1898–99a	Rangers	36	Hearts	26	Celtic	24
1899–1900a	Rangers	32	Celtic	25	Hibernian	24
1900–01c	Rangers	35	Celtic	29	Hibernian	25
1901–02a	Rangers	28	Celtic	26	Hearts	22
1902–03b	Hibernian	37	Dundee	31	Rangers	29
1903–04d	Third Lanark	43	Hearts	39	Celtic*	38
1904–05d	Celtic‡	41	Rangers	41	Third Lanark	35
1905–06e	Celtic	49	Hearts	43	Airdrieonians	38
1906–07f	Celtic	55	Dundee	48	Rangers	45
1907–08f	Celtic	55	Falkirk	51	Rangers	50
1908–09f	Celtic	51	Dundee	50	Clyde	48
1909–10f	Celtic	54	Falkirk	52	Rangers	46
1910–11f	Rangers	52	Aberdeen	48	Falkirk	44
1911–12f	Rangers	51	Celtic	45	Clyde	42
1912–13f	Rangers	53	Celtic	49	Hearts*	41

First	Pts	Second	Pts	Third	Pts
1913–14g Celtic	65	Rangers	59	Hearts*	54
1914–15g Celtic	65	Hearts	61	Rangers	50
1915–16g Celtic	67	Rangers	56	Morton	51
1916–17g Celtic	64	Morton	54	Rangers	53
1917–18f Rangers	56	Celtic	55	Kilmarnock*	43
1918–19f Celtic	58	Rangers	57	Morton	47
1919–20h Rangers	71	Celtic	68	Motherwell	57
1920–21h Rangers	76	Celtic	66	Hearts	50
1921–22h Celtic	67	Rangers	66	Raith R	51
1922–23g Rangers	55	Airdrieonians	50	Celtic	46
1923–24g Rangers	59	Airdrieonians	50	Celtic	46
1924–25g Rangers	60	Airdrieonians	57	Hibernian	52
1925–26g Celtic	58	Airdrieonians*	50	Hearts	50
1926–27g Rangers	56	Motherwell	51	Celtic	49
1927–28g Rangers	60	Celtic*	55	Motherwell	55
1928–29g Rangers	67	Celtic	51	Motherwell	50
1929–30g Rangers	60	Motherwell	55	Aberdeen	53
1930–31g Rangers	60	Celtic	58	Motherwell	56
1931–32g Motherwell	66	Rangers	61	Celtic	48
1932–33g Rangers	62	Motherwell	59	Hearts	50
1933–34g Rangers	66	Motherwell	62	Celtic	47
1934–35g Rangers	55	Celtic	52	Hearts	50
1935–36g Celtic	66	Rangers*	61	Aberdeen	61
1936–37g Rangers	61	Aberdeen	54	Celtic	52
1937–38g Celtic	61	Hearts	58	Rangers	49
1938–39g Rangers	59	Celtic	48	Aberdeen	46
1946–47e Rangers	46	Hibernian	44	Aberdeen	39
1947–48e Hibernian	48	Rangers	46	Partick Th	36
1948–49e Rangers	46	Dundee	45	Hibernian	39
1949–50e Rangers	50	Hibernian	49	Hearts	43
1950–51e Hibernian	48	Rangers*	38	Dundee	38
1951–52e Hibernian	45	Rangers	41	East Fife	37
1952–53e Rangers*	43	Hibernian	43	East Fife	39
1953–54e Celtic	43	Hearts	38	Partick Th	35
1954–55e Aberdeen	49	Celtic	46	Rangers	41
1955–56f Rangers	52	Aberdeen	46	Hearts*	45
1956–57f Rangers	55	Hearts	53	Kilmarnock	42
1957–58f Hearts	62	Rangers	49	Celtic	46
1958–59f Rangers	50	Hearts	48	Motherwell	44
1959–60f Hearts	54	Kilmarnock	50	Rangers*	42
1960–61f Rangers	51	Kilmarnock	50	Third Lanark	42
1961–62f Dundee	54	Rangers	51	Celtic	46
1962–63f Rangers	57	Kilmarnock	48	Partick Th	46
1963–64f Rangers	55	Kilmarnock	49	Celtic*	47
1964–65f Kilmarnock*	50	Hearts	50	Dunfermline Ath	49
1965–66f Celtic	57	Rangers	55	Kilmarnock	45
1966–67f Celtic	58	Rangers	55	Clyde	46
1967–68f Celtic	63	Rangers	61	Hibernian	45

	First	Pts	Second	Pts	Third	Pts
1968–69f	Celtic	54	Rangers	49	Dunfermline Ath	45
1969–70f	Celtic	57	Rangers	45	Hibernian	44
1970–71f	Celtic	56	Aberdeen	54	St Johnstone	44
1971–72f	Celtic	60	Aberdeen	50	Rangers	44
1972–73f	Celtic	57	Rangers	56	Hibernian	45
1973–74f	Celtic	53	Hibernian	49	Rangers	48
1974–75f	Rangers	56	Hibernian	49	Celtic	45

DIVISION 2 to 1974–75

Maximum points: a 76; b 72; c 68; d 52; e 60; f 36; g 44.

	First	Pts	Second	Pts	Third	Pts
1893–94f	Hibernian	29	Cowlairs	27	Clyde	24
1894–95f	Hibernian	30	Motherwell	22	Port Glasgow	20
1895–96f	Abercorn	27	Leith Ath	23	Renton	21
1896–97f	Partick Th	31	Leith Ath	27	Kilmarnock*	21
1897–98f	Kilmarnock	29	Port Glasgow	25	Morton	22
1898–99f	Kilmarnock	32	Leith Ath	27	Port Glasgow	25
1899–1900f	Partick Th	29	Morton	28	Port Glasgow	20
1900–01f	St Bernard's	25	Airdrieonians	23	Abercorn	21
1901–02g	Port Glasgow	32	Partick Th	31	Motherwell	26
1902–03g	Airdrieonians	35	Motherwell	28	Ayr U*	27
1903–04g	Hamilton A	37	Clyde	29	Ayr U	28
1904–05g	Clyde	32	Falkirk	28	Hamilton A	27
1905–06g	Leith Ath	34	Clyde	31	Albion R	27
1906–07g	St Bernard's	32	Vale of Leven*	27	Arthurlie	27
1907–08g	Raith R	30	Dumbarton‡‡	27	Ayr U	27
1908–09g	Abercorn	31	Raith R*	28	Vale of Leven	28
1909–10g	Leith Ath‡	33	Raith R	33	St Bernard's	27
1910–11g	Dumbarton	31	Ayr U	27	Albion R	25
1911–12g	Ayr U	35	Abercorn	30	Dumbarton	27
1912–13d	Ayr U	34	Dunfermline Ath	33	East Stirling	32
1913–14g	Cowdenbeath	31	Albion R	27	Dunfermline Ath*	26
1914–15d	Cowdenbeath*	37	St Bernard's*	37	Leith Ath	37
1921–22a	Alloa Ath	60	Cowdenbeath	47	Armadale	45
1922–23a	Queen's Park	57	Clydebank ¶	50	St Johnstone ¶	45
1923–24a	St Johnstone	56	Cowdenbeath	55	Bathgate	44
1924–25a	Dundee U	50	Clydebank	48	Clyde	47
1925–26a	Dunfermline Ath	59	Clyde	53	Ayr U	52
1926–27a	Bo'ness	56	Raith R	49	Clydebank	45
1927–28a	Ayr U	54	Third Lanark	45	King's Park	44
1928–29b	Dundee U	51	Morton	50	Arbroath	47
1929–30a	Leith Ath*	57	East Fife	57	Albion R	54
1930–31a	Third Lanark	61	Dundee U	50	Dunfermline Ath	47
1931–32a	East Stirling*	55	St Johnstone	55	Raith R*	46
1932–33c	Hibernian	54	Queen of the S	49	Dunfermline Ath	47
1933–34c	Albion R	45	Dunfermline Ath*	44	Arbroath	44
1934–35c	Third Lanark	52	Arbroath	50	St Bernard's	47
1935–36c	Falkirk	59	St Mirren	52	Morton	48
1936–37c	Ayr U	54	Morton	51	St Bernard's	48

	First	Pts	Second	Pts	Third	Pts
1937–38c	Raith R	59	Albion R	48	Airdrieonians	47
1938–39c	Cowdenbeath	60	Alloa Ath*	48	East Fife	48
1946–47d	Dundee	45	Airdrieonians	42	East Fife	31
1947–48e	East Fife	53	Albion R	42	Hamilton A	40
1948–49e	Raith R*	42	Stirling Alb	42	Airdrieonians*	41
1949–50e	Morton	47	Airdrieonians	44	Dunfermline Ath*	36
1950–51e	Queen of the S*	45	Stirling Alb	45	Ayr U*	36
1951–52e	Clyde	44	Falkirk	43	Ayr U	39
1952–53e	Stirling Alb	44	Hamilton A	43	Queen's Park	37
1953–54e	Motherwell	45	Kilmarnock	42	Third Lanark*	36
1954–55e	Airdrieonians	46	Dunfermline Ath	42	Hamilton A	39
1955–56b	Queen's Park	54	Ayr U	51	St Johnstone	49
1956–57b	Clyde	64	Third Lanark	51	Cowdenbeath	45
1957–58b	Stirling Alb	55	Dunfermline Ath	53	Arbroath	47
1958–59b	Ayr U	60	Arbroath	51	Stenhousemuir	46
1959–60b	St Johnstone	53	Dundee U	50	Queen of the S	49
1960–61b	Stirling Alb	55	Falkirk	54	Stenhousemuir	50
1961–62b	Clyde	54	Queen of the S	53	Morton	44
1962–63b	St Johnstone	55	East Stirling	49	Morton	48
1963–64b	Morton	67	Clyde	53	Arbroath	46
1964–65b	Stirling Alb	59	Hamilton A	50	Queen of the S	45
1965–66b	Ayr U	53	Airdrieonians	50	Queen of the S	47
1966–67a	Morton	69	Raith R	58	Arbroath	57
1967–68b	St Mirren	62	Arbroath	53	East Fife	49
1968–69b	Motherwell	64	Ayr U	53	East Fife*	48
1969–70b	Falkirk	56	Cowdenbeath	55	Queen of the S	50
1970–71b	Partick Th	56	East Fife	51	Arbroath	46
1971–72b	Dumbarton*	52	Arbroath	52	Stirling Alb	50
1972–73b	Clyde	56	Dumfermline Ath	52	Raith R*	47
1973–74b	Airdrieonians	60	Kilmarnock	58	Hamilton A	55
1974–75a	Falkirk	54	Queen of the S*	53	Montrose	53

Elected to Division 1: 1894 Clyde; 1895 Hibernian; 1896 Abercorn; 1897 Partick Th; 1899 Kilmarnock; 1900 Morton and Partick Th; 1902 Port Glasgow and Partick Th; 1903 Airdrieonians and Motherwell; 1905 Falkirk and Aberdeen; 1906 Clyde and Hamilton A; 1910 Raith R; 1913 Ayr U and Dumbarton.

From 1946–47 to 1955–56 the two divisions were known as A and B. A division 3 had existed for three years from 1923–24 and was revived for three more seasons from 1946–47 as Division C when it included reserve teams.

RELEGATED CLUBS

From Premier League

1998–99	Dunfermline Ath
1999–00	*No relegated team*
2000–01	St Mirren
2001–02	St Johnstone
2002–03	*No relegated team*
2003–04	Partick Th
2004–05	Dundee
2005–06	Livingston
2006–07	Dunfermline Ath
2007–08	Gretna
2008–09	Inverness CT
2009–10	Falkirk
2010–11	Hamilton A

From Premier Division

1974–75	*No relegation due to League reorganisation*
1975–76	Dundee, St Johnstone
1976–77	Hearts, Kilmarnock
1977–78	Ayr U, Clydebank
1978–79	Hearts, Motherwell
1979–80	Dundee, Hibernian
1980–81	Kilmarnock, Hearts
1981–82	Partick Th, Airdrieonians
1982–83	Morton, Kilmarnock
1983–84	St Johnstone, Motherwell
1984–85	Dumbarton, Morton
1985–86	*No relegation due to League reorganisation*
1986–87	Clydebank, Hamilton A
1987–88	Falkirk, Dunfermline Ath, Morton
1988–89	Hamilton A
1989–90	Dundee
1990–91	None
1991–92	St Mirren, Dunfermline Ath
1992–93	Falkirk, Airdrieonians
1993–94	*See footnote*
1994–95	Dundee U
1995–96	Partick Th, Falkirk
1996–97	Raith R
1997–98	Hibernian

From Division 1

1974–75	*No relegation due to League reorganisation*
1975–76	Dunfermline Ath, Clyde
1976–77	Raith R, Falkirk
1977–78	Alloa Ath, East Fife
1978–79	Montrose, Queen of the S
1979–80	Arbroath, Clyde
1980–81	Stirling Alb, Berwick R
1981–82	East Stirling, Queen of the S
1982–83	Dunfermline Ath, Queen's Park
1983–84	Raith R, Alloa Ath
1984–85	Meadowbank Th, St Johnstone
1985–86	Ayr U, Alloa Ath
1986–87	Brechin C, Montrose
1987–88	East Fife, Dumbarton
1988–89	Kilmarnock, Queen of the S
1989–90	Albion R, Alloa Ath
1990–91	Clyde, Brechin C
1991–92	Montrose, Forfar Ath
1992–93	Meadowbank Th, Cowdenbeath
1993–94	*See footnote*
1994–95	Ayr U, Stranraer
1995–96	Hamilton A, Dumbarton
1996–97	Clydebank, East Fife
1997–98	Partick Th, Stirling Alb
1998–99	Hamilton A, Stranraer
1999–00	Clydebank
2000–01	Morton, Alloa Ath
2001–02	Raith R
2002–03	Alloa Ath, Arbroath
2003–04	Ayr U, Brechin C
2004–05	Partick Th, Raith R
2005–06	Stranraer, Brechin C
2006–07	Airdrie U, Ross Co
2007–08	Stirling Alb
2008–09	Clyde
2009–10	Airdrie U, Ayr U
2010–11	Cowdenbeath, Stirling Alb

From Division 2

1994–95	Meadowbank Th, Brechin C
1995–96	Forfar Ath, Montrose
1996–97	Dumbarton, Berwick R
1997–98	Stenhousemuir, Brechin C
1998–99	East Fife, Forfar Ath
1999–00	Hamilton A**
2000–01	Queen's Park, Stirling Alb
2001–02	Morton
2002–03	Stranraer, Cowdenbeath
2003–04	East Fife, Stenhousemuir
2004–05	Arbroath, Berwick R
2005–06	Dumbarton
2006–07	Stranraer, Forfar Ath
2007–08	Cowdenbeath, Berwick R
2008–09	Stranraer, Queen's Park
2009–10	Arbroath, Clyde
2010–11	Alloa Ath, Peterhead

From Division 1 1973–74

1921–22 *Queen's Park, Dumbarton,
    Clydebank
1922–23 Albion R, Alloa Ath
1923–24 Clyde, Clydebank
1924–25 Third Lanark, Ayr U
1925–26 Raith R, Clydebank
1926–27 Morton, Dundee U
1927–28 Dunfermline Ath, Bo'ness
1928–29 Third Lanark, Raith R
1929–30 St Johnstone, Dundee U
1930–31 Hibernian, East Fife
1931–32 Dundee U, Leith Ath
1932–33 Morton, East Stirling
1933–34 Third Lanark, Cowdenbeath
1934–35 St Mirren, Falkirk
1935–36 Airdrieonians, Ayr U
1936–37 Dunfermline Ath, Albion R
1937–38 Dundee, Morton
1938–39 Queen's Park, Raith R
1946–47 Kilmarnock, Hamilton A
1947–48 Airdrieonians, Queen's Park
1948–49 Morton, Albion R
1949–50 Queen of the S, Stirling Alb
1950–51 Clyde, Falkirk

1951–52 Morton, Stirling Alb
1952–53 Motherwell, Third Lanark
1953–54 Airdrieonians, Hamilton A
1954–55 *No clubs relegated*
1955–56 Stirling Alb, Clyde
1956–57 Dunfermline Ath, Ayr U
1957–58 East Fife, Queen's Park
1958–59 Queen of the S, Falkirk
1959–60 Arbroath, Stirling Alb
1960–61 Ayr U, Clyde
1961–62 St Johnstone, Stirling Alb
1962–63 Clyde, Raith R
1963–64 Queen of the S, East Stirling
1964–65 Airdrieonians, Third Lanark
1965–66 Morton, Hamilton A
1966–67 St Mirren, Ayr U
1967–68 Motherwell, Stirling Alb
1968–69 Falkirk, Arbroath
1969–70 Raith R, Partick Th
1970–71 St Mirren, Cowdenbeath
1971–72 Clyde, Dunfermline Ath
1972–73 Kilmarnock, Airdrieonians
1973–74 East Fife, Falkirk

*Season 1921–22 – only 1 club promoted, 3 clubs relegated.
**15 pts deducted for failing to field a team.*

Scottish League championship wins: Rangers 54, Celtic 41, Aberdeen 4, Hearts 4, Hibernian 4, Dumbarton 2, Dundee 1, Dundee U 1, Kilmarnock 1, Motherwell 1, Third Lanark 1.

The Scottish Football League was reconstructed into three divisions at the end of the 1974–75 season, so the usual relegation statistics do not apply. Further reorganization took place at the end of the 1985–86 season. From 1986–87, the Premier and First Division had 12 teams each. The Second Division remained at 14. From 1988–89, the Premier Division reverted to 10 teams, and the First Division to 14 teams but in 1991–92 the Premier and First Division reverted to 12. At the end of the 1997–98 season, the top nine clubs in Premier Division broke away from the Scottish League to form a new competition, the Scottish Premier League, with the club promoted from Division One. At the end of the 1999–2000 season two teams were added to the Scottish League. There was no relegation from the Premier League but two promoted from the First Division and three from each of the Second and Third Divisions. One team was relegated from the First Division and one from the Second Division, leaving 12 teams in each division. In season 2002–03, Falkirk were not promoted to the Premier League due to the failure of their ground to meet League standards. Inverness CT were promoted after a previous refusal in 2003–04 because of ground sharing. At the end of 2005–06 the Scottish League introduced play-offs for the team finishing second from the bottom of Division 1 against the winners of the second, third and fourth finishing teams in Division 2 and with a similar procedure for Division 2 and Division 3.

SCOTTISH LEAGUE PLAY-OFFS 2010–2011

DIVISION 1 SEMI-FINALS FIRST LEG

Brechin C	(0) 2	Cowdenbeath	(2) 2
Forfar Ath	(1) 1	Ayr U	(2) 4

DIVISION 1 SEMI-FINALS SECOND LEG

Ayr U	(1) 3	Forfar Ath	(1) 3
Cowdenbeath	(0) 0	Brechin C	(0) 2

DIVISION 1 FINAL FIRST LEG Wednesday, 18 May 2011

Ayr U (1) 1 *(Moffat 31)*

Brechin C (0) 1 *(Janczyk 86)*   2020

Ayr U: Martin; Lauchlan, Smith, Malone, Campbell, Bannigan (Easton), McLaughlin, Trouten, Moffat, Roberts (Rodgers), McCann (Tiffoney).
Brechin C: Nelson; Cook, McLean, McLauchlan, Moyes, Redman, Molloy, McKenna (Byers), McAllister, Megginson (Janczyk), Kirkpatrick (Fusco).

DIVISION 1 FINAL SECOND LEG Sunday, 22 May 2011

Brechin C (1) 1 *(Tiffoney 44 (og))*

Ayr U (0) 2 *(Roberts 77, Moffat 88)*   2404

Brechin C: Nelson; Cook, McBain, McLauchlan, Moyes, Janczyk (Kirkpatrick), Fusco (McLean), Molloy, Redman, McAllister, McKenna (Megginson).
Ayr U: Martin; Lauchlan (Tiffoney), Smith, Malone, Campbell, McLaughlin, Trouten, Bannigan (Rodgers), McCann (Robertson), Moffat, Roberts.

DIVISION 2 SEMI-FINALS FIRST LEG

Annan Ath	(1) 2	Alloa Ath	(0) 1
Queen's Park	(1) 1	Albion R	(0) 1

DIVISION 2 SEMI-FINALS SECOND LEG

Albion R	(0) 2	Queen's Park	(0) 0
Alloa Ath	(0) 0	Annan Ath	(0) 0

DIVISION 2 FINAL FIRST LEG Wednesday, 18 May 2011

Albion R (1) 3 *(Love 14, 67, 76)*

Annan Ath (1) 1 *(Harty 42)*   1014

Albion R: Gaston; Lumsden, McGowan, Stevenson, Reid, Donnelly, Canning, Chaplain, Love (Innes), Gemmell, Lawless (Ferry).
Annan Ath: Summersgill; Neilson, Aitken, Muirhead (Felvus), Steele, Watson, Docherty, Macfarlane (Gilfillan), Sloan S, Harty, O'Connor.

DIVISION 2 FINAL SECOND LEG Sunday, 22 May 2011

Annan Ath (0) 2 *(Gilfillan 51, 65)*

Albion R (1) 1 *(Donnelly 24)*   1165

Annan Ath: Summersgill; Muirhead, Neilson, Aitken, Steele (MacBeth), Gilfillan▪, Docherty (Watson), Sloan S, Macfarlane, Harty, O'Connor (Felvus).
Albion R: Gaston; Lumsden, McGowan, Stevenson, Reid, Donnelly, Canning, Love, Lawless (Boyle), Gemmell, Chaplain.

PAST SCOTTISH LEAGUE CUP FINALS

1946–47	Rangers	4	Aberdeen	0
1947–48	East Fife	0 4	Falkirk	0* 1
1948–49	Rangers	2	Raith Rovers	0
1949–50	East Fife	3	Dunfermline	0
1950–51	Motherwell	3	Hibernian	0
1951–52	Dundee	3	Rangers	2
1952–53	Dundee	2	Kilmarnock	0
1953–54	East Fife	3	Partick Th	2
1954–55	Hearts	4	Motherwell	2
1955–56	Aberdeen	2	St Mirren	1
1956–57	Celtic	0 3	Partick Th	0 0
1957–58	Celtic	7	Rangers	1
1958–59	Hearts	5	Partick Th	1
1959–60	Hearts	2	Third Lanark	1
1960–61	Rangers	2	Kilmarnock	0
1961–62	Rangers	1 3	Hearts	1 1
1962–63	Hearts	1	Kilmarnock	0
1963–64	Rangers	5	Morton	0
1964–65	Rangers	2	Celtic	1
1965–66	Celtic	2	Rangers	1
1966–67	Celtic	1	Rangers	0
1967–68	Celtic	5	Dundee	3
1968–69	Celtic	6	Hibernian	2
1969–70	Celtic	1	St Johnstone	0
1970–71	Rangers	1	Celtic	0
1971–72	Partick Th	4	Celtic	1
1972–73	Hibernian	2	Celtic	1
1973–74	Dundee	1	Celtic	0
1974–75	Celtic	6	Hibernian	3
1975–76	Rangers	1	Celtic	0
1976–77	Aberdeen	2	Celtic	1
1977–78	Rangers	2	Celtic	1*
1978–79	Rangers	2	Aberdeen	1
1979–80	Aberdeen	0 0	Dundee U	0* 3
1980–81	Dundee	0	Dundee U	3
1981–82	Rangers	2	Dundee U	1
1982–83	Celtic	2	Rangers	1
1983–84	Rangers	3	Celtic	2
1984–85	Rangers	1	Dundee U	0
1985–86	Aberdeen	3	Hibernian	0
1986–87	Rangers	2	Celtic	1
1987–88	Rangers†	3	Aberdeen	3*
1988–89	Aberdeen	2	Rangers	3*
1989–90	Aberdeen	2	Rangers	1
1990–91	Rangers	2	Celtic	1
1991–92	Hibernian	2	Dunfermline Ath	0
1992–93	Rangers	2	Aberdeen	1*
1993–94	Rangers	2	Hibernian	1
1994–95	Raith R†	2	Celtic	2*
1995–96	Aberdeen	2	Dundee	0
1996–97	Rangers	4	Hearts	3
1997–98	Celtic	3	Dundee U	0
1998–99	Rangers	2	St Johnstone	1

1999–2000	Celtic	2	Aberdeen	0
2000–01	Celtic	3	Kilmarnock	0
2001–02	Rangers	4	Ayr U	0
2002–03	Rangers	2	Celtic	1
2003–04	Livingston	2	Hibernian	0
2004–05	Rangers	5	Motherwell	1
2005–06	Celtic	3	Dunfermline Ath	0
2006–07	Hibernian	5	Kilmarnock	1
2007–08	Rangers†	2	Dundee U	2*
2008–09	Celtic	2	Rangers	0*
2009–10	Rangers	1	St Mirren	0
2010–11	Rangers	2	Celtic	1*

†*Won on penalties *After extra time*

PAST LEAGUE CHALLENGE FINALS

1990–91	Dundee	3	Ayr U	2
1991–92	Hamilton A	1	Ayr U	0
1992–93	Hamilton A	3	Morton	2
1993–94	St Mirren	9	Falkirk	3
1994–95	Airdrieonians	3	Dundee	2
1995–96	Stenhousemuir	0	Dundee U	0
	(aet; Stenhousemuir won 5-4 on penalties.)			
1996–97	Stranraer	1	St Johnstone	0
1997–98	Falkirk	1	Qeeen of the S	0
1998–99	no competition			
1999–2000	Alloa Ath	4	Inverness CT	4
	(aet; Alloa Ath won 5-4 on penalties.)			
2000–01	Airdrieonians	2	Livingston	2
	(aet; Airdrieonians won 3-2 on penalties.)			
2001–02	Airdrieonians	2	Alloa Ath	1
2002–03	Queen of the S	2	Brechin C	0
2003–04	Inverness CT	2	Airdrie U	0
2004–05	Falkirk	2	Ross Co	1
2005–06	St Mirren	2	Hamilton A	1
2006–07	Ross Co	1	Clyde	1
	(aet; Ross Co won 5-4 on penalties.)			
2007–08	St Johnstone	3	Dunfermline Ath	2
2008–09	Airdrie	2	Ross Co	2
	(aet; Airdrie U won 3-2 on penalties.)			
2009–10	Dundee	3	Inverness CT	2
2010–11	Ross Co	2	Queen of the S	0

CIS SCOTTISH LEAGUE CUP 2010–2011

FIRST ROUND

Albion R	(0) 0	Airdrie U	(0) 1
Annan Ath	(0) 0	Partick Th	(0) 1
Clyde	(0) 2	Cowdenbeath	(0) 1
Dundee	(1) 3	Montrose	(0) 0
Dunfermline Ath	(1) 5	Arbroath	(1) 2
Elgin C	(1) 3	Ayr U	(1) 2
(aet.)			
Inverness CT	(1) 3	Queen's Park	(0) 0
Peterhead	(0) 1	Berwick R	(0) 0
Queen of the S	(2) 5	Dumbarton	(0) 1
Raith R	(3) 4	East Fife	(0) 1
Ross Co	(1) 2	Livingston	(0) 1
Stenhousemuir	(1) 1	Brechin C	(2) 3
Stirling Alb	(0) 1	Forfar Ath	(1) 2
Stranraer	(0) 1	Morton	(2) 7
East Stirling	(1) 1	Alloa Ath	(1) 2

SECOND ROUND

Alloa Ath	(0) 0	Aberdeen	(2) 3
Brechin C	(0) 2	Dundee	(0) 2
(aet; Brechin C won 3-1 on penalties.)			
Dunfermline Ath	(1) 3	Clyde	(2) 2
Hearts	(2) 4	Elgin C	(0) 0
Partick Th	(0) 0	Falkirk	(0) 1
Raith R	(0) 1	Hamilton A	(0) 0
St Johnstone	(1) 2	Morton	(0) 0
Inverness CT	(2) 3	Peterhead	(0) 0
Kilmarnock	(3) 6	Airdrie U	(1) 2
Queen of the S	(2) 4	Forfar Ath	(0) 1
Ross Co	(0) 3	St Mirren	(1) 3
(aet; Ross Co won 4-3 on penalties.)			

THIRD ROUND

Brechin C	(0) 0	Motherwell	(1) 2
Falkirk	(2) 4	Hearts	(0) 3
Rangers	(3) 7	Dunfermline Ath	(1) 2
St Johnstone	(0) 3	Queen of the S	(0) 0
Aberdeen	(1) 3	Raith R	(2) 2
Celtic	(3) 6	Inverness CT	(0) 0
Kilmarnock	(1) 3	Hibernian	(1) 1
Ross Co	(0) 1	Dundee U	(0) 2
(aet.)			

QUARTER-FINALS

Aberdeen	(0) 2	Falkirk	(1) 1
Motherwell	(0) 1	Dundee U	(0) 0
Kilmarnock	(0) 0	Rangers	(1) 2
St Johnstone	(1) 2	Celtic	(3) 3

SEMI-FINAL

Aberdeen	(0) 1	Celtic	(4) 4
Rangers	(1) 2	Motherwell	(0) 1

FINAL

Celtic	(1) 1	Rangers	(1) 2
(aet.)			

ALBA LEAGUE CHALLENGE CUP 2010–2011

FIRST ROUND NORTH EAST

Dundee	(0) 2	Alloa Ath	(0) 1
Dunfermline Ath	(0) 1	Arbroath	(0) 0
East Fife	(0) 4	Brechin C	(1) 3
(aet.)			
Elgin C	(0) 1	Ross Co	(0) 2
Peterhead	(1) 5	Montrose	(0) 0
Raith R	(0) 0	Cowdenbeath	(0) 1
Stirling Alb	(0) 0	Falkirk	(0) 0
(aet; Stirling Alb won 3-1 on penalties.)			

FIRST ROUND SOUTH WEST

Airdrie U	(0) 1	Ayr U	(0) 2
Partick Th	(1) 2	Clyde	(1) 1
Queen of the S	(1) 2	Albion R	(0) 1
Queen's Park	(1) 3	Livingston	(1) 2
(aet.)			
Stenhousemuir	(3) 3	Annan Ath	(0) 2
Stranraer	(0) 1	East Stirling	(0) 2
(aet.)			
Dumbarton	(0) 0	Morton	(0) 0
(aet; Morton won 4-3 on penalties.)			

SECOND ROUND

Ayr U	(0) 2	Cowdenbeath	(0) 0
Dunfermline Ath	(0) 1	Queen of the S	(0) 1
(aet; Queen of the S won 6-5 on penalties.)			
East Fife	(1) 3	Stirling Alb	(1) 1
Partick Th	(1) 2	Berwick R	(1) 1
Peterhead	(1) 6	East Stirling	(1) 1
Queen's Park	(1) 2	Forfar Ath	(0) 3
Ross Co	(1) 3	Morton	(1) 1
Stenhousemuir	(2) 4	Dundee	(0) 1

QUARTER-FINALS

Forfar Ath	(0) 0	Ross Co	(1) 2
Partick Th	(2) 2	Ayr U	(1) 1
Queen of the S	(1) 5	East Fife	(0) 0
Peterhead	(2) 3	Stenhousemuir	(0) 1

SEMI-FINALS

Peterhead	(0) 1	Queen of the S	(0) 2
Ross Co	(0) 2	Partick Th	(1) 2
(aet; Ross Co won 4-3 on penalties.)			

FINAL

Queen of the S	(0) 0	Ross Co	(2) 2

ACTIVE NATION SCOTTISH CUP 2010–2011

FIRST ROUND

Beith v Linlithgow Rose	2-0
Civil Service Strollers v Wigtown & Bladnoch	1-2
Coldstream v Forres Mechanics	1-3
Deveronvale v Inverurie Loco Works	0-0, 5-0
Edinburgh City v Clachnacuddin	1-0
Edinburgh Univ v Brora R	2-2, 1-2
Fraserburgh v St Cuthbert W	3-3, 1-3
Gala Fairydean v Sunnybank	1-6
Glasgow Univ v Burntisland	1-0
Golspie Sutherland v Fort William	2-2, 3-2
Hawick Royal Albert v Dalbeattie Star	0-3
Huntly v Girvan	2-2, 1-2
Lossiemouth v Whitehill Welfare	0-2
Newton Stewart v Preston Athletic	1-1, 0-3
Rothes v Nairn Co	2-2, 1-4
Selkirk v Bo'ness	1-6
Vale of Leithen v Keith	1-3

SECOND ROUND

Deveronvale v Dalbeattie Star	1-0
Forres Mechanics v East Stirling	0-0, 0-4
Preston Ath v Annan Ath	0-0, 0-5
Clyde v Berwick R	1-2
Wigtown & Bladnoch v Buckie Th	1-7
Beith v Glasgow Univ	8-1
Nairn Co v Cove R	0-1
Keith v Spartans	0-3
Stranraer v St Cuthbert W	9-0
Bo'ness v Queen's Park	2-1
Golspie Sutherland v Girvan	2-2, 0-4
Montrose v Arbroath	1-1, 3-2
Edinburgh C v Threave R	2-4
Albion R v Sunnybank	0-1
Elgin C v Brora R	5-3
Whitehill Welfare v Wick Academy	4-3

THIRD ROUND

Airdrie U	(0) 2	Beith	(1) 2
Alloa Ath	(2) 4	Raith R	(1) 2
Ayr U	(2) 5	Sunnybank	(0) 0
Bo'ness	(0) 0	Buckie Th	(1) 2
Brechin C	(1) 2	Annan Ath	(0) 2
Cove R	(0) 0	Berwick R	(2) 3
Dumbarton	(1) 1	Morton	(1) 2
East Fife	(2) 3	Forfar Ath	(0) 1
Elgin C	(0) 2	Livingston	(0) 1
Montrose	(2) 3	Whitehill Welfare	(1) 1
Peterhead	(1) 2	Cowdenbeath	(0) 0
Ross Co	(2) 4	Deveronvale	(0) 1
Spartans	(0) 1	East Stirling	(1) 2
Stenhousemuir	(0) 2	Threave R	(1) 2
Stirling Alb	(0) 1	Partick Th	(0) 3
Stranraer	(2) 4	Girvan	(1) 2

THIRD ROUND REPLAYS

Annan Ath	(1) 2	Brechin C	(4) 5
Beith	(0) 3	Airdrie U	(3) 4
Threave R	(0) 1	Stenhousemuir	(2) 5

FOURTH ROUND

Aberdeen	(4) 6	East Fife	(0) 0
Dundee U	(0) 0	Ross Co	(0) 0
Hamilton A	(1) 2	Alloa Ath	(0) 0
Hibernian	(0) 0	Ayr U	(0) 0
Inverness CT	(0) 2	Elgin C	(0) 0
Montrose	(1) 2	Dunfermline Ath	(0) 2
St Mirren	(0) 0	Peterhead	(0) 0
Berwick R	(0) 0	Celtic	(1) 2
Dundee	(0) 0	Motherwell	(1) 4
Rangers	(2) 3	Kilmarnock	(0) 0
Falkirk	(1) 2	Partick Th	(1) 2
Hearts	(0) 0	St Johnstone	(0) 1
Queen of the S	(0) 1	Brechin C	(2) 2
Morton	(0) 2	Airdrie U	(1) 2
Stenhousemuir	(0) 0	Stranraer	(0) 0
East Stirling	(0) 1	Buckie Th	(0) 0

(East Stirling fielded an ineligible player; Buckie Th awarded the tie.)

FOURTH ROUND REPLAYS

Ayr U	(1) 1	Hibernian	(0) 0
Dunfermline Ath	(2) 5	Montrose	(0) 3
Partick Th	(1) 1	Falkirk	(0) 0
Peterhead	(0) 1	St Mirren	(4) 6
Ross Co	(0) 0	Dundee U	(0) 0

(Dundee U won 4-3 on penalties.)

Airdrie U	(0) 2	Morton	(1) 5
Stranraer	(2) 4	Stenhousemuir	(2) 3

FIFTH ROUND

Ayr U	(0) 1	St Mirren	(2) 2
Buckie Th	(0) 0	Brechin C	(2) 2
Hamilton A	(0) 1	Dundee U	(2) 3
Inverness CT	(2) 5	Morton	(0) 1
Stranraer	(0) 0	Motherwell	(1) 2
Aberdeen	(0) 1	Dunfermline Ath	(0) 0
Rangers	(2) 2	Celtic	(1) 2
St Johnstone	(1) 2	Partick Th	(0) 0

FIFTH ROUND REPLAY

Celtic	(0) 1	Rangers	(0) 0

QUARTER-FINALS

Brechin C	(1) 2	St Johnstone	(0) 2
St Mirren	(0) 1	Aberdeen	(0) 1
Dundee U	(1) 2	Motherwell	(1) 2
Inverness CT	(1) 1	Celtic	(1) 2

QUARTER-FINAL REPLAYS

Aberdeen	(2) 2	St Mirren	(0) 1
St Johnstone	(1) 1	Brechin C	(0) 0
Motherwell	(2) 3	Dundee U	(0) 0

SEMI-FINALS

Motherwell	(3) 3	St Johnstone	(0) 0
Aberdeen	(0) 0	Celtic	(0) 4

FINAL

Motherwell	(0) 0	Celtic	(1) 3

PAST SCOTTISH CUP FINALS

1874	Queen's Park	2	Clydesdale	0
1875	Queen's Park	3	Renton	0
1876	Queen's Park	1 2	Third Lanark	1 0
1877	Vale of Leven	0 1 3	Rangers	0 1 2
1878	Vale of Leven	1	Third Lanark	0
1879	Vale of Leven	1	Rangers	1

Vale of Leven awarded cup, Rangers did not appear for replay

1880	Queen's Park	3	Thornlibank	0
1881	Queen's Park	2 3	Dumbarton	1 1

Replayed because of protest

1882	Queen's Park	2 4	Dumbarton	2 1
1883	Dumbarton	2 2	Vale of Leven	2 1

1884 Queen's Park awarded cup when Vale of Leven did not appear for the final

1885	Renton	0 3	Vale of Leven	0 1
1886	Queen's Park	3	Renton	1
1887	Hibernian	2	Dumbarton	1
1888	Renton	6	Cambuslang	1
1889	Third Lanark	3 2	Celtic	0 1

Replayed because of protest

1890	Queen's Park	1 2	Vale of Leven	1 1
1891	Hearts	1	Dumbarton	0
1892	Celtic	1 5	Queen's Park	0 1

Replayed because of protest

1893	Queen's Park	2	Celtic	1
1894	Rangers	3	Celtic	1
1895	St Bernards	3	Renton	1
1896	Hearts	3	Hibernian	1
1897	Rangers	5	Dumbarton	1
1898	Rangers	2	Kilmarnock	0
1899	Celtic	2	Rangers	0
1900	Celtic	4	Queen's Park	3
1901	Hearts	4	Celtic	3
1902	Hibernian	1	Celtic	0
1903	Rangers	1 0 2	Hearts	1 0 0
1904	Celtic	3	Rangers	2
1905	Third Lanark	0 3	Rangers	0 1
1906	Hearts	1	Third Lanark	0
1907	Celtic	3	Hearts	0
1908	Celtic	5	St Mirren	1

1909 *After two drawn games between Celtic and Rangers, 2-2, 1-1, there was a riot and the cup was withheld*

1910	Dundee	2 0 2	Clyde	2 0 1
1911	Celtic	0 2	Hamilton Acad	0 0
1912	Celtic	2	Clyde	0
1913	Falkirk	2	Raith R	0
1914	Celtic	0 4	Hibernian	0 1
1920	Kilmarnock	3	Albion R	2
1921	Partick Th	1	Rangers	0
1922	Morton	1	Rangers	0
1923	Celtic	1	Hibernian	0
1924	Airdrieonians	2	Hibernian	0
1925	Celtic	2	Dundee	1
1926	St Mirren	2	Celtic	0
1927	Celtic	3	East Fife	1
1928	Rangers	4	Celtic	0
1929	Kilmarnock	2	Rangers	0
1930	Rangers	0 2	Partick Th	0 1

1931	Celtic	2 4	Motherwell	2 2
1932	Rangers	1 3	Kilmarnock	1 0
1933	Celtic	1	Motherwell	0
1934	Rangers	5	St Mirren	0
1935	Rangers	2	Hamilton A	1
1936	Rangers	1	Third Lanark	0
1937	Celtic	2	Aberdeen	1
1938	East Fife	1 4	Kilmarnock	1 2
1939	Clyde	4	Motherwell	0
1947	Aberdeen	2	Hibernian	1
1948	Rangers	1 1	Morton	1 0
1949	Rangers	4	Clyde	1
1950	Rangers	3	East Fife	0
1951	Celtic	1	Motherwell	0
1952	Motherwell	4	Dundee	0
1953	Rangers	1 1	Aberdeen	1 0
1954	Celtic	2	Aberdeen	1
1955	Clyde	1 1	Celtic	1 0
1956	Hearts	3	Celtic	1
1957	Falkirk	1 2	Kilmarnock	1 1
1958	Clyde	1	Hibernian	0
1959	St Mirren	3	Aberdeen	1
1960	Rangers	2	Kilmarnock	0
1961	Dunfermline Ath	0 2	Celtic	0 0
1962	Rangers	2	St Mirren	0
1963	Rangers	1 3	Celtic	1 0
1964	Rangers	3	Dundee	1
1965	Celtic	3	Dunfermline Ath	2
1966	Rangers	0 1	Celtic	0 0
1967	Celtic	2	Aberdeen	0
1968	Dunfermline Ath	3	Hearts	1
1969	Celtic	4	Rangers	0
1970	Aberdeen	3	Celtic	1
1971	Celtic	1 2	Rangers	1 1
1972	Celtic	6	Hibernian	1
1973	Rangers	3	Celtic	2
1974	Celtic	3	Dundee U	0
1975	Celtic	3	Airdrieonians	1
1976	Rangers	3	Hearts	1
1977	Celtic	1	Rangers	0
1978	Rangers	2	Aberdeen	1
1979	Rangers	0 0 3	Hibernian	0 0 2
1980	Celtic	1	Rangers	0
1981	Rangers	0 4	Dundee U	0 1
1982	Aberdeen	4	Rangers	1 (aet)
1983	Aberdeen	1	Rangers	0 (aet)
1984	Aberdeen	2	Celtic	1 (aet)
1985	Celtic	2	Dundee U	1
1986	Aberdeen	3	Hearts	0
1987	St Mirren	1	Dundee U	0 (aet)
1988	Celtic	2	Dundee U	1
1989	Celtic	1	Rangers	0
1990	Aberdeen	0	Celtic	0
	(aet; Aberdeen won 9-8 on penalties)			
1991	Motherwell	4	Dundee U	3
	(aet.)			
1992	Rangers	2	Airdrieonians	1
1993	Rangers	2	Aberdeen	1
1994	Dundee U	1	Rangers	0

1995	Celtic	1	Airdrieonians	0
1996	Rangers	5	Hearts	1
1997	Kilmarnock	1	Falkirk	0
1998	Hearts	2	Rangers	1
1999	Rangers	1	Celtic	0
2000	Rangers	4	Aberdeen	0
2001	Celtic	3	Hibernian	0
2002	Rangers	3	Celtic	2
2003	Rangers	1	Dundee	0
2004	Celtic	3	Dunfermline Ath	1
2005	Celtic	1	Dundee U	0
2006	Hearts	1	Gretna	1
	(aet; Hearts won 4-2 on penalties)			
2007	Celtic	1	Dunfermline Ath	0
2008	Rangers	3	Queen of the S	2
2009	Rangers	1	Falkirk	0
2010	Dundee U	3	Ross Co	0
2011	Celtic	3	Motherwell	0

SCOTS-ADS HIGHLAND LEAGUE 2010–2011

			Total				Home					Away					
		P	W	D	L	F	A	W	D	L	F	A	W	D	L	F	A	GD	Pts
1	Buckie Thistle	34	24	5	5	84	42	14	2	1	43	14	10	3	4	41	28	42	77
2	Deveronvale	34	23	3	8	100	45	13	2	2	57	15	10	1	6	43	30	55	72
3	Cove Rangers	34	22	5	7	100	43	11	1	5	59	23	11	4	2	41	20	57	71
4	Keith	34	22	4	8	93	46	12	3	2	56	23	10	1	6	37	31	39	70
5	Nairn County	34	18	9	7	86	49	11	4	2	52	25	7	5	5	34	24	37	63
6	Forres Mechanics	34	19	6	9	72	56	12	4	1	44	22	7	2	8	28	34	16	63
7	Inverurie Loco Works	34	19	5	10	81	50	13	1	3	42	17	6	4	7	39	33	31	62
8	Turriff United	34	15	8	11	89	60	11	4	2	57	22	4	4	9	32	38	29	53
9	Formartine United	34	15	3	16	71	68	7	3	7	44	32	8	0	9	27	36	3	48
10	Huntly	34	13	6	15	63	72	8	1	8	36	37	5	5	7	27	35	–9	45
11	Brora Rangers	34	13	6	15	51	64	6	4	7	24	26	7	2	8	27	38	–13	45
12	Lossiemouth	34	12	8	14	52	63	8	5	4	33	23	4	3	10	19	40	–11	44
13	Fraserburgh	34	11	9	14	69	65	8	4	5	41	25	3	5	9	28	40	4	42
14	Wick Academy	34	12	3	19	75	78	8	1	8	39	37	4	2	11	36	41	–3	39
15	Clachnacuddin	34	9	7	18	68	89	4	6	7	37	39	5	1	11	31	50	–21	34
16	Rothes	34	6	4	24	43	92	3	2	12	25	47	3	2	12	18	45	–49	22
17	Strathspey Thistle	34	2	4	28	36	131	2	1	14	22	61	0	3	14	14	70	–95	10
18	Fort William	34	2	3	29	36	148	2	1	14	18	52	0	2	15	18	96	–112	9

CENTRAL TAXIS EAST OF SCOTLAND LEAGUE PREMIER DIVISION 2010–2011

		P	W	D	L	F	A	GD	Pts
1	Spartans	22	17	4	1	62	18	44	55
2	Stirling University	22	12	5	5	58	28	30	41
3	Lothian Thistle	22	10	4	8	40	36	4	34
4	Whitehill Welfare	22	9	5	8	32	29	3	32
5	Edinburgh University	22	8	8	6	27	26	1	32
6	Edinburgh City	22	6	13	3	32	30	2	31
7	Vale of Leithen	22	7	9	6	30	29	1	30
8	Civil Service Strollers	22	8	5	9	29	37	–8	29
9	Tynecastle	22	6	6	10	32	35	–3	24
10	Selkirk	22	4	5	13	31	54	–23	17
11	Preston Athletic	22	4	5	13	30	61	–31	17
12	Heriot-Watt University	22	3	7	12	27	47	–20	16

PRINCIPALITY BUILDING SOCIETY
WELSH PREMIER LEAGUE 2010–2011

		Total					Home					Away					
		P	W	D	L	F	A	W	D	L	F	A	W	D	L	F	A	GD	Pts
1	Bangor C	32	22	4	6	80	44	12	1	3	51	21	10	3	3	29	23	36	70
2	The New Saints	32	20	8	4	87	34	13	2	1	57	15	7	6	3	30	19	53	68
3	Neath Ath	32	16	10	6	62	41	7	6	3	27	18	9	4	3	35	23	21	58
4	Llanelli	32	15	8	9	58	41	8	3	5	32	25	7	5	4	26	16	17	53
5	Prestatyn T	32	10	10	12	44	46	6	7	3	22	14	4	3	9	22	32	–2	40
6	Port Talbot T	32	8	12	12	37	48	4	5	7	18	19	4	7	5	19	29	–11	36
7	Aberystwyth T	32	11	9	12	42	54	6	5	5	21	23	5	4	7	21	31	–12	42
8	Airbus UK Broughton	32	11	8	13	53	52	5	6	5	33	26	6	2	8	20	26	1	41
9	Newtown	32	8	11	13	40	55	4	7	5	18	21	4	4	8	22	34	–15	35
10	Carmarthen T	32	10	5	17	39	64	5	2	9	22	30	5	3	8	17	34	–25	35
11	Bala T	32	10	3	19	41	57	6	1	9	24	25	4	2	10	17	32	–16	33
12	Haverfordwest Co	32	5	4	23	30	77	3	1	12	17	34	2	3	11	13	43	–47	19

Top 6 teams split after 22 games.

NORTHERN IRELAND
CARLING PREMIERSHIP 2010–2011

		Total					Home					Away					
		P	W	D	L	F	A	W	D	L	F	A	W	D	L	F	A	GD	Pts
1	Linfield	38	26	7	5	80	29	14	4	1	39	9	12	3	4	41	20	51	85
2	Crusaders	38	23	5	10	78	59	13	2	4	43	26	10	3	6	35	33	19	74
3	Glentoran	38	20	6	12	63	41	9	5	5	28	17	11	1	7	35	24	22	66
4	Cliftonville	38	17	7	14	60	56	10	2	7	38	31	7	5	7	22	25	4	58
5	Portadown	38	15	5	18	49	58	9	3	7	26	24	6	2	11	23	34	–9	50
6	Lisburn Distillery	38	14	6	18	50	66	6	3	9	25	39	8	3	9	25	27	–16	48
7	Coleraine	38	17	5	16	50	50	10	2	9	32	31	7	3	7	18	19	0	56
8	Dungannon Swifts	38	14	9	15	50	53	7	4	7	22	23	7	5	8	28	30	–3	51
9	Ballymena U	38	12	13	13	48	56	5	6	8	21	31	7	7	5	27	25	–8	49
10	Glenavon	38	12	9	17	60	58	8	2	9	25	24	4	7	8	35	34	2	45
11	Donegal Celtic	38	8	8	22	55	89	3	6	9	27	41	5	2	13	28	48	–34	32
12	Newry C	38	6	8	24	37	65	5	5	10	24	34	1	3	14	13	31	–28	26

Top 6 teams split after 33 games.

REPUBLIC OF IRELAND LEAGUE 2010

		Total					Home					Away					
		P	W	D	L	F	A	W	D	L	F	A	W	D	L	F	A	GD	Pts
1	Shamrock R	36	19	10	7	57	34	11	4	3	31	12	8	6	4	26	22	23	67
2	Bohemians	36	19	10	7	50	29	9	7	2	23	10	10	3	5	27	19	21	67
3	Sligo R	36	17	12	7	61	36	11	4	3	37	16	6	8	4	24	20	25	63
4	Sporting Fingal	36	16	14	6	60	38	7	7	4	31	23	9	7	2	29	15	22	62
5	St Patrick's Ath	36	16	9	11	55	33	10	3	5	27	14	6	6	6	28	19	22	57
6	Dundalk	36	14	6	16	46	50	7	4	7	26	24	7	2	9	20	26	–4	48
7	UCD	36	11	8	17	47	54	7	3	8	22	21	4	5	9	25	33	–7	41
8	Galway U	36	9	11	16	38	59	4	8	6	23	27	5	3	10	15	32	–21	38
9	Bray Wanderers	36	6	9	21	35	72	3	5	10	20	39	3	4	11	15	33	–37	27
10	Drogheda U	36	4	9	23	30	74	2	4	12	15	38	2	5	11	15	36	–44	21

UEFA CHAMPIONS LEAGUE 2010–2011

■ *Denotes player sent off.* * *Winner after extra time.*

FIRST QUALIFYING ROUND FIRST LEG

Santa Coloma	(0) 0	Birkirkara	(0) 0

(Match forfeited, result given as 0-3 by UEFA.)

Tre Fiori	(0) 0	Rudar	(2) 3

FIRST QUALIFYING ROUND SECOND LEG

Birkirkara	(4) 4	Santa Coloma	(2) 3
Rudar	(1) 4	Tre Fiori	(1) 1

SECOND QUALIFYING ROUND FIRST LEG

AIK Stockholm	(0) 1	Jeunesse Esch	(0) 0
Birkirkara	(1) 1	Zilina	(0) 0
Bohemians	(0) 1	The New Saints	(0) 0
Dinamo Zagreb	(2) 5	Koper	(1) 1
Hapoel Tel Aviv	(5) 5	Zeljeznicar	(0) 0
Inter Baku	(0) 0	Lech	(0) 1
Levadia	(0) 1	Debrecen	(0) 1
Litex	(1) 1	Rudar	(0) 0
Metalurgs Liepaya	(0) 0	Sparta Prague	(1) 3
Omonia	(2) 3	Renova	(0) 0
Salzburg	(2) 5	HB Torshavn	(0) 0
Aktobe	(1) 2	Olimpi	(0) 0
BATE Borisov	(0) 5	Hafnarfjordur	(0) 1
Ekranas	(1) 1	HJK Helsinki	(0) 0
Linfield	(0) 0	Rosenborg	(0) 0
Partizan Belgrade	(2) 3	Pyunik	(1) 1
Serif	(1) 3	Dinamo Tirana	(1) 1

Tuesday, 13 July 2010
Bohemians (0) 1 *(Brennan 66)*
The New Saints (0) 0   2314

Bohemians: Murphy B; Heary, Powell, Oman, Higgins, Brennan, Shelley, Cretaro (Byrne 75), Keegan, Quigley, Madden.
The New Saints: Harrison; Evans, Baker, Holmes D, Marriott, Jones C, Hogan, Ruscoe, Berkeley (Wood 77), Williams M (Darlington 83), Sharp.

Wednesday, 14 July 2010
Linfield (0) 0
Rosenborg (0) 0   1715

Linfield: Blayney; Bailie, Lindsay, Burns B (Ervin 76), Burns A, Garrett, Mulgrew, Curran, Lowry (McAllister 70), McCaul (Carvill 61), Thompson.
Rosenborg: Orlund; Dorsin, Stadsgaard, Lustig, Demidov, Annan, Traore (Strand 46), Winsnes, Henriksen, Iversen, Moldskred (Olsen 87).

SECOND QUALIFYING ROUND SECOND LEG

Dinamo Tirana	(1) 1	Serif	(0) 0
HB Torshavn	(0) 1	Salzburg	(0) 0

Koper	(1) 3	Dinamo Zagreb	(0) 0
Renova	(0) 0	Omonia	(2) 2
Rudar	(0) 0	Litex	(2) 4
The New Saints	(3) 4	Bohemians	(0) 0
Debrecen	(2) 3	Levadia	(1) 2
Hafnarfjordur	(0) 0	BATE Borisov	(1) 1
HJK Helsinki	(0) 2	Ekranas	(0) 0
(aet.)			
Jeunesse Esch	(0) 0	AIK Stockholm	(0) 0
Lech	(0) 0	Inter Baku	(0) 1
(aet; Lech won 9-8 on penalties.)			
Olimpi	(1) 1	Aktobe	(0) 1
Pyunik	(0) 0	Partizan Belgrade	(1) 1
Rosenborg	(1) 2	Linfield	(0) 0
Sparta Prague	(2) 2	Metalurgs Liepaya	(0) 0
Zeljeznicar	(0) 0	Hapoel Tel Aviv	(0) 1
Zilina	(1) 3	Birkirkara	(0) 0

Tuesday, 20 July 2010

The New Saints (3) 4 *(Jones C 6, Williams M 14, 73, Sharp 20)*

Bohemians (0) 0   1056

The New Saints: Harrison; Evans, Baker, Holmes D, Marriott, Jones C, Hogan, Ruscoe, Berkeley (Wood 89), Williams M, Sharp.
Bohemians: Murphy B; Heary, Powell (McGuinness 46), Oman, Higgins (Cronin 46), Brennan, Shelley, Keegan, Quigley, Byrne (Greene 67), Madden.

Wednesday, 21 July 2010

Rosenborg (1) 2 *(Prica 32, Henriksen 87)*

Linfield (0) 0   6645

Rosenborg: Orlund; Dorsin, Stadsgaard, Lustig, Demidov, Annan, Skjelbred (Strand 82), Henriksen, Iversen, Moldskred (Winsnes 74), Prica (Olsen 74).
Linfield: Blayney; Bailie, Lindsay, Burns B, Burns A (Munster 81), Garrett, Mulgrew, Curran, Lowry (Carvill 68), McCaul (Allen 63), Thompson.

THIRD QUALIFYING ROUND FIRST LEG

Dynamo Kiev	(1) 3	Gent	(0) 0
Litex	(0) 1	Zilina	(0) 1
Omonia	(0) 1	Salzburg	(1) 1
Sparta Prague	(0) 1	Lech	(0) 0
The New Saints	(0) 1	Anderlecht	(2) 3
Unirea	(0) 0	Zenit	(0) 0
AIK Stockholm	(0) 0	Rosenborg	(1) 1
Ajax	(1) 1	PAOK Salonika	(0) 1
Aktobe	(0) 1	Hapoel Tel Aviv	(0) 0
BATE Borisov	(0) 0	FC Copenhagen	(0) 0
Braga	(1) 3	Celtic	(0) 0
Debrecen	(0) 0	Basle	(1) 2
Partizan Belgrade	(2) 3	HJK Helsinki	(0) 0
Serif	(1) 1	Dinamo Zagreb	(1) 1
Young Boys	(1) 2	Fenerbahce	(2) 2

Tuesday, 27 July 2010

The New Saints (0) 1 *(Jones C 52)*

Anderlecht (2) 3 *(Kljestan 7, Legear 18, Suarez 73)* 2486

The New Saints: Harrison; Evans, Baker, Holmes D, Marriott (Holmes T 21), Jones C, Hogan, Ruscoe, Berkeley (Seargeant 78), Williams M, Sharp (Darlington 84).
Anderlecht: Proto; Juhasz, Deschacht, Mazuch (Lecjaks 83), Biglia, Kljestan (Kanu 87), Boussoufa, Gillet, Legear, Kouyate, Suarez (De Sutter 76).

Wednesday, 28 July 2010

Braga (1) 3 *(Alan 26 (pen), Elderson 76, Matheus 88)*

Celtic (0) 0 12,295

Braga: Mario Felgueiras; Rodriguez, Miguel Garcia, Elderson, Andres Madrid, Vandinho, Moises, Salino, Alan (Helder Barbosa 90), Lima (Matheus 66), Paulo Cesar.
Celtic: Zaluska; Cha, Hooiveld, Mulgrew, Loovens, Juarez (Forrest 79), Brown, Ki, Ledley, Maloney (Murphy 71), Samaras.

THIRD QUALIFYING ROUND SECOND LEG

Anderlecht	(1) 3	The New Saints	(0) 0
Hapoel Tel Aviv	(3) 3	Aktobe	(0) 1
Basle	(1) 3	Debrecen	(0) 1
Celtic	(0) 2	Braga	(1) 1
Dinamo Zagreb	(0) 1	Serif	(1) 1
(aet; Serif won 6-5 on penalties.)			
FC Copenhagen	(2) 3	BATE Borisov	(2) 2
Fenerbahce	(0) 0	Young Boys	(1) 1
Gent	(0) 1	Dynamo Kiev	(1) 3
HJK Helsinki	(1) 1	Partizan Belgrade	(1) 2
Lech	(0) 0	Sparta Prague	(0) 1
PAOK Salonika	(1) 3	Ajax	(0) 3
Rosenborg	(0) 3	AIK Stockholm	(0) 0
Salzburg	(3) 4	Omonia	(0) 1
Zenit	(1) 1	Unirea	(0) 0
Zilina	(0) 3	Litex	(0) 1

Tuesday, 3 August 2010

Anderlecht (1) 3 *(De Sutter 17, Lukaku 69, 74)*

The New Saints (0) 0 19,338

Anderlecht: Proto; Juhasz, Lecjaks, Bernardez, Rnic, Kljestan (Gillet 73), Chatelle, Marecek, De Sutter (Lukaku 59), Suarez (Diandy 46), Chavarria.
The New Saints: Harrison; Evans (Edwards 74), Baker, Holmes T, Holmes D, Jones C, Hogan, Ruscoe, Wood (Seargeant 87), Williams M, Sharp (Darlington 83).

Wednesday, 4 August 2010

Celtic (0) 2 *(Hooper 52, Juarez 79)*

Braga (1) 1 *(Paulo Cesar 20)* 53,592

Celtic: Zaluska; Cha, Hooiveld, Mulgrew (Fortune 47), Loovens, Juarez, Brown (McCourt 88), Ledley, Maloney (Murphy 64), Samaras, Hooper.
Braga: Mario Felgueiras; Rodriguez, Miguel Garcia, Elderson, Andres Madrid (Paulao 86), Vandinho, Moises, Salino (Meyong 90), Alan, Paulo Cesar, Matheus (Lima 67).

PLAY-OFF ROUND FIRST LEG

Dynamo Kiev	(0) 1	Ajax	(0) 1
Rosenborg	(1) 2	FC Copenhagen	(0) 1
Sparta Prague	(0) 0	Zilina	(0) 2
Young Boys	(3) 3	Tottenham H	(1) 2
Zenit	(1) 1	Auxerre	(0) 0
Basle	(0) 1	Serif	(0) 0
Braga	(0) 1	Sevilla	(0) 0
Partizan Belgrade	(0) 2	Anderlecht	(0) 2
Salzburg	(1) 2	Hapoel Tel Aviv	(2) 3
Werder Bremen	(0) 3	Sampdoria	(0) 1

Tuesday, 17 August 2010

Young Boys (3) 3 *(Lulic 4, N'Tsama 13, Hochstrasser 28)*

Tottenham H (1) 2 *(Bassong 42, Pavlyuchenko 83)*   30,166

Young Boys: Wolfli; Spycher, Sutter, El Jemal, Affolter, Degen (Raimondi 90), Hochstrasser, Doubai, Lulic, Costanzo (Schneuwly C 65), N'Tsama.
Tottenham H: Gomes; Corluka, Assou-Ekotto (Huddlestone 36), Palacios, Dawson, Bassong, Giovani, Modric (Kranjcar 46), Pavlyuchenko, Defoe (Keane 66), Bale.

PLAY-OFF ROUND SECOND LEG

Anderlecht	(0) 2	Partizan Belgrade	(1) 2
(aet; Partizan Belgrade won 3-2 on penalties.)			
Hapoel Tel Aviv	(0) 1	Salzburg	(1) 1
Sampdoria	(2) 3	Werder Bremen	(0) 2
(aet.)			
Serif	(0) 0	Basle	(0) 3
Sevilla	(0) 3	Braga	(1) 4
Ajax	(1) 2	Dynamo Kiev	(0) 1
Auxerre	(1) 2	Zenit	(0) 0
FC Copenhagen	(1) 1	Rosenborg	(0) 0
Tottenham H	(2) 4	Young Boys	(0) 0
Zilina	(1) 1	Sparta Prague	(0) 0

Wednesday, 25 August 2010

Tottenham H (2) 4 *(Crouch 5, 61, 78 (pen), Defoe 32)*

Young Boys (0) 0   34,709

Tottenham H: Gomes (Cudicini 46); Corluka, Assou-Ekotto, Palacios, Dawson, King, Lennon, Huddlestone, Crouch, Defoe (Pavlyuchenko 62), Bale (Kranjcar 82).
Young Boys: Wolfli; Spycher, Sutter (Schneuwly M 62), El Jemal, Affolter, Degen, Hochstrasser, Doubai (Schneuwly C 82), Lulic■, Costanzo (Regazzoni 62), N'Tsama.

GROUP A

Twente	(2) 2	Internazionale	(2) 2
Werder Bremen	(1) 2	Tottenham H	(2) 2
Internazionale	(3) 4	Werder Bremen	(0) 0
Tottenham H	(0) 4	Twente	(0) 1
Internazionale	(4) 4	Tottenham H	(0) 3
Twente	(0) 1	Werder Bremen	(0) 1
Tottenham H	(1) 3	Internazionale	(0) 1
Werder Bremen	(0) 0	Twente	(0) 2
Internazionale	(0) 1	Twente	(0) 0
Tottenham H	(2) 3	Werder Bremen	(0) 0

| Twente | (1) 3 | Tottenham H | (1) 3 |
| Werder Bremen | (1) 3 | Internazionale | (0) 0 |

Tuesday, 14 September 2010

Werder Bremen (1) 2 *(Hugo Almeida 43, Marin 47)*

Tottenham H (2) 2 *(Pasanen 12 (og), Crouch 18)* 30,344

Werder Bremen: Wiese; Silvestre, Pasanen, Fritz, Prodl, Frings, Marin, Bargfrede (Hunt 37), Wesley (Borowski 67), Hugo Almeida (Wagner 79), Arnautovic.
Tottenham H: Cudicini; Corluka, Assou-Ekotto, Huddlestone, Kaboul, King, Lennon (Palacios 76), Jenas, Crouch, Van der Vaart (Keane 49), Bale.

Wednesday, 29 September 2010

Tottenham H (0) 4 *(Van der Vaart 48, Pavlyuchenko 51 (pen), 65 (pen), Bale 85)*

Twente (0) 1 *(Chadli 57)* 32,518

Tottenham H: Gomes; Hutton, Assou-Ekotto, Huddlestone, Bassong, King, Van der Vaart■, Modric (Lennon 82), Crouch (Jenas 66), Pavlyuchenko (Keane 89), Bale.
Twente: Mihaylov; Wisgerhof, Rosales, Douglas, Kuiper, Landzaat (De Jong 69), Janssen, Brama, Bajrami (Chadli 28), Ruiz, Janko.

Wednesday, 20 October 2010

Internazionale (4) 4 *(Zanetti 2, Eto'o 11, 35, Stankovic 14)*

Tottenham H (0) 3 *(Bale 52, 89, 90)* 49,551

Internazionale: Julio Cesar; Lucio, Zanetti, Maicon, Samuel, Chivu (Pandev 61), Sneijder, Stankovic (Santon 50), Philippe Coutinho, Eto'o, Biabiany (Cordoba 75).
Tottenham H: Gomes■; Hutton, Assou-Ekotto, Huddlestone (Palacios 80), Bassong, Gallas, Lennon, Jenas, Crouch (Keane 67), Modric (Cudicini 10), Bale.

Tuesday, 2 November 2010

Tottenham H (1) 3 *(Van der Vaart 18, Crouch 61, Pavlyuchenko 89)*

Internazionale (0) 1 *(Eto'o 80)* 34,103

Tottenham H: Cudicini; Hutton, Assou-Ekotto, Huddlestone, Gallas, Kaboul, Lennon (Palacios 84), Modric, Crouch (Pavlyuchenko 76), Van der Vaart (Jenas 46), Bale.
Internazionale: Castellazzi; Lucio, Zanetti, Maicon, Samuel, Chivu, Sneijder, Muntari (Nwankwo 53), Eto'o, Pandev (Milito 71), Biabiany (Philippe Coutinho 64).

Wednesday, 24 November 2010

Tottenham H (2) 3 *(Kaboul 6, Modric 45, Crouch 79)*

Werder Bremen (0) 0 33,546

Tottenham H: Gomes; Hutton, Assou-Ekotto, Modric, Gallas, Kaboul, Lennon, Jenas (Palacios 20), Crouch, Pavlyuchenko (Defoe 57), Bale (Kranjcar 81).
Werder Bremen: Wiese; Mertesacker, Fritz, Prodl, Schmidt, Jensen (Pasanen 86), Marin, Bargfrede, Hunt (Thy 80), Wagner, Kroos (Ayik 55).

Tuesday, 7 December 2010

Twente (1) 3 *(Landzaat 22 (pen), Rosales 56, Chadli 64)*

Tottenham H (1) 3 *(Wisgerhof 12 (og), Defoe 47, 59)* 24,000

Twente: Boschker; Wisgerhof, Tiendalli, Rosales, Douglas, Landzaat, Janssen, Brama, Chadli, Janko (Vujicevic 73), De Jong.
Tottenham H: Gomes; Corluka, Assou-Ekotto, Palacios, Gallas, Bassong, Kranjcar (Crouch 86), Jenas (Lennon 34), Pavlyuchenko (Keane 73), Defoe, Bale.

Group A Table	P	W	D	L	F	A	Pts
Tottenham H	6	3	2	1	18	11	11
Internazionale	6	3	1	2	12	11	10
Twente	6	1	3	2	9	11	6
Werder Bremen	6	1	2	3	6	12	5

GROUP B

Benfica	(1) 2	Hapoel Tel Aviv	(0) 0
Lyon	(1) 1	Schalke	(0) 0
Hapoel Tel Aviv	(0) 1	Lyon	(2) 3
Schalke	(0) 2	Benfica	(0) 0
Lyon	(1) 2	Benfica	(0) 0
Schalke	(1) 3	Hapoel Tel Aviv	(0) 1
Benfica	(3) 4	Lyon	(0) 3
Hapoel Tel Aviv	(0) 0	Schalke	(0) 0
Hapoel Tel Aviv	(1) 3	Benfica	(0) 0
Schalke	(2) 3	Lyon	(0) 0
Benfica	(0) 1	Schalke	(1) 2
Lyon	(0) 2	Hapoel Tel Aviv	(0) 2

Group B Table	P	W	D	L	F	A	Pts
Schalke	6	4	1	1	10	3	13
Lyon	6	3	1	2	11	10	10
Benfica	6	2	0	4	7	12	6
Hapoel Tel Aviv	6	1	2	3	7	10	5

GROUP C

Bursa	(0) 0	Valencia	(2) 4
Manchester U	(0) 0	Rangers	(0) 0
Rangers	(1) 1	Bursa	(0) 0
Valencia	(0) 0	Manchester U	(0) 1
Manchester U	(1) 1	Bursa	(0) 0
Rangers	(1) 1	Valencia	(0) 1
Bursa	(0) 0	Manchester U	(0) 3
Valencia	(1) 3	Rangers	(0) 0
Rangers	(0) 0	Manchester U	(0) 1
Valencia	(4) 6	Bursa	(0) 1
Bursa	(0) 1	Rangers	(1) 1
Manchester U	(0) 1	Valencia	(1) 1

Tuesday, 14 September 2010

Manchester U (0) 0

Rangers (0) 0 74,408

Manchester U: Kuszczak; Fabio (Evans J 75), Smalling, Fletcher, Brown, Ferdinand, Valencia (Giggs 63), Gibson, Hernandez, Rooney, Park (Owen 75).
Rangers: McGregor; Whittaker, Papac, Broadfoot, Weir, Bougherra, Davis, Edu, Naismith, Miller (Lafferty 81), McCulloch.

Wednesday, 29 September 2010

Rangers (1) 1 *(Naismith 18)*

Bursa (0) 0 41,905

Rangers: McGregor; Whittaker, Papac, McCulloch, Weir, Bougherra, Broadfoot, Davis, Naismith, Miller (Lafferty 87), Edu.
Bursa: Ivankov; Ali, Stepanov, Omer, Vederson, Ergic (Insua 39), Svensson, Batalla (Nunez 71), Volkan, Ozan, Sercan (Turgay 72).

Valencia (0) 0

Manchester U (0) 1 *(Hernandez 85)* 34,946

Valencia: Cesar; Maduro, Miguel, Mathieu, David Navarro, Albelda (Mehmet Topal 88), Tino Costa (Manuel Fernandes 74), Pablo Hernandez, Soldado, Chori Dominguez (Aduriz 59), Mata.
Manchester U: Van der Sar; Rafael (O'Shea 90), Evra, Carrick, Ferdinand, Vidic, Nani, Fletcher, Berbatov (Macheda 85), Anderson (Hernandez 77), Park.

Wednesday, 20 October 2010

Manchester U (1) 1 *(Nani 7)*

Bursa (0) 0 72,610

Manchester U: Kuszczak; Rafael, Evra, Carrick, Smalling, Vidic, Park (Obertan 71), Fletcher, Macheda, Anderson (Hernandez 78), Nani.
Bursa: Ivankov; Ali (Mustafa 71), Stepanov (Turgay 46), Omer, Vederson, Ergic, Insua, Svensson, Volkan, Ozan, Sercan (Ibrahim 46).

Rangers (1) 1 *(Edu 34)*

Valencia (0) 1 *(Edu 46 (og))* 45,153

Rangers: McGregor; Whittaker, Papac, Foster, Weir, Bougherra, Davis, Edu, Naismith, Miller, Weiss (Lafferty 88).
Valencia: Cesar; Ricardo Costa, Mathieu, David Navarro, Bruno, Mehmet Topal, Tino Costa (Manuel Fernandes 76), Pablo Hernandez, Aduriz, Chori Dominguez (Soldado 46), Mata (Vicente 85).

Tuesday, 2 November 2010

Bursa (0) 0

Manchester U (0) 3 *(Fletcher 48, Obertan 73, Ali 77 (og))* 19,050

Bursa: Ivankov; Ali, Omer, Ibrahim, Vederson, Ergic, Insua (Nunez 75), Svensson, Volkan (Ismail 82), Turgay, Sercan (Ozan 75).
Manchester U: Van der Sar; Rafael, Evra (Fabio 81), Carrick, Smalling, Vidic, Fletcher (Bebe 62), Scholes, Berbatov, Obertan, Nani (Park 29).

Valencia (1) 3 *(Soldado 33, 71, Tino Costa 90)*

Rangers (0) 0 26,821

Valencia: Cesar; Ricardo Costa, Miguel, Mathieu, David Navarro, Albelda, Joaquin (Pablo Hernandez 85), Banega (Tino Costa 70), Aduriz, Soldado (Manuel Fernandes 77), Mata.
Rangers: McGregor; Whittaker, Papac, Broadfoot, Weir, Bougherra, Davis, Edu (Lafferty 83), Naismith, Miller, McCulloch.

Wednesday, 24 November 2010

Rangers (0) 0

Manchester U (0) 1 *(Rooney 87 (pen))* 49,764

Rangers: McGregor; Hutton (Beattie 88), Whittaker, Foster, Weir, Broadfoot, Davis, McCulloch, Naismith, Miller, Weiss (Fleck 79).
Manchester U: Van der Sar; Fabio, O'Shea, Carrick, Smalling, Evans J, Nani (Obertan 77), Scholes (Anderson 67), Berbatov (Hernandez 76), Rooney, Giggs.

Tuesday, 7 December 2010

Bursa (0) 1 *(Sercan 79)*

Rangers (1) 1 *(Miller 20)*   9673

Bursa: Yavuz; Mustafa, Stepanov, Serdar (Omer 46), Vederson, Insua, Bekir, Ozan, Huseyin (Batalla 46), Nunez (Turgay 62), Sercan.
Rangers: McGregor; Whittaker, Foster, McCulloch, Weir, Bougherra, Davis, Hutton, Naismith (Weiss 71), Miller (Beattie 63), Cole (McMillan 82).

Manchester U (0) 1 *(Anderson 62)*

Valencia (1) 1 *(Pablo Hernandez 32)*   74,513

Manchester U: Amos; Rafael, Fabio, Carrick, Ferdinand (Smalling 50), Vidic, Nani (Giggs 81), Anderson (Fletcher 90), Berbatov, Rooney, Park.
Valencia: Guaita; Ricardo Costa, Miguel, Mathieu, Dealbert, Albelda, Banega, Pablo Hernandez (Sofiane 81), Jordi Alba (Mata 68), Aduriz, Chori Dominguez (Isco 54).

Group C Table	P	W	D	L	F	A	Pts
Manchester U	6	4	2	0	7	1	14
Valencia	6	3	2	1	15	4	11
Rangers	6	1	3	2	3	6	6
Bursa	6	0	1	5	2	16	1

GROUP D

Barcelona	(3) 5	Panathinaikos	(1) 1
FC Copenhagen	(0) 1	Rubin	(0) 0
Panathinaikos	(0) 0	FC Copenhagen	(2) 2
Rubin	(1) 1	Barcelona	(0) 1
Barcelona	(1) 2	FC Copenhagen	(0) 0
Panathinaikos	(0) 0	Rubin	(0) 0
FC Copenhagen	(1) 1	Barcelona	(1) 1
Rubin	(0) 0	Panathinaikos	(0) 0
Panathinaikos	(0) 0	Barcelona	(1) 3
Rubin	(1) 1	FC Copenhagen	(0) 0
Barcelona	(0) 2	Rubin	(0) 0
FC Copenhagen	(1) 3	Panathinaikos	(0) 1

Group D Table	P	W	D	L	F	A	Pts
Barcelona	6	4	2	0	14	3	14
FC Copenhagen	6	3	1	2	7	5	10
Rubin	6	1	3	2	2	4	6
Panathinaikos	6	0	2	4	2	13	2

GROUP E

Bayern Munich	(0) 2	Roma	(0) 0
Cluj	(2) 2	Basle	(1) 1
Basle	(1) 1	Bayern Munich	(0) 2
Roma	(0) 2	Cluj	(0) 1
Bayern Munich	(2) 3	Cluj	(1) 2
Roma	(1) 1	Basle	(2) 3
Basle	(0) 2	Roma	(2) 3
Cluj	(0) 0	Bayern Munich	(2) 4
Basle	(1) 1	Cluj	(0) 0
Roma	(0) 3	Bayern Munich	(2) 2
Bayern Munich	(2) 3	Basle	(0) 0
Cluj	(0) 1	Roma	(1) 1

Group E Table	P	W	D	L	F	A	Pts
Bayern Munich	6	5	0	1	16	6	15
Roma	6	3	1	2	10	11	10
Basle	6	2	0	4	8	11	6
Cluj	6	1	1	4	6	12	4

GROUP F

Marseille	(0) 0	Spartak Moscow	(0) 1
Zilina	(0) 1	Chelsea	(3) 4
Chelsea	(2) 2	Marseille	(0) 0
Spartak Moscow	(1) 3	Zilina	(0) 0
Marseille	(0) 1	Zilina	(0) 0
Spartak Moscow	(0) 0	Chelsea	(2) 2
Chelsea	(0) 4	Spartak Moscow	(0) 1
Zilina	(0) 0	Marseille	(4) 7
Chelsea	(0) 2	Zilina	(1) 1
Spartak Moscow	(0) 0	Marseille	(1) 3
Marseille	(0) 1	Chelsea	(0) 0
Zilina	(0) 1	Spartak Moscow	(0) 2

Wednesday, 15 September 2010

Zilina (0) 1 *(Oravec 55)*

Chelsea (3) 4 *(Essien 13, Anelka 24, 28, Sturridge 48)*   10,829

Zilina: Dubravka; Guldan (Angelovic 79), Pecalka, Piacek, Jez, Vladavic, Mraz, Rilke (Poliacek 57), Oravec, Ceesay (Majtan 62), Bello.
Chelsea: Cech; Ivanovic, Zhirkov, Mikel, Terry, Alex, Benayoun (McEachran 79), Essien, Anelka, Sturridge (Kakuta 62), Malouda (Van Aanholt 88).

Tuesday, 28 September 2010

Chelsea (2) 2 *(Terry 7, Anelka 28 (pen))*

Marseille (0) 0   40,675

Chelsea: Cech; Ivanovic, Cole, Mikel (McEachran 88), Terry, Alex, Malouda, Essien, Anelka, Kakuta (Ramires 61), Zhirkov (Sturridge 73).
Marseille: Mandanda; Heinze, Diawara, Gonzalez, Cheyrou (Valbuena 59), M'Bia, Cisse, Kabore, Gignac (Ayew A 59), Remy, Brandao.

Tuesday, 19 October 2010

Spartak Moscow (0) 0

Chelsea (2) 2 *(Zhirkov 23, Anelka 43)*   75,000

Spartak Moscow: Dikan; Pareja, Parshivlyuk, Suchy, Sheshukov, Makeev, McGeady, Ibson, Kombarov D, Ari (Ananidze 85), Welliton.
Chelsea: Cech; Paulo Ferreira, Cole (Van Aanholt 87), Mikel, Terry, Ivanovic, Malouda (Kakuta 82), Essien, Anelka, Kalou (McEachran 74), Zhirkov.

Wednesday, 3 November 2010

Chelsea (0) 4 *(Anelka 49, Drogba 62 (pen), Ivanovic 66, 90)*

Spartak Moscow (0) 1 *(Bazhenov 86)*   40,477

Chelsea: Cech; Paulo Ferreira, Cole, Mikel (McEachran 69), Ivanovic, Alex, Ramires, Kalou, Anelka (Sturridge 76), Drogba (Kakuta 76), Zhirkov.
Spartak Moscow: Dikan; Pareja, Suchy, Ivanov, Sheshukov (Drincic 68), Makeev, McGeady (Bazhenov 80), Ibson, Kombarov D, Alex (Kozlov 69), Welliton.

Tuesday, 23 November 2010

Chelsea (0) 2 *(Sturridge 51, Malouda 86)*

Zilina (1) 1 *(Bello 19)*   40,266

Chelsea: Turnbull; Paulo Ferreira, Van Aanholt, McEachran (Mellis 90), Ivanovic, Bruma, Ramires, Kakuta (Kalou 46), Sturridge (Anelka 74), Drogba, Malouda.
Zilina: Dubravka; Guldan, Pecalka, Angelovic, Piacek, Jez, Vladavic (Rilke 90), Gergel, Bello, Oravec (Ceesay 64), Majtan (Poliacek 85).

Wednesday, 8 December 2010

Marseille (0) 1 *(Brandao 81)*

Chelsea (0) 0   50,604

Marseille: Mandanda; Heinze, Diawara, Taiwo, Abriel (Ayew A 63), Cheyrou, Valbuena (Gonzalez 62), N'Diaye (Ayew J 85), Kabore, Remy, Brandao.
Chelsea: Cech; Bosingwa (Van Aanholt 79), Paulo Ferreira, McEachran, Terry (Bruma 72), Ivanovic, Essien, Ramires, Kalou, Drogba (Sturridge 62), Malouda.

Group F Table	P	W	D	L	F	A	Pts
Chelsea	6	5	0	1	14	4	15
Marseille	6	4	0	2	12	3	12
Spartak Moscow	6	3	0	3	7	10	9
Zilina	6	0	0	6	3	19	0

GROUP G

AC Milan	(0) 2	Auxerre	(0) 0
Real Madrid	(1) 2	Ajax	(0) 0
Ajax	(1) 1	AC Milan	(1) 1
Auxerre	(0) 0	Real Madrid	(0) 1
Ajax	(2) 2	Auxerre	(0) 1
Real Madrid	(2) 2	AC Milan	(0) 0
AC Milan	(0) 2	Read Madrid	(1) 2
Auxerre	(1) 2	Ajax	(0) 1
Ajax	(0) 0	Real Madrid	(2) 4
Auxerre	(0) 0	AC Milan	(0) 2
AC Milan	(0) 0	Ajax	(0) 2
Real Madrid	(1) 4	Auxerre	(0) 0

Group G Table	P	W	D	L	F	A	Pts
Real Madrid	6	5	1	0	15	2	16
AC Milan	6	2	2	2	7	7	8
Ajax	6	2	1	3	6	10	7
Auxerre	6	1	0	5	3	12	3

GROUP H

Arsenal	(3) 6	Braga	(0) 0
Shakhter Donetsk	(0) 1	Partizan Belgrade	(0) 0
Braga	(0) 0	Shakhter Donetsk	(0) 3
Partizan Belgrade	(1) 1	Arsenal	(1) 3
Arsenal	(2) 5	Shakhtar Donetsk	(0) 1
Braga	(1) 2	Partizan Belgrade	(0) 0
Partizan Belgrade	(0) 0	Braga	(1) 1
Shakhtar Donetsk	(2) 2	Arsenal	(1) 1
Braga	(0) 2	Arsenal	(0) 0

Partizan Belgrade	(0) 0	Shakhtar Donetsk	(0) 3
Arsenal	(1) 3	Partizan Belgrade	(0) 1
Shakhtar Donetsk	(0) 2	Braga	(0) 0

Wednesday, 15 September 2010

Arsenal (3) 6 *(Fabregas 9 (pen), 53, Arshavin 30, Chamakh 34, Vela 68, 84)*

Braga (0) 0 59,333

Arsenal: Almunia; Sagna, Clichy, Song Billong (Vela 63), Squillaci, Koscielny, Wilshere, Fabregas, Chamakh (Denilson 63), Arshavin (Eboue 70), Nasri.
Braga: Felipe; Rodriguez, Miguel Garcia, Silvio, Hugo Viana (Marcio Mossoro 55), Vandinho, Moises, Aguiar, Alan, Paulo Cesar (Helder Barbosa 70), Matheus (Lima 60).

Tuesday, 28 September 2010

Partizan Belgrade (1) 1 *(Cleo 33 (pen))*

Arsenal (1) 3 *(Arshavin 15, Chamakh 71, Squillaci 82)* 29,348

Partizan Belgrade: Stojkovic; Krstajic, Jovanovic M■, Lazevski, Stevanovic, Ilic S, Kamara, Petrovic (Smiljanic 69), Tomic (Savic 60), Boya (Iliev 83), Cleo.
Arsenal: Fabianski; Sagna, Gibbs, Denilson, Squillaci, Djourou, Song Billong, Wilshere (Nasri 74), Chamakh (Vela 75), Arshavin (Clichy 85), Rosicky.

Tuesday, 19 October 2010

Arsenal (2) 5 *(Song Billong 19, Nasri 42, Fabregas 59 (pen), Wilshere 66, Chamakh 69)*

Shakhtar Donetsk (0) 1 *(Eduardo Da Silva 82)* 60,016

Arsenal: Fabianski; Djourou, Squillaci, Clichy, Rosicky, Eboue, Fabregas (Denilson 63), Song Billong, Wilshere, Chamakh (Walcott 72), Nasri (Arshavin 72).
Shakhtar Donetsk: Pyatov; Srna, Kucher, Rat, Hubschman, Rakitskiy, Willian (Douglas Costa 46), Alex Teixeira, Mkhitaryan, Gai (Jadson 68), Luiz Adriano (Eduardo Da Silva 63).

Wednesday, 3 November 2010

Shakhtar Donetsk (2) 2 *(Chygrynskiy 28, Eduardo Da Silva 45)*

Arsenal (1) 1 *(Walcott 10)* 51,153

Shakhtar Donetsk: Pyatov; Srna, Chygrynskiy, Rat, Hubschman, Rakitskiy, Willian, Jadson (Douglas Costa 74), Gai (Alex Texeira 62), Luiz Adriano (Moreno 88), Eduardo Da Silva.
Arsenal: Fabianski; Eboue, Clichy, Eastmond (Vela 59), Squillaci, Djourou, Walcott (Emmanuel-Thomas 82), Wilshere, Bendtner (Chamakh 73), Rosicky, Nasri.

Tuesday, 23 November 2010

Braga (0) 2 *(Matheus 83, 90)*

Arsenal (0) 0 14,809

Braga: Felipe; Rodriguez, Miguel Garcia, Elderson, Vandinho (Hugo Viana 89), Moises, Aguiar (Andres Madrid 80), Salino, Alan, Lima (Elton 81), Matheus.
Arsenal: Fabianski; Eboue, Gibbs, Denilson, Squillaci, Djourou, Walcott (Vela 77), Fabregas (Nasri 69), Bendtner (Chamakh 74), Wilshere, Rosicky.

Wednesday, 8 December 2010

Arsenal (1) 3 *(Van Persie 30 (pen), Walcott 73, Nasri 77)*

Partizan Belgrade (0) 1 *(Cleo 52)* 58,845

Arsenal: Fabianski; Sagna■, Gibbs (Eboue 24), Denilson, Squillaci, Koscielny, Song Billong, Van Persie, Chamakh (Bendtner 76), Arshavin (Walcott 67), Nasri.
Partizan Belgrade: Stojkovic; Krstajic, Jovanovic M, Lazevski, Savic, Ilic S, Kamara, Babovic (Davidov 81), Almami Moreira (Brasanac 90), Petrovic, Cleo.

Group H Table	P	W	D	L	F	A	Pts
Shakhtar Donetsk	6	5	0	1	12	6	15
Arsenal	6	4	0	2	18	7	12
Braga	6	3	0	3	5	11	9
Partizan Belgrade	6	0	0	6	2	13	0

KNOCK-OUT ROUND FIRST LEG

AC Milan	(0) 0	Tottenham H	(0) 1
Valencia	(1) 1	Schalke	(0) 1
Arsenal	(0) 2	Barcelona	(1) 1
Roma	(1) 2	Shakhtar Donetsk	(3) 3
FC Copenhagen	(0) 0	Chelsea	(1) 2
Lyon	(0) 1	Real Madrid	(0) 1
Internazionale	(0) 0	Bayern Munich	(0) 1
Marseille	(0) 0	Manchester U	(0) 0

Tuesday, 15 February 2011

AC Milan (0) 0

Tottenham H (0) 1 *(Crouch 80)*   75,652

AC Milan: Abbiati (Amelia 18); Nesta, Yepes, Antonini, Thiago Silva, Gattuso, Flamini, Seedorf (Alexandre Pato 46), Abate, Robinho, Ibrahimovic.
Tottenham H: Gomes; Corluka (Woodgate 59), Assou-Ekotto, Palacios, Gallas, Dawson, Lennon, Pienaar (Kranjcar 76), Crouch, Sandro, Van der Vaart (Modric 62).

Wednesday, 16 February 2011

Arsenal (0) 2 *(Van Persie 78, Arshavin 83)*

Barcelona (1) 1 *(David Villa 26)*   59,927

Arsenal: Sczcesny; Eboue, Clichy, Song Billong (Arshavin 69), Djourou, Koscielny, Walcott (Bendtner 77), Fabregas, Van Persie, Wilshere, Nasri.
Barcelona: Valdes; Abidal, Dani Alves, Maxwell, Pique, Iniesta (Adriano 89), Xavi, Sergio Busquets, Messi, David Villa (Keita 68), Pedro.

Tuesday, 22 February 2011

FC Copenhagen (0) 0

Chelsea (1) 2 *(Anelka 17, 54)*   36,713

FC Copenhagen: Wiland; Wendt (Bengtsson 75), Antonsson, Kvist Jorgensen, Pospech, Zanka Jorgensen, Gronkjaer (Zohore 87), Claudemir, Cesar Santin (Vingaard 46), N'Doye, Bolanos.
Chelsea: Cech; Bosingwa, Cole, Ramires, Terry, Ivanovic, Essien, Lampard, Torres (Kalou 90), Anelka (Drogba 73), Malouda (Zhirkov 85).

Wednesday, 23 February 2011

Marseille (0) 0

Manchester U (0) 0   57,957

Marseille: Mandanda; Heinze, Fanni, Diawara, Gonzalez, M'Bia, Cisse (Cheyrou 70), Kabore, Remy (Valbuena 79), Brandao, Ayew A.
Manchester U: Van der Sar; O'Shea, Evra, Carrick, Smalling, Vidic, Gibson (Scholes 73), Fletcher, Berbatov, Rooney, Nani.

KNOCK-OUT ROUND SECOND LEG

Barcelona	(1) 3	Arsenal	(0) 1
Shakhtar Donetsk	(1) 3	Roma	(0) 0
Schalke	(1) 3	Valencia	(1) 1
Tottenham H	(0) 0	AC Milan	(0) 0
Bayern Munich	(2) 2	Internazionale	(1) 3
Manchester U	(1) 2	Marseille	(0) 1
Chelsea	(0) 0	FC Copenhagen	(0) 0
Real Madrid	(1) 3	Lyon	(0) 0

Tuesday, 8 March 2011

Barcelona (1) 3 *(Messi 45, 71 (pen), Xavi 69)*

Arsenal (0) 1 *(Sergio Busquets 53 (og))*   95,486

Barcelona: Valdes; Abidal, Dani Alves, Adriano (Maxwell 90), Mascherano (Keita 89), Iniesta, Xavi, Sergio Busquets, Messi, David Villa (Afellay 82), Pedro.
Arsenal: Szczesny (Almunia 19); Sagna, Clichy, Diaby, Djourou, Koscielny, Wilshere, Fabregas (Bendtner 78), Van Persie■, Rosicky (Arshavin 74), Nasri.

Wednesday, 9 March 2011

Tottenham H (0) 0

AC Milan (0) 0   34,320

Tottenham H: Gomes; Corluka, Assou-Ekotto, Modric, Gallas, Dawson, Lennon, Sandro, Crouch (Pavlyuchenko 83), Van der Vaart (Bale 66), Pienaar (Jenas 71).
AC Milan: Abbiati; Nesta, Jankulovski (Antonini 70), Thiago Silva, Boateng (Merkel 76), Flamini (Strasser 87), Seedorf, Abate, Robinho, Ibrahimovic, Alexandre Pato.

Tuesday, 15 March 2011

Manchester U (1) 2 *(Hernandez 5, 75)*

Marseille (0) 1 *(Brown 81 (og))*   73,996

Manchester U: Van der Sar; O'Shea (Rafael 37) (Fabio 70), Evra, Carrick, Brown, Smalling, Nani (Valencia 62), Scholes, Hernandez, Rooney, Giggs.
Marseille: Mandanda; Heinze, Fanni, Diawara, Taiwo, Gonzalez, Cheyrou, M'Bia (Ayew J 80), Gignac (Valbuena 69), Remy, Ayew A.

Wednesday, 16 March 2011

Chelsea (0) 0

FC Copenhagen (0) 0   36,454

Chelsea: Cech; Bosingwa, Cole, Mikel (Essien 83), Terry, Ivanovic, Ramires, Lampard, Anelka (Torres 68), Drogba, Zhirkov (Malouda 75).
FC Copenhagen: Wiland; Wendt, Bengtsson (Zohore 61), Antonsson, Kvist Jorgensen, Zanka Jorgensen, Gronkjaer, Vingaard (Cesar Santin 74), Claudemir, N'Doye, Bolanos (Kristensen 90).

QUARTER-FINALS FIRST LEG

Internazionale	(2) 2	Schalke	(2) 5
Real Madrid	(1) 4	Tottenham H	(0) 0
Barcelona	(2) 5	Shakhtar Donetsk	(0) 1
Chelsea	(0) 0	Manchester U	(1) 1

Tuesday, 5 April 2011

Real Madrid (1) 4 *(Adebayor 5, 57, Di Maria 72, Cristiano Ronaldo 87)*

Tottenham H (0) 0   71,657

Real Madrid: Casillas; Sergio Ramos, Ricardo Carvalho, Pepe, Marcelo, Xabi Alonso, Ozil, Khedira (Diarra L 61), Di Maria (Kaka 77), Cristiano Ronaldo, Adebayor (Higuain 75).

Tottenham H: Gomes; Corluka (Bassong 79), Assou-Ekotto, Modric, Gallas, Dawson, Van der Vaart (Defoe 46), Jenas, Crouch▪, Sandro, Bale.

Wednesday, 6 April 2011

Chelsea (0) 0

Manchester U (1) 1 *(Rooney 24)*   37,915

Chelsea: Cech; Bosingwa (Mikel 78), Cole, Essien, Terry, Ivanovic, Ramires, Lampard, Torres, Drogba (Anelka 71), Zhirkov (Malouda 70).

Manchester U: Van der Sar; Rafael (Nani 51), Evra, Carrick, Ferdinand, Vidic, Valencia, Park (Smalling 90), Hernandez (Berbatov 78), Rooney, Giggs.

QUARTER-FINALS SECOND LEG

Manchester U	(1) 2	Chelsea	(0) 1
Shakhtar Donetsk	(0) 0	Barcelona	(1) 1
Schalke	(1) 2	Internazionale	(0) 1
Tottenham H	(0) 0	Real Madrid	(0) 1

Tuesday, 12 April 2011

Manchester U (1) 2 *(Hernandez 43, Park 77)*

Chelsea (0) 1 *(Drogba 76)*   74,672

Manchester U: Van der Sar; O'Shea, Evra, Carrick, Ferdinand, Vidic, Park, Giggs, Hernandez, Rooney, Nani (Valencia 75).

Chelsea: Cech; Ivanovic, Cole, Essien, Terry, Alex (Paulo Ferreira 82), Ramires▪, Lampard, Torres (Drogba 46), Anelka (Kalou 60), Malouda.

Wednesday, 13 April 2011

Tottenham H (0) 0

Real Madrid (0) 1 *(Cristiano Ronaldo 50)*   34,311

Tottenham H: Gomes; Corluka, Assou-Ekotto, Huddlestone (Sandro 71), Gallas, Dawson, Lennon (Defoe 61), Modric (Kranjcar 83), Pavlyuchenko, Van der Vaart, Bale.

Real Madrid: Casillas; Sergio Ramos (Granero 57), Ricardo Carvalho, Albiol, Arbeloa, Marcelo, Xabi Alonso (Benzema 75), Ozil, Khedira, Cristiano Ronaldo (Kaka 65), Adebayor.

SEMI-FINALS FIRST LEG

Schalke	(0) 0	Manchester U	(0) 2
Real Madrid	(0) 0	Barcelona	(0) 2

Tuesday, 26 April 2011

Schalke (0) 0

Manchester U (0) 2 *(Giggs 67, Rooney 69)*   54,142

Schalke: Neuer; Metzelder, Sarpei (Sergio 72), Uchida, Papadopoulos, Baumjohann (Kluge 53), Jurado (Draxler 83), Matip, Raul, Edu, Farfan.

Manchester U: Van der Sar; Fabio, Evra, Carrick, Ferdinand, Vidic, Valencia, Park (Anderson 73), Hernandez (Scholes 73), Rooney (Nani 83), Giggs.

Barcelona	(0) 1	Real Madrid	(0) 1
Manchester U	(2) 4	Schalke	(1) 1

Wednesday, 4 May 2011

Manchester U (2) 4 *(Valencia 26, Gibson 31, Anderson 72, 76)*

Schalke (1) 1 *(Jurado 35)*   74,687

Manchester U: Van der Sar; O'Shea, Rafael (Evra 60), Anderson, Smalling, Evans J, Valencia, Scholes (Fletcher 73), Berbatov (Owen 77), Gibson, Nani.

Schalke: Neuer; Metzelder, Uchida, Howedes (Huntelaar 70), Papadopoulos, Sergio, Baumjohann (Edu 46), Jurado, Draxler, Raul, Farfan (Matip 75).

UEFA CHAMPIONS LEAGUE FINAL 2011

Saturday, 28 May 2011

(at Wembley, attendance 87,695)

Barcelona (1) 3 *(Pedro 27, Messi 54, David Villa 70)*

Manchester U (1) 1 *(Rooney 34)*

Barcelona: Valdes; Abidal, Dani Alves (Puyol 88), Pique, Mascherano, Iniesta, Xavi, Sergio Busquets, Messi, David Villa (Keita 86), Pedro (Afellay 90).

Manchester U: Van der Sar; Fabio (Nani 69), Evra, Carrick (Scholes 77), Ferdinand, Vidic, Valencia, Giggs, Hernandez, Rooney, Park.

Referee: V. Kassai (Hungary).

Did You Know?

The 2011 final will go down in history as one of the great football finals of any competition. It also produced some interesting statistics. Barcelona's Lionel Messi became the first player to be outright Champions League top goal scorer in three consecutive seasons in the European Cup and Champions League. His 12 goals also equalled Ruud Van Nistelrooy's tally for Manchester United in 2002–03. The opening goal for Barcelona scored by Pedro was Barcelona's 150th in all competitions and the one by Messi took his total to 53 in similar tournaments. This was also the Argentine player's first in the Champions League on English soil. That pass master in midfield Xavi successfully completed 141 of 148 such attempts to find a colleague, a record for the final. Referee Viktor Kassai became the youngest to officiate in the competition's final stage at the age of 35 years and 260 days.

UEFA CHAMPIONS LEAGUE 2011–2012

PARTICIPATING CLUBS
This list is provisional and subject to final confirmation from UEFA.

UEFA CHAMPIONS LEAGUE GROUP STAGE
FC Barcelona (ESP) – holders
Manchester United FC (ENG)
Chelsea FC (ENG)
Real Madrid CF (ESP)
FC Porto (POR)
FC Internazionale Milano (ITA)
AC Milan (ITA)
FC Shakhtar Donetsk (UKR)
Valencia CF (ESP)
PFC CSKA Moskva (RUS)
Olympique de Marseille (FRA)
FC Zenit St Petersburg (RUS)
AFC Ajax (NED)
Bayer 04 Leverkusen (GER)
Olympiacos FC (GRE)
Fenerbahçe SK (TUR)
Manchester City FC (ENG)
LOSC Lille Métropole (FRA)
FC Basel 1893 (SUI)
Borussia Dortmund (GER)
SSC Napoli (ITA)
FC O elul Gala i (ROU)

UEFA CHAMPIONS LEAGUE PLAY-OFF – LEAGUE ROUTE
FC Bayern München (GER)
Arsenal FC (ENG)
Olympique Lyonnais (FRA)
Villarreal CF (ESP)
Udinese Calcio (ITA)

UEFA CHAMPIONS LEAGUE THIRD QUALIFYING ROUND – LEAGUE ROUTE
SL Benfica (POR)
FC Dynamo Kyiv (UKR)
Panathinaikos FC (GRE)
FC Twente (NED)
R. Standard de Liège (BEL)
FC Rubin Kazan (RUS)
FC Zürich (SUI)
Odense BK (DEN)
Trabzonspor A (TUR)
FC Vaslui (ROU)

UEFA CHAMPIONS LEAGUE THIRD QUALIFYING ROUND – CHAMPIONS ROUTE
Rangers FC (SCO)
FC København (DEN)
KRC Genk (BEL)

UEFA CHAMPIONS LEAGUE SECOND QUALIFYING ROUND
FC BATE Borisov (BLR)
Macabi Haifa FC (ISR)
NK Dinamo Zagreb (CRO)
Rosenborg BK (NOR)
FK Partizan (SRB)
APOEL FC (CYP)
Wisła Kraków (POL)
SK Sturm Graz (AUT)
PFC Litex Lovech (BUL)
ŠK Slovan Bratislava (SVK)
FC Viktoria Plze (CZE)
NK Maribor (SVN)
HJK Helsinki (FIN)
FK Ekranas (LTU)
FC Zestafoni (GEO)
Malmö FF (SWE)
Shamrock Rovers FC (IRL)
FC Dacia Chisinau (MDA)
FC Pyunik (ARM)
FK Borac Banja Luka (BIH)
FK Mogren (MNE)
Skonto FC (LVA)
Videoton FC (HUN)
Bangor City FC (WAL)
HB Tórshavn (FRO)
Linfield FC (NIR)
FC Tobol Kostanay (KAZ)
FC Flora Tallinn (EST)
Breidablik (ISL)
Neftçi PFK (AZE)
FK Skendija 79 (MKD)
KS Skënderbeu (ALB)

UEFA CHAMPIONS LEAGUE FIRST QUALIFYING ROUND
F91 Dudelange (LUX)
Valletta FC (MLT)
FC Santa Coloma (AND)
SP Tre Fiori (SMR)

UEFA EUROPA LEAGUE 2010–2011

■ *Denotes player sent off.* * *Winner after extra time.*

FIRST QUALIFYING ROUND FIRST LEG

Anorthosis	(2) 3	Banants	(0) 0
Dinamo Tbilisi	(1) 2	Flora	(1) 1
Grevenmacher	(0) 3	Dundalk	(1) 3
Kalmar	(0) 1	EB/Streymur	(0) 0
Karabakh	(2) 4	Metalurg	(0) 1
KR Reykjavik	(2) 3	Glentoran	(0) 0
Laci	(1) 1	Dnepr Mogilev	(0) 1
Llanelli	(1) 2	Tauras	(2) 2
Nitra	(1) 2	Gyor	(1) 2
NSI	(0) 0	Gefle	(1) 2
Olimpia	(0) 0	Xazar	(0) 0
Olimpija	(0) 0	Siroki	(1) 2
Portadown	(1) 1	Skonto Riga	(0) 1
Rabotnicki	(2) 5	Lusitanos	(0) 0
Randers	(3) 6	F91 Dudelange	(0) 1
Shakhter Karagandy	(1) 1	Ruch	(1) 2
Sibenik	(0) 0	Sliema Wanderers	(0) 0
SK Tirana	(0) 0	Zalaegerszegi	(0) 0
Tobol	(1) 1	Zrinjski	(0) 2
Torpedo Zhodino	(0) 3	Fylkir	(0) 0
TPS Turku	(3) 3	Port Talbot Town	(0) 1
Trans	(0) 0	MyPa	(0) 2
UE Santa Coloma	(0) 0	Mogren	(1) 3
Ulisses	(0) 0	Bnei Yehuda	(0) 0
Zestafoni	(3) 5	Faetano	(0) 0
Zeta	(0) 1	Dacia	(1) 1

Thursday, 1 July 2010

Grevenmacher (0) 3 *(Heinz 63, Gaspar 73, Almeida 76)*

Dundalk (1) 3 *(Kudozovic 26, Hatswell 51, Benichou 80 (og))*   731

Grevenmacher: Pleimling; Heinz, Mendes (Almeida 67), Furst, Louadj, Hartung, Benichou, Baur (Stojadinovic 90), Gaspar, Hoffmann, Muller (Braun 83).
Dundalk: Gregg; Hatswell, Kelly, Breen G, Murphy N (McGuigan 62), Cawley, Maher, Miller, Fenn, Kudozovic, Gaynor (McGowan 79).

KR Reykjavik (2) 3 *(Gunnarsson 12, Finnbogason 32, Takefusa 62)*

Glentoran (0) 0   813

KR Reykjavik: Moldskred; Fridgeirsson, Gunnarsson, Sigurdarson, Rutgers, Amarsson, Gudjonsson, Sigurdsson B, Hauksson (Kristjansson 84), Takefusa (Baldvinsson 81), Finnbogason (Jonsson G 88).
Glentoran: Morris; Hill, Ward, McGovern, Johnny Taylor, Fordyce, Gawley (Southam 66), McCabe (Gardiner 46), Clarke, Hamilton, Waterworth (Black 66).

Llanelli (1) 2 *(Thomas D 17, Jones S 47)*

Tauras (2) 2 *(Kizys 9, 20)*   556

Llanelli: Morris; Jones S, Thomas D, Giles, Thomas C, Llewellyn (Legg 77), Corbisiero, Holloway■, Venables, Follows (Griffiths 62), Moses.
Tauras: Kilijonas; Regelskis, Vaitkus, Mockus, Kizys, Jasaitis, Maciulis, Buitkus, Savastas (Gedgaudas 66), Lekis, Daunoravicius (Jose Vide 46).

Portadown (1) 1 *(Lecky 38)*
Skonto Riga (0) 1 *(Laizans 90)* 571

Portadown: Armstrong; Kelly, O'Hara, Redman, Ramsey∎, McCafferty (Mackle 73), Mouncey, Boyle, Clarke, Lecky, Teggart (Haire 83).
Skonto Riga: Ikstens (Malins 46); Smirnovs, Rode, Laizans, Tarasovs, Fertovs, Dubra, Sinelnikovs (Petersons 16), Maksimenko, Karasausks, Nathan Junior.

TPS Turku (3) 3 *(Riku Riski 24, 35, Wusu 30)*
Port Talbot Town (0) 1 *(Rose 70)* 1405

TPS Turku: Moisander; Rahmonen, Jovanovic, Nyberg, Manninen, Riku Riski (Virtanen 75), Cleaver, Kolehmainen, Johansson, Aaritalo (Roope Riski 78), Wusu.
Port Talbot Town: Kendall; De Vulgt (Holland 46), Surman, Rees, Barrow, Phillips, Lewis, Grist, John (Bowen 87), McCreesh, Rose (Fahiya 87).

FIRST QUALIFYING ROUND SECOND LEG

Banants	(0) 0	Anorthosis	(1) 1
Bnei Yehuda	(1) 1	Ulisses	(0) 0
Dacia	(0) 0	Zeta	(0) 0
Dnepr Mogilev	(3) 7	Laci	(0) 1
Dundalk	(2) 2	Grevenmacher	(0) 1
EB/Streymur	(0) 0	Kalmar	(1) 3
F91 Dudelange	(1) 2	Randers	(1) 1
Faetano	(0) 0	Zestafoni	(0) 0
Flora	(0) 0	Dinamo Tbilisi	(0) 0
Fylkir	(1) 1	Torpedo Zhodino	(1) 3
Gefle	(1) 2	NSI	(0) 1
Glentoran	(1) 2	KR Reykjavik	(1) 2
Gyor	(1) 3	Nitra	(1) 1
Lusitanos	(0) 0	Rabotnicki	(3) 6
Metalurg	(0) 1	Karabakh	(0) 1
Mogren	(2) 2	UE Santa Coloma	(0) 0
MyPa	(0) 5	Trans	(0) 0
Port Talbot Town	(0) 0	TPS Turku	(2) 4
Ruch	(0) 1	Shakhter Karagandy	(0) 0
Siroki	(0) 3	Olimpija	(0) 0
Skonto Riga	(0) 0	Portadown	(1) 1
Sliema Wanderers	(0) 0	Sibenik	(0) 3
Tauras	(2) 3	Llanelli	(2) 2
(aet.)			
Xazar	(0) 1	Olimpia	(1) 1
Zalaegerszegi	(0) 0	SK Tirana	(0) 1
(aet.)			
Zrinjski	(1) 2	Tobol	(0) 1

Thursday, 8 July 2010

Dundalk (2) 2 *(Fenn 5 (pen), Kudozovic 16)*
Grevenmacher (0) 1 *(Muller 90)* 2000

Dundalk: Gregg; Hatswell, Kelly, Breen G, Cawley, Maher (McDonnell 77), Miller, Fenn, Kudozovic (Breen J 90), Mulvenna (McGowan 71), Gaynor.
Grevenmacher: Pleimling; Heinz, Mendes (Almeida 61), Furst, Louadj, Hartung, Benichou (Lorig 46), Baur, Gaspar (Brzyski 72), Hoffmann, Muller.

Glentoran (1) 2 *(Callacher 22, Hamilton 56 (pen))*

KR Reykjavik (1) 2 *(Finnbogason 45, Black 54 (og))* 771

Glentoran: Morris; Nixon, Ward, McGovern, Black, Gawley, Clarke, Gardiner (Martyn 56), Callacher (Fordyce 75), Hamilton, Waterworth.

KR Reykjavik: Moldskred; Fridgeirsson■, Gunnarsson (Jonsson G 80), Sigurdarson, Rutgers, Amarsson (Eggert Einarsson 56), Gudjonsson, Sigurdsson B, Hauksson, Takefusa (Jordao Diogo 66), Finnbogason.

Port Talbot Town (0) 0

TPS Turku (2) 4 *(Wusu 26, Kolehmainen 32, Riku Riski 69, Roope Riski 90)* 676

Port Talbot Town: Kendall; Holland (Brooks 46), Surman, Palmer (Thomas D 67), Rees, Barrow, Lewis, Grist, John, McCreesh (Bowen 76), Rose.

TPS Turku: Moisander; Rahmonen, Heinikangas (Jovanovic 63), Nyberg, Manninen (Milsom 46), Riku Riski, Cleaver, Kolehmainen, Johansson, Aaritalo, Wusu (Roope Riski 55).

Skonto Riga (0) 0

Portadown (1) 1 *(Lecky 29)* 6000

Skonto Riga: Ikstens; Smirnovs, Rode, Laizans, Tarasovs (Petersons 33), Fertovs, Dubra, Maksimenko (Astafjevs 59), Pereplotkins, Karasausks (Turkovs 46), Nathan Junior.

Portadown: Miskelly; Kelly, O'Hara, Redman, Mackle, Mouncey, Boyle, Clarke (McCafferty 85), Braniff, Lecky, Teggart (Haire 79).

Tauras (2) 3 *(Irkha 17, 31, Regelskis 104)*

Llanelli (2) 2 *(Llewellyn 19, Bowen 36)* 350

Tauras: Kilijonas; Regelskis, Vaitkus, Mockus, Kizys, Jasaitis (Jose Vide 69), Maciulis, Savastas, Lekis■, Daunoravicius (Gedgaudas 38), Irkha.

Llanelli: Morris; Jones S (Follows 114), Thomas D, Giles, Thomas C, Bowen, Llewellyn (Legg 106), Corbisiero, Venables, Griffiths■, Moses■.

SECOND QUALIFYING ROUND FIRST LEG

Anorthosis	(0) 0	Sibenik	(1) 2
Atyrau	(0) 0	Gyor	(1) 2
Baku	(0) 2	Buducnost	(1) 1
Besa	(0) 0	Olympiakos	(2) 5
Besiktas	(1) 3	Vikingur	(0) 0
Brondby	(0) 3	Vaduz	(0) 0
Cliftonville	(0) 1	Cibalia	(0) 0
CS Brugge	(0) 0	TPS Turku	(1) 1
Differdange	(2) 3	Spartak Subotica	(2) 3
Dynamo Minsk	(2) 5	Sillamae	(0) 1
Elfsborg	(0) 2	Iskra-Stal	(0) 1
FK Austria	(0) 2	Siroki	(1) 2
(Behind closed doors.)			
Gefle	(0) 1	Dinamo Tbilisi	(1) 2
Gorica	(0) 0	Randers	(0) 3
Honka	(1) 1	Bangor City	(0) 1
Kalmar	(0) 0	Dacia	(0) 0
KR Reykjavik	(0) 0	Karpaty	(0) 3
Lausanne	(1) 1	Borac	(0) 0
Levski	(3) 6	Dundalk	(0) 0
Maccabi Tel Aviv	(0) 2	Mogren	(0) 0

Maritimo	(0) 3	Sporting Fingal	(1) 2
Molde	(0) 1	Jelgava	(0) 0
Motherwell	(0) 1	Breidablik	(0) 0
MyPa	(1) 3	Sant Julia	(0) 0
OFK Belgrade	(1) 2	Torpedo Zhodino	(1) 2
Olimpia	(0) 0	Dinamo Bucharest	(1) 2
Portadown	(1) 1	Karabakh	(0) 2
Rabotnicki	(0) 1	Mika	(0) 0
Shamrock Rovers	(0) 1	Bnei Yehuda	(1) 1
Siauliai	(0) 0	Wilsa	(0) 2
Stabaek	(1) 2	Dnepr Mogliev	(2) 2
Suduva	(0) 0	Rapid Vienna	(1) 2
Tauras	(0) 0	Apoel	(0) 3
Utrecht	(3) 4	SK Tirana	(0) 0
Valletta	(0) 1	Ruch	(1) 1
Ventspils	(0) 0	Teteks	(0) 0
Videoton	(0) 1	Maribor	(1) 1
WIT Georgia	(0) 0	Banik Ostrava	(1) 6
Zestafoni	(1) 3	Bystrica	(0) 0
Zrinjski	(4) 4	Tre Penne	(1) 1

Thursday, 15 July 2010

Cliftonville (0) 1 *(Caldwell 82)*

Cibalia (0) 0   775

Cliftonville: Connolly; Scannell R, Donaghy, Holland B, Catney, McMullan, Caldwell, Holland M, Scannell C (O'Connor 83), Garrett, Boyce (Patterson 90).
Cibalia: Matkovic; Parmakovic, Bozic, Lucic, Tomic, Radotic (Prgomet 86), Juric, Grgic (Kvesic 89), Mazalovic, Baraban (Simunac 81), Kresinger.

Honka (1) 1 *(Savage 43)*

Bangor City (0) 1 *(Jones C 58)*   1279

Honka: Peltonen; Koskinen, Heikkila, Aalto (Otaru 79), Koskimaa, Lepola, Paatelainen (Vasara 65), Schuller, Vuorinen (Rasimus 71), Puustinen, Savage.
Bangor City: Smith; Morley, Roberts, Brewerton (Edwards 52), Hoy, Johnston, Garside, Davies (Williams 79), Ward, Jebb (Bull 61), Jones C.

Levski (3) 6 *(Yovov 12, Mladenov 14, 46, Dembele 42, Isa 86, 90)*

Dundalk (0) 0   8655

Levski: Petkov; Minev, Stanchev, Miliev, Ivanov, Gadzhev, Joazinho, Tasevski (Aleksandrov 64), Yovov (Baltanov 52), Dembele (Isa 77), Mladenov.
Dundalk: Cherrie; Hatswell, Kelly, Breen G, McGuigan, Cawley, Maher, Miller, Fenn (Lennon 60), Kudozovic (McGowan 80), Gaynor.

Maritimo (0) 3 *(Ricardo Esteves 78, Cherrad 85, Tcho 90)*

Sporting Fingal (1) 2 *(Crowe 33, Fitzgerald 87)*   1961

Maritimo: Pecanha; Robson, Alonso, Joao Guilherme, Roberto De Sousa, Ricardo Esteves, Tcho, Kanu (Danilo Dias 46), Djalma Campos (Luciano Amaral 74), Baba, Marquinho (Cherrad 46).
Sporting Fingal: Clarke; Browne, O'Brien, Hawkins (Maher 73), Fitzgerald, Kirby, McFaul, Byrne (Cahill 88), Finn, Williams, Crowe (Zayed 64).

Motherwell (0) 1 *(Forbes 63)*

Breidablik (0) 0 5990

Motherwell: Randolph; Craigan, Reynolds, Hammell, Lasley, Forbes (Saunders 72), Humphrey (Smith 59), Jennings, Hateley, Sutton, Murphy.
Breidablik: Kale; Adalsteinsson, Jonsson, Helgason, Arsaelsson, Kristjansson, Elisabetarson, Steindorsson (Sigurgeirsson 73), Margeirsson, Petursson, Finnbogason.

Portadown (1) 1 *(Lecky 29)*

Karabakh (0) 2 *(Ismayilov 67, 86)* 765

Portadown: Miskelly; Kelly, O'Hara, Redman, Ramsey, McCafferty, Mouncey, Boyle, Braniff (Haire 80), Lecky, Teggart.
Karabakh: Veliyev; Rashad F Sadygov, Abbasov, Medvedev, Gashimov, Garayev, Rashad A Sadygov, Imamaliyev (Aliyev 46), Mammadov E (Kerimov 76), Ismayilov, Adamia (Nadirov 82).

Shamrock Rovers (0) 1 *(Bayly 90)*

Bnei Yehuda (1) 1 *(Afek 26)* 4850

Shamrock Rovers: Mannus; Murray, Price (Dennehy W 64), Sives, Stevens, Rice, Turner (Bayly 71), Kavanagh, Chambers, Stewart, Twigg.
Bnei Yehuda: Aiyenugba; Garrido, Azoz, Hadad, Linic, Edri, Baldut, Zairi, Menashe (Abu Zaid 73), Biton (Afek 19), Yavruyan (Rali 57).

SECOND QUALIFYING ROUND SECOND LEG

Apoel	(1) 3	Tauras	(0) 1
Bangor City	(0) 2	Honka	(1) 1
(At Wrexham.)			
Banik Ostrava	(0) 0	WIT Georgia	(0) 0
Bnei Yehuda	(0) 0	Shamrock Rovers	(0) 1
Borac	(0) 1	Lausanne	(0) 1
Breidablik	(0) 0	Motherwell	(1) 1
Buducnost	(0) 1	Baku	(2) 2

(Baku given two match suspension for fielding an ineligible player; tie awarded to Buducnost.)

Bystrica	(1) 1	Zestafoni	(0) 0
Cibalia	(0) 0	Cliftonville	(0) 0
Dacia	(0) 0	Kalmar	(1) 2
Dinamo Bucharest	(3) 5	Olimpia	(0) 1
Dinamo Tbilisi	(0) 2	Gefle	(0) 1
Dnepr Mogilev	(0) 1	Stabaek	(1) 1
Dundalk	(0) 0	Levski	(2) 2
Gyor	(0) 2	Atyrau	(0) 0
Iskra-Stal	(0) 0	Elfsborg	(0) 1
Jelgava	(2) 2	Molde	(1) 1
Karabakh	(0) 1	Portadown	(0) 1
Karpaty	(2) 3	KR Reykjavik	(0) 2
Maribor	(1) 2	Videoton	(0) 0
Mika	(0) 0	Rabotnicki	(0) 0
Mogren	(0) 2	Maccabi Tel Aviv	(1) 1
Olympiakos	(0) 6	Besa	(0) 1
Randers	(1) 1	Gorica	(0) 1
Rapid Vienna	(1) 4	Suduva	(0) 2

Ruch	(0) 0	Valletta	(0) 0
Sibenik	(0) 0	Anorthosis	(2) 3
(aet.)			
Sillamae	(0) 0	Dynamo Minsk	(3) 5
Siroki	(0) 0	FK Austria	(0) 1
SK Tirana	(1) 1	Utrecht	(1) 1
Spartak Subotica	(1) 2	Differdange	(0) 0
Sporting Fingal	(0) 2	Maritimo	(1) 3
Teteks	(2) 3	Ventspils	(0) 1
Torpedo Zhodino	(0) 0	OFK Belgrade	(0) 1
TPS Turku	(1) 1	CS Brugge	(0) 2
Tre Penne	(1) 2	Zrinjski	(4) 9
Vaduz	(0) 0	Brondby	(0) 0
Vikingur	(0) 0	Besiktas	(4) 4
Wisla	(1) 5	Siauliai	(0) 0
Sant Julia	(0) 0	MyPa	(2) 5

(Original match on 22 July suspended at 0-1 due to thunderstorms.)

Thursday, 22 July 2010

Bangor City (0) 2 *(Morley 84, Jones C 90)*

Honka (1) 1 *(Koskinen 21)* 954

Bangor City: Smith; Morley, Roberts, Brewerton, Hoy, Johnston, Edwards, Davies, Ward, Jebb (Bull 62), Jones C.
Honka: Peltonen; Koskinen, Heilala, Koskimaa, Otaru, Lepola, Paatelainen (Vasara 70), Schuller, Vuorinen, Puustinen, Savage.
At Wrexham.

Bnei Yehuda (0) 0

Shamrock Rovers (0) 1 *(Stewart 70)* 1784

Bnei Yehuda: Aiyenugba; Garrido, Azoz (Baldut 79), Hadad, Linic (Menashe 74), Edri, Rali, Zairi, Afek, Abu Zaid (Levi 90), Yavruyan.
Shamrock Rovers: Mannus; Murray, Price, Sives, Stevens, Rice, Turner (Bradley 84), Chambers (Dennehy W 64), Bayly (Kavanagh 58), Stewart, Twigg.

Breidablik (0) 0

Motherwell (1) 1 *(Murphy 42)* 1700

Breidablik: Kale; Adalsteinsson, Jonsson (Gunnarsson 78), Helgason, Arsaelsson, Kristjansson, Elisabetarson, Steindorsson, Margeirsson (Baldvinsson 72), Petursson (Yeoman 61), Finnbogason.
Motherwell: Randolph; Craigan, Reynolds, Hammell, Saunders, Lasley, Forbes (Humphrey 74), Jennings, Hateley, Sutton (Pollock 83), Murphy (McHugh 87).

Cibalia (0) 0

Cliftonville (0) 0 5200

Cibalia: Matkovic; Parmakovic, Bozic (Culjak 68), Lucic, Tomic, Radotic, Juric, Mazalovic (Grgic 46), Baraban, Malcic (Prgomet 46), Kresinger.
Cliftonville: Connolly; Scannell R, Donaghy, Holland B, Catney, McMullan, Caldwell (Smyth 85), Holland M (O'Hara 40), Scannell C (Patterson 81), Garrett, Boyce.

Dundalk (0) 0

Levski (2) 2 *(Dembele 4, 33)* 1000

Dundalk: Cherrie; Hatswell, Kelly, Breen G, McGuigan, Maher, Lennon (Mulvenna 59), Miller, McDonnell, Kudozovic, Gaynor.
Levski: Petkov; Mulder, Minev, Miliev, Ivanov, Gadzhev (Ognyanov 61), Baltanov, Joaozinho (Kirov 71), Tasevski, Dembele (Isa 56), Mladenov.

Karabakh (0) 1 *(Ismayilov 83)*

Portadown (0) 1 *(Braniff 71)* 20,000

Karabakh: Veliyev; Rashad F Sadygov, Abbasov, Teli, Medvedev, Agolli, Rashad A Sadygov, Mammadov E (Nadirov 63), Ismayilov, Adamia, Aliyev (Kerimov 76).
Portadown: Miskelly; O'Hara, Redman, Ramsey, McCafferty, Mackle (Coleman 90), Mouncey, Boyle, Clarke (McCullough 85), Braniff, Teggart (Haire 70).

Sporting Fingal (0) 2 *(Zayed 81, 90)*

Maritimo (1) 3 *(Alonso 20 (pen), Marquinho 67, Kanu 87)* 2150

Sporting Fingal: Clarke; Browne, O'Brien, Maher, Fitzgerald, Kirby, McFaul (Zayed 64), Byrne, Finn, Williams, Crowe.
Maritimo: Pecanha; Robson, Alonso, Joao Guilherme, Roberto De Sousa, Ricardo Esteves, Tcho (Kanu 81), Cherrad (Fidelis 90), Baba, Marquinho (Luciano Amaral 72), Danilo Dias.

THIRD QUALIFYING ROUND FIRST LEG

CSKA Sofia	(1) 3	Cliftonville	(0) 0
Aalesund	(0) 1	Motherwell	(0) 1
Apoel	(0) 1	Jablonec	(0) 0
AZ	(0) 2	IFK Gotheburg	(0) 0
Beroe	(0) 1	Rapid Vienna	(1) 1
Buducnost	(0) 1	Brondby	(0) 2
CS Brugge	(0) 1	Anorthosis	(0) 0
Dinamo Bucharest	(2) 3	Hajduk Split	(0) 1
Dnepr Mogliev	(0) 1	Banik Ostrava	(0) 0
Elfsborg	(1) 5	Teteks	(0) 0
Galatasaray	(1) 2	OFK Belgrade	(0) 2
Gyor	(0) 0	Montpellier	(1) 1
Inter Turku	(0) 1	Genk	(2) 5
Jagiellonia	(1) 1	Aris Salonika	(2) 2
Kalmar	(0) 1	Levski	(1) 1
Karpaty	(1) 1	Zestafoni	(0) 0
Maccabi Haifa	(1) 1	Dynamo Minsk	(0) 0
Maribor	(1) 3	Hibernian	(0) 0
Maritimo	(2) 8	Bangor City	(0) 2
Molde	(0) 2	Stuttgart	(1) 3
MyPa	(0) 1	Timisoara	(1) 2
Nordsjaelland	(0) 0	Sporting Lisbon	(1) 1
Odense	(4) 5	Zrinjski	(1) 3
Olympiakos	(0) 2	Maccabi Tel Aviv	(1) 1
(Behind closed doors.)			
Rabotnicki	(0) 0	Liverpool	(1) 2
Randers	(1) 2	Lausanne	(1) 3
Red Star Belgrade	(0) 1	Slovan Bratislava	(1) 2
Ruch	(1) 1	FK Austria	(2) 3
Shamrock Rovers	(0) 0	Juventus	(1) 2

Sibir	(0) 1	Apollon	(0) 0
Spartak Subotica	(1) 2	Dnepr	(1) 1
Sturm Graz	(0) 2	Dinamo Tbilisi	(0) 0
Utrecht	(1) 1	Lucerne	(0) 0
Viktoria Plzen	(1) 1	Besiktas	(1) 1
Wisla	(0) 0	Karabakh	(0) 1

Tuesday, 27 July 2010

CSKA Sofia (1) 3 *(Vidanov 9, Marquinhos 72, Trifonov 74)*

Cliftonville (0) 0   2500

CSKA Sofia: Karadzhov; Minev, Trifonov, Vidanov, Aquaro, Stoyanov K, Marquinhos, Yanchev, Galchev (Yanev 86), Tonev (Kostadinov 70), Rui Miguel (Iliev 59).
Cliftonville: Connolly; Hutton, Scannell R, Donaghy, Holland B, Catney, McMullan, Caldwell, Scanell C (O'Connor 78), Garrett■, Boyce.

Thursday, 29 July 2010

Aalesund (0) 1 *(Mathisen 90 (pen))*

Motherwell (0) 1 *(Murphy 48)*   8450

Aalesund: Lindegaard; Arnefjord, Jaager, Jalasto, Arneng, Larsen (Fredriksen 56), Herrera (Mathisen 57), Phillips, Aaroy, Parr, Olsen (Carlsen 70).
Motherwell: Randolph; Craigan, Reynolds, Hammell, Saunders, Lasley, Forbes (Humphrey 46), Jennings, Hateley, Sutton (McHugh 46), Murphy.

Maribor (1) 3 *(Ilicic 31, 52, Marcos Tavares 60)*

Hibernian (0) 0   9200

Maribor: Pridigar; Rajcevic, Viler, Andelkovic, Mejac, Mezga (Cvijanovic 71), Bacinovic, Mertelj, Ilicic (Pavlicic 79), Marcos Tavares, Volas (Plut 90).
Hibernian: Stack; Murray, Hogg, Hart, Hanlon, McBride (Stokes 68), Rankin, De Graaf, Miller, Wotherspoon (Galbraith 77), Nish (Riordan 68).

Maritimo (2) 8 *(Tcho 33, 79, Danilo Dias 38, 75, Baba 51, 78, Kanu 80, Fidelis 89)*

Bangor City (0) 2 *(Ward 73, Jebb 90)*   2000

Maritimo: Marcelo Boeck; Robson, Alonso, Joao Guilherme, Roberto De Sousa, Ricardo Esteves, Tcho (Fidelis 83), Cherrad (Rafael Miranda 70), Baba, Marquinho (Kanu 64), Danilo Dias.
Bangor City: Smith; Morley, Roberts, Brewerton■, Hoy, Johnston, Williams (Jebb 66), Bull, Edwards, Davies (Ward 46), Jones C (Hurdman 81).

Rabotnicki (0) 0

Liverpool (1) 2 *(N'Gog 17, 59)*   23,000

Rabotnicki: Bogatinov; Dimovski, Sekulovski (Adem 44), Fernando, Belica, Gligorov, Todorovski, Ze Carlos (Mojsov 57), Tuneski (Petkovski 78), Wandeir, Fabio.
Liverpool: Cavalieri; Kyrgiakos, Agger (Darby 72), Skrtel, Kelly, Aquilani (Dalla Valle 83), Lucas, Spearing, N'Gog, Jovanovic, Amoo (Eccleston 84).

Shamrock Rovers (0) 0

Juventus (1) 2 *(Amauri 3, 75)*   5800

Shamrock Rovers: Mannus; Murray, Price, Sives, Stevens, Rice (Dennehy W 66), Turner, Chambers (Kavanagh 78), Bayly (Bradley 90), Stewart, Twigg.
Juventus: Storari; Bonucci, Motta, Chiellini, De Ceglie, Diego (Del Piero 82), Sissoko, Pepe, Marchisio (Ekdal 89), Amauri, Lanzafame (Martinez 52).

THIRD QUALIFYING ROUND SECOND LEG

Rapid Vienna	(1) 3	Beroe	(0) 0
Anorthosis	(1) 3	CS Brugge	(0) 1
Apollon	(1) 2	Sibir	(0) 1
Aris Salonika	(1) 2	Jagiellonia	(1) 2
Bangor City	(1) 1	Maritimo	(0) 2
(At Wrexham.)			
Banik Ostrava	(1) 1	Dnepr Mogilev	(1) 2
Besiktas	(1) 3	Viktoria Plzen	(0) 0
Brondby	(1) 1	Buducnost	(0) 0
Cliftonville	(1) 1	CSKA Sofia	(0) 2
Dinamo Tbilisi	(1) 1	Sturm Graz	(1) 1
Dnepr	(1) 2	Spartak Subotica	(0) 0
Dynamo Minsk	(1) 3	Maccabi Haifa	(1) 1
FK Austria	(3) 3	Ruch	(0) 0
Genk	(1) 3	Inter Turku	(1) 2
Hajduk Split	(3) 3	Dinamo Bucharest	(0) 0
Hibernian	(0) 2	Maribor	(1) 3
IFK Gothenburg	(0) 1	AZ	(0) 0
Jablonec	(1) 1	Apoel	(3) 3
Juventus	(0) 1	Shamrock Rovers	(0) 0
Karabakh	(3) 3	Wisla	(0) 2
Lausanne	(0) 1	Randers	(0) 1
Levski	(2) 5	Kalmar	(0) 2
Liverpool	(2) 2	Rabotnicki	(0) 0
Lucerne	(0) 1	Utrecht	(3) 3
Maccabi Tel Aviv	(1) 1	Olympiakos	(0) 0
Montpellier	(0) 0	Gyor	(1) 1
(aet; Gyor won 4-3 on penalties.)			
Motherwell	(2) 3	Aalesund	(0) 0
OFK Belgrade	(1) 1	Galatasaray	(2) 5
Slovan Bratislava	(1) 1	Red Star Belgrade	(0) 1
Sporting Lisbon	(1) 2	Nordsjaelland	(0) 1
Stuttgart	(0) 2	Molde	(1) 2
Teteks	(1) 1	Elfsborg	(1) 2
Timisoara	(0) 3	MyPa	(3) 3
Zestafoni	(0) 0	Karpaty	(0) 1
Zrinjski	(0) 0	Odense	(0) 0

Thursday, 5 August 2010

Bangor City (1) 1 *(Bull 9)*

Maritimo (0) 2 *(Adilson 48, Marquinho 58)* 556

Bangor City: Smith; Morley, Roberts, Hoy, Johnston, Bull, Garside (Hurdman 67), Edwards (Williams 77), Ward, Jebb (Davies 66), Jones C.

Maritimo: Marcelo Boeck; Briguel, Luciano Amaral, Robson, Joao Guilherme, Rafael Miranda, Tcho, Baba, Marquinho (Dylan 80), Danilo Dias (Luis Olim 63), Adilson (Fidelis 72).

At Wrexham.

Cliftonville (1) 1 *(Boyce 42)*

CSKA Sofia (0) 2 *(Kostadinov 85, Marquinhos 88)* 776

Cliftonville: Connolly; Hutton, Scannell R, Donaghy■, Holland B, Catney (Patterson 80), McMullan, O'Connor (Smyth 74), Caldwell, Scannell C, Boyce.
CSKA Sofia: Karadzhov; Popov, Trifonov, Vidanov, Aquaro, Grandin, Yanev, Marquinhos, Yanchev (Galchev 67), Iliev (Rui Miguel 58), Delev (Kostadinov 81).

Hibernian (0) 2 *(De Graaf 54, 89)*

Maribor (1) 3 *(Marcos Tavares 20, 73, Mezga 67 (pen))* 13,500

Hibernian: Smith; Murray (Wotherspoon 70), Hogg, Hart (Galbraith 70), Bamba, McBride, De Graaf, Miller, Riodan, Nish, Stokes.
Maribor: Pridigar; Rajcevic, Viler, Andelkovic, Mejac, Mezga (Cvijanovic 90), Bacinovic, Mertelj, Ilicic, Marcos Tavares, Volas (Plut 90).

Juventus (0) 1 *(Del Piero 74)*

Shamrock Rovers (0) 0 17,579

Juventus: Storari; Bonucci, Motta, Chiellini, De Ceglie, Diego (Del Piero 46), Sissoko, Pepe, Marchisio, Amauri (Trezeguet 81), Lanzafame.
Shamrock Rovers: Mannus; Flynn, Murray, Price, Murphy, Rice (Bayly 59), Bradley, Kavanagh (Stewart 46), Chambers (Turner 46), Dennehy W, Twigg.

Liverpool (2) 2 *(N'Gog 22, Gerrard 40 (pen))*

Rabotnicki (0) 0 31,202

Liverpool: Cavalieri; Carragher, Johnson, Skrtel, Kelly, Cole, Gerrard (Aquilani 62), Lucas (Spearing 73), N'Gog, Jovanovic (Rodriguez 67), Pacheco.
Rabotnicki: Bogatinov; Dimovski, Adem, Fernando, Belica, Gligorov, Todorovski (Petkovski 88), Ze Carlos (Mojsov 62), Tuneski, Wandeir, Fabio (Marcio 81).

Motherwell (2) 3 *(Murphy 4, Sutton 13, Page 89)*

Aalesund (0) 0 7721

Motherwell: Randolph; Craigan, Reynolds, Hammell, Saunders, Lasley (Fitzpatrick 74), Humphrey, Jennings (Forbes 90), Hateley, Sutton (Page 86), Murphy.
Aalesund: Lindegaard; Jalasto, Tollas, Arneng, Fredriksen, Mathisen (Flotre 65), Larsen (Karlsen 70), Herrera, Aaroy, Parr, Olsen.

PLAY-OFF ROUND FIRST LEG

Aris Salonika	(0) 1	FK Austria	(0) 0
Besiktas	(1) 2	HJK Helsinki	(0) 0
AIK Stockholm	(0) 0	Levski	(0) 0
AZ	(2) 2	Aktobe	(0) 0
BATE Borisov	(0) 3	Maritimo	(0) 0
Borussia Dortmund	(4) 4	Karabakh	(0) 0
Celtic	(2) 2	Utrecht	(0) 0
Club Brugge	(0) 2	Dynamo Minsk	(1) 1
CSKA Moscow	(2) 4	Anorthosis	(0) 0
CSKA Sofia	(0) 3	The New Saints	(0) 0
Debrecen	(2) 2	Litex	(0) 0
Dnepr	(0) 0	Lech	(1) 1
Dundee U	(0) 0	AEK Athens	(1) 1
Feyenoord	(0) 1	Gent	(0) 0
Galatasaray	(0) 2	Karpaty	(2) 2
Genk	(0) 0	Porto	(1) 3

Getafe	(1) 1	Apoel	(0) 0
Gyor	(0) 0	Dinamo Zagreb	(2) 2
Hajduk Split	(1) 4	Unirea	(1) 1
Lausanne	(1) 1	Lokomotiv Moscow	(0) 1
Leverkusen	(1) 3	Tavriya	(0) 0
Liverpool	(1) 1	Trabzonspor	(0) 0
Napoli	(1) 1	Elfsborg	(0) 0
Odense	(1) 2	Motherwell	(0) 1
Omonia	(0) 0	Metalist Kharkiv	(1) 1
Palermo	(2) 3	Maribor	(0) 0
PAOK Salonika	(1) 1	Fenerbahce	(0) 0
Paris St Germain	(1) 2	Maccabi Tel Aviv	(0) 0
Rapid Vienna	(1) 1	Aston Villa	(1) 1
Sibir	(0) 1	PSV Eindhoven	(0) 0
Slovan Bratislava	(0) 0	Stuttgart	(0) 1
Sporting Lisbon	(0) 0	Brondby	(1) 2
Steaua	(0) 1	Grasshoppers	(0) 0
Sturm Graz	(0) 1	Juventus	(1) 2
Timisoara	(0) 0	Manchester C	(0) 1
Vaslui	(0) 0	Lille	(0) 0
Villarreal	(4) 5	Dnepr Mogilev	(0) 0

Thursday, 19 August 2010

Celtic (2) 2 *(Juarez 19, Samaras 34)*

Utrecht (0) 0   35,755

Celtic: Zaluska; Cha, Juarez, Brown, Majstorovic, Loovens, Kayal (Forrest 69), Ledley, Samaras, Maloney, Fortune.
Utrecht: Vorm; Wuytens, Schut, Cornelisse, Nesu, Silberbauer, Lensky (Nijholt 82), Asare, Mulenga (Duplan 17), Mertens, Van Wolfswinkel.

Dundee U (0) 0

AEK Athens (1) 1 *(Djebbour 11)*   12,116

Dundee U: Pernis; Dillon, Dixon, Buaben, Kenneth, Watson, Robertson S (Cadamarteri 81), Gomis, Daly, Goodwillie, Conway.
AEK Athens: Saja; Dallas, Jahic, Manolas, Makos, Leonardo (Burns 71), Kafes, Lagos, Liberopoulos (Eder 89), Nacho Scocco, Djebbour (Bouba Diop 82).

Liverpool (1) 1 *(Babel 45)*

Trabzonspor (0) 0   40,941

Liverpool: Reina; Kelly, Kyrgiakos, Poulsen, Carragher, Fabio Aurelio, Lucas, Rodriguez (N'Gog 73), Jovanovic, Cole, Babel (Torres 46).
Trabzonspor: Onur; Egemen, Glowacki, Cale, Serkan, Burak (Alanzinho 56), Selcuk, Colman (Remzi 77), Ceyhun, Umut (Yattara 86), Gutierrez.

Odense (1) 2 *(Sorensen 31, Utaka 78)*

Motherwell (0) 1 *(Hateley 90)*   5127

Odense: Carroll; Haland, Ruud, Moller Christensen, Sorensen, Gislason (Johansson 74), Djemba-Djemba, Caca (Hansen H 46), Andreasen, Absalonsen, Utaka.
Motherwell: Randolph; Saunders, Hammell, Reynolds, Craigan, Hateley, Humphrey, Jennings■, Sutton (McHugh 85), Murphy (Blackman 73), Lasley (Forbes 72).

Rapid Vienna (1) 1 *(Nuhiu 33)*
Aston Villa (1) 1 *(Bannan 12)*   17,500
Rapid Vienna: Hedl; Soma, Katzer, Sonnleitner, Hofmann, Kavlak, Heikkinen, Hinum (Drazan 86), Kayhan, Salihi (Gartler 73), Nuhiu.
Aston Villa: Guzan; Beye, Warnock, Reo-Coker, Davies, Lichaj, Albrighton (Weimann 79) (Osbourne 86), Bannan (Delfouneso 74), Hogg, Heskey, Downing.

Timisoara (0) 0
Manchester C (0) 1 *(Balotelli 72)*   24,695
Timisoara: Pantilimo; Sepsi, Scutaru (Zicu 71), Luchin, Cisovsky, Contra (Mera 80), Alexa, Curtean, Bourceanu, Magera (Goga 83), Axente.
Manchester C: Hart; Toure K, Lescott, De Jong, Zabaleta, Kompany, Toure Y, Barry (Balotelli 57), Silva (Johnson A 66), Adebayor, Tevez (Jo 77).

PLAY-OFF ROUND SECOND LEG

Anorthosis	(0) 1	CSKA Moscow	(0) 2
AEK Athens	(1) 1	Dundee U	(0) 1
Aktobe	(0) 2	AZ	(1) 1
Apoel	(1) 1	Getafe	(0) 1
(aet.)			
Aston Villa	(1) 2	Rapid Vienna	(0) 3
Brondby	(0) 0	Sporting Lisbon	(1) 3
Dinamo Zagreb	(1) 2	Gyor	(1) 1
Dnepr Mogilev	(1) 1	Villarreal	(1) 2
Dynamo Minsk	(0) 2	Club Brugge	(3) 3
Elfsborg	(0) 0	Napoli	(2) 2
Fenerbahce	(0) 1	PAOK Salonika	(0) 1
(aet.)			
FK Austria	(0) 1	Aris Salonika	(1) 1
Gent	(1) 2	Feyenoord	(0) 0
Grasshoppers	(0) 1	Steaua	(0) 0
(aet; Steaua won 4-3 on penalties.)			
HJK Helsinki	(0) 0	Besiktas	(1) 4
Juventus	(0) 1	Sturm Graz	(0) 0
Karabakh	(0) 0	Borussia Dortmund	(0) 1
Karpaty	(0) 1	Galatasaray	(0) 1
Lech	(0) 0	Dnepr	(0) 0
Levski	(0) 2	AIK Stockholm	(1) 1
Lille	(0) 2	Vaslui	(0) 0
Litex	(0) 1	Debrecen	(0) 2
Lokomotiv Moscow	(0) 1	Lausanne	(1) 1
(aet; Lausanne won 4-3 on penalties.)			
Maccabi Tel Aviv	(0) 4	Paris St Germain	(1) 3
Manchester C	(1) 2	Timisoara	(0) 0
Maribor	(1) 3	Palermo	(0) 2
Maritimo	(0) 1	BATE Borisov	(0) 2
Metalist Kharkiv	(0) 2	Omonia	(0) 2
Motherwell	(0) 0	Odense	(1) 1
Porto	(1) 4	Genk	(1) 2
PSV Eindhoven	(1) 5	Sibir	(0) 0
Stuttgart	(0) 2	Slovan Bratislava	(1) 2
Tavirya	(1) 1	Leverkusen	(0) 3
The New Saints	(1) 2	CSKA Sofia	(1) 2
(at Wrexham.)			

Trabzonspor	(1) 1	Liverpool	(0) 2
Unirea	(1) 1	Hajduk Split	(0) 1
Utrecht	(2) 4	Celtic	(0) 0

Thursday, 26 August 2010

AEK Athens (1) 1 *(Bouba Diop 23)*

Dundee U (0) 1 *(Daly 78)* 700

AEK Athens: Saja; Georgeas (Gentzoglou 46), Jahic, Manolas, Bouba Diop, Makos, Leonardo (Karabelas 89), Kafes, Lagos, Nacho Scocco, Djebbour (Blanco 58).
Dundee U: Pernis; Dillon, Dixon, Buaben, Kenneth, Watson, Robertson D, Gomis (Daly 63), Robertson S (Swanson 59), Cadamarteri (Goodwillie 49), Conway.

Aston Villa (1) 2 *(Agbonlahor 22, Heskey 77)*

Rapid Vienna (0) 3 *(Nuhiu 52, Sonnleitner 78, Gartler 81)* 29,980

Aston Villa: Guzan; Beye, Collins JM, Petrov, Cuellar, Davies, Ireland, Reo-Coker (Delfouneso 82), Agbonlahor (Albrighton 40), Heskey, Young A.
Rapid Vienna: Hedl; Soma, Dober, Katzer, Sonnleitner, Saurer (Trimmel 73), Hofmann (Patocka 90), Kavlak, Heikkinen, Pehlivan (Gartler 78), Nuhiu.

Manchester C (1) 2 *(Wright-Phillips 43, Boyata 59)*

Timisoara (0) 0 23,542

Manchester C: Hart; Richards, Zabaleta, De Jong (Cunningham 64), Boyata, Kompany, Wright-Phillips, Vieira, Adebayor, Jo, Silva.
Timisoara: Pantilimon; Sepsi, Burca, Luchin, Mera, Contra, Alexa (Chiacu 82), Curtean (Goga 57), Bourceanu, Magera (Zicu 46), Axente.

Motherwell (0) 0

Odense (1) 1 *(Utaka 28)* 9105

Motherwell: Randolph; Saunders, Hammell, Reynolds, Craigan, Hateley, Humphrey, Lasley, Sutton, Murphy, Blackman.
Odense: Carroll; Haland (Johansson 53), Ruud■, Moller Christensen■, Sorensen, Gislason, Djemba-Djemba, Andreasen, Traore, Toft (Demba-Nyren 66), Utaka (Kadrii 88).

Trabzonspor (1) 1 *(Gutierrez 4)*

Liverpool (0) 2 *(Remzi Giray 83 (og), Kuyt 88)* 18,630

Trabzonspor: Onur; Egemen, Remzi, Cale (Jaja Coelho 87), Serkan, Burak, Yattara (Alanzinho 46), Selcuk, Colman, Ceyhun (Baris 65), Gutierrez.
Liverpool: Reina; Johnson, Kyrgiakos, Fabio Aurelio (Pacheco 77), Carragher, Kelly, Poulsen (Skrtel 90), Lucas, N'Gog (Babel 86), Kuyt, Cole.

Utrecht (2) 4 *(Van Wolfswinkel 11 (pen), 18 (pen), 46, Maguire 62)*

Celtic (0) 0 18,000

Utrecht: Vorm; Wuytens, Schut, Cornelisse, Nesu, Silberbauer, Lensky, Asare (Maguire 53), Duplan, Mertens (Nijholt 75), Van Wolfswinkel (Oar 90).
Celtic: Zaluska; Cha, Juarez (Ki 65), Brown (Maloney 51), Majstorovic, Hooiveld, Kayal, Ledley, Samaras (McCourt 72), Fortune, Forrest.

GROUP A

Juventus	(1) 3	Lech	(2) 3
Salzburg	(0) 0	Manchester C	(1) 2
Lech	(0) 2	Salzburg	(0) 0
Manchester C	(1) 1	Juventus	(1) 1
Manchester C	(2) 3	Lech	(0) 1
Salzburg	(1) 1	Juventus	(0) 1
Juventus	(0) 0	Salzburg	(0) 0
Lech	(2) 3	Manchester C	(0) 1
Lech	(1) 1	Juventus	(0) 1
Manchester C	(1) 3	Salzburg	(0) 0
Juventus	(1) 1	Manchester C	(0) 1
Salzburg	(0) 0	Lech	(1) 1

Thursday, 16 September 2010

Salzburg (0) 0

Manchester C (1) 2 *(Silva 8, Jo 63)*   25,100

Salzburg: Tremmel; Afolabi, Schiemer, Sekagya, Schwegler, Mendes da Silva (Augustinussen 74), Svento, Pokrivac (Jantscher 55), Leitgeb, Zarate, Boghossian (Wallner 54).
Manchester C: Hart; Zabaleta, Bridge (Boyata 68), De Jong, Toure K, Kompany, Silva (Wright-Phillips 84), Toure Y, Jo, Tevez (Vieira 79), Barry.

Thursday, 30 September 2010

Manchester C (1) 1 *(Johnson A 37)*

Juventus (1) 1 *(Iaquinta 11)*   35,212

Manchester C: Hart; Boateng (Milner 84), Zabaleta (Boyata 46), Vieira, Toure K, Kompany, Barry, Toure Y, Adebayor (Silva 74), Tevez, Johnson A.
Juventus: Manninger; Grygera, Bonucci, Chiellini, De Ceglie (Motta 72), Sissoko, Krasic (Felipe Melo 75), Martinez (Pepe 54), Marchisio, Iaquinta, Del Piero.

Thursday, 21 October 2010

Manchester C (2) 3 *(Adebayor 13, 25, 73)*

Lech (0) 1 *(Tshibamba 50)*   33,388

Manchester C: Hart; Richards, Zabaleta (Bridge 85), De Jong, Boyata, Lescott, Wright-Phillips (Jo 77), Vieira, Adebayor, Silva (Toure Y 74), Johnson A.
Lech: Buric; Bosacki, Henriquez, Arboleda (Djurdjevic 70), Injac, Wilk (Stilic 56), Peszko, Krivets, Kikut, Drygas (Rudnevs 55), Tshibamba.

Thursday, 4 November 2010

Lech (1) 3 *(Injac 30, Arboleda 36, Mozdzen 90)*

Manchester C (0) 1 *(Adebayor 51)*   43,000

Lech: Buric; Bosacki, Henriquez, Arboleda, Djurdjevic, Injac (Kielb 52), Peszko (Wilk 73), Krivets, Kikut, Stilic (Mozdzen 62), Rudnevs.
Manchester C: Given; Richards, Bridge (Kolarov 70), Vieira, Lescott, Zabaleta, Wright-Phillips (Silva 46), Boyata, Milner (Kompany 78), Adebayor, Johnson A.

Wednesday, 1 December 2010

Manchester C (1) 3 *(Balotelli 18, 65, Johnson 78)*

Salzburg (0) 0   37,552

Manchester C: Given; Zabaleta, Boateng, Vieira, Toure K (Richards 81), Lescott, Wright-Phillips, Milner, Balotelli (Adebayor 71), Jo, Johnson.

Salzburg: Tremmel; Afolabi, Schiemer, Sekagya, Hinteregger (Svento 46), Cziommer (Alan 57), Mendes da Silva (Augustinussen 67), Jantscher, Leitgeb, Hierlander, Boghossian.

Thursday, 16 December 2010

Juventus (1) 1 *(Giannetti 43)*

Manchester C (0) 1 *(Jo 77)*   6992

Juventus: Manninger; Grygera, Traore (Boniperti 67), Chiellini, Legrottaglie, Sissoko, Felipe Melo, Pepe, Krasic (Camilleri 57), Del Piero, Giannetti (Buchel 79).

Manchester C: Given; Boateng, Bridge, Vieira, Richards, Boyata, Wright-Phillips (Chantler 90), Milner, Jo, Tchuimeni-Nimely (Zabaleta 61), Johnson A.

Group A Table	P	W	D	L	F	A	Pts
Manchester C	6	3	2	1	11	6	11
Lech	6	3	2	1	11	8	11
Juventus	6	0	6	0	7	7	6
Salzburg	6	0	2	4	1	9	2

GROUP B

Aris Salonika	(0) 1	Atletico Madrid	(0) 0
Leverkusen	(2) 4	Rosenborg	(0) 0
Atletico Madrid	(0) 1	Leverkusen	(1) 1
Rosenborg	(1) 2	Aris	(1) 1
Aris Salonika	(0) 0	Leverkusen	(0) 0
Atletico Madrid	(1) 3	Rosenborg	(0) 0
Leverkusen	(0) 1	Aris Salonika	(0) 0
Rosenborg	(0) 1	Atletico Madrid	(1) 2
Atletico Madrid	(2) 2	Aris Salonika	(1) 3
Rosenborg	(0) 0	Leverkusen	(1) 1
Aris Salonika	(1) 2	Rosenborg	(0) 0
Leverkusen	(0) 1	Atletico Madrid	(0) 1

Group B Table	P	W	D	L	F	A	Pts
Leverkusen	6	3	3	0	8	2	12
Aris Salonika	6	3	1	2	7	5	10
Atletico Madrid	6	2	2	2	9	7	8
Rosenborg	6	1	0	5	3	13	3

GROUP C

Levski	(1) 3	Gent	(1) 2
Lille	(0) 1	Sporting Lisbon	(2) 2
Gent	(1) 1	Lille	(1) 1
Sporting Lisbon	(2) 5	Levski	(0) 0
Lille	(0) 1	Levski	(0) 0
Sporting Lisbon	(4) 5	Gent	(1) 1

Gent	(1) 3	Sporting Lisbon	(1) 1
Levski	(1) 2	Lille	(1) 2
Gent	(0) 1	Levski	(0) 0
Sporting Lisbon	(1) 1	Lille	(0) 0
Levski	(1) 1	Sporting Lisbon	(0) 0
Lille	(1) 3	Gent	(0) 0

Group C Table	P	W	D	L	F	A	Pts
Sporting Lisbon	6	4	0	2	14	6	12
Lille	6	2	2	2	8	6	8
Gent	6	2	1	3	8	13	7
Levski	6	2	1	3	6	11	7

GROUP D

Club Brugge	(0) 1	PAOK Salonika	(0) 1
Dinamo Zagreb	(1) 2	Villarreal	(0) 0
PAOK Salonika	(0) 1	Dinamo Zagreb	(0) 0
Villarreal	(1) 2	Club Brugge	(1) 1
Dinamo Zagreb	(0) 0	Club Brugge	(0) 0
Villarreal	(1) 1	PAOK Salonika	(0) 0
Club Brugge	(0) 0	Dinamo Zagreb	(0) 2
PAOK Salonika	(0) 1	Villarreal	(0) 0
PAOK Salonika	(1) 1	Club Brugge	(0) 1
Villarreal	(1) 3	Dinamo Zagreb	(0) 0
Club Brugge	(1) 1	Villarreal	(2) 2
Dinamo Zagreb	(0) 0	PAOK Salonika	(0) 1

Group D Table	P	W	D	L	F	A	Pts
Villarreal	6	4	0	2	8	5	12
PAOK Salonika	6	3	2	1	5	3	11
Dinamo Zagreb	6	2	1	3	4	5	7
Club Brugge	6	0	3	3	4	8	3

GROUP E

AZ	(1) 2	Serif	(0) 1
Dynamo Kiev	(2) 2	BATE Borisov	(1) 2
BATE Borisov	(1) 4	AZ	(0) 1
Serif	(2) 2	Dynamo Kiev	(0) 0
AZ	(1) 1	Dynamo Kiev	(2) 2
Serif	(0) 0	BATE Borisov	(1) 1
BATE Borisov	(1) 3	Serif	(1) 1
Dynamo Kiev	(0) 2	AZ	(0) 0
BATE Borisov	(0) 1	Dynamo Kiev	(2) 4
Serif	(0) 1	AZ	(1) 1
AZ	(1) 3	BATE Borisov	(0) 0
Dynamo Kiev	(0) 0	Serif	(0) 0

Group E Table	P	W	D	L	F	A	Pts
Dynamo Kiev	6	3	2	1	10	6	11
BATE Borisov	6	3	1	2	11	11	10
AZ	6	2	1	3	8	10	7
Serif	6	1	2	3	5	7	5

GROUP F

Lausanne	(0) 0	CSKA Moscow	(1) 3
Sparta Prague	(1) 3	Palermo	(1) 2
CSKA Moscow	(0) 3	Sparta Prague	(0) 0
Palermo	(0) 1	Lausanne	(0) 0
Palermo	(0) 0	CSKA Moscow	(1) 3
Sparta Prague	(3) 3	Lausanne	(1) 3
CSKA Moscow	(0) 3	Palermo	(1) 1
Lausanne	(1) 1	Sparta Prague	(1) 3
CSKA Moscow	(3) 5	Lausanne	(0) 1
(Played in Khimki.)			
Palermo	(1) 2	Sparta Prague	(0) 2
Lausanne	(0) 0	Palermo	(0) 1
Sparta Prague	(1) 1	CSKA Moscow	(1) 1

Group F Table	P	W	D	L	F	A	Pts
CSKA Moscow	6	5	1	0	18	3	16
Sparta Prague	6	2	3	1	12	12	9
Palermo	6	2	1	3	7	11	7
Lausanne	6	0	1	5	5	16	1

GROUP G

AEK Athens	(1) 3	Hajduk Split	(1) 1
Anderlecht	(0) 1	Zenit	(3) 3
Hajduk Split	(0) 1	Anderlecht	(0) 0
Zenit	(3) 4	AEK Athens	(1) 2
Anderlecht	(1) 3	AEK Athens	(0) 0
Zenit	(1) 2	Hajduk Split	(0) 0
AEK Athens	(0) 1	Anderlecht	(0) 1
Hajduk Split	(0) 2	Zenit	(1) 3
Hajduk Split	(0) 1	AEK Athens	(0) 3
Zenit	(1) 3	Anderlecht	(0) 1
AEK Athens	(0) 0	Zenit	(1) 3
Anderlecht	(2) 2	Hajduk Split	(0) 0

Group G Table	P	W	D	L	F	A	Pts
Zenit	6	6	0	0	18	6	18
Anderlecht	6	2	1	3	8	8	7
AEK Athens	6	2	1	3	9	13	7
Hajduk Split	6	1	0	5	5	13	3

GROUP H

Getafe	(0) 2	Odense	(1) 1
Stuttgart	(1) 3	Young Boys	(0) 0
Odense	(0) 1	Stuttgart	(0) 2
Young Boys	(1) 2	Getafe	(0) 0
Stuttgart	(1) 1	Getafe	(0) 0
Young Boys	(2) 4	Odense	(0) 2
Getafe	(0) 0	Stuttgart	(1) 3
Odense	(1) 2	Young Boys	(0) 0
Odense	(0) 1	Getafe	(1) 1

Young Boys		(1) 4	Stuttgart				(0) 2
Getafe		(1) 1	Young Boys				(0) 0
Stuttgart		(1) 5	Odense				(0) 1

Group H Table	P	W	D	L	F	A	Pts
Stuttgart	6	5	0	1	16	6	15
Young Boys	6	3	0	3	10	10	9
Getafe	6	2	1	3	4	8	7
Odense	6	1	1	4	8	14	4

GROUP I

Debrecen		(0) 0	Metalist Kharkiv				(2) 5
PSV Eindhoven		(0) 1	Sampdoria				(1) 1
Metalist Kharkiv		(0) 0	PSV Eindhoven				(2) 2
Sampdoria		(1) 1	Debrecen				(0) 0
Debrecen		(1) 1	PSV Eindhoven				(1) 2
Metalist Kharkiv		(1) 2	Sampdoria				(1) 1
PSV Eindhoven		(2) 3	Debrecen				(0) 0
Sampdoria		(0) 0	Metalist Kharkiv				(0) 0
Metalist Kharkiv		(0) 2	Debrecen				(0) 1
Sampdoria		(1) 1	PSV Eindhoven				(0) 2
Debrecen		(0) 2	Sampdoria				(0) 0
PSV Eindhoven		(0) 0	Metalist Kharkiv				(0) 0

Group I Table	P	W	D	L	F	A	Pts
PSV Eindhoven	6	4	2	0	10	3	14
Metalist Kharkiv	6	3	2	1	9	4	11
Sampdoria	6	1	2	3	4	7	5
Debrecen	6	1	0	5	4	13	3

GROUP J

Karpaty		(1) 3	Borussia Dortmund				(2) 4
Sevilla		(0) 0	Paris St Germain				(0) 1
Borussia Dortmund		(0) 0	Sevilla				(1) 1
Paris St Germain		(2) 2	Karpaty				(0) 0
Borussia Dortmund		(0) 1	Paris St Germain				(0) 1
Karpaty		(0) 0	Sevilla				(1) 1
Paris St Germain		(0) 0	Borussia Dortmund				(0) 0
Sevilla		(3) 4	Karpaty				(0) 0
Borussia Dortmund		(1) 3	Karpaty				(0) 0
Paris St Germain		(3) 4	Sevilla				(2) 2
Karpaty		(1) 1	Paris St Germain				(1) 1
Sevilla		(2) 2	Borussia Dortmund				(1) 2

Group J Table	P	W	D	L	F	A	Pts
Paris St Germain	6	3	3	0	9	4	12
Sevilla	6	3	1	2	10	7	10
Borussia Dortmund	6	2	3	1	10	7	9
Karpaty	6	0	1	5	4	15	1

GROUP K

Liverpool	(1) 4	Steaua	(1) 1
Napoli	(0) 0	Utrecht	(0) 0
Steaua	(3) 3	Napoli	(1) 3
Utrecht	(0) 0	Liverpool	(0) 0
Napoli	(0) 0	Liverpool	(0) 0
Utrecht	(0) 1	Steaua	(0) 1
Liverpool	(0) 3	Napoli	(1) 1
Steaua	(1) 3	Utrecht	(1) 1
Steaua	(0) 1	Liverpool	(1) 1
Utrecht	(3) 3	Napoli	(2) 3
Liverpool	(0) 0	Utrecht	(0) 0
Napoli	(0) 1	Steaua	(0) 0

Thursday, 16 September 2010

Liverpool (1) 4 *(Cole 1, N'Gog 55 (pen), 90, Lucas 81)*

Steaua (1) 1 *(Tanase 13)* 25,605

Liverpool: Reina; Kyrgiakos, Konchesky, Raul Meireles, Agger, Kelly, Rodriguez (Pacheco 85), Spearing, N'Gog, Cole (Eccleston 88), Babel (Lucas 79).
Steaua: Tatarusanu; Emeghara (Nicolita 20), Abrudan, Latovlevici, Geraldo Alves, Angelov (Eder Bonfim 52), Bicfalvi, Tanase, Radut (Surdu 73), Kapetanos, Stancu.

Thursday, 30 September 2010

Utrecht (0) 0

Liverpool (0) 0 23,662

Utrecht: Vorm; Wuytens, Schut, Cornelisse, Nesu, Silberbauer, Lensky (Nijholt 82), Duplan (Maguire 69), Mulenga, Mertens, Van Wolfswinkel.
Liverpool: Reina; Johnson, Kelly, Raul Meireles, Carragher, Skrtel, Lucas, Poulsen, Torres, Kuyt, Cole (Rodriguez 81).

Thursday, 21 October 2010

Napoli (0) 0

Liverpool (0) 0 52,910

Napoli: De Sanctis; Dossena, Aronica, Cannavaro, Campagnaro, Pazienza, Maggio (Zuniga 75), Gargano (Yebda 83), Hansik (Sosa 85), Cavani, Lavezzi.
Liverpool: Reina; Kelly, Konchesky (Fabio Aurelio 65), Poulsen, Carragher (Kyrgiakos 46), Skrtel, Spearing, Shelvey, N'Gog, Jovanovic, Babel (Cole 77).

Thursday, 4 November 2010

Liverpool (0) 3 *(Gerrard 76, 88 (pen), 89)*

Napoli (1) 1 *(Lavezzi 28)* 33,895

Liverpool: Reina; Johnson, Konchesky, Raul Meireles, Carragher, Kyrgiakos, Spearing, Poulsen (Eccleston 65), N'Gog (Lucas 82), Jovanovic (Gerrard 46), Shelvey.
Napoli: De Sanctis; Dossena, Aronica, Cannavaro, Campagnaro, Pazienza, Maggio, Gargano, Hamsik (Yebda 84), Cavani, Lavezzi.

Wednesday, 1 December 2010

Steaua (0) 1 *(Eder Bonfim 61)*

Liverpool (1) 1 *(Jovanovic 19)*   13,639

Steaua: Tatarusanu; Latolevici, Geraldo Alves, Eder Bonfim, Gardos, Nicolita, Bicfalvi (Angelov 46), Ricardo, Tanase, Surdu (Szekely 80), Stancu.
Liverpool: Reina; Kelly, Fabio Aurelio, Poulsen, Kyrgiakos, Wilson, Shelvey, Cole (N'Gog 75), Jovanovic (Eccleston 79), Pacheco (Lucas 89), Babel.

Wednesday, 15 December 2010

Liverpool (0) 0

Utrecht (0) 0   37,800

Liverpool: Jones; Kelly, Fabio Aurelio, Poulsen, Skrtel (Kyrgiakos 46), Wilson, Shelvey, Eccleston (Pacheco 56), Jovanovic (Kuyt 73), Cole, Babel.
Utrecht: Vorm; Wuytens, Cornelisse, Keller, Nesu, Silberbauer, Nijholt, Maguire (Sarota 84), Duplan (Oar 71), Mertens, Van Wolfswinkel (De Kogel 46).

Group K Table	P	W	D	L	F	A	Pts
Liverpool	6	2	4	0	8	3	10
Napoli	6	1	4	1	8	9	7
Steaua	6	1	3	2	9	11	6
Utrecht	6	0	5	1	5	7	5

GROUP L

Besiktas	(0) 1	CSKA Sofia	(0) 0
Porto	(1) 3	Rapid Vienna	(0) 0
CSKA Sofia	(0) 0	Porto	(1) 1
Rapid Vienna	(0) 1	Besiktas	(0) 2
Besiktas	(0) 1	Porto	(1) 3
CSKA Sofia	(0) 0	Rapid Vienna	(2) 2
Porto	(1) 1	Besiktas	(0) 1
Rapid Vienna	(0) 1	CSKA Sofia	(0) 2
CSKA Sofia	(0) 1	Besiktas	(0) 2
Rapid Vienna	(1) 1	Porto	(1) 3
Besiktas	(2) 2	Rapid Vienna	(0) 0
Porto	(1) 3	CSKA Sofia	(0) 1

Group L Table	P	W	D	L	F	A	Pts
Porto	6	5	1	0	14	4	16
Besiktas	6	4	1	1	9	6	13
Rapid Vienna	6	1	0	5	5	12	3
CSKA Sofia	6	1	0	5	4	10	3

SECOND ROUND FIRST LEG

Aris Salonika	(0) 0	Manchester C	(0) 0
Anderlecht	(0) 0	Ajax	(1) 3
Basle	(2) 2	Spartak Moscow	(0) 3
BATE Borisov	(1) 2	Paris St Germain	(1) 2
Benfica	(0) 2	Stuttgart	(1) 1
Besiktas	(1) 1	Dynamo Kiev	(1) 4
Lech	(0) 1	Braga	(0) 0

Lille	(2) 2	PSV Eindhoven	(0) 2
Metalist Kharkiv	(0) 0	Leverkusen	(1) 4
Napoli	(0) 0	Villarreal	(0) 0
PAOK Salonika	(0) 0	CSKA Moscow	(1) 1
Rangers	(0) 1	Sporting	(0) 1
Rubin	(0) 0	Twente	(0) 2
Sevilla	(0) 1	Porto	(0) 2
Sparta Prague	(0) 0	Liverpool	(0) 0
Young Boys	(0) 2	Zenit	(1) 1

Tuesday, 15 February 2011

Aris Salonika (0) 0

Manchester C (0) 0   21,000

Aris Salonika: Sifakis; Michel, Neto (Castillo 88), Ronaldo, Vangjeli, Lazaridis, Faty, Toja, Prittas, Sakata, Bobadilla (Cesarec 72).
Manchester C: Hart; Boateng, Kolarov, Barry, Toure K, Richards, Silva, Toure Y, Dzeko (Zabaleta 84), Tevez, Wright-Phillips (Balotelli 77).

Thursday, 17 February 2011

Rangers (0) 1 *(Whittaker 66)*

Sporting (0) 1 *(Fernandez 89)*   34,095

Rangers: McGregor; Whittaker, Papac, Foster, Weir, Bougherra, Davis, Edu, Lafferty, Diouf, Weiss.
Sporting: Rui Patricio; Anderson Polga, Joao Pereira, Evaldo, Daniel Carrico, Maniche (Fernandez 77), Pedro Mendes, Alberto Zapater, Cristiano (Carlos Saleiro 74), Helder Postiga (Diogo Salomao 85), Yannick Djalo.

Sparta Prague (0) 0

Liverpool (0) 0   17,569

Sparta Prague: Blazek; Brabec, Kusnir, Repka, Pamic, Vacek, Matejovsky (Pekhart 90), Abena, Keric (Sionko 73), Kweuke, Kadlec (Zeman 89).
Liverpool: Reina; Johnson, Wilson, Raul Meireles, Carragher, Kyrgiakos, Rodriguez, Lucas, N'Gog (Skrtel 83), Kuyt, Fabio Aurelio (Cole 37).

SECOND ROUND SECOND LEG

CSKA Moscow	(0) 1	PAOK Salonika	(0) 1
(Played in Khimki.)			
Porto	(0) 0	Sevilla	(0) 1
Ajax	(2) 2	Anderlecht	(0) 0
Braga	(2) 2	Lech	(0) 0
Dynamo Kiev	(1) 4	Besiktas	(0) 0
Leverkusen	(0) 2	Metalist Kharkiv	(0) 0
Liverpool	(0) 1	Sparta Prague	(0) 0
Manchester C	(2) 3	Aris Salonika	(0) 0
Paris St Germain	(0) 0	BATE Borisov	(0) 0
PSV Eindhoven	(0) 3	Lille	(1) 1
Spartak Moscow	(0) 1	Basle	(1) 1
Sporting	(1) 2	Rangers	(1) 2
Stuttgart	(0) 0	Benfica	(1) 2
Twente	(1) 2	Rubin	(2) 2
Villarreal	(2) 2	Napoli	(1) 1
Zenit	(1) 3	Young Boys	(1) 1

Thursday, 24 February 2011

Liverpool (0) 1 *(Kuyt 86)*

Sparta Prague (0) 0   42,949

Liverpool: Reina; Wilson, Kelly (Carragher 46), Raul Meireles, Kyrgiakos, Agger (Skrtel 85), Poulsen (Spearing 65), Lucas, N'Gog, Kuyt, Cole.
Sparta Prague: Blazek; Brabec, Kusnir, Repka, Pamic (Keric 90), Sionko (Podany 74), Vacek, Matejovsky, Abena (Pekhart 78), Kweuke, Kadlec.

Manchester C (2) 3 *(Dzeko 7, 12, Toure Y 75)*

Aris Salonika (0) 0   36,748

Manchester C: Hart; Boateng, Kolarov, Barry, Lescott, Kompany (Zabaleta 35), Balotelli, Toure Y, Dzeko, Tevez (Vieira 79), Silva (Wright-Phillips 80).
Aris Salonika: Sifakis; Michel, Neto (Kaznaferis 80), Ronaldo, Vangjeli, Lazaridis, Faty, Toja, Prittas, Sakata (Mendrinos 46), Bobadilla (Koke 61).

Sporting (1) 2 *(Pedro Mendes 42, Yannick Djalo 83)*

Rangers (1) 2 *(Diouf 20, Edu 90)*   15,375

Sporting: Rui Patricio; Anderson Polga, Torsiglieri, Abel, Joao Pereira, Evaldo, Pedro Mendes (Carlos Saleiro 81), Alberto Zapater, Fernandez (Nuno Coelho 90), Helder Postiga (Andre Santos 87), Yannick Djalo.
Rangers: McGregor; Whittaker, Papac, Foster, Weir (Lafferty 71), Bougherra, Davis, Edu, Fleck (Weiss 72), Diouf (Healy 82), Bartley.

THIRD ROUND FIRST LEG

Ajax	(0) 0	Spartak Moscow	(0) 1
Benfica	(1) 2	Paris St Germain	(1) 1
Braga	(1) 1	Liverpool	(0) 0
CSKA Moscow	(0) 0	Porto	(0) 1
Dynamo Kiev	(1) 2	Manchester C	(0) 0
Leverkusen	(1) 2	Villarreal	(1) 3
PSV Eindhoven	(0) 0	Rangers	(0) 0
Twente	(1) 3	Zenit	(0) 0

Thursday, 10 March 2011

Braga (1) 1 *(Alan 18 (pen))*

Liverpool (0) 0   12,991

Braga: Artur Moraes; Rodriguez, Kaka, Miguel Garcia, Silvio, Hugo Viana, Marcio Mossoro (Paulao 69), Salino, Alan, Lima (Meyong 77), Paulo Cesar (Helder Barbosa 90).
Liverpool: Reina; Johnson, Kyrgiakos, Raul Meireles, Carragher, Skrtel, Lucas, Poulsen (Carroll 57), Spearing, Kuyt, Cole.

Dynamo Kiev (1) 2 *(Shevchenko 25, Gusev 77)*

Manchester C (0) 0   16,315

Dynamo Kiev: Shovkovskiy; Popov, Danilo Silva, Khacheridi, Gusev, Yussuf, Eremenko, Vukojevic, Milevskiy, Shevchenko (Ninkovic 88), Yarmolenko.
Manchester C: Hart; Richards, Kolarov (Wright-Phillips 82), Barry, Lescott, Kompany, Silva, Toure Y, Balotelli (Tevez 57), Dzeko, Zabaleta.

PSV Eindhoven (0) 0

Rangers (0) 0   26,000

PSV Eindhoven: Isaksson; Pieters, Bouma, Marcelo, Manolev, Engelaar, Hutchinson, Dzsudzsak, Lens, Berg (Koevermans 70), Toivonen (Bakkal 84).
Rangers: Alexander; Whittaker, Foster, Bartley, Weir, Bougherra, Davis, Edu, Lafferty (Wylde 80), Diouf (Weiss 64), Hutton.

THIRD ROUND SECOND LEG

Liverpool	(0) 0	Braga	(0) 0
Manchester C	(1) 1	Dynamo Kiev	(0) 0
Paris St Germain	(1) 1	Benfica	(1) 1
Porto	(2) 2	CSKA Moscow	(1) 1
Rangers	(0) 0	PSV Eindhoven	(1) 1
Spartak Moscow	(2) 3	Ajax	(0) 0
Villarreal	(1) 2	Leverkusen	(0) 1
Zenit	(2) 2	Twente	(0) 0

Thursday, 17 March 2011

Liverpool (0) 0

Braga (0) 0   37,494

Liverpool: Reina; Johnson, Wilson, Raul Meireles, Carragher, Skrtel, Rodriguez (N'Gog 75), Cole (Spearing 75), Carroll, Kuyt, Lucas.
Braga: Artur Moraes; Rodriguez, Paulao, Miguel Garcia, Silvio, Hugo Viana, Vandinho (Kaka 74), Salino (Marcio Mossoro 89), Alan, Lima (Meyong 85), Paulo Cesar.

Manchester C (1) 1 *(Kolarov 39)*

Dynamo Kiev (0) 0   27,816

Manchester C: Hart; Richards, Kolarov (Milner 88), Barry (Johnson A 71), Lescott, Kompany, De Jong, Silva (Dzeko 76), Balotelli■, Tevez, Toure Y.
Dynamo Kiev: Shovkovskiy; Leandro Almeida, Popov, Danilo Silva, Gusev, Yussuf, Eremenko, Ninkovic (Zozulya 46), Vukojevic, Shevchenko (Garmash 62), Yarmolenko (Betao 90).

Rangers (0) 0

PSV Eindhoven (1) 1 *(Lens 14)*   35,373

Rangers: Alexander; Whittaker, Papac, Foster (Healy 86), Weir (Naismith 46), Bougherra, Davis, Edu, Lafferty (Diouf 66), Bartley, Wylde.
PSV Eindhoven: Isaksson; Pieters, Bouma, Marcelo, Engelaar, Hutchinson, Dzsudzsak, Tamata, Lens, Berg (Bakkal 66), Toivonen.

QUARTER-FINALS FIRST LEG

Benfica	(2) 4	PSV Eindhoven	(0) 1
Dynamo Kiev	(1) 1	Braga	(1) 1
Porto	(1) 5	Spartak Moscow	(0) 1
Villarreal	(3) 5	Twente	(0) 1

QUARTER-FINALS SECOND LEG

Braga	(0) 0	Dynamo Kiev	(0) 0
PSV Eindhoven	(2) 2	Benfica	(1) 2
Spartak Moscow	(0) 2	Porto	(2) 5
Twente	(1) 1	Villarreal	(0) 3

SEMI-FINALS FIRST LEG

Benfica	(0) 2	Braga	(0) 1
Porto	(0) 5	Villarreal	(1) 1

SEMI-FINALS SECOND LEG

Braga	(1) 1	Benfica	(0) 0
Villarreal	(1) 3	Porto	(1) 2

UEFA EUROPA LEAGUE FINAL 2011

Wednesday, 18 May 2011

(in Dublin, attendance 45,391)

Porto (1) 1 *(Falcao 44)*   Braga (0) 0

Porto: Helton; Sapunaru, Rolando, Otamendi, Joao Moutinho, Silvestre Varela (James Rodriguez 79), Pereira, Guarin (Belluschi 73), Fernando, Falcao, Hulk.

Braga: Artur; Rodriguez (Kaka 46), Paulao, Miguel Garcia, Silvio, Hugo Viana (Marcio Mossoro 46), Vandinho, Custodio, Alan, Lima (Meyong 66), Paulo Cesar.

Referee: Velasco (Spain).

Did You Know?

The youngest of the European tournaments but the fastest growing one ever initiated by UEFA, in 2010–11 it encompassed 481 matches and involved well over 200 different teams. In addition to the original entries, some eliminated teams from the group stages of the Champions League filtered their way down to the Europa League. The competition also provided a place for a team that has been considered to have the best disciplinary record in Europe. For the new season, Fulham who had been runners-up in 2010–11, was awarded this recognition for its outstanding behaviour in domestic matches. It was one of 50 teams entering the first qualifying round for the new season. Though the 2010–11 campaign began on 1 July after the Champions League and ended before its older companion, it had completed 276 matches before even the group stages had started in mid-September!

UEFA EUROPA LEAGUE 2011–2012

PARTICIPATING CLUBS
This list is provisional and subject to final confirmation from UEFA

UEFA EUROPA LEAGUE PLAY-OFFS
Sevilla FC (ESP)
AS Roma (ITA)
Tottenham Hotspur FC (ENG)
PSV Eindhoven (NED)
Sporting Clube de Portugal (POR)
SC Braga(POR)
FC Schalke 04 (GER)*
FC Spartak Moskva (RUS)
Paris Saint-Germain FC (FRA)
RSC Anderlecht (BEL)
Celtic FC (SCO)*
Be ikta JK (TUR)*
FC Metalist Kharkiv (UKR)
AEK Athens FC (GRE)*
FC Steaua Bucure ti (ROU)*
Athletic Club (ESP)
S.S. Lazio (ITA)
FC Lokomotiv Moskva (RUS)
Birmingham City FC (ENG)
FC Rapid Bucure ti (ROU)
Hannover 96 (GER)
FC Sochaux-Montbéliard (FRA)
FC Dnipro Dnipropetrovsk (UKR)
PFC CSKA Sofia (BUL)*
FC Sion (SUI)*
FC Nordsjælland (DEN)*

UEFA EUROPA LEAGUE THIRD QUALIFYING ROUND
Club Atlético de Madrid (ESP)
AZ Alkmaar (NED)
Hapoel Tel-Aviv FC (ISR)*
Club Brugge KV (BEL)
AC Sparta Praha (CZE)
US Città di Palermo (ITA)†
FC Dinamo Bucure ti (ROU)
PAOK FC (GRE)
Stoke City FC (ENG)†
Stade Rennais FC (FRA)
BSC Young Boys (SUI)
PFC Levski Sofia (BUL)
1. FSV Mainz 05 (GER)

FK Mladá Boleslav (CZE)*
Bursaspor (TUR)
Vitória SC (POR)
Helsingborgs IF (SWE)*
FC Karpaty Lviv (UKR)
Brøndby IF (DEN)
FK Crvena zvezda (SRB)
FC Alania Vladikavkaz (RUS)†
Heart of Midlothian FC (SCO)
HNK Hajduk Split (CRO)
AC Omonia (CYP)*
Legia Warszawa (POL)*
SV Ried (AUT)
FC Gomel (BLR)*
FK Senica (SVK)
Strømsgodset IF (NOR)*
Sligo Rovers FC (IRL)*

UEFA EUROPA LEAGUE SECOND QUALIFYING ROUND
FC Salzburg (AUT)
FK Austria Wien (AUT)
Anorthosis Famagusta FC (CYP)
MŠK Žilina (SVK)
CD Nacional (POR)
FC Vorskla Poltava (UKR)
FC Sheriff (MDA)
ADO Den Haag (NED)
PFC Lokomotiv Sofia (BUL)
Gaziantepspor (TUR)
Olympiacos Volou FC (GRE)
Dundee United FC (SCO)
Bnei Yehuda Tel-Aviv FC (ISR)
FC Midtjylland (DEN)
Maccabi Tel-Aviv FC (ISR)
KVC Westerlo (BEL)†
FK Jablonec (CZE)
AS Gaz Metan Media (ROU)
FK Ventspils (LVA)*
FC Thun (SUI)
Vålerenga Fotball (NOR)
FC Aktobe (KAZ)
FK Vojvodina (SRB)
Bohemian FC (IRL)

AEK Larnaca FC (CYP)
FK Sarajevo (BIH)
FC Levadia Tallinn (EST)
RNK Split (CRO)
FC Shakhtyor Soligorsk (BLR)
WKS 1 sk Wrocław (POL)
FH Hafnarfjördur (ISL)*
SK Liep jas Metalurgs (LVA)
Örebro SK (SWE)
FK Željezni ar (BIH)*
FC Iskra-Stal (MDA)*
FK S duva (LTU)
FC Vaduz (LIE)*
TPS Turku (FIN)*
KF Tirana (ALB)*
FK Tauras (LTU)
KuPS Kuopio (FIN)
FK Rudar Pljevlja (MNE)*
Kecskeméti TE (HUN)*
UE Sant Julià (AND)*
EB/Streymur (FRO)*
Xäzär Länkäran FK (AZE)*
FC Gagra (GEO)*
FC Metalurg Skopje (MKD)*
FC Differdange 03 (LUX)*
FC Mika (ARM)*
NK Domžale (SVN)
Llanelli AFC (WAL)*
Crusaders FC (NIR)
AC Juvenese-Dogana (SMR)*
Floriana FC (MLT)*

FC Spartak Trnava (SVK)
FC Dinamo Tbilisi (GEO)
FC Honka Espoo (FIN)
NK Varaždin (CRO)†
FC Minsk (BLR)
Metalurgi Rustavi (GEO)
FK Rad (SRB)
BK Häcken (SWE)¶
NK Široki Brijeg (BIH)
FK Budu nost Podgorica (MNE)
KR Reykjavík (ISL)
The New Saints FC (WAL)
FK Renova (MKD)
FC Koper (SVN)
Birkirkara FC (MLT)
Ferencvárosi TC (HUN)
Paksi SE (HUN)
Glentoran FC (NIR)
FC Milsami Orhei (MDA)
FK Banga (LTU)†
FC Daugava Daugavpils (LVA)
NK Olimpija Ljubljana (SVN)
Cliftonville FC (NIR)
KS Flaumurtari (ALB)
KS Vllaznia (ALB)
JK Trans Narva (EST)
Olimpik- üvälan PFK (AZE)
FC Irtysh Pavlodar (KAZ)
FC Shakhter Karagandy (KAZ)†
FK Zeta (MNE)
FC Banants (ARM)
JK Nõmme Kalju (EST)
ÍBV Vestmannaeyjar (ISL)
NSÍ Runavík (FRO)
Ulisses FC (ARM)
SP Tre Penne (SMR)
Neath FC (WAL)
UN Käerjéng 97 (LUX)
FC Lusitans (AND)
UE Santa Coloma (AND)
ÍF Fuglafjørdur (FRO)
CS Fola Esch (LUX)

UEFA EUROPA LEAGUE FIRST QUALIFYING ROUND
Fulham FC (ENG)¶
IL Elfsborg (SWE)
Tromsø IL (NOR)
Saint Patrick's Athletic FC (IRL)
Qaraba FK (AZE)
Jagiellonia Białystok (POL)
FK Rabotnicki (MKD)
Aalesunds FK (NOR)¶¶

* – cup winners; † – losing cup finalists; ¶ – Fair Play winners.

PAST EUROPEAN CUP FINALS

Year	Winner	Score	Runner-up	Score
1956	Real Madrid	4	Stade de Rheims	3
1957	Real Madrid	2	Fiorentina	0
1958	Real Madrid*	3	AC Milan	2
1959	Real Madrid	2	Stade de Rheims	0
1960	Real Madrid	7	Eintracht Frankfurt	3
1961	Benfica	3	Barcelona	2
1962	Benfica	5	Real Madrid	3
1963	AC Milan	2	Benfica	1
1964	Internazionale	3	Real Madrid	1
1965	Internazionale	1	SL Benfica	0
1966	Real Madrid	2	Partizan Belgrade	1
1967	Celtic	2	Internazionale	1
1968	Manchester U*	4	Benfica	1
1969	AC Milan	4	Ajax	1
1970	Feyenoord*	2	Celtic	1
1971	Ajax	2	Panathinaikos	0
1972	Ajax	2	Internazionale	0
1973	Ajax	1	Juventus	0
1974	Bayern Munich	1 4	Atletico Madrid	1 0
1975	Bayern Munich	2	Leeds U	0
1976	Bayern Munich	1	St Etienne	0
1977	Liverpool	3	Borussia Moenchengladbach	1
1978	Liverpool	1	FC Brugge	0
1979	Nottingham F	1	Malmö	0
1980	Nottingham F	1	Hamburg	0
1981	Liverpool	1	Real Madrid	0
1982	Aston Villa	1	Bayern Munich	0
1983	Hamburg	1	Juventus	0
1984	Liverpool†	1	Roma	1
1985	Juventus	1	Liverpool	0
1986	Steaua Bucharest†	0	Barcelona	0
1987	Porto	2	Bayern Munich	1
1988	PSV Eindhoven†	0	Benfica	0
1989	AC Milan	4	Steaua Bucharest	0
1990	AC Milan	1	Benfica	0
1991	Red Star Belgrade†	0	Marseille	0
1992	Barcelona	1	Sampdoria	0

PAST UEFA CHAMPIONS LEAGUE FINALS

Year	Winner	Score	Runner-up	Score
1993	Marseille	1	AC Milan	0

(Marseille subsequently stripped of title)

Year	Winner	Score	Runner-up	Score
1994	AC Milan	4	Barcelona	0
1995	Ajax	1	AC Milan	0
1996	Juventus†	1	Ajax	1
1997	Borussia Dortmund	3	Juventus	1
1998	Real Madrid	1	Juventus	0
1999	Manchester U	2	Bayern Munich	1
2000	Real Madrid	3	Valencia	0
2001	Bayern Munich†	1	Valencia	1
2002	Real Madrid	2	Leverkusen	1
2003	AC Milan†	0	Juventus	0
2004	Porto	3	Monaco	0
2005	Liverpool†	3	AC Milan	3
2006	Barcelona	2	Arsenal	1
2007	AC Milan	2	Liverpool	1
2008	Manchester U†	1	Chelsea	1
2009	Barcelona	2	Manchester U	0
2010	Internazionale	2	Bayern Munich	0
2011	Barcelona	3	Manchester U	1

† aet; won on penalties.   * aet.

PAST UEFA CUP FINALS

Year	Winner	Score	Runner-up	Score
1972	Tottenham H	2 1	Wolverhampton W	1 1
1973	Liverpool	3 0	Borussia Moenchengladbach	0 2
1974	Feyenoord	2 2	Tottenham H	2 0
1975	Borussia Moenchengladbach	0 5	Twente Enschede	0 1
1976	Liverpool	3 1	FC Brugge	2 1
1977	Juventus**	1 1	Athletic Bilbao	0 2
1978	PSV Eindhoven	0 3	SEC Bastia	0 0
1979	Borussia Moenchengladbach	1 1	Red Star Belgrade	1 0
1980	Borussia Moenchengladbach	3 0	Eintracht Frankfurt**	2 1
1981	Ipswich T	3 2	AZ 67 Alkmaar	0 4
1982	IFK Gothenburg	1 3	SV Hamburg	0 0
1983	Anderlecht	1 1	Benfica	0 1
1984	Tottenham H†	1 1	RSC Anderlecht	1 1
1985	Real Madrid	3 0	Videoton	0 1
1986	Real Madrid	5 0	Cologne	1 2
1987	IFK Gothenburg	1 1	Dundee U	0 1
1988	Bayer Leverkusen†	0 3	Espanol	0 3
1989	Napoli	2 3	Stuttgart	1 3
1990	Juventus	3 0	Fiorentina	1 0
1991	Internazionale	2 0	AS Roma	0 1
1992	Ajax**	0 2	Torino	0 2
1993	Juventus	3 3	Borussia Dortmund	1 0
1994	Internazionale	1 1	Salzburg	0 0
1995	Parma	1 1	Juventus	0 1
1996	Bayern Munich	2 3	Bordeaux	0 1
1997	Schalke*†	1 0	Internazionale	0 1
1998	Internazionale	3	Lazio	0
1999	Parma	3	Marseille	0
2000	Galatasaray†	0	Arsenal	0
2001	Liverpool§	5	Alaves	4
2002	Feyenoord	3	Borussia Dortmund	2
2003	Porto*	3	Celtic	2
2004	Valencia	2	Marseille	0
2005	CSKA Moscow	3	Sporting Lisbon	1
2006	Sevilla	4	Middlesbrough	0
2007	Sevilla*†	2	Espanyol	2
2008	Zenit St Petersburg	2	Rangers	0
2009	Shakhtar Donetsk*	2	Werder Bremen	1

UEFA EUROPA LEAGUE FINALS

Year	Winner	Score	Runner-up	Score
2010	Atletico Madrid*	2	Fulham	1
2011	Porto	1	Braga	0

*After extra time **Won on away goals †Won on penalties §Won on sudden death.*

PAST EUROPEAN CHAMPIONSHIP FINALS

Year	Winners		Runners-up		Venue	Attendance
1960	USSR	2	Yugoslavia	1	Paris	17,966
1964	Spain	2	USSR	1	Madrid	120,000
1968	Italy	2	Yugoslavia	0	Rome	60,000
	(After 1-1 draw)					75,000
1972	West Germany	3	USSR	0	Brussels	43,437
1976	Czechoslovakia	2	West Germany	2	Belgrade	45,000
	(Czechoslovakia won on penalties)					
1980	West Germany	2	Belgium	1	Rome	47,864
1984	France	2	Spain	0	Paris	48,000
1988	Holland	2	USSR	0	Munich	72,308
1992	Denmark	2	Germany	0	Gothenburg	37,800
1996	Germany	2	Czech Republic	1	Wembley	73,611
	(Germany won on sudden death)					
2000	France	2	Italy	1	Rotterdam	50,000
	(France won on sudden death)					
2004	Greece	1	Portugal	0	Lisbon	62,865
2008	Spain	1	Germany	0	Vienna	51,428

PAST WORLD CUP FINALS

Year	Winners		Runners-up		Venue	Att.	Referee
1930	Uruguay	4	Argentina	2	Montevideo	90,000	Langenus (B)
1934	Italy*	2	Czechoslovakia	1	Rome	50,000	Eklind (Se)
1938	Italy	4	Hungary	2	Paris	45,000	Capdeville (F)
1950	Uruguay	2	Brazil	1	Rio de Janeiro	199,854	Reader (E)
1954	West Germany	3	Hungary	2	Berne	60,000	Ling (E)
1958	Brazil	5	Sweden	2	Stockholm	49,737	Guigue (F)
1962	Brazil	3	Czechoslovakia	1	Santiago	68,679	Latychev (USSR)
1966	England*	4	West Germany	2	Wembley	93,802	Dienst (Sw)
1970	Brazil	4	Italy	1	Mexico City	107,412	Glockner (EG)
1974	West Germany	2	Holland	1	Munich	77,833	Taylor (E)
1978	Argentina*	3	Holland	1	Buenos Aires	77,000	Gonella (I)
1982	Italy	3	West Germany	1	Madrid	90,080	Coelho (Br)
1986	Argentina	3	West Germany	2	Mexico City	114,580	Filho (Br)
1990	West Germany	1	Argentina	0	Rome	73,603	Mendez (Mex)
1994	Brazil*	0	Italy	0	Los Angeles	94,194	Puhl (H)
	(Brazil won 3-2 on penalties)						
1998	France	3	Brazil	0	St-Denis	75,000	Belqola (Mor)
2002	Brazil	2	Germany	0	Yokohama	69,029	Collina (I)
2006	Italy*	1	France	1	Berlin	69,000	Elizondo (Arg)
	(Italy won 5-3 on penalties)						
2010	Spain*	1	Holland	0	Johannesburg	84,490	Webb (E)

*After extra time.

EURO 2012 QUALIFYING RESULTS

■ *Denotes player sent off.*

GROUP A

Belgium	(0) 0	Germany	(0) 1
Kazakhstan	(0) 0	Turkey	(2) 3
Austria	(0) 2	Kazakhstan	(0) 0
Germany	(3) 6	Azerbaijan	(0) 1
Turkey	(0) 3	Belgium	(1) 2
Austria	(1) 3	Azerbaijan	(0) 0
Germany	(1) 3	Turkey	(0) 0
Kazakhstan	(0) 0	Belgium	(0) 2
Azerbaijan	(1) 1	Turkey	(0) 0
Belgium	(1) 4	Austria	(2) 4
Kazakhstan	(0) 0	Germany	(0) 3
Austria	(0) 0	Belgium	(1) 2
Germany	(3) 4	Kazakhstan	(0) 0
Belgium	(3) 4	Azerbaijan	(1) 1
Turkey	(1) 2	Austria	(0) 0
Austria	(0) 1	Germany	(1) 2
Belgium	(1) 1	Turkey	(1) 1
Kazakhstan	(0) 2	Azerbaijan	(0) 1
Azerbaijan	(0) 1	Germany	(2) 3

Group A Table	P	W	D	L	F	A	Pts
Germany	7	7	0	0	22	3	21
Belgium	7	3	2	2	15	10	11
Turkey	6	3	1	2	9	7	10
Austria	6	2	1	3	10	10	7
Azerbaijan	6	1	0	5	5	18	3
Kazakhstan	6	1	0	5	2	15	3

GROUP B

Andorra	(0) 0	Russia	(1) 2
Armenia	(0) 0	Republic of Ireland	(0) 1
Slovakia	(0) 1	Macedonia	(0) 0
Macedonia	(1) 2	Armenia	(1) 2
Republic of Ireland	(2) 3	Andorra	(1) 1
Russia	(0) 0	Slovakia	(1) 1
Andorra	(0) 0	Macedonia	(1) 2
Armenia	(1) 3	Slovakia	(1) 1
Republic of Ireland	(0) 2	Russia	(2) 3
Armenia	(3) 4	Andorra	(0) 0
Macedonia	(0) 0	Russia	(1) 1
Slovakia	(1) 1	Republic of Ireland	(1) 1
Andorra	(0) 0	Slovakia	(1) 1
Armenia	(0) 0	Russia	(0) 0
Republic of Ireland	(2) 2	Macedonia	(1) 1
Macedonia	(0) 0	Republic of Ireland	(2) 2
Russia	(1) 3	Armenia	(1) 1
Slovakia	(0) 1	Andorra	(0) 0

Erevan, 3 September 2010, 8600

Armenia (0) 0

Republic of Ireland (0) 1 *(Fahey 76)*

Armenia: Berezovskiy; Arzumanian, Arakelian, Hovespian, Artur Yedigarian (Manoian 68), Artak Yedigarian (Hambardzumian 71), Pachajian, Mkhitarian, Malakian (Manucharian 78), Mkrtchian K, Movsisian.
Republic of Ireland: Given; Dunne, Kilbane, Whelan, St Ledger-Hall, O'Shea, Lawrence, Green, Keane (Keogh 85), Doyle, McGeady (Fahey 68).
Referee: Szabo (Hungary).

Dublin, 7 September 2010, 40,283

Republic of Ireland (2) 3 *(Kilbane 15, Doyle 41, Keane 54)*

Andorra (1) 1 *(Martinez 45)*

Republic of Ireland: Given; Dunne, Kilbane, Whelan (Gibson 61), St Ledger-Hall, O'Shea (Kelly 75), Lawrence, Green, Keane, Doyle (Keogh 82), McGeady.
Andorra: Gomes; Lima I, Escura, Marc Bernaus, Martinez, Josep Ayala (Andorra 71), Vieira, Moreno (Manolo Jimenez 59), Pujol (Oscar Sonejee 86), Silva, Gomez.
Referee: Trattou (Cyprus).

Dublin, 8 October 2010, 50,411

Republic of Ireland (0) 2 *(Keane 72 (pen), Long 78)*

Russia (2) 3 *(Kerzhakov 10, Dzagoev 28, Shirokov 51)*

Republic of Ireland: Given; O'Shea, Kilbane, Whelan (Gibson 66), Dunne, St Ledger-Hall, Lawrence (Long 62), Green, Doyle (Fahey 71), Keane, McGeady.
Russia: Akinfeev; Berezutski V, Ignashevich, Anyukov, Zhirkov, Shirokov, Zyryanov (Semshov 68), Denisov, Dzagoev (Berezutski A 85), Kerzhakov (Pogrebnyak 80), Arshavin.
Referee: Blom (Holland).

Zilina, 12 October 2010, 10,892

Slovakia (1) 1 *(Durica 36)*

Republic of Ireland (1) 1 *(St Ledger-Hall 16)*

Slovakia: Mucha; Zabavnik, Hubocan, Salata, Durica, Karhan, Hamsik, Kucka, Weiss (Holosko 70), Jendrisek (Oravec 84), Sestak (Stoch 70).
Republic of Ireland: Given; O'Shea, Kilbane, Whelan, Dunne, St Ledger-Hall, Green (Gibson 41), Fahey (Keogh 71), Long, Keane, McGeady.
Referee: Mallenco (Spain).

Dublin, 26 March 2011, 33,200

Republic of Ireland (2) 2 *(McGeady 2, Keane 21)*

Macedonia (1) 1 *(Trichkovski 45)*

Republic of Ireland: Westwood; Dunne, O'Dea, Foley, Whelan, McGeady, Kilbane, Gibson (Fahey 77), Doyle (Long 20), Keane (McCarthy 87), Duff.
Macedonia: Nuredinoski; Novevski, Grncharov, Shikov, Popov, Shumulikoski, Demiri (Georgievski 84), Tasevski (Durovski 61), Pandev, Naumoski (Ristic 68), Trichkovski.
Referee: Vad II (Hungary).

Skopje, 4 June 2011, 29,500

Macedonia (0) 0

Republic of Ireland (2) 2 *(Keane 8, 36)*

Macedonia: Bogatinov; Noveski, Grncharov, Shikov, Popov, Shumulikoski, Despotovski (Durovski 57), Demiri (Savic 72), Pandev, Naumoski (Hasani 10), Trichkovski.
Republic of Ireland: Given; O'Dea, O'Shea, Kelly, McGeady, Hunt, Kilbane, Whelan, Andrews, Keane, Cox (Long 64).
Referee: Meyer (Germany).

Group B Table	P	W	D	L	F	A	Pts
Republic of Ireland	6	4	1	1	11	6	13
Russia	6	4	1	1	9	4	13
Slovakia	6	4	1	1	6	4	13
Armenia	6	2	2	2	10	7	8
Macedonia	6	1	1	4	5	8	4
Andorra	6	0	0	6	1	13	0

GROUP C

Estonia	(0) 2	Faeroes	(1) 1
Estonia	(1) 1	Italy	(0) 2
Faeroes	(0) 0	Serbia	(2) 3
Slovenia	(0) 0	Northern Ireland	(0) 1
Italy	(3) 5	Faeroes	(0) 0
Serbia	(0) 1	Slovenia	(0) 1
Northern Ireland	(0) 0	Italy	(0) 0
Serbia	(0) 1	Estonia	(0) 3
Slovenia	(2) 5	Faeroes	(0) 1
Estonia	(0) 0	Slovenia	(0) 1
Faeroes	(0) 1	Northern Ireland	(0) 1
Italy	(0) 0	Serbia	(0) 0

(Abandoned 7 minutes; crowd trouble. Italy awarded the match 3-0.)

Serbia	(0) 2	Northern Ireland	(1) 1
Slovenia	(0) 0	Italy	(0) 1
Estonia	(0) 1	Serbia	(1) 1
Northern Ireland	(0) 0	Slovenia	(0) 0
Faeroes	(0) 0	Slovenia	(1) 2
Italy	(2) 3	Estonia	(0) 0
Faeroes	(1) 2	Estonia	(0) 0

Maribor, 3 September 2010, 12,000

Slovenia (0) 0

Northern Ireland (0) 1 *(Evans C 70)*

Slovenia: Handanovic; Cesar, Jokic, Brecko, Mavric, Koren, Kirm (Dedic 74), Radosavljevic, Birsa, Novakovic (Ilicic 74), Ljubijankic (Matavz 88).
Northern Ireland: Taylor; Baird, McAuley, McCann (Lafferty 67), Hughes, Craigan, Cathcart, Davis, Healy (Evans C 67), Feeney, Brunt (Gorman 89).
Referee: Balaj (Romania).

Belfast, 8 October 2010, 15,200

Northern Ireland (0) 0

Italy (0) 0

Northern Ireland: Taylor; Baird, McAuley, Craigan, Hughes, Evans J, Davis, McCann (Evans C 80), Healy (Lafferty 66), Brunt (McGinn 71), Feeney.
Italy: Viviano; Bonucci, Cassani, Chiellini, Criscito, De Rossi, Pirlo, Mauri (Marchisio 79), Pepe (Rossi 84), Cassano, Borriello (Pazzini 74).
Referee: Chapron (France).

Toftir, 12 October 2010, 1921

Faeroes (0) 1 *(Holst 60)*

Northern Ireland (0) 1 *(Lafferty 76)*

Faeroes: Mikkelsen; Gregersen, Davidsen, Naes, Samuelsen (Hansen A 78), Benjaminsen, Jacobsen, Udsen (Petersen J 68), Holst (Hansen J 85), Edmundsson, Elttor.
Northern Ireland: Taylor; Baird, McAuley, Craigan, Hughes, Evans J, Davis, McGinn (Evans C 83), Lafferty, Feeney (Healy 50), Brunt.
Referee: Zimmermann (Switzerland).

Belgrade, 25 March 2011, 350

Serbia (0) 2 *(Pantelic 65, Tosic 74)*

Northern Ireland (1) 1 *(McAuley 40)*

Serbia: Brkic; Ivanovic, Bisevac, Subotic, Kolarov, Stankovic, Krasic (Petrovic 86), Milijas (Jovanovic 47), Tosic, Ljajic (Ninkovic 47), Pantelic.
Northern Ireland: Camp; Baird, Cathcart, McAuley, Hughes, Evans J (McCourt 86), Evans C, Clingan, Lafferty (Healy 46), Gorman (Feeney 78), Brunt.
Referee: Gumienny (Belgium).

Belfast, 29 March 2011, 14,200

Northern Ireland (0) 0

Slovenia (0) 0

Northern Ireland: Camp; Baird, Cathcart, Craigan, McAuley, Evans J, Evans C (Boyce 90), McCann (McQuoid 72), Brunt, Feeney (McCourt 82), Clingan.
Slovenia: Handanovic; Jokic, Brecko, Mavric, Suler, Koren, Kirm, Bacinovic (Sukalo 90), Ilicic (Ljubijankic 29), Birsa, Novakovic (Dedic 84).
Referee: Kuipers (Holland).

Group C Table	P	W	D	L	F	A	Pts
Italy	6	5	1	0	14	1	16
Slovenia	7	3	2	2	9	4	11
Serbia	6	2	2	2	8	9	8
Estonia	7	2	1	4	7	11	7
Northern Ireland	5	1	3	1	3	3	6
Faeroes	7	1	1	5	5	18	4

GROUP D

France	(0) 0	Belarus	(0) 1
Luxembourg	(0) 0	Bosnia	(3) 3
Romania	(0) 1	Albania	(0) 1
Albania	(1) 1	Luxembourg	(0) 0
Belarus	(0) 0	Romania	(0) 0

Bosnia	(0) 0	France	(0) 2
Albania	(1) 1	Bosnia	(1) 1
Luxembourg	(0) 0	Belarus	(0) 0
France	(0) 2	Romania	(0) 0
Belarus	(1) 2	Albania	(0) 0
France	(1) 2	Luxembourg	(0) 0
Luxembourg	(0) 0	France	(1) 2
Albania	(0) 1	Belarus	(0) 0
Bosnia	(0) 2	Romania	(1) 1
Romania	(1) 3	Luxembourg	(1) 1
Belarus	(1) 1	France	(1) 1
Romania	(2) 3	Bosnia	(0) 0
Belarus	(0) 2	Luxembourg	(0) 0
Bosnia	(0) 2	Albania	(0) 0

Group D Table	P	W	D	L	F	A	Pts
France	6	4	1	1	9	2	13
Belarus	7	3	3	1	6	2	12
Bosnia	6	3	1	2	8	7	10
Romania	6	2	2	2	8	6	8
Albania	6	2	2	2	4	6	8
Luxembourg	7	0	1	6	1	13	1

GROUP E

Moldova	(0) 2	Finland	(0) 0
San Marino	(0) 0	Holland	(2) 5
Sweden	(0) 2	Hungary	(0) 0
Holland	(2) 2	Finland	(1) 1
Hungary	(0) 2	Moldova	(0) 1
Sweden	(3) 6	San Marino	(0) 0
Hungary	(4) 8	San Marino	(0) 0
Moldova	(0) 0	Holland	(1) 1
Finland	(0) 1	Hungary	(0) 2
Holland	(2) 4	Sweden	(0) 1
San Marino	(0) 0	Moldova	(1) 2
Finland	(1) 8	San Marino	(0) 0
Hungary	(0) 0	Holland	(2) 4
Holland	(1) 5	Hungary	(0) 3
Sweden	(2) 2	Moldova	(0) 1
Moldova	(0) 1	Sweden	(2) 4
San Marino	(0) 0	Finland	(1) 1
San Marino	(0) 0	Hungary	(1) 3
Sweden	(3) 5	Finland	(0) 0

Group E Table	P	W	D	L	F	A	Pts
Holland	6	6	0	0	21	5	18
Sweden	6	5	0	1	20	6	15
Hungary	7	4	0	3	18	13	12
Finland	6	2	0	4	11	11	6
Moldova	6	2	0	4	7	9	6
San Marino	7	0	0	7	0	33	0

GROUP F

Israel	(1) 3	Malta	(1) 1
Greece	(0) 1	Georgia	(1) 1
Latvia	(0) 0	Croatia	(1) 3
Croatia	(0) 0	Greece	(0) 0
Georgia	(0) 0	Israel	(0) 0
Malta	(0) 0	Latvia	(1) 2
Georgia	(0) 1	Malta	(0) 0
Greece	(0) 1	Latvia	(0) 0
Israel	(0) 1	Croatia	(2) 2
Greece	(1) 2	Israel	(0) 1
Latvia	(0) 1	Georgia	(0) 1
Croatia	(2) 3	Malta	(0) 0
Georgia	(0) 1	Croatia	(0) 0
Israel	(1) 2	Latvia	(0) 1
Malta	(0) 0	Greece	(0) 1
Israel	(0) 1	Georgia	(0) 0
Croatia	(0) 2	Georgia	(1) 1
Greece	(2) 3	Malta	(0) 1
Latvia	(0) 1	Israel	(2) 2

Group F Table	P	W	D	L	F	A	Pts
Greece	6	4	2	0	8	3	14
Croatia	6	4	1	1	10	3	13
Israel	7	4	1	2	10	7	13
Georgia	7	2	3	2	5	5	9
Latvia	6	1	1	4	5	9	4
Malta	6	0	0	6	2	13	0

GROUP G

England	(1) 4	Bulgaria	(0) 0
Montenegro	(1) 1	Wales	(0) 0
Bulgaria	(0) 0	Montenegro	(1) 1
Switzerland	(0) 1	England	(1) 3
Montenegro	(0) 1	Switzerland	(0) 0
Wales	(0) 0	Bulgaria	(0) 1
England	(0) 0	Montenegro	(0) 0
Switzerland	(2) 4	Wales	(1) 1
Bulgaria	(0) 0	Switzerland	(0) 0
Wales	(0) 0	England	(2) 2
England	(1) 2	Switzerland	(2) 2
Montenegro	(0) 1	Bulgaria	(0) 1

Wembley, 3 September 2010, 73,426

England (1) 4 *(Defoe 3, 61, 86, Johnson A 83)*

Bulgaria (0) 0

England: Hart; Johnson G, Cole, Barry, Dawson (Cahill 56), Jagielka, Walcott (Johnson A 74), Gerrard, Defoe (Young A 87), Rooney, Milner.
Bulgaria: Mihaylov; Milanov, Stoyanov, Ivanov, Manolev (Minev 66), Petrov S, Yankov, Petrov M, Angelov, Popov (Peev 79), Bozhinov (Rangelov 63).
Referee: Kassai (Hungary).

Podgorica, 3 September 2010, 7442

Montenegro (1) 1 *(Vucinic 30)*

Wales (0) 0

Montenegro: Bozovic M; Basa, Dzudovic, Jovanovic, Zverotic, Pavicevic, Boskovic B (Bozovic V 74), Pekovic, Vukcevic (Beciraj 87), Vucinic, Dalovic (Novakovic 83).
Wales: Hennessey; Gunter, Bale, Collins J (Morgan C 75), Williams A, Ricketts, Edwards D (Earnshaw 68), Ledley, Morison (Church 78), Bellamy, Vaughan.
Referee: Kakos (Greece).

Basle, 7 September 2010, 37,500

Switzerland (0) 1 *(Shaqiri 71)*

England (1) 3 *(Rooney 10, Johnson A 69, Bent 88)*

Switzerland: Benaglio; Grichting, Lichtsteiner■, Ziegler, Von Bergen, Degen (Streller 64), Schwegler (Costanzo 83), Inler, Margairaz (Shaqiri 46), Frei, Derdiyok.
England: Hart; Johnson G, Cole, Barry, Lescott, Jagielka, Walcott (Johnson A 13), Gerrard, Defoe (Bent 70), Rooney (Wright-Phillips 79), Milner.
Referee: Rizzoli (Italy).

Cardiff, 8 October 2010, 14,061

Wales (0) 0

Bulgaria (0) 1 *(Popov 48)*

Wales: Hennessey; Gunter■, Bale, Collins D, Williams A, Collins J, Ricketts, Edwards D (Church 69), Morison (Robson-Kanu 82), Ledley (King 59), Vaughan.
Bulgaria: Mihaylov; Iliev (Vidanov 37), Ivanov, Bodurov, Zanev, Petrov S, Petrov M, Peev (Rangelov 72), Georgiev, Popov, Makriev (Yankov 87).
Referee: Eriksson (Sweden).

Wembley, 12 October 2010, 73,451

England (0) 0

Montenegro (0) 0

England: Hart; Johnson G, Cole, Barry, Ferdinand, Lescott, Young A (Wright-Phillips 74), Gerrard, Crouch (Davies 70), Rooney, Johnson A.
Montenegro: Bozovic M; Basa, Dzudovic, Jovanovic, Savic, Boskovic B (Beciraj 82), Pekovic, Vukcevic, Zverotic, Novakovic (Kascelan 62), Dalovic (Delibasic 77).
Referee: Grafe (Germany).

Basle, 12 October 2010, 26,000

Switzerland (2) 4 *(Stocker 9, 89, Streller 22, Inler 82 (pen))*

Wales (1) 1 *(Bale 13)*

Switzerland: Benaglio (Wolfli 8); Grichting, Lichtsteiner, Ziegler, Von Bergen, Barnetta, Schwegler (Gelson 90), Inler, Stocker, Frei (Derdiyok 79), Streller.
Wales: Hennessey; Blake (Ribeiro 54), Bale, Collins J, Williams A, Collins D, Edwards D (Morison 77), King, Church, Crofts, Vaughan (MacDonald 89).
Referee: Hamer (Luxembourg).

Cardiff, 26 March 2011, 68,959

Wales (0) 0

England (2) 2 *(Lampard 7 (pen), Bent 15)*

Wales: Hennessey; Gunter, Collins D, King (Vaughan 65), Collins J, Williams A, Crofts, Ramsey, Morison (Evans C 65), Bellamy, Ledley.

England: Hart; Johnson G, Cole, Parker (Jagielka 88), Terry, Dawson, Young A, Lampard, Bent, Rooney (Milner 70), Wilshere (Downing 82).
Referee: Benquerenca (Portugal).

Wembley, 4 June 2011, 84,459

England (1) 2 *(Lampard 37 (pen), Young A 51)*

Switzerland (2) 2 *(Barnetta 32, 35)*

England: Hart; Johnson G, Cole (Baines 30), Parker, Terry, Ferdinand, Walcott (Downing 77), Wilshere, Bent, Lampard (Young A 46), Milner.
Switzerland: Benaglio; Djourou, Senderos, Lichtsteiner, Ziegler, Barnetta (Emeghara 90), Behrami (Dzemaili 58), Inler, Shaqiri, Xhaka, Derdiyok (Mehmedi 74).
Referee: Skomina (Slovenia).

Group G Table	P	W	D	L	F	A	Pts
England	5	3	2	0	11	3	11
Montenegro	5	3	2	0	4	1	11
Switzerland	5	1	2	2	7	7	5
Bulgaria	5	1	2	2	2	6	5
Wales	4	0	0	4	1	8	0

GROUP H

Iceland	(1) 1	Norway	(0) 2
Portugal	(2) 4	Cyprus	(2) 4
Denmark	(0) 1	Iceland	(0) 0
Norway	(1) 1	Portugal	(0) 0
Cyprus	(0) 1	Norway	(2) 2
Portugal	(2) 3	Denmark	(0) 1
Denmark	(0) 2	Cyprus	(0) 0
Iceland	(1) 1	Portugal	(2) 3
Cyprus	(0) 0	Iceland	(0) 0
Norway	(0) 1	Denmark	(1) 1
Iceland	(0) 0	Denmark	(0) 2
Portugal	(0) 1	Norway	(0) 0

Group H Table	P	W	D	L	F	A	Pts
Portugal	5	3	1	1	11	7	10
Denmark	5	3	1	1	7	4	10
Norway	5	3	1	1	6	4	10
Cyprus	4	0	2	2	5	8	2
Iceland	5	0	1	4	2	8	1

GROUP I

Liechtenstein	(0) 0	Spain	(2) 4
Lithuania	(0) 0	Scotland	(0) 0
Czech Republic	(0) 0	Lithuania	(1) 1
Scotland	(0) 2	Liechtenstein	(0) 1
Czech Republic	(0) 1	Scotland	(0) 0
Spain	(0) 3	Lithuania	(0) 1
Liechtenstein	(0) 0	Czech Republic	(2) 2
Scotland	(0) 2	Spain	(1) 3
Spain	(0) 2	Czech Republic	(1) 1

Czech Republic	(1) 2	Liechtenstein	(0) 0
Lithuania	(0) 1	Spain	(1) 3
Liechtenstein	(2) 2	Lithuania	(0) 0

Kaunas, 3 September 2010, 5248

Lithuania (0) 0

Scotland (0) 0

Lithuania: Karcemarskas; Stankevicius, Skerla, Kijanskas, Mikoliunas (Poskus 71), Semberas, Cesnauskis E, Panka, Sernas (Luksa 80), Radavicius, Danilevicius (Ivaskevicius 90).
Scotland: McGregor; Hutton, Whittaker (Berra 90), McCulloch, Weir, McManus, Robson (McFadden 69), Brown (Morrison 76), Fletcher D, Miller, Naismith.
Referee: Cuneyt (Turkey).

Hampden Park, 7 September 2010, 37,050

Scotland (0) 2 *(Miller 62, McManus 90)*

Liechtenstein (0) 1 *(Frick M 46)*

Scotland: McGregor; Hutton, Wallace L (Robson 54), McCulloch, Weir, McManus, Fletcher D, Brown, Boyd (Naismith 66), Miller, McFadden (Morrison 46).
Liechtenstein: Jehle; Martin Stocklasa, Oehri, Michael Stocklasa, Rechsteiner, Burgmeier, Polverino, Wieser (Buchel R 71), Frick M (D'Elia 79), Erne, Hasler D (Hasler N 90).
Referee: Shvetsov (Ukraine).

Prague, 8 October 2010, 14,922

Czech Republic (0) 1 *(Hubnik 69)*

Scotland (0) 0

Czech Republic: Cech; Hubschman, Hubnik, Suchy, Pospech, Kadlec M, Plasil (Rajnoch 90), Polak, Rosicky, Necid (Holek 84), Magera (Bednar 59).
Scotland: McGregor; Hutton, Whittaker, Morrison (Robson 84), Caldwell G (Iwelumo 76), Weir, McManus, Fletcher D, Mackie (Miller 78), Naismith, Dorrans.
Referee: Bebek (Croatia).

Glasgow, 12 October 2010, 51,322

Scotland (0) 2 *(Naismith 58, Pique 66 (og))*

Spain (1) 3 *(David Villa 44 (pen), Iniesta 56, Llorente 79)*

Scotland: McGregor; Whittaker[a], Bardsley, McCulloch (Adam 46), Weir, McManus, Morrison (Maloney 88), Fletcher D, Naismith, Miller, Dorrans (Mackie 80).
Spain: Casillas; Puyol, Sergio Ramos, Pique, Capdevila, Iniesta, Xabi Alonso, David Silva (Llorente 76), Cazorla (Pablo Hernandez 70), Sergio Busquets (Marchena 90), David Villa.
Referee: Busacca (Switzerland).

Group I Table	P	W	D	L	F	A	Pts
Spain	5	5	0	0	15	5	15
Czech Republic	5	3	0	2	6	3	9
Scotland	4	1	1	2	4	5	4
Lithuania	5	1	1	3	3	8	4
Liechtenstein	5	1	0	4	3	10	3

EURO 2012 REMAINING FIXTURES

10 AUGUST 2011
Group C Northern Ireland v Faeroe Islands

02 SEPTEMBER 2011
Group A Germany v Austria
Group A Turkey v Kazakhstan
Group A Azerbaijan v Belgium
Group B Russia v FYR Macedonia
Group B Republic of Ireland v Slovakia
Group B Andorra v Armenia
Group C Northern Ireland v Serbia
Group C Slovenia v Estonia
Group C Faeroe Islands v Italy
Group D Belarus v Bosnia-Herzegovina
Group D Albania v France
Group D Luxembourg v Romania
Group E Holland v San Marino
Group E Finland v Moldova
Group E Hungary v Sweden
Group F Israel v Greece
Group F Georgia v Latvia
Group F Malta v Croatia
Group G Bulgaria v England
Group G Wales v Montenegro
Group H Norway v Iceland
Group H Cyprus v Portugal
Group I Lithuania v Liechtenstein

03 SEPTEMBER 2011
Group I Scotland v Czech Republic

06 SEPTEMBER 2011
Group A Austria v Turkey
Group A Azerbaijan v Kazakhstan
Group B Russia v Republic of Ireland
Group B Slovakia v Armenia
Group B FYR Macedonia v Andorra
Group C Italy v Slovenia
Group C Serbia v Faeroe Islands
Group C Estonia v Northern Ireland
Group D Romania v France
Group D Bosnia-Herzegovina v Belarus
Group D Luxembourg v Albania
Group E Finland v Holland
Group E Moldova v Hungary
Group E San Marino v Sweden
Group F Croatia v Israel
Group F Latvia v Greece
Group F Malta v Georgia
Group G England v Wales
Group G Switzerland v Bulgaria
Group H Denmark v Norway
Group H Iceland v Cyprus
Group I Spain v Liechtenstein
Group I Scotland v Lithuania

07 OCTOBER 2011
Group A Turkey v Germany
Group A Belgium v Kazakhstan
Group A Azerbaijan v Austria
Group E Holland v Moldova
Group E Finland v Sweden
Group B Slovakia v Russia
Group B Armenia v FYR Macedonia
Group B Andorra v Republic of Ireland
Group C Serbia v Italy
Group C Northern Ireland v Estonia
Group D France v Albania
Group D Romania v Belarus
Group D Bosnia-Herzegovina v Luxembourg
Group F Greece v Croatia
Group F Latvia v Malta
Group G Wales v Switzerland
Group G Montenegro v England
Group H Portugal v Iceland
Group H Cyprus v Denmark
Group I Czech Republic v Spain

08 OCTOBER 2011
Group I Liechtenstein v Scotland

11 OCTOBER 2011
Group A Germany v Belgium
Group A Turkey v Azerbaijan
Group A Kazakhstan v Austria
Group B Russia v Andorra
Group B Republic of Ireland v Armenia
Group B FYR Macedonia v Slovakia
Group C Italy v Northern Ireland
Group C Slovenia v Serbia
Group D France v Bosnia-Herzegovina
Group D Albania v Romania
Group E Sweden v Holland
Group E Hungary v Finland
Group E Moldova v San Marino
Group F Croatia v Latvia
Group F Georgia v Greece
Group F Malta v Israel
Group G Switzerland v Montenegro
Group G Bulgaria v Wales
Group H Denmark v Portugal
Group H Norway v Cyprus
Group I Spain v Scotland
Group I Lithuania v Czech Republic

EUROPEAN SUPER CUP FINAL 2010

27 August 2010, Monaco (attendance 17,265)

Internazionale (0) 0   Atletico Madrid (0) 2 *(Reyes 62, Aguero 83)*

Internazionale: Julio Cesar; Maicon, Samuel, Lucio, Chivu, Stankovic (Pandev 68), Zanetti, Cambiasso, Sneijder (Coutinho 79), Eto'o, Milito.

Atletico Madrid: De Gea; Ujfalusi, Perea, Godin, Alvaro Dominguez, Paulo Assuncao, Reyes (Merida 69), Garcia, Simao (Camacho 90), Aguero, Forlan (Jurado 82).

Referee: M. Busacca (Switzerland).

FIFA CLUB WORLD CUP FINAL 2010

18 December 2010, Abu Dhabi (attendance 42,174)

TP Mazembe Englebert (0) 0

Internazionale (2) 3 *(Pandev 13, Eto'o 17, Biabiany 85)*

TP Mazembe Englebert: Kidiaba; Kimwaki, Kasusula, Nkulukuta, Singuluma, Kabangu, Bedi, Kaluyituka (Ndonga 90), Mihayo, Ekanga, Kasongo (Kanda 46).

Internazionale: Julio Cesar; Cordoba, Zanetti, Lucio, Thiago Motta (Mariga 87), Eto'o, Maicon, Cambiasso, Milito (Biabiany 70), Chievu (Stankovic 54), Pandev.

COPA SUDAMERICANA 2010

FINAL First Leg:
Goias 2   Independiente 0

FINAL Second Leg:
Independiente 3   Goias 1
Independendiente won 5-3 on penalties.

COPA LIBERTADORES 2010

FINAL First Leg:
Guadalajara 1   Internacionale 2

FINAL Second Leg:
Internacionale 3   Guadalajara 2

COPA SANTANDER LIBERTADORES 2011

FINAL First Leg:
Penarol 0   Santos 0

FINAL Second Leg:
Santos 2   Penarol 1

MLS CUP 2010

FINAL
Dallas 1   Colorado Rapids 2

ASIAN CUP 2011

FINAL
Australia 0   Japan 1

GULF CUP 2011

FINAL
Kuwait 1   Saudi Arabia 0

OTHER BRITISH AND IRISH INTERNATIONAL MATCHES 2010–2011

■ *Denotes player sent off.*

FRIENDLIES

Wembley, 11 August 2010, 72,024

England (0) 2 *(Gerrard 69, 73)*

Hungary (0) 1 *(Jagielka 63 (og))*

England: Hart; Johnson G, Cole A (Gibbs 46), Barry, Terry (Dawson 46), Jagielka, Walcott (Young A 46), Lampard (Zamora 46), Rooney (Milner 66), Gerrard (Wilshere 82), Johnson A.
Hungary: Kiraly; Liptak (Komlosi 55), Vanczak (Laczko 46), Juhasz, Szelesi, Vadocz, Dzsudzsak (Koman 46), Rudolf (Priskin 83), Elek (Toth 59), Gera, Huszti (Hajnal 46).
Referee: S. Lannoy (France).

Wembley, 17 November 2010, 85,495

England (0) 1 *(Crouch 86)*

France (1) 2 *(Benzema 16, Valbuena 55)*

England: Foster; Jagielka, Gibbs (Warnock 72), Gerrard (Crouch 84), Ferdinand (Richards 46), Lescott, Walcott (Johnson A 46), Henderson, Carroll (Bothroyd 72), Barry (Young A 46), Milner.
France: Lloris; Sagna (Reveillere 86), Abidal, Rami, Mexes (Sakho 46), Gourcuff (Hoarau 85), Malouda (Payet 77), M'Vila, Valbuena (Diarra 68), Benzema (Remy 67), Nasri.
Referee: Bo Larsen (Denmark).

Copenhagen, 9 February 2011, 21,523

Denmark(1) 1 *(Agger 7)*

England (1) 2 *(Bent 10, Young A 68)*

Denmark: Sorensen; Poulsen C, Jorgensen (Kjaer 46), Agger, Poulsen S (Wass 46), Jacobsen (Silberbauer 60), Kvist (Vingaard 90), Eriksen, Krohn-Delhi (Pedersen 70), Rommedahl (Enevoldsen 82), Bendtner.
England: Hart; Johnson G, Cole A (Baines 81), Wilshere (Parker 46), Terry, Dawson (Cahill 60), Walcott (Downing 67), Lampard (Barry 46), Rooney (Young A 46), Bent, Milner.
Referee: J. Eriksson (Sweden).

Wembley, 29 March 2011, 80,102

England (1) 1 *(Carroll 43)*

Ghana (0) 1 *(Gyan 90)*

England: Hart; Johnson G, Baines, Barry, Cahill, Jagielka (Lescott 46), Milner, Wilshere (Jarvis 46), Carroll (Defoe 59), Young A (Welbeck 81), Downing.
Ghana: Kingson; Pantsil, Addy (Jonathan Mensah 46), Vorsah (Boateng 46), John Mensah, Annan (Opare 46), Agyemang-Badu, Adiyiah (Tagoe 69), Gyan, Muntari (Ayew-Dede 59), Asamoah (Inkoom 84).
Referee: C. Cuneyt (Turkey).

Stockholm, 11 August 2010, 25,249

Sweden (2) 3 *(Ibrahimovic 4, Bajrami 39, Toivonen 56)*

Scotland (0) 0

Sweden: Isaksson; Lustig (Larsson 46), Mellberg, Majstorovic, Safari, Svensson (Wendt 73), Wernbloom (Kallstrom 46), Elmander (Berg 78), Toivonen, Bajrami (Wilhelmsson 64), Ibrahimovic (Hysen 59).
Scotland: McGregor; Broadfoot (Whittaker 74), Kenneth, Berra, Wallace L, Robson (Iwelumo 78), Fletcher D, Thomson (Robertson S 54), Adam (Morrison 64), McFadden, Fletcher S (Boyd 64).
Referee: G. Rocchi (Italy).

Aberdeen, 16 November 2010, 25,064

Scotland (3) 3 *(Wilson 24, Commons 31, Mackie 45)*

Faeroes (0) 0

Scotland: Gordon (Bell 68); Bardsley (Saunders 71), Caldwell S, Wilson (Kenneth 60), Crainey, Commons (Goodwillie 76), Bannan, Fletcher D (Bryson 68), Adam (McArthur 55), Maloney, Mackie.
Faeroes: Nielsen; Naes, Davidsen, Gregersen, Jacobsen, Udsen (Juspinusen 86), Petersen (Mouritsen 60), Lokin, Elttor, Holst (Poulsen 56), Edmundsson.
Referee: P. van Boekel (Holland)

Emirates Stadium, 27 March 2011, 53,087

Scotland (0) 0

Brazil (1) 2 *(Neymar 42, 77 (pen))*

Scotland: McGregor; Hutton, Crainey, Brown, Caldwell G, Berra (Wilson D 73), Morrison (Cowie 90), Adam (Snodgrass 78), Miller K (Mackail-Smith 87), McArthur (Bannan 56), Whittaker (Commons 64).
Brazil: Julio Cesar; Dani Alves, Lucio, Thiago Silva, Andre Santos, Lucas (Sandro 86), Elano (Elias 82), Ramires, Jadson (Lucas Rodriguez 72), Neymar (Renato Augusto 89), Leandro Damiao (Oliveira 78).
Referee: H. Webb (England).

Llanelli, 11 August 2010, 10,000

Wales (1) 5 *(Cotterill 35, Ledley 48 (pen), King 55, Williams A 78, Bellamy 82)*

Luxembourg (1) 1 *(Kitenge 44)*

Wales: Hennessey (Myhill 46); Ricketts, Morgan, Williams A (Eardley 85), Gunter, Ledley, Cotterill (Crofts 81), Stock (King 46), Bellamy, Morison, Earnshaw (Vaughan 46).
Luxembourg: Joubert; Mutsch ▪, Janisch (Collette 79), Kintziger, Hoffmann, Schnell, Peters, Krogh Gerson (Pedro 60), Bettmer (Bernard 86), Da Mota (Laterza 68), Kitenge.
Referee: M. Gestranius (Finland).

Podgorica, 11 August 2010, 5000

Montenegro (1) 2 *(Djalovic 43, 59)*

Northern Ireland (0) 0

Montenegro: Bozovic M; Pavicevic (Bozovic D 52), Djudovic, Jovanovic (Savic 75), Pekovic M (Novakovic 62), Vukcevic, Pejovic (Tomasevic 56), Zverotic (Beciraj 83), Bozovic V, Vucinic, Djalovic (Delibasic 77).
Northern Ireland: Taylor; Little, McGivern (Healy 68), Evans J, Craigan, Baird (Feeney 46), Davis, Clingan (Norwood 64), Paterson (Evans C 46), Lafferty (Gorman 58), Brunt (McCann 46).
Referee: B. Jovanetic (Serbia).

Belfast, 17 November 2010, 15,000

Northern Ireland (0) 1 *(Patterson 86 (pen))*

Morocco (0) 1 *(Chamakh 55)*

Northern Ireland: Tuffey (Blayney 46); Hodson, McGivern (Coates 62), Barton, Evans J, Hughes (McArdle 46), McCourt (O'Connor 46), McGinn (Magennis 69), Patterson, Gorman, Brunt (McQuoid 47).
Morocco: Lamyaghri; Soulaimani, El Kaddouri, Kantari, Mehdi Benatia (Mohamed Berrabeh 78), Hermach (El Ahmadi 89), Belhanda (Benzoukane 75), Kharja, Hadji (El Zhar 80), Chadli, Chamakh (El Arabi 71).
Referee: T. Hagen (Norway).

Dublin, 11 August 2010, 49,500

Republic of Ireland (0) 0

Argentina (1) 1 *(Di Maria 20)*

Republic of Ireland: Given; McShane, Dunne, O'Shea, Kilbane (Cunningham 57), Fahey (Treacy 77), Andrews (Gibson 67), Green, Duff, Keane, Sheridan (Keogh 56).
Argentina: Romero; Demichelis, Burdisso (Zabaleta 46), Samuel (Coloccini 83), Heinze (Insua 72), Mascherano, Gago, Banega, Messi (Lavezzi 58), Di Maria (Gutierrez 75), Higuain (Milito 46).
Referee: P. Rasmussen (Denmark).

Dublin, 17 November 2010, 25,000

Republic of Ireland (1) 1 *(Long 5 (pen))*

Norway (1) 2 *(Pedersen 34, Huseklepp 86)*

Republic of Ireland: Given; Kelly, Cunningham, O'Shea, O'Dea (Foley 67), Whelan, Lawrence (Walters 46), Fahey, Long, Doyle (McGeady 46), Duff (Hunt S 74).
Norway: Knudsen (Pettersen 46); Hogli, Waehler, Hangeland, Riise J, Hauger, Pedersen, Grindheim (Yettergard Jenssen 55), Moen (Haestad 78), Helstad (Riise B 46), Huseklepp (Moldskred 90).
Referee: K. Jakobsson (Iceland).

Dublin, 29 March 2011, 25,611

Republic of Ireland (1) 2 *(Long 15, Fahey 48 (pen))*

Uruguay (3) 3 *(Lugano 12, Cavani 22, Hernandez 39)*

Republic of Ireland: Westwood; Foley, O'Dea, Kelly, Clark (Delaney 75), Lawrence (McGeady 78), Green, Fahey (Gibson 66), Keogh (Stokes 85), McCarthy (Treacy 66), Long.
Uruguay: Muslera; Lugano, Godin, Caceres, Maxi Pereira, Arevalo Rios (Gargano 64), Perez (Scotti 90), Pereira, Hernandez (Eguren 84), Forlan, Cavani.
Referee: S. Ennjimi (France).

Liege, 7 June 2011, 21,516

Italy (0) 0

Republic of Ireland (1) 2 *(Andrews 36, Cox 90)*

Italy: Viviano; Cassani, Gamberini, Criscito (Balzaretti 66), Chiellini, Marchisio, Pirlo (Palombo 46), Nocerino (Giovinco 59), Montolivo, Rossi (Matri 46), Pazzini (Gilardino 59).
Republic of Ireland: Forde; McShane, Ward (Delaney 90), St Ledger-Hall, O'Dea (Kelly 83), Foley (Whelan 60), Coleman, Andrews, Hunt, Long (Cox 60), Keogh (Treacy 74).
Referee: S. Gumienny (Belgium).

CARLING NATIONS CUP

Dublin, 8 February 2011, 19,783

Republic of Ireland (0) 3 *(Gibson 60, Duff 67, Fahey 83)*

Wales (0) 0

Republic of Ireland: Given; O'Shea (O'Dea 85), St Ledger-Hall, Dunne, Clark, Coleman (Fahey 58), Whelan (Green 76), Gibson (Wilson 81), Duff (Keogh 71), Walters, Doyle (Long 46).
Wales: Hennessey; Eardley (Gunter 46), Collins D, Collins JM, Ricketts (Nyatanga 83), Crofts, Vaughan (Ledley 61), King, Robson-Kanu (Eastwood 68), Church, Earnshaw (Easter 80).
Referee: M. Courtney (N. Ireland).

Dublin, 9 February 2011, 18,742

Northern Ireland (0) 0

Scotland (2) 3 *(Miller K 19, McArthur 32, Commons 51)*

Northern Ireland: Tuffey; McArdle (Hodson 46), Baird, McAuley, Craigan (Thompson 66), McCourt, Evans J, Davis (Norwood 58), McCann (Healy 46), McGinn (Boyce 72), Patterson.
Scotland: McGregor; Hutton, Caldwell S, Berra, Bardsley (Wilson M 57), Morrison (Maguire 79), Adam (Bannan 57), Commons (Conway 72), McArthur, Naismith (Snodgrass 58), Miller K (Wilson D 90).
Referee: T. Connolly (Republic of Ireland).

Dublin, 24 May 2011, 12,083

Republic of Ireland (3) 5 *(Ward 24, Keane 37, 54 (pen), Cathcart 45 (og), Cox 80)*

Northern Ireland (0) 0

Republic of Ireland: Given (Forde 72); McShane, Ward, Kelly, Delaney, Coleman (Lawrence 55), Andrews, Foley (Hunt 70), Treacy, Keane (Keogh 62), Cox.
Northern Ireland: Blayney; Thompson■, Cathcart, McAuley, Hodson, Carson (McGinn 73), Clingan, Davis (Garrett 76), Gorman (Coates 55), Feeney (Boyce 73), McQuoid (Norwood 46).
Referee: C. Thomson (Scotland).

Dublin, 25 May 2011, 6036

Wales (1) 1 *(Earnshaw 36)*

Scotland (0) 3 *(Morrison 55, Miller K 64, Berra 70)*

Wales: Myhill; Eardley (Matthews 61), Morgan, Blake, Taylor (Gunter 46), Tudur Jones (Vaughan 72), Dorman (Cotterill 60), King (Ramsey 61), Vokes (Morison 72), Earnshaw, Easter.
Scotland: McGregor; Whittaker (Bardsley 81), Caldwell G (Hanley 84), Berra, Crainey (Martin 81), Naismith, Brown, Adam (McArthur 88), Morrison (Robson 74), McCormack (Bannan 73), Miller, K.
Referee: R. Crangle (Northern Ireland).

Dublin, 27 May 2011, 529

Wales (1) 2 *(Ramsey 35, Earnshaw 68)*

Northern Ireland (0) 0

Wales: Hennessey (Price 74); Gunter (Matthews 72), Taylor, Collison (Tudur Jones 61), Collins D, Gabbidon, Cotterill, Bellamy (Earnshaw 61), Morison (Vokes 80), Ramsey (Dorman 89), Vaughan.
Northern Ireland: Tuffey; Hodson, Coates, Cathcart (Dallas 61), McAuley, Norwood, Carson, Garrett (Winchester 75), McGinn (Owens 80), Feeney (Boyce 72), Gorman.
Referee: A. Kelly (Republic of Ireland).

Dublin, 29 May 2011, 17,694

Repbulic of Ireland (1) 1 *(Keane 23)*

Scotland (0) 0

Republic of Ireland: Given; McShane, O'Dea (Foley 66), Kelly, Ward, Lawrence (Coleman 62), Andrews, Fahey, Hunt, Keane (Treacy 83), Cox.
Scotland: McGregor; Whittaker, Hanley, Berra, Bardsley, Forrest (McCormack 85), Brown, Adam (Bannan 63), Robson (Maguire 75), Naismith, Miller K.
Referee: M. Whitby (Wales).

	P	W	D	L	F	A	Pts
Republic of Ireland	3	3	0	0	9	0	9
Scotland	3	2	0	1	6	2	6
Wales	3	1	0	2	3	6	3
Northern Ireland	3	0	0	3	0	10	0

ENGLAND UNDER-21 TEAMS 2010–2011

■Denotes player sent off.

Bristol, 10 August 2010, 9821

England (0) 2 *(Rose 64, Kelly 78)*

Uzbekistan (0) 0

England: Fielding (McCarthy 77); Walker, Smalling, Jones (Kelly 46), Mancienne, Henderson (Cork 46), Rodwell (Lansbury 61), Rose, Cleverley, Sturridge (Albrighton 71), Moses (Welbeck 46).

Colchester, 7 September 2010, 7240

England (0) 3 *(Welbeck 51, 90, Albrighton 79)*

Lithuania (0) 0

England: Fielding; Bertrand, Mancienne, Smalling, Walker (Wilshere 46), Cleverley (Albrighton 64), Sturridge (Cork 78), Welbeck, Jones, Henderson, Rose.

Barcelos, 3 September 2010, 6821

Portugal (0) 0

England (1) 1 *(Sturridge 32)*

England: Fielding; Bertrand (Cork 84), Mancienne (Muamba 74), Smalling, Walker, Cleverley, Sturridge (Delfounesco 90), Welbeck, Jones, Henderson, Rose.

Norwich, 8 October 2010, 25,794

England (0) 2 *(Henderson 63, Smalling 83)*

Romania (0) 1 *(Bertrand 71 (og))*

England: Fielding; Jones, Bertrand, Muamba, Mancienne, Smalling, Cleverley (Albrighton 75), Wilshere (Cork 90), Welbeck (Sturridge 81), Henderson, Rose.

Botosani, 12 October 2010, 6400

Romania (0) 0

England (0) 0

England: Fielding; Mancienne, Bertrand, Smalling, Jones, Muamba, Henderson, Welbeck (Delfouneso 90), Sturridge (Lansbury 62), Rose (Cork 82), Cleverley.

Wiesbaden, 16 November 2010, 5600

Germany (1) 2 *(Rausch 37, Tosun 59 (pen))*

England (0) 0

England: Loach (Steele ■ 46); Trippier, Bertrand, Rodwell (Mee 66), Mancienne, Cork, Kelly (Caulker 77), Lansbury, Delfouneso (McEachran 87), Sinclair (Wickham 66), Rose.

Empoli, 8 February 2011, 3700

Italy (0) 1 *(Macheda 88 (pen))*

England (0) 0

England: Fielding; Naughton, Bennett, Rodwell (Cork 12), Mee ■, Muamba, Albrighton (Sinclair 73), Lansbury (Oxlade-Chamberlain 60), McEachran (Trippier 83), Vaughan (Rodriguez 60), Delfouneso (Howson 60).

Viborg, 24 March 2011

Denmark (0) 0

England (1) 4 *(Welbeck 23, Sinclair 58, Sturridge 62, Henderson 72)*

England: McCarthy; Naughton, Bertrand, Muamba (Albrighton 87), Richards (Tomkins 5), Smalling, Cleverley (Delfouneso 79), Henderson (Cork 79), Sturridge (Wickham 87), Welbeck (McEachran 67), Sinclair (Rose 67).

Preston, 28 March 2011, 14,622

England (1) 1 *(Delfouneso 13)*

Iceland (1) 2 *(Smarason 41, Eyjolfsson 67)*

England: McCarthy (Loach 46); Naughton (Spence 73), Bertrand (Bennett 74), Tomkins, Albrighton (Sinclair 83), McEachran (Mutch 83), Rose, Cork (Cleverley 46), Wickham, Delfouneso (Hammill 74), Baker.

Southampton, 5 June 2011, 17,996

England (2) 2 *(Sturridge 9, Rose 40)*

Norway (0) 0

England: Fielding; Mancienne, Bertrand (Cleverley 46), Muamba (Gibbs 46), Smalling, Jones P (Tomkins 83), Sturridge (Delfouneso 65), Henderson (Cork 46), Welbeck (Albrighton 46), Rodwell, Rose (Lansbury 46).

Herning, 12 June 2011, 8046

Spain (1) 1 *(Herrera 14)*

England (0) 1 *(Welbeck 88)*

England: Fielding; Mancienne (Lansbury 67), Bertrand, Smalling, Jones P, Henderson, Welbeck, Sturridge, Walker, Cleverley (Sinclair 81), Rose (Rodwell 67).

Herning, 15 June 2011, 3495

Ukraine (0) 0

England (0) 0

England: Fielding; Mancienne (Muamba 89), Bertrand, Smalling, Jones P, Henderson, Welbeck, Sturridge, Walker, Rodwell (Lansbury 57), Rose (Sinclair 58).

Viborg, 19 June 2011, 5262

Czech Republic (0) 2 *(Chramosta 89, Pekhart 90)*

England (0) 1 *(Welbeck 76)*

England: Fielding; Bertrand, Muamba, Smalling, Jones P, Henderson (Lansburg 64), Welbeck, Sturridge, Sinclair (Rose 87), Walker, Cleverley (Albrighton 77).

ENGLAND C 2010–2011

14 Sept (in Newtown)

Wales Under-23 2 *(Moses 78, Jones 82)*   **England C 2** *(McFadzean 2, Rodman 45)*

Wales: Cann (Idzi 46); Pearson, McDonald, Johnston (Surman 65), Mike Williams, Williams A, Reed (Christopher 55), Jones (Moses 55), Sherbon (Williams R 76), Darlington (Marc Williams 55), Barrow.
England: Roberts (Brown 46); Hatton, Taylor, Flint (Saah 46), Gregory (Rose 46), McFadzean, Henry, Porter, Barnes-Homer (Gash 32), Howells, Rodman (Wright 46).

FA XI
20 Oct (in Hallam)

Hallam 1 *(Preece 87 (pen))*

FA XI 6 *(Taylor 17 (og), Walshaw 28, Mooney 33, Duncum 45, Waterfall 62, Mills 90)*

FA XI: Evans; Law, Brownhill, Murphy, Storer (Church 46), Waterfall, Duncum, Dillon (Thorley 46), Walshaw (Mills 46), Mooney (Marsden 46), Holden.

INTERNATIONAL CHALLENGE TROPHY
12 Oct (in Tallinn)

Estonia Under-23 0   England 1 *(Votti 52 (og))*

England: Brown; Hatton, Newton, Flint, Gregory, Wylde, Henry, Porter, Barnes-Homer (Wright), Howells, Rodman (Nix).

9 Feb (at Luton)

England 1 *(Barnes-Homer 7)*   **Belgium 0**   2315

England: Brown; Hatton (Bignot 70), Day, Atkinson, Gregory, Wylde, Morgan-Smith (Mangan 74), Simpson, Barnes-Homer, Porter, Howells.

18 May (at Northampton)

England 0   Portugal 1 *(Tavares 63)*   1517

England: Edwards; Vaughan, Franklin (Blair 65), Atkinson, Porter, Wylde (Coulson 73), Mangan, Rose (Byrne 81), Donnelly, Simpson (Styche 71), Clancy.

ENGLAND UNDER-16 2010–2011

VICTORY SHIELD

15 October *(at Haverfordwest).*

Wales 4 *(O'Sullivan 7, John 21 (pen), 28 (pen), James 31)*   **England 0**

Wales: Stephens; Watkins (Miles 46), Strong (Barrow 41), Dalley, Yorwerth, Weeks, Holden (Williams L 66), Jones G, James (Reid 41), O'Sullivan (Bowen 53), John.
England: Rose; Facey, Johns (Clark 41), Graham, Hayden (Swift 41), Houghton, Poyet, Ward (Woodland 69), Long (Lipman 41), Moli (Mitchell 71), Chambers.

23 March *(in Ballymena).*

Northern Ireland 0   England 3 *(Cole 39, Jebb 55, Rothwell 71)*

England: Gunn; Rothwell, Jebb (Glendon 70), Houghton, Campbell (Lewis 41), Cole (Mitchell 65), Dabo, Gorman (Akpom 41), Hayden, Wilson, Ormonde-Ottewill (Johns 68).

30 March *(at Morecambe).*

England 2 *(Moli 7, Inniss 30)*   **Scotland 1** *(Kirwan 71)*   2352

England: Willis; Chambers, Facey (Pearson 48), Graham (Long 62), Inniss, Lipman (Gordon 41), Moli (Thomas 62), Poyet (Robinson 41), Shaw, Wallace, Rothwell.
Scotland: Crump; Ramsay, Madden (Lunday 38), Turnbull, Findlay, Lindsay, Storie (Murdoch 64), Munn (Kirwan 28), Johnstone (Sibbald 73), Kidd, Smith (Finnie 40).

	P	W	D	L	F	A	Pts
England	3	2	0	1	5	5	6
Wales	3	1	1	1	5	2	4
Scotland	3	1	1	1	5	3	4
Northern Ireland	3	1	0	2	1	6	3

UEFA UNDER-21 CHAMPIONSHIP 2009–2011

QUALIFYING ROUND

GROUP 1
Romania 2, Andorra 0; Russia 4, Andorra 0; Latvia 4, Andorra 0; Faeroes 0, Romania 4; Faeroes 1, Russia 0; Andorra 0, Romania 2; Moldova 1, Latvia 0; Faeroes 1, Moldova 1; Latvia 0, Russia 4; Andorra 0, Russia 4; Romania 3, Moldova 0; Faeroes 1, Latvia 3; Latvia 5, Romania 1; Russia 2, Faeroes 0; Moldova 1, Andorra 0; Romania 3, Faeroes 0; Russia 3, Moldova 1; Romania 4, Latvia 1; Moldova 0, Russia 3; Latvia 0, Faeroes 1; Andorra 1, Faeroes 1; Andorra 1, Moldova 3; Russia 2, Latvia 1; Moldova 0, Romania 1; Faeroes 3, Andorra 1; Romania 3, Russia 0; Andorra 0, Latvia 1; Moldova 1, Faeroes 0; Latvia 1, Moldova 1; Russia 0, Romania 0

GROUP 2
Republic of Ireland 0, Turkey 3; Switzerland 2, Armenia 1; Armenia 2, Turkey 5; Switzerland 0, Estonia 1; Armenia 1, Switzerland 3; Estonia 2, Georgia 0; Georgia 4, Turkey 0; Estonia 1, Republic of Ireland 1; Estonia 1, Switzerland 4; Republic of Ireland 1, Georgia 1; Turkey 1, Armenia 0; Republic of Ireland 1, Switzerland 1; Georgia 1, Republic of Ireland 1; Armenia 1, Estonia 1; Turkey 1, Switzerland 3; Armenia 4, Republic of Ireland 1; Turkey 0, Estonia 0; Switzerland 1, Georgia 0; Georgia 2, Estonia 0; Republic of Ireland 1, Armenia 2; Estonia 2, Armenia 3; Estonia 1, Turkey 0; Switzerland 0, Turkey 2; Georgia 0, Switzerland 0; Republic of Ireland 5, Estonia 0; Armenia 2, Georgia 3; Switzerland 1, Republic of Ireland 0; Turkey 0, Georgia 1; Turkey 1, Republic of Ireland 0; Georgia 0, Armenia 2

GROUP 3
Luxembourg 0, Wales 0; Wales 4, Luxembourg 1; Hungary 3, Luxembourg 0; Luxembourg 0, Hungary 1; Wales 4, Hungary 1; Bosnia 0, Luxembourg 1; Wales 2, Italy 1; Italy 2, Luxembourg 0; Wales 2, Bosnia 0; Italy 1, Bosnia 1; Hungary 2, Italy 0; Luxembourg 0, Italy 4; Bosnia 2, Wales 1; Luxembourg 0, Bosnia 1; Italy 2, Hungary 0; Bosnia 0, Hungary 2; Bosnia 0, Italy 1; Hungary 0, Wales 1; Italy 1, Wales 0; Hungary 0, Bosnia 0

GROUP 4
Poland 2, Liechtenstein 0; Spain 2, Poland 0; Holland 2, Finland 0; Liechtenstein 0, Spain 4; Poland 2, Finland 1; Liechtenstein 0, Poland 5; Finland 0, Holland 1; Poland 0, Holland 4; Liechtenstein 0, Finland 4; Spain 1, Finland 0; Holland 3, Liechtenstein 0; Holland 2, Spain 1; Spain 3, Liechtenstein 1; Holland 3, Poland 2; Liechtenstein 0, Holland 3; Finland 1, Spain 1; Spain 2, Holland 1; Finland 2, Poland 0; Finland 3, Liechtenstein 0; Poland 0, Spain 1

GROUP 5
San Marino 0, Czech Republic 8; Iceland 0, Czech Republic 2; Germany 6, San Marino 0; Czech Republic 2, Northern Ireland 0; Germany 1, Czech Republic 2; Northern Ireland 2, Iceland 6; Iceland 8, San Marino 0; Iceland 2, Northern Ireland 1; San Marino 0, Iceland 6; Northern Ireland 1, Germany 1; San Marino 0, Germany 11; Northern Ireland 1, Czech Republic 2; Germany 2, Iceland 2; San Marino 0, Northern Ireland 3; Czech Republic 5, San Marino 0; Iceland 4, Germany 1; Czech Republic 1, Germany 1; Northern Ireland 4, San Marino 0; Germany 3, Northern Ireland 0; Czech Republic 3, Iceland 1

GROUP 6
Israel 1, Kazakhstan 1; Kazakhstan 2, Bulgaria 0; Kazakhstan 0, Montenegro 2; Bulgaria 3, Israel 4; Bulgaria 3, Kazakhstan 0; Montenegro 0, Sweden 2; Kazakhstan 1, Israel 2; Sweden 2, Bulgaria 1; Bulgaria 1, Montenegro 1; Kazakhstan 1, Sweden 1; Montenegro 3, Kazakhstan 1; Montenegro 1, Israel 0; Sweden 5, Kazakhstan 1; Israel 4, Bulgaria 0; Montenegro 2, Bulgaria 0; Israel 0, Sweden 1; Sweden 2, Montenegro 0; Sweden 1, Israel 2; Bulgaria 0, Sweden 1; Israel 5, Montenegro 0

GROUP 7

Croatia 0, Cyprus 2; Norway 2, Slovakia 2; Cyprus 1, Norway 3; Serbia 1, Slovakia 2; Norway 1, Croatia 3; Slovakia 1, Cyprus 0; Norway 0, Serbia 1; Serbia 2, Cyprus 0; Croatia 3, Serbia 1; Cyprus 0, Slovakia 1; Cyprus 1, Croatia 2; Serbia 3, Norway 2; Slovakia 1, Croatia 2; Croatia 1, Slovakia 1; Slovakia 2, Serbia 1; Croatia 4, Norway 1; Norway 1, Cyprus 3; Serbia 2, Croatia 2; Cyrpus 1, Serbia 3; Slovakia 1, Norway 4

GROUP 8

Malta 0, Slovenia 2; Ukraine 1, Malta 0; Malta 0, Belgium 1; Slovenia 1, France 3; Belgium 2, Slovenia 0; France 2, Ukraine 2; Ukraine 1, Belgium 1; Malta 0, France 2; Belgium 0, France 0; Slovenia 0, Ukraine 2; Slovenia 1, Malta 0; Belgium 0, Ukraine 2; France 1, Slovenia 0; Belgium 1, Malta 0; Malta 0, Ukraine 3; France 0, Belgium 1; Slovenia 2, Belgium 2; Ukraine 2, France 2; France 2, Malta 0; Ukraine 0, Slovenia 0

GROUP 9

Greece 3, Macedonia 1; Lithuania 0, Greece 1; Macedonia 1, England 2; Portugal 4, Lithuania 1; Greece 1, England 1; Macedonia 1, Lithuania 1; Greece 2, Portugal 1; England 6, Macedonia 3; Macedonia 1, Portugal 1; Greece 1, Lithuania 0; Lithuania 1, Macedonia 0; England 1, Portugal 0; Lithuania 0, England 0; Portugal 2, Greece 1; England 1, Greece 2; Lithuania 0, Portugal 1; Portugal 0, England 1; Macedonia 1, Greece 2; England 3, Lithuania 0; Portugal 3, Macedonia 1

GROUP 10

Albania 0, Scotland 1; Scotland 5, Albania 2; Belarus 2, Austria 1; Albania 1, Azerbaijan 0; Austria 1, Scotland 0; Azerbaijan 2, Belarus 3; Austria 3, Albania 1; Azerbaijan 1, Austria 2; Scotland 1, Belarus 0; Belarus 4, Albania 2; Albania 2, Austria 2; Azerbaijan 0, Scotland 4; Albania 1, Belarus 2; Austria 4, Azerbaijan 0; Scotland 2, Azerbaijan 2; Austria 3, Belarus 3; Belarus 1, Scotland 1; Azerbaijan 3, Albania 2; Belarus 1, Azerbaijan 0; Scotland 2, Austria 1

PLAY-OFFS FIRST LEG

Switzerland 4, Sweden 1; Iceland 2, Scotland 1; Czech Republic 3, Greece 0; Italy 2, Belarus 0; England 2, Romania 1; Holland 1, Ukraine 3; Spain 2, Croatia 1

PLAY-OFFS SECOND LEG

Sweden 1, Switzerland 1; Scotland 1, Iceland 2; Greece 0, Czech Republic 2; Belarus 3, Italy 0; Romania 0, England 0; Ukraine 0, Holland 2; Croatia 0, Spain 3

FINALS (in Denmark)

GROUP A

Belarus 2, Iceland 0; Denmark 0, Switzerland 1; Switzerland 2, Iceland 0; Denmark 2, Belarus 1; Iceland 3, Denmark 1; Switzerland 3, Belarus 0

GROUP B

Czech Republic 2, Ukraine 1; Spain 1, England 1; Czech Republic 0, Spain 2; Ukraine 0, England 0; England 1, Czech Republic 2; Ukraine 0, Spain 3

SEMI-FINALS

Spain 3, Belarus 1; Switzerland 1, Czech Republic 0

MATCH FOR THIRD PLACE

Czech Republic 0, Belarus 1

FINAL

Spain (1) 2 *(Herrera 41, Alcantara 81)*   **Switzerland (0) 0**

Spain: De Gea; Alvaro Dominguez, Javi Martinez, Adrian Lopez (Suarez 80), Mata, Montoya, Vila, Herrera (Capel 90), Alcantara, Botia, Muniain (Parejo 85).
Switzerland: Sommer; Koch, Rossini, Lustenberger, Emeghara (Gavranovic 53), Frei (Abrashi 54), Shaqiri, Mehmedi, Xhaka (Kasami 67), Klose, Berardi.
Referee: Tagliavento (Italy).

UEFA UNDER-17 CHAMPIONSHIP 2010–2011

ELITE ROUND

GROUP 1
Italy 0, Scotland 0
Slovakia 0, Czech Republic 1
Italy 1, Czech Republic 2
Scotland 2, Slovakia 0
Slovakia 1, Italy 1
Czech Republic 1, Scotland 1

GROUP 2
Portugal 0, Croatia 0
Holland 2, Austria 1
Portugal 0, Austria 2
Croatia 0, Holland 0
Holland 1, Portugal 0
Austria 0, Croatia 2

GROUP 3
Greece 2, Latvia 0
Denmark 2, Republic of Ireland 2
Republic of Ireland 1, Greece 1
Denmark 1, Latvia 0
Greece 0, Denmark 1
Latvia 1, Republic of Ireland 4

GROUP 4
Germany 2, Turkey 0
Switzerland 1, Ukraine 0

Turkey 2, Switzerland 1
Germany 2, Ukraine 0
Switzerland 0, Germany 2
Ukraine 2, Turkey 2

GROUP 5
England 3, Northern Ireland 2
Spain 3, Belgium 1
Spain 5, Northern Ireland 1
Belgium 1, England 2
England 2, Spain 1
Northern Ireland 2, Belgium 1

GROUP 6
Norway 5, Belarus 1
Georgia 0, France 2
Belarus 1, Georgia 0
Norway 2, France 2
Georgia 0, Norway 5
France 9, Belarus 0

GROUP 7
Romania 0, Iceland 0
Hungary 1, Russia 2
Romania 2, Russia 1
Iceland 0, Hungary 2
Hungary 1, Romania 2
Russia 2, Iceland 0

FINAL TOURNAMENT IN SERBIA

GROUP A
Serbia 2, Denmark 3
France 2, England 2
Serbia 1, France 1
Denmark 2, England 0
England 3, Serbia 0
Denmark 1, France 0

GROUP B
Germany 0, Holland 2
Czech Republic 1, Romania 1
Germany 1, Czech Republic 1
Holland 1, Romania 0
Romania 0, Germany 1
Holland 0, Czech Republic 0

SEMI-FINALS
Holland 1, England 0
Denmark 0, Germany 2

FINAL (in Novi Sad)

15 May

Germany (2) 2 *(Yesil 8, Aydin 32)*

Holland (3) 5 *(Trindade de Vilhena 23, 34, Depay 43, Kongolo 52, Ebecilio 77)*

Germany: Vlachodimos; Weiser, Rocker (Toljan 65), Gunter, Perrey (Weihrauch 73), Yalcin, Can, Yesil, Aydin, Mende (Berko 57), Schnelhardt.
Holland: De Jong; Disveld, Kongolo, Rekik, Willens, Ebecilio, Ayoub, Achahbar, Trindade de Vilhena, Depay (Gravenberch 71), De Bondt (Ake 64).

UEFA UNDER-19 CHAMPIONSHIP 2010

Final tournament in France

GROUP A

Austria v England	2-3
France v Holland	4-1
France v Austria	5-0
Holland v England	1-0
England v France	1-1
Holland v Austria	0-1

Croatia v Italy	0-0
Portugal v Croatia	0-5
Spain v Italy	3-0

SEMI-FINALS

Spain v England	3-1
France v Croatia	2-1

GROUP B

Croatia v Spain	1-2
Italy v Portugal	0-2
Spain v Portugal	2-1

FINAL (in Caen)

30 July

France (0) 2 *(Sunu 49, Lacazette 85)*

Spain (1) 1 *(Rodrigo 18)* 20,188

France: Diallo; Nego, Mavinga, Faure, Kakuta, Fofana, Sunu (Lacazette 69), Griezmann (Tafer 46), Coquelin, Kolodziejczak, Bakambu.
Spain: Alex; Montoya, Planas, Bartra, Pulido (Calvente 87), Romeu, Keko (Muniain 64), Thiago Alcantara, Rodrigo (Rochina 73), Canales, Pacheco.
Referee: S. Studer (Switzerland).

UEFA REGIONS CUP 2011

GROUP A

Braga 3, Zlin 1
Yednyst Plysky 0, Wurttemberg 2
Braga 2, Yednyst Plysky 1
Zlin 1, Wurttemberg 0
Wurttenberg 1, Braga 3
Zlin 2, Yednyst Plysky 1

GROUP B

Ankara 0, Leinster & Munster 0
South Region Russia 2, Belgrade 3
South Region Russia 1, Ankara 2
Belgrade 0, Leinster & Munster 1
Leinster & Munster 2, South Region Russia 1
Belgrade 2, Ankara 0

The two group winners advanced to the Final; the runners-up receiving medals.

FINAL

Braga 2, Leinster & Munster 1

FIFA UNDER-17 WORLD CUP 2011

Finals in Mexico

GROUP A
Congo 1, Holland 0
Mexico 3, South Korea 1
South Korea 1, Holland 1
Mexico 2, Congo 1
South Korea 1, Congo 1
Mexico 3, Holland 2

GROUP B
France 3, Argentina 0
Japan 1, Jamaica 0
Japan 1, France 1
Jamaica 1, Argentina 2
Japan 3, Argentina 1
Jamaica 1, France 1

GROUP C
Rwanda 0, England 2
Uruguay 3, Canada 0
Uruguay 1, Rwanda 0
Canada 2, England 2
Uruguay 0, England 2
Canada 0, Rwanda 0

GROUP D
Uzbekistan 1, New Zealand 4
USA 3, Czech Republic 0
USA 1, Uzbekistan 2
Czech Republic 1, New Zealand 0
USA 0, New Zealand 0
Czech Republic 1, Uzbekistan 2

GROUP E
Germany 6, Ecuador 1
Burkina Faso 0, Panama 1
Burkina Faso 0, Germany 3
Panama 1, Ecuador 2
Burkina Faso 0, Ecuador 2
Panama 0, Germany 2

GROUP F
Brazil 3, Denmark 0
Australia 2, Ivory Coast 1
Australia 0, Brazil 1
Ivory Coast 4, Denmark 2
Australia 1, Denmark 1
Ivory Coast 3, Brazil 3

FIRST ROUND
Congo 1, Uruguay 2
Uzbekistan 4, Australia 0
Japan 6, New Zealand 0
Brazil 2, Ecudador 0
Germany 4, USA 0
England 1, Argentina 1
England won 4-2 on penalties.
France 3, Ivory Coast 2
Mexico 2, Panama 0

QUARTER-FINALS
Uruguay 2, Uzbekistan 0
Japan 2, Brazil 3
Germany 3, England 2
France 1, Mexico 2

SEMI-FINALS
Uruguay 3, Brazil 0
Germany 2, Mexico 3

MATCH FOR THIRD PLACE
Brazil 3, Germany 4

FINAL
Uruguay 0, Mexico 2

POST-WAR INTERNATIONAL APPEARANCES

As at July 2011 *(Season of first cap given)*

ENGLAND

A'Court, A. (5) 1957/8 Liverpool
Adams, T. A. (66) 1986/7 Arsenal
Agbonlahor, G. (3) 2008/09 Aston Villa
Allen, C. (5) 1983/4 QPR, Tottenham H
Allen, R. (5) 1951/2 WBA
Allen, T. (3) 1959/60 Stoke C
Anderson, S. (2) 1961/2 Sunderland
Anderson, V. (30) 1978/9 Nottingham F, Arsenal, Manchester U
Anderton, D. R. (30) 1993/4 Tottenham H
Angus, J. (1) 1960/1 Burnley
Armfield, J. (43) 1958/9 Blackpool
Armstrong, D. (3) 1979/80 Middlesbrough, Southampton
Armstrong, K. (1) 1954/5 Chelsea
Ashton, D. (1) 2007/08 West Ham U
Astall, G. (2) 1955/6 Birmingham C
Astle, J. (5) 1968/9 WBA
Aston, J. (17) 1948/9 Manchester U
Atyeo, J. (6) 1955/6 Bristol C

Bailey, G. R. (2) 1984/5 Manchester U
Bailey, M. (2) 1963/4 Charlton
Baily, E. (9) 1949/50 Tottenham H
Baines, L. J. (5) 2009/10 Everton
Baker, J. (8) 1959/60 Hibernian, Arsenal
Ball, A. (72) 1964/5 Blackpool, Everton, Arsenal
Ball, M. J. (1) 2000/01 Everton
Banks, G. (73) 1962/3 Leicester C, Stoke C
Banks, T. (6) 1957/8 Bolton W
Bardsley, D. (2) 1992/3 QPR
Barham, M. (2) 1982/3 Norwich C
Barlow, R. (1) 1954/5 WBA
Barmby, N. J. (23) 1994/5 Tottenham H, Middlesbrough, Everton, Liverpool
Barnes, J. (79) 1982/3 Watford, Liverpool
Barnes, P. (22) 1977/8 Manchester C, WBA, Leeds U
Barrass, M. (3) 1951/2 Bolton W
Barrett, E. D. (3) 1990/1 Oldham Ath, Aston Villa
Barry, G. (46) 1999/00 Aston Villa, Manchester C
Barton, J. (1) 2006/07 Manchester C

Barton, W. D. (3) 1994/5 Wimbledon, Newcastle U
Batty, D. (42) 1990/1 Leeds U, Blackburn R, Newcastle U, Leeds U
Baynham, R. (3) 1955/6 Luton T
Beardsley, P. A. (59) 1985/6 Newcastle U, Liverpool, Newcastle U
Beasant, D. J. (2) 1989/90 Chelsea
Beattie, J. S. (5) 2002/03 Southampton
Beattie, T. K. (9) 1974/5 Ipswich T
Beckham, D. R. J. (115) 1996/7 Manchester U, Real Madrid, LA Galaxy
Bell, C. (48) 1967/8 Manchester C
Bent, D. A. (10) 2005/06 Charlton Ath, Tottenham H, Sunderland, Aston Villa
Bentley, D. M. (7) 2007/08 Blackburn R, Tottenham H
Bentley, R. (12) 1948/9 Chelsea
Berry, J. (4) 1952/3 Manchester U
Birtles, G. (3) 1979/80 Nottingham F
Blissett, L. (14) 1982/3 Watford, AC Milan
Blockley, J. (1) 1972/3 Arsenal
Blunstone, F. (5) 1954/5 Chelsea
Bonetti, P. (7) 1965/6 Chelsea
Bothroyd, J. (1) 2010/11 Cardiff C
Bould, S. A. (2) 1993/4 Arsenal
Bowles, S. (5) 1973/4 QPR
Bowyer, L. D. (1) 2002/03 Leeds U
Boyer, P. (1) 1975/6 Norwich C
Brabrook, P. (3) 1957/8 Chelsea
Bracewell, P. W. (3) 1984/5 Everton
Bradford, G. (1) 1955/6 Bristol R
Bradley, W. (3) 1958/9 Manchester U
Bridge, W. M. (36) 2001/02 Southampton, Chelsea, Manchester C
Bridges, B. (4) 1964/5 Chelsea
Broadbent, P. (7) 1957/8 Wolverhampton W
Broadis, I. (14) 1951/2 Manchester C, Newcastle U
Brooking, T. (47) 1973/4 West Ham U
Brooks, J. (3) 1956/7 Tottenham H
Brown, A. (1) 1970/1 WBA
Brown, K. (1) 1959/60 West Ham U
Brown, W. M. (23) 1998/9 Manchester U

Bull, S. G. (13) 1988/9 Wolverhampton W
Butcher, T. (77) 1979/80 Ipswich T, Rangers
Butt, N. (39) 1996/7 Manchester U, Newcastle U
Byrne, G. (2) 1962/3 Liverpool
Byrne, J. (11) 1961/2 Crystal P, West Ham U
Byrne, R. (33) 1953/4 Manchester U

Cahill, G. J. (3) 2010/11 Bolton W
Callaghan, I. (4) 1965/6 Liverpool
Campbell, S. (73) 1995/6 Tottenham H, Arsenal, Portsmouth
Carragher, J. L. (38) 1998/9 Liverpool
Carrick, M. (22) 2000/01 West Ham U, Tottenham H, Manchester U
Carroll, A. T. (2) 2010/11 Newcastle U, Liverpool
Carson, S. P. (3) 2007/08 Liverpool, WBA
Carter, H. (7) 1946/7 Derby Co
Chamberlain, M. (8) 1982/3 Stoke C
Channon, M. (46) 1972/3 Southampton, Manchester C
Charles, G. A. (2) 1990/1 Nottingham F
Charlton, J. (35) 1964/5 Leeds U
Charlton, R. (106) 1957/8 Manchester U
Charnley, R. (1) 1962/3 Blackpool
Cherry, T. (27) 1975/6 Leeds U
Chilton, A. (2) 1950/1 Manchester U
Chivers, M. (24) 1970/1 Tottenham H
Clamp, E. (4) 1957/8 Wolverhampton W
Clapton, D. (1) 1958/9 Arsenal
Clarke, A. (19) 1969/70 Leeds U
Clarke, H. (1) 1953/4 Tottenham H
Clayton, R. (35) 1955/6 Blackburn R
Clemence, R. (61) 1972/3 Liverpool, Tottenham H
Clement, D. (5) 1975/6 QPR
Clough, B. (2) 1959/60 Middlesbrough
Clough, N. H. (14) 1988/9 Nottingham F
Coates, R. (4) 1969/70 Burnley, Tottenham H
Cockburn, H. (13) 1946/7 Manchester U
Cohen, G. (37) 1963/4 Fulham
Cole, Andy (15) 1994/5 Manchester U
Cole, Ashley (89) 2000/01 Arsenal, Chelsea
Cole, C. (7) 2008/09 West Ham U
Cole, J. J. (56) 2000/01 West Ham U, Chelsea
Collymore, S. V. (3) 1994/5 Nottingham F, Aston Villa
Compton, L. (2) 1950/1 Arsenal

Connelly, J. (20) 1959/60 Burnley, Manchester U
Cooper, C. T. (2) 1994/5 Nottingham F
Cooper, T. (20) 1968/9 Leeds U
Coppell, S. (42) 1977/8 Manchester U
Corrigan, J. (9) 1975/6 Manchester C
Cottee, A. R. (7) 1986/7 West Ham U, Everton
Cowans, G. (10) 1982/3 Aston Villa, Bari, Aston Villa
Crawford, R. (2) 1961/2 Ipswich T
Crouch, P. J. (42) 2004/05 Southampton, Liverpool, Portsmouth, Tottenham H
Crowe, C. (1) 1962/3 Wolverhampton W
Cunningham, L. (6) 1978/9 WBA, Real Madrid
Curle, K. (3) 1991/2 Manchester C
Currie, A. (17) 1971/2 Sheffield U, Leeds U

Daley, A. M. (7) 1991/2 Aston Villa
Davenport, P. (1) 1984/5 Nottingham F
Davies, K. C. (1) 2010/11 Bolton W
Dawson, M. R. (4) 2010/11 Tottenham H
Deane, B. C. (3) 1990/1 Sheffield U
Deeley, N. (2) 1958/9 Wolverhampton W
Defoe, J. C. (46) 2003/04 Tottenham H, Portsmouth, Tottenham H
Devonshire, A. (8) 1979/80 West Ham U
Dickinson, J. (48) 1948/9 Portsmouth
Ditchburn, E. (6) 1948/9 Tottenham H
Dixon, K. M. (8) 1984/5 Chelsea
Dixon, L. M. (22) 1989/90 Arsenal
Dobson, M. (5) 1973/4 Burnley, Everton
Dorigo, A. R. (15) 1989/90 Chelsea, Leeds U
Douglas, B. (36) 1957/8 Blackburn R
Downing, S. (27) 2004/05 Middlesbrough, Aston Villa
Doyle, M. (5) 1975/6 Manchester C
Dublin, D. (4) 1997/8 Coventry C, Aston Villa
Dunn, D. J. I. (1) 2002/03 Blackburn R
Duxbury, M. (10) 1983/4 Manchester U
Dyer, K. C. (33) 1999/00 Newcastle U, West Ham U

Eastham, G. (19) 1962/3 Arsenal
Eckersley, W. (17) 1949/50 Blackburn R
Edwards, D. (18) 1954/5 Manchester U
Ehiogu, U. (4) 1995/6 Aston Villa, Middlesbrough
Ellerington, W. (2) 1948/9 Southampton
Elliott, W. H. (5) 1951/2 Burnley

Fantham, J. (1) 1961/2 Sheffield W
Fashanu, J. (2) 1988/9 Wimbledon
Fenwick, T. (20) 1983/4 QPR, Tottenham H
Ferdinand, L. (17) 1992/3 QPR, Newcastle U, Tottenham H
Ferdinand, R. G. (81) 1997/8 West Ham U, Leeds U, Manchester U
Finney, T. (76) 1946/7 Preston NE
Flowers, R. (49) 1954/5 Wolverhampton W
Flowers, T. (11) 1992/3 Southampton, Blackburn R
Foster, B. (5) 2006/07 Manchester U, Birmingham C
Foster, S. (3) 1981/2 Brighton
Foulkes, W. (1) 1954/5 Manchester U
Fowler, R. B. (26) 1995/6 Liverpool, Leeds U
Francis, G. (12) 1974/5 QPR
Francis, T. (52) 1976/7 Birmingham C, Nottingham F, Manchester C, Sampdoria
Franklin, N. (27) 1946/7 Stoke C
Froggatt, J. (13) 1949/50 Portsmouth
Froggatt, R. (4) 1952/3 Sheffield W

Gardner, A. (1) 2003/04 Tottenham H
Garrett, T. (3) 1951/2 Blackpool
Gascoigne, P. J. (57) 1988/9 Tottenham H, Lazio, Rangers, Middlesbrough
Gates, E. (2) 1980/1 Ipswich T
George, F. C. (1) 1976/7 Derby Co
Gerrard, S. G. (89) 1999/00 Liverpool
Gibbs, K. J. R. (2) 2010/11 Arsenal
Gidman, J. (1) 1976/7 Aston Villa
Gillard, I. (3) 1974/5 QPR
Goddard, P. (1) 1981/2 West Ham U
Grainger, C. (7) 1955/6 Sheffield U, Sunderland
Gray, A. A. (1) 1991/2 Crystal P
Gray, M. (3) 1998/9 Sunderland
Greaves, J. (57) 1958/9 Chelsea, Tottenham H
Green, R. P. (11) 2004/05 Norwich C, West Ham U
Greenhoff, B. (18) 1975/6 Manchester U, Leeds U
Gregory, J. (6) 1982/3 QPR
Guppy, S. (1) 1999/00 Leicester C

Hagan, J. (1) 1948/9 Sheffield U
Haines, J. (1) 1948/9 WBA
Hall, J. (17) 1955/6 Birmingham C

Hancocks, J. (3) 1948/9 Wolverhampton W
Hardwick, G. (13) 1946/7 Middlesbrough
Harford, M. G. (2) 1987/8 Luton T
Hargreaves, O. (42) 2001/02 Bayern Munich, Manchester U
Harris, G. (1) 1965/6 Burnley
Harris, P. (2) 1949/50 Portsmouth
Hart, C. (11) 2007/08 Manchester C
Harvey, C. (1) 1970/1 Everton
Hassall, H. (5) 1950/1 Huddersfield T, Bolton W
Hateley, M. (32) 1983/4 Portsmouth, AC Milan, Monaco, Rangers
Haynes, J. (56) 1954/5 Fulham
Hector, K. (2) 1973/4 Derby Co
Hellawell, M. (2) 1962/3 Birmingham C
Henderson, J. B. (1) 2010/11 Sunderland
Hendrie, L. A. (1) 1998/9 Aston Villa
Henry, R. (1) 1962/3 Tottenham H
Heskey, E. W. (62) 1998/9 Leicester C, Liverpool, Birmingham C, Wigan Ath, Aston Villa
Hill, F. (2) 1962/3 Bolton W
Hill, G. (6) 1975/6 Manchester U
Hill, R. (3) 1982/3 Luton T
Hinchcliffe, A. G. (7) 1996/7 Everton, Sheffield W
Hinton, A. (3) 1962/3 Wolverhampton W, Nottingham F
Hirst, D. E. (3) 1990/1 Sheffield W
Hitchens, G. (7) 1960/1 Aston Villa, Internazionale
Hoddle, G. (53) 1979/80 Tottenham H, Monaco
Hodge, S. B. (24) 1985/6 Aston Villa, Tottenham H, Nottingham F
Hodgkinson, A. (5) 1956/7 Sheffield U
Holden, D. (5) 1958/9 Bolton W
Holliday, E. (3) 1959/60 Middlesbrough
Hollins, J. (1) 1966/7 Chelsea
Hopkinson, E. (14) 1957/8 Bolton W
Howe, D. (23) 1957/8 WBA
Howe, J. (3) 1947/8 Derby Co
Howey, S. N. (4) 1994/5 Newcastle U
Huddlestone, T. A. (3) 2009/10 Tottenham H
Hudson, A. (2) 1974/5 Stoke C
Hughes, E. (62) 1969/70 Liverpool, Wolverhampton W
Hughes, L. (3) 1949/50 Liverpool
Hunt, R. (34) 1961/2 Liverpool
Hunt, S. (2) 1983/4 WBA
Hunter, N. (28) 1965/6 Leeds U
Hurst, G. (49) 1965/6 West Ham U

Ince, P. (53) 1992/3 Manchester U, Internazionale, Liverpool, Middlesbrough

Jagielka, P. N. (9) 2007/08 Everton
James, D. B. (53) 1996/7 Liverpool, Aston Villa, West Ham U, Manchester C, Portsmouth
Jarvis, M. T. (1) 2010/11 Wolverhampton W
Jeffers, F. (1) 2002/03 Arsenal
Jenas, J. A. (21) 2002/03 Newcastle U, Tottenham H
Jezzard, B. (2) 1953/4 Fulham
Johnson, A. (8) 2004/05 Crystal P, Everton
Johnson, A. (6) 2009/10 Manchester C
Johnson, D. (8) 1974/5 Ipswich T, Liverpool
Johnson, G. M. C. (34) 2003/04 Chelsea, Portsmouth, Liverpool
Johnson, S. A. M. (1) 2000/01 Derby Co
Johnston, H. (10) 1946/7 Blackpool
Jones, M. (3) 1964/5 Sheffield U, Leeds U
Jones, R. (8) 1991/2 Liverpool
Jones, W. H. (2) 1949/50 Liverpool

Kay, A. (1) 1962/3 Everton
Keegan, K. (63) 1972/3 Liverpool, SV Hamburg, Southampton
Kennedy, A. (2) 1983/4 Liverpool
Kennedy, R. (17) 1975/6 Liverpool
Keown, M. R. (43) 1991/2 Everton, Arsenal
Kevan, D. (14) 1956/7 WBA
Kidd, B. (2) 1969/70 Manchester U
King, L. B. (21) 2001/02 Tottenham H
Kirkland, C. E. (1) 2006/07 Liverpool
Knight, Z. (2) 2004/05 Fulham
Knowles, C. (4) 1967/8 Tottenham H
Konchesky, P. M. (2) 2002/03 Charlton Ath, West Ham U

Labone, B. (26) 1962/3 Everton
Lampard, F. J. (86) 1999/00 West Ham U, Chelsea
Lampard, F. R. G. (2) 1972/3 West Ham U
Langley, J. (3) 1957/8 Fulham
Langton, R. (11) 1946/7 Blackburn R, Preston NE, Bolton W
Latchford, R. (12) 1977/8 Everton
Lawler, C. (4) 1970/1 Liverpool
Lawton, T. (15) 1946/7 Chelsea, Notts Co
Lee, F. (27) 1968/9 Manchester C

Lee, J. (1) 1950/1 Derby C
Lee, R. M. (21) 1994/5 Newcastle U
Lee, S. (14) 1982/3 Liverpool
Lennon, A. J. (19) 2005/06 Tottenham H
Lescott, J. P. (13) 2007/08 Everton, Manchester C
Le Saux, G. P. (36) 1993/4 Blackburn R, Chelsea
Le Tissier, M. P. (8) 1993/4 Southampton
Lindsay, A. (4) 1973/4 Liverpool
Lineker, G. (80) 1983/4 Leicester C, Everton, Barcelona, Tottenham H
Little, B. (1) 1974/5 Aston Villa
Lloyd, L. (4) 1970/1 Liverpool, Nottingham F
Lofthouse, N. (33) 1950/1 Bolton W
Lowe, E. (3) 1946/7 Aston Villa

Mabbutt, G. (16) 1982/3 Tottenham H
Macdonald, M. (14) 1971/2 Newcastle U
Madeley, P. (24) 1970/1 Leeds U
Mannion, W. (26) 1946/7 Middlesbrough
Mariner, P. (35) 1976/7 Ipswich T, Arsenal
Marsh, R. (9) 1971/2 QPR, Manchester C
Martin, A. (17) 1980/1 West Ham U
Martyn, A. N. (23) 1991/2 Crystal P, Leeds U
Marwood, B. (1) 1988/9 Arsenal
Matthews, R. (5) 1955/6 Coventry C
Matthews, S. (37) 1946/7 Stoke C, Blackpool
McCann, G. P. (1) 2000/01 Sunderland
McDermott, T. (25) 1977/8 Liverpool
McDonald, C. (8) 1957/8 Burnley
McFarland, R. (28) 1970/1 Derby C
McGarry, W. (4) 1953/4 Huddersfield T
McGuinness, W. (2) 1958/9 Manchester U
McMahon, S. (17) 1987/8 Liverpool
McManaman, S. (37) 1994/5 Liverpool, Real Madrid
McNab, R. (4) 1968/9 Arsenal
McNeil, M. (9) 1960/1 Middlesbrough
Meadows, J. (1) 1954/5 Manchester C
Medley, L. (6) 1950/1 Tottenham H
Melia, J. (2) 1962/3 Liverpool
Merrick, G. (23) 1951/2 Birmingham C
Merson, P. C. (21) 1991/2 Arsenal, Middlesbrough, Aston Villa
Metcalfe, V. (2) 1950/1 Huddersfield T
Milburn, J. (13) 1948/9 Newcastle U
Miller, B. (1) 1960/1 Burnley
Mills, D. J. (19) 2000/01 Leeds U
Mills, M. (42) 1972/3 Ipswich T

Milne, G. (14) 1962/3 Liverpool

Milner, J. P. (19) 2009/10 Aston Villa, Manchester C

Milton, C. A. (1) 1951/2 Arsenal

Moore, R. (108) 1961/2 West Ham U

Morley, A. (6) 1981/2 Aston Villa

Morris, J. (3) 1948/9 Derby Co

Mortensen, S. (25) 1946/7 Blackpool

Mozley, B. (3) 1949/50 Derby Co

Mullen, J. (12) 1946/7 Wolverhampton W

Mullery, A. (35) 1964/5 Tottenham H

Murphy, D. B. (9) 2001/02 Liverpool

Neal, P. (50) 1975/6 Liverpool

Neville, G. A. (85) 1994/5 Manchester U

Neville, P. J. (59) 1995/6 Manchester U, Everton

Newton, K. (27) 1965/6 Blackburn R, Everton

Nicholls, J. (2) 1953/4 WBA

Nicholson, W. (1) 1950/1 Tottenham H

Nish, D. (5) 1972/3 Derby Co

Norman, M. (23) 1961/2 Tottenham H

Nugent, D. J. (1) 2006/07 Preston NE

O'Grady, M. (2) 1962/3 Huddersfield T, Leeds U

Osgood, P. (4) 1969/70 Chelsea

Osman, R. (11) 1979/80 Ipswich T

Owen, M. J. (89) 1997/8 Liverpool, Real Madrid, Newcastle U

Owen, S. (3) 1953/4 Luton T

Paine, T. (19) 1962/3 Southampton

Pallister, G. (22) 1987/8 Middlesbrough, Manchester U

Palmer, C. L. (18) 1991/2 Sheffield W

Parker, P. A. (19) 1988/9 QPR, Manchester U

Parker, S. M. (6) 2003/04 Charlton Ath, Chelsea, Newcastle U, West Ham U

Parkes, P. (1) 1973/4 QPR

Parlour, R. (10) 1998/9 Arsenal

Parry, R. (2) 1959/60 Bolton W

Peacock, A. (6) 1961/2 Middlesbrough, Leeds U

Pearce, S. (78) 1986/7 Nottingham F, West Ham U

Pearson, Stan (8) 1947/8 Manchester U

Pearson, Stuart (15) 1975/6 Manchester U

Pegg, D. (1) 1956/7 Manchester U

Pejic, M. (4) 1973/4 Stoke C

Perry, W. (3) 1955/6 Blackpool

Perryman, S. (1) 1981/2 Tottenham H

Peters, M. (67) 1965/6 West Ham U, Tottenham H

Phelan, M. C. (1) 1989/90 Manchester U

Phillips, K. (8) 1998/9 Sunderland

Phillips, L. (3) 1951/2 Portsmouth

Pickering, F. (3) 1963/4 Everton

Pickering, N. (1) 1982/3 Sunderland

Pilkington, B. (1) 1954/5 Burnley

Platt, D. (62) 1989/90 Aston Villa, Bari, Juventus, Sampdoria, Arsenal

Pointer, R. (3) 1961/2 Burnley

Powell, C. G. (5) 2000/01 Charlton Ath

Pye, J. (1) 1949/50 Wolverhampton W

Quixall, A. (5) 1953/4 Sheffield W

Radford, J. (2) 1968/9 Arsenal

Ramsey, A. (32) 1948/9 Southampton, Tottenham H

Reaney, P. (3) 1968/9 Leeds U

Redknapp, J. F. (17) 1995/6 Liverpool

Reeves, K. (2) 1979/80 Norwich C, Manchester C

Regis, C. (5) 1981/2 WBA, Coventry C

Reid, P. (13) 1984/5 Everton

Revie, D. (6) 1954/5 Manchester C

Richards, J. (1) 1972/3 Wolverhampton W

Richards, M. (12) 2006/07 Manchester C

Richardson, K. (1) 1993/4 Aston Villa

Richardon, K. E. (8) 2004/05 Manchester U

Rickaby, S. (1) 1953/4 WBA

Ricketts, M. B. (1) 2001/02 Bolton W

Rimmer, J. (1) 1975/6 Arsenal

Ripley, S. E. (2) 1993/4 Blackburn R

Rix, G. (17) 1980/1 Arsenal

Robb, G. (1) 1953/4 Tottenham H

Roberts, G. (6) 1982/3 Tottenham H

Robinson, P. W. (41) 2002/03 Leeds U, Tottenham H

Robson, B. (90) 1979/80 WBA, Manchester U

Robson, R. (20) 1957/8 WBA

Rocastle, D. (14) 1988/9 Arsenal

Rooney, W. (70) 2002/03 Everton, Manchester U

Rowley, J. (6) 1948/9 Manchester U

Royle, J. (6) 1970/1 Everton, Manchester C

Ruddock, N. (1) 1994/5 Liverpool

Sadler, D. (4) 1967/8 Manchester U

Salako, J. A. (5) 1990/1 Crystal P

Sansom, K. (86) 1978/9 Crystal P, Arsenal

Scales, J. R. (3) 1994/5 Liverpool
Scholes, P. (66) 1996/7 Manchester U
Scott, L. (17) 1946/7 Arsenal
Seaman, D. A. (75) 1988/9 QPR, Arsenal
Sewell, J. (6) 1951/2 Sheffield W
Shackleton, L. (5) 1948/9 Sunderland
Sharpe, L. S. (8) 1990/1 Manchester U
Shaw, G. (5) 1958/9 Sheffield U
Shearer, A. (63) 1991/2 Southampton, Blackburn R, Newcastle U
Shellito, K. (1) 1962/3 Chelsea
Sheringham, E. (51) 1992/3 Tottenham H, Manchester U, Tottenham H
Sherwood, T. A. (3) 1998/9 Tottenham H
Shilton, P. (125) 1970/1 Leicester C, Stoke C, Nottingham F, Southampton, Derby Co
Shimwell, E. (1) 1948/9 Blackpool
Shorey, N, (2) 2006/07 Reading
Sillett, P. (3) 1954/5 Chelsea
Sinclair, T. (12) 2001/02 West Ham U, Manchester C
Sinton, A. (12) 1991/2 QPR, Sheffield W
Slater, W. (12) 1954/5 Wolverhampton W
Smith, A. (19) 2000/01 Leeds U, Manchester U, Newcastle U
Smith, A. M. (13) 1988/9 Arsenal
Smith, L. (6) 1950/1 Arsenal
Smith, R. (15) 1960/1 Tottenham H
Smith, Tom (1) 1970/1 Liverpool
Smith, Trevor (2) 1959/60 Birmingham C
Southgate, G. (57) 1995/6 Aston Villa, Middlesbrough
Spink, N. (1) 1982/3 Aston Villa
Springett, R. (33) 1959/60 Sheffield W
Staniforth, R. (8) 1953/4 Huddersfield T
Statham, D. (3) 1982/3 WBA
Stein, B. (1) 1983/4 Luton T
Stepney, A. (1) 1967/8 Manchester U
Sterland, M. (1) 1988/9 Sheffield W
Steven, T. M. (36) 1984/5 Everton, Rangers, Marseille
Stevens, G. A. (7) 1984/5 Tottenham H
Stevens, M. G. (46) 1984/5 Everton, Rangers
Stewart, P. A. (3) 1991/2 Tottenham H
Stiles, N. (28) 1964/5 Manchester U
Stone, S. B. (9) 1995/6 Nottingham F
Storey-Moore, I. (1) 1969/70 Nottingham F
Storey, P. (19) 1970/1 Arsenal
Streten, B. (1) 1949/50 Luton T
Summerbee, M. (8) 1967/8 Manchester C
Sunderland, A. (1) 1979/80 Arsenal
Sutton, C. R. (1) 1997/8 Blackburn R

Swan, P. (19) 1959/60 Sheffield W
Swift, F. (19) 1946/7 Manchester C

Talbot, B. (6) 1976/7 Ipswich T, Arsenal
Tambling, R. (3) 1962/3 Chelsea
Taylor, E. (1) 1953/4 Blackpool
Taylor, J. (2) 1950/1 Fulham
Taylor, P. H. (3) 1947/8 Liverpool
Taylor, P. J. (4) 1975/6 Crystal P
Taylor, T. (19) 1952/3 Manchester U
Temple, D. (1) 1964/5 Everton
Terry, J. G. (68) 2002/03 Chelsea
Thomas, Danny (2) 1982/3 Coventry C
Thomas, Dave (8) 1974/5 QPR
Thomas, G. R. (9) 1990/1 Crystal P
Thomas, M. L. (2) 1988/9 Arsenal
Thompson, A. (1) 2003/04 Celtic
Thompson, P. (16) 1963/4 Liverpool
Thompson, P. B. (42) 1975/6 Liverpool
Thompson, T. (2) 1951/2 Aston Villa, Preston NE
Thomson, R. (8) 1963/4 Wolverhampton W
Todd, C. (27) 1971/2 Derby Co
Towers, T. (3) 1975/6 Sunderland
Tueart, D. (6) 1974/5 Manchester C

Ufton, D. (1) 1953/4 Charlton Ath
Unsworth, D. G. (1) 1994/5 Everton
Upson, M. J. (21) 2002/03 Birmingham C, West Ham U

Vassell, D. (22) 2001/02 Aston Villa
Venables, T. (2) 1964/5 Chelsea
Venison, B. (2) 1994/5 Newcastle U
Viljoen, C. (2) 1974/5 Ipswich T
Viollet, D. (2) 1959/60 Manchester U

Waddle, C. R. (62) 1984/5 Newcastle U, Tottenham H, Marseille
Waiters, A. (5) 1963/4 Blackpool
Walcott, T. J. (17) 2005/06 Arsenal
Walker, D. S. (59) 1988/9 Nottingham F, Sampdoria, Sheffield W
Walker, I. M. (4) 1995/6 Tottenham H, Leicester C
Wallace, D. L. (1) 1985/6 Southampton
Walsh, P. (5) 1982/3 Luton T
Walters, K. M. (1) 1990/1 Rangers
Ward, P. (1) 1979/80 Brighton
Ward, T. (2) 1947/8 Derby C
Warnock, S. (2) 2007/08 Blackburn R, Aston Villa
Watson, D. (12) 1983/4 Norwich C, Everton

299

Watson, D. V. (65) 1973/4 Sunderland, Manchester C, Werder Bremen, Southampton, Stoke C

Watson, W. (4) 1949/50 Sunderland

Webb, N. (26) 1987/8 Nottingham F, Manchester U

Welbeck, D. (1) 2010/11 Manchester U

Weller, K. (4) 1973/4 Leicester C

West, G. (3) 1968/9 Everton

Wheeler, J. (1) 1954/5 Bolton W

White, D. (1) 1992/3 Manchester C

Whitworth, S. (7) 1974/5 Leicester C

Whymark, T. (1) 1977/8 Ipswich T

Wignall, F. (2) 1964/5 Nottingham F

Wilcox, J. M. (3) 1995/6 Blackburn R, Leeds U

Wilkins, R. (84) 1975/6 Chelsea, Manchester U, AC Milan

Williams, B. (24) 1948/9 Wolverhampton W

Williams, S. (6) 1982/3 Southampton

Willis, A. (1) 1951/2 Tottenham H

Wilshaw, D. (12) 1953/4 Wolverhampton W

Wilshere, J. A. (5) 2010/11 Arsenal

Wilson, R. (63) 1959/60 Huddersfield T, Everton

Winterburn, N. (2) 1989/90 Arsenal

Wise, D. F. (21) 1990/1 Chelsea

Withe, P. (11) 1980/1 Aston Villa

Wood, R. (3) 1954/5 Manchester U

Woodcock, A. (42) 1977/8 Nottingham F, FC Cologne, Arsenal

Woodgate, J. S. (8) 1998/9 Leeds U, Newcastle U, Real Madrid, Tottenham H

Woods, C. C. E. (43) 1984/5 Norwich C, Rangers, Sheffield W

Worthington, F. (8) 1973/4 Leicester C

Wright, I. E. (33) 1990/1 Crystal P, Arsenal, West Ham U

Wright, M. (45) 1983/4 Southampton, Derby C, Liverpool

Wright, R. I. (2) 1999/00 Ipswich T, Arsenal

Wright, T. (11) 1967/8 Everton

Wright, W. (105) 1946/7 Wolverhampton W

Wright-Phillips, S. C. (36) 2004/05 Manchester C, Chelsea, Manchester C

Young, A. S. (15) 2007/08 Aston Villa

Young, G. (1) 1964/5 Sheffield W

Young, L. P. (7) 2004/05 Charlton Ath

Zamora, R. L. (1) 2010/11 Fulham

NORTHERN IRELAND

Aherne, T. (4) 1946/7 Belfast Celtic, Luton T

Anderson, T. (22) 1972/3 Manchester U, Swindon T, Peterborough U

Armstrong, G. (63) 1976/7 Tottenham H, Watford, Real Mallorca, WBA, Chesterfield

Baird, C. P. (51) 2002/03 Southampton, Fulham

Barr, H. H. (3) 1961/2 Linfield, Coventry C

Barton, A. J, (1) 2010/11 Preston NE

Best, G. (37) 1963/4 Manchester U, Fulham

Bingham, W. (56) 1950/1 Sunderland, Luton T, Everton, Port Vale

Black, K. (30) 1987/8 Luton T, Nottingham F

Blair, R. (5) 1974/5 Oldham Ath

Blanchflower, D. (54) 1949/50 Barnsley, Aston Villa, Tottenham H

Blanchflower, J. (12) 1953/4 Manchester U

Blayney, A. (5) 2005/06 Doncaster R, Linfield

Bowler, G. C. (3) 1949/50 Hull C

Boyce, L. (4) 2010/11 Werder Bremen

Braithwaite, R. (10) 1961/2 Linfield, Middlesbrough

Braniff, K. R. (2) 2009/10 Portadown

Brennan, R. (5) 1948/9 Luton T, Birmingham C, Fulham

Briggs, R. (2) 1961/2 Manchester U, Swansea

Brotherston, N. (27) 1979/80 Blackburn R

Bruce, W. (2) 1960/1 Glentoran

Brunt, C. (33) 2004/05 Sheffield W, WBA

Bryan, M. A. (2) 2009/10 Watford

Camp, L. M. J. (2) 2010/11 Nottingham F

Campbell, A. (2) 1962/3 Crusaders

Campbell, D. A. (10) 1985/6 Nottingham F, Charlton Ath

Campbell, J. (2) 1950/1 Fulham

Campbell, R. M. (2) 1981/2 Bradford C

Campbell, W. (6) 1967/8 Dundee

Capaldi, A. C. (22) 2003/04 Plymouth Arg, Cardiff C
Carey, J. (7) 1946/7 Manchester U
Carroll, R. E. (19) 1996/7 Wigan Ath, Manchester U, West Ham U
Carson, J. G. (2) 2010/11 Ipswich T
Carson, S. (1) 2008/09 Coleraine
Casement, C. (1) 2008/09 Ipswich T
Casey, T. (12) 1954/5 Newcastle U, Portsmouth
Caskey, A. (8) 1978/9 Derby C, Tulsa Roughnecks
Cassidy, T. (24) 1970/1 Newcastle U, Burnley
Cathcart, C. G. (5) 2010/11 Blackpool
Caughey, M. (2) 1985/6 Linfield
Clarke, C. J. (38) 1985/6 Bournemouth, Southampton, Portsmouth
Cleary, J. (5) 1981/2 Glentoran
Clements, D. (48) 1964/5 Coventry C, Sheffield W, Everton, New York Cosmos
Clingan, S. G. (28) 2005/06 Nottingham F, Norwich C, Coventry C
Clyde, M.G. (3) 2004/05 Wolverhampon W
Coates, C. (6) 2008/09 Crusaders
Cochrane, D. (10) 1946/7 Leeds U
Cochrane, T. (26) 1975/6 Coleraine, Burnley, Middlesbrough, Gillingham
Connell, T. E. (1) 1977/8 Coleraine
Coote, A. (6) 1998/9 Norwich C
Cowan, J. (1) 1969/70 Newcastle U
Coyle, F. (4) 1955/6 Coleraine, Nottingham F
Coyle, L. (1) 1988/9 Derry C
Coyle, R. (5) 1972/3 Sheffield W
Craig, D. (25) 1966/7 Newcastle U
Craigan, S. J. (54) 2002/03 Partick T, Motherwell
Crossan, E. (3) 1949/50 Blackburn R
Crossan, J. (24) 1959/60 Sparta Rotterdam, Sunderland, Manchester C, Middlesbrough
Cunningham, W. (30) 1950/1 St Mirren, Leicester C, Dunfermline Ath
Cush, W. (26) 1950/1 Glentoran, Leeds U, Portadown

Dallas, S. (1) 2010/11 Crusaders
D'Arcy, S. (5) 1951/2 Chelsea, Brentford
Davis, S. (46) 2004/05 Aston Villa, Fulham, Rangers
Davison, A. J. (3) 1995/6 Bolton W, Bradford C, Grimsby T

Dennison, R. (18) 1987/8 Wolverhampton W
Devine, J. (1) 1989/90 Glentoran
Dickson, D. (4) 1969/70 Coleraine
Dickson, T. (1) 1956/7 Linfield
Dickson, W. (12) 1950/1 Chelsea, Arsenal
Doherty, L. (2) 1984/5 Linfield
Doherty, P. (6) 1946/7 Derby Co, Huddersfield T, Doncaster R
Doherty, T. E. (9) 2002/03 Bristol C
Donaghy, M. (91) 1979/80 Luton T, Manchester U, Chelsea
Donnelly, M. (1) 2008/09 Crusaders
Dougan, D. (43) 1957/8 Portsmouth, Blackburn R, Aston Villa, Leicester C, Wolverhampton W
Douglas, J. P. (1) 1946/7 Belfast Celtic
Dowd, H. (3) 1973/4 Glenavon, Sheffield W
Dowie, I. (59) 1989/90 Luton T, West Ham U, Southampton, Crystal P, West Ham U, QPR
Duff, M. J. (22) 2001/02 Cheltenham T, Burnley
Dunlop, G. (4) 1984/5 Linfield

Eglington, T. (6) 1946/7 Everton
Elder, A. (40) 1959/60 Burnley, Stoke C
Elliott, S. (39) 2000/01 Motherwell, Hull C
Evans, C. J. (11) 2008/09 Manchester U
Evans, J. G. (26) 2006/07 Manchester U

Farrell, P. (7) 1946/7 Everton
Feeney, J. (2) 1946/7 Linfield, Swansea T
Feeney, W. (1) 1975/6 Glentoran
Feeney, W. J. (42) 2001/02 Bournemouth, Luton T, Cardiff C, Oldham Ath
Ferguson, G. (5) 1998/9 Linfield
Ferguson, S. (1) 2008/09 Newcastle U
Ferguson, W. (2) 1965/6 Linfield
Ferris, R. (3) 1949/50 Birmingham C
Fettis, A. (25) 1991/2 Hull C, Nottingham F, Blackburn R
Finney, T. (14) 1974/5 Sunderland, Cambridge U
Fleming, J. G. (31) 1986/7 Nottingham F, Manchester C, Barnsley
Forde, T. (4) 1958/9 Ards

Gallogly, C. (2) 1950/1 Huddersfield T
Garrett, R. (5) 2008/09 Linfield
Garton, R. (1) 1968/9 Oxford U
Gault, M. (1) 2007/08 Linfield

Gillespie, K. R. (86) 1994/5
Manchester U, Newcastle U, Blackburn R, Leicester C, Sheffield U
Gorman, R. J. (8) 2009/10
Wolverhampton W
Gorman, W. (4) 1946/7 Brentford
Graham, W. (14) 1950/1 Doncaster R
Gray, P. (26) 1992/3 Luton T, Sunderland, Nancy, Luton T, Burnley, Oxford U
Gregg, H. (25) 1953/4 Doncaster R, Manchester U
Griffin, D. J. (29) 1995/6 St Johnstone, Dundee U, Stockport Co

Hamill, R. (1) 1998/9 Glentoran
Hamilton, B. (50) 1968/9 Linfield, Ipswich T, Everton, Millwall, Swindon T
Hamilton, G. (5) 2002/03 Portadown
Hamilton, W. (41) 1977/8 QPR, Burnley, Oxford U
Harkin, T. (5) 1967/8 Southport, Shrewsbury T
Harvey, M. (34) 1960/1 Sunderland
Hatton, S. (2) 1962/3 Linfield
Healy, D. J. (86) 1999/00 Manchester U, Preston NE, Leeds U, Fulham, Sunderland, Rangers
Healy, P. J. (4) 1981/2 Coleraine, Glentoran
Hegan, D. (7) 1969/70 WBA, Wolverhampton W
Hill, C. F. (27) 1989/90 Sheffield U, Leicester C, Trelleborg, Northampton T
Hill, J. (7) 1958/9 Norwich C, Everton
Hinton, E. (7) 1946/7 Fulham, Millwall
Hodson, L. J. S. (4) 2010/11 Watford
Holmes, S. P. (1) 2001/02 Wrexham
Horlock, K. (32) 1994/5 Swindon T, Manchester C
Hughes, A. W. (76) 1997/8 Newcastle U, Aston Villa, Fulham
Hughes, J. (2) 2005/06 Lincoln C
Hughes, M. A. (2) 2005/06 Oldham Ath
Hughes, M. E. (71) 1991/2 Manchester C, Strasbourg, West Ham U, Wimbledon, Crystal P
Hughes, P. (3) 1986/7 Bury
Hughes, W. (1) 1950/1 Bolton W
Humphries, W. (14) 1961/2 Ards, Coventry C, Swansea T
Hunter, A. (53) 1969/70 Blackburn R, Ipswich T
Hunter, B. V. (15) 1994/5 Wrexham, Reading

Hunter, V. (2) 1961/2 Coleraine

Ingham, M. G. (3) 2004/05 Sunderland, Wrexham
Irvine, R. (8) 1961/2 Linfield, Stoke C
Irvine, W. (23) 1962/3 Burnley, Preston NE, Brighton & HA

Jackson, T. (35) 1968/9 Everton, Nottingham F, Manchester U
Jamison, A. (1) 1975/6 Glentoran
Jenkins, I. (6) 1996/7 Chester C, Dundee U
Jennings, P. (119) 1963/4 Watford, Tottenham H, Arsenal, Tottenham H
Johnson, D. M. (56) 1998/9 Blackburn R, Birmingham C
Johnston, W. (2) 1961/2 Glenavon, Oldham Ath
Jones, J. (3) 1955/6 Glenavon
Jones, S. G. (29) 2002/03 Crewe Alex, Burnley

Keane, T. (1) 1948/9 Swansea T
Kee, P. V. (9) 1989/90 Oxford U, Ards
Keith, R. (23) 1957/8 Newcastle U
Kelly, H. (4) 1949/50 Fulham, Southampton
Kelly, P. (1) 1949/50 Barnsley
Kennedy, P. H. (20) 1998/9 Watford, Wigan Ath
Kirk, A. R. (11) 1999/00 Heart of Midlothian, Boston U, Northampton T, Dunfermline Ath

Lafferty, K. (29) 2005/06 Burnley, Rangers
Lawrie, J. (3) 2008/09 Port Vale
Lawther, I. (4) 1959/60 Sunderland, Blackburn R
Lennon, N. F. (40) 1993/4 Crewe Alex, Leicester C, Celtic
Little, A. (6) 2008/09 Rangers
Lockhart, N. (8) 1946/7 Linfield, Coventry C, Aston Villa
Lomas, S. M. (45) 1993/4 Manchester C, West Ham U
Lutton, B. (6) 1969/70 Wolverhampton W, West Ham U

Magennis, J. B. D. (3) 2009/10 Cardiff C, Aberdeen
Magill, E. (26) 1961/2 Arsenal, Brighton & HA

Magilton, J. (52) 1990/1 Oxford U, Southampton, Sheffield W, Ipswich T

Mannus, A. (4) 2003/04 Linfield

Martin, C. (6) 1946/7 Glentoran, Leeds U, Aston Villa

McAdams, W. (15) 1953/4 Manchester C, Bolton W, Leeds U

McAlinden, J. (2) 1946/7 Portsmouth, Southend U

McArdle, R. A. (4) 2009/10 Rochdale, Aberdeen

McAuley, G. (30) 2004/05 Lincoln C, Leicester C, Ipswich T

McBride, S. (4) 1990/1 Glenavon

McCabe, J. (6) 1948/9 Leeds U

McCann, G. S. (33) 2001/02 West Ham U, Cheltenham T, Barnsley, Scunthorpe U, Peterborough U

McCarthy, J. D. (18) 1995/6 Port Vale, Birmingham C

McCartney, G. (34) 2001/02 Sunderland, West Ham U, Sunderland

McCavana, T. (3) 1954/5 Coleraine

McCleary, J. W. (1) 1954/5 Cliftonville

McClelland, J. (6) 1960/1 Arsenal, Fulham

McClelland, J. (53) 1979/80 Mansfield T, Rangers, Watford, Leeds U

McCourt, F. (6) 1951/2 Manchester C

McCourt, P. J. (7) 2001/02 Rochdale, Celtic

McCoy, R. (1) 1986/7 Coleraine

McCreery, D. (67) 1975/6 Manchester U, QPR, Tulsa Roughnecks, Newcastle U, Heart of Midlothian

McCrory, S. (1) 1957/8 Southend U

McCullough, W. (10) 1960/1 Arsenal, Millwall

McCurdy, C. (1) 1979/80 Linfield

McDonald, A. (52) 1985/6 QPR

McElhinney, G. (6) 1983/4 Bolton W

McEvilly, L. R. (1) 2001/02 Rochdale

McFaul, I. (6) 1966/7 Linfield, Newcastle U

McGarry, J. K. (3) 1950/1 Cliftonville

McGaughey, M. (1) 1984/5 Linfield

McGibbon, P. C. G. (7) 1994/5 Manchester U, Wigan Ath

McGinn, N. (13) 2009/10 Celtic

McGivern, R. (13) 2008/09 Manchester C

McGovern, M. (1) 2009/10 Ross Co

McGrath, R. (21) 1973/4 Tottenham H, Manchester U

McIlroy, J. (55) 1951/2 Burnley, Stoke C

McIlroy, S. B. (88) 1971/2 Manchester U, Stoke C, Manchester C

McKeag, W. (2) 1967/8 Glentoran

McKenna, J. (7) 1949/50 Huddersfield T

McKenzie, R. (1) 1966/7 Airdrieonians

McKinney, W. (1) 1965/6 Falkirk

McKnight, A. (10) 1987/8 Celtic, West Ham U

McLaughlin, J. (12) 1961/2 Shrewsbury T, Swansea T

McLean, B. S. (1) 2005/06 Rangers

McMahon, G. J. (17) 1994/5 Tottenham H, Stoke C

McMichael, A. (39) 1949/50 Newcastle U

McMillan, S. (2) 1962/3 Manchester U

McMordie, E. (21) 1968/9 Middlesbrough

McMorran, E. (15) 1946/7 Belfast Celtic, Barnsley, Doncaster R

McNally, B. A. (5) 1985/6 Shrewsbury T

McParland, P. (34) 1953/4 Aston Villa, Wolverhampton W

McQuoid, J. J. (3) 2010/11 Millwall

McVeigh, P. (20) 1998/9 Tottenham H, Norwich C

Montgomery, F. J. (1) 1954/5 Coleraine

Moore, C. (1) 1948/9 Glentoran

Moreland, V. (6) 1978/9 Derby Co

Morgan, S. (18) 1971/2 Port Vale, Aston Villa, Brighton & HA, Sparta Rotterdam

Morrow, S. J. (39) 1989/90 Arsenal, QPR

Mulgrew, J. (2) 2009/10 Linfield

Mullan, G. (4) 1982/3 Glentoran

Mulryne, P. P. (27) 1996/7 Manchester U, Norwich C, Cardiff C

Murdock, C. J. (34) 1999/00 Preston NE, Hibernian, Crewe Alex, Rotherham U

Napier, R. (1) 1965/6 Bolton W

Neill, T. (59) 1960/1 Arsenal, Hull C

Nelson, S. (51) 1969/70 Arsenal, Brighton & HA

Nicholl, C. (51) 1974/5 Aston Villa, Southampton, Grimsby T

Nicholl, J. M. (73) 1975/6 Manchester U, Toronto Blizzard, Sunderland, Rangers, WBA

Nicholson, J. (41) 1960/1 Manchester U, Huddersfield T

Nolan, I. R. (18) 1996/7 Sheffield W, Bradford C, Wigan Ath

Norwood, O. J. (4) 2010/11 Manchester U

O'Boyle, G. (13) 1993/4 Dunfermline Ath, St Johnstone

O'Connor, M. J. (10) 2007/08 Crewe Alex, Scunthorpe U

O'Doherty, A. (2) 1969/70 Coleraine

O'Driscoll, J. (3) 1948/9 Swansea T

O'Kane, L. (20) 1969/70 Nottingham F

O'Neill, C. (3) 1988/9 Motherwell

O'Neill, H. M. (64) 1971/2 Distillery, Nottingham F, Norwich C, Manchester C, Norwich C, Notts Co

O'Neill, J. (1) 1961/2 Sunderland

O'Neill, J. P. (39) 1979/80 Leicester C

O'Neill, M. A. (31) 1987/8 Newcastle U, Dundee U, Hibernian, Coventry C

Owens, J. (1) 2010/11 Crusaders

Parke, J. (13) 1963/4 Linfield, Hibernian, Sunderland

Paterson, M. A. (12) 2007/08 Scunthorpe U, Burnley

Patterson, D. J. (17) 1993/4 Crystal P, Luton T, Dundee U

Patterson, R. (5) 2009/10 Coleraine, Plymouth Arg

Peacock, R. (31) 1951/2 Celtic, Coleraine

Penney, S. (17) 1984/5 Brighton & HA

Platt, J. A. (23) 1975/6 Middlesbrough, Ballymena U, Coleraine

Quinn, J. M. (46) 1984/5 Blackburn R, Swindon T, Leicester, Bradford C, West Ham U, Bournemouth, Reading

Quinn, S. J. (50) 1995/6 Blackpool, WBA, Willem II, Sheffield U, Peterborough U, Northampton T

Rafferty, P. (1) 1979/80 Linfield

Ramsey, P. (14) 1983/4 Leicester C

Rice, P. (49) 1968/9 Arsenal

Robinson, S. (7) 1996/7 Bournemouth, Luton T

Rogan, A. (18) 1987/8 Celtic, Sunderland, Millwall

Ross, E. (1) 1968/9 Newcastle U

Rowland, K. (19) 1994/5 West Ham U, QPR

Russell, A. (1) 1946/7 Linfield

Ryan, R. (1) 1949/50 WBA

Sanchez, L. P. (3) 1986/7 Wimbledon

Scott, J. (2) 1957/8 Grimsby T

Scott, P. (10) 1974/5 Everton, York C, Aldershot

Sharkey, P. (1) 1975/6 Ipswich T

Shields, J. (1) 1956/7 Southampton

Shiels, D. (9) 2005/06 Hibernian, Doncaster R

Simpson, W. (12) 1950/1 Rangers

Sloan, D. (2) 1968/9 Oxford

Sloan, T. (3) 1978/9 Manchester U

Sloan, W. (1) 1946/7 Arsenal

Smith, A. W. (18) 2002/03 Glentoran, Preston NE

Smyth, S. (9) 1947/8 Wolverhampton W, Stoke C

Smyth, W. (4) 1948/9 Distillery

Sonner, D. J. (13) 1997/8 Ipswich T, Sheffield W, Birmingham C, Nottingham F, Peterborough U

Spence, D. (29) 1974/5 Bury, Blackpool, Southend U

Sproule, I. (11) 2005/06 Hibernian, Bristol C

Stevenson, A. (3) 1946/7 Everton

Stewart, A. (7) 1966/7 Glentoran, Derby

Stewart, D. (1) 1977/8 Hull C

Stewart, I. (31) 1981/2 QPR, Newcastle U

Stewart, T. (1) 1960/1 Linfield

Taggart, G. P. (51) 1989/90 Barnsley, Bolton W, Leicester C

Taylor, M. S. (87) 1998/9 Fulham, Birmingham C

Thompson, P. (8) 2005/06 Linfield, Stockport Co

Thompson, A. L. (2) 2010/11 Watford

Todd, S, (11) 1965/6 Burnley, Sheffield W

Toner, C. (2) 2002/03 Leyton Orient

Trainor, D. (1) 1966/7 Crusaders

Tuffey, J. (3) 2008/09 Partick T, Inverness CT

Tully, C. (10) 1948/9 Celtic

Uprichard, N. (18) 1951/2 Swindon T, Portsmouth

Vernon, J. (17) 1946/7 Belfast Celtic, WBA

Walker, J. (1) 1954/5 Doncaster R

Walsh, D. (9) 1946/7 WBA

Walsh, W. (5) 1947/8 Manchester C

Watson, P. (1) 1970/1 Distillery

Webb, S. M. (4) 2005/06 Ross Co

Welsh, S. (4) 1965/6 Carlisle U

Whiteside, N. (38) 1981/2 Manchester U, Everton

Whitley, Jeff (20) 1996/7 Manchester C, Sunderland, Cardiff C

Whitley, Jim (3) 1997/8 Manchester C

Williams, M. S. (36) 1998/9 Chesterfield, Watford, Wimbledon, Stoke C, Wimbledon, Milton Keynes D
Williams, P. (1) 1990/1 WBA
Wilson, D. J. (24) 1986/7 Brighton & HA, Luton, Sheffield W
Wilson, K. J. (42) 1986/7 Ipswich T, Chelsea, Notts C, Walsall

Wilson, S. (12) 1961/2 Glenavon, Falkirk, Dundee
Winchester, C. (1) 2010/11 Oldham Ath
Wood, T. J. (1) 1995/6 Walsall
Worthington, N. (66) 1983/4 Sheffield W, Leeds U, Stoke C
Wright, T. J. (31) 1988/9 Newcastle U, Nottingham F, Manchester C

SCOTLAND

Adam, C. G. (11) 2006/07 Rangers, Blackpool
Aird, J. (4) 1953/4 Burnley
Aitken, G. G. (8) 1948/9 East Fife, Sunderland
Aitken, R. (57) 1979/80 Celtic, Newcastle U, St Mirren
Albiston, A. (14) 1981/2 Manchester U
Alexander, G. (40) 2001/02 Preston NE, Burnley
Alexander, N. (3) 2005/06 Cardiff C
Allan, T. (2) 1973/4 Dundee
Anderson, J. (1) 1953/4 Leicester C
Anderson, R. (11) 2002/03 Aberdeen, Sunderland
Archibald, S. (27) 1979/80 Aberdeen, Tottenham H, Barcelona
Auld, B. (3) 1958/9 Celtic

Baird, H. (1) 1955/6 Airdrieonians
Baird, S. (7) 1956/7 Rangers
Bannan, B. (5) 2010/11 Aston Villa
Bannon, E. (11) 1979/80 Dundee U
Bardsley, P. A. (5) 2010/11 Sunderland
Barr, D. (1) 2008/09 Falkirk
Bauld, W. (3) 1949/50 Heart of Midlothian
Baxter, J. (34) 1960/1 Rangers, Sunderland
Beattie, C. (7) 2005/06 Celtic, WBA
Bell, C. (1) 2010/11 Kilmarnock
Bell, W. (2) 1965/6 Leeds U
Bernard, P. R. (2) 1994/5 Oldham Ath
Berra, C. (13) 2007/08 Heart of Midlothian, Wolverhampton W
Bett, J. (25) 1981/2 Rangers, Lokeren, Aberdeen
Black, E. (2) 1987/8 Metz
Black, I. (1) 1947/8 Southampton
Blacklaw, A. (3) 1962/3 Burnley
Blackley, J. (7) 1973/4 Hibernian
Blair, J. (1) 1946/7 Blackpool
Blyth, J. (2) 1977/8 Coventry C

Bone, J. (2) 1971/2 Norwich C
Booth, S. (21) 1992/3 Aberdeen, Borussia Dortmund, Twente
Bowman, D. (6) 1991/2 Dundee U
Boyd, K. (18) 2005/06 Rangers, Middlesbrough
Boyd, T. (72) 1990/1 Motherwell, Chelsea, Celtic
Brand, R. (8) 1960/1 Rangers
Brazil, A. (13) 1979/80 Ipswich T, Tottenham H
Bremner, D. (1) 1975/6 Hibernian
Bremner, W. (54) 1964/5 Leeds U
Brennan, F. (7) 1946/7 Newcastle U
Broadfoot, K. (4) 2008/09 Rangers
Brogan, J. (4) 1970/1 Celtic
Brown, A. (14) 1949/50 East Fife, Blackpool
Brown, H. (3) 1946/7 Partick Th
Brown, J. (1) 1974/5 Sheffield U
Brown, R. (3) 1946/7 Rangers
Brown, S. (25) 2005/06 Hibernian, Celtic
Brown, W. (28) 1957/8 Dundee, Tottenham H
Brownlie, J. (7) 1970/1 Hibernian
Bryson, C. (1) 2010/11 Kilmarnock
Buchan, M. (34) 1971/2 Aberdeen, Manchester U
Buckley, P. (3) 1953/4 Aberdeen
Burchill, M. J. (6) 1999/00 Celtic
Burke, C. (2) 2005/06 Rangers
Burley, C. W. (46) 1994/5 Chelsea, Celtic, Derby Co
Burley, G. (11) 1978/9 Ipswich T
Burns, F. (1) 1969/70 Manchester U
Burns, K. (20) 1973/4 Birmingham C, Nottingham F
Burns, T. (8) 1980/1 Celtic

Calderwood, C. (36) 1994/5 Tottenham H, Aston Villa
Caldow, E. (40) 1956/7 Rangers

Caldwell, G. (40) 2001/02 Newcastle U, Hibernian, Celtic, Wigan Ath

Caldwell, S. (12) 2000/01 Newcastle U, Sunderland, Burnley, Wigan Ath

Callaghan, W. (2) 1969/70 Dunfermline

Cameron, C. (28) 1998/9 Heart of Midlothian, Wolverhampton W

Campbell, R. (5) 1946/7 Falkirk, Chelsea

Campbell, W. (5) 1946/7 Morton

Canero, P. (1) 2003/04 Leicester C

Carr, W. (6) 1969/70 Coventry C

Chalmers, S. (5) 1964/5 Celtic

Clark, J. (4) 1965/6 Celtic

Clark, R. (17) 1967/8 Aberdeen

Clarke, S. (6) 1987/8 Chelsea

Clarkson, D. (2) 2007/08 Motherwell

Collins, J. (58) 1987/8 Hibernian, Celtic, Monaco, Everton

Collins, R. (31) 1950/1 Celtic, Everton, Leeds U

Colquhoun, E. (9) 1971/2 Sheffield U

Colquhoun, J. (2) 1987/8 Heart of Midlothian

Combe, R. (3) 1947/8 Hibernian

Commons, K. (9) 2008/09 Derby Co, Celtic

Conn, A. (1) 1955/6 Heart of Midlothian

Conn, A. (2) 1974/5 Tottenham H

Connachan, E. (2) 1961/2 Dunfermline Ath

Connelly, G. (2) 1973/4 Celtic

Connolly, J. (1) 1972/3 Everton

Connor, R. (4) 1985/6 Dundee, Aberdeen

Conway, C. (2) 2009/10 Dundee U

Cooke, C. (16) 1965/6 Dundee, Chelsea

Cooper, D. (22) 1979/80 Rangers, Motherwell

Cormack, P. (9) 1965/6 Hibernian, Nottingham F

Cowan, J. (25) 1947/8 Morton

Cowie, D. (20) 1952/3 Dundee

Cowie, D. M. (3) 2009/10 Watford

Cox, C. (1) 1947/8 Heart of Midlothian

Cox, S. (24) 1947/8 Rangers

Craig, J. (1) 1976/7 Celtic

Craig, J. P. (1) 1967/8 Celtic

Craig, T. (1) 1975/6 Newcastle U

Crainey, S. D. (9) 2001/02 Celtic, Southampton, Blackpool

Crawford, S. (25) 1994/5 Raith R, Dunfermline Ath, Plymouth Arg

Crerand, P. (16) 1960/1 Celtic, Manchester U

Cropley, A. (2) 1971/2 Hibernian

Cruickshank, J. (6) 1963/4 Heart of Midlothian

Cullen, M. (1) 1955/6 Luton T

Cumming, J. (9) 1954/5 Heart of Midlothian

Cummings, W. (1) 2001/02 Chelsea

Cunningham, W. (8) 1953/4 Preston NE

Curran, H. (5) 1969/70 Wolverhampton W

Dailly, C. (67) 1996/7 Derby Co, Blackburn R, West Ham U, Rangers

Dalglish, K. (102) 1971/2 Celtic, Liverpool

Davidson, C. I. (19) 1998/9 Blackburn R, Leicester C, Preston NE

Davidson, J. (8) 1953/4 Partick Th

Dawson, A. (5) 1979/80 Rangers

Deans, D. (2) 1974/5 Celtic

Delaney, J. (4) 1946/7 Manchester U

Devlin, P. J. (10) 2002/03 Birmingham C

Dick, J. (1) 1958/9 West Ham U

Dickov, P. (10) 2000/01 Manchester C, Leicester C, Blackburn R

Dickson, W. (5) 1969/70 Kilmarnock

Dobie, R. S. (6) 2001/02 WBA

Docherty, T. (25) 1951/2 Preston NE, Arsenal

Dodds, D. (2) 1983/4 Dundee U

Dodds, W. (26) 1996/7 Aberdeen, Dundee U, Rangers

Donachie, W. (35) 1971/2 Manchester C

Donnelly, S. (10) 1996/7 Celtic

Dorrans, G. (5) 2009/10 WBA

Dougall, C. (1) 1946/7 Birmingham C

Dougan, R. (1) 1949/50 Heart of Midlothian

Douglas, R. (19) 2001/02 Celtic, Leicester C

Doyle, J. (1) 1975/6 Ayr U

Duncan, A. (6) 1974/5 Hibernian

Duncan, D. (3) 1947/8 East Fife

Duncanson, J. (1) 1946/7 Rangers

Durie, G. S. (43) 1987/8 Chelsea, Tottenham H, Rangers

Durrant, I. (20) 1987/8 Rangers, Kilmarnock

Elliott, M. S. (18) 1997/8 Leicester C

Evans, A. (4) 1981/2 Aston Villa

Evans, R. (48) 1948/9 Celtic, Chelsea

Ewing, T. (2) 1957/8 Partick Th

Farm, G. (10) 1952/3 Blackpool

Ferguson, B. (45) 1998/9 Rangers, Blackburn R, Rangers

Ferguson, Derek (2) 1987/8 Rangers

Ferguson, Duncan (7) 1991/2 Dundee U, Everton

Ferguson, I. (9) 1988/9 Rangers

Ferguson, R. (7) 1965/6 Kilmarnock

Fernie, W. (12) 1953/4 Celtic

Flavell, R. (2) 1946/7 Airdrieonians

Fleck, R. (4) 1989/90 Norwich C

Fleming, C. (1) 1953/4 East Fife

Fletcher, D. B. (53) 2003/04 Manchester U

Fletcher, S. (8) 2007/08 Hibernian, Burnley, Wolverhampton W

Forbes, A. (14) 1946/7 Sheffield U, Arsenal

Ford, D. (3) 1973/4 Heart of Midlothian

Forrest, J. (1) 1957/8 Motherwell

Forrest, J. (5) 1965/6 Rangers, Aberdeen

Forrest, J. (1) 2010/11 Celtic

Forsyth, A. (10) 1971/2 Partick Th, Manchester U

Forsyth, C. (4) 1963/4 Kilmarnock

Forsyth, T. (22) 1970/1 Motherwell, Rangers

Fox, D. (1) 2009/10 Burnley

Fraser, D. (2) 1967/8 WBA

Fraser, W. (2) 1954/5 Sunderland

Freedman, D. A. (2) 2001/02 Crystal P

Gabriel, J. (2) 1960/1 Everton

Gallacher, K. W. (53) 1987/8 Dundee U, Coventry C, Blackburn R, Newcastle U

Gallacher, P. (8) 2001/02 Dundee U

Gallagher, P. (1) 2003/04 Blackburn R

Galloway, M. (1) 1991/2 Celtic

Gardiner, W. (1) 1957/8 Motherwell

Gemmell, T. (2) 1954/5 St Mirren

Gemmell, T. (18) 1965/6 Celtic

Gemmill, A. (43) 1970/1 Derby Co, Nottingham F, Birmingham C

Gemmill, S. (26) 1994/5 Nottingham F, Everton

Gibson, D. (7) 1962/3 Leicester C

Gillespie, G. T. (13) 1987/8 Liverpool

Gilzean, A. (22) 1963/4 Dundee, Tottenham H

Glass, S. (1) 1998/9 Newcastle U

Glavin, R. (1) 1976/7 Celtic

Glen, A. (2) 1955/6 Aberdeen

Goodwillie, D. (2) 2010/11 Dundee U

Goram, A. L. (43) 1985/6 Oldham Ath, Hibernian, Rangers

Gordon, C. S. (40) 2003/04 Heart of Midlothian, Sunderland

Gough, C. R. (61) 1982/3 Dundee U, Tottenham H, Rangers

Gould, J. (2) 1999/00 Celtic

Govan, J. (6) 1947/8 Hibernian

Graham, A. (11) 1977/8 Leeds U

Graham, G. (12) 1971/2 Arsenal, Manchester U

Grant, J. (2) 1958/9 Hibernian

Grant, P. (2) 1988/9 Celtic

Gray, A. (20) 1975/6 Aston Villa, Wolverhampton W, Everton

Gray, A. D. (2) 2002/03 Bradford C

Gray, E. (12) 1968/9 Leeds U

Gray F. (32) 1975/6 Leeds U, Nottingham F, Leeds U

Green, A. (6) 1970/1 Blackpool, Newcastle U

Greig, J. (44) 1963/4 Rangers

Gunn, B. (6) 1989/90 Norwich C

Haddock, H. (6) 1954/5 Clyde

Haffey, F. (2) 1959/60 Celtic

Hamilton, A. (24) 1961/2 Dundee

Hamilton, G. (5) 1946/7 Aberdeen

Hamilton, W. (1) 1964/5 Hibernian

Hammell, S. (1) 2004/05 Motherwell

Hanley, G. (2) 2010/11 Blackburn R

Hansen, A. (26) 1978/9 Liverpool

Hansen, J. (2) 1971/2 Partick Th

Harper, J. (4) 1972/3 Aberdeen, Hibernian, Aberdeen

Hartford, A. (50) 1971/2 WBA, Manchester C, Everton, Manchester C

Hartley, P. J. (25) 2004/05 Heart of Midlothian, Celtic, Bristol C

Harvey, D. (16) 1972/3 Leeds U

Haughney, M. (1) 1953/4 Celtic

Hay, D. (27) 1969/70 Celtic

Hegarty, P. (8) 1978/9 Dundee U

Henderson, J. (7) 1952/3 Portsmouth, Arsenal

Henderson, W. (29) 1962/3 Rangers

Hendry, E. C. J. (51) 1992/3 Blackburn R, Rangers, Coventry C, Bolton W

Herd, D. (5) 1958/9 Arsenal

Herd, G. (5) 1957/8 Clyde

Herriot, J. (8) 1968/9 Birmingham C

Hewie, J. (19) 1955/6 Charlton Ath

Holt, D. D. (5) 1962/3 Heart of Midlothian

Holt, G. J. (10) 2000/01 Kilmarnock, Norwich C

Holton, J. (15) 1972/3 Manchester U

Hope, R. (2) 1967/8 WBA

Hopkin, D. (7) 1996/7 Crystal P, Leeds U

Houliston, W. (3) 1948/9 Queen of the South

Houston, S. (1) 1975/6 Manchester U

Howie, H. (1) 1948/9 Hibernian

Hughes, J. (8) 1964/5 Celtic

Hughes, R. D. (5) 2003/04 Portsmouth

Hughes, S. D. (1) 2009/10 Norwich C

Hughes, W. (1) 1974/5 Sunderland

Humphries, W. (1) 1951/2 Motherwell

Hunter, A. (4) 1971/2 Kilmarnock, Celtic

Hunter, W. (3) 1959/60 Motherwell

Husband, J. (1) 1946/7 Partick Th

Hutchison, D. (26) 1998/9 Everton, Sunderland, West Ham U

Hutchison, T. (17) 1973/4 Coventry C

Hutton, A. (20) 2006/07 Rangers, Tottenham H

Imlach, S. (4) 1957/8 Nottingham F

Irvine, B. (9) 1990/1 Aberdeen

Iwelumo, C. R. (4) 2008/09 Wolverhampton W, Burnley

Jackson, C. (8) 1974/5 Rangers

Jackson, D. (28) 1994/5 Hibernian, Celtic

Jardine, A. (38) 1970/1 Rangers

Jarvie, A. (3) 1970/1 Airdrieonians

Jess, E. (18) 1992/3 Aberdeen, Coventry C, Aberdeen

Johnston, A. (18) 1998/9 Sunderland, Rangers, Middlesbrough

Johnston, M. (38) 1983/4 Watford, Celtic, Nantes, Rangers

Johnston, L. (2) 1947/8 Clyde

Johnston, W. (22) 1965/6 Rangers, WBA

Johnstone, D. (14) 1972/3 Rangers

Johnstone, J. (23) 1964/5 Celtic

Johnstone, R. (17) 1950/1 Hibernian, Manchester C

Jordan, J. (52) 1972/3 Leeds U, Manchester U, AC Milan

Kelly, H. (1) 1951/2 Blackpool

Kelly, J. (2) 1948/9 Barnsley

Kennedy, Jim (6) 1963/4 Celtic

Kennedy, John (1) 2003/04 Celtic

Kennedy, S. (5) 1974/5 Rangers

Kennedy, S. (8) 1977/8 Aberdeen

Kenneth, G. (2) 2010/11 Dundee U

Kerr, A. (2) 1954/5 Partick Th

Kerr, B. (3) 2002/03 Newcastle U

Kyle, K. (10) 2001/02 Sunderland, Kilmarnock

Lambert, P. (40) 1994/5 Motherwell, Borussia Dortmund, Celtic

Law, D. (55) 1958/9 Huddersfield T, Manchester C, Torino, Manchester U, Manchester C

Lawrence, T. (3) 1962/3 Liverpool

Leggat, G. (18) 1955/6 Aberdeen, Fulham

Leighton, J. (91) 1982/3 Aberdeen, Manchester U, Hibernian, Aberdeen

Lennox, R. (10) 1966/7 Celtic

Leslie, L. (5) 1960/1 Airdrieonians

Levein, C. (16) 1989/90 Heart of Midlothian

Liddell, W. (28) 1946/7 Liverpool

Linwood, A. (1) 1949/50 Clyde

Little, R. J. (1) 1952/3 Rangers

Logie, J. (1) 1952/3 Arsenal

Long, H. (1) 1946/7 Clyde

Lorimer, P. (21) 1969/70 Leeds U

Macari, L. (24) 1971/2 Celtic, Manchester U

Macaulay, A. (7) 1946/7 Brentford, Arsenal

MacDougall, E. (7) 1974/5 Norwich C

Mackay, D. (22) 1956/7 Heart of Midlothian, Tottenham H

Mackay, G. (4) 1987/8 Heart of Midlothian

Mackay, M. (5) 2003/04 Norwich C

Maloney, S. R. (19) 2005/06 Celtic, Aston Villa, Celtic

Malpas, M. (55) 1983/4 Dundee U

Marshall, D. J. (5) 2004/05 Celtic, Cardiff C

Marshall, G. (1) 1991/2 Celtic

Martin, B. (2) 1994/5 Motherwell

Martin, F. (6) 1953/4 Aberdeen

Martin, N. (3) 1964/5 Hibernian, Sunderland

Martin, R. K. A. (1) 2010/11 Norwich C

Martis, J. (1) 1960/1 Motherwell

Mason, J. (7) 1948/9 Third Lanark

Masson, D. (17) 1975/6 QPR, Derby C

Mathers, D. (1) 1953/4 Partick Th

Matteo, D. (6) 2000/01 Leeds U

McAllister, B. (3) 1996/7 Wimbledon

McAllister, G. (57) 1989/90 Leicester C, Leeds U, Coventry C

McAllister, J. R. (1) 2003/04 Livingston

McArthur, J. (4) 2010/11 Wigan Ath

McAvennie, F. (5) 1985/6 West Ham U, Celtic

McBride, J. (2) 1966/7 Celtic

McCall, S. M. (40) 1989/90 Everton, Rangers
McCalliog, J. (5) 1966/7 Sheffield W, Wolverhampton W
McCann, N. D. (26) 1998/9 Heart of Midlothian, Rangers, Southampton
McCann, R. (5) 1958/9 Motherwell
McClair, B. (30) 1986/7 Celtic, Manchester U
McCloy, P. (4) 1972/3 Rangers
McCoist, A. (61) 1985/6 Rangers, Kilmarnock
McColl, I. (14) 1949/50 Rangers
McCormack, R. (7) 20007/08 Motherwell, Cardiff C, Leeds U
McCreadie, E. (23) 1964/5 Chelsea
McCulloch, L. (18) 2004/05 Wigan Ath, Rangers
MacDonald, A. (1) 1975/6 Rangers
McDonald, J. (2) 1955/6 Sunderland
McEveley, J. (3) 2007/08 Derby Co
McFadden, J. (48) 2001/02 Motherwell, Everton, Birmingham C
McFarlane, W. (1) 1946/7 Heart of Midlothian
McGarr, E. (2) 1969/70 Aberdeen
McGarvey, F. (7) 1978/9 Liverpool, Celtic
McGhee, M. (4) 1982/3 Aberdeen
McGinlay, J. (13) 1993/4 Bolton W
McGrain, D. (62) 1972/3 Celtic
McGregor, A. (13) 2006/07 Rangers
McGrory, J. (3) 1964/5 Kilmarnock
McInally, A. (8) 1988/9 Aston Villa, Bayern Munich
McInally, J. (10) 1986/7 Dundee U
McInnes, D. (2) 2002/03 WBA
MacKay, D. (14) 1958/9 Celtic
McKean, R. (1) 1975/6 Rangers
MacKenzie, J. (9) 1953/4 Partick Th
McKimmie, S. (40) 1988/9 Aberdeen
McKinlay, T. (22) 1995/6 Celtic
McKinlay, W. (29) 1993/4 Dundee U, Blackburn R
McKinnon, Rob (3) 1993/4 Motherwell
McKinnon, Ronnie (28) 1965/6 Rangers
McLaren, Alan (24) 1991/2 Heart of Midlothian, Rangers
McLaren, Andy (4) 1946/7 Preston NE
McLaren, Andy (1) 2000/01 Kilmarnock
McLean, G. (1) 1967/8 Dundee
McLean, T. (6) 1968/9 Kilmarnock
McLeish, A. (77) 1979/80 Aberdeen
McLeod, J. (4) 1960/1 Hibernian
MacLeod, M. (20) 1984/5 Celtic, Borussia Dortmund, Hibernian

McLintock, F. (9) 1962/3 Leicester C, Arsenal
McManus, S. (26) 2006/07 Celtic, Middlesbrough
McMillan, I. (6) 1951/2 Airdrieonians, Rangers
McNamara, J. (33) 1996/7 Celtic, Wolverhampton W
McNamee, D. (4) 2003/04 Livingston
McNaught, W. (5) 1950/1 Raith R
McNaughton, K. (4) 2001/02 Aberdeen, Cardiff C
McNeill, W. (29) 1960/1 Celtic
McPhail, J. (5) 1949/50 Celtic
McPherson, D. (27) 1988/9 Heart of Midlothian, Rangers
McQueen, G. (30) 1973/4 Leeds U, Manchester U
McStay, P. (76) 1983/4 Celtic
McSwegan, G. (2) 1999/00 Heart of Midlothian
Mackail-Smith, C. (1) 2010/11 Peterborough U
Mackie, J. C. (3) 2010/11 QPR
Maguire, C. (2) 2010/11 Aberdeen
Millar, J. (2) 1962/3 Rangers
Miller, C. (1) 2000/01 Dundee U
Miller, K. (55) 2000/01 Rangers, Wolverhampton W, Celtic, Derby Co, Rangers, Bursa
Miller, L. (3) 2005/06 Dundee U, Aberdeen
Miller, W. (6) 1946/7 Celtic
Miller, W. (65) 1974/5 Aberdeen
Mitchell, R. (2) 1950/1 Newcastle U
Mochan, N. (3) 1953/4 Celtic
Moir, W. (1) 1949/50 Bolton W
Moncur, R. (16) 1967/8 Newcastle U
Morgan, W. (21) 1967/8 Burnley, Manchester U
Morris, H. (1) 1949/50 East Fife
Morrison, J. C. (13) 2007/08 WBA
Mudie, J. (17) 1956/7 Blackpool
Mulhall, G. (3) 1959/60 Aberdeen, Sunderland
Munro, F. (9) 1970/1 Wolverhampton W
Munro, I. (7) 1978/9 St Mirren
Murdoch, R. (12) 1965/6 Celtic
Murray, I. (6) 2002/03 Hibernian, Rangers
Murray, J. (5) 1957/8 Heart of Midlothian
Murray, S. (1) 1971/2 Aberdeen
Murty, G. S. (4) 2003/04 Reading

Naismith, S. J. (10) 2006/07 Kilmarnock, Rangers

Narey, D. (35) 1976/7 Dundee U

Naysmith, G. A. (46) 1999/00 Heart of Midlothian, Everton, Sheffield U

Neilson, R. (1) 2006/07 Heart of Midlothian

Nevin, P. K. F. (28) 1985/6 Chelsea, Everton, Tranmere R

Nicholas, C. (20) 1982/3 Celtic, Arsenal, Aberdeen

Nicholson, B. (3) 2000/01 Dunfermline Ath

Nicol, S. (27) 1984/5 Liverpool

O'Connor, G. (16) 2001/02 Hibernian, Lokomotiv Moscow, Birmingham C

O'Donnell, P. (1) 1993/4 Motherwell

O'Hare, J. (13) 1969/70 Derby Co

O'Neil, B. (7) 1995/6 Celtic, Wolfsburg, Derby Co, Preston NE

O'Neil, J. (1) 2000/01 Hibernian

Ormond, W. (6) 1953/4 Hibernian

Orr, T. (2) 1951/2 Morton

Parker, A. (15) 1954/5 Falkirk, Everton

Parlane, D. (12) 1972/3 Rangers

Paton, A. (2) 1951/2 Motherwell

Pearson, S. P. (10) 2003/04 Motherwell, Celtic, Derby Co

Pearson, T. (2) 1946/7 Newcastle U

Penman, A. (1) 1965/6 Dundee

Pettigrew, W. (5) 1975/6 Motherwell

Plenderleith, J. (1) 1960/1 Manchester C

Pressley, S. J. (32) 1999/00 Heart of Midlothian

Provan, David (10) 1979/80 Celtic

Provan, Davie (5) 1963/4 Rangers

Quashie, N. F. (14) 2003/04 Portsmouth, Southampton, WBA

Quinn, P. (4) 1960/1 Motherwell

Rae, G. P. (14) 2000/01 Dundee, Rangers, Cardiff C

Redpath, W. (9) 1948/9 Motherwell

Reilly, L. (38) 1948/9 Hibernian

Ring, T. (12) 1952/3 Clyde

Rioch, B. (24) 1974/5 Derby Co, Everton, Derby Co

Riordan, D. G. (3) 2005/06 Hibernian

Ritchie, P. S. (7) 1998/9 Heart of Midlothian, Bolton W, Walsall

Ritchie, W. (1) 1961/2 Rangers

Robb, D. (5) 1970/1 Aberdeen

Robertson, A. (5) 1954/5 Clyde

Robertson, D. (3) 1991/2 Rangers

Robertson, H. (1) 1961/2 Dundee

Robertson, J. (16) 1990/1 Heart of Midlothian

Robertson, J. G. (1) 1964/5 Tottenham H

Robertson, J. N. (28) 1977/8 Nottingham F, Derby Co

Robertson, S. (2) 2008/09 Dundee U

Robinson, B. (4) 1973/4 Dundee

Robson, B. G. G. (14) 2007/08 Dundee U, Celtic, Middlesbrough

Ross, M. (13) 2001/02 Rangers

Rough, A. (53) 1975/6 Partick Th, Hibernian

Rougvie, D. (1) 1983/4 Aberdeen

Rutherford, E. (1) 1947/8 Rangers

St John, I. (21) 1958/9 Motherwell, Liverpool

Saunders, S. (1) 2010/11 Motherwell

Schaedler, E. (1) 1973/4 Hibernian

Scott, A. (16) 1956/7 Rangers, Everton

Scott, Jimmy (1) 1965/6 Hibernian

Scott, Jocky (2) 1970/1 Dundee

Scoular, J. (9) 1950/1 Portsmouth

Severin, S. D. (15) 2001/02 Heart of Midlothian, Aberdeen

Sharp, G. M. (12) 1984/5 Everton

Shaw, D. (8) 1946/7 Hibernian

Shaw, J. (4) 1946/7 Rangers

Shearer, D. (7) 1993/4 Aberdeen

Shearer, R. (4) 1960/1 Rangers

Simpson, N. (4) 1982/3 Aberdeen

Simpson, R. (5) 1966/7 Celtic

Sinclair, J. (1) 1965/6 Leicester C

Smith, D. (2) 1965/6 Aberdeen, Rangers

Smith, E. (2) 1958/9 Celtic

Smith, G. (18) 1946/7 Hibernian

Smith, H. G. (3) 1987/8 Heart of Midlothian

Smith, J. (4) 1967/8 Aberdeen, Newcastle U

Smith, J. E. (2) 2002/03 Celtic

Snodgrass, R. (2) 2010/11 Leeds U

Souness, G. (54) 1974/5 Middlesbrough, Liverpool, Sampdoria

Speedie, D. R. (10) 1984/5 Chelsea, Coventry C

Spencer, J. (14) 1994/5 Chelsea, QPR

Stanton, P. (16) 1965/6 Hibernian

Steel, W. (30) 1946/7 Morton, Derby C, Dundee

Stein, C. (21) 1968/9 Rangers, Coventry C

Stephen, J. (2) 1946/7 Bradford PA

Stewart, D. (1) 1977/8 Leeds U
Stewart, J. (2) 1976/7 Kilmarnock, Middlesbrough
Stewart, M. J. (4) 2001/02 Manchester U, Heart of Midlothian
Stewart, R. (10) 1980/1 West Ham U
Stockdale, R. K. (5) 2001/02 Middlesbrough
Strachan, G. (50) 1979/80 Aberdeen, Manchester U, Leeds U
Sturrock, P. (20) 1980/1 Dundee U
Sullivan, N. (28) 1996/7 Wimbledon, Tottenham H

Teale, G. (13) 2005/06 Wigan Ath, Derby Co
Telfer, P. N. (1) 1999/00 Coventry C
Telfer, W. (1) 1953/4 St Mirren
Thompson, S. (16) 2001/02 Dundee U, Rangers
Thomson, K. (3) 2008/09 Rangers, Middlesbrough
Thomson, W. (7) 1979/80 St Mirren
Thornton, W. (7) 1946/7 Rangers
Toner, W. (2) 1958/9 Kilmarnock
Turnbull, E. (8) 1947/8 Hibernian

Ure, I. (11) 1961/2 Dundee, Arsenal

Waddell, W. (17) 1946/7 Rangers
Walker, A. (3) 1987/8 Celtic
Walker, J. N. (2) 1992/3 Heart of Midlothian, Partick Th
Wallace, I. A. (3) 1977/8 Coventry C
Wallace, L. (5) 2009/10 Heart of Midlothian
Wallace, R. (1) 2009/10 Preston NE
Wallace, W. S. B. (7) 1964/5 Heart of Midlothian, Celtic
Wardhaugh, J. (2) 1954/5 Heart of Midlothian

Wark, J. (29) 1978/9 Ipswich T, Liverpool
Watson, J. (2) 1947/8 Motherwell, Huddersfield T
Watson, R. (1) 1970/1 Motherwell
Webster, A. (23) 2002/03 Heart of Midlothian, Dundee U
Weir, A. (6) 1958/9 Motherwell
Weir, D. G. (69) 1996/7 Heart of Midlothian, Everton, Rangers
Weir, P. (6) 1979/80 St Mirren, Aberdeen
White, J. (22) 1958/9 Falkirk, Tottenham H
Whittaker, S. G. (12) 2009/10 Rangers
Whyte, D. (12) 1987/8 Celtic, Middlesbrough, Aberdeen
Wilkie, L. (11) 2001/02 Dundee
Williams, G. (5) 2001/02 Nottingham F
Wilson, A. (1) 1953/4 Portsmouth
Wilson, D. (22) 1960/1 Rangers
Wilson, D. (3) 2010/11 Liverpool
Wilson, I. A. (5) 1986/7 Leicester C, Everton
Wilson, M. (1) 2010/11 Celtic
Wilson, P. (1) 1974/5 Celtic
Wilson, R. (2) 1971/2 Arsenal
Winters, R. (1) 1998/9 Aberdeen
Wood, G. (4) 1978/9 Everton, Arsenal
Woodburn, W. (24) 1946/7 Rangers
Wright, K. (1) 1991/2 Hibernian
Wright, S. (2) 1992/3 Aberdeen
Wright, T. (3) 1952/3 Sunderland

Yeats, R. (2) 1964/5 Liverpool
Yorston, H. (1) 1954/5 Aberdeen
Young, A. (8) 1959/60 Heart of Midlothian, Everton
Young, G. (53) 1946/7 Rangers
Younger, T. (24) 1954/5 Hibernian, Liverpool

WALES

Aizlewood, M. (39) 1985/6 Charlton Ath, Leeds U, Bradford C, Bristol C, Cardiff C
Allchurch, I. (68) 1950/1 Swansea T, Newcastle U, Cardiff C, Swansea T
Allchurch, L. (11) 1954/5 Swansea T, Sheffield U
Allen, B. (2) 1950/1 Coventry C
Allen, J. M. (2) 2008/09 Swansea C
Allen, M. (14) 1985/6 Watford, Norwich C, Millwall, Newcastle U

Baker, C. (7) 1957/8 Cardiff C
Baker, W. (1) 1947/8 Cardiff C
Bale, G. (27) 2005/06 Southampton, Tottenham H
Barnard, D. S. (22) 1997/8 Barnsley, Grimsby T
Barnes, W. (22) 1947/8 Arsenal
Bellamy, C. D. (62) 1997/8 Norwich C, Coventry C, Newcastle U, Blackburn R, Liverpool, West Ham U, Manchester C

Berry, G. (5) 1978/9 Wolverhampton W, Stoke C
Blackmore, C. G. (39) 1984/5 Manchester U, Middlesbrough
Blake, D. J. (2) 2010/11 Cardiff C
Blake, N. A. (29) 1993/4 Sheffield U, Bolton W, Blackburn R, Wolverhampton W
Bodin, P. J. (23) 1989/90 Swindon T, Crystal P, Swindon T
Bowen, D. (19) 1954/5 Arsenal
Bowen, J. P. (2) 1993/4 Swansea C, Birmingham C
Bowen, M. R. (41) 1985/6 Tottenham H, Norwich C, West Ham U
Boyle, T. (2) 1980/1 Crystal P
Bradley, M. S. (1) 2009/10 Walsall
Brown, J. R. (2) 2005/06 Gillingham, Blackburn R
Browning, M. T. (5) 1995/6 Bristol R, Huddersfield T
Burgess, R. (32) 1946/7 Tottenham H
Burton, O. (9) 1962/3 Norwich C, Newcastle U

Cartwright, L. (7) 1973/4 Coventry C, Wrexham
Charles, J. (38) 1949/50 Leeds U, Juventus, Leeds U, Cardiff C
Charles, J. M. (19) 1980/1 Swansea C, QPR, Oxford U
Charles, M. (31) 1954/5 Swansea T, Arsenal, Cardiff C
Church, S. R. (12) 2008/09 Reading
Clarke, R. (22) 1948/9 Manchester C
Coleman, C. (32) 1991/2 Crystal P, Blackburn R, Fulham
Collins, D. L. (12) 2004/05 Sunderland, Stoke C
Collins, J. M. (39) 2003/04 Cardiff C, West Ham U, Aston Villa
Collison, J. D. (8) 2007/08 West Ham U
Cornforth, J. M. (2) 1994/5 Swansea C
Cotterill, D. R. G. B. (19) 2005/06 Bristol C, Wigan Ath, Sheffield U, Swansea C
Coyne, D. (16) 1995/6 Tranmere R, Grimsby T, Leicester C, Burnley, Tranmere R
Crofts, A. L. (17) 2005/06 Gillingham, Brighton & HA, Norwich C
Crossley, M. G. (8) 1996/7 Nottingham F, Middlesbrough, Fulham
Crowe, V. (16) 1958/9 Aston Villa

Curtis, A. (35) 1975/6 Swansea C, Leeds U, Swansea C, Southampton, Cardiff C

Daniel, R. (21) 1950/1 Arsenal, Sunderland
Davies, A. (13) 1982/3 Manchester U, Newcastle U, Swansea C, Bradford C
Davies, A. R. (1) 2005/06 Yeovil T
Davies, C. (1) 1971/2 Charlton Ath
Davies, C. M. (5) 2005/06 Oxford U, Verona, Oldham Ath
Davies, D. (52) 1974/5 Everton, Wrexham, Swansea C
Davies, G. (16) 1979/80 Fulham, Manchester C
Davies, R. Wyn (34) 1963/4 Bolton W, Newcastle U, Manchester C, Manchester U, Blackpool
Davies, Reg (6) 1952/3 Newcastle U
Davies, Ron (29) 1963/4 Norwich C, Southampton, Portsmouth
Davies, S. (58) 2000/01 Tottenham H, Everton, Fulham
Davies, S. I. (1) 1995/6 Manchester U
Davis, G. (3) 1977/8 Wrexham
Deacy, N. (12) 1976/7 PSV Eindhoven, Beringen
Delaney, M. A. (36) 1999/00 Aston Villa
Derrett, S. (4) 1968/9 Cardiff C
Dibble, A. (3) 1985/6 Luton T, Manchester C
Dorman, A. (3) 2009/10 St Mirren, Crystal Palace
Duffy, R. M. (13) 2005/06 Portsmouth
Durban, A. (27) 1965/6 Derby C
Dwyer, P. (10) 1977/8 Cardiff C

Eardley, N. (16) 2007/08 Oldham Ath, Blackpool
Earnshaw, R. (54) 2001/02 Cardiff C, WBA, Norwich C, Derby Co, Nottingham F
Easter, J. M. (10) 2006/07 Wycombe W, Plymouth Arg, Milton Keynes D, Crystal Palace
Eastwood, F. (11) 2007/08 Wolverhampton W, Coventry C
Edwards, C. N. H. (1) 1995/6 Swansea C
Edwards, D. (22) 2007/08 Luton T, Wolverhampton W
Edwards, G. (12) 1946/7 Birmingham C, Cardiff C
Edwards, I. (4) 1977/8 Chester, Wrexham

Edwards, R. O. (15) 2002/03 Aston Villa, Wolverhampton W

Edwards, R. W. (4) 1997/8 Bristol C

Edwards, T. (2) 1956/7 Charlton Ath

Emanuel, J. (2) 1972/3 Bristol C

England, M. (44) 1961/2 Blackburn R, Tottenham H

Evans, B. (7) 1971/2 Swansea C, Hereford U

Evans, C. M. (13) 2007/08 Manchester C, Sheffield U

Evans, I. (13) 1975/6 Crystal P

Evans, P. S. (2) 2001/02 Brentford, Bradford C

Evans, R. (1) 1963/4 Swansea T

Evans, S. J. (7) 2006/07 Wrexham

Felgate, D. (1) 1983/4 Lincoln C

Fletcher, C. N. (36) 2003/04 Bournemouth, West Ham U, Crystal P

Flynn, B. (66) 1974/5 Burnley, Leeds U, Burnley

Ford, T. (38) 1946/7 Swansea T, Aston Villa, Sunderland, Cardiff C

Foulkes, W. (11) 1951/2 Newcastle U

Freestone, R. (1) 1999/00 Swansea C

Gabbidon, D. L. (44) 2001/02 Cardiff C, West Ham U

Garner, G. (1) 2005/06 Leyton Orient

Giggs, R. J. (64) 1991/2 Manchester U

Giles, D. (12) 1979/80 Swansea C, Crystal P

Godfrey, B. (3) 1963/4 Preston NE

Goss, J. (9) 1990/1 Norwich C

Green, C. (15) 1964/5 Birmingham C

Green, R. M. (2) 1997/8 Wolverhampton W

Griffiths, A. (17) 1970/1 Wrexham

Griffiths, H. (1) 1952/3 Swansea T

Griffiths, M. (11) 1946/7 Leicester C

Gunter, C. R. (29) 2006/07 Cardiff C, Tottenham H, Nottingham F

Hall, G. D. (9) 1987/8 Chelsea

Harrington, A. (11) 1955/6 Cardiff C

Harris, C. (24) 1975/6 Leeds U

Harris, W. (6) 1953/4 Middlesbrough

Hartson, J. (51) 1994/5 Arsenal, West Ham U, Wimbledon, Coventry C, Celtic

Haworth, S. O. (5) 1996/7 Cardiff C, Coventry C

Hennessey, T. (39) 1961/2 Birmingham C, Nottingham F, Derby Co

Hennessey, W. R. (32) 2006/07 Wolverhampton W

Hewitt, R. (5) 1957/8 Cardiff C

Hill, M. (2) 1971/2 Ipswich T

Hockey, T. (9) 1971/2 Sheffield U, Norwich C, Aston Villa

Hodges, G. (18) 1983/4 Wimbledon, Newcastle U, Watford, Sheffield U

Holden, A. (1) 1983/4 Chester C

Hole, B. (30) 1962/3 Cardiff C, Blackburn R, Aston Villa, Swansea C

Hollins, D. (11) 1961/2 Newcastle U

Hopkins, J. (16) 1982/3 Fulham, Crystal P

Hopkins, M. (34) 1955/6 Tottenham H

Horne, B. (59) 1987/8 Portsmouth, Southampton, Everton, Birmingham C

Howells, R. (2) 1953/4 Cardiff C

Hughes, C. M. (8) 1991/2 Luton T, Wimbledon

Hughes, I. (4) 1950/1 Luton T

Hughes, L. M. (72) 1983/4 Manchester U, Barcelona, Manchester U, Chelsea, Southampton

Hughes, W. (3) 1946/7 Birmingham C

Hughes, W. A. (5) 1948/9 Blackburn R

Humphreys, J. (1) 1946/7 Everton

Jackett, K. (31) 1982/3 Watford

James, G. (9) 1965/6 Blackpool

James, L. (54) 1971/2 Burnley, Derby C, QPR, Burnley, Swansea C, Sunderland

James, R. M. (47) 1978/9 Swansea C, Stoke C, QPR, Leicester C, Swansea C

Jarvis, A. (3) 1966/7 Hull C

Jenkins, S. R. (16) 1995/6 Swansea C, Huddersfield T

Johnson, A. J. (15) 1998/9 Nottingham F, WBA

Johnson, M. (1) 1963/4 Swansea T

Jones, A. (6) 1986/7 Port Vale, Charlton Ath

Jones, Barrie (15) 1962/3 Swansea T, Plymouth Argyle, Cardiff C

Jones, Bryn (4) 1946/7 Arsenal

Jones, C. (59) 1953/4 Swansea T, Tottenham H, Fulham

Jones, D. (8) 1975/6 Norwich C

Jones, E. (4) 1947/8 Swansea T, Tottenham H

Jones, J. (72) 1975/6 Liverpool, Wrexham, Chelsea, Huddersfield T

Jones, K. (1) 1949/50 Aston Villa

Jones, M. A. (2) 2006/07 Wrexham

Jones, M. G. (13) 1999/00 Leeds U, Leicester C

Jones, P. L. (2) 1996/7 Liverpool, Tranmere R

Jones, P. S. (50) 1996/7 Stockport Co, Southampton, Wolverhampton W, QPR

Jones, R. (1) 1993/4 Sheffield W

Jones, T. G. (13) 1946/7 Everton

Jones, V. P. (9) 1994/5 Wimbledon

Jones, W. (1) 1970/1 Bristol R

Kelsey, J. (41) 1953/4 Arsenal

King, A. (9) 2008/09 Leicester C

King, J. (1) 1954/5 Swansea T

Kinsey, N. (7) 1950/1 Norwich C, Birmingham C

Knill, A. R. (1) 1988/9 Swansea C

Koumas, J. (34) 2000/01 Tranmere R, WBA, Wigan Ath

Krzywicki, R. (8) 1969/70 WBA, Huddersfield T

Lambert, R. (5) 1946/7 Liverpool

Law, B. J. (1) 1989/90 QPR

Lea, C. (2) 1964/5 Ipswich T

Ledley, J. C. (37) 2005/06 Cardiff C, Celtic

Leek, K. (13) 1960/1 Leicester C, Newcastle U, Birmingham C, Northampton T

Legg, A. (6) 1995/6 Birmingham C, Cardiff C

Lever, A. (1) 1952/3 Leicester C

Lewis, D. (1) 1982/3 Swansea C

Llewellyn, C. M. (6) 1997/8 Norwich C, Wrexham

Lloyd, B. (3) 1975/6 Wrexham

Lovell, S. (6) 1981/2 Crystal P, Millwall

Lowndes, S. (10) 1982/3 Newport Co, Millwall, Barnsley

Lowrie, G. (4) 1947/8 Coventry C, Newcastle U

Lucas, M. (4) 1961/2 Leyton Orient

Lucas, W. (7) 1948/9 Swansea T

MacDonald, S. B. (1) 2010/11 Swansea C

Maguire, G. T. (7) 1989/90 Portsmouth

Mahoney, J. (51) 1967/8 Stoke C, Middlesbrough, Swansea C

Mardon, P. J. (1) 1995/6 WBA

Margetson, M. W. (1) 2003/04 Cardiff C

Marriott, A. (5) 1995/6 Wrexham

Marustik, C. (6) 1981/2 Swansea C

Matthews, A. J. (2) 2010/11 Cardiff C

Medwin, T. (30) 1952/3 Swansea T, Tottenham H

Melville, A. K. (65) 1989/90 Swansea C, Oxford U, Sunderland, Fulham, West Ham U

Mielczarek, R. (1) 1970/1 Rotherham U

Millington, A. (21) 1962/3 WBA, Crystal P, Peterborough U, Swansea C

Moore, G. (21) 1959/60 Cardiff C, Chelsea, Manchester U, Northampton T, Charlton Ath

Morgan, C. (23) 2006/07 Milton Keynes D, Peterborough U, Preston NE

Morison, S. W. (7) 2010/11 Millwall

Morris, W. (5) 1946/7 Burnley

Myhill, G. O. (10) 2007/08 Hull C, WBA

Nardiello, D. (2) 1977/8 Coventry C

Nardiello, D. A. (3) 2006/07 Barnsley, QPR

Neilson, A. B. (5) 1991/2 Newcastle U, Southampton

Nicholas, P. (73) 1978/9 Crystal P, Arsenal, Crystal P, Luton T, Aberdeen, Chelsea, Watford

Niedzwiecki, E. A. (2) 1984/5 Chelsea

Nogan, L. M. (2) 1991/2 Watford, Reading

Norman, A. J. (5) 1985/6 Hull C

Nurse, M. T. G. (12) 1959/60 Swansea T, Middlesbrough

Nyatanga, L. J. (34) 2005/06 Derby Co, Bristol C

O'Sullivan, P. (3) 1972/3 Brighton & HA

Oster, J. M. (13) 1997/8 Everton, Sunderland

Page, M. (28) 1970/1 Birmingham C

Page, R. J. (41) 1996/7 Watford, Sheffield U, Cardiff C, Coventry C

Palmer, D. (3) 1956/7 Swansea T

Parry, J. (1) 1950/1 Swansea T

Parry, P. I. (12) 2003/04 Cardiff C

Partridge, D. W. (7) 2004/05 Motherwell, Bristol C

Pascoe, C. (10) 1983/4 Swansea C, Sunderland

Paul, R. (33) 1948/9 Swansea T, Manchester C

Pembridge, M. A. (54) 1991/2 Luton T, Derby C, Sheffield W, Benfica, Everton, Fulham

Perry, J. (1) 1993/4 Cardiff C

Phillips, D. (62) 1983/4 Plymouth Argyle, Manchester C, Coventry C, Norwich C, Nottingham F

Phillips, J. (4) 1972/3 Chelsea

Phillips, L. (58) 1970/1 Cardff C,
Aston Villa, Swansea C, Charlton Ath

Pipe, D. R. (1) 2002/03 Coventry C

Pontin, K. (2) 1979/80 Cardiff C

Powell, A. (8) 1946/7 Leeds U, Everton,
Birmingham C

Powell, D. (11) 1967/8 Wrexham,
Sheffield U

Powell, I. (8) 1946/7 QPR, Aston Villa

Price, L. P. (8) 2005/06 Ipswich T,
Derby Co, Crystal Palace

Price, P. (25) 1979/80 Luton T,
Tottenham H

Pring, K. (3) 1965/6 Rotherham U

Pritchard, H. K. (1) 1984/5 Bristol C

Ramsey, A. (14) 2008/09 Arsenal

Rankmore, F. (l) 1965/6 Peterborough U

Ratcliffe, K. (59) 1980/1 Everton,
Cardiff C

Ready, K. (5) 1996/7 QPR

Reece, G. (29) 1965/6 Sheffield U,
Cardiff C

Reed, W. (2) 1954/5 Ipswich T

Rees, A. (1) 1983/4 Birmingham C

Rees, J. M. (1) 1991/2 Luton T

Rees, R. (39) 1964/5 Coventry C, WBA,
Nottingham F

Rees, W. (4) 1948/9 Cardiff C,
Tottenham H

Ribeiro, C. M. (2) 2009/10 Bristol C

Richards, S. (1) 1946/7 Cardiff C

Ricketts, S. (42) 2004/05 Swansea C,
Hull C, Bolton W

Roberts, A. M. (2) 1992/3 QPR

Roberts, D. (17) 1972/3 Oxford U, Hull C

Roberts, G. W. (9) 1999/00 Tranmere R

Roberts, I. W. (15) 1989/90 Watford,
Huddersfield T, Leicester C, Norwich C

Roberts, J. G. (22) 1970/1 Arsenal,
Birmingham C

Roberts, J. H. (1) 1948/9 Bolton W

Roberts, N. W. (4) 1999/00 Wrexham,
Wigan Ath

Roberts, P. (4) 1973/4 Portsmouth

Roberts, S. W. (1) 2004/05 Wrexham

Robinson, C. P. (52) 1999/00
Wolverhampton W, Portsmouth,
Sunderland, Norwich C, Toronto Lynx

Robinson, J. R. C. (30) 1995/6
Charlton Ath

Robson-Kanu, T. H. (3) 2009/10 Reading

Rodrigues, P. (40) 1964/5 Cardiff C,
Leicester C, Sheffield W

Rouse, V. (1) 1958/9 Crystal P

Rowley, T. (1) 1958/9 Tranmere R

Rush, I. (73) 1979/80 Liverpool, Juventus,
Liverpool

Saunders, D. (75) 1985/6 Brighton & HA,
Oxford U, Derby C, Liverpool, Aston
Villa, Galatasaray, Nottingham F,
Sheffield U, Benfica, Bradford C

Savage, R. W. (39) 1995/6 Crewe
Alexandra, Leicester C, Birmingham C

Sayer, P. (7) 1976/7 Cardiff C

Scrine, F. (2) 1949/50 Swansea T

Sear, C. (1) 1962/3 Manchester C

Sherwood, A. (41) 1946/7 Cardiff C,
Newport C

Shortt, W. (12) 1946/7 Plymouth Argyle

Showers, D. (2) 1974/5 Cardiff C

Sidlow, C. (7) 1946/7 Liverpool

Slatter, N. (22) 1982/3 Bristol R,
Oxford U

Smallman, D. (7) 1973/4 Wrexham,
Everton

Southall, N. (92) 1981/2 Everton

Speed, G. A. (85) 1989/90 Leeds U,
Everton, Newcastle U, Bolton W

Sprake, G. (37) 1963/4 Leeds U,
Birmingham C

Stansfield, F. (1) 1948/9 Cardiff C

Stevenson, B. (15) 1977/8 Leeds U,
Birmingham C

Stevenson, N. (4) 1981/2 Swansea C

Stitfall, R. (2) 1952/3 Cardiff C

Stock, B. B. (3) 2009/10 Doncaster R

Sullivan, D. (17) 1952/3 Cardiff C

Symons, C. J. (37) 1991/2 Portsmouth,
Manchester C, Fulham, Crystal P

Tapscott, D. (14) 1953/4 Arsenal,
Cardiff C

Taylor, G. K. (15) 1995/6 Crystal P,
Sheffield U, Burnley, Nottingham F

Taylor, N. J. (3) 2009/10 Wrexham,
Swansea C

Thatcher, B. D. (7) 2003/04 Leicester C,
Manchester C

Thomas, D. (2) 1956/7 Swansea T

Thomas, M. (51) 1976/7 Wrexham,
Manchester U, Everton,
Brighton & HA, Stoke C, Chelsea,
WBA

Thomas, M. R. (1) 1986/7 Newcastle U

Thomas, R. (50) 1966/7 Swindon T,
Derby C, Cardiff C

Thomas, S. (4) 1947/8 Fulham

Toshack, J. (40) 1968/9 Cardiff C, Liverpool, Swansea C

Trollope, P. J. (9) 1996/7 Derby Co, Fulham, Coventry C, Northampton T

Tudur-Jones, O. (6) 2007/08 Swansea C, Norwich C

Van Den Hauwe, P. W. R. (13) 1984/5 Everton

Vaughan, D. O. (25) 2002/03 Crewe Alex, Real Sociedad, Blackpool

Vaughan, N. (10) 1982/3 Newport Co, Cardiff C

Vearncombe, G. (2) 1957/8 Cardiff C

Vernon, R. (32) 1956/7 Blackburn R, Everton, Stoke C

Villars, A. (3) 1973/4 Cardiff C

Vokes, S. M. (18) 2007/08 Bournemouth, Wolverhampton W

Walley, T. (1) 1970/1 Watford

Walsh, I. (18) 1979/80 Crystal P, Swansea C

Ward, D. (2) 1958/9 Bristol R, Cardiff C

Ward, D. (5) 1999/00 Notts Co, Nottingham F

Webster, C. (4) 1956/7 Manchester U

Weston, R. D. (7) 1999/00 Arsenal, Cardiff C

Williams, A. (13) 1993/4 Reading, Wolverhampton W, Reading

Williams, A. E. (25) 2007/08 Stockport Co, Swansea C

Williams, A. P. (2) 1997/8 Southampton

Williams, D. G. 1987/8 13, Derby Co, Ipswich T

Williams, D. M. (5) 1985/6 Norwich C

Williams, G. (1) 1950/1 Cardiff C

Williams, G. E. (26) 1959/60 WBA

Williams, G. G. (5) 1960/1 Swansea T

Williams, G. J. (2) 2005/06 West Ham U, Ipswich T

Williams, H. (4) 1948/9 Newport Co, Leeds U

Williams, Herbert (3) 1064/5 Swansea T

Williams, S. (43) 1953/4 WBA, Southampton

Witcomb, D. (3) 1946/7 WBA, Sheffield W

Woosnam, P. (17) 1958/9 Leyton Orient, West Ham U, Aston Villa

Yorath, T. (59) 1969/70 Leeds U, Coventry C, Tottenham H, Vancouver Whitecaps

Young, E. (21) 1989/90 Wimbledon, Crystal P, Wolverhampton W

REPUBLIC OF IRELAND

Aherne, T. (16) 1945/6 Belfast Celtic, Luton T

Aldridge, J. W. (69) 1985/6 Oxford U, Liverpool, Real Sociedad, Tranmere R

Ambrose, P. (5) 1954/5 Shamrock R

Anderson, J. (16) 1979/80 Preston NE, Newcastle U

Andrews, K. J. (20) 2008/09 Blackburn R

Babb, P. (35) 1993/4 Coventry C, Liverpool, Sunderland

Bailham, E. (1) 1963/4 Shamrock R

Barber, E. (2) 1965/6 Shelbourne, Birmingham C

Barrett, G. (6) 2002/03 Arsenal, Coventry C

Beglin, J. (15) 1983/4 Liverpool

Bennett, A. J. (2) 2006/07 Reading

Best, L. J. B. (7) 2008/09 Coventry C, Newcastle U

Bonner, P. (80) 1980/1 Celtic

Braddish, S. (1) 1977/8 Dundalk

Brady, T. R. (6) 1963/4 QPR

Brady, W. L. (72) 1974/5 Arsenal, Juventus, Sampdoria, Internazionale, Ascoli, West Ham U

Branagan, K. G. (1) 1996/7 Bolton W

Breen, G. (63) 1995/6 Birmingham C, Coventry C, West Ham U, Sunderland

Breen, T. (3) 1946/7 Shamrock R

Brennan, F. (1) 1964/5 Drumcondra

Brennan, S. A. (19) 1964/5 Manchester U, Waterford

Browne, W. (3) 1963/4 Bohemians

Bruce, A. (2) 2006/07 Ipswich T

Buckley, L. (2) 1983/4 Shamrock R, Waregem

Burke, F. (1) 1951/2 Cork Ath

Butler, P. J. (1) 1999/00 Sunderland

Butler, T. (2) 2002/03 Sunderland

Byrne, A. B. (14) 1969/70 Southampton

Byrne, J. (23) 1984/5 QPR, Le Havre, Brighton & HA, Sunderland, Millwall
Byrne, J. (2) 2003/04 Shelbourne
Byrne, P. (8) 1983/4 Shamrock R

Campbell, A. (3) 1984/5 Santander
Campbell, N. (11) 1970/1 St Patrick's Ath, Fortuna Cologne
Cantwell, N. (36) 1953/4 West Ham U, Manchester U
Carey, B. P. (3) 1991/2 Manchester U, Leicester C
Carey, J. J. (21) 1945/6 Manchester U
Carolan, J. (2) 1959/60 Manchester U
Carr, S. (44) 1998/9 Tottenham H, Newcastle U
Carroll, B. (2) 1948/9 Shelbourne
Carroll, T. R. (17) 1967/8 Ipswich T, Birmingham C
Carsley, L. K. (39) 1997/8 Derby Co, Blackburn R, Coventry C, Everton
Cascarino, A. G. (88) 1985/6 Gillingham, Millwall, Aston Villa, Celtic, Chelsea, Marseille, Nancy
Chandler, J. (2) 1979/80 Leeds U
Clark, C. (2) 2010/11 Aston Villa
Clarke, C. R. (2) 2003/04 Stoke C
Clarke, J. (1) 1977/8 Drogheda U
Clarke, K. (2) 1947/8 Drumcondra
Clarke, M. (1) 1949/50 Shamrock R
Clinton, T. J. (3) 1950/1 Everton
Coad, P. (11) 1946/7 Shamrock R
Coffey, T. (1) 1949/50 Drumcondra
Coleman, S. (4) 2010/11 Everton
Colfer, M. D. (2) 1949/50 Shelbourne
Colgan, N. (9) 2001/02 Hibernian, Barnsley
Conmy, O. M. (5) 1964/5 Peterborough U
Connolly, D. J. (41) 1995/6 Watford, Feyenoord, Wolverhampton W, Excelsior, Wimbledon, West Ham U, Wigan Ath
Conroy, G. A. (27) 1969/70 Stoke C
Conway, J. P. (20) 1966/7 Fulham, Manchester C
Corr, P. J. (4) 1948/9 Everton
Courtney, E. (1) 1945/6 Cork U
Cox, S. R. (4) 2010/11 WBA
Coyle, O. (1) 1993/4 Bolton W
Coyne, T. (22) 1991/2 Celtic, Tranmere R, Motherwell
Crowe, G. (2) 2002/03 Bohemians

Cummins, G. P. (19) 1953/4 Luton T
Cuneen, T. (1) 1950/1 Limerick
Cunningham, G. R. (3) 2009/10 Manchester C
Cunningham, K. (72) 1995/6 Wimbledon, Birmingham C
Curtis, D. P. (17) 1956/7 Shelbourne, Bristol C, Ipswich T, Exeter C
Cusack, S. (1) 1952/3 Limerick

Daish, L. S. (5) 1991/2 Cambridge U, Coventry C
Daly, G. A. (48) 1972/3 Manchester U, Derby C, Coventry C, Birmingham C, Shrewsbury T
Daly, M. (2) 1977/8 Wolverhampton W
Daly, P. (1) 1949/50 Shamrock R
Deacy, E. (4) 1981/2 Aston Villa
Delaney, D. F. (5) 2007/08 QPR, Ipswich T
Delap, R. J. (11) 1997/8 Derby Co, Southampton
De Mange, K. J. P. P. (2) 1986/7 Liverpool, Hull C
Dempsey, J. T. (19) 1966/7 Fulham, Chelsea
Dennehy, J. (11) 1971/2 Cork Hibernian, Nottingham F, Walsall
Desmond, P. (4) 1949/50 Middlesbrough
Devine, J. (13) 1979/80 Arsenal, Norwich C
Doherty, G. M. T. (34) 1999/00 Luton T, Tottenham H, Norwich C
Donovan, D. C. (5) 1954/5 Everton
Donovan, T. (1) 1979/80 Aston Villa
Douglas, J. (8) 2003/04 Blackburn R, Leeds U
Doyle, C. (1) 1958/9 Shelbourne
Doyle, Colin (1) 2006/07 Birmingham C
Doyle, K. E. (41) 2005/06 Reading, Wolverhampton W
Doyle, M. P. (1) 2003/04 Coventry C
Duff, D. A. (87) 1997/8 Blackburn R, Chelsea, Newcastle U, Fulham
Duffy, B. (1) 1949/50 Shamrock R
Dunne, A. P. (33) 1961/2 Manchester U, Bolton W
Dunne, J. C. (1) 1970/1 Fulham
Dunne, P. A. J. (5) 1964/5 Manchester U
Dunne, R. P. (65) 1999/00 Everton, Manchester C, Aston Villa
Dunne, S. (15) 1952/3 Luton T

Dunne, T. (3) 1955/6 St Patrick's Ath
Dunning, P. (2) 1970/1 Shelbourne
Dunphy, E. M. (23) 1965/6 York C,
Millwall
Dwyer, N. M. (14) 1959/60 West Ham U,
Swansea T

Eccles, P. (1) 1985/6 Shamrock R
Eglington, T. J. (24) 1945/6 Shamrock R,
Everton
Elliott, S. W. (9) 2004/05 Sunderland
Evans, M. J. (1) 1997/8 Southampton

Fagan, E. (1) 1972/3 Shamrock R
Fagan, F. (8) 1954/5 Manchester C,
Derby C
Fahey, K. D. (11) 2009/10 Birmingham C
Fairclough, M. (2) 1981/2 Dundalk
Fallon, S. (8) 1950/1 Celtic
Farrell, P. D. (28) 1945/6 Shamrock R,
Everton
Farrelly, G. (6) 1995/6 Aston Villa,
Everton, Bolton W
Finnan, S. (53) 1999/00 Fulham,
Liverpool
Finucane, A. (11) 1966/7 Limerick
Fitzgerald, F. J. (2) 1954/5 Waterford
Fitzgerald, P. J. (5) 1960/1 Leeds U,
Chester
Fitzpatrick, K. (1) 1969/70 Limerick
Fitzsimons, A. G. (26) 1949/50
Middlesbrough, Lincoln C
Fleming, C. (10) 1995/6 Middlesbrough
Fogarty, A. (11) 1959/60 Sunderland,
Hartlepool U
Folan, C. C. (7) 2008/09 Hull C
Foley, D. J. (6) 1999/00 Watford
Foley, K. P. (8) 2008/09
Wolverhampton W
Foley, T. C. (9) 1963/4 Northampton T
Forde, D. (2) 2010/11 Millwall
Fullam, J. 1960/1 Preston NE,
Shamrock R

Gallagher, C. (2) 1966/7 Celtic
Gallagher, M. (1) 1953/4 Hibernian
Galvin, A. (29) 1982/3 Tottenham H,
Sheffield W, Swindon T
Gamble, J. (2) 2006/07 Cork C
Gannon, E. (14) 1948/9 Notts Co,
Sheffield W, Shelbourne K
Gannon, M. (1) 1971/2 Shelbourne

Gavin, J. T. (7) 1949/50 Norwich C,
Tottenham H, Norwich C
Gibbons, A. (4) 1951/2 St Patrick's Ath
Gibson, D. T. D. (16) 2007/08
Manchester U
Gilbert, R. (1) 1965/6 Shamrock R
Giles, C. (1) 1950/1 Doncaster R
Giles, M. J. (59) 1959/60 Manchester U,
Leeds U, WBA, Shamrock R
Given, S. J. J. (113) 1995/6 Blackburn R,
Newcastle U, Manchester C
Givens, D. J. (56) 1968/9 Manchester U,
Luton T, QPR, Birmingham C,
Neuchatel Xamax
Gleeson, S. M. (2) 2006/07
Wolverhampton W
Glynn, D. (2) 1951/2 Drumcondra
Godwin, T. F. (13) 1948/9 Shamrock R,
Leicester C, Bournemouth
Goodman, J. (4) 1996/7 Wimbledon
Goodwin, J. (1) 2002/03 Stockport Co
Gorman, W. C. (2) 1946/7 Brentford
Grealish, A. (45) 1975/6 Orient, Luton T,
Brighton & HA, WBA
Green, P. J. (9) 2009/10 Derby Co
Gregg, E. (8) 1977/8 Bohemians
Grimes, A. A. (18) 1977/8 Manchester U,
Coventry C, Luton T

Hale, A. (13) 1961/2 Aston Villa,
Doncaster R, Waterford
Hamilton, T. (2) 1958/9 Shamrock R
Hand, E. K. (20) 1968/9 Portsmouth
Harte, I. P. (64) 1995/6 Leeds U, Levante
Hartnett, J. B. (2) 1948/9 Middlesbrough
Haverty, J. (32) 1955/6 Arsenal,
Blackburn R, Millwall, Celtic,
Bristol R, Shelbourne
Hayes, A. W. P. (1) 1978/9 Southampton
Hayes, W. E. (2) 1946/7 Huddersfield T
Hayes, W. J. (1) 1948/9 Limerick
Healey, R. (2) 1976/7 Cardiff C
Healy, C. (13) 2001/02 Celtic, Sunderland
Heighway, S. D. (34) 1970/1 Liverpool,
Minnesota Kicks
Henderson, B. (2) 1947/8 Drumcondra
Henderson, W. C. P. (6) 2005/06
Brighton & HA, Preston NE
Hennessy, J. (5) 1964/5 Shelbourne, St
Patrick's Ath
Herrick, J. (3) 1971/2 Cork Hibernians,
Shamrock R

318

Higgins, J. (1) 1950/1 Birmingham C

Holland, M. R. (49) 1999/00 Ipswich T, Charlton Ath

Holmes, J. (30) 1970/1 Coventry C, Tottenham H, Vancouver Whitecaps

Hoolahan, W. (1) 2007/08 Blackpool

Houghton, R. J. (73) 1985/6 Oxford U, Liverpool, Aston Villa, Crystal P, Reading

Howlett, G. (1) 1983/4 Brighton & HA

Hughton, C. (53) 1979/80 Tottenham H, West Ham U

Hunt, N. (3) 2008/09 Reading

Hunt, S. P. (30) 2006/07 Reading, Hull C, Wolverhampton W

Hurley, C. J. (40) 1956/7 Millwall, Sunderland, Bolton W

Ireland, S. J. (6) 2005/06 Manchester C

Irwin, D. J. (56) 1990/1 Manchester U

Kavanagh, G. A. (16) 1997/8 Stoke C, Cardiff C, Wigan Ath

Keane, R. D. (108) 1997/8 Wolverhampton W, Coventry C, Internazionale, Leeds U, Tottenham H, Liverpool, Tottenham H

Keane, R. M. (67) 1990/1 Nottingham F, Manchester U

Keane, T. R. (4) 1948/9 Swansea T

Kearin, M. (1) 1971/2 Shamrock R

Kearns, F. T. (1) 1953/4 West Ham U

Kearns, M. (18) 1969/70 Oxford U, Walsall, Wolverhampton W

Kelly, A. T. (34) 1992/3 Sheffield U, Blackburn R

Kelly, D. T. (26) 1987/8 Walsall, West Ham U, Leicester C, Newcastle U, Wolverhampton W, Sunderland, Tranmere R

Kelly, G. (52) 1993/4 Leeds U

Kelly, J. A. (48) 1956/7 Drumcondra, Preston NE

Kelly, J. P. V. (5) 1960/1 Wolverhampton W

Kelly, M. J. (4) 1987/8 Portsmouth

Kelly, N. (1) 1953/4 Nottingham F

Kelly, S. M. (24) 2005/06 Tottenham H, Birmingham C, Fulham

Kenna, J. J. (27) 1994/5 Blackburn R

Kennedy, M. (34) 1995/6 Liverpool, Wimbledon, Manchester C, Wolverhampton W

Kennedy, M. F. (2) 1985/6 Portsmouth

Kenny, P. (7) 2003/04 Sheffield U

Keogh, A. D. (21) 2006/07 Wolverhampton W

Keogh, J. (1) 1965/6 Shamrock R

Keogh, S. (1) 1958/9 Shamrock R

Kernaghan, A. N. (22) 1992/3 Middlesbrough, Manchester C

Kiely, D. L. (11) 1999/00 Charlton Ath, WBA

Kiernan, F. W. (5) 1950/1 Shamrock R, Southampton

Kilbane, K. D. (110) 1997/8 WBA, Sunderland, Everton, Wigan Ath, Hull C

Kinnear, J. P. (26) 1966/7 Tottenham H, Brighton & HA

Kinsella, M. A. (48) 1997/8 Charlton Ath, Aston Villa, WBA

Langan, D. (26) 1977/8 Derby Co, Birmingham C, Oxford U

Lapira, J. (1) 2006/07 Notre Dame

Lawler, J. F. (8) 1952/3 Fulham

Lawlor, J. C. (3) 1948/9 Drumcondra, Doncaster R

Lawlor, M. (5) 1970/1 Shamrock R

Lawrence, L. (15) 2008/09 Stoke C, Portsmouth

Lawrenson, M. (39) 1976/7 Preston NE, Brighton & HA, Liverpool

Lee, A. L. (10) 2002/03 Rotherham U, Cardiff C, Ipswich T

Leech, M. (8) 1968/9 Shamrock R

Long, S. P. (21) 2006/07 Reading

Lowry, D. (1) 1961/2 St Patrick's Ath

McAlinden, J. (2) 1945/6 Portsmouth

McAteer, J. W. (52) 1993/4 Bolton W, Liverpool, Blackburn R, Sunderland

McCann, J. (1) 1956/7 Shamrock R

McCarthy, J. (3) 2009/10 Wigan Ath

McCarthy, M. (57) 1983/4 Manchester C, Celtic, Lyon, Millwall

McConville, T. (6) 1971/2 Dundalk, Waterford

McDonagh, Jim (25) 1980/1 Everton, Bolton W, Notts C

McDonagh, Jacko (3) 1983/4 Shamrock R

McEvoy, M. A. (17) 1960/1 Blackburn R

McGeady, A. (40) 2003/04 Celtic, Spartak Moscow

McGee, P. (15) 1977/8 QPR, Preston NE

McGoldrick, E. J. (15) 1991/2 Crystal P, Arsenal

McGowan, D. (3) 1948/9 West Ham U

McGowan, J. (1) 1946/7 Cork U

McGrath, M. (22) 1957/8 Blackburn R, Bradford Park Avenue

McGrath, P. (83) 1984/5 Manchester U, Aston Villa, Derby C

McLoughlin, A. F. (42) 1989/90 Swindon T, Southampton, Portsmouth

McMillan, W. (2) 1945/6 Belfast Celtic

McNally, J. B. (3) 1958/9 Luton T

McPhail, S. (10) 1999/00 Leeds U

McShane, P. D. (26) 2006/07 WBA, Sunderland, Hull C

Macken, A. (1) 1976/7 Derby Co

Macken, J. P. (1) 2004/05 Manchester C

Mackey, G. (3) 1956/7 Shamrock R

Mahon, A. J. (2) 1999/00 Tranmere R

Malone, G. (1) 1948/9 Shelbourne

Mancini, T. J. (5) 1973/4 QPR, Arsenal

Martin, C. J. (30) 1945/6 Glentoran, Leeds U, Aston Villa

Martin, M. P. (52) 1971/2 Bohemians, Manchester U, WBA, Newcastle U

Maybury, A. (10) 1997/8 Leeds U, Heart of Midlothian, Leicester C

Meagan, M. K. (17) 1960/1 Everton, Huddersfield T, Drogheda

Miller, L. W. P. (21) 2003/04 Celtic, Manchester U, Sunderland, Hibernian

Milligan, M. J. (1) 1991/2 Oldham Ath

Mooney, J. (2) 1964/5 Shamrock R

Moore, A. (8) 1995/6 Middlesbrough

Moran, K. (71) 1979/80 Manchester U, Sporting Gijon, Blackburn R

Moroney, T. (12) 1947/8 West Ham U, Evergreen U

Morris, C. B. (35) 1987/8 Celtic, Middlesbrough

Morrison, C. H. (36) 2001/02 Crystal P, Birmingham C, Crystal P

Moulson, G. B. (3) 1947/8 Lincoln C

Mucklan, C. (1) 1977/8 Drogheda

Mulligan, P. M. (50) 1968/9 Shamrock R, Chelsea, Crystal P, WBA, Shamrock R

Munroe, L. (1) 1953/4 Shamrock R

Murphy, A. (1) 1955/6 Clyde

Murphy, B. (1) 1985/6 Bohemians

Murphy, D. (9) 2006/07 Sunderland

Murphy, Jerry (1) 1979/80 Crystal P

Murphy, Joe (2) 2003/04 WBA, Scunthorpe U

Murphy, P. M. (1) 2006/07 Carlisle U

Murray, T. (1) 1949/50 Dundalk

Newman, W. (1) 1968/9 Shelbourne

Nolan, E. W. (3) 2008/09 Preston NE

Nolan, R. (10) 1956/7 Shamrock R

O'Brien, A. (5) 2006/07 Newcastle U

O'Brien, A. J. (26) 2000/01 Newcastle U, Portsmouth

O'Brien, F. (3) 1979/80 Philadelphia Fury

O'Brien, J. M. (3) 2005/06 Bolton W

O'Brien, L. (16) 1985/6 Shamrock R, Manchester U, Newcastle U, Tranmere R

O'Brien, R. (5) 1975/6 Notts Co

O'Byrne, L. B. (1) 1948/9 Shamrock R

O'Callaghan, B. R. (6) 1978/9 Stoke C

O'Callaghan, K. (21) 1980/1 Ipswich T, Portsmouth

O'Cearuill, J. (2) 2006/07 Arsenal

O'Connnell, A. (2) 1966/7 Dundalk, Bohemians

O'Connor, T. (4) 1949/50 Shamrock R

O'Connor, T. (7) 1967/8 Fulham, Dundalk, Bohemians

O'Dea, D. (9) 2009/10 Celtic, Ipswich T

O'Driscoll, J. F. (3) 1948/9 Swansea T

O'Driscoll, S. (3) 1981/2 Fulham

O'Farrell, F. (9) 1951/2 West Ham U, Preston NE

O'Flanagan, K. P. (3) 1946/7 Arsenal

O'Flanagan, M. (1) 1946/7 Bohemians

O'Halloran, S. E. (2) 2006/07 Aston Villa

O'Hanlon, K. G. (1) 1987/8 Rotherham U

O'Keefe, E. (5) 1980/1 Everton, Port Vale

O'Leary, D. (68) 1976/7 Arsenal

O'Leary, P. (7) 1979/80 Shamrock R

O'Neill, F. S. (20) 1961/2 Shamrock R

O'Neill, J. (17) 1951/2 Everton

O'Neill, J. (1) 1960/1 Preston NE

O'Neill, K. P. (13) 1995/6 Norwich C, Middlesbrough

O'Regan, K. (4) 1983/4 Brighton & HA

O'Reilly, J. (2) 1945/6 Cork U
O'Shea, J. F. (70) 2001/02 Manchester U

Peyton, G. (33) 1976/7 Fulham, Bournemouth, Everton
Peyton, N. (6) 1956/7 Shamrock R, Leeds U
Phelan, T. (42) 1991/2 Wimbledon, Manchester C, Chelsea, Everton, Fulham
Potter, D. M. (5) 2006/07 Wolverhampton W

Quinn, A. (8) 2002/03 Sheffield W, Sheffield U
Quinn, B. S. (4) 1999/00 Coventry C
Quinn, N. J. (91) 1985/6 Arsenal, Manchester C, Sunderland

Reid, A. M. (27) 2003/04 Nottingham F, Tottenham H, Charlton Ath, Sunderland
Reid, S. J. (23) 2001/02 Millwall, Blackburn R
Richardson, D. J. (3) 1971/2 Shamrock R, Gillingham
Ringstead, A. (20) 1950/1 Sheffield U
Robinson, M. (24) 1980/1 Brighton & HA, Liverpool, QPR
Roche, P. J. (8) 1971/2 Shelbourne, Manchester U
Rogers, E. (19) 1967/8 Blackburn R, Charlton Ath
Rowlands, M. C. (5) 2003/04 QPR
Ryan, G. (18) 1977/8 Derby Co, Brighton & HA
Ryan, R. A. (16) 1949/50 WBA, Derby C

Sadlier, R. T. (1) 2001/02 Millwall
Savage, D. P. T. (5) 1995/6 Millwall
Saward, P. (18) 1953/4 Millwall, Aston Villa, Huddersfield T
Scannell, T. (1) 1953/4 Southend U
Scully, P. J. (1) 1988/9 Arsenal
Sheedy, K. (46) 1983/4 Everton, Newcastle U
Sheridan, C. (3) 2009/10 Celtic, CSKA Sofia
Sheridan, J. J. (34) 1987/8 Leeds U, Sheffield W
Slaven, B. (7) 1989/90 Middlesbrough

Sloan, J. W. (2) 1945/6 Arsenal
Smyth, M. (1) 1968/9 Shamrock R
Stapleton, F. (71) 1976/7 Arsenal, Manchester U, Ajax, Le Havre, Blackburn R
Staunton, S. (102) 1988/9 Liverpool, Aston Villa, Liverpool, Aston Villa
St. Ledger-Hall, S. P. (18) 2008/09 Preston NE
Stevenson, A. E. (6) 1946/7 Everton
Stokes, A. (4) 2006/07 Sunderland, Celtic
Strahan, F. (5) 1963/4 Shelbourne
Swan, M. M. G. (1) 1959/60 Drumcondra
Synott, N. (3) 1977/8 Shamrock R

Taylor T. (1) 1958/9 Waterford
Thomas, P. (2) 1973/4 Waterford
Thompson, J. (1) 2003/04 Nottingham F
Townsend, A. D. (70) 1988/9 Norwich C, Chelsea, Aston Villa, Middlesbrough
Traynor, T. J. (8) 1953/4 Southampton
Treacy, K. (5) 2010/11 Preston NE
Treacy, R. C. P. (42) 1965/6 WBA, Charlton Ath, Swindon T, Preston NE, WBA, Shamrock R
Tuohy, L. (8) 1955/6 Shamrock R, Newcastle U, Shamrock R
Turner, P. (2) 1962/3 Celtic

Vernon, J. (2) 1945/6 Belfast Celtic

Waddock, G. (21) 1979/80 QPR, Millwall
Walsh, D. J. (20) 1945/6 Linfield, WBA, Aston Villa
Walsh, J. (1) 1981/2 Limerick
Walsh, M. (21) 1975/6 Blackpool, Everton, QPR, Porto
Walsh, M. (4) 1981/2 Everton
Walsh, W. (9) 1946/7 Manchester C
Walters, J. R. (2) 2010/11 Stoke C
Ward. S. R. (3) 2010/11 Wolverhampton W
Waters, J. (2) 1976/7 Grimsby T
Westwood, K. (7) 2008/09 Coventry C
Whelan, G. D. (29) 2007/08 Stoke C
Whelan, R. (2) 1963/4 St Patrick's Ath
Whelan, R. (53) 1980/1 Liverpool, Southend U
Whelan, W. (4) 1955/6 Manchester U
Whittaker, R. (1) 1958/9 Chelsea
Wilson, M. D. (1) 2010/11 Stoke C

BRITISH ISLES INTERNATIONAL GOALSCORERS SINCE 1946

ENGLAND

A'Court, A.	1	Cole, J.J.	10	Ince P.E.C.	2
Adams, T.A.	5	Connelly, J.M.	7		
Allen, R.	2	Coppell, S.J.	7	Jeffers, F.	1
Anderson, V.	2	Cowans, G.	2	Jenas, J.A.	1
Anderton, D.R.	7	Crawford, R.	1	**Johnson, A.**	**2**
Astall, G.	1	**Crouch, P.J.**	**22**	Johnson, D.E.	6
Atyeo, P.J.W.	5	Currie, A.W.	3	Johnson, G.M.C.	1
Baily, E.F.	5	**Defoe, J.C.**	**15**	Kay, A.H.	1
Baker, J.H.	3	Dixon, L.M.	1	Keegan, J.K.	21
Ball, A.J.	8	Dixon, K.M.	4	Kennedy, R.	3
Barmby, N.J.	4	Douglas, B.	11	Keown, M.R.	2
Barnes, J.	11			Kevan, D.T.	8
Barnes, P.S.	4	Eastham, G.	2	Kidd, B.	1
Barry, G.	2	Edwards, D.	5	King, L.B.	2
Beardsley, P.A.	9	Ehiogu, U.	1		
Beattie, J.K.	1	Elliott, W.H.	3	**Lampard, F.J.**	**22**
Beckham, D.R.J.	17			Langton, R.	1
Bell, C.	9	Ferdinand, L.	5	Latchford, R.D.	5
Bent, D.A.	**3**	Ferdinand, R.G.	3	Lawler, C.	1
Bentley, R.T.F.	9	Finney, T.	30	Lawton, T.	16
Blissett, L.	3	Flowers, R.	10	Lee, F.	10
Bowles, S.	1	Fowler, R.B.	7	Lee, J.	1
Bradford, G.R.W.	1	Francis, G.C.J.	3	Lee, R.M.	2
Bradley, W.	2	Francis, T.	12	Lee, S.	2
Bridge, W.M.	1	Froggatt, J.	2	Le Saux, G.P.	1
Bridges, B.J.	1	Froggatt, R.	2	Lineker, G.	48
Broadbent, P.F.	2			Lofthouse, N.	30
Broadis, I.A.	8	Gascoigne, P.J.	10		
Brooking, T.D.	5	**Gerrard, S.G.**	**19**	Mabbutt, G.	1
Brooks, J.	2	Goddard, P.	1	McDermott, T.	3
Brown, W.M.	1	Grainger, C.	3	Macdonald, M.	6
Bull, S.G.	4	Greaves, J.	44	McManaman, S.	3
Butcher, T.	3			Mannion, W.J.	11
Byrne, J.J.	8	Haines, J.T.W.	2	Mariner, P.	13
		Hancocks, J.	2	Marsh, R.W.	1
Campbell, S.J.	1	Hassall, H.W.	4	Matthews, S.	3
Carroll, A.T.	**1**	Hateley, M.	9	Medley, L.D.	1
Carter, H.S.	5	Haynes, J.N.	18	Melia, J.	1
Chamberlain, M.	1	Heskey, E.W.	7	Merson, P.C.	3
Channon, M.R.	21	Hirst, D.E.	1	Milburn, J.E.T.	10
Charlton, J.	6	Hitchens, G.A.	5	Moore, R.F.	2
Charlton, R.	49	Hoddle, G.	8	Morris, J.	3
Chivers, M.	13	Hughes, E.W.	1	Mortensen, S.H.	23
Clarke, A.J.	10	Hunt, R.	18	Mullen, J.	6
Cole, A.	1	Hunter, N.	2	Mullery, A.P.	1
		Hurst, G.C.	24	Murphy, D.B.	1

Neal, P.G. 5
Nicholls, J. 1
Nicholson, W.E. 1
Nugent, D.J. 1

O'Grady, M. 3
Owen, M.J. 40
Own goals 31

Paine, T.L. 7
Palmer, C.L. 1
Parry, R.A. 1
Peacock, A. 3
Pearce, S. 5
Pearson, J.S. 5
Pearson, S.C. 5
Perry, W. 2
Peters, M. 20
Pickering, F. 5
Platt, D. 27
Pointer, R. 2

Ramsay, A.E. 3
Redknapp, J.F. 1
Revie, D.G. 4
Richards, M. 1
Richardson, K.E. 2
Robson, B. 26
Robson, R. 4
Rooney, W. 26
Rowley, J.F. 6
Royle, J. 2

Sansom, K. 1
Scholes, P. 14
Sewell, J. 3
Shackleton, L.F. 1
Shearer, A. 30
Sheringham, E.P. 11
Smith, A. 1
Smith, A.M. 2
Smith, R. 13
Southgate, G. 2
Steven, T.M. 4
Stiles, N.P. 1
Stone, S.B. 2
Summerbee, M.G. 1

Tambling, R.V. 1
Taylor, P.J. 2
Taylor, T. 16
Terry, J.G. 6

Thompson, P.B. 1
Tueart, D. 2

Upson, M.J. 2

Vassell, D. 6
Viollet, D.S. 1

Waddle, C.R. 6
Walcott, T.J. 3
Wallace, D.L. 1
Walsh, P. 1
Watson, D.V. 4
Webb, N. 4
Weller, K. 1
Wignall, F. 2
Wilkins, R.G. 3
Wilshaw, D.J. 10
Wise, D.F. 1
Withe, P. 1
Woodcock, T. 16
Worthington, F.S. 2
Wright, I.E. 9
Wright, M. 1
Wright, W.A. 3
Wright-Phillips, S.C. 6

Young, A. S. 2

SCOTLAND

Aitken, R. 1
Archibald, S. 4

Baird, S. 2
Bannon, E. 1
Bauld, W. 2
Baxter, J.C. 3
Beattie, C. 1
Berra, C. 1
Bett, J. 1
Bone, J. 1
Booth, S. 6
Boyd, K. 7
Boyd, T. 1
Brand, R. 8
Brazil, A. 1
Bremner, W.J. 3
Broadfoot, K. 1
Brown, A.D. 6
Brown, S. 2
Buckley, P. 1
Burke, C. 2

Burley, C.W. 3
Burns, K. 1

Caldwell, G. 2
Calderwood, C. 1
Caldow, E. 4
Cameron, C. 2
Campbell, R. 1
Chalmers, S. 3
Clarkson, D. 1
Collins, J. 12
Collins, R.V. 10
Combe, J.R. 1
Commons, K. 2
Conn, A. 1
Cooper, D. 6
Craig, J. 1
Crawford, S. 4
Curran, H.P. 1

Dailly, C. 6
Dalglish, K. 30
Davidson, J.A. 1
Dickov, P. 1
Dobie, R.S. 1
Docherty, T.H. 1
Dodds, D. 1
Dodds, W. 7
Duncan, D.M. 1
Durie, G.S. 7

Elliott, M.S. 1

Ferguson, B. 3
Fernie, W. 1
Flavell, R. 2
Fleming, C. 2
Fletcher, D. 4
Fletcher, S. 1
Freedman, D.A. 1

Gallacher, K.W. 9
Gemmell, T.K *(St Mirren)* 1
Gemmell, T.K *(Celtic)* 1
Gemmill, A. 8
Gemmill, S. 1
Gibson, D.W. 3
Gilzean, A.J. 12
Gough, C.R. 6
Graham, A. 2
Graham, G. 3

Gray, A.	7	MacKay, D.C.	4	Nevin, P.K.F.	5
Gray, E.	3	Mackay, G.	1	Nicholas, C.	5
Gray, F.	1	MacKenzie, J.A.	1		
Greig, J.	3	**Mackie, J.C.**	**1**	O'Connor, G.	4
		MacLeod, M.	1	O'Hare, J.	5
Hamilton, G.	4	McAllister, G.	5	Ormond, W.E.	2
Harper, J.M.	2	**McArthur, J.**	**1**	Orr, T.	1
Hartford, R.A.	4	McAvennie, F.	1	**Own goals**	**10**
Hartley, P.J.	1	McCall, S.M.	1		
Henderson, J.G.	1	McCalliog, J.	1	Parlane, D.	1
Henderson, W.	5	McCann, N.	3	Pettigrew, W.	2
Hendry, E.C.J.	3	McClair, B.	2	Provan, D.	1
Herd, D.G.	3	McCoist, A.	19		
Herd, G.	1	McCormack, R.	1	Quashie, N.F.	1
Hewie, J.D.	2	McCulloch, L.	1	Quinn, J.	7
Holt, G.J.	1	McFadden, J.	15*	Quinn, P.	1
Holton, J.A.	2	McGhee, M.	2		
Hopkin, D.	2	McGinlay, J.	3	Reilly, L.	22
Houliston, W.	2	McInally, A.	3	Ring, T.	2
Howie, H.	1	McKimmie, S.I.	1	Rioch, B.D.	6
Hughes, J.	1	McKinlay, W.	4	Ritchie, P.S.	1
Hunter, W.	1	McKinnon, R.	1	Robertson, A.	2
Hutchison, D.	6	McLaren, A.	4	Robertson, J.	3
Hutchison, T.	1	McLean, T.	1	Robertson, J.N.	8
		McLintock, F.	1	Robson, B.	1
Jackson, C.	1	**McManus S.**	**2**		
Jackson, D.	4	McMillan, I.L.	2	St John, I.	9
Jardine, A.	1	McNeill, W.	3	Scott, A.S.	5
Jess, E.	2	McPhail, J.	3	Sharp, G.	1
Johnston, A.	2	McQueen, G.	5	Shearer, D.	2
Johnston, L.H.	1	McStay, P.	9	Smith, G.	4
Johnston, M.	14	McSwegan, G.J.	1	Souness, G.J.	4
Johnstone, D.	2	Maloney, S.	1	Steel, W.	12
Johnstone, J.	4	Mason, J.	4	Stein, C.	10
Johnstone, R.	10	Masson, D.S.	5	Stewart, R.	1
Jordan, J.	11	**Miller, K.**	**14**	Strachan, G.	5
		Miller, W.	1	Sturrock, P.	3
Kyle, K.	1	Mitchell, R.C.	1		
		Morgan, W.	1	Thompson, S.	3
Lambert, P.	1	Morris, H.	3	Thornton, W.	1
Law, D.	30	**Morrison, J.C.**	**1**		
Leggat, G.	8	Mudie, J.K.	9	Waddell, W.	6
Lennox, R.	3	Mulhall, G.	1	Wallace, I.A.	1
Liddell, W.	6	Murdoch, R.	5	Wark, J.	7
Linwood, A.B.	1	Murray, J.	1	Webster, A.	1
Lorimer, P.	4			Weir, A.	1
		Narey, D.	1	Weir, D.	1
Macari, L.	5	**Naismith, S.**	**1**	White, J.A.	3
MacDougall, E.J.	3	Naysmith, G.A.	1	Wilkie, L.	1

* The Scottish FA officially changed Robsons's goal against Iceland on 10 September 2008 to McFadden.

Wilson, D. *(Liverpool)* 1
Wilson, D. *(Rangers)* 9

Young, A. 2

WALES

Allchurch, I.J. 23
Allen, M. 3

Bale, G. 3
Barnes, W. 1
Bellamy, C.D. 18
Blackmore, C.G. 1
Blake, N.A. 4
Bodin, P.J. 3
Bowen, D.I. 3
Bowen, M. 2
Boyle, T. 1
Burgess, W.A.R. 1

Charles, J. 1
Charles, M. 6
Charles, W.J. 15
Church, S.R. 1
Clarke, R.J. 5
Coleman, C. 4
Collins, J. 2
Cotterill, D. 1
Curtis, A. 6

Davies, G. 2
Davies, R.T. 9
Davies, R.W. 6
Davies, Simon 6
Deacy, N. 4
Durban, A. 2
Dwyer, P. 2

Earnshaw, R. 16
Eastwood, F. 4
Edwards, D. 3
Edwards, G. 2
Edwards, R.I. 4
England, H.M. 4
Evans, C. 2
Evans, I. 1

Fletcher, C. 1
Flynn, B. 7
Ford, T. 23
Foulkes, W.J. 1

Giggs, R.J. 12
Giles, D. 2
Godfrey, B.C. 2
Griffiths, A.T. 6
Griffiths, M.W. 2

Harris, C.S. 1
Hartson, J. 14
Hewitt, R. 1
Hockey, T. 1
Hodges, G. 2
Horne, B. 2
Hughes, L.M. 16

James, L. 10
James, R. 7
Jones, A. 1
Jones, B.S. 2
Jones, Cliff 16
Jones, D.E. 1
Jones, J.P. 1

King, A. 1
Koumas, J. 10
Kryzwicki, R.I. 1

Ledley, J. 3
Leek, K. 5
Llewelyn, C.M 1
Lovell, S. 1
Lowrie, G. 2

Mahoney, J.F. 1
Medwin, T.C. 6
Melville, A.K. 3
Moore, G. 1

Nicholas, P. 2

O'Sullivan, P.A. 1
Own goals 8

Palmer, D. 1
Parry, P.I. 1
Paul, R. 1
Pembridge, M.A. 6
Phillips, D. 2
Powell, A. 1
Powell, D. 1
Price, P. 1

Ramsay, A. 3

Reece, G.I. 2
Rees, R.R. 3
Roberts, P.S. 1
Robinson, C.P. 1
Robinson, J.R.C. 3
Rush, I. 28

Saunders, D. 22
Savage R.W. 2
Slatter, N. 2
Smallman, D.P. 1
Speed, G.A. 7
Symons, C.J. 2

Tapscott, D.R. 4
Taylor, G.J. 1
Thomas, M. 4
Toshack, J.B. 12

Vaughan, D.O. 1
Vernon, T.R. 8
Vokes, S.M. 2

Walsh, I. 7
Williams, A. 2
Williams, G.E. 1
Williams, G.G. 1
Woosnam, A.P. 3

Yorath, T.C. 2
Young, E. 1

NORTHERN IRELAND

Anderson, T. 4
Armstrong, G. 12

Barr, H.H. 1
Best, G. 9
Bingham, W.L. 10
Black, K. 1
Blanchflower, D. 2
Blanchflower, J. 1
Brennan, R.A. 1
Brotherston, N. 3
Brunt, C. 1

Campbell, W.G. 1
Casey, T. 2
Caskey, W. 1
Cassidy, T. 1
Clarke, C.J. 13

Clements, D.	2	McAdams, W.J.	7	Taggart, G.P.	7
Cochrane, T.	1	**McAuley, G.**	**2**	Tully, C.P.	3
Crossan, E.	1	McCann, G.S.	4		
Crossan, J.A.	10	McCartney, G.	1	Walker, J.	1
Cush, W.W.	5	McClelland, J.	1	Walsh, D.J.	5
		McCrory, S.	1	Welsh, E.	1
Davis S.	2	McCurdy, C.	1	Whiteside, N.	9
D'Arcy, S.D.	1	McDonald, A.	3	Whitley, Jeff	2
Doherty, I.	1	McGarry, J.K.	1	Williams, M.S.	1
Doherty, P.D.	2	McGrath, R.C.	4	Wilson, D.J.	1
Dougan, A.D.	8	McIlroy, J.	10	Wilson, K.J.	6
Dowie, I.	12	McIlroy, S.B.	5	Wilson, S.J.	7
		McLaughlin, J.C.	6		
Elder, A.R.	1	McMahon, G.J.	2	**REPUBLIC OF**	
Elliott, S.	4	McMordie, A.S.	3	**IRELAND**	
Evans, C.	**1**	McMorran, E.J.	4	Aldridge, J.	19
Evans, J.G.	1	McParland, P.J.	10	Ambrose, P.	1
		Moreland, V.	1	Anderson, J.	1
Feeney, W.	1	Morgan, S.	3	**Andrews, K.**	**2**
Feeney, W.J.	5	Morrow, S.J.	1		
Ferguson, W.	1	Mulryne, P.P.	3	Barrett, G.	2
Ferris, R.O.	1	Murdoch, C.J.	1	Brady, L.	9
Finney, T.	2			Breen, G.	7
		Neill, W.J.T.	2	Byrne, J.	4
Gibson, W.	1	Nelson, S.	1		
Gillespie, K.R.	2	Nicholl, C.J.	3	Cantwell, J.	14
Gray, P.	6	Nicholl, J.M.	1	Carey, J.	3
Griffin, D.J.	1	Nicholson, J.J.	6	Carroll, T.	1
				Cascarino, A.	19
Hamilton, B.	4	O'Boyle, G.	1	Coad, P.	3
Hamilton, W.	5	O'Kane, W.J.	1	Connolly, D.J.	9
Harkin, J.T.	2	O'Neill, J.	2	Conroy, T.	2
Harvey, M.	3	O'Neill, M.A.	4	Conway, J.	3
Healy, D.J.	35	O'Neill, M.H.	8	**Cox, S.R.**	**2**
Hill, C.F.	1	Own goals	9	Coyne, T.	6
Humphries, W.	1			Cummins, G.	5
Hughes, M.E.	5	Patterson, D.J.	1	Curtis, D.	8
Hunter, A.	1	**Patterson, R.**	**1**		
Hunter, B.V.	1	Peacock, R.	2	Daly, G.	13
		Penney, S.	2	Dempsey, J.	1
Irvine, W.J.	8			Dennehy, M.	2
		Quinn, J.M.	12	Doherty, G.M.T.	4
Johnston, W.C.	1	Quinn, S.J.	4	**Doyle, K.E.**	**9**
Jones, J.	1			**Duff, D.A.**	**8**
Jones, S.	1	Rowland, K.	1	Duffy, B.	1
				Dunne, R.P.	7
Lafferty, K.	**8**	Simpson, W.J.	5		
Lennon, N.F.	2	Smyth, S.	5	Eglinton, T.	2
Lockhart, N.	3	Spence, D.W.	3	Elliott, S.W.	1
Lomas, S.M.	3	Sproule, I.	1		
		Stewart, I.	2	Fagan, F.	5
Magilton, J.	5			Fallon, S.	2

BLUE SQUARE PREMIER 2010–2011

(P) *Promoted into division at end of 2009–10 season.*
(R) *Relegated into division at end of 2009–10 season.*

			Total					Home					Away					
	P	W	D	L	F	A	W	D	L	F	A	W	D	L	F	A	GD	Pts
1 Crawley T	46	31	12	3	93	30	18	3	2	57	19	13	9	1	36	11	63	105
2 AFC Wimbledon¶	46	27	9	10	83	47	17	3	3	46	15	10	6	7	37	32	36	90
3 Luton T	46	23	15	8	85	37	14	7	2	57	17	9	8	6	28	20	48	84
4 Wrexham	46	22	15	9	66	49	13	7	3	36	24	9	8	6	30	25	17	81
5 Fleetwood T (P)	46	22	12	12	68	42	12	8	3	35	19	10	4	9	33	23	26	78
6 Kidderminster H	46	20	17	9	74	60	13	6	4	40	27	7	11	5	34	33	14	72
7 Darlington (R)	46	18	17	11	61	42	13	6	4	37	14	5	11	7	24	28	19	71
8 York C	46	19	14	13	55	50	14	6	3	31	13	5	8	10	24	37	5	71
9 Newport Co (P)	46	18	15	13	78	60	11	7	5	44	29	7	8	8	34	31	18	69
10 Bath C (P)	46	16	15	15	64	68	10	10	3	38	27	6	5	12	26	41	–4	63
11 Grimsby T (R)	46	15	17	14	72	62	7	12	4	37	28	8	5	10	35	34	10	62
12 Rushden & D*	46	16	14	16	65	62	10	6	7	37	27	6	8	9	28	35	3	62
13 Mansfield T	46	17	10	19	73	75	9	6	8	40	37	8	4	11	33	38	–2	61
14 Kettering T	46	15	13	18	64	75	8	8	7	33	32	7	5	11	31	43	–11	58
15 Gateshead	46	14	15	17	65	68	8	9	6	28	28	6	6	11	37	40	–3	57
16 Hayes & Yeading U	46	15	6	25	57	81	10	2	11	34	38	5	4	14	23	43	–24	51
17 Cambridge U	46	11	17	18	53	61	7	7	9	32	28	4	10	9	21	33	–8	50
18 Barrow	46	12	14	20	52	67	9	6	8	31	22	3	8	12	21	45	–15	50
19 Tamworth	46	12	13	21	62	83	6	8	9	34	41	6	5	12	28	42	–21	49
20 Forest Green R	46	10	16	20	53	72	7	10	6	28	25	3	6	14	25	47	–19	46
21 Southport (P)†	46	11	13	22	56	77	9	6	8	39	33	2	7	14	17	44	–21	46
22 Altrincham	46	11	11	24	47	87	6	8	9	29	38	5	3	15	18	49	–40	44
23 Eastbourne B	46	10	9	27	62	104	6	5	12	36	46	4	4	15	26	58	–42	39
24 Histon	46	8	9	29	41	90	4	3	16	18	45	4	6	13	23	45	–49	28

*Kidderminster H deducted 5 points. Histon deducted 5 points. ¶AFC Wimbledon promoted via play-offs. *Rushden & D expelled from Blue Square Premier. †Southport reprieved from relegation. Altrincham and Histon relegated to Blue Square North, Eastbourne B relegated to Blue Square South.*

Leading Goalscorers 2010–2011

	Club	League	Play-Offs	FA Cup	Total
Matt Tubbs	(Crawley T)	37	0	3	40
Alan Connell	(Grimsby T)	25	0	1	26
Danny Kedwell	(AFC Wimbledon)	23	1	0	24
Magno Vieira	(Fleetwood T)	22	0	0	22
Jean-Paul Marna	(Kettering T)	19	0	0	19
Craig Reid	(Newport Co)	18	0	0	18
Kyle Perry	(Tamworth)	17	0	1	18
Chris McPhee	(Kidderminster H)	17	0	0	17
Jon Shaw	(Gateshead)	17	0	0	17
Matthew Barnes-Homer	(Luton T)	16	0	2	18

BLUE SQUARE PREMIER RESULTS 2010–2011

	York C	Wrexham	Tamworth	Southport	Rushden & D	Newport Co	Mansfield T	Luton T	Kidderminster H	Kettering T	Histon	Hayes & Yeading U	Grimsby T	Gateshead	Forest Green R	Fleetwood T	Eastbourne B	Darlington	Crawley T	Cambridge U	Bath C	Barrow	Altrincham	AFC Wimbledon
AFC Wimbledon	1-0	0-1	3-0	5-0	2-2	2-2	2-1	0-0	1-2	3-2	2-0	3-1	2-1	1-0	1-1	1-0	3-0	0-2	2-1	3-0	4-0	2-0	4-1	—
Altrincham	0-0	0-0	2-0	1-1	2-2	1-3	0-4	0-1	1-2	3-2	0-3	4-2	2-2	1-1	2-1	1-0	3-4	2-2	0-1	2-2	0-3	2-0	—	1-0
Barrow	0-0	0-0	0-2	1-1	2-1	2-2	2-0	0-1	2-0	5-0	1-1	2-0	0-2	1-3	3-0	0-2	4-0	1-1	1-2	1-2	0-1	—	1-0	2-0
Bath C	2-2	0-2	2-0	1-2	2-1	2-1	0-0	0-0	1-2	1-1	0-0	3-1	2-1	1-0	2-4	1-1	0-3	2-2	0-2	4-0	—	1-2	1-2	2-2
Cambridge U	2-1	1-3	2-1	0-0	4-0	0-1	0-0	0-0	2-0	3-0	5-0	1-0	1-1	5-0	1-1	0-1	2-0	0-1	2-2	—	1-2	3-1	4-0	1-2
Crawley T	1-1	3-2	3-3	1-0	2-0	2-3	0-0	1-1	2-0	1-1	3-1	5-2	0-1	2-0	1-0	0-1	3-1	1-0	—	3-0	2-1	3-2	7-0	3-1
Darlington	2-1	1-1	3-1	1-0	0-2	4-0	1-3	2-2	2-0	1-3	1-1	5-0	2-3	0-3	3-0	4-0	6-1	—	1-2	1-0	3-1	3-1	3-1	0-0
Eastbourne B	2-1	4-3	1-0	4-1	1-1	0-2	3-0	2-4	3-0	4-1	2-2	1-1	3-0	0-0	0-0	0-6	—	1-1	1-2	0-2	2-1	0-2	5-0	2-3
Fleetwood T	2-1	1-0	1-4	2-0	2-2	0-0	2-1	0-3	1-2	0-2	1-1	1-0	3-3	0-0	2-0	—	0-1	1-0	0-3	2-2	0-0	1-0	3-1	1-1
Forest Green R	2-1	3-0	2-1	0-0	3-3	1-1	1-1	1-1	2-2	2-1	0-1	1-0	0-0	1-1	—	1-0	3-4	2-2	0-0	1-1	2-1	2-3	1-0	0-0
Gateshead	0-3	0-1	4-0	1-1	0-2	1-7	7-2	1-0	3-3	0-0	0-0	1-2	1-0	—	1-1	0-2	3-0	0-1	0-0	2-3	1-2	3-0	3-0	0-2
Grimsby T	0-0	0-1	3-1	1-0	1-0	2-0	4-0	2-0	0-4	2-1	2-1	1-2	—	2-2	3-4	1-2	0-0	3-2	0-3	1-0	2-2	1-1	1-1	2-1
Hayes & Yeading U	1-2	0-3	1-2	3-1	3-0	0-0	2-3	0-4	1-1	3-2	1-2	—	0-3	3-1	0-3	1-0	2-2	0-0	2-0	2-0	1-0	1-0	0-1	0-0
Histon	1-2	1-1	2-1	3-4	2-1	2-0	0-2	4-0	1-1	0-3	—	0-1	1-6	1-4	1-0	2-1	2-1	0-0	0-0	0-2	2-0	2-0	3-0	0-4
Kettering T	0-0	1-1	1-2	6-0	1-3	2-3	1-3	1-3	0-1	—	4-3	2-1	1-2	2-1	6-1	2-1	3-0	2-1	0-0	2-2	2-1	3-1	3-3	1-2
Kidderminster H	5-0	0-0	0-1	2-0	3-0	1-1	0-2	3-3	—	4-1	2-2	3-1	3-2	2-2	3-1	6-1	4-0	1-1	1-4	0-0	1-0	2-1	2-1	3-3
Luton T	5-0	1-0	1-1	2-2	1-0	0-3	1-0	—	1-1	2-2	5-1	1-0	0-2	3-2	2-2	1-3	3-3	2-1	0-1	2-0	3-1	0-0	2-1	2-0
Mansfield T	4-0	1-1	2-1	0-1	1-1	2-3	—	0-0	3-0	1-1	1-0	3-2	2-1	0-2	4-0	2-5	1-3	1-1	0-4	1-0	1-1	1-1	0-1	3-0
Newport Co	0-4	2-2	2-1	2-1	1-3	—	1-2	1-1	2-1	1-2	3-1	2-1	4-1	5-1	2-1	1-3	1-3	0-4	1-1	1-1	5-1	5-0	2-1	2-5
Rushden & D	4-0	0-1	1-2	2-0	—	1-1	1-1	2-1	2-2	1-2	0-1	4-1	2-0	1-1	2-1	2-2	4-2	1-1	0-3	1-1	2-3	2-4	1-2	3-3
Southport	1-3	0-1	2-1	—	2-2	3-2	2-1	2-1	2-2	3-1	4-0	0-0	2-1	2-7	3-1	4-0	2-1	0-3	0-0	3-1	1-1	2-2	1-0	1-0
Tamworth	1-1	4-2	—	0-1	1-0	1-0	1-1	3-1	2-2	2-0	1-0	2-3	2-0	2-1	2-1	2-1	2-1	0-0	0-0	2-0	1-1	1-1	1-1	0-1
Wrexham	1-1	—	4-2	2-1	1-1	2-1	2-1	1-0	1-2	2-0	2-1	0-2	3-1	0-3	2-1	1-1	2-0	1-1	0-0	1-0	2-0	2-1	2-5	1-2
York C	—	1-1	1-2	1-0	2-1	1-0	2-1	1-0	2-2	0-1	1-0	2-0	2-0	0-3	2-1	1-0	2-1	0-0	1-1	0-0	1-1	0-0	1-2	4-1

BLUE SQUARE PREMIER PLAY-OFFS 2010–2011

SEMI-FINALS FIRST LEG

Wrexham	(0) 0	Luton T	(3) 3
Fleetwood T	(0) 0	AFC Wimbledon	(1) 2

SEMI-FINALS SECOND LEG

Luton T	(1) 2	Wrexham	(1) 1
AFC Wimbledon	(3) 6	Fleetwood T	(0) 1

FINAL (at Eastlands)
Saturday, 21 May 2011

AFC Wimbledon (0) 0

Luton T (0) 0   18,195

AFC Wimbledon: Brown; Hatton, Gwillim (Yakubu), Gregory (Minshull), Stuart, Johnson, Yussuff, Wellard (Mulley), Kedwell, Mohamed, Moore L.
Luton T: Tyler; Gleeson, Asafu-Adjaye, Keane, Kroca, Pilkington G, Lawless, Howells, Walker J, Gnakpa (Newton), Willmott (Barnes-Homer).
aet; AFC Wimbledon won 4-3 on penalties.

ATTENDANCES BY CLUB 2010–2011

	Aggregate 2010–2011	Average 2010–2011	Highest Attendance 2010–2011
Luton Town	143,562	6,242	7,283 v AFC Wimbledon
AFC Wimbledon	77,979	3,390	4,287 v Luton Town
Grimsby Town	70,672	3,073	5,037 v York City
Wrexham	70,398	3,061	4,630 v Crawley Town
Crawley Town	58,297	2,535	4,054 v AFC Wimbledon
Cambridge United	57,822	2,514	3,225 v Histon
York City	57,166	2,485	3,176 v Darlington
Mansfield Town	48,825	2,123	3,266 v Wrexham
Newport County	48,078	2,090	3,462 v AFC Wimbledon
Darlington	43,384	1,886	2,966 v York City
Fleetwood Town	40,295	1,752	2,831 v Luton Town
Kidderminster Harriers	37,504	1,631	3,028 v Wrexham
Kettering Town	31,535	1,371	2,906 v Luton Town
Rushden & Diamonds	28,856	1,255	2,459 v Luton Town
Barrow	27,925	1,214	1,718 v Darlington
Southport	26,541	1,154	1,866 v Darlington
Eastbourne Borough	25,406	1,105	2,518 v Luton Town
Tamworth	25,077	1,090	1,717 v Forest Green Rovers
Bath City	24,606	1,070	2,301 v Luton Town
Altrincham	23,919	1,040	1,982 v Wrexham
Forest Green Rovers	21,845	950	1,824 v AFC Wimbledon
Gateshead	17,318	753	1,231 v York City
Histon	14,176	616	1,903 v Cambridge United
Hayes & Yeading United	8,877	386	801 v Luton Town

APPEARANCES AND GOALSCORERS 2010–2011

AFC WIMBLEDON

League Appearances: Blackman, 12(1); Broughton, 3(5); Brown, 45; Bush, 12(1); Franks, 15(9); Gregory, 41(1); Gwillim, 20; Harris, 15(1); Hatton, 40; Hudson, 11(3); Jackson, 23(14); Johnson, 21(2); Jolley, 22(10); Jones, 1(2); Kedwell, 43(2); Kiernan, 1(1); Main, 7(9); Minshull, 9(10); Mohamed, 6(1); Moore, S. 27(1); Moore, L. 19(14); Mulley, 19(3); Nwokeji, 6(12); Stuart, 18(3); Turner, 1; Wellard, 22(3); Yakubu, 26(1); Yussuff, 21(17).

Goals – League (83): Kedwell 23 (5 pens), Jolley 12, Moore L 7 (1 pen), Yussuff 6, Hatton 5 (1 pen), Moore S 5, Mulley 5, Johnson 4, Broughton 2, Franks 2, Jackson 2, Minshull 2, Wellard 2, Yakubu 2, Hudson 1, Mohamed 1, Nwokeji 1, Stuart 1.

FA Cup (4): Moore S 2, Harris 1, Nwokeji 1.

ALTRINCHAM

League Appearances: Bateson, 6(3); Baynes, 20(6); Beesley, 8(10); Brown, 24(9); Clee, 33(5); Coates, 9; Coburn, 25; Connors, 11; Crowell, 7(2); Danylyk, 15(13); Denham, 11(5); Densmore, 32; Dootson, 12; Foster, (1); Hewson, 10(8); Holmes, 2(3); Holsgrove, 4(9); Johnson, 7(6); Jones, 1; Joseph, 38(1); Lawton, 37(2); McCarthy, 5(3); McCready, (2); Milne, 9; Piergianni, 21; Reeves, 33(10); Smith, 32; Somner, 9; Twiss, 16(16); Wedgbury, 6; Welch, 8(3); Williams, 44(1); Young, 11.

Goals – League (47): Reeves 15 (3 pens), Clee 4, Johnson 4, Joseph 4, Twiss 4, Denham 3, Densmore 3 (2 pens), Baynes 2, Beesley 2, Hewson 1, Lawton 1, Milne 1, Wedgbury 1, Williams 1, Young 1.

FA Cup (0).

BARROW

League Appearances: Almond, 17(3); Baker, 12(2); Blundell, 7(2); Bolland, 40; Boyd, 11(2); Chadwick, 10(5); Clay, 1; Cook, 7(26); Curtis, 15; Darwikwa, 1; Donnelly, 6(10); Edwards, 43; Ferrell, 8; Forrest, 10(4); Goodfellow, 9(10); Grant, 3(2); Halstead, 1; Hulbert, 17(3); Jones, 14(2); Martin, 14; Masters, 25; Milne, 2; Nicholas, 3(7); Owen, 30(2); Pearson, M. 40(4); Pearson, S. 6(1); Rutherford, 41(1); Sheridan, 23(1); Smith, 13; Spender, 45(1); Wainwright, 6; Walker, 18; Wiles, 8(2).

Goals – League (52): Walker 11 (5 pens), Rutherford 7, Almond 6 (1 pen), Baker 5, Chadwick 3, Ferrell 2, Forrest 2, Owen 2, Pearson M 2, Smith 2, Wiles 2, Boyd 1, Cook 1, Curtis 1, Goodfellow 1, Spender 1 (1 pen), own goals 3.

FA Cup (0).

BATH C

League Appearances: Badman, (1); Borhy, 2; Brown, (2); Burnell, 21(4); Canham, 44(1); Clough, 9(2); Connolly, 43(2); Coupe, 1; Edwards, D. 5(8); Edwards, J. 8(2); Egan, (1); Harris, 17(8); Hart, 1(2); Henry, 3(1); Hogg, 10(10); Jeanne, (3); Jombati, 43; Jones, 36(3); Lennox, (3); Mackie, 3(16); Mohamed, 28(6); Murray, 13(20); Pentney, 13; Phillips, 41(2); Reid, (4); Robinson, 31; Rollo, 26(12); Ruddick, 9; Russell, 12; Simpson, 35(1); Watkins, 20(2); Watson, 5(2); Webb, 27(2).

Goals – League (64): Phillips 15, Mohamed 13 (5 pens), Murray 7 (1 pen), Canham 4, Jones 3, Watkins 3, Clough 2, Connolly 2, Edwards D 2, Hogg 2, Jombati 2, Mackie 2, Russell 2, Webb 2, Harris 1, Watson 1, own goal 1.

FA Cup (3): Connolly 1, Jombati 1, Mackie 1.

CAMBRIDGE U

League Appearances: Bentley, 6; Berry, 12(2); Brighton, (1); Brown, 32; Carden, 24; Clare, 10(10); Coakley, 3(2); Coulson, 35(3); Eades, (1); Gray, 14(9); Herbert, (1); Hudson, (2); Hughes, 10(8); Ives, 4(11); Jeffers, (2); Jennings, 38; Marriott, 9(24); McAuley, 28(7); Miller, 5; Naisbitt, 14; Partridge, 27(2); Patrick, 14(12); Platt, 19(9); Roberts, 37(1); Russell, 31; Saah, 36(2); Sinclair, 5(1); Stavrinou, 7; Thorpe, 2(3); Walker, 4(2); Wellard, 9; Willmott, 26(1); Wright, 45.

Goals – League (53): Willmott 10 (2 pens), Wright 10, Gray 7, Russell 6, Coulson 4, Marriott 3, Saah 3, Hughes 2, Patrick 2, Bentley 1, Berry 1, Clare 1, Jennings 1, Sinclair 1, own goal 1.

FA Cup (4): Gray 1, McAuley 1, Russell 1, Wright 1.

CRAWLEY T

League Appearances: Brodie, 25(13); Bulman, 31; Cogan, 2(1); Cook, 6(15); Dance, 2(5); Dempster, 8(2); Enver-Marum, 1(2); Flood, (3); Gibson, 11(3); Hall, 9(5); Howell, 35; Hunt, 22(3); Hutchinson, (1); Jordan, 5(2); Kuipers, 26; Malcolm, (3); Masterton, 12(1); McAllister, 27(14); McFadzean, 34(3); Mills, 32; Neilson, 23(4); Quinn, 11; Reason, (4); Rents, 4(1); Rusk, 9(7); Shearer, 15(1); Simpson, 20(6); Smith, 22(7); Torres, 34(5); Tubbs, 38(3); Wassmer, 10(2); Wilson, 32(7); Wright, (9).

Goals – League (93): Tubbs 37 (11 pens), McAllister 12 (1 pen), Brodie 11 (1 pen), Neilson 5, Smith 4, Torres 4, McFadzean 3, Mills 3, Simpson 3, Cook 2, Wassmer 2, Bulman 1, Dance 1, Dempster 1, Gibson 1, Howell 1, Hunt 1, Masterton 1.

FA Cup (13): Tubbs 3, McAllister 2, Smith 2, Torres 2, Brodie 1, Hall 1, Neilson 1, own goal 1.

DARLINGTON

League Appearances: Arnison, 34(3); Austin, 13; Bridge-Wilkinson, 27; Brough, 5; Brown, 40; Burn, 9(1); Campbell, 7(5); Chandler, 23(5); Clarke, 7(3); Gillespie, 1; Gray, P. 2(3); Gray, J. 3(10); Hatch, 37; Hone, 21; Louis, 4(2); Main, 5(11); McReady, 8(7); Miller, 37; Modest, 6(7); Moore, 9(5); Offiong, 3(3); Powell, 3(2); Quinn, 14; Russell, 43; Senior, 16(13); Smith, G. 37; Smith, M. 20(9); St Louis-Hamilton, 3; Taylor, 14(2); Terry, 20(4); Verma, 25(1); Waite, 1(4); Wright, 9(13).

Goals – League (61): Hatch 11, Bridge-Wilkinson 9 (3 pens), Smith M 5, Campbell 4, Miller 4, Senior 4, Verma 4, Wright 4, Brown 2, Chandler 2, Terry 2, Arnison 1, Clarke 1, Hone 1, McReady 1, Moore 1, Powell 1, Smith G 1, own goals 3.

FA Cup (8): Smith G 2, Senior 2, Austin 1, Bridge-Wilkinson 1, Brough 1, Wright 1 (pen).

EASTBOURNE BOR

League Appearances: Atkin, 5(6); Austin, 40(1); Baker, 27(6); Banks, 41; Brinkhurst, 19(18); Brown, 7(4); Cook, 7; Crabb, M. 37(3); Crabb, N. 2(16); Demetriou, 5(5); Elphick, 21(2); Forecast, 5; Hutchinson, 17(1); Jenkins, 35(2); Jenkinson, 3(1); Johnson, 26(9); Kelly, 12; Langston, 18; Mambo, 3(2); Masterton, 4(1); Nelson, 8; Norwood, 3(1); Pacquette, 29(4); Partington, 4; Purcell, 10(7); Rooney, 4; Smart, 22(11); Spencer, 1; Strevett, 8(12); Taylor, 42(3); Treleavan, 9; Walker, 6(1); Weatherstone, 25(8); Wills, 1.

Goals – League (62): Taylor 15, Pacquette 10, Elphick 5, Weatherstone 5 (4 pens), Crabb M 4, Purcell 3, Smart 3, Treleavan 3, Johnson 2, Langston 2, Walker 2, Atkin 1, Austin 1, Baker 1, Brinkhurst 1, Cook 1, Crabb N 1, Rooney 1, own goal 1.

FA Cup (2): Taylor 2.

FLEETWOOD T

League Appearances: Barry, 44; Beeley, 38; Beesley, 1(4); Brown, 20(1); Camozzi, 1; Cavanagh, 15(1); Clancy, 20(11); Connors, 2(6); Craney, 19; Curtis, 18(2); Davies, 30(1);

Donnelly, 13(7); Grand, 4; Gregan, 26; Haining, 7; Harvey, 1(3); Horne, 1; Hurst, 16; Linwood, 18; McGuire, 30(7); McNulty, 38; Miles, 6(2); Milligan, 8(4); Mullan, 14(14); Parker, 7(6); Pond, 16(7); Rogan, 1(2); Rowe, 2(3); Seddon, 29(5); Thorpe, 4(14); Vieira, 38(2); Warlow, 1(2); Worthington, 3; Wright, 15(3).

Goals – League (68): Vieira 22 (2 pens), Seddon 10 (1 pen), McGuire 6, Donnelly 4, Clancy 3, Craney 3, Curtis 3, Barry 2, Beeley 2, Brown 2, Parker 2, Pond 2, Harvey 1, McNulty 1, Mullan 1, Rogan 1, Wright 1, own goals 2.

FA Cup (3): Mullan 1, Seddon 1, Warlow 1.

FOREST GREEN R

League Appearances: Allen, 3(2); Armstrong, 24; Baldwin, 1(3); Bartlett, 6(4); Bittner, 46; Caines, 36(7); Cleaver, (1); Davies, 1(9); Dyer, 26(5); Else, 5(12); Enver-Marum, 7(11); Flood, 5; Forbes, 23(2); Fowler, L. 11; Fowler, M. 18(2); Gill, 2(1); Gray, 4(9); Grimes, 4(1); Guinan, 10(8); Hall, 16(1); Head, (4); Henry, (1); Herring, 10(3); Hodgkiss, 21(2); Imudia, 2(1); Jones, L. 45; Kamara, 1(1); Klukowski, 30(7); Matthews, 4(3); McDonald, 22(1); Mills, 1(1); Norwood, 11; Quinn, 6; Smith, 6(4); Somner, 14(2); Stokes, 14; Styche, 41(2); Turk, 23(2); Watson, 6(1); Young, 1.

Goals – League (53): Styche 15 (1 pen), Klukowski 7 (2 pens), Dyer 5, Guinan 5, McDonald 4, Caines 3, Forbes 2, Jones 2, Norwood 2, Davies 1, Else 1, Herring 1 (1 pen), Matthews 1, Quinn 1, Somner 1, Watson 1, own goal 1.

FA Cup (1): Styche 1.

GATESHEAD

League Appearances: Allan, (3); Baptist, (2); Baxter, 24(4); Brittain, 39(2); Clark, 43; Clarke, 1(1); Curtis, 35; Deasy, 41; Edmundsson, 5; Farman, 5(1); Ferrell, 13(7); Fisher, 19(21); Francis, 1; Gate, 34; Gillies, 4(14); Heckingbottom, 21; Jones, 14(5); Kay, 8; Liddle, 23; Marwood, 10(11); Mulligan, 24(7); Nelthorpe, 24(10); Offiong, 5(6); Rundle, 7; Shaw, 36(1); Tavernier, 13; Turnbull, 46; Wake, (12); White, 3; Winn, 8(5).

Goals – League (65): Shaw 17, Brittain 9 (5 pens), Fisher 9, Mulligan 7, Nelthorpe 4, Ferrell 3, Gate 3, Clark 2, Turnbull 2, Winn 2, Curtis 1, Gillies 1, Kay 1, Liddle 1, Offiong 1, own goals 2.

FA Cup (2): Fisher 1, Turnbull 1.

GRIMSBY T

League Appearances: Ademeno, 6(6); Arthur, 28; Atkinson, 24(1); Bore, 34(3); Carlton, 6; Connell, 46; Corner, 2(9); Coulson, 29; Croudson, 8; Cummins, 32(4); Dixon, (2); Duffy, 14(3); Eagle, 29(10); Garner, 13(4); Gobern, 7(2); Hudson, 24(16); Hughes, 9; Kempson, 34; L'Anson, 4; Leary, 13(7); Makofo, 4(6); Mulreade, 1(1); O'Donnell, 10; Peacock, 15(21); Ridley, 30; Samuels, 9(2); Sinclair, 10(2); Southwell, (3); Stockdale, 1; Thanoj, 4(3); Watt, 21(4); Wood, 36(7); Wright, 9.

Goals – League (72): Connell 25 (4 pens), Eagle 9, Coulson 8, Hudson 5, Atkinson 4, Bore 4, Peacock 3, Sinclair 3, Ademeno 2, Duffy 2, Watt 2, Cummins 1, Kempson 1, L'Anson 1, Leary 1, Wright 1.

FA Cup (1): Connell 1.

HAYES & YEADING U

League Appearances: Appiah, 3(17); Brown, 28; Buchanan, 21(14); Bulmer, 5; Bygrave, 44; Cadmore, 40; Deen, 8(6); Enver-Marum, 3(5); Ferrell, 32(2); Green, 23(1); Hand, 40; Harrison, 25(1); Holmes, 44; Hyde, 7(2); Joseph-Dubois, (4); Lennie, 7(2); Louis, 10; Malcolm, 15(1); Masterton, 8; McLean, (5); McWeeney, 1; Montgomery, 3; Mulley, 10(3); Patulea, 8(1); Preddie, 8; Pritchard, 46; Rents, 8; Wassmer, 17(2); Webb, 11(5); Wishart, (13); Wright, 15(7); Yiadom, 16(20).

Goals – League (57): Pritchard 14, Buchanan 12, Wright 6 (1 pen), Brown 3 (3 pens), Holmes 3, Patulea 3 (1 pen), Cadmore 2, Hand 2, Hyde 2, Malcolm 2, Deen 1, Enver-Marum 1, Ferrell 1, Louis 1, Masterton 1, Rents 1, Yiadom 1, own goal 1.
FA Cup (4): Brown 3 (1 pen), Holmes 1.

HISTON
League Appearances: Adjei, 2(8); Ainsley, 2; Asafu-Adjaye, 5; Asensi, (1); Attwood, 16(10); Clarke, 2(2); Clerima, 43; Cox, 2(3); Day, 1(2); Diarra, 1(1); Dowie, 3(3); Fitzsimons, 6; Foderingham, 9; Hawkins, 2(2); Ilesanmi, 15(1); Lawton, 1(2); Livermore, 11(3); McCrae, 17(1); Mills, D. 13(5); Mills, Z. 38(1); Murray, 35(1); Okay, 37(2); Okojie, 5(6); Oyebanjo, 38; Pavett, 3(1); Riza, 34(1); Sagna, (1); Sessions, (1); Smith, 32(6); Sparkes, 27(6); Stevenson, 21(8); Stewart, 8(2); Taaffe, 10(15); Welch, 36; Wootton, 31(1); York, (2).
Goals – League (41): Riza 12 (5 pens), Murray 9, Clerima 5, Attwood 3, Sparkes 3, McCrae 2, Oyebanjo 2 (1 pen), Stevenson 2, Mills D 1, Okay 1, Wootton 1.
FA Cup (0).

KETTERING T
League Appearances: Abbey, 11; Ashikodi, 2(4); Boucaud, 19(1); Bussey, 7; Challinor, 4(9); Christie, 12(7); Collins, 3(2); Cunnington, 11(3); Dance, 21(1); Davis, 16(6); Dempster, 17(1); Flanagan, 22; Furlong, 10(17); Graham, 22(3); Green, 5; Gueret, 14; Halstead, 3; Harding, (1); Harper, 1; Jack, 9; Jaszczun, 1; John, 3; Kelly, 28(12); Makofo, 17(6); Marna, 43(3); McCrae, 3(5); McDonald, 14(5); McKoy, 25(5); Mills, 11(6); Noubissie, 30(3); O'Leary, 1; O'Neill, 18(1); Raynor, 1(1); Roper, 24(7); Smith, (1); Solkhon, 34(9); St Aimie, 3(3); Taylor, 13; Towers, (1); Westwood, 12; Wilson, 16(1).
Goals – League (64): Marna 19 (6 pens), Solkhon 7, Christie 6, Mills 6, Dance 4, Furlong 4, McKoy 3, Kelly 2, Makofo 2, O'Neill 2, Ashikodi 1, Challinor 1, Cunnington 1, Dempster 1, Flanagan 1, Green 1, St Aimie 1, Wilson 1, own goal 1.
FA Cup (1): Furlong 1.

KIDDERMINSTER H
League Appearances: Albrighton, 28(2); Blair, 30(12); Briggs, 43; Briscoe, 43(2); Byrne, 32(5); Canham, 10(2); Gittings, 25(19); Griffiths, 2(3); Hadley, (1); Hankin, 17(10); Lewis, 46; Lindfield, (1); Lowe, 1; Matt, 8(14); McPhee, 43(2); McPike, (2); Morris, 23(5); Sharpe, 14; Shaw, 26(16); Thompson-Brown, (1); Thorne, 9; Vaughan, 33(1); Verma, 1; Williams, Mike 41(1); Williams, Marc 7(10); Wright, 24(15).
Goals – League (74): McPhee 17 (7 pens), Blair 11, Wright 8, Byrne 7, Briggs 6, Shaw 6 (2 pens), Morris 5, Gittings 4, Matt 3, Williams, Marc 3; Canham 2, Briscoe 1, Williams, Mike 1.
FA Cup (0).

LUTON T
League Appearances: Asafu-Adjaye, 3(2); Atieno, 6(7); Barnes-Homer, 39(5); Besta, 3(3); Blackett, 7(1); Carden, 8(2); Craddock, 1(3); Crow, 17(11); Drury, A. 23; Gallen, 4(2); Gleeson, 33(1); Gnakpa, 33(9); Graham, 6(4); Howells, 34(8); Keane, 39; Kroca, 45; Lacey, (1); Lawless, 15(5); Morgan-Smith, 15(5); Murray, F. 28; Murray, A. 6(1); Newton, 14(5); Owusu, 13; Pilkington, G. 45; Pilkington, K. 3; Poku, 2(7); Tyler, 43; Walker, J. 8(12); Walker, D. 1(11); Watkins, (3); Willmott, 12(3).
Goals – League (85): Barnes-Homer 16 (2 pens), Gnakpa 13, Crow 7 (1 pen), Drury 6 (2 pens), Owusu 6, Willmott 6, Kroca 5, Morgan-Smith 5, Pilkington G 4, Walker J 4 (1 pen), Atieno 3, Howells 3, Lawless 3, Craddock 2, Murray F 1, Walker D 1.
FA Cup (12): Morgan-Smith 3, Atieno 2, Barnes-Homer 2, Drury 2, Crow 1, Gnakpa 1, Kroca 1.
Play-Offs (5): Asafu-Adjaye 1, Gnakpa 1, Kroca 1, Lawless 1, Walker J 1.

MANSFIELD T

League Appearances: Aksalu, 2; Briscoe, 36(6); Cain, 17(3); Collett, 5; Connor, 34(6); Cook, 8; Day, 8; Duffy, 8(11); Foster, 33; Grand, 6; Gregory, 2; Grof, 12(1); Hall, (3); Higginson, 5(3); Istead, 18(11); Marriott, 17; Medley, 11(20); Mills, 15(3); Mitchley, 8(9); Moult, 3; Murray, 32; Naylor, 16(1); Nix, 15(10); O'Rafferty, 4(3); Parker, 13(7); Pilkington, 10; Preece, 4(1); Sandwith, 32(1); Silk, 33(1); Smith, C. 15; Smith, A. 27(4); Spence, 6; Stonehouse, 20(3); Thompson, 26(1); Vincenti, 3; Williams, 2.

Goals – League (73): Briscoe 13 (1 pen), Connor 11, Medley 6, Murray 6, Smith A 6, Duffy 5 (1 pen), Parker 5 (3 pens), Nix 3, Higginson 2, Mitchley 2, Moult 2, Thompson 2, Cain 1, Foster 1, Gregory 1, Istead 1, Mills 1, Naylor 1, Sandwith 1, Smith C 1, own goals 2.

FA Cup (1): Briscoe 1.

NEWPORT CO

League Appearances: Baker, (1); Bignot, 41; Burns, 1; Challinor, (3); Clough, (2); Collins, 44(1); Deering, 3; Foley, 22(18); Fowler, 1(2); Garner, 7(1); Goodall, 8; Griffin, 13(2); Hatswell, 11; Henry, 16(3); Hughes, 10; John, 9; Knights, 27(14); Lennon, 6(3); Matthews, 19(16); McDonald, 2(2); Miller, 9(4); Montgomery, 5(3); Morgan, 15(18); Odhiambo, 26(8); Odubade, 4(7); Reid, 29; Rogers, 10(10); Rose, 46; Smith, (1); Sole, 1(1); Taggart, (3); Thompson, 39; Todd, 40(1); Warren, 39(2); Wright, 3(2).

Goals – League (78): Reid 18 (5 pens), Collins 10 (3 pens), Knights 7, Rose 6, Warren 6, Foley 5, Matthews 5, Todd 5, Griffin 3, Henry 2, Baker 1, Bignot 1, Hatswell 1, Hughes 1, Miller 1, Morgan 1, Odubade 1, Rogers 1, Wright 1, own goals 2.

FA Cup (0).

RUSHDEN & D

League Appearances: Charles, 22(17); Corcoran, 22(5); Cousins, (6); Cowan-Hall, 2(1); Day, Jamie 34(4); Day, Joe 32; Evans, 6; Farrell, 11(16); Gash, 18; Green, 7(2); Howe, 18(1); Huke, 29(2); Johnson, 22(22); Keehan, 3(3); King, (1); Koranteng, (4); Miller, 27(5); Mills, 19(1); O'Connor, 35(1); Osano, 39(1); Oshodi, 11(1); Porter, 43; Power, 40(1); Prosser, 6; Roberts, 8; Robinson, 6(6); Shariff, 5(6); Sills, 9(2); Simmonds, 1(1); Smith, 3(4); Spence, 5(10); Stuart, 21; Thorne, 2; Woolley, (1).

Goals – League (65): O'Connor 14 (2 pens), Charles 7, Gash 6, Howe 6 (1 pen), Porter 4, Shariff 4, Johnson 3, Miller 3, Power 3 (1 pen), Smith 3, Corcoran 2, Huke 2, Cowan-Hall 1, Day, Jamie 1, Farrell 1, Oshodi 1, Prosser 1, Sills 1, Stuart 1, own goal 1.

FA Cup (2): Howe 1 (pen), Spence 1.

SOUTHPORT

League Appearances: Barratt, 17(21); Blakeman, 16(6); Collins, (6); Daly, 17(13); Davis, 39(3); Dickinson, 1(1); Flynn, 23(5); Gray, T. 20(18); Gray, S. 3; Kissock, 22(12); Ledsham, 21(3); Lee, 33(1); Lever, 27(3); Lloyd-McGoldrick, (4); Marsh-Evans, 26(2); McGinn, 28(5); McMillan, 45; McNeil, 31(4); Moogan, 40(1); Morley, (1); Powell, 14(13); Simm, 7(1); Turner, 19; Whalley, 15(2); Williams, 29(4); Winn, 13(1).

Goals – League (56): Whalley 8 (1 pen), Daly 6, Lee 5, McGinn 5 (4 pens), McNeil 5, Gray T 4 (1 pen), Ledsham 4, Barratt 3, Kissock 3, Marsh-Evans 3, Blakeman 2, Davis 2, Powell 2, Lever 1 (1 pen), Moogan 1, Simm 1, Turner 1.

FA Cup (4): Barratt 1, McGinn 1, own goals 2.

TAMWORTH

League Appearances: Atkins, 29; Barrow, 41(1); Belford, (1); Bojang, (2); Bradley, D. 37(6); Bradley, J. 9(9); Christie, (2); Connor, 2; Courtney, 17(1); Farrell, 4(7); Hendrie, 2(2); Kamara, (8); Lake-Gaskin, 13(12); Lyttle, 2(1); MacKenzie, 16(10); Marshall, 37(2); Mitchell, A. 11(6); Mitchell, L. 11; Oakes, 3(7); Perry, 35(5); Rodman, A. 25;

335

Severn, J. 3; Sheridan, 22(12); Smith, 35(1); Tait, 41; Thomas, 44(1); Ward, 1; Wilkinson, 22(6); Wylde, 38(2); Yussuf, 6(4).

Goals – League (62): Perry 17 (2 pens), Rodman 9 (2 pens), Thomas 7, Bradley D 4, Wylde 4, Barrow 3, Marshall 3, Smith 3, Bradley J 2, Wilkinson 2, Yussuf 2, Lake-Gaskin 1, MacKenzie 1, Sheridan 1, Tait 1, own goals 2.

FA Cup (6): Thomas 2, McKenzie 1, Marshall 1, Perry 1, Rodman 1.

WREXHAM

League Appearances: Andrews, 20(9); Ashton, 41; Blackburn, 43; Brown, 6(3); Cieslewicz, 3(17); Creighton, 27; Fowler, 7(5); Gall, 3(2); Harris, 38(2); Hunt, 2(1); Keates, 40; Knight-Percival, 11(21); Mangan, 40(2); Maxwell, 36; Mayebi, 1; McMillan, 4(1); Morrell, 40(1); Moss, 1; Obeng, 32(2); Pogba, 19(10); Salathiel, (1); Shearer, 9; Sinclair, 37(2); Smith, 5(1); Stevens, (1); Taylor, G. 20(13); Tolley, 15(9); Tomassen, (1); Walker, 5(1); Williams, M. 1(3).

Goals – League (66): Mangan 15 (1 pen), Morrell 10, Keates 6, Taylor 6 (1 pen), Harris 4, Knight-Percival 4, Pogba 4, Tolley 4, Smith 3, Andrews 2, Cieslewicz 2, Blackburn 1, Brown 1, Fowler 1, Moss 1, Obeng 1, own goal 1.

FA Cup (1): Tolley 1.

YORK C

League Appearances: Barrett, 19(3); Beesley, 2(1); Boucaud, 10(9); Brodie, 6; Carruthers, 14(12); Chambers, 22(4); Constantine, 13(13); Courtney, 4(3); Darville, 17; Dowson, (5); Fyfield, 9(2); Gash, 12(5); Hatfield, 1(3); Ingham, 45; Kerr, 16; Knight, 1; Lawless, 16; Mackin, 6(6); McDermott, 8(9); McGurk, 34; Meredith, 43(2); Parslow, 41(1); Purcell, (1); Racchi, 15(2); Rankine, 34(8); Reed, 12(11); Sangare, 9(1); Smith, J. 30(8); Smith, C. 24; Till, 29(12); Weir, 5; Young, 9(3).

Goals – League (55): Rankine 12 (5 pens), Reed 9, Constantine 8 (2 pens), Smith J 4, Till 4, Lawless 3, Barrett 2, Chambers 2, Brodie 1 (1 pen), Carruthers 1, Fyfield 1, Gash 1, Mackin 1, McDermott 1, Parslow 1, Racchi 1, Young 1, own goal 1.

FA Cup (7): Rankine 2 (1 pen), Chambers 1, Racchi 1, Sangare 1, Smith C 1, Smith J 1.

BLUE SQUARE NORTH AND SOUTH PLAY-OFFS 2010–2011

BLUE SQUARE NORTH

SEMI-FINALS FIRST LEG

Nuneaton T 1 *(Storer 74)*
AFC Telford U 1 *(Trainer 90)*   2089

Guiseley 1 *(Peyton 75)*
Boston U 0   1022

SEMI-FINALS SECOND LEG

AFC Telford U 2 *(Adams 16, Newton 44 (pen))*
Nuneaton T 1 *(Spencer 56)*   3442

Boston U 3 *(Pearson 19, Church 79, Davidson 113)*
Guiseley 2 *(Rothery 60, Stamp 108)*   2640
aet.

FINAL

AFC Telford U 3 *(Newton 9 (pen), Murray 79, Trainer 90)*
Guiseley 2 *(Walshaw 44 (pen), Stamp 45)* 5436

BLUE SQUARE SOUTH

SEMI-FINALS FIRST LEG

Chelmsford C 1 *(Modeste 45)*
Ebbsfleet U 4 *(West 22, 26, Shakes 78, 88)* 1701

Woking 0
Farnborough T 1 *(Holloway 71)*   2726

SEMI-FINALS SECOND LEG

Ebbsfleet U 2 *(West 27, 35)*
Chelmsford C 1 *(Gray 62)*   1538

Farnborough T 1 *(McDonald 111)*
Woking 1 *(Hammond 45)*   2137
aet.

FINAL

Farnborough T 2 *(McMahon 88, Booth 90)*
Ebbsfleet U 4 *(West 29, 74, Shakes 53, Willock 90)*   4267

BLUE SQUARE NORTH 2010–2011

(P) *Promoted into division at end of 2009–10 season.*
(R) *Relegated into division at end of 2009–10 season.*

	Total						Home					Away						
	P	W	D	L	F	A	W	D	L	F	A	W	D	L	F	A	GD	Pts
1 Alfreton T	40	29	5	6	97	33	16	3	1	55	11	13	2	5	42	22	64	92
2 AFC Telford U¶	40	23	13	4	71	29	12	6	2	42	17	11	7	2	29	12	42	82
3 Boston U (P)	40	23	10	7	72	33	13	4	3	34	14	10	6	4	38	19	39	79
4 Eastwood T	40	22	7	11	82	50	13	2	5	40	23	9	5	6	42	27	32	73
5 Guiseley (P)	40	20	13	7	56	41	9	6	5	29	21	11	7	2	27	20	15	73
6 Nuneaton T (P)	40	21	9	10	66	44	10	5	5	30	21	11	4	5	36	23	22	72
7 Solihull Moors	40	18	10	12	66	49	11	4	5	36	24	7	6	7	30	25	17	64
8 Droylsden	40	17	9	14	69	67	11	2	7	41	36	6	7	7	28	31	2	60
9 Blyth Spartans	40	16	10	14	61	54	9	5	6	30	22	7	5	8	31	32	7	58
10 Stalybridge Celtic	40	16	9	15	64	55	8	6	6	28	23	8	3	9	36	32	9	57
11 Workington	40	16	6	18	52	60	10	3	7	32	28	6	3	11	20	32	−8	54
12 Harrogate T	40	13	11	16	53	66	9	7	4	34	24	4	4	12	19	42	−13	50
13 Corby T	40	13	10	17	58	80	7	5	8	28	33	6	5	9	30	47	−22	49
14 Gloucester C	40	14	5	21	49	63	7	3	10	26	31	7	2	11	23	32	−14	47
15 Hinckley U	40	13	7	20	76	76	9	4	7	47	29	4	3	13	29	47	0	46
16 Worcester C (S)	40	12	10	18	49	55	7	4	9	29	29	5	6	9	20	26	−6	46
17 Vauxhall Motors	40	12	9	19	52	71	7	5	8	28	34	5	4	11	24	37	−19	45
18 Gainsborough Trinity	40	12	5	23	50	74	4	4	12	20	40	8	1	11	30	34	−24	41
19 Hyde U	40	10	6	24	44	73	4	3	13	18	38	6	3	11	26	35	−29	36
20 Stafford Rangers	40	8	8	24	39	78	5	3	12	20	43	3	5	12	19	35	−39	32
21 Redditch U	40	2	8	30	30	105	1	6	13	16	52	1	2	17	14	53	−75	9

Redditch U deducted 5 points. ¶AFC Telford U promoted via play-offs.

BLUE SQUARE SOUTH 2010–2011

	Total						Home					Away						
	P	W	D	L	F	A	W	D	L	F	A	W	D	L	F	A	GD	Pts
1 Braintree T	42	27	8	7	78	33	15	4	2	45	17	12	4	5	33	16	45	89
2 Farnborough (P)	42	25	7	10	83	47	12	5	4	37	22	13	2	6	46	25	36	82
3 Ebbsfleet U¶ (R)	42	22	12	8	75	51	9	7	5	34	26	13	5	3	41	25	24	78
4 Chelmsford C	42	23	8	11	82	50	14	3	4	48	16	9	5	7	34	34	32	77
5 Woking	42	22	10	10	62	42	13	5	3	35	17	9	5	7	27	25	20	76
6 Welling U	42	24	8	10	81	47	14	3	4	44	20	10	5	6	37	27	34	75
7 Dover Ath	42	22	8	12	80	51	9	5	7	36	26	13	3	5	44	25	29	74
8 Eastleigh	42	22	6	14	74	53	12	1	8	39	30	10	5	6	35	23	21	72
9 Havant & Waterlooville	42	16	10	16	56	51	8	5	8	31	27	8	5	8	25	24	5	58
10 Dartford (P)	42	15	12	15	60	60	9	7	5	37	28	6	5	10	23	32	0	57
11 Bromley	42	15	12	15	49	61	7	6	8	24	30	8	6	7	25	31	−12	57
12 Weston Super Mare	42	15	8	19	56	67	12	3	6	34	24	3	5	13	22	43	−11	53
13 Basingstoke T	42	13	10	19	50	63	8	4	9	34	32	5	6	10	16	31	−13	49
14 Boreham Wood (P)	42	12	11	19	56	67	8	5	8	35	33	4	6	11	21	34	−11	47
15 Staines T	42	11	14	17	48	63	7	5	9	25	30	4	9	8	23	33	−15	47
16 Bishop's Stortford	42	13	6	23	48	79	6	3	12	19	38	7	3	11	29	41	−31	45
17 Dorchester T	42	10	14	18	49	59	5	9	7	23	28	5	5	11	26	31	−10	44
18 Hampton & Richmond B	42	9	15	18	43	60	3	8	10	19	30	6	7	8	24	30	−17	42
19 Maidenhead U	42	10	10	22	43	70	3	6	12	16	34	7	4	10	27	36	−27	40
20 Thurrock	42	8	13	21	50	77	5	7	9	28	40	3	6	12	22	37	−27	37
21 Lewes	42	9	9	24	34	70	5	5	11	19	38	4	4	13	15	32	−36	36
22 St Albans C	42	7	13	22	39	72	4	7	10	24	42	3	6	12	15	30	−33	24

Welling U deducted 5 points. St Albans City deducted 10 points.
¶Ebbsfleet U promoted via play-offs.

EVO-STIK PREMIER DIVISION 2010–2011

			Total				Home				Away					
	P	W	D	L	F	A	W	D	L	F	A	W	D	L	F	A	GD	Pts
1 FC Halifax T	42	30	8	4	108	36	15	5	1	54	18	15	3	3	54	18	72	98
2 Colwyn Bay¶	42	24	7	11	67	56	12	2	7	33	30	12	5	4	34	26	11	79
3 Bradford Park Avenue	42	23	8	11	84	55	14	2	5	50	24	9	6	6	34	31	29	77
4 FC United	42	24	4	14	76	53	14	1	6	44	25	10	3	8	32	28	23	76
5 North Ferriby U	42	22	7	13	78	51	12	1	8	45	24	10	6	5	33	27	27	73
6 Buxton	42	20	10	12	71	52	10	7	4	38	20	10	3	8	33	32	19	70
7 Kendal T	42	21	5	16	80	77	12	3	6	42	34	9	2	10	38	43	3	68
8 Marine	42	20	7	15	74	64	9	4	8	41	43	11	3	7	33	21	10	67
9 Worksop T	42	21	6	15	72	54	11	5	5	38	20	10	1	10	34	34	18	66
10 Chasetown	42	20	6	16	76	59	11	4	6	40	24	9	2	10	36	35	17	66
11 Matlock T	42	20	6	16	74	59	10	3	8	35	28	10	3	8	39	31	15	66
12 Northwich Victoria	42	18	9	15	66	55	11	3	7	35	27	7	6	8	31	28	11	63
13 Stocksbridge PS	42	17	6	19	75	75	10	2	9	40	34	7	4	10	35	41	0	57
14 Ashton U	42	16	5	21	57	62	11	0	10	36	34	5	5	11	21	28	–5	53
15 Mickleover Sports	42	15	7	20	70	76	7	3	11	41	42	8	4	9	29	34	–6	52
16 Whitby T	42	14	9	19	58	77	8	5	8	31	34	6	4	11	27	43	–19	51
17 Nantwich T	42	13	7	22	68	90	10	3	8	34	41	3	4	14	34	49	–22	46
18 Frickley Ath	42	11	11	20	43	68	6	7	8	18	19	5	4	12	25	49	–25	44
19 Burscough†	42	12	7	23	56	73	7	3	11	28	32	5	4	12	28	41	–17	43
20 Hucknall T	42	11	10	21	57	80	6	7	8	35	37	5	3	13	22	43	–23	43
21 Ossett T	42	9	5	28	45	103	1	4	16	15	56	8	1	12	30	47	–58	32
22 Retford U	42	5	2	35	31	111	2	2	17	14	53	3	0	18	17	58	–80	17

Worksop T deducted 3 points. ¶Colwyn Bay promoted via play-offs. †Burscough not relegated.

ZAMARETTO PREMIER DIVISION 2010–2011

			Total				Home				Away					
	P	W	D	L	F	A	W	D	L	F	A	W	D	L	F	A	GD	Pts
1 Truro C	40	27	6	7	91	35	16	2	2	48	15	11	4	5	43	20	56	87
2 Hednesford T	40	26	5	9	82	38	14	3	3	43	17	12	2	6	39	21	44	83
3 Salisbury C¶	40	23	10	7	82	45	15	2	3	52	26	8	8	4	30	19	37	79
4 Cambridge C	40	24	7	9	74	40	12	4	4	46	21	12	3	5	28	19	34	79
5 Leamington	40	24	6	10	68	39	16	1	3	42	19	8	5	7	26	20	29	78
6 Chesham U	40	20	11	9	64	35	14	4	5	1	38	10	6	6	8	26	25	29	71
7 Chippenham T	40	18	14	8	54	41	12	5	3	31	13	6	9	5	23	28	13	68
8 Stourbridge	40	18	8	14	72	61	12	4	4	46	27	6	4	10	26	34	11	62
9 Brackley T	40	16	10	14	67	47	10	7	3	38	19	6	3	11	29	28	20	58
10 Swindon Supermarine	40	17	7	16	56	58	10	3	7	29	23	7	4	9	27	35	–2	58
11 Bashley	40	14	10	16	55	63	8	5	7	24	31	6	5	9	31	32	–8	52
12 Evesham U	40	14	9	17	54	49	8	6	6	32	24	6	3	11	22	25	5	51
13 Cirencester T	40	13	8	19	59	67	8	3	9	31	29	5	5	10	28	38	–8	47
14 Oxford C	40	11	12	17	48	54	4	9	7	26	27	7	3	10	22	27	–6	45
15 Hemel Hempstead T	40	13	6	21	50	59	6	3	11	16	26	7	3	10	34	33	–9	45
16 Banbury U	40	11	8	21	44	67	6	5	9	21	30	5	3	12	23	37	–23	40
17 Bedford T	40	10	7	23	41	76	6	4	10	20	33	4	3	13	21	43	–35	37
18 Weymouth	40	12	8	20	55	85	8	5	7	33	33	4	3	13	22	52	–30	34
19 Didcot T	40	7	11	22	39	69	3	5	12	16	36	4	6	10	23	33	–30	32
20 Tiverton T	40	7	8	25	33	77	5	6	9	21	31	2	2	16	12	46	–44	29
21 Halesowen T	40	5	9	26	24	107	3	3	14	14	55	2	6	12	10	52	–83	24

Banbury U deducted 1 point. Weymouth deducted 10 points.
¶Salisbury C promoted via play-offs.
Windsor & Eton record expunged following Winding Up Order on 2 February 2011.

RYMAN PREMIER LEAGUE 2010–2011

			Total				Home					Away					
	P	W	D	L	F	A	W	D	L	F	A	W	D	L	F	A	GD	Pts
1 Sutton U	42	26	9	7	76	33	17	4	0	48	16	9	5	7	28	17	43	87
2 Tonbridge Angels¶	42	22	10	10	71	45	12	5	4	41	24	10	5	6	30	21	26	76
3 Bury T	42	22	10	10	67	49	11	5	5	33	25	11	5	5	34	24	18	76
4 Lowestoft T	42	20	15	7	68	30	9	10	2	37	12	11	5	5	31	18	38	75
5 Harrow Borough	42	22	7	13	77	51	12	5	4	40	18	10	2	9	37	33	26	73
6 Canvey Island	42	21	10	11	69	51	13	4	4	39	24	8	6	7	30	27	18	73
7 Kingstonian	42	21	9	12	66	50	13	2	6	36	25	8	7	6	30	25	16	72
8 Concord Rangers	42	21	8	13	72	55	11	5	5	33	25	10	3	8	39	30	17	71
9 Cray Wanderers	42	20	9	13	72	46	12	2	7	35	20	8	7	6	37	26	26	69
10 AFC Hornchurch	42	19	12	11	58	46	12	6	3	32	16	7	6	8	26	30	12	69
11 Billericay T	42	20	9	13	56	45	14	2	5	31	17	6	7	8	25	28	11	69
12 Wealdstone	42	16	10	16	58	54	9	6	6	27	25	7	4	10	31	29	4	58
13 Carshalton Ath	42	14	10	18	49	57	7	6	8	24	28	7	4	10	25	29	–8	52
14 Tooting & Mitcham	42	13	10	19	63	85	9	4	8	36	43	4	6	11	27	42	–22	49
15 Hendon	42	12	10	20	61	81	7	5	9	32	35	5	5	11	29	46	–20	46
16 Margate	42	11	12	19	52	64	6	6	9	31	33	5	6	10	21	31	–12	45
17 Horsham	42	11	11	20	43	77	4	8	9	21	37	7	3	11	22	40	–34	44
18 Hastings U	42	9	11	22	50	65	6	4	11	27	30	3	7	11	23	35	–15	38
19 Aveley	42	10	8	24	35	62	4	5	12	17	34	6	3	12	18	28	–27	38
20 Maidstone U	42	9	10	23	43	75	2	5	14	17	37	7	5	9	26	38	–32	37
21 Croydon Ath	42	10	4	28	44	95	5	2	14	24	49	5	2	14	20	46	–51	31
22 Folkestone Invicta	42	5	12	25	34	68	3	7	11	19	31	2	5	14	15	37	–34	27

Croydon Ath deducted 3 points. ¶ Tonbridge Angels promoted via play-offs.

MACWHIRTER WELSH LEAGUE 2010–2011

	P	W	D	L	F	A	GD	Pts
1 Bryntirion Ath	30	23	1	6	76	27	49	70
2 Afan Lido	30	20	5	5	63	28	35	65
3 Cambrian & Clydach	30	17	6	7	68	37	31	57
4 Pontardawe T	30	15	6	9	54	44	10	51
5 Caerau (Ely)	30	15	4	11	66	52	14	49
6 Bridgend T	30	14	5	11	60	47	13	47
7 West End	30	13	6	11	57	47	10	45
8 Cardiff Corinthians	30	12	4	14	58	52	6	40
9 Taffs Well	30	12	3	15	47	57	–10	39
10 Aberaman Ath	30	12	3	15	58	74	–16	39
11 Goytre U	30	10	8	12	47	53	–6	38
12 Cwmbran Celtic	30	10	7	13	45	50	–5	37
13 Barry T	30	9	8	13	39	55	–16	35
14 Caldicot T	30	8	3	19	37	48	–11	27
15 Garden Village	30	6	7	17	41	75	–34	25
16 Penrhiwceiber Rangers	30	4	4	22	27	97	–70	16

FA PREMIER RESERVE LEAGUE 2010–2011

With the reserve teams of Premier League clubs Birmingham City, Fulham, Stoke City and Tottenham Hotspur, deciding not to enter the 2010–11 season, the organizers had to come up with an ingenious system to replace the North and South sections that had hitherto been in operation.

The 16 remaining teams were split into three sections. The North had two groups A and B consisting of five teams in each, while the South had one section of six teams. Each team in Group A played each other twice and met the five from Group B and the South section just once for a total of 19 matches. The same criteria applied to the teams in Group B and the South, though the latter played 20 games in total because of their superiority in numbers – six opposed to five in each of the Northern sections.

NORTHERN GROUP A	P	W	D	L	GD	Pts	NORTHERN GROUP B	P	W	D	L	GD	Pts
Manchester U	19	9	8	2	14	35	Blackburn R	19	7	5	7	1	26
Manchester C	19	10	3	6	10	33	Sunderland	19	6	6	7	2	24
Wigan Ath	19	9	4	6	–1	31	Liverpool	19	5	8	6	–1	23
Newcastle U	19	8	4	7	0	28	Everton	19	4	3	12	–11	15
Bolton W	19	8	3	8	–8	27	Blackpool	19	4	2	13	–26	14

Manchester United – Appearances and Goals
Wootton 18, Vermijl 15+4, Brown R 15, Dudgeon 13, Gill 13, Norwood 13+1, Obertan 13, King 11, Bebe 10, Brady 8+3, Tunnicliffe 8+2, Devlin 8+1, Amos 7, Keane W 6+3, Morrison 6+2, Eikrem 5, Brown W 4, Johnstone 4, Stewart 4, Thorpe 3+2, Keane M 3+1, Cofie +4, Evans C 3, De Laet 3, Petrucci 2+7, Pogba 2+1, Fabio 2, Blackett 1+2, Lingard 1+2, Ajose 1+1, Anderson 1+1, Ekangamene +2, McGinty +2, Rudge +2, Cole 1, Fletcher 1, Fryers 1, James 1, O'Shea 1, Fornasier +1, Van Velzen +1.
Goals: Obertan 6, Bebe 5, Keane W 4 (1 pen), King 4, Anderson 2, Brady 2 (1 pen), Keane M 2 (1 pen), Morrison 2, Norwood 2 (1 pen), Ajose 1, Cofie 1, Eikrem 1, Fornasier 1, Stewart 1, Thorpe 1, Tunnicliffe 1, Vermijl 1, own goal 1.

Blackburn Rovers – Appearances and Goals
Pearson 16+1, Morris 16, Potts 12+3, Ramm 11+4, Parry 11+1, O'Connor 10+3, Henley 9+1, Kean 9, Aley 8+2, Hitchcock 7+6, MacLaren 7+5, Evans 7+2, Knowles 7+2, Hoilett 7, Lowe 7, Bunn 6, Gunning 6, Linganzi 6, O'Connor A 5+2, O'Connor C 5+1, Hanley G 5, Goulon 4, Roberts 4, Rochina 4, Fernandez 3+2, Cogan 3, Dunn 3, Formica 3, Mwaruwari 2, Nzonzi 2, Urwin 2, Hanley R +2, Osawe 1+4, Ajagbe 1, Andrews 1, Biram Diouf 1, Chimbonda 1, Dilo 1, Emerton 1, Fielding 1, Jones P 1, Judge 1, Kalinic 1, Rigters 1, Edwards +1, O'Sullivan +1, Vastic +1, Wylie +1.
Goals: Rochina 5, Hitchcock 4, Morris 3, Pearson 3, Potts 3, Roberts 3 (1 pen), Dunn 2, Hoilett 2 (1 pen), Biram Diouf 1, Cogan 1, Goulon 1, Evans 1, Gunning 1, Kalinic 1, Knowles 1, MacLaren 1, Mwaruwari 1, Osawe 1, Rigters 1, Roberts 1, own goals 2.

NORTHERN GROUP A AND B PLAY-OFF

Manchester U (0) 1 *(Petrucci 65 (pen))*   **Blackburn R (2) 2** *(Rochina 21, 31)*
(at Old Trafford.
Manchester U: Amos; Vermijl, Wootton, Gill, Brady, Rafael (Petrucci), Brown R, Fletcher (Cofie), Norwood (Ajose), Obertan, King.
Blackburn R: Bunn; Henley, Morris, Lowe, Hanley G, Parry, Formica, Potts, Kalinic (Hitchcock), Rochina (Evans), Aley (Ramm).

SOUTHERN GROUP

	P	W	D	L	GD	Pts
Chelsea	20	11	3	6	3	36
Arsenal	20	10	5	5	7	35
Aston Villa	20	8	6	6	16	30
West Ham U	20	8	4	8	1	28
WBA	20	5	10	5	1	25

Chelsea – Appearances and Goals

Lalkovic 13+1, Chalobah 13, Clifford B 13, Tore 13, Djalo 11+5, Sala 11+1, Phillip 10+5, Pappoe 9, Sebek 9, Borini 8, Clifford C 8, McEachran 8, Kane 7+4, Kalas 7, Bertrand 6, Mellis 6, Walker 6, Deen-Conteh 5+6, Ince 5+1, Woods 4+4, Bruma 4, Nkumu 3+1, Van Aanholt 3, Magnay 2+1, Kakuta 2, Saville 1+6, Mitrovic 1+5, Sampayo 1+3, Philliskirk 1+2, Devyne 1+1, Affane 1, Blackman 1, Bosingwa 1, Gordon 1, Hilario 1, Mancienne 1, Turnbull 1, Davey +1, Figuerira +1, Jones +1.

Goals: Borini 12 (1 pen), Phillip 8 (1 pen), Lalkovic 6, Tore 4, Chalobah 2, Clifford B 2, Kane 2, Djalo 1, Magnay 1, Mellis 1, Nkumu 1, own goal 1.

PREMIER RESERVE LEAGUE PLAY-OFF FINAL

Chelsea (0) 1 *(Kane 80)*   **Blackburn R (1) 1** *(Formica 20))*

(at Stamford Bridge, Chelsea won 5-4 on penalties, attendance 799)

Chelsea: Turnbull, Kane, Kalas, Magnay, Bertrand (Devyne), Chalobah (Deen-Conteh), Tore, Clifford C, Lalkovic, Saville (Woods), Phillip.
Substitutes not used: Walker, Gordon.
Blackburn R: Kean, Henley, Morris, Lowe, Pearson, Parry, Evans (Ramm), Potts, Hitch-cock (Osawe), Formica (Knowles), Aley.
Substitutes not used: Urwin, O'Connor.

FA ACADEMY UNDER-18 LEAGUE 2010–2011

SOUTHERN SECTION

GROUP A

	P	W	D	L	GD	Pts
Fulham	28	15	6	7	20	51
Southampton	28	15	5	8	17	50
West Ham U	27	14	1	12	8	43
Norwich C	28	12	5	11	0	41
Arsenal	28	12	3	13	–5	39
Crystal Palace	28	12	3	13	–6	39
Ipswich T	28	9	7	12	–10	34
Chelsea	25	9	5	11	–5	32
Charlton Ath	27	8	5	14	–8	29
Portsmouth	28	4	5	19	–31	17

GROUP B

	P	W	D	L	GD	Pts
Aston Villa	27	17	6	4	37	57
Leicester C	28	17	5	6	28	56
Watford	27	16	5	6	16	53
Tottenham H	28	13	6	9	4	45
Reading	27	13	2	12	8	41
Birmingham C	27	11	5	11	–4	38
Bristol C	28	10	3	15	–15	33
Coventry C	28	6	12	10	–4	30
Cardiff C	28	7	6	15	–19	27
Milton Keynes D	27	2	4	21	–49	10

NORTHERN SECTION

GROUP C

	P	W	D	L	GD	Pts
Everton	28	17	7	4	25	58
Liverpool	28	17	6	5	35	57
Manchester C	27	14	10	3	11	52
Bolton W	28	14	4	10	6	46
Manchester U	27	12	5	10	8	41
WBA	28	11	8	9	5	41
Wolverhampton W	28	11	5	12	1	38
Blackburn R	28	10	6	12	1	36
Crewe Alex	28	11	3	14	–5	36
Stoke C	28	5	3	20	–31	18

GROUP D

	P	W	D	L	GD	Pts
Sunderland	27	15	7	5	19	52
Nottingham F	27	15	3	9	18	48
Barnsley	28	12	5	11	7	41
Newcastle U	27	11	7	9	6	40
Sheffield U	28	11	6	11	–3	39
Middlesbrough	28	11	4	13	–7	37
Leeds U	27	10	4	13	–16	34
Huddersfield T	28	7	5	16	–23	26
Derby Co	28	7	3	18	–6	24
Sheffield W	28	6	6	16	–33	24

ACADEMY PLAY-OFF SEMI-FINALS
Everton 3, Aston Villa 2
Fulham 3, Sunderland 3
Fulham won 4-1 on penalties.

ACADEMY FINAL
Fulham 1, Everton 2

TOTESPORT.COM LEAGUE 2010–2011

CENTRAL DIVISION

	P	W	D	L	GD	Pts
Derby Co	14	11	0	3	20	33
Sheffield U	14	9	0	5	13	27
Nottingham F	14	8	1	5	2	25
Port Vale	14	7	2	5	0	23
Rotherham U	14	7	1	6	0	22
Barnsley	14	5	2	7	8	17
Bradford C	14	4	2	8	–8	14
Sheffield W	14	0	2	12	–35	2

EAST DIVISION

	P	W	D	L	GD	Pts
Middlesbrough	14	10	1	3	18	31
Hartlepool U	14	8	4	2	7	28
Leeds U	14	7	2	5	13	23
Hull C	14	5	5	4	4	20
Lincoln C	14	6	2	6	2	20
Scunthorpe U	14	5	2	7	–5	17
Gateshead	14	3	1	10	–20	10
Grimsby T	14	1	5	8	–19	8

WEST DIVISION

	P	W	D	L	GD	Pts
Preston NE	18	14	1	3	37	43
Burnley	18	11	3	4	20	36
Wrexham	18	10	2	6	6	32
Oldham Ath	18	10	2	6	6	32
Morecambe	18	8	2	8	0	26
Shrewsbury T	18	5	6	7	–5	21
Tranmere R	18	5	5	8	–5	20
Macclesfield T	18	6	1	11	–17	19
Accrington S	18	5	2	11	–18	17
Bury	18	3	2	13	–24	11

TOTESPORT.COM COMBINATION 2010–2011

CENTRAL DIVISION

	P	W	D	L	GD	Pts
Brighton & HA	12	8	4	0	15	28
Leyton Orient	12	5	5	2	5	20
Wycombe W	12	4	5	3	1	17
Brentford	12	4	3	5	1	15
Gillingham	12	4	3	5	–5	15
Crawley T	11	2	2	7	–6	8
Aldershot	11	2	2	7	–11	8

EAST DIVISION

	P	W	D	L	GD	Pts
Ipswich T	12	6	3	3	11	21
Oxford U	12	6	3	3	9	21
Watford	12	5	4	3	3	19
Southend U	12	4	5	3	3	17
Luton T	11	5	0	6	–1	15
Colchester U	12	3	2	7	–11	11
Stevenage	11	2	3	6	–14	9

WALES & WEST DIVISION

	P	W	D	L	GD	Pts
Torquay U	12	9	2	1	16	29
Swansea C	12	5	3	4	–1	18
Exeter C	12	5	2	5	2	17
Swindon T	12	5	2	5	2	17
Forest Green R	12	4	4	4	4	16
AFC Bournemouth	12	4	2	6	–4	14
Plymouth Arg	12	2	1	9	–19	7

TOTESPORT.COM LEAGUE CUP 2010–2011

GROUP ONE

	P	W	D	L	GD	Pts
Preston NE	3	2	0	1	0	6
Tranmere R	3	1	1	1	2	4
Carlisle U	3	1	1	1	1	4
Morecambe	3	1	0	2	–3	3

GROUP TWO

	P	W	D	L	GD	Pts
Walsall	3	2	0	1	8	6
Derby Co	3	1	1	1	–1	4
Rotherham U	3	1	1	1	–2	4
Lincoln C	3	1	0	2	–5	3

GROUP THREE

	P	W	D	L	GD	Pts
Sunderland	4	3	1	0	10	10
Scunthorpe U	4	2	0	2	–4	6
Gateshead	4	1	1	2	–1	4
Middlesbrough	4	1	1	2	–2	4
Hartlepool U	4	1	1	2	–3	4

SEMI-FINALS

Sunderland 5, Preston NE 3
Walsall 5, Scunthorpe U 1

FINAL

Sunderland v Walsall
(Match to be played in August.)

WOMEN'S FOOTBALL 2010–2011

FA WOMEN'S PREMIER LEAGUE 2010–11

NATIONAL DIVISION

	P	W	D	L	GD	Pts
Sunderland WFC	14	9	3	2	14	30
Nottingham F LFC	14	6	5	3	3	23
Reading FC Women	14	6	2	6	3	20
Leeds U LFC	14	5	3	6	0	18
Barnet FC Ladies	14	4	4	6	–2	16
Watford LFC	14	3	7	4	–5	16
Blackburn R LFC	14	4	4	6	–6	16
Millwall Lionesses LFC	14	3	4	7	–7	13

SOUTHERN DIVISION

	P	W	D	L	GD	Pts
Charlton Ath WFC	18	11	3	4	18	36
Cardiff C LFC	18	11	3	4	7	36
West Ham U LFC	18	10	3	5	12	33
Portsmouth FC Ladies	18	10	1	7	3	31
Keynsham T LFC	18	9	3	6	4	30
Colchester U FC	18	6	3	9	–1	21
Brighton & HA WFC	18	5	4	9	–10	19
QPR LFC	18	5	3	10	–10	18
Gillingham LFC	18	5	2	11	–10	17
Yeovil T LFC	18	3	5	10	–13	14

NORTHERN DIVISION

	P	W	D	L	GD	Pts
Aston Villa LFC	18	14	0	4	22	42
Coventry C LFC	18	13	2	3	23	41
Leicester C WFC	18	12	1	5	39	37
Manchester C LFC	18	12	1	5	19	37
Derby Co LFC	18	8	3	7	–1	27
Leeds City Vixens LFC	18	5	2	11	–15	17
Rochdale AFC Ladies	18	5	1	12	–21	16
Preston NE WFC	18	4	3	11	–24	15
Newcastle U WFC	18	4	3	11	–26	15
Curzon Ashton LFC	18	3	4	11	–16	13

WOMEN'S LEAGUE CUP FINAL 2010–2011

Thursday, 24 March 2011

(at Wycombe)

Barnet 0

Nottingham F 0   1281

Barnet won 4-3 on penalties.

Barnet: Rowlands; Dempster, Wade, Prosser, Reidy (O'Leary 120), Rudman, Murphy, Sowden, Trimnell, Boardman, Pond (Lance 77).

Nottingham F: Wallhead; Gilliatt, Tomkins, Bailey, Bell, Connor-Iommi, Lawson, Clarke, Davies (Hinton 116), Stainthorpe (Howard 83), Murray (Waddell 61).

aet.

WOMEN'S FA CUP FINAL 2010–2011

Saturday, 21 May 2011

(at Coventry)

Arsenal (2) 2 *(Little 19, Fleeting 32)*

Bristol Acad (0) 0   13,885

Arsenal: Byrne; Houghton, Grant, Flaherty, Fahey, Nobbs, Chapman, White, Little, Yankey (Carter 90), Fleeting (Beattie 80).

Bristol Acad: Chamberlain; McCatty, Rose, Yorston, Culvin (Clark 68), Hoogendijk, Daley, Dykes, Fishlock (Billson 46), Bleazard, Heatherson.

Referee: S. Massey (West Midlands).

UEFA WOMEN'S CHAMPIONS LEAGUE 2010–2011

QUALIFYING ROUND – GROUP 1
NSA Sofia 7, Gazi Univ 0
Brondby 6, Roma Calfa 0
Brondby 12, Gazi Univ 0
Roma Calfa 0, NSA Sofia 4
NSA Sofia 0, Brondby 3
Gazi Univ 3, Roma Calfa 3

GROUP 2
Everton 6, Klaksvik 0
Gintra 4, Borec 0
Everton 10, Borec 0
Klaksvik 0, Gintra 0
Gintra 0, Everton 7
Borec 0, Klaksvik 2

GROUP 3
Umea 3, Tel Aviv 0
Sarajevo 1, Apollon 6
Umea 1, Apollon 4
Tel Aviv 3, Sarajevo 1
Sarajevo 0, Umea 1
Apollon 3, Tel Aviv 0

GROUP 4
Juvisy Essonne 5, Targu Mures 1
Breidablik 8, Levadia 1
Juvisy Essonne 12, Levadia 0
Targu Mures 0, Breidablik 7
Breidablik 3, Juvisy Essonne 3
Levadia 1, Targu Mures 2

GROUP 5
Bardolino 7, Swansea 0
Bardolino 3, Baia Zugdidi 0
Swansea 0, Krka 4
Krka 4, Baia Zugdidi 0
Krka 1, Bardolino 4
Baia Zugdidi 1, Swansea 2

GROUP 6
Rossiyanka 5, Osijek 0
1st Dezembro 1, St Francis 4
Rossiyanka 9, St Francis 0
Osijek 1, 1st Dezembro 4
1st Dezembro 1, Rossiyanka 4
St Francis 5, Osijek 3

GROUP 7
Duisburg 3, Slovan Bratislava 0
Glasgow 8, Newtonabbey 0
Slovan Bratislava 0, Glasgow 4
Duisburg 6, Newtonabbey 1
Glasgow 0, Duisburg 4
Newtonabbey 0, Slovan Bratislava 1

FIRST ROUND FIRST LEG
Zorka-BDU 1, Roa 2
Masinac 1, Arsenal 3
Apollon 1, Zvezda-2005 2
Unia 1, Brondby 2
Legenda Chernigiv 1, Rossiyanka 3
Krka 0, Linkoping 7
PAOK 1, Neulengbach 0
Aland United 0, Potsdam 9
AZ 1, Lyon 2
Fortuna 8, Bardolino 0

Zurich 2, Torres 3
CSHVSM 0, Duisburg 5
Breidablik 0, Juvisy Essonne 3
MTK 0, Everton 0
Rayo 3, Valur 0
St Truiden 0, Sparta Prague 3

FIRST ROUND SECOND LEG
Duisburg 6, CSHVSM 0
Roa 0, Zorka-BDU 0
Zvezda-2005 2, Apollon 1
Torres 4, Zurich 1
Potsdam 6, Aland United 0
Valur 1, Rayo 1
Neulengbach 3, PAOK 0
Brondby 0, Unia 1
Bardolino 1, Fortuna 6
Rossiyanka 4, Legenda Chernigiv 0
Arsenal 9, Masinac 0
Sparta Prague 7, St Truiden 0
Lyon 8, AZ 0
Linkoping 5, Krka 0
Juvisy Essonne 6, Breidablik 0
Everton 7, MTK 1

SECOND ROUND FIRST LEG
Linkoping 2, Sparta Prague 0
Potsdam 7, Neulengbach 0
Duisburg 4, Fortuna 0
Roa 1, Zvezda-2005 1
Brondby 1, Everton 4
Torres 1, Juvisy Essonne 2
Rossiyanka 1, Lyon 6
Rayo 2, Arsenal 0

SECOND ROUND SECOND LEG
Sparta Prague 1, Linkoping 1
Zvezda-2005 4, Roa 0
Lyon 5, Rossiyanka 0
Fortuna 0, Duisburg 3
Neulengbach 0, Potsdam 9
Juvisy Essonne 2, Torres 2
Arsenal 4, Rayo 1
Everton 1, Brondby 1

QUARTER-FINALS FIRST LEG
Juvisy Essonne 0, Potsdam 3
Zvezda-2005 0, Lyon 0
Arsenal 1, Linkoping 1
Everton 1, Duisburg 3

QUARTER-FINALS SECOND LEG
Duisburg 2, Everton 1
Lyon 1, Zvezda-2005 0
Linkoping 2, Arsenal 2
Potsdam 6, Juvisy Essonne 2

SEMI-FINALS FIRST LEG
Duisburg 2, Potsdam 2
Lyon 2, Arsenal 0

SEMI-FINALS SECOND LEG
Arsenal 2, Lyon 3
Potsdam 1, Duisburg 0

FINAL
Lyon 2, Potsdam 0

ENGLAND WOMEN'S INTERNATIONAL MATCHES 2010–2011

FRIENDLIES

2 Apr, at Leyton Orient

England 2 *(Clarke 8, Yankey 26)*   **USA 1** *(Rapinoe 39)*

England: Bardsley; Scott A, Stoney, Unitt, White F (Bradley 68), Scott J, Williams F, Yankey (Carney 75), Clarke, White E, Smith K.

17 May, at Oxford

England 2 *(Scott J 46, Carney 70 (pen))*   **Sweden 0**   5167

England: Bardsley (Chamberlain 78); Scott A, Unitt (Aluko 46), Asante (Carney 46), Bradley, Stoney (Whelan 87), Clarke, Scott J, White E (Houghton 46), Smith K (Rafferty 46), Yankey.

CYPRUS CUP

2 Mar, in Larnaca

Italy 0   England 2 *(White E 3, Smith K 38 (pen))*

England: Bardsley; Susi (Smith S 80), Unitt, White F, Yankey, Clarke (Scott A 66), White E, Stoney, Smith K, Houghton, Asante.

4 Mar, in Nicosia

Scotland 2 *(Little 26, Beattie 52)*   **England 0**

England: Chamberlain; Johnson, Scott A, Stoney, Unitt, Scott J, Williams F, Clarke (Susi 68), Aluko, Bassett, Smith S.

7 Mar, in Nicosia

Canada 2 *(Sinclair 45, Timko 55)*   **England 0**

England: Bardsley; Scott A, Susi, White F, Williams F, Yankey, White E, Bradley (Stoney 73), Smith K, Houghton, Asante.

9 Mar, in Larnaca

England 2 *(Smith S 16, 80)*   **South Korea 0**

England: Bardsley (Chamberlain 46); Johnson, Stoney, Susi (Scott A 46), Unitt (Houghton 58), Scott J, Clarke (White E 62), Aluko, Smith K, Bassett, Smith S.

THE PEACE CUP

19 Oct, in South Korea

South Korea 0   England 0

England: Brown; Scott A, Stoney, Scott J, Williams F, Yankey, Clarke (Aluko 74), Bradley, Houghton, Smith K (White E 60), Rafferty.

21 Oct, in South Korea

England 0   New Zealand 0

England: Bardsley; Johnson, Scott A, Susi (White E 75), Unitt, White F, Clarke, Aluko (Yankey 86), Smith K (Williams F 84), Bassett, Asante.

FIFA 2011 WOMEN'S WORLD CUP – QUALIFYING COMPETITION

■*Denotes player sent off.*

29 July, at Walsall

England 3 *(Yankey 22, White E 58, Clarke 76)*   **Turkey 0**

England: Brown; Scott A, Stoney, Unitt, White F, Chapman, Scott J, Williams F (Bassett 77), Yankey, Clarke (Susi 77), Aluko (White E 46).

21 Aug, in Krems
Austria 0   England 4 *(Scott A 40, Smith K 7, 30, White E 80)*
England: Brown; Scott A, Stoney, Unitt, White F (White E 46), Chapman (Houghton 60), Scott J, Williams F, Yankey, Smith K (Bradley 46), Carney.

12 Sept, at Shrewsbury
England 2 *(Williams F 44, Smith K 45)*   **Switzerland 0**   4119
England: Brown; Scott A, Stoney, Unitt, White F, Chapman, Scott J, Williams F, Yankey (Clarke 89), Aluko, Smith K.

16 Sept, in Wahlen
Switzerland 2 *(Bachmann 41, Zumbuhl 65)*
England 3 *(Smith K 32, Aluko 34, Williams F 50 (pen))*   1800
England: Brown■; Scott A, Stoney, Unitt, White F, Chapman, Scott J, Williams F, Yankey (Clarke 78), Aluko (Chamberlain 42), Smith K (White E 88).

FIFA WOMEN'S WORLD CUP FINALS GERMANY 2011

27 June, in Wolfsburg
Mexico 1 *(Ocampo 34)*   **England 1** *(Williams F 21)*   18,702
England: Bardsley; Scott A, Unitt, Scott J, White F (Bradley 83), Stoney, Williams F, Smith K, Yankey, Carney (White E 72), Aluko.

1 July, in Dresden
New Zealand 1 *(Gregorius 18)*   **England 2** *(Scott J 63, Clarke 81)*   19,110
England: Bardsley; Scott A, Unitt, Scott J, White F (Bradley 86), Stoney, Williams F, White E, Smith K, Yankey (Clarke 66), Aluko (Carney 46).

5 July, in Augsburg
England 2 *(White E 15, Yankey 66)*   **Japan 0**   20,777
England: Bardsley; Scott A, Unitt, Scott J, Stoney, Clarke (Yankey 46), White E (Bassett 90), Smith K (Aluko 63), Carney, Bradley, Asante.

QUARTER-FINALS

9 July, in Leverkusen
France 1 *(Bussaglia 88)*   **England 1** *(Scott J 59)*   26,395
France won 4-3 on penalties.
France: Deville; Georges, Soubeyrand (Thomis 67), Bompastor, Abily, Lepailleur, Necib (Bretigny 79) (Le Sommer 106), Bussaglia, Thiney, Delie, Viguier.
England: Bardsley; Scott A (Houghton 81), Unitt (Rafferty 81), Scott J, White F, Stoney, Williams F, White E, Smith K, Yankey (Asante 84), Carney.
Penalties: Abily (saved); Smith K (scored); Bussaglia (scored); Carney (scored); Thiney (scored); Stoney (scored); Bompastor (scored); Rafferty (missed); Le Sommer (scored); White F (hit bar).

GROUP A
Nigeria 0, France 1
Germany 2, Canada 1
Canada 0, France 4
Germany 1, Nigeria 0
France 2, Germany 4
Canada 0, Nigeria 1

GROUP B
Japan 2, New Zealand 1
Mexico 1, England 1
Japan 4, Mexico 0
New Zealand 1, England 2

England 2, Japan 0
New Zealand 2, Mexico 2

GROUP C
Colombia 0, Sweden 1
USA 2, North Korea 0
North Korea 0, Sweden 1
USA 3, Colombia 0
Sweden 2, USA 1
North Korea 0, Colombia 0

GROUP D
Norway 1,
   Equatorial Guinea 0

Brazil 1, Australia 0
Australia 3,
   Equatorial Guinea 2
Brazil 3, Norway 0
Equatorial Guinea 0, Brazil 3
Australia 2, Norway 1

QUARTER-FINALS
Germany 0, Japan 1
England 1, France 1
France won 4-3 on penalties.
Sweden v Australia
Brazil v USA

THE FA TROPHY 2010–2011

FINAL (at Wembley) – Saturday, 7 May 2011

Darlington (0) 1 *(Senior 119)*

Mansfield T (0) 0 24,668

Darlington: Russell; Arnison, Brown, Chandler, Miller, Wright, Moore, Bridge-Wilkinson (Terry), Campbell (Senior), Hatch, Smith G (Verma).
Mansfield T: Marriott; Silk, Spence, Murray (Mitchley), Foster, Naylor, Briscoe, Thompson, Connor, Nix, Smith A (Cain).
aet.
Referee: S. Attwell (Warwickshire).

THE FA VASE 2010–2011

FINAL (at Wembley) – Sunday, 8 May 2011

Coalville T (0) 2 *(Moore 58, Goodby 80)*

Whitley Bay (1) 3 *(Chow 28, 86, Kerr 61)* 8778

Coalville T: Bowles; Brown (Gardner), Stuart, Goodby, Costello, Woodward, Miveld, Moore, Murdock, Carney (Attwood), Robbins (Wells).
Whitley Bay: Burke; McFarlane (Gibson), Anderson, Timmons, Williams (Coulson), Robson, Kerr, Chow, Robinson, Pounder (Smith), Ormston.
Referee: S. Mathieson (Cheshire).

THE FA YOUTH CUP 2010–2011

FINAL FIRST LEG – Tuesday, 17 May 2011

Sheffield U (1) 2 *(McFadzean 45, Slew 74)*

Manchester U (1) 2 *(Lingard 14, Keane W 70)* 29,977

Sheffield U: Long; Montgomery, Maguire (Pomares 86), Kennedy, Barry, Gregory (Wilkinson 72), Harriott, Whitehouse, McFadzean, Ironside (Martin 74), Slew.
Manchester U: Johnstone; Keane M, Thorpe, Fornasier, McGinty, Lingard, Pogba, Tunnicliffe, Van Velzen (Cofie 76), Morrison, Keane W.

FINAL SECOND LEG – Monday, 23 May 2011

Manchester U (2) 4 *(Morrison 38, 70, Keane W 45, 80)*

Sheffield U (0) 1 *(Ironside 73)* 24,916

Manchester U: Johnstone; Keane M, McGinty, Thorpe, Fornasier, Lingard (Cole 78), Pogba, Tunnicliffe, Morrison (Cofie 90), Van Velzen (Blackett 84), Keane W.
Sheffield U: Long; Montgomery, Barry, Harriott, Maguire (Pomares 57), Kennedy, Gregory (Martin 68), Whitehouse, Ironside (Wilkinson 76), Slew, McFadzean.

THE FA SUNDAY CUP 2010–2011

FINAL (at Prenton Park) – Sunday, 1 May 2011

Oyster Martyrs (0) 1 *(McGivern 76)*

Paddock (0) 0 1105

Oyster Martyrs: Eastham; Rooney I, Latham, Dames, Rendell, Smith I (Smith II), Forshaw, Lipson, Rooney II, McGivern, Rimmers.
Paddock: O'Connor; Shinks, Dolan, Marsden (Kearns), Shaw, Hussey, Brown (Riley), Wheeler, Henders, Duncan, Langley.
Referee: R. Booth (Nottinghamshire).

THE FA COUNTY YOUTH CUP 2010–2011

FINAL (at Stoke) – Saturday, 30 April 2011

Staffordshire (1) 2 *(Timmins 6, Sherratt 81)*

Norfolk (1) 4 *(Marsden 26, Howard 45, 48, Cunningham 62 (og))* 580

Staffordshire: Wiggins; Cunningham, Burnett (Moyo), Hulin, Brown, Horton (Glover), Barnett, Southall (Kirby), Plimmer, Timmins, Sherratt.
Norfolk: Hewitt; Manning, McLiesh, Southgate (Livoti), Savory, Fryatt, Marsden (Sturman), Borrer, Butcher (George), Howard, Jones.
Referee: J. Adcock (Nottinghamshire).

FOOTBALL TITLES FOR YOUR LIBRARY

SUNK WITHOUT TRACE: THE CHINGFORD TOWN STORY
by Jack Rollin
An account of the brief rise and fall of the East London club in the Southern League
from 1947 to 1950. ISBN 978-1-905891-46-7. £8.

THE MEN WHO NEVER WERE
by Jack Rollin and Tony Brown
An account of the expunged Football League season of 1939-40, with results and line-ups
and details of all the players that took part.
ISBN 978-1-905891-11-5. £12.

THE FORGOTTEN CUP
by Jack Rollin and Tony Brown
The FA Cup competition of 1945-46, which was a transitional season for English football
following the end of WWII. Full results, line-ups and player details.
ISBN 978-1-899468-86-7. £10.

ASHINGTON AFC IN THE FOOTBALL LEAGUE
by Garth Dykes
Full match details and a comprehensive Who's Who of the club's players during their
time in the League.
ISBN 978-1-905891-48-1. £10.
Also, by the same author, similar books on Nelson and Durham City (each priced at £10).

FOOTBALL IN EUROPE 2010/11
by Graeme Riley
Now in its ninth edition, the book gives results of major League and Cup competitions
for the 2010–11 season in all 53 European countries and includes full line-ups for the
Champions League, Europa League and international matches.
ISBN 978-1-905891-50-4. £19.50.

FOOTBALL LEAGUE PLAYERS' RECORDS 1888-1939
by Michael Joyce
Career details of all Football League players during this period.
ISBN 978-1-899468-67-6. £25.

THE DEFINITIVE NEWTON HEATH
by Alan Shury and Brian Landamore
The story of the club that became Manchester United in 1902, with contemporary press
reports, results, line-ups and player details.
ISBN 978-1-899468-16-4. £8.99.

THE FOOTBALL LEAGUE MATCH BY MATCH 1888-1970
55 volumes giving detailed results, scorers and line-up grids for all Football League
seasons from 1888–89 to 1969–70. £12 per volume, £500 for the set.

Please send orders to Tony Brown, 4 Adrian Close, Toton, Nottingham NG9 6FL. The
web site is www.soccerdata.com. 10% of the value of your order (to a maximum of £4)
will be a welcome contribution to postage costs. Please make cheques payable to Tony
Brown.

NATIONAL LIST OF REFEREES FOR SEASON 2011–2012

Adcock, James
Atkinson, Martin
Attwell, Stuart
Bates, Anthony
Berry, Carl
Booth, Russell
Boyeson, Carl
Brown, Mark
Clattenburg, Mark
Collins, Lee
Coote, David
Deadman, Darren
Dean, Mike
Dowd, Phil
Drysdale, Darren
D'Urso, Andrew
East, Roger
Eltringham, Geoff
Foster, David
Foy, Chris
Friend, Kevin
Gibbs, Philip
Graham, Frederick
Haines, Andy
Hall, Andrew
Halsey, Mark
Haywood, Mark
Hegley, Grant
Heywood, Mark
Hooper, Simon
Ilderton, Eddie
Jones, Michael
Kettle, Trevor
Langford, Oliver
Lewis, Robert
Linington, James
Madley, Andrew
Madley, Robert
Malone, Brendan

Marriner, Andre
Mason, Lee
Mathieson, Scott
McDermid, Danny
Miller, Nigel
Miller, Patrick
Mohareb, Dean
Moss, Jonathan
Naylor, Michael
Oliver, Michael
Pawson, Craig
Penn, Andrew
Phillips, David
Probert, Lee
Quinn, Peter
Rushton, Steven
Russell, Michael
Salisbury, Graham
Sarginson, Christopher
Scott, Graham
Sheldrake, Darren
Shoebridge, Robert
Stroud, Keith
Sutton, Gary
Swarbrick, Neil
Tanner, Stephen
Taylor, Anthony
Tierney, Paul
Walton, Peter
Ward, Gavin
Waugh, Jock
Webb, David
Webb, Howard
Webster, Colin
Whitestone, Dean
Williamson, Iain
Woolmer, Andy
Wright, Kevin

ENGLISH LEAGUE FIXTURES 2011–2012

*Sky Sports   †ESPN   §BBC   All fixtures subject to change.

Friday, 5 August 2011
npower Football League Championship
Hull C v Blackpool* (7.45)

Saturday, 6 August 2011
npower Football League Championship
Brighton & HA v Doncaster R
Bristol C v Ipswich T
Burnley v Watford
Coventry C v Leicester C
Derby Co v Birmingham C
Middlesbrough v Portsmouth
Nottingham F v Barnsley
Peterborough U v Crystal Palace
Reading v Millwall
Southampton v Leeds U* (5.20)

npower Football League One
Brentford v Yeovil T
Carlisle U v Notts Co
Charlton Ath v Bournemouth
Huddersfield T v Bury
Milton Keynes D v Hartlepool U
Oldham Ath v Sheffield U
Preston NE v Colchester U
Sheffield W v Rochdale
Stevenage v Exeter C
Tranmere R v Chesterfield
Walsall v Leyton Orient
Wycombe W v Scunthorpe U

npower Football League Two
AFC Wimbledon v Bristol R* (12.45)
Bradford C v Aldershot T
Gillingham v Cheltenham T
Macclesfield T v Dagenham & R
Morecambe v Barnet
Northampton T v Accrington S
Port Vale v Crawley T
Rotherham U v Oxford U

Shrewsbury T v Plymouth Arg
Southend U v Hereford U
Swindon T v Crewe Alex
Torquay U v Burton Alb

Sunday, 7 August 2011
Community Shield
Manchester C v Manchester U* (3.00)

npower Football League Championship
West Ham U v Cardiff C§ (1.00)

Saturday, 13 August 2011
Barclays Premier League
Blackburn R v Wolverhampton W
Fulham v Aston Villa
Liverpool v Sunderland
Newcastle U v Arsenal† (5.30)
QPR v Bolton W
Tottenham H v Everton
Wigan Ath v Norwich C

npower Football League Championship
Barnsley v Southampton
Birmingham C v Coventry C
Blackpool v Peterborough U
Cardiff C v Bristol C
Crystal Palace v Burnley
Doncaster R v West Ham U
Ipswich T v Hull C
Leeds U v Middlesbrough
Leicester C v Reading
Millwall v Nottingham F
Portsmouth v Brighton & HA
Watford v Derby Co

npower Football League One
Bournemouth v Sheffield W
Bury v Carlisle U
Chesterfield v Stevenage
Colchester U v Wycombe W

Exeter C v Milton Keynes D
Hartlepool U v Walsall
Leyton Orient v Tranmere R
Notts Co v Charlton Ath
Rochdale v Huddersfield T
Scunthorpe U v Preston NE
Sheffield U v Brentford
Yeovil T v Oldham Ath

npower Football League Two
Accrington S v Southend U
Aldershot T v Northampton T
Barnet v Port Vale
Bristol R v Torquay U
Burton Alb v Shrewsbury T
Cheltenham T v Swindon T
Crawley T v Macclesfield T
Crewe Alex v Gillingham
Dagenham & R v AFC Wimbledon
Hereford U v Morecambe
Oxford U v Bradford C
Plymouth Arg v Rotherham U

Sunday, 14 August 2011
Barclays Premier League
Stoke C v Chelsea* (1.30)
WBA v Manchester U* (4.00)

Monday, 15 August 2011
Barclays Premier League
Manchester C v Swansea C* (8.00)

Tuesday, 16 August 2011
npower Football League Championship
Barnsley v Middlesbrough
Birmingham C v Burnley
Blackpool v Derby Co
Cardiff C v Brighton & HA
Crystal Palace v Coventry C
Doncaster R v Nottingham F
Ipswich T v Southampton
Leeds U v Hull C
Leicester C v Bristol C
Millwall v Peterborough U
Portsmouth v Reading
Watford v West Ham U

npower Football League One
Bournemouth v Stevenage
Bury v Sheffield W
Chesterfield v Preston NE
Colchester U v Charlton Ath
Exeter C v Brentford
Hartlepool U v Huddersfield T
Leyton Orient v Wycombe W
Notts Co v Tranmere R

Rochdale v Carlisle U
Scunthorpe U v Oldham Ath
Sheffield U v Walsall
Yeovil T v Milton Keynes D

npower Football League Two
Accrington S v Bradford C
Aldershot T v Torquay U
Barnet v Gillingham
Bristol R v Northampton T
Burton Alb v Port Vale
Cheltenham T v Morecambe
Crawley T v Southend U
Crewe Alex v Rotherham U
Dagenham & R v Swindon T
Hereford U v Macclesfield T
Oxford U v Shrewsbury T
Plymouth Arg v AFC Wimbledon

Saturday, 20 August 2011
Barclays Premier League
Arsenal v Liverpool* (12.45)
Aston Villa v Blackburn R
Chelsea v WBA† (5.30)
Everton v QPR
Norwich C v Stoke C
Sunderland v Newcastle U (12.00)
Swansea C v Wigan Ath
Wolverhampton W v Fulham

npower Football League Championship
Brighton & HA v Blackpool
Bristol C v Portsmouth
Burnley v Cardiff C
Coventry C v Watford
Derby Co v Doncaster R
Hull C v Crystal Palace
Middlesbrough v Birmingham C
Nottingham F v Leicester C
Peterborough U v Ipswich T* (5.20)
Reading v Barnsley
Southampton v Millwall

npower Football League One
Brentford v Leyton Orient
Carlisle U v Bournemouth
Charlton Ath v Scunthorpe U
Huddersfield T v Colchester U
Milton Keynes D v Chesterfield
Oldham Ath v Rochdale
Preston NE v Exeter C
Sheffield W v Notts Co
Stevenage v Hartlepool U
Tranmere R v Sheffield U
Walsall v Yeovil T
Wycombe W v Bury

npower Football League Two
AFC Wimbledon v Hereford U
Bradford C v Dagenham & R
Gillingham v Plymouth Arg
Macclesfield T v Bristol R
Morecambe v Aldershot T
Northampton T v Cheltenham T
Port Vale v Accrington S
Rotherham U v Barnet
Shrewsbury T v Crewe Alex
Southend U v Burton Alb
Swindon T v Oxford U
Torquay U v Crawley T

Sunday, 21 August 2011
Barclays Premier League
Bolton W v Manchester C* (4.00)

npower Football League Championship
West Ham U v Leeds U* (1.15)

Monday, 22 August 2011
Barclays Premier League
Manchester U v Tottenham H* (8.00)

Saturday, 27 August 2011
Barclays Premier League
Aston Villa v Wolverhampton W* (12.05)
Blackburn R v Everton
Chelsea v Norwich C
Liverpool v Bolton W* (5.30)
Newcastle U v Fulham
Swansea C v Sunderland
WBA v Stoke C
Wigan Ath v QPR

npower Football League Championship
Brighton & HA v Peterborough U
Crystal Palace v Blackpool
Derby Co v Burnley
Doncaster R v Bristol C
Hull C v Reading
Ipswich T v Leeds U
Leicester C v Southampton
Middlesbrough v Coventry C
Millwall v Barnsley
Portsmouth v Cardiff C
Watford v Birmingham C

npower Football League One
Bournemouth v Walsall
Brentford v Tranmere R
Bury v Charlton Ath
Colchester U v Oldham Ath
Exeter C v Chesterfield
Huddersfield T v Wycombe W

Leyton Orient v Carlisle U
Milton Keynes D v Stevenage
Preston NE v Notts Co
Rochdale v Hartlepool U
Sheffield W v Scunthorpe U
Yeovil T v Sheffield U

npower Football League Two
Accrington S v Burton Alb
Bradford C v Barnet
Bristol R v Hereford U
Cheltenham T v Crawley T
Dagenham & R v Torquay U
Macclesfield T v AFC Wimbledon
Northampton T v Morecambe
Oxford U v Aldershot T
Plymouth Arg v Crewe Alex
Port Vale v Southend U
Rotherham U v Gillingham
Shrewsbury T v Swindon T

Sunday, 28 August 2011
Barclays Premier League
Manchester U v Arsenal* (4.00)
Tottenham H v Manchester C† (1.30)

npower Football League Championship
Nottingham F v West Ham U* (1.15)

Saturday, 3 September 2011
npower Football League One
Carlisle U v Milton Keynes D
Chesterfield v Leyton Orient
Hartlepool U v Exeter C
Notts Co v Bournemouth
Oldham Ath v Huddersfield T
Scunthorpe U v Colchester U
Sheffield U v Bury
Stevenage v Rochdale
Tranmere R v Yeovil T
Walsall v Brentford
Wycombe W v Preston NE

npower Football League Two
AFC Wimbledon v Port Vale
Aldershot T v Cheltenham T
Barnet v Accrington S
Burton Alb v Plymouth Arg
Crawley T v Bristol R
Crewe Alex v Oxford U
Gillingham v Shrewsbury T
Hereford U v Dagenham & R
Morecambe v Bradford C
Southend U v Northampton T
Swindon T v Rotherham U* (12.15)
Torquay U v Macclesfield T

Monday, 5 September 2011
npower Football League One
Charlton Ath v Sheffield W* (7.45)

Saturday, 10 September 2011
Barclays Premier League
Arsenal v Swansea C
Bolton W v Manchester U† (5.30)
Everton v Aston Villa
Manchester C v Wigan Ath
Stoke C v Liverpool
Sunderland v Chelsea
Wolverhampton W v Tottenham H

npower Football League Championship
Barnsley v Leicester C
Birmingham C v Millwall
Blackpool v Ipswich T
Bristol C v Brighton & HA
Burnley v Middlesbrough
Cardiff C v Doncaster R
Coventry C v Derby Co* (5.20)
Leeds U v Crystal Palace
Peterborough U v Hull C
Reading v Watford
Southampton v Nottingham F
West Ham U v Portsmouth

npower Football League One
Bournemouth v Chesterfield
Bury v Rochdale
Carlisle U v Hartlepool U
Charlton Ath v Exeter C
Colchester U v Leyton Orient
Huddersfield T v Tranmere R
Notts Co v Walsall
Oldham Ath v Stevenage
Preston NE v Yeovil T
Scunthorpe U v Sheffield U
Sheffield W v Milton Keynes D
Wycombe W v Brentford

npower Football League Two
Aldershot T v AFC Wimbledon
Bradford C v Bristol R
Cheltenham T v Macclesfield T
Crewe Alex v Barnet
Gillingham v Accrington S
Morecambe v Crawley T
Northampton T v Torquay U
Oxford U v Burton Alb
Plymouth Arg v Port Vale
Rotherham U v Dagenham & R
Shrewsbury T v Hereford U
Swindon T v Southend U

Sunday, 11 September 2011
Barclays Premier League
Norwich C v WBA* (1.30)
Fulham v Blackburn R* (4.00)

Monday, 12 September 2011
Barclays Premier League
QPR v Newcastle U* (8.00)

Tuesday, 13 September 2011
npower Football League One
Brentford v Colchester U
Chesterfield v Bury
Exeter C v Notts Co
Hartlepool U v Preston NE
Leyton Orient v Bournemouth
Milton Keynes D v Charlton Ath
Rochdale v Scunthorpe U
Sheffield U v Huddersfield T
Stevenage v Sheffield W
Tranmere R v Carlisle U
Walsall v Oldham Ath
Yeovil T v Wycombe W

npower Football League Two
AFC Wimbledon v Northampton T
Accrington S v Rotherham U
Barnet v Plymouth Arg
Bristol R v Shrewsbury T
Burton Alb v Crewe Alex
Crawley T v Swindon T
Dagenham & R v Oxford U
Hereford U v Aldershot T
Macclesfield T v Morecambe
Port Vale v Bradford C
Southend U v Gillingham
Torquay U v Cheltenham T

Saturday, 17 September 2011
Barclays Premier League
Aston Villa v Newcastle U
Blackburn R v Arsenal* (12.45)
Bolton W v Norwich C
Everton v Wigan Ath
Fulham v Manchester C
Sunderland v Stoke C
Swansea C v WBA
Wolverhampton W v QPR

npower Football League Championship
Barnsley v Watford
Blackpool v Cardiff C
Crystal Palace v Middlesbrough
Hull C v Portsmouth
Ipswich T v Coventry C
Leeds U v Bristol C

Leicester C v Brighton & HA
Millwall v West Ham U
Nottingham F v Derby Co
Peterborough U v Burnley
Reading v Doncaster R
Southampton v Birmingham C* (5.20)

npower Football League One
Brentford v Preston NE
Chesterfield v Carlisle U
Exeter C v Bournemouth
Hartlepool U v Bury
Leyton Orient v Oldham Ath
Milton Keynes D v Huddersfield T
Rochdale v Charlton Ath
Sheffield U v Colchester U
Stevenage v Notts Co
Tranmere R v Wycombe W
Walsall v Scunthorpe U
Yeovil T v Sheffield W

npower Football League Two
AFC Wimbledon v Cheltenham T
Accrington S v Crewe Alex
Barnet v Oxford U
Bristol R v Aldershot T
Burton Alb v Swindon T
Crawley T v Bradford C
Dagenham & R v Morecambe
Hereford U v Gillingham
Macclesfield T v Northampton T
Port Vale v Shrewsbury T
Southend U v Plymouth Arg
Torquay U v Rotherham U

Sunday, 18 September 2011
Barclays Premier League
Tottenham H v Liverpool* (1.30)
Manchester U v Chelsea* (4.00)

Friday, 23 September 2011
npower Football League Championship
Brighton & HA v Leeds U* (7.45)

Saturday, 24 September 2011
Barclays Premier League
Arsenal v Bolton W
Chelsea v Swansea C
Liverpool v Wolverhampton W
Manchester C v Everton* (12.45)
Newcastle U v Blackburn R
Stoke C v Manchester U† (5.30)
WBA v Fulham
Wigan Ath v Tottenham H

npower Football League Championship
Birmingham C v Barnsley
Bristol C v Hull C
Burnley v Southampton
Coventry C v Reading
Derby Co v Millwall
Doncaster R v Crystal Palace
Middlesbrough v Ipswich T
Portsmouth v Blackpool
Watford v Nottingham F§ (5.15)
West Ham U v Peterborough U

npower Football League One
Bournemouth v Hartlepool U
Bury v Milton Keynes D
Carlisle U v Stevenage
Charlton Ath v Chesterfield
Colchester U v Walsall
Huddersfield T v Leyton Orient
Notts Co v Rochdale
Oldham Ath v Brentford
Preston NE v Tranmere R
Scunthorpe U v Yeovil T
Sheffield W v Exeter C
Wycombe W v Sheffield U

npower Football League Two
Aldershot T v Crawley T
Bradford C v AFC Wimbledon
Cheltenham T v Hereford U
Crewe Alex v Port Vale
Gillingham v Burton Alb
Morecambe v Bristol R
Northampton T v Dagenham & R
Oxford U v Accrington S
Plymouth Arg v Macclesfield T
Rotherham U v Southend U
Shrewsbury T v Torquay U
Swindon T v Barnet

Sunday, 25 September 2011
Barclays Premier League
QPR v Aston Villa* (4.00)

npower Football League Championship
Cardiff C v Leicester C* (1.30)

Monday, 26 September 2011
Barclays Premier League
Norwich C v Sunderland* (8.00)

Tuesday, 27 September 2011
npower Football League Championship
Birmingham C v Leeds U
Brighton & HA v Crystal Palace
Bristol C v Reading

Burnley v Nottingham F
Cardiff C v Southampton
Coventry C v Blackpool
Derby Co v Barnsley
Doncaster R v Hull C
Middlesbrough v Leicester C
Portsmouth v Peterborough U
Watford v Millwall
West Ham U v Ipswich T

Saturday, 1 October 2011
Barclays Premier League
Aston Villa v Wigan Ath
Blackburn R v Manchester C
Everton v Liverpool* (12.45)
Fulham v QPR
Manchester U v Norwich C
Sunderland v WBA
Swansea C v Stoke C
Wolverhampton W v Newcastle U

npower Football League Championship
Barnsley v Coventry C
Blackpool v Bristol C
Crystal Palace v West Ham U
Hull C v Cardiff C
Ipswich T v Brighton & HA
Leeds U v Portsmouth
Leicester C v Derby Co
Millwall v Burnley
Nottingham F v Birmingham C* (5.20)
Peterborough U v Doncaster R
Reading v Middlesbrough
Southampton v Watford

npower Football League One
Brentford v Huddersfield T
Chesterfield v Colchester U
Exeter C v Oldham Ath
Hartlepool U v Sheffield W
Leyton Orient v Preston NE
Milton Keynes D v Notts Co
Rochdale v Wycombe W
Sheffield U v Charlton Ath
Stevenage v Scunthorpe U
Tranmere R v Bournemouth
Walsall v Carlisle U
Yeovil T v Bury

npower Football League Two
AFC Wimbledon v Gillingham
Accrington S v Aldershot T
Barnet v Northampton T
Bristol R v Cheltenham T
Burton Alb v Bradford C
Crawley T v Plymouth Arg

Dagenham & R v Crewe Alex
Hereford U v Oxford U
Macclesfield T v Swindon T
Port Vale v Rotherham U
Southend U v Shrewsbury T
Torquay U v Morecambe

Sunday, 2 October 2011
Barclays Premier League
Bolton W v Chelsea* (1.30)
Tottenham H v Arsenal* (4.00)

Saturday, 8 October 2011
npower Football League One
Bournemouth v Rochdale
Bury v Exeter C
Carlisle U v Brentford
Charlton Ath v Tranmere R
Colchester U v Yeovil T
Huddersfield T v Stevenage
Notts Co v Hartlepool U
Oldham Ath v Milton Keynes D
Preston NE v Sheffield U
Scunthorpe U v Leyton Orient
Sheffield W v Chesterfield
Wycombe W v Walsall

npower Football League Two
Aldershot T v Macclesfield T
Bradford C v Torquay U
Cheltenham T v Dagenham & R
Crewe Alex v Southend U
Gillingham v Port Vale
Morecambe v AFC Wimbledon
Northampton T v Crawley T
Oxford U v Bristol R
Plymouth Arg v Accrington S
Rotherham U v Burton Alb
Shrewsbury T v Barnet
Swindon T v Hereford U

Friday, 14 October 2011
npower Football League Championship
Doncaster R v Leeds U* (7.45)

Saturday, 15 October 2011
Barclays Premier League
Arsenal v Sunderland
Chelsea v Everton† (5.30)
Liverpool v Manchester U* (12.45)
Manchester C v Aston Villa
Norwich C v Swansea C
QPR v Blackburn R
Stoke C v Fulham
WBA v Wolverhampton W (12.00)
Wigan Ath v Bolton W

npower Football League Championship
Brighton & HA v Hull C
Bristol C v Peterborough U
Burnley v Reading
Cardiff C v Ipswich T
Coventry C v Nottingham F
Derby Co v Southampton
Middlesbrough v Millwall
Portsmouth v Barnsley* (5.20)
Watford v Crystal Palace
West Ham U v Blackpool

npower Football League One
Brentford v Scunthorpe U
Chesterfield v Notts Co
Exeter C v Huddersfield T
Hartlepool U v Wycombe W
Leyton Orient v Bury
Milton Keynes D v Bournemouth
Rochdale v Colchester U
Sheffield U v Sheffield W
Stevenage v Charlton Ath
Tranmere R v Oldham Ath
Walsall v Preston NE
Yeovil T v Carlisle U

npower Football League Two
AFC Wimbledon v Crewe Alex
Accrington S v Swindon T
Barnet v Aldershot T
Bristol R v Rotherham U
Burton Alb v Cheltenham T
Crawley T v Shrewsbury T
Dagenham & R v Plymouth Arg
Hereford U v Bradford C
Macclesfield T v Oxford U
Port Vale v Northampton T
Southend U v Morecambe
Torquay U v Gillingham

Sunday, 16 October 2011
Barclays Premier League
Manchester C v Aston Villa* (1.30)
Newcastle U v Tottenham H* (4.00)

npower Football League Championship
Birmingham C v Leicester C§ (1.00)

Tuesday, 18 October 2011
npower Football League Championship
Barnsley v Burnley
Blackpool v Doncaster R
Crystal Palace v Bristol C
Hull C v Birmingham C
Ipswich T v Portsmouth
Leeds U v Coventry C

Leicester C v Watford
Millwall v Brighton & HA
Nottingham F v Middlesbrough
Peterborough U v Cardiff C
Reading v Derby Co
Southampton v West Ham U

Saturday, 22 October 2011
Barclays Premier League
Arsenal v Stoke C
Aston Villa v WBA
Blackburn R v Tottenham H
Bolton W v Sunderland
Fulham v Everton
Liverpool v Norwich C† (5.30)
Newcastle U v Wigan Ath
Wolverhampton W v Swansea C* (12.45)

npower Football League Championship
Blackpool v Nottingham F
Brighton & HA v West Ham U
Bristol C v Birmingham C
Cardiff C v Barnsley
Coventry C v Burnley
Hull C v Watford
Ipswich T v Crystal Palace
Leicester C v Millwall
Middlesbrough v Derby Co
Peterborough U v Leeds U
Portsmouth v Doncaster R
Reading v Southampton* (5.20)

npower Football League One
Bournemouth v Bury
Charlton Ath v Carlisle U
Chesterfield v Hartlepool U
Exeter C v Rochdale
Huddersfield T v Preston NE
Leyton Orient v Sheffield U
Milton Keynes D v Scunthorpe U
Notts Co v Brentford
Oldham Ath v Wycombe W
Sheffield W v Colchester U
Stevenage v Yeovil T
Tranmere R v Walsall

npower Football League Two
AFC Wimbledon v Crawley T
Accrington S v Cheltenham T
Bradford C v Northampton T
Burton Alb v Bristol R
Crewe Alex v Macclesfield T
Dagenham & R v Aldershot T
Gillingham v Oxford U
Hereford U v Barnet
Plymouth Arg v Swindon T

Port Vale v Morecambe
Rotherham U v Shrewsbury T
Southend U v Torquay U

Sunday, 23 October 2011
Barclays Premier League
Manchester U v Manchester C* (1.30)
QPR v Chelsea* (4.00)

Tuesday, 25 October 2011
npower Football League One
Brentford v Stevenage
Bury v Notts Co
Carlisle U v Sheffield W
Colchester U v Bournemouth
Hartlepool U v Tranmere R
Preston NE v Oldham Ath
Rochdale v Chesterfield
Scunthorpe U v Huddersfield T
Sheffield U v Milton Keynes D
Walsall v Exeter C
Wycombe W v Charlton Ath
Yeovil T v Leyton Orient

npower Football League Two
Aldershot T v Burton Alb
Barnet v Southend U
Bristol R v Port Vale
Cheltenham T v Crewe Alex
Crawley T v Dagenham & R
Macclesfield T v Bradford C
Morecambe v Rotherham U
Northampton T v Hereford U
Oxford U v Plymouth Arg
Shrewsbury T v Accrington S
Swindon T v Gillingham
Torquay U v AFC Wimbledon

Saturday, 29 October 2011
Barclays Premier League
Chelsea v Arsenal* (12.45)
Everton v Manchester U (12.00)
Manchester C v Wolverhampton W
Norwich C v Blackburn R
Sunderland v Aston Villa
Swansea C v Bolton W
WBA v Liverpool† (5.30)
Wigan Ath v Fulham

npower Football League Championship
Barnsley v Bristol C
Birmingham C v Brighton & HA
Burnley v Blackpool* (5.20)
Crystal Palace v Reading
Derby Co v Portsmouth
Doncaster R v Coventry C

Millwall v Ipswich T
Nottingham F v Hull C
Southampton v Middlesbrough
Watford v Peterborough U
West Ham U v Leicester C

npower Football League One
Brentford v Chesterfield
Bury v Stevenage
Carlisle U v Oldham Ath
Colchester U v Notts Co
Hartlepool U v Charlton Ath
Preston NE v Bournemouth
Rochdale v Leyton Orient
Scunthorpe U v Tranmere R
Sheffield U v Exeter C
Walsall v Milton Keynes D
Wycombe W v Sheffield W
Yeovil T v Huddersfield T

npower Football League Two
Aldershot T v Crewe Alex
Barnet v Burton Alb
Bristol R v Dagenham & R
Cheltenham T v Plymouth Arg
Crawley T v Accrington S
Macclesfield T v Southend U
Morecambe v Gillingham
Northampton T v Rotherham U
Oxford U v Port Vale
Shrewsbury T v AFC Wimbledon
Swindon T v Bradford C
Torquay U v Hereford U

Sunday, 30 October 2011
Barclays Premier League
Tottenham H v QPR* (4.00)

npower Football League Championship
Leeds U v Cardiff C* (1.15)

Monday, 31 October 2011
Barclays Premier League
Stoke C v Newcastle U* (8.00)

Tuesday, 1 November 2011
npower Football League Championship
Barnsley v Hull C
Birmingham C v Ipswich T
Burnley v Leicester C
Crystal Palace v Portsmouth
Derby Co v Cardiff C
Doncaster R v Middlesbrough
Leeds U v Blackpool
Millwall v Coventry C
Nottingham F v Reading

Southampton v Peterborough U
Watford v Brighton & HA
West Ham U v Bristol C

Saturday, 5 November 2011
Barclays Premier League
Arsenal v WBA
Aston Villa v Norwich C
Blackburn R v Chelsea
Bolton W v Stoke C
Liverpool v Swansea C
Manchester U v Sunderland
Newcastle U v Everton* (12.45)
QPR v Manchester C† (5.30)

npower Football League Championship
Blackpool v Millwall
Brighton & HA v Barnsley
Bristol C v Burnley
Cardiff C v Crystal Palace
Coventry C v Southampton
Hull C v West Ham U
Ipswich T v Doncaster R
Leicester C v Leeds U
Middlesbrough v Watford* (1.15)
Peterborough U v Derby Co
Portsmouth v Nottingham F
Reading v Birmingham C

npower Football League One
Bournemouth v Scunthorpe U
Charlton v Preston NE
Chesterfield v Yeovil T
Exeter C v Carlisle U
Huddersfield T v Walsall
Leyton Orient v Hartlepool U
Milton Keynes D v Rochdale
Notts Co v Wycombe W
Oldham Ath v Bury
Sheffield W v Brentford
Stevenage v Sheffield U
Tranmere R v Colchester U

npower Football League Two
AFC Wimbledon v Barnet
Accrington S v Bristol R
Bradford C v Cheltenham T
Burton Alb v Macclesfield T
Crewe Alex v Torquay U
Dagenham & R v Shrewsbury T
Gillingham v Northampton T
Hereford U v Crawley T
Plymouth Arg v Morecambe
Port Vale v Swindon T
Rotherham U v Aldershot T
Southend U v Oxford U

Sunday, 6 November 2011
Barclays Premier League
Wolverhampton W v Wigan Ath* (1.30)
Fulham v Tottenham H* (4.00)

Saturday, 19 November 2011
Barclays Premier League
Everton v Wolverhampton W
Manchester C v Newcastle U
Norwich C v Arsenal* (12.45)
Stoke C v QPR
Sunderland v Fulham
Swansea C v Manchester U† (5.30)
WBA v Bolton W
Wigan Ath v Blackburn R

npower Football League Championship
Barnsley v Doncaster R
Birmingham C v Peterborough U
Burnley v Leeds U§ (12.45)
Coventry C v West Ham U
Derby Co v Hull C
Leicester C v Crystal Palace
Middlesbrough v Blackpool
Millwall v Bristol C
Nottingham F v Ipswich T
Reading v Cardiff C
Southampton v Brighton & HA
Watford v Portsmouth

npower Football League One
Brentford v Charlton Ath
Colchester U v Milton Keynes D
Huddersfield T v Notts Co
Leyton Orient v Stevenage
Oldham Ath v Chesterfield
Preston NE v Rochdale
Scunthorpe U v Hartlepool U
Sheffield U v Carlisle U
Tranmere R v Sheffield W
Walsall v Bury
Wycombe W v Bournemouth
Yeovil T v Exeter C

npower Football League Two
AFC Wimbledon v Swindon T
Aldershot T v Gillingham
Bradford C v Rotherham U
Bristol R v Barnet
Cheltenham T v Port Vale
Crawley T v Oxford U
Dagenham & R v Southend U
Hereford U v Burton Alb
Macclesfield T v Accrington S
Morecambe v Crewe Alex
Northampton T v Shrewsbury T

Torquay U v Plymouth Arg

Sunday, 20 November 2011
Barclays Premier League
Chelsea v Liverpool* (4.00)

Monday, 21 November 2011
Barclays Premier League
Tottenham H v Aston Villa* (8.00)

Saturday, 26 November 2011
Barclays Premier League
Arsenal v Fulham† (5.30)
Bolton W v Everton
Chelsea v Wolverhampton W
Manchester U v Newcastle U
Norwich C v QPR
Sunderland v Wigan Ath
WBA v Tottenham H

npower Football League Championship
Blackpool v Birmingham C
Brighton & HA v Coventry C
Bristol C v Southampton
Cardiff C v Nottingham F
Crystal Palace v Millwall
Doncaster R v Watford
Hull C v Burnley
Ipswich T v Reading
Leeds U v Barnsley
Peterborough U v Middlesbrough
Portsmouth v Leicester C
West Ham U v Derby Co

npower Football League One
Bournemouth v Oldham Ath
Bury v Preston NE
Carlisle U v Colchester U
Charlton Ath v Huddersfield T
Chesterfield v Sheffield U
Exeter C v Tranmere R
Hartlepool U v Yeovil T
Milton Keynes D v Wycombe W
Notts Co v Scunthorpe U
Rochdale v Brentford
Sheffield W v Leyton Orient
Stevenage v Walsall

npower Football League Two
Accrington S v Dagenham & R
Barnet v Macclesfield T
Burton Alb v AFC Wimbledon
Crewe Alex v Hereford U
Gillingham v Bradford C
Oxford U v Cheltenham T
Plymouth Arg v Northampton T

Port Vale v Torquay U
Rotherham U v Crawley T
Shrewsbury T v Morecambe
Southend U v Bristol R
Swindon T v Aldershot T

Sunday, 27 November 2011
Barclays Premier League
Swansea C v Aston Villa* (1.30)
Liverpool v Manchester C* (4.00)

Monday, 28 November 2011
Barclays Premier League
Stoke C v Blackburn R* (8.00)

Tuesday, 29 November 2011
npower Football League Championship
Barnsley v Crystal Palace
Birmingham C v Portsmouth
Burnley v Ipswich T
Coventry C v Cardiff C
Derby Co v Brighton & HA
Leicester C v Blackpool
Middlesbrough v West Ham U
Millwall v Doncaster R
Nottingham F v Leeds U
Reading v Peterborough U
Southampton v Hull C
Watford v Bristol C

Saturday, 3 December 2011
Barclays Premier League
Aston Villa v Manchester U
Blackburn R v Swansea C
Everton v Stoke C
Fulham v Liverpool
Manchester C v Norwich C
Newcastle U v Chelsea
QPR v WBA
Tottenham H v Bolton W
Wigan Ath v Arsenal
Wolverhampton W v Sunderland

npower Football League Championship
Blackpool v Reading
Brighton & HA v Nottingham F
Bristol C v Middlesbrough
Cardiff C v Birmingham C
Crystal Palace v Derby Co
Doncaster R v Southampton
Hull C v Leicester C
Ipswich T v Watford
Leeds U v Millwall
Peterborough U v Barnsley
Portsmouth v Coventry C
West Ham U v Burnley

Saturday, 10 December 2011

Barclays Premier League
Arsenal v Everton
Bolton W v Aston Villa
Chelsea v Manchester C
Liverpool v QPR
Manchester U v Wolverhampton W
Norwich C v Newcastle U
Stoke C v Tottenham H
Sunderland v Blackburn R
Swansea C v Fulham
WBA v Wigan Ath

npower Football League Championship
Barnsley v Ipswich T
Birmingham C v Doncaster R
Burnley v Portsmouth
Coventry C v Hull C
Derby Co v Bristol C
Leicester C v Peterborough U
Middlesbrough v Brighton & HA
Millwall v Cardiff C
Nottingham F v Crystal Palace
Reading v West Ham U
Southampton v Blackpool
Watford v Leeds U

npower Football League One
Brentford v Hartlepool U
Colchester U v Bury
Huddersfield T v Bournemouth
Leyton Orient v Exeter C
Oldham Ath v Sheffield W
Preston NE v Stevenage
Scunthorpe U v Carlisle U
Sheffield U v Rochdale
Tranmere R v Milton Keynes D
Walsall v Charlton Ath
Wycombe W v Chesterfield
Yeovil T v Notts Co

npower Football League Two
AFC Wimbledon v Accrington S
Aldershot T v Shrewsbury T
Bradford C v Plymouth Arg
Bristol R v Swindon T
Cheltenham T v Southend U
Crawley T v Burton Alb
Dagenham & R v Port Vale
Hereford U v Rotherham U
Macclesfield T v Gillingham
Morecambe v Oxford U
Northampton T v Crewe Alex
Torquay U v Barnet

Saturday, 17 December 2011

Barclays Premier League
Aston Villa v Liverpool
Blackburn R v WBA
Everton v Norwich C
Fulham v Bolton W
Manchester C v Arsenal
Newcastle U v Swansea C
QPR v Manchester U
Tottenham H v Sunderland
Wigan Ath v Chelsea
Wolverhampton W v Stoke C

npower Football League Championship
Blackpool v Watford
Brighton & HA v Burnley
Bristol C v Nottingham F
Cardiff C v Middlesbrough
Crystal Palace v Birmingham C
Doncaster R v Leicester C
Hull C v Millwall
Ipswich T v Derby Co
Leeds U v Reading
Peterborough U v Coventry C
Portsmouth v Southampton
West Ham U v Barnsley

npower Football League One
Bournemouth v Sheffield U
Bury v Brentford
Carlisle U v Wycombe W
Charlton Ath v Oldham Ath
Chesterfield v Walsall
Exeter C v Scunthorpe U
Hartlepool U v Colchester U
Milton Keynes D v Preston NE
Notts Co v Leyton Orient
Rochdale v Yeovil T
Sheffield W v Huddersfield T
Stevenage v Tranmere R

npower Football League Two
Accrington S v Torquay U
Barnet v Cheltenham T
Burton Alb v Dagenham & R
Crewe Alex v Crawley T
Gillingham v Bristol R
Oxford U v Northampton T
Plymouth Arg v Hereford U
Port Vale v Aldershot T
Rotherham U v AFC Wimbledon
Shrewsbury T v Macclesfield T
Southend U v Bradford C
Swindon T v Morecambe

Tuesday, 20 December 2011
Barclays Premier League
QPR v Sunderland
Tottenham H v Chelsea
Wigan Ath v Liverpool
Wolverhampton W v Norwich C

Wednesday, 21 December 2011
Barclays Premier League
Aston Villa v Arsenal
Blackburn R v Bolton W
Everton v Swansea C
Fulham v Manchester U
Manchester C v Stoke C
Newcastle U v WBA

Monday, 26 December 2011
Barclays Premier League
Arsenal v Wolverhampton W
Bolton W v Newcastle U
Chelsea v Fulham (1.00)
Liverpool v Blackburn R
Manchester U v Wigan Ath
Norwich C v Tottenham H
Stoke C v Aston Villa
Sunderland v Everton
Swansea C v QPR
WBA v Manchester C

npower Football League Championship
Barnsley v Blackpool
Birmingham C v West Ham U
Burnley v Doncaster R
Coventry C v Bristol C
Derby Co v Leeds U
Leicester C v Ipswich T
Middlesbrough v Hull C
Millwall v Portsmouth
Nottingham F v Peterborough U
Reading v Brighton & HA
Southampton v Crystal Palace
Watford v Cardiff C

npower Football League One
Brentford v Bournemouth
Colchester U v Stevenage
Huddersfield T v Chesterfield
Leyton Orient v Milton Keynes D
Oldham Ath v Hartlepool U
Preston NE v Carlisle U
Scunthorpe U v Bury
Sheffield U v Notts Co
Tranmere R v Rochdale
Walsall v Sheffield W
Wycombe W v Exeter C
Yeovil T v Charlton Ath

npower Football League Two
AFC Wimbledon v Oxford U
Aldershot T v Southend U
Bradford C v Crewe Alex
Bristol R v Plymouth Arg
Cheltenham T v Shrewsbury T
Crawley T v Gillingham
Dagenham & R v Barnet
Hereford U v Port Vale
Macclesfield T v Rotherham U
Morecambe v Accrington S
Northampton T v Burton Alb
Torquay U v Swindon T

Saturday, 31 December 2011
Barclays Premier League
Arsenal v QPR
Bolton W v Wolverhampton W
Chelsea v Aston Villa
Liverpool v Newcastle U (12.45)
Manchester U v Blackburn R
Norwich C v Fulham
Stoke C v Wigan Ath
Sunderland v Manchester C
Swansea C v Tottenham H
WBA v Everton

npower Football League Championship
Barnsley v Leeds U
Birmingham C v Blackpool
Burnley v Hull C
Coventry C v Brighton & HA
Derby Co v West Ham U
Leicester C v Portsmouth
Middlesbrough v Peterborough U
Millwall v Crystal Palace
Nottingham F v Cardiff C
Reading v Ipswich T
Southampton v Bristol C
Watford v Doncaster R

npower Football League One
Brentford v Milton Keynes D
Colchester U v Exeter C
Huddersfield T v Carlisle U
Leyton Orient v Charlton Ath
Oldham Ath v Notts Co
Preston NE v Sheffield W
Scunthorpe U v Chesterfield
Sheffield U v Hartlepool U
Tranmere R v Bury
Walsall v Rochdale
Wycombe W v Stevenage
Yeovil T v Bournemouth

npower Football League Two
AFC Wimbledon v Southend U
Aldershot T v Plymouth Arg
Bradford C v Shrewsbury T
Bristol R v Crewe Alex
Cheltenham T v Rotherham U
Crawley T v Barnet
Dagenham & R v Gillingham
Hereford U v Accrington S
Macclesfield T v Port Vale
Morecambe v Burton Alb
Northampton T v Swindon T
Torquay U v Oxford U

Monday, 2 January 2012
Barclays Premier League
Aston Villa v Swansea C
Blackburn R v Stoke C
Everton v Bolton W
Fulham v Arsenal
Manchester C v Liverpool
Newcastle U v Manchester U
QPR v Norwich C
Tottenham H v WBA
Wigan Ath v Sunderland
Wolverhampton W v Chelsea

npower Football League Championship
Blackpool v Middlesbrough
Brighton & HA v Southampton
Bristol C v Millwall
Cardiff C v Reading
Crystal Palace v Leicester C
Doncaster R v Barnsley
Hull C v Derby Co
Ipswich T v Nottingham F
Leeds U v Burnley
Peterborough U v Birmingham C
Portsmouth v Watford
West Ham U v Coventry C

npower Football League One
Bournemouth v Wycombe W
Bury v Walsall
Carlisle U v Sheffield U
Charlton Ath v Brentford
Chesterfield v Oldham Ath
Exeter C v Yeovil T
Hartlepool U v Scunthorpe U
Milton Keynes D v Colchester U
Notts Co v Huddersfield T
Rochdale v Preston NE
Sheffield W v Tranmere R
Stevenage v Leyton Orient

npower Football League Two
Accrington S v Macclesfield T
Barnet v Bristol R
Burton Alb v Hereford U
Crewe Alex v Morecambe
Gillingham v Aldershot T
Oxford U v Crawley T
Plymouth Arg v Torquay U
Port Vale v Cheltenham T
Rotherham U v Bradford C
Shrewsbury T v Northampton T
Southend U v Dagenham & R
Swindon T v AFC Wimbledon

Saturday, 7 January 2012
npower Football League One
Carlisle U v Leyton Orient
Charlton Ath v Bury
Chesterfield v Exeter C
Hartlepool U v Rochdale
Notts Co v Preston NE
Oldham Ath v Colchester U
Scunthorpe U v Sheffield W
Sheffield U v Yeovil T
Stevenage v Milton Keynes D
Tranmere R v Brentford
Walsall v Bournemouth
Wycombe W v Huddersfield T

npower Football League Two
AFC Wimbledon v Macclesfield T
Aldershot T v Oxford U
Barnet v Bradford C
Burton Alb v Accrington S
Crawley T v Cheltenham T
Crewe Alex v Plymouth Arg
Gillingham v Rotherham U
Hereford U v Bristol R
Morecambe v Northampton T
Southend U v Port Vale
Swindon T v Shrewsbury T
Torquay U v Dagenham & R

Saturday, 14 January 2012
Barclays Premier League
Aston Villa v Everton
Blackburn R v Fulham
Chelsea v Sunderland
Liverpool v Stoke C
Manchester U v Bolton W
Newcastle U v QPR
Swansea C v Arsenal
Tottenham H v Wolverhampton W
WBA v Norwich C
Wigan Ath v Manchester C

npower Football League Championship

Brighton & HA v Bristol C
Crystal Palace v Leeds U
Derby Co v Coventry C
Doncaster R v Cardiff C
Hull C v Peterborough U
Ipswich T v Blackpool
Leicester C v Barnsley
Middlesbrough v Burnley
Millwall v Birmingham C
Nottingham F v Southampton
Portsmouth v West Ham U
Watford v Reading

npower Football League One

Bournemouth v Notts Co
Brentford v Walsall
Bury v Sheffield U
Colchester U v Scunthorpe U
Exeter C v Hartlepool U
Huddersfield T v Oldham Ath
Leyton Orient v Chesterfield
Milton Keynes D v Carlisle U
Preston NE v Wycombe W
Rochdale v Stevenage
Sheffield W v Charlton Ath
Yeovil T v Tranmere R

npower Football League Two

Accrington S v Barnet
Bradford C v Morecambe
Bristol R v Crawley T
Cheltenham T v Aldershot T
Dagenham & R v Hereford U
Macclesfield T v Torquay U
Northampton v Southend U
Oxford U v Crewe Alex
Plymouth Arg v Burton Alb
Port Vale v AFC Wimbledon
Rotherham U v Swindon T
Shrewsbury T v Gillingham

Saturday, 21 January 2012
Barclays Premier League

Arsenal v Manchester U
Bolton W v Liverpool
Everton v Blackburn R
Fulham v Newcastle U
Manchester C v Tottenham H
Norwich C v Chelsea
QPR v Wigan Ath
Stoke C v WBA
Sunderland v Swansea C
Wolverhampton W v Aston Villa

npower Football League Championship

Barnsley v Millwall
Birmingham C v Watford
Blackpool v Crystal Palace
Bristol C v Doncaster R
Burnley v Derby Co
Cardiff C v Portsmouth
Coventry C v Middlesbrough
Leeds U v Ipswich T
Peterborough U v Brighton & HA
Reading v Hull C
Southampton v Leicester C
West Ham U v Nottingham F

npower Football League One

Bournemouth v Tranmere R
Bury v Yeovil T
Carlisle U v Walsall
Charlton Ath v Sheffield U
Colchester U v Chesterfield
Huddersfield T v Brentford
Notts Co v Milton Keynes D
Oldham Ath v Exeter C
Preston NE v Leyton Orient
Scunthorpe U v Stevenage
Sheffield W v Hartlepool U
Wycombe W v Rochdale

npower Football League Two

Aldershot T v Accrington S
Bradford C v Burton Alb
Cheltenham T v Bristol R
Crewe Alex v Dagenham & R
Gillingham v AFC Wimbledon
Morecambe v Torquay U
Northampton T v Barnet
Oxford U v Hereford U
Plymouth Arg v Crawley T
Rotherham U v Port Vale
Shrewsbury T v Southend U
Swindon T v Macclesfield T

Saturday, 28 January 2012
npower Football League One

Brentford v Wycombe W
Chesterfield v Bournemouth
Exeter C v Charlton Ath
Hartlepool U v Carlisle U
Leyton Orient v Colchester U
Milton Keynes D v Sheffield W
Rochdale v Bury
Sheffield U v Scunthorpe U
Stevenage v Oldham Ath
Tranmere R v Huddersfield T
Walsall v Notts Co
Yeovil T v Preston NE

npower Football League Two
AFC Wimbledon v Aldershot T
Accrington S v Gillingham
Barnet v Crewe Alex
Bristol R v Bradford C
Burton Alb v Oxford U
Crawley T v Morecambe
Dagenham & R v Rotherham U
Hereford U v Shrewsbury T
Macclesfield T v Cheltenham T
Port Vale v Plymouth Arg
Southend U v Swindon T
Torquay U v Northampton T

Tuesday, 31 January 2012
Barclays Premier League
Bolton W v Arsenal
Manchester U v Stoke C
Sunderland v Norwich C
Swansea C v Chelsea
Tottenham H v Wigan Ath
Wolverhampton W v Liverpool

npower Football League Championship
Barnsley v Derby Co
Blackpool v Coventry C
Crystal Palace v Brighton & HA
Hull C v Doncaster R
Ipswich T v West Ham U
Leeds U v Birmingham C
Leicester C v Middlesbrough
Millwall v Watford
Nottingham F v Burnley
Peterborough U v Portsmouth
Reading v Bristol C
Southampton v Cardiff C

Wednesday, 1 February 2012
Barclays Premier League
Aston Villa v QPR
Blackburn R v Newcastle U
Everton v Manchester C
Fulham v WBA

Saturday, 4 February 2012
Barclays Premier League
Arsenal v Blackburn R
Chelsea v Manchester U
Liverpool v Tottenham H
Manchester C v Fulham
Newcastle U v Aston Villa
Norwich C v Bolton W
QPR v Wolverhampton W
Stoke C v Sunderland
WBA v Swansea C
Wigan Ath v Everton

npower Football League Championship
Birmingham C v Southampton
Brighton & HA v Leicester C
Bristol C v Leeds U
Burnley v Peterborough U
Cardiff C v Blackpool
Coventry C v Ipswich T
Derby Co v Nottingham F
Doncaster R v Reading
Middlesbrough v Crystal Palace
Portsmouth v Hull C
Watford v Barnsley
West Ham U v Millwall

npower Football League One
Bournemouth v Exeter C
Bury v Hartlepool U
Carlisle U v Chesterfield
Charlton Ath v Rochdale
Colchester U v Sheffield U
Huddersfield T v Milton Keynes D
Notts Co v Stevenage
Oldham Ath v Leyton Orient
Preston NE v Brentford
Scunthorpe U v Walsall
Sheffield W v Yeovil T
Wycombe W v Tranmere R

npower Football League Two
Aldershot T v Bristol R
Bradford C v Crawley T
Cheltenham T v AFC Wimbledon
Crewe Alex v Accrington S
Gillingham v Hereford U
Morecambe v Dagenham & R
Northampton T v Macclesfield T
Oxford U v Barnet
Plymouth Arg v Southend U
Rotherham U v Torquay U
Shrewsbury T v Port Vale
Swindon T v Burton Alb

Saturday, 11 February 2012
Barclays Premier League
Aston Villa v Manchester C
Blackburn R v QPR
Bolton W v Wigan Ath
Everton v Chelsea
Fulham v Stoke C
Manchester U v Liverpool
Sunderland v Arsenal
Swansea C v Norwich C
Tottenham H v Newcastle U

npower Football League Championship
Barnsley v Birmingham C

Blackpool v Portsmouth
Crystal Palace v Doncaster R
Hull C v Bristol C
Ipswich T v Middlesbrough
Leeds U v Brighton & HA
Leicester C v Cardiff C
Millwall v Derby Co
Nottingham F v Watford
Peterborough U v West Ham U
Reading v Coventry C
Southampton v Burnley

npower Football League One
Brentford v Oldham Ath
Chesterfield v Charlton Ath
Exeter C v Sheffield W
Hartlepool U v Bournemouth
Leyton Orient v Huddersfield T
Milton Keynes D v Bury
Rochdale v Notts Co
Sheffield U v Wycombe W
Stevenage v Carlisle U
Tranmere R v Preston NE
Walsall v Colchester U
Yeovil T v Scunthorpe U

npower Football League Two
AFC Wimbledon v Bradford C
Accrington S v Oxford U
Barnet v Swindon T
Bristol R v Morecambe
Burton Alb v Gillingham
Crawley T v Aldershot T
Dagenham & R v Northampton T
Hereford U v Cheltenham T
Macclesfield T v Plymouth Arg
Port Vale v Crewe Alex
Southend U v Rotherham U
Torquay U v Shrewsbury T

Sunday, 12 February 2012
Barclays Premier League
Wolverhampton W v WBA (1.00)

Tuesday, 14 February 2012
npower Football League Championship
Birmingham C v Hull C
Brighton & HA v Millwall
Bristol C v Crystal Palace
Burnley v Barnsley
Cardiff C v Peterborough U
Coventry C v Leeds U
Derby Co v Reading
Doncaster R v Blackpool
Middlesbrough v Nottingham F
Portsmouth v Ipswich T

Watford v Leicester C
West Ham U v Southampton

npower Football League One
Bournemouth v Leyton Orient
Bury v Chesterfield
Carlisle U v Tranmere R
Charlton Ath v Milton Keynes D
Colchester U v Brentford
Huddersfield T v Sheffield U
Notts Co v Exeter C
Oldham Ath v Walsall
Preston NE v Hartlepool U
Scunthorpe U v Rochdale
Sheffield W v Stevenage
Wycombe W v Yeovil T

npower Football League Two
Aldershot T v Hereford U
Bradford C v Port Vale
Cheltenham T v Torquay U
Crewe Alex v Burton Alb
Gillingham v Southend U
Morecambe v Macclesfield T
Northampton T v AFC Wimbledon
Oxford U v Dagenham & R
Plymouth Arg v Barnet
Rotherham U v Accrington S
Shrewsbury T v Bristol R
Swindon T v Crawley T

Saturday, 18 February 2012
npower Football League Championship
Barnsley v Portsmouth
Blackpool v West Ham U
Crystal Palace v Watford
Hull C v Brighton & HA
Ipswich T v Cardiff C
Leeds U v Doncaster R
Leicester C v Birmingham C
Millwall v Middlesbrough
Nottingham F v Coventry C
Peterborough U v Bristol C
Reading v Burnley
Southampton v Derby Co

npower Football League One
Brentford v Carlisle U
Chesterfield v Sheffield W
Exeter C v Bury
Hartlepool U v Notts Co
Leyton Orient v Scunthorpe U
Milton Keynes D v Oldham Ath
Rochdale v Bournemouth
Sheffield U v Preston NE
Stevenage v Huddersfield T

Tranmere R v Charlton Ath
Walsall v Wycombe W
Yeovil T v Colchester U

npower Football League Two
AFC Wimbledon v Morecambe
Accrington S v Plymouth Arg
Barnet v Shrewsbury T
Bristol R v Oxford U
Burton Alb v Rotherham U
Crawley T v Northampton T
Dagenham & R v Cheltenham T
Hereford U v Swindon T
Macclesfield T v Aldershot T
Port Vale v Gillingham
Southend U v Crewe Alex
Torquay U v Bradford C

Saturday, 25 February 2012
Barclays Premier League
Arsenal v Tottenham H
Chelsea v Bolton W
Liverpool v Everton
Manchester C v Blackburn R
Newcastle U v Wolverhampton W
Norwich C v Manchester U
QPR v Fulham
Stoke C v Swansea C
WBA v Sunderland
Wigan Ath v Aston Villa

npower Football League Championship
Birmingham C v Nottingham F
Brighton & HA v Ipswich T
Bristol C v Blackpool
Burnley v Millwall
Cardiff C v Hull C
Coventry C v Barnsley
Derby Co v Leicester C
Doncaster R v Peterborough U
Middlesbrough v Reading
Portsmouth v Leeds U
Watford v Southampton
West Ham U v Crystal Palace

npower Football League One
Bournemouth v Milton Keynes D
Bury v Leyton Orient
Carlisle U v Yeovil T
Charlton Ath v Stevenage
Colchester U v Rochdale
Huddersfield T v Exeter C
Notts Co v Chesterfield
Oldham Ath v Tranmere R
Preston NE v Walsall
Scunthorpe U v Brentford

Sheffield W v Sheffield U
Wycombe W v Hartlepool U

npower Football League Two
Aldershot T v Barnet
Bradford C v Hereford U
Cheltenham T v Burton Alb
Crewe Alex v AFC Wimbledon
Gillingham v Torquay U
Morecambe v Southend U
Northampton T v Port Vale
Oxford U v Macclesfield T
Plymouth Arg v Dagenham & R
Rotherham U v Bristol R
Shrewsbury T v Crawley T
Swindon T v Accrington S

Saturday, 3 March 2012
Barclays Premier League
Blackburn R v Aston Villa
Fulham v Wolverhampton W
Liverpool v Arsenal
Manchester C v Bolton W
Newcastle U v Sunderland
QPR v Everton
Stoke C v Norwich C
Tottenham H v Manchester U
WBA v Chelsea
Wigan Ath v Swansea C

npower Football League Championship
Barnsley v Nottingham F
Birmingham C v Derby Co
Blackpool v Hull C
Cardiff C v West Ham U
Crystal Palace v Peterborough U
Doncaster R v Brighton & HA
Ipswich T v Bristol C
Leeds U v Southampton
Leicester C v Coventry C
Millwall v Reading
Portsmouth v Middlesbrough
Watford v Burnley

npower Football League One
Bournemouth v Charlton Ath
Bury v Huddersfield T
Chesterfield v Tranmere R
Colchester U v Preston NE
Exeter C v Stevenage
Hartlepool U v Milton Keynes D
Leyton Orient v Walsall
Notts Co v Carlisle U
Rochdale v Sheffield W
Scunthorpe U v Wycombe W
Sheffield U v Oldham Ath

Yeovil T v Brentford

npower Football League Two
Accrington S v Port Vale
Aldershot T v Morecambe
Barnet v Rotherham U
Bristol R v Macclesfield T
Burton Alb v Southend U
Cheltenham T v Northampton T
Crawley T v Torquay U
Crewe Alex v Shrewsbury T
Dagenham & R v Bradford C
Hereford U v AFC Wimbledon
Oxford U v Swindon T
Plymouth Arg v Gillingham

Tuesday, 6 March 2012
npower Football League Championship
Brighton & HA v Cardiff C
Bristol C v Leicester C
Burnley v Birmingham C
Coventry C v Crystal Palace
Derby Co v Blackpool
Hull C v Leeds U
Middlesbrough v Barnsley
Nottingham F v Doncaster R
Peterborough U v Millwall
Reading v Portsmouth
Southampton v Ipswich T
West Ham U v Watford

npower Football League One
Brentford v Exeter C
Carlisle U v Rochdale
Charlton Ath v Colchester U
Huddersfield T v Hartlepool U
Milton Keynes D v Yeovil T
Oldham Ath v Scunthorpe U
Preston NE v Chesterfield
Sheffield W v Bury
Stevenage v Bournemouth
Tranmere R v Notts Co
Walsall v Sheffield U
Wycombe W v Leyton Orient

npower Football League Two
AFC Wimbledon v Plymouth Arg
Bradford C v Accrington S
Gillingham v Barnet
Macclesfield T v Hereford U
Morecambe v Cheltenham T
Northampton T v Bristol R
Port Vale v Burton Alb
Rotherham U v Crewe Alex
Shrewsbury T v Oxford U
Southend U v Crawley T

Swindon T v Dagenham & R
Torquay U v Aldershot T

Saturday, 10 March 2012
Barclays Premier League
Arsenal v Newcastle U
Aston Villa v Fulham
Bolton W v QPR
Chelsea v Stoke C
Everton v Tottenham H
Manchester U v WBA
Norwich C v Wigan Ath
Sunderland v Liverpool
Swansea C v Manchester C
Wolverhampton W v Blackburn R

npower Football League Championship
Brighton & HA v Portsmouth
Bristol C v Cardiff C
Burnley v Crystal Palace
Coventry C v Birmingham C
Derby Co v Watford
Hull C v Ipswich T
Middlesbrough v Leeds U
Nottingham F v Millwall
Peterborough U v Blackpool
Reading v Leicester C
Southampton v Barnsley
West Ham U v Doncaster R

npower Football League One
Brentford v Sheffield U
Carlisle U v Bury
Charlton Ath v Notts Co
Huddersfield T v Rochdale
Milton Keynes D v Exeter C
Oldham Ath v Yeovil T
Preston NE v Scunthorpe U
Sheffield W v Bournemouth
Stevenage v Chesterfield
Tranmere R v Leyton Orient
Walsall v Hartlepool U
Wycombe W v Colchester U

npower Football League Two
AFC Wimbledon v Dagenham & R
Bradford C v Oxford U
Gillingham v Crewe Alex
Macclesfield T v Crawley T
Morecambe v Hereford U
Northampton T v Aldershot T
Port Vale v Barnet
Rotherham U v Plymouth Arg
Shrewsbury T v Burton Alb
Southend U v Accrington S
Swindon T v Cheltenham T

Torquay U v Bristol R

Saturday, 17 March 2012
Barclays Premier League
Aston Villa v Bolton W
Blackburn R v Sunderland
Everton v Arsenal
Fulham v Swansea C
Manchester C v Chelsea
Newcastle U v Norwich C
QPR v Liverpool
Tottenham H v Stoke C
Wigan Ath v WBA
Wolverhampton W v Manchester U

npower Football League Championship
Barnsley v Reading
Birmingham C v Middlesbrough
Blackpool v Brighton & HA
Cardiff C v Burnley
Crystal Palace v Hull C
Doncaster R v Derby Co
Ipswich T v Peterborough U
Leeds U v West Ham U
Leicester C v Nottingham F
Millwall v Southampton
Portsmouth v Bristol C
Watford v Coventry C

npower Football League One
Bournemouth v Carlisle U
Bury v Wycombe W
Chesterfield v Milton Keynes D
Colchester U v Huddersfield T
Exeter C v Preston NE
Hartlepool U v Stevenage
Leyton Orient v Brentford
Notts Co v Sheffield W
Rochdale v Oldham Ath
Scunthorpe U v Charlton Ath
Sheffield U v Tranmere R
Yeovil T v Walsall

npower Football League Two
Accrington S v Northampton T
Aldershot T v Bradford C
Barnet v Morecambe
Bristol R v AFC Wimbledon
Burton Alb v Torquay U
Cheltenham T v Gillingham
Crawley T v Port Vale
Crewe Alex v Swindon T
Dagenham & R v Macclesfield T
Hereford U v Southend U
Oxford U v Rotherham U
Plymouth Arg v Shrewsbury T

Tuesday, 20 March 2012
npower Football League Championship
Blackpool v Leicester C
Brighton & HA v Derby Co
Bristol C v Watford
Cardiff C v Coventry C
Crystal Palace v Barnsley
Doncaster R v Millwall
Hull C v Southampton
Ipswich T v Burnley
Leeds U v Nottingham F
Peterborough U v Reading
Portsmouth v Birmingham C
West Ham U v Middlesbrough

npower Football League One
Bournemouth v Brentford
Bury v Scunthorpe U
Carlisle U v Preston NE
Charlton Ath v Yeovil T
Chesterfield v Huddersfield T
Exeter C v Wycombe W
Hartlepool U v Oldham Ath
Milton Keynes D v Leyton Orient
Notts Co v Sheffield U
Rochdale v Tranmere R
Sheffield W v Walsall
Stevenage v Colchester U

npower Football League Two
Accrington S v Morecambe
Barnet v Dagenham & R
Burton Alb v Northampton T
Crewe Alex v Bradford C
Gillingham v Crawley T
Oxford U v AFC Wimbledon
Plymouth Arg v Bristol R
Port Vale v Hereford U
Rotherham U v Macclesfield T
Shrewsbury T v Cheltenham T
Southend U v Aldershot T
Swindon T v Torquay U

Saturday, 24 March 2012
Barclays Premier League
Arsenal v Aston Villa
Bolton W v Blackburn R
Chelsea v Tottenham H
Liverpool v Wigan Ath
Manchester U v Fulham
Norwich C v Wolverhampton W
Stoke C v Manchester C
Sunderland v QPR
Swansea C v Everton
WBA v Newcastle U

npower Football League Championship
Barnsley v Peterborough U
Birmingham C v Cardiff C
Burnley v West Ham U
Coventry C v Portsmouth
Derby Co v Crystal Palace
Leicester C v Hull C
Middlesbrough v Bristol C
Millwall v Leeds U
Nottingham F v Brighton & HA
Reading v Blackpool
Southampton v Doncaster R
Watford v Ipswich T

npower Football League One
Brentford v Rochdale
Colchester U v Carlisle U
Huddersfield T v Charlton Ath
Leyton Orient v Sheffield W
Oldham Ath v Bournemouth
Preston NE v Bury
Scunthorpe U v Notts Co
Sheffield U v Chesterfield
Tranmere R v Exeter C
Walsall v Stevenage
Wycombe W v Milton Keynes D
Yeovil T v Hartlepool U

npower Football League Two
AFC Wimbledon v Burton Alb
Aldershot T v Swindon T
Bradford C v Gillingham
Bristol R v Southend U
Cheltenham T v Oxford U
Crawley T v Rotherham U
Dagenham & R v Accrington S
Hereford U v Crewe Alex
Macclesfield T v Barnet
Morecambe v Shrewsbury T
Northampton T v Plymouth Arg
Torquay U v Port Vale

Saturday, 31 March 2012
Barclays Premier League
Aston Villa v Chelsea
Blackburn R v Manchester U
Everton v WBA
Fulham v Norwich C
Manchester C v Sunderland
Newcastle U v Liverpool
QPR v Arsenal
Tottenham H v Swansea C
Wigan Ath v Stoke C
Wolverhampton W v Bolton W

npower Football League Championship
Blackpool v Southampton
Brighton & HA v Middlesbrough
Bristol C v Derby Co
Cardiff C v Millwall
Crystal Palace v Nottingham F
Doncaster R v Birmingham C
Hull C v Coventry C
Ipswich T v Barnsley
Leeds U v Watford
Peterborough U v Leicester C
Portsmouth v Burnley
West Ham U v Reading

npower Football League One
Bournemouth v Yeovil T
Bury v Tranmere R
Carlisle U v Huddersfield T
Charlton Ath v Leyton Orient
Chesterfield v Scunthorpe U
Exeter C v Colchester U
Hartlepool U v Sheffield U
Milton Keynes D v Brentford
Notts Co v Oldham Ath
Rochdale v Walsall
Sheffield W v Preston NE
Stevenage v Wycombe W

npower Football League Two
Accrington S v AFC Wimbledon
Barnet v Torquay U
Burton Alb v Crawley T
Crewe Alex v Northampton T
Gillingham v Macclesfield T
Oxford U v Morecambe
Plymouth Arg v Bradford C
Port Vale v Dagenham & R
Rotherham U v Hereford U
Shrewsbury T v Aldershot T
Southend U v Cheltenham T
Swindon T v Bristol R

Saturday, 7 April 2012
Barclays Premier League
Arsenal v Manchester C
Bolton W v Fulham
Chelsea v Wigan Ath
Liverpool v Aston Villa
Manchester U v QPR
Norwich C v Everton
Stoke C v Wolverhampton W
Sunderland v Tottenham H
Swansea C v Newcastle U
WBA v Blackburn R

npower Football League Championship

Barnsley v West Ham U
Birmingham C v Crystal Palace
Burnley v Brighton & HA
Coventry C v Peterborough U
Derby Co v Ipswich T
Leicester C v Doncaster R
Middlesbrough v Cardiff C
Millwall v Hull C
Nottingham F v Bristol C
Reading v Leeds U
Southampton v Portsmouth
Watford v Blackpool

npower Football League Championship

Blackpool v Barnsley
Brighton & HA v Reading
Bristol C v Coventry C
Cardiff C v Watford
Crystal Palace v Southampton
Doncaster R v Burnley
Hull C v Middlesbrough
Ipswich T v Leicester C
Leeds U v Derby Co
Peterborough U v Nottingham F
Portsmouth v Millwall
West Ham U v Birmingham C

npower Football League One

Brentford v Bury
Colchester U v Hartlepool U
Huddersfield T v Sheffield W
Leyton Orient v Notts Co
Oldham Ath v Charlton Ath
Preston NE v Milton Keynes D
Scunthorpe U v Exeter C
Sheffield U v Bournemouth
Tranmere R v Stevenage
Walsall v Chesterfield
Wycombe W v Carlisle U
Yeovil T v Rochdale

npower Football League One

Bournemouth v Huddersfield T
Bury v Colchester U
Carlisle U v Scunthorpe U
Charlton Ath v Walsall
Chesterfield v Wycombe W
Exeter C v Leyton Orient
Hartlepool U v Brentford
Milton Keynes D v Tranmere R
Notts Co v Yeovil T
Rochdale v Sheffield U
Sheffield W v Oldham Ath
Stevenage v Preston NE

npower Football League Two

AFC Wimbledon v Rotherham U
Aldershot T v Port Vale
Bradford C v Southend U
Bristol R v Gillingham
Cheltenham T v Barnet
Crawley T v Crewe Alex
Dagenham & R v Burton Alb
Hereford U v Plymouth Arg
Macclesfield T v Shrewsbury T
Morecambe v Swindon T
Northampton T v Oxford U
Torquay U v Accrington S

npower Football League Two

Accrington S v Hereford U
Barnet v Crawley T
Burton Alb v Morecambe
Crewe Alex v Bristol R
Gillingham v Dagenham & R
Oxford U v Torquay U
Plymouth Arg v Aldershot T
Port Vale v Macclesfield T
Rotherham U v Cheltenham T
Shrewsbury T v Bradford C
Southend U v AFC Wimbledon
Swindon T v Northampton T

Monday, 9 April 2012

Barclays Premier League

Aston Villa v Stoke C
Blackburn R v Liverpool
Everton v Sunderland
Fulham v Chelsea
Manchester C v WBA
Newcastle U v Bolton W
QPR v Swansea C
Tottenham H v Norwich C
Wigan Ath v Manchester U
Wolverhampton W v Arsenal

Saturday, 14 April 2012

Barclays Premier League

Arsenal v Wigan Ath
Bolton W v Tottenham H
Chelsea v Newcastle U
Liverpool v Fulham (12.45)
Manchester U v Aston Villa
Norwich C v Manchester C
Stoke C v Everton
Sunderland v Wolverhampton W
Swansea C v Blackburn R
WBA v QPR

npower Football League Championship
Barnsley v Cardiff C
Birmingham C v Bristol C
Burnley v Coventry C
Crystal Palace v Ipswich T
Derby Co v Middlesbrough
Doncaster R v Portsmouth
Leeds U v Peterborough U
Millwall v Leicester C
Nottingham F v Blackpool
Southampton v Reading
Watford v Hull C
West Ham U v Brighton & HA

npower Football League One
Brentford v Notts Co
Bury v Bournemouth
Carlisle U v Charlton Ath
Colchester U v Sheffield W
Hartlepool U v Chesterfield
Preston NE v Huddersfield T
Rochdale v Exeter C
Scunthorpe U v Milton Keynes D
Sheffield U v Leyton Orient
Walsall v Tranmere R
Wycombe W v Oldham Ath
Yeovil T v Stevenage

npower Football League Two
Aldershot T v Dagenham & R
Barnet v Hereford U
Bristol R v Burton Alb
Cheltenham T v Accrington S
Crawley T v AFC Wimbledon
Macclesfield T v Crewe Alex
Morecambe v Port Vale
Northampton T v Bradford C
Oxford U v Gillingham
Shrewsbury T v Rotherham U
Swindon T v Plymouth Arg
Torquay U v Southend U

Tuesday, 17 April 2012
npower Football League Championship
Blackpool v Leeds U
Brighton & HA v Watford
Bristol C v West Ham U
Cardiff C v Derby Co
Coventry C v Millwall
Hull C v Barnsley
Ipswich T v Birmingham C
Leicester C v Burnley
Middlesbrough v Doncaster R
Peterborough U v Southampton
Portsmouth v Crystal Palace
Reading v Nottingham F

Saturday, 21 April 2012
Barclays Premier League
Arsenal v Chelsea
Aston Villa v Sunderland
Blackburn R v Norwich C
Bolton W v Swansea C
Fulham v Wigan Ath
Liverpool v WBA
Manchester U v Everton
Newcastle U v Stoke C
QPR v Tottenham H
Wolverhampton W v Manchester C

npower Football League Championship
Blackpool v Burnley
Brighton & HA v Birmingham C
Bristol C v Barnsley
Cardiff C v Leeds U
Coventry C v Doncaster R
Hull C v Nottingham F
Ipswich T v Millwall
Leicester C v West Ham U
Middlesbrough v Southampton
Peterborough U v Watford
Portsmouth v Derby Co
Reading v Crystal Palace

npower Football League One
Bournemouth v Colchester U
Charlton Ath v Wycombe W
Chesterfield v Rochdale
Exeter C v Walsall
Huddersfield T v Scunthorpe U
Leyton Orient v Yeovil T
Milton Keynes D v Sheffield U
Notts Co v Bury
Oldham Ath v Preston NE
Sheffield W v Carlisle U
Stevenage v Brentford
Tranmere R v Hartlepool U

npower Football League Two
AFC Wimbledon v Torquay U
Accrington S v Shrewsbury T
Bradford C v Macclesfield T
Burton Alb v Aldershot T
Crewe Alex v Cheltenham T
Dagenham & R v Crawley T
Gillingham v Swindon T
Hereford U v Northampton T
Plymouth Arg v Oxford U
Port Vale v Bristol R
Rotherham U v Morecambe
Southend U v Barnet

Saturday, 28 April 2012
Barclays Premier League
Chelsea v QPR
Everton v Fulham
Manchester C v Manchester U
Norwich C v Liverpool
Stoke C v Arsenal
Sunderland v Bolton W
Swansea C v Wolverhampton W
Tottenham H v Blackburn R
WBA v Aston Villa
Wigan Ath v Newcastle U

npower Football League Championship
Barnsley v Brighton & HA
Birmingham C v Reading
Burnley v Bristol C
Crystal Palace v Cardiff C
Derby Co v Peterborough U
Doncaster R v Ipswich T
Leeds U v Leicester C
Millwall v Blackpool
Nottingham F v Portsmouth
Southampton v Coventry C
Watford v Middlesbrough
West Ham U v Hull C

npower Football League One
Brentford v Sheffield W
Bury v Oldham Ath
Carlisle U v Exeter C
Colchester U v Tranmere R
Hartlepool U v Leyton Orient
Preston NE v Charlton Ath
Rochdale v Milton Keynes D
Scunthorpe U v Bournemouth
Sheffield U v Stevenage
Walsall v Huddersfield T
Wycombe W v Notts Co
Yeovil T v Chesterfield

npower Football League Two
Aldershot v Rotherham U
Barnet v AFC Wimbledon
Bristol R v Accrington S
Cheltenham T v Bradford C
Crawley T v Hereford U
Macclesfield T v Burton Alb
Morecambe v Plymouth Arg
Northampton T v Gillingham
Oxford U v Southend U
Shrewsbury T v Dagenham & R
Swindon T v Port Vale
Torquay U v Crewe Alex

Saturday, 5 May 2012
Barclays Premier League
Arsenal v Norwich C
Aston Villa v Tottenham H
Blackburn R v Wigan Ath
Bolton W v WBA
Fulham v Sunderland
Liverpool v Chelsea
Manchester U v Swansea C
Newcastle U v Manchester C
QPR v Stoke C
Wolverhampton W v Everton

npower Football League One
Bournemouth v Preston NE
Charlton Ath v Hartlepool U
Chesterfield v Brentford
Exeter C v Sheffield U
Huddersfield T v Yeovil T
Leyton Orient v Rochdale
Milton Keynes D v Walsall
Notts Co v Colchester U
Oldham Ath v Carlisle U
Sheffield W v Wycombe W
Stevenage v Bury
Tranmere R v Scunthorpe U

npower Football League Two
AFC Wimbledon v Shrewsbury T
Accrington S v Crawley T
Bradford C v Swindon T
Burton Alb v Barnet
Crewe Alex v Aldershot T
Dagenham & R v Bristol R
Gillingham v Morecambe
Hereford U v Torquay U
Plymouth Arg v Cheltenham T
Port Vale v Oxford U
Rotherham U v Northampton T
Southend U v Macclesfield T

Sunday, 13 May 2012
Barclays Premier League
Chelsea v Blackburn R
Everton v Newcastle U
Manchester C v QPR
Norwich C v Aston Villa
Stoke C v Bolton W
Sunderland v Manchester U
Swansea C v Liverpool
Tottenham H v Fulham
WBA v Arsenal
Wigan Ath v Wolverhampton W

BLUE SQUARE PREMIER FIXTURES 2011–2012

Saturday, 13 August 2011
AFC Telford v Luton T
Barrow v Tamworth
Darlington v Braintree T
Ebbsfleet U v York C
Forest Green R v Stockport Co
Grimsby T v Fleetwood T
Hayes & Yeading U v Alfreton T
Kettering T v Newport Co
Kidderminster H v Gateshead
Mansfield T v Bath C
Southport v Lincoln C
Wrexham v Cambridge U

Tuesday, 16 August 2011
Alfreton T v Southport
Bath C v Wrexham
Braintree T v Grimsby T
Cambridge U v AFC Telford
Fleetwood T v Darlington
Gateshead v Mansfield T
Lincoln C v Kidderminster H
Luton T v Forest Green R
Newport Co v Hayes & Yeading U
Stockport Co v Kettering T
Tamworth v Ebbsfleet U
York C v Barrow

Saturday, 20 August 2011
Alfreton T v Forest Green R
Bath C v Barrow
Braintree T v Mansfield T
Cambridge U v Kidderminster H
Fleetwood T v Hayes & Yeading U
Gateshead v Kettering T
Lincoln C v Wrexham
Luton T v Southport
Newport Co v Grimsby T
Stockport Co v Ebbsfleet U
Tamworth v Darlington
York C v AFC Telford

Tuesday, 23 August 2011
AFC Telford v Lincoln C
Barrow v Fleetwood T

Darlington v Alfreton T
Ebbsfleet U v Newport Co
Forest Green R v Braintree T
Grimsby T v Cambridge U
Hayes & Yeading U v Bath C
Kettering T v York C
Kidderminster H v Stockport Co
Mansfield T v Luton T
Southport v Gateshead
Wrexham v Tamworth

Saturday, 27 August 2011
AFC Telford v Newport Co
Alfreton T v Wrexham
Barrow v Gateshead
Bath C v Tamworth
Cambridge U v Hayes & Yeading U
Ebbsfleet U v Forest Green R
Fleetwood T v York C
Grimsby T v Darlington
Kidderminster H v Southport
Lincoln C v Stockport Co
Luton T v Braintree T
Mansfield T v Kettering T

Monday, 29 August 2011
Braintree T v Ebbsfleet U
Darlington v Lincoln C
Forest Green R v Bath C
Gateshead v Grimsby T
Hayes & Yeading U v Luton T
Kettering T v Cambridge U
Newport Co v Kidderminster H
Southport v Barrow
Stockport Co v Mansfield T
Tamworth v AFC Telford
Wrexham v Fleetwood T
York C v Alfreton T

Saturday, 3 September 2011
Braintree T v Lincoln C
Darlington v Mansfield T
Ebbsfleet U v Barrow
Forest Green R v Grimsby T
Gateshead v Alfreton T

Hayes & Yeading U v Tamworth
Kettering T v Fleetwood T
Newport Co v Cambridge U
Southport v AFC Telford
Stockport Co v Luton T
Wrexham v Kidderminster H
York C v Bath C

Saturday, 10 September 2011
AFC Telford v Stockport Co
Alfreton T v Braintree T
Barrow v Wrexham
Bath C v Southport
Cambridge U v Forest Green R
Fleetwood T v Gateshead
Grimsby T v Hayes & Yeading U
Kidderminster H v Ebbsfleet U
Lincoln C v Kettering T
Luton T v Darlington
Mansfield T v Newport Co
Tamworth v York C

Saturday, 17 September 2011
AFC Telford v Bath C
Barrow v Mansfield T
Braintree T v Newport Co
Darlington v Hayes & Yeading U
Ebbsfleet U v Fleetwood T
Forest Green R v Southport
Gateshead v Cambridge U
Kettering T v Tamworth
Kidderminster H v Alfreton T
Luton T v Lincoln C
Stockport Co v Grimsby T
Wrexham v York C

Tuesday, 20 September 2011
Alfreton T v Barrow
Bath C v Luton T
Cambridge U v Ebbsfleet U
Fleetwood T v Kidderminster H
Grimsby T v Kettering T
Hayes & Yeading U v Braintree T
Lincoln C v Gateshead
Mansfield T v AFC Telford
Newport Co v Stockport Co
Southport v Wrexham
Tamworth v Forest Green R
York C v Darlington

Saturday, 24 September 2011
Alfreton T v Ebbsfleet U
Bath C v Kettering T
Cambridge U v Darlington
Fleetwood T v AFC Telford
Grimsby T v Wrexham
Hayes & Yeading U v Gateshead
Lincoln C v Forest Green R
Mansfield T v Kidderminster H
Newport Co v Barrow
Southport v Braintree T
Tamworth v Stockport Co
York C v Luton T

Tuesday, 27 September 2011
AFC Telford v Alfreton T
Barrow v Lincoln C
Braintree T v Tamworth
Darlington v Southport
Ebbsfleet U v Bath C
Forest Green R v Newport Co
Gateshead v York C
Kettering T v Hayes & Yeading U
Kidderminster H v Grimsby T
Luton T v Cambridge U
Stockport Co v Fleetwood T
Wrexham v Mansfield T

Saturday, 1 October 2011
AFC Telford v Hayes & Yeading U
Braintree T v Fleetwood T
Darlington v Newport Co
Forest Green R v Mansfield T
Gateshead v Tamworth
Grimsby T v Alfreton T
Kettering T v Kidderminster H
Lincoln C v Bath C
Luton T v Barrow
Southport v Cambridge U
Stockport Co v York C
Wrexham v Ebbsfleet U

Saturday, 8 October 2011
Alfreton T v Kettering T
Barrow v AFC Telford
Bath C v Darlington
Cambridge U v Stockport Co
Ebbsfleet U v Gateshead
Fleetwood T v Forest Green R

Kidderminster H v Luton T
Mansfield T v Grimsby T
Newport Co v Southport
Tamworth v Lincoln C
York C v Braintree T

Sunday, 9 October 2011
Hayes & Yeading U v Wrexham

Tuesday, 11 October 2011
Alfreton T v Lincoln C
Bath C v Cambridge U
Ebbsfleet U v Luton T
Fleetwood T v Newport Co
Gateshead v Wrexham
Grimsby T v Barrow
Hayes & Yeading U v Forest Green R
Kettering T v Braintree T
Kidderminster H v AFC Telford
Southport v York C
Stockport Co v Darlington

Saturday, 15 October 2011
AFC Telford v Ebbsfleet U
Barrow v Hayes & Yeading U
Braintree T v Bath C
Cambridge U v Alfreton T
Darlington v Kidderminster H
Forest Green R v Kettering T
Lincoln C v Fleetwood T
Luton T v Gateshead
Mansfield T v Southport
Newport Co v Tamworth
Wrexham v Stockport Co
York C v Grimsby T

Tuesday, 18 October 2011
Alfreton T v Fleetwood T
Bath C v Stockport Co
Darlington v Barrow
Ebbsfleet U v Grimsby T
Forest Green R v AFC Telford
Gateshead v Southport
Kidderminster H v Braintree T
Lincoln C v Mansfield T
Luton T v Wrexham
Newport Co v Kettering T
Tamworth v Hayes & Yeading U
York C v Cambridge U

Saturday, 22 October 2011
AFC Telford v Gateshead
Barrow v Kidderminster H
Braintree T v Darlington
Cambridge U v Lincoln C
Fleetwood T v Bath C
Grimsby T v Luton T
Hayes & Yeading U v York C
Kettering T v Ebbsfleet U
Mansfield T v Alfreton T
Southport v Tamworth
Stockport Co v Forest Green R
Wrexham v Newport Co

Saturday, 5 November 2011
Bath C v Grimsby T
Darlington v AFC Telford
Forest Green R v Alfreton T
Gateshead v Braintree T
Kettering T v Southport
Kidderminster H v Tamworth
Lincoln C v Barrow
Luton T v Fleetwood T
Mansfield T v Cambridge U
Newport Co v Ebbsfleet U
Stockport Co v Hayes & Yeading U
York C v Wrexham

Saturday, 19 November 2011
AFC Telford v Mansfield T
Alfreton T v Gateshead
Barrow v York C
Braintree T v Forest Green R
Cambridge U v Luton T
Ebbsfleet U v Darlington
Fleetwood T v Stockport Co
Grimsby T v Newport Co
Hayes & Yeading U v Kidderminster H
Southport v Bath C
Tamworth v Kettering T
Wrexham v Lincoln C

Saturday, 26 November 2011
AFC Telford v Barrow
Alfreton T v Hayes & Yeading U
Bath C v Mansfield T
Braintree T v Wrexham
Darlington v Tamworth
Forest Green R v York C

Gateshead v Fleetwood T
Kettering T v Grimsby T
Kidderminster H v Cambridge U
Lincoln C v Ebbsfleet U
Newport Co v Luton T
Stockport Co v Southport

Tuesday, 29 November 2011
Barrow v Alfreton T
Cambridge U v Bath C
Ebbsfleet U v Kidderminster H
Fleetwood T v Kettering T
Grimsby T v Stockport Co
Hayes & Yeading U v Newport Co
Luton T v AFC Telford
Mansfield T v Gateshead
Southport v Forest Green R
Tamworth v Braintree T
Wrexham v Darlington
York C v Lincoln C

Saturday, 3 December 2011
Barrow v Ebbsfleet U
Bath C v AFC Telford
Cambridge U v Grimsby T
Darlington v Forest Green R
Gateshead v Kidderminster H
Luton T v Stockport Co
Mansfield T v Braintree T
Newport Co v Lincoln C
Southport v Alfreton T
Tamworth v Wrexham
York C v Kettering T

Sunday, 4 December 2011
Hayes & Yeading U v Fleetwood T

Tuesday, 6 December 2011
AFC Telford v York C
Alfreton T v Newport Co
Braintree T v Hayes & Yeading U
Ebbsfleet U v Cambridge U
Fleetwood T v Barrow
Forest Green R v Tamworth
Grimsby T v Mansfield T
Kettering T v Darlington
Kidderminster H v Bath C
Lincoln C v Luton T
Stockport Co v Gateshead

Wrexham v Southport

Saturday, 17 December 2011
Braintree T v AFC Telford
Darlington v Cambridge U
Forest Green R v Lincoln C
Grimsby T v Ebbsfleet U
Hayes & Yeading U v Barrow
Kettering T v Bath C
Newport Co v Fleetwood T
Southport v Mansfield T
Stockport Co v Alfreton T
Tamworth v Luton T
Wrexham v Gateshead
York C v Kidderminster H

Monday, 26 December 2011
AFC Telford v Wrexham
Alfreton T v Tamworth
Barrow v Stockport Co
Bath C v Newport Co
Cambridge U v Braintree T
Ebbsfleet U v Hayes & Yeading U
Fleetwood T v Southport
Gateshead v Darlington
Kidderminster H v Forest Green R
Lincoln C v Grimsby T
Luton T v Kettering T
Mansfield T v York C

Sunday, 1 January 2012
Braintree T v Cambridge U
Darlington v Gateshead
Forest Green R v Kidderminster H
Grimsby T v Lincoln C
Hayes & Yeading U v Ebbsfleet U
Kettering T v Luton T
Newport Co v Bath C
Southport v Fleetwood T
Stockport Co v Barrow
Tamworth v Alfreton T
Wrexham v AFC Telford
York C v Mansfield T

Saturday, 7 January 2012
AFC Telford v Kettering T
Alfreton T v Grimsby T
Barrow v Darlington
Bath C v Braintree T

376

Cambridge U v Southport
Ebbsfleet U v Wrexham
Fleetwood T v Tamworth
Gateshead v Stockport Co
Kidderminster H v Hayes & Yeading U
Lincoln C v York C
Luton T v Newport Co
Mansfield T v Forest Green R

Saturday, 21 January 2012
AFC Telford v Cambridge U
Alfreton T v Kidderminster H
Braintree T v Stockport Co
Darlington v Fleetwood T
Gateshead v Lincoln C
Grimsby T v Bath C
Mansfield T v Hayes & Yeading U
Newport Co v Forest Green R
Southport v Luton T
Tamworth v Barrow
Wrexham v Kettering T
York C v Ebbsfleet U

Tuesday, 24 January 2012
Barrow v Grimsby T
Bath C v Alfreton T
Cambridge U v Newport Co
Ebbsfleet U v Tamworth
Fleetwood T v Braintree T
Forest Green R v Wrexham
Hayes & Yeading U v Darlington
Kettering T v Gateshead
Kidderminster H v York C
Lincoln C v Southport
Luton T v Mansfield T
Stockport Co v AFC Telford

Saturday, 28 January 2012
Braintree T v Barrow
Cambridge U v Tamworth
Darlington v York C
Ebbsfleet U v Mansfield T
Forest Green R v Fleetwood T
Gateshead v Newport Co
Grimsby T v AFC Telford
Hayes & Yeading U v Southport
Kettering T v Lincoln C
Luton T v Alfreton T

Stockport Co v Kidderminster H
Wrexham v Bath C

Saturday, 4 February 2012
AFC Telford v Forest Green R
Alfreton T v Stockport Co
Barrow v Luton T
Bath C v Hayes & Yeading U
Fleetwood T v Ebbsfleet U
Kidderminster H v Wrexham
Lincoln C v Cambridge U
Mansfield T v Darlington
Newport Co v Braintree T
Southport v Kettering T
Tamworth v Grimsby T
York C v Gateshead

Tuesday, 7 February 2012
AFC Telford v Kidderminster H
Alfreton T v Mansfield T
Gateshead v Hayes & Yeading U
Kettering T v Forest Green R

Saturday, 11 February 2012
Braintree T v Southport
Cambridge U v Barrow
Darlington v Wrexham
Ebbsfleet U v Alfreton T
Forest Green R v Luton T
Gateshead v Bath C
Grimsby T v York C
Hayes & Yeading U v Lincoln C
Kettering T v AFC Telford
Mansfield T v Fleetwood T
Stockport Co v Newport Co
Tamworth v Kidderminster H

Tuesday, 14 February 2012
Lincoln C v Braintree T
Southport v Darlington

Saturday, 18 February 2012
AFC Telford v Braintree T
Alfreton T v Darlington
Barrow v Kettering T
Bath C v Ebbsfleet U
Fleetwood T v Cambridge U
Forest Green R v Gateshead
Kidderminster H v Lincoln C
Luton T v Tamworth

Newport Co v Mansfield T
Southport v Grimsby T
Wrexham v Hayes & Yeading U
York C v Stockport Co

Tuesday, 21 February 2012
Tamworth v Newport Co

Saturday, 25 February 2012
Barrow v Forest Green R
Bath C v Kidderminster H
Braintree T v Kettering T
Cambridge U v Gateshead
Darlington v Luton T
Ebbsfleet U v Southport
Fleetwood T v Alfreton T
Hayes & Yeading U v Grimsby T
Lincoln C v AFC Telford
Mansfield T v Tamworth
Newport Co v York C
Stockport Co v Wrexham

Saturday, 3 March 2012
Alfreton T v AFC Telford
Darlington v Stockport Co
Forest Green R v Cambridge U
Gateshead v Ebbsfleet U
Grimsby T v Braintree T
Kettering T v Wrexham
Kidderminster H v Barrow
Luton T v Bath C
Mansfield T v Lincoln C
Southport v Newport Co
Tamworth v Fleetwood T
York C v Hayes & Yeading U

Tuesday, 6 March 2012
Barrow v Bath C
Cambridge U v Mansfield T
Ebbsfleet U v Stockport Co
Fleetwood T v Grimsby T
Wrexham v Luton T
York C v Tamworth

Saturday, 10 March 2012
AFC Telford v Southport
Bath C v York C
Braintree T v Gateshead
Grimsby T v Forest Green R
Hayes & Yeading U v Kettering T

Kidderminster H v Fleetwood T
Lincoln C v Alfreton T
Luton T v Ebbsfleet U
Newport Co v Darlington
Stockport Co v Cambridge U
Tamworth v Mansfield T
Wrexham v Barrow

Saturday, 17 March 2012
AFC Telford v Fleetwood T
Bath C v Lincoln C
Braintree T v Kidderminster H
Cambridge U v York C
Darlington v Ebbsfleet U
Forest Green R v Hayes & Yeading U
Gateshead v Luton T
Grimsby T v Tamworth
Kettering T v Alfreton T
Mansfield T v Barrow
Newport Co v Wrexham
Southport v Stockport Co

Saturday, 24 March 2012
Alfreton T v Cambridge U
Barrow v Braintree T
Ebbsfleet U v Kettering T
Fleetwood T v Mansfield T
Hayes & Yeading U v AFC Telford
Kidderminster H v Darlington
Lincoln C v Newport Co
Luton T v Grimsby T
Stockport Co v Bath C
Tamworth v Gateshead
Wrexham v Forest Green R
York C v Southport

Saturday, 31 March 2012
AFC Telford v Darlington
Bath C v Fleetwood T
Braintree T v Alfreton T
Cambridge U v Wrexham
Forest Green R v Barrow
Grimsby T v Kidderminster H
Kettering T v Stockport Co
Lincoln C v Tamworth
Luton T v York C
Mansfield T v Ebbsfleet U
Newport Co v Gateshead
Southport v Hayes & Yeading U

Saturday, 7 April 2012
Braintree T v Luton T
Darlington v Grimsby T
Forest Green R v Ebbsfleet U
Gateshead v Barrow
Hayes & Yeading U v Cambridge U
Kettering T v Mansfield T
Newport Co v AFC Telford
Southport v Kidderminster H
Stockport Co v Lincoln C
Tamworth v Bath C
Wrexham v Alfreton T
York C v Fleetwood T

Monday, 9 April 2012
AFC Telford v Tamworth
Alfreton T v York C
Barrow v Southport
Bath C v Forest Green R
Cambridge U v Kettering T
Ebbsfleet U v Braintree T
Fleetwood T v Wrexham
Grimsby T v Gateshead
Kidderminster H v Newport Co
Lincoln C v Darlington
Luton T v Hayes & Yeading U
Mansfield T v Stockport Co

Saturday, 14 April 2012
Alfreton T v Luton T
Barrow v Cambridge U
Darlington v Bath C
Ebbsfleet U v AFC Telford
Fleetwood T v Lincoln C
Gateshead v Forest Green R

Hayes & Yeading U v Mansfield T
Kidderminster H v Kettering T
Stockport Co v Braintree T
Tamworth v Southport
Wrexham v Grimsby T
York C v Newport Co

Saturday, 21 April 2012
AFC Telford v Grimsby T
Bath C v Gateshead
Braintree T v York C
Cambridge U v Fleetwood T
Forest Green R v Darlington
Kettering T v Barrow
Lincoln C v Hayes & Yeading U
Luton T v Kidderminster H
Mansfield T v Wrexham
Newport Co v Alfreton T
Southport v Ebbsfleet U
Stockport Co v Tamworth

Saturday, 28 April 2012
Alfreton T v Bath C
Barrow v Newport Co
Darlington v Kettering T
Ebbsfleet U v Lincoln C
Fleetwood T v Luton T
Gateshead v AFC Telford
Grimsby T v Southport
Hayes & Yeading U v Stockport Co
Kidderminster H v Mansfield T
Tamworth v Cambridge U
Wrexham v Braintree T
York C v Forest Green R

OTHER FIXTURES — SEASON 2011–2012

July 2011

12 Tue	UEFA CL 2 Q (1)
13 Wed	UEFA CL 2 Q (1)
14 Thu	UEFA EL Q 2 (1)
19 Tue	UEFA CL 2 Q (2)
20 Wed	UEFA CL 2 Q (2)
21 Thu	UEFA EL Q 2 (2)
26 Tue	UEFA CL 3 Q (1)
27 Wed	UEFA CL Q 3 (1)
28 Thu	UEFA EL Q 3 (1)

August 2011

02 Tue	UEFA CL 3 (2)
03 Wed	UEFA CL 3 Q (2)
04 Thu	UEFA EL Q 3 (2)
06 Sat	Football League Commences
10 Wed	ENGLAND v HOLLAND – Friendly
	FL Cup 1
13 Sat	Premier League Commences
16 Tue	UEFA CL PO (1)
17 Wed	UEFA CL PO (1)
18 Thu	UEFA EL PO (1)
20 Sat	FA Cup EP
23 Tue	UEFA CL PO (2)
24 Wed	UEFA CL PO (2)
	FL Cup 2
25 Thu	UEFA EL PO (2)
26 Fri	UEFA Super Cup
31 Wed	FL JPT 1

September 2011

02 Fri	BULGARIA v ENGLAND – UEFA Championship
03 Sat	FA Cup P
05 Mon	FA Youth Cup P†
06 Tue	ENGLAND v WALES – UEFA Championship
10 Sat	FA Vase 1Q
13 Tue	UEFA CL MD1
14 Wed	UEFA CL MD1
15 Thu	UEFA EL MD1
17 Sat	FA Cup 1Q
19 Mon	FA Youth Cup 1Q†
21 Wed	FL Cup 3
24 Sat	FA Vase 2Q
25 Sun	FA Sunday Cup P
27 Tue	UEFA CL MD2
28 Wed	UEFA CL MD2
29 Thu	UEFA EL MD

October 2011

01 Sat	FA Cup 2Q
03 Mon	FA Youth Cup 2Q†
05 Wed	FL JPT 2
06 Thu	Iceland v England – UEFA U21 Qualifier
07 Fri	MONTENEGRO v ENGLAND – UEFA Championship
08 Sat	FA Trophy P
10 Mon	Norway v England – UEFA U21 Qualifier
11 Tue	International Qualifier (England no game)
15 Sat	FA Cup 3Q
	FA County Youth 1*
16 Sun	FA Sunday Cup 1
17 Mon	FA Youth Cup 3Q†
18 Tue	UEFA CL MD3
19 Wed	UEFA CL MD3
20 Thu	UEFA EL MD3
22 Sat	FA Trophy 1Q
	FA Vase 1P
26 Wed	FL Cup 4
29 Sat	FA Cup 4Q

November 2011

01 Tue	UEFA CL MD4
02 Wed	UEFA CL MD4
03 Thu	UEFA EL MD4
05 Sat	FA Trophy 2Q
	FA Youth Cup 1P*
09 Wed	FL JPT QF
11 Fri	International Play-off/Friendly
12 Sat	FA Cup 1P
	FA County Youth 2*
14 Mon	Belgium v England – UEFA U21 Qualifier
15 Tue	International Play Off/Friendly
19 Sat	FA Vase 2P
	FA Youth Cup 2P*
20 Sun	FA Sunday Cup 2
22 Tue	UEFA CL MD 5
23 Wed	FA Cup 1P Replay
	UEFA CL MD 5
26 Sat	FA Trophy 3Q
30 Wed	UEFA EL MD5
	FL Cup 5

December 2011

01 Thu	UEFA EL MD5
03 Sat	FA Cup 2P
	FA Vase 3P

06 Tue	UEFA CL MD6
07 Wed	UEFA CL MD6
	FL JPT SF
10 Sat	FA Trophy 1P
11 Sun	FA Sunday Cup 3
14 Wed	UEFA EL MD6
	FA Cup 2P Replay
17 Sat	UEFA EL MD6
	FA Youth Cup 3P*
19 Sat	FA County Youth 3*
26 Mon	Bank Holiday

January 2012

07 Sat	FA Cup 3P
11 Wed	FL Cup SF1
14 Sat	FA Trophy 2P
18 Wed	FA Cup 3P Replay
	FL JPT F1
21 Sat	FA Vase 4P
	FA Youth Cup 4P*
22 Sun	FA Sunday Cup 4
25 Wed	FL Cup SF 2
28 Sat	FA Cup 4P
	FA County Youth 4*

February 2012

04 Sat	FA Trophy 3P
08 Wed	FA Cup 4P Replay
	FL JPT F2
11 Sat	FA Vase 5P
	FA Youth Cup 5P*
14 Tue	UEFA CL 16 (1)
15 Wed	UEFA CL 16 (1)
16 Thu	UEFA EL 32 (2)
18 Sat	FA Cup 5
19 Sun	FA Sunday Cup 5
21 Tue	UEFA CL 16 (1)
22 Wed	UEFA CL 16 (1)
23 Thu	UEFA EL 32 (2)
25 Sat	FA Trophy 4P
	FA Youth Cup 6P*
	FA County Youth SF*
26 Sun	FL Cup Final
29 Wed	International Friendly
	FA Cup 5P Replay

March 2012

| 03 Sat | FA Vase 6P |
| 06 Tue | UEFA CL16 (2) |

07 Wed	UEFA CL 16 (2)
08 Thu	UEFA EL 16 (1)
10 Sat	FA Trophy SF1
13 Tue	UEFA CL 16 (2)
14 Wed	UEFA CL 16 (2)
15 Thu	UEFA EL 16 (2)
17 Sat	FA Cup 6P
	FA Trophy SF2
	FA Youth Cup SF1*
18 Sun	FA Sunday Cup SF
24 Sat	FA Vase SF1
25 Sun	FL JPT Final
27 Tue	UEFA CL QF (1)
28 Wed	UEFA CL QF (1)
	FA Cup 6P Replay
29 Thu	UEFA EL QF (1)
31 Sat	FA Vase SF2
	FA Youth Cup SF2*

April 2012

03 Tue	UEFA CL QF (2)
04 Wed	UEFA CL QF (2)
05 Thu	UEFA EL QF (2)
14 Sat	FA Cup SF1
15 Sun	FA Cup SF1
17 Tue	UEFA CL SF (1)
18 Wed	UEFA CL SF (1)
19 Thu	UEFA EL SF (1)
21 Sat	FA Youth Cup Final 1*
24 Tue	UEFA CL SF (2)
25 Wed	UEFA CL SF (2)
26 Thu	UEFA EL SF (2)
27 Sat	FA County Youth Final (prov)
28 Sun	FA Sunday Cup Final (prov)
	FL Championship Finish

May 2012

05 Sat	FA Cup Final
	FL 1&2 Finish
	FA Youth Cup Final 2*
09 Wed	UEFA EL Cup Final
12 Sat	FA Trophy Final
13 Sun	FA Vase Final
	Premier League Finish
19 Sat	FL Championship Play-off Final
	UEFA CL Final
26 Sat	FL 1 Play-off Final
27 Sun	FL 2 Play-off Final

† *Ties to be played in week commencing.*

* *Closing date of round.*
FA Youth Cup Final 1st and 2nd leg – dates to be confirmed.
FA Women's Cup – dates to be confirmed.

STOP PRESS

Summer transfers completed and pending:
Premier League: Bolton W: Darren Pratley (Swansea C) Free. **Liverpool:** Charlie Adam (Blackpool) £8,500,000; Jordan Henderson (Sunderland) £20,000,000. **Manchester C:** Stefan Savic (Partizan Belgrade) £6,000,000; Gael Clichy (Arsenal) £7,000,000. **Manchester U:** David De Gea (Atletico Madrid) undisclosed; Ashley Young (Aston Villa) £17,000,000; Phil Jones (Blackburn R) £16,000,000. **Newcastle U:** Sylvain Marveaux (Rennes) Free; Demba Ba (West Ham U) Free; Yohan Cabaye (Lille) undisclosed. **Norwich C:** Anthony Pilkington (Huddersfield T) undisclosed; Elliott Bennett (Brighton & HA) undisclosed; Bradley Johnson (Leeds U) Free; James Vaughan (Everton) £2,500,000; Ritchie De Laet (Manchester U) Loan; Steve Morison (Millwall) undisclosed. **Stoke C:** Jonathan Woodgate (Tottenham H) Free. **Sunderland:** David Vaughan (Blackpool) Free; John O'Shea (Manchester U) undisclosed; Wes Brown (Manchester U) undisclosed; Keiren Westwood (Coventry C) Free; Sebastian Larsson (Birmingham C) Free; Craig Gardner (Birmingham C) undisclosed; Connor Wickham (Ipswich T) £8,100,000; Ahmed Elmohamady (ENPPI Club) £2,000,000. **Swansea C:** Steven Caulker (Tottenham H) Loan; Danny Graham (Watford) £3,500,000. **Tottenham:** Brad Friedel (Aston Villa) Free. **WBA:** Gareth McAuley (Ipswich T) Free; Billy Jones (Preston NE) Free. **Wigan Ath:** Al Habsi (Bolton W) undisclosed. **Wolverhampton W:** Dorus De Vries (Swansea C) Free; Jamie O'Hara (Tottenham H) £5,000,000.

Football League Championship: Barnsley: Scott Wiseman (Rochdale) undisclosed; Jim McNulty (Brighton & HA) undisclosed; Rob Edwards (Blackpool) Free; Miles Addison (Derby Co) Loan. **Birmingham C:** Steven Caldwell (Wigan Ath) Free; Adam Rooney (Inverness CT) Free. **Blackpool:** Kevin Phillips (Birmingham C) Free. **Brighton & HA:** Craig Mackail-Smith (Peterborough U) undisclosed; Roland Bergkamp (Excelsior) undisclosed; Will Buckley (Watford) £1,000,000; Will Hoskins (Bristol R) undisclosed. **Bristol C:** Ryan Taylor (Rotherham U) undisclosed. **Cardiff C:** Aron Gunnarsson (Coventry C) Free; Robert Earnshaw (Nottingham F) Free; Andrew Taylor (Middlesbrough) Free; Don Cowie (Watford) Free; Joe Mason (Plymouth Arg) undisclosed. **Coventry C:** Joe Murphy (Scunthorpe U) Free. **Crystal Palace:** Kagisho Dikgacoi (Fulham) undisclosed; Mile Jedinak (Genclerbirligi) Free. **Derby Co:** Adam Legzdins (Burton Alb) undisclosed; Chris Maguire (Aberdeen) undisclosed; Theo Robinson (Millwall) undisclosed; Jason Shackell (Barnsley) undisclosed; Jamie Ward (Sheffield U) undisclosed; Frank Fielding (Blackburn R) undisclosed. **Doncaster R:** Kyle Bennett (Bury) undisclosed; Richard Naylor (Leeds U) Free. **Hull C:** Paul McKenna (Nottingham F) Free; Dele Adebola (Nottingham F) Free; Joe Dudgeon (Manchester U) undisclosed. **Ipswich T:** Nathan Ellington (Watford) Free; Michael Chopra (Cardiff C) undisclosed. **Leeds U:** Paul Rachubka (Blackpool) Free; Michael Brown (Portsmouth) Free. **Leicester C:** Matthew Mills (Reading) undisclosed; David Nugent (Portsmouth) Free; Sean St Ledger-Hall (Preston NE) undisclosed; Lee Peltier (Huddersfield T) undisclosed; Kasper Schmeichel (Leeds U) undisclosed. **Middlesbrough:** Curtis Main (Darlington) Free. **Millwall:** Jordan Stewart (Xanthi) Free; Ryan Allsop (WBA) undisclosed; Darius Henderson (Sheffield U) undisclosed. **Nottingham F:** Andy Reid (Blackpool) Free. **Peterborough U:** Craig Alcock (Yeovil T) undisclosed; Paul Jones (Exeter C) Free; Ryan Tunnicliffe (Manchester U) Loan; Nicky Ajose (Manchester U) undisclosed. **Portsmouth:** Stephen Henderson (Bristol C) undisclosed; Luke Varney (Derby Co) undisclosed; Jason Pearce (Bournemouth) undisclosed; David Norris (Ipswich T) Free; Greg Halford (Wolverhampton W) undisclosed. **Southampton:** Jack Cork (Chelsea) undisclosed. **Watford:** David Mirfin (Scunthorpe U) Free; Craig Forsyth (Dundee) undisclosed. **West Ham U:** Kevin Nolan (Newcastle U) undisclosed; Abdoulaye Faye (Stoke C) Free.

Football League 1: Bournemouth: Darryl Flahavan (Portsmouth) Free. **Brentford:** Jonathan Douglas (Swindon T) Free. **Bury:** Mark Hughes (North Queensland Fury) Free. **Carlisle U:** Stephen O'Halloran (Coventry C) Free; Andy Welsh (Yeovil T) Free; Jon-Paul McGovern (Swindon T) Free. **Charlton Ath:** Bradley Pritchard (Hayes & Yeading U) Free; Danny Hollands (Bournemouth) Free. **Chesterfield:** Mark Randall

Arsenal) Free. **Exeter C:** Lenny Pidgeley (Bradford C) undisclosed; Danny Coles (Bristol R) Free. **Hartlepool U:** Colin Nish (Hibernian) Free. **Huddersfield T:** Tommy ...r (Sheffield W) Free. **Leyton Orient:** Jamie Cureton (Exeter C) Free. **Milton ...es D:** Dean Bowditch (Yeovil T) Free; Darren Potter (Sheffield W) Free. **Notts ...eff Hughes (Bristol R) Free; Charlie Allen (Dagenham & R) Free; Hamza ...herif (Macclesfield T) Free; Alan Sheehan (Swindon T) Free; Jude Stirling ...n Keynes D) Free; Julian Kelly (Reading) Free; Ishmel Demontagnac ...kpool) Free. **Oldham Ath:** Matt Smith (Solihull Moors) undisclosed. **Rochdale:** ...rew Tutte (Manchester C) Free; Ashley Grimes (Millwall) Free; Stephen Darby ...erpool) Loan. **Scunthorpe U:** Andy Barcham (Gillingham) Free; Jimmy Ryan (Accrington S) undisclosed; Jordan Robertson (St Johnstone) Free. **Sheffield W:** Julian Bennett (Nottingham F) Free; Rob Jones (Scunthorpe U) Free. **Stevenage:** Phil Edwards (Accrington S) Free. **Walsall:** Ryan Jarvis (Leyton Orient) Free; Kevan Hurst (Carlisle U) Free. **Wycombe W:** Elliot Benyon (Swindon T) Loan; Scott Donnelly (Swansea C) Loan; James Tunnicliffe (Brighton & HA) Free; John Halls (Aldershot T) Free; Joel Grant (Crewe Alex) Free; Ben Harding (Aldershot T) Free. **Yeovil T:** Gavin Williams (Bristol R) Free.

Football League 2: **AFC Wimbledon:** Mat Mitchel-King (Crewe Alex) Free; Jack Midson (Oxford U) undisclosed; Max Porter (Rushden & D) undisclosed. **Accrington S:** Danny Coid (Blackpool) Free. **Aldershot T:** Bradley Bubb (Farnborough T) undisclosed; Ross Worner (Charlton Ath) Free; Jamie Collins (Newport Co) undisclosed; Aaron Brown (Leyton Orient) Free. **Bradford C:** Guy Branston (Torquay U) Free; Ross Hannah (Matlock T) Free. **Bristol R:** Lance Cronin (Gillingham) Free; Scott McGleish (Leyton Orient) Free; Matt Harrold (Shrewsbury T) undisclosed; Lee Brown (QPR) Free; Adam Virgo (Yeovil T) Free; Craig Stanley (Morecambe) Free; Matthew Gill (Norwich C) Free; Scott Bevan (Torquay U) Free; Cian Bolger (Leicester C) Loan. **Cheltenham T:** Sido Jombati (Bath C) nominal; Alan Bennett (Wycombe W) Free; Marlon Pack (Portsmouth) Free; Russell Penn (Burton Alb) Free. **Crawley T:** Scott Davies (Reading) undisclosed; Wesley Thomas (Cheltenham T) undisclosed; John Akinde (Bristol C) undisclosed; Jamie Day (Rushden & D) Free; Charlie Wassmer (Hayes & Yeading U) undisclosed; Hope Akpan (Everton) Free; David Hunt (Brentford) Free. **Dagenham & R:** Medy Elito (Colchester U) Free; Robert Edmans (Chelmsford C) undisclosed. **Gillingham:** Lewis Montrose (Wycombe W) Free; Dean Rance (Bishop's Stortford) undisclosed. **Hereford U:** Delroy Facey (Lincoln C) undisclosed. **Macclesfield T:** Scott Kay (Manchester C) Free. **Morecambe:** Lewis Alessandra (Oldham Ath) Free; Izak Reid (Macclesfield T) Free; Kevin Ellison (Rotherham U) Free. **Oxford U:** Jon-Paul Pittman (Wycombe W) Free; Tony Capaldi (Morecambe) Free. **Rotherham U:** Gareth Evans (Bradford C) Free. **Shrewsbury T:** Reuben Hazell (Oldham Ath) Free; Marvin Morgan (Aldershot T) Free. **Swindon T:** Jonathan Smith (York C) £30,000; Adam Birchall (Dover Ath) undisclosed. **Torquay U:** Chris McPhee (Kidderminster H) undisclosed.

Scottish Premier League: **Aberdeen:** David Gonzalez (Manchester C) Loan; Isaac Osbourne (Coventry C) Free; Chris Clark (Plymouth Arg) Free. **Celtic:** Victor Wanyama (Beerschot) undisclosed; Adam Matthews (Cardiff C) Free; Kelvin Wilson (Nottingham F) Free. **Dundee U:** Willo Flood (Middlesbrough) Free. **Dunfermline Ath:** Jason Thomson (Hearts) Loan; Patrick Boyle (Partick Th) Free. **Hearts:** Mehdi Taouil (Kilmarnock) Free. **Hibernian:** Garry O'Connor (Barnsley) Free. **Kilmarnock:** Paul Heffernan (Sheffield W) Free. **Motherwell:** Nicky Law (Rotherham U) Free; Michael Higdon (St Mirren) Free. **Rangers:** David Healy (Sunderland) Free. **St Johnstone:** Callum Davidson (Preston NE) Free. **St Mirren:** Graham Carey (Celtic) undisclosed; Gary Teale (Sheffield W) Free; Graeme Smith (St Johnstone) Free.

Leaving the country: **Chelsea:** Jeffrey Bruma (Hamburg) Loan; Michael Mancienne (Hamburg). **Fulham:** Diomansy Kamara (Eskisehir) Free. **Liverpool:** Dean Bouzanis (Melbourne Victory) Free. **Manchester U:** Bebe Besiktas (Loan). **WBA:** Gianni Zuiverloon (Mallorca) undisclosed; Scott Carson (Bursa) undisclosed; Abdoulaye Meite (Dijon) Free. **Portsmouth:** Nadir Ciftci (Kayseri) Free. **West Ham U:** Radoslav Kovac (Basle).

Now you can buy any of these other bestselling sports titles from your bookshop or *direct from the publisher*.